THE WRITINGS OF MARGARET FULLER

By Mason Wade

MARGARET FULLER: Whetstone of Genius

The Writings of

MARGARET FULLER

Selected and Edited by

MASON WADE

NEW YORK

The Viking Press

1941

Introduction

This book has been put together in the belief that the merit of Margaret Fuller's work has been obscured by the richness of her personality and the melodrama of her life. She was by no means a great writer. She wrote too much, with necessity driving her pen; she wrote too hastily, with a constitutional impatience of organization and detail; she wrote awkwardly, for conversation and not the written word was her natural medium. Her life was cut short only a few years after she had determined to devote her energies to a literary career, and just as she was entering upon what promised to be a period of emotional and intellectual maturity. The tragedy of her early death and the romantic story of her last years in Europe received more attention from her contemporaries than did her works, which were never properly edited or collected. The "Margaret Myth" grew apace as those who had felt the force of her remarkable personality contributed their reminiscences, but her literary reputation grew dim. Then the Civil War altered the intellectual climate of New England. The myth survived the change, and the personality was remembered, but the work was largely neglected, although reprints appeared as late as 1874. In recent years her work has been practically inaccessible.

Vernon Parrington complained that "the written record that Margaret Fuller left is quite inadequate to explain her contemporary reputation." In her able study, "Margaret Fuller as a Literary Critic," Helen Neill McMaster offered the explanation of inadequate publication and editorial blundering. Margaret Fuller published five books during her lifetime. The first two were translations from the German, radically abridged to meet the exigencies of publication in an era when there was only a minute audience for German literature in America. Her first original book, *Summer on the Lakes,* was revised from a journal kept during her tour of the Middle West in 1843, and, like Thoreau's *Week on the Concord and Merrimack Rivers,* in its original form was almost a selected edition of her works. It contained long extracts from books she had read and criticisms of them, translations, verses, and sketches, which destroy the unity of the book but indicate the range of her interests and talents. Her best-known book, *Woman in the Nineteenth Century,* was revised from an article in the *Dial* and expanded into book form at a time when Margaret was breaking with the past and was apprehensive about her future in a larger world than that of Boston and Cambridge. Her *Papers on Literature and Art* was put together hastily as she was leaving New York to go abroad, and the plan she had proposed for the collection was not followed by her publisher. She never had the opportunity to make "the more complete selection from my miscellanies" which she promised in the preface of this book, or the chance to revise work she had done to meet the need of the moment. Much of her best critical work has remained buried in the files of the periodicals to which it was contributed.

Her history of the Roman Revolution, which she considered her best work, was lost in the shipwreck in which she perished with her husband and child. The posthumous volumes of her writings which were edited by her brother, the Reverend Arthur Buckminster Fuller, suffer from his lack of qualifications for the task. The editorial emphasis is religious rather than literary; the selection was poorly made, and there are numerous major alterations and omissions. Her letters and journals are scattered or lost, and in many instances the original text cannot be recovered because of mutilation by her first biographers, Emerson, William Henry Channing, and James Freeman Clarke, who brought out their *Memoirs of Margaret Fuller Ossoli* in 1852. In their concern for the memory of their dead friend and to avoid offense to the living, they took unpardonable liberties with the materials before them. Channing, through whose hands all the material passed, with the exception of Emerson's and Clarke's private contributions, and who was responsible for most of the work, was the leading offender in this process of bowdlerizing. Arthur Fuller took similar liberties when transcribing his sister's works and letters into the five large manuscript volumes now preserved in the Harvard College Library as the *Works of Sarah Margaret Fuller Ossoli.*

This book, then, is an attempt to rescue Margaret Fuller the writer from the obscurity and neglect to which fate and the well-meant attentions of her friends and relatives have brought her. It is not intended to establish her as a great figure in American literature, for that she clearly was not,

but rather as a literary journalist of no mean ability with a double claim
upon the attention of the modern reader. Her work reveals the constantly
expanding horizons of one who began as a Cambridge prodigy and ended,
despite grave handicaps of environment and temperament, as a citizen of
the world. It mirrors the ideas and interests of her era, and links the mi-
crocosm of Boston and Concord with the macrocosm of Europe. And
some of her work has more than a historical interest and is not without
application to our own times, which it curiously anticipates.

It has been difficult to bring within the compass of one volume all of
Margaret Fuller's work that deserves to be made available to the modern
reader. *Summer on the Lakes* appears, stripped of some of its forays and
excursions, because it is entertaining and revealing in its picture of East
meeting West. Horace Greeley, something of an authority in this matter,
judged it "one of the best works in this department ever issued from the
American press." *Woman in the Nineteenth Century* demands inclusion
as one of the sacred books of American feminism, and because there is
still much to be said for Julia Ward Howe's estimate of it in 1883: "Nothing that has been written or said in later days has made its teaching superfluous." A section has been devoted to criticism, because Margaret Fuller
was one of the best of the earlier American critics and did much to shape
our critical tradition. Since *Things and Thoughts in Europe,* her letters
from abroad to Horace Greeley's *Tribune,* is too long to be given entire,
and since the incidents of her travels in Great Britain and France have become familiar in biographical accounts, a selection from her Italian letters
has been made, because of her insight into European life at one of its most
interesting periods and because they contain the materials of her lost *mag-
num opus.* And finally there is a selection from her letters which are not
readily available in print, because she was happiest in this free form of literary expression and one of the great letter-writers of her day. Since the
book is designed for the general reader, the prefatory notes provide only
the minimum of information essential to help those who wish to make
further acquaintance of a writer and a woman worth remembering. The
text, wherever possible, is as Margaret Fuller wrote it, not as others re-
made it, although punctuation and spelling have been modernized. (In
the Letters, Part V, the spelling and punctuation of the originals have
been followed.) Since this book is designed as a companion volume to my

biography, *Margaret Fuller: Whetstone of Genius,* no biographical details beyond the scope of the chronological table are given.

This book owes its very existence to the generous interest of Mrs. Paul Mellon. The editor is also greatly indebted to Mrs. Arthur B. Nichols of Cambridge, Mass., for her kind permission to publish or republish any of her aunt's writings; to the Harvard College Library and the Boston Public Library, for the right to print certain items from their collections of Fuller manuscripts; to Mrs. Pierre Jay of New York City, Mrs. Gorham Brooks of Brookline, Mass., and Mrs. Edward W. Forbes and the Ralph Waldo Emerson Memorial Association, for permission to publish letters of Margaret Fuller in their possession; to the Rowfant Club of Cleveland, Ohio, for permission to use material from George Willis Cooke's bibliography of the *Dial;* and to the Dartmouth College Library, for many courtesies.

MASON WADE

Cornish, N.H.
December 1940

Contents

Chronological Table

1810 Sarah Margaret Fuller born at Cambridgeport, Mass., May 23.

1823–4 Attended the Misses Prescott's school at Groton, Mass.

1824–33 Lived in Cambridge. Knew many members of the Harvard College class of 1829 and Divinity School class of 1833: W. H. Channing, James Freeman Clarke, Frederick Henry Hedge.

1833 The Fullers moved to a farm at Groton, where Margaret taught the four younger children: Arthur, Ellen, Richard, Lloyd.

1835 Margaret's father Timothy Fuller died suddenly and she assumed burdens of head of family.

1836 First visit to Emerson at Concord.

1836–37 Taught at Bronson Alcott's Temple School. Read German with Dr. William Ellery Channing.

1837–39 Taught at Greene St. School in Providence.

1839 *Eckermann's Conversations with Goethe* (translation).

1839 Moved to Jamaica Plain. Began conducting Conversation classes in Boston and Cambridge, which continued until 1844.

1840 Edited the *Dial* from July of this year until July 1842.

1841 Brook Farm launched in April.

1842 *Correspondence of Fräulein Günderode with Bettina von Arnim* (translation).

1843 Made trip to the West with James and Sarah Clarke.

1844 *Summer on the Lakes.* Went to New York in December as literary critic of Horace Greeley's *Tribune*.

1845 *Woman in the Nineteenth Century.*

1846 *Papers on Literature and Art.* Sailed for Europe with Marcus and Rebecca Spring in August. Traveled in England, Scotland, and France.

1847 First stay in Rome. Met Ossoli. Traveled in northern Italy and Switzerland. Returned to Rome in autumn and married Ossoli.

1848 Spent summer in Aquila and Rieti in the Abruzzi. Her son Angelo born on September 5.

1849 Roman Republic proclaimed in February. Siege of Rome by French, April–June. Margaret Fuller director of a hospital.

1850 In Florence. Sailed for America, May 17. Died in shipwreck at Fire Island, July 19, with her husband and child.

PART I

Summer on the Lakes

Prefatory Note

Margaret Fuller's first original book was the record of a trip which she took for change and relaxation in the company of her friends, the Reverend James Freeman Clarke and his sister Sarah—the J. and S. of the dialogue in Chapter II. All three travelers had a personal interest in the regions they visited during the summer of 1843. Margaret's uncle, William Williams Fuller, had long been a lawyer in Oregon, Illinois. As early as December 1838, she wrote to William Henry Channing, in discussing an unrealized plan of establishing a school in Cincinnati: "I have always had some desire to be meddling with the West, and have only been checked in my tendencies thitherward by the mood to fancy that [if] the East was not at a sufficiently advanced step of culture for my plans, how then should her younger sister be!!!" (Fuller MSS., Boston Public Library, letter dated "Providence, Dec. 9, '38.") James Clarke, one of Margaret's oldest friends, had held pulpits in St. Louis and Louisville after graduating from the Harvard Divinity School in 1833 and was the chief editor of the *Western Messenger* until his return to Boston in 1840, where he organized the Church of the Disciples. Sarah Clarke, who was something of an artist, had taken part in Margaret's Conversations and shared her interest in Dante. Two of her brothers had settled in Chicago in 1835, and one of them, William, acted as guide to the party on their trip through northern Illinois.

The book was based upon a journal kept during the expedition, which helps to explain its episodic character. A transcript of this journal, from which a few footnotes were drawn by Arthur Fuller, may be found in *Works of S. M. F. Ossoli,* Harvard College Library, Vol. V, pp. 41–79. In revising her notes and making a book out of them, Margaret found it necessary to consult reference works, and for this purpose she was the first woman reader admitted to the Harvard College Library. Though she began work on the book soon after her return home, the writing went slowly in the rare intervals of leisure allowed by the Conversation classes, and the book was not finished until the following spring. She wrote the last line on her birthday, May 23, 1844, and the book was published early that summer. In a letter to her close friend William Henry Channing, she tells of its reception and of her publishing arrangements (Fuller MSS., Boston Public Library, letter of June 1844): "As to my book, there are complimentary notices in the papers and I receive good letters about it. It is much read already, & esteemed very entertaining. Little and Brown take the risk and allow a percentage. My bargain with them is only for one edition: if this succeeds, I shall make a better. They take their own measures about circulating the work, but any effort from my friends helps, of course. Short notices by you, distributed at Phila., New York, and even Cincinnati, would attract attention & buyers!! Outward success in this way is very desirable to me, not so much on account of present profit to be derived, as because it would give me advantage in making future bargains, and offer the way to ransom more time for writing."

The text used is that found in *At Home and Abroad; or, Things and Thoughts in America and Europe,* edited by her brother, Arthur B. Fuller (Boston: Crosby, Nichols and Co., 1856). Arthur Fuller did a good job of editing in this case. His deletions, aside from verbal omissions, were: "extracts from books which she read in relation to the Indians; an account of and translation from the *Seeress of Prevorst,* a German work which had not then, but has since, been translated into English, and republished in this country; a few extracts from letters and poems sent to her by friends while she was in the West, one of which poems has since been published elsewhere by its author; and the story of Marianna (a great proportion of which may be found in my sister's *Memoirs*) and also 'Lines to Edith,' a short poem."

Summer on the Lakes

Summer days of busy leisure,
Long summer days of dear-bought pleasure,
You have done your teaching well;
Had the scholar means to tell
How grew the vine of bittersweet,
What made the path for truant feet,
Winter nights would quickly pass,
Gazing on the magic glass
O'er which the new-world shadows pass.
But, in fault of wizard spell,
Moderns their tale can only tell
In dull words, with a poor reed
Breaking at each time of need.
Yet those to whom a hint suffices
Mottoes find for all devices,
See the knights behind their shields,
Through dried grasses, blooming fields.

Some dried grass-tufts from the wide flowery field,
A muscle-shell from the lone fairy shore,
Some antlers from tall woods which never more
To the wild deer a safe retreat can yield,
An eagle's feather which adorned a brave,
Well-nigh the last of his despairing band—
For such slight gifts wilt thou extend thy hand
When weary hours a brief refreshment crave?
I give you what I can, not what I would
If my small drinking-cup would hold a flood,
As Scandinavia sung those must contain
With which the giants gods may entertain;
In our dwarf day we drain few drops, and soon must thirst again.

Chapter 1

Niagara, June 10, 1843

Since you are to share with me such footnotes as may be made on the pages of my life during this summer's wanderings, I should not be quite silent as to this magnificent prologue to the as yet unknown drama. Yet I, like others, have little to say, where the spectacle is for once great enough to fill the whole life and supersede thought, giving us only its own presence. "It is good to be here," is the best, as the simplest, expression that occurs to the mind.

We have been here eight days, and I am quite willing to go away. So great a sight soon satisfies, making us content with itself and with what is less than itself. Our desires, once realized, haunt us again less readily. Having "lived one day," we would depart, and become worthy to live another.

We have not been fortunate in weather, for there cannot be too much or too warm sunlight for this scene, and the skies have been lowering, with cold, unkind winds. My nerves, too much braced up by such an atmosphere, do not well bear the continual stress of sight and sound. For here there is no escape from the weight of a perpetual creation; all other forms and motions come and go, the tide rises and recedes, the wind, at its mightiest, moves in gales and gusts, but here is really an incessant, an indefatigable motion. Awake or asleep, there is no escape, still this rushing round you and through you. It is in this way I have most felt the grandeur—somewhat eternal, if not infinite.

At times a secondary music rises; the cataract seems to seize its own rhythm and sing it over again, so that the ear and soul are roused by a double vibration. This is some effect of the wind, causing echoes to the thundering anthem. It is very sublime, giving the effect of a spiritual repetition through all the spheres.

When I first came, I felt nothing but a quiet satisfaction. I found that drawings, the panorama, &c., had given me a clear notion of the position and proportions of all objects here; I knew where to look for everything, and everything looked as I thought it would.

Long ago, I was looking from a hillside with a friend at one of the finest sunsets that ever enriched this world. A little cowboy, trudging along, wondered what we could be gazing at. After spying about some time, he found it could only be the sunset, and looking, too, a moment, he said approvingly, "That sun looks well enough"; a speech worthy of Shakespeare's Cloten, or the infant Mercury, up to everything from the cradle, as you please to take it.

Even such a familiarity, worthy of Jonathan, our national hero, in a prince's palace, or "stumping," as he boasts to have done, "up the Vatican stairs, into the Pope's presence, in my old boots," I felt here; it looks really *well enough,* I felt, and was inclined, as you suggested, to give my approbation as to the one object in the world that would not disappoint.

But all great expression, which on a superficial survey seems so easy as well as so simple, furnishes after a while, to the faithful observer, its own standard by which to appreciate it. Daily these proportions widened and towered more and more upon my sight, and I got at last a proper foreground for these sublime distances. Before coming away, I think I really saw the full wonder of the scene. After a while it so drew me into itself as to inspire an undefined dread, such as I never knew before, such as may be felt when death is about to usher us into a new existence. The perpetual trampling of the waters seized my senses. I felt that no other sound, however near, could be heard, and would start and look behind me for a foe. I realized the identity of that mood of nature in which these waters were poured down with such absorbing force, with that in which the Indian was shaped on the same soil. For continually upon my mind came unsought and unwelcome images, such as never haunted it before, of naked savages stealing behind me with uplifted tomahawks; again and again this illusion recurred, and even after I had thought it over, and tried to shake it off, I could not help starting and looking behind me.

As picture, the falls can only be seen from the British side. There they are seen in their veils, and at sufficient distance to appreciate the magical effects of these, and the light and shade. From the boat, as you cross, the effects and contrasts are more melodramatic. On the road back from the whirlpool, we saw them as a reduced picture with delight. But what I liked best was to sit on Table Rock, close to the great fall. There all power of observing details, all separate consciousness, was quite lost.

Once, just as I had seated myself there, a man came to take his first look. He walked close up to the fall, and after looking at it a moment, with an air as if thinking how he could best appropriate it to his own use, he spat into it.

This trait seemed wholly worthy of an age whose love of *utility* is such that the Prince Pückler-Muskau suggests the probability of men coming to put the bodies of their dead parents in the fields to fertilize them, and of a country such as Dickens has described; but these will not, I hope, be seen on the historic page to be truly the age or truly the America. A little leaven is leavening the whole mass for other bread.

The whirlpool I like very much. It is seen to advantage after the great falls; it is so sternly solemn. The river cannot look more imperturbable, almost sullen in its marble green, than it does just below the great fall; but the slight circles that mark the hidden vortex seem to whisper mysteries the thundering voice above could not proclaim—a meaning as untold as ever.

It is fearful, too, to know as you look that whatever has been swallowed by the cataract is like to rise suddenly to light here, whether uprooted tree or body of man or bird.

The rapids enchanted me far beyond what I expected; they are so swift that they cease to seem so; you can think only of their beauty. The fountain beyond the Moss Islands I discovered for myself, and thought it for some time an accidental beauty which it would not do to leave, lest I might never see it again. After I found it permanent, I returned many times to watch the play of its crest. In the little waterfall beyond, Nature seems, as she often does, to have made a study for some larger design. She delights in this— a sketch within a sketch, a dream within a dream. Wherever we see it, the lines of the great buttress in the fragment of stone, the hues of the water- fall copied in the flowers that star its bordering mosses, we are delighted; for all the lineaments become fluent, and we mold the scene in con‚ nial thought with its genius.

People complain of the buildings at Niagara, and fear to see it further deformed. I cannot sympathize with such an apprehension: the spectacle is capable of swallowing up all such objects; they are not seen in the great whole, more than an earthworm in a wide field.

The beautiful wood on Goat Island is full of flowers; many of the fairest love to do homage here. The wake-robin and may-apple are in bloom now; the former, white, pink, green, purple, copying the rainbow of the fall and fit to make a garland for its presiding deity when he walks the land, for they are of imperial size and shaped like stones for a diadem. Of the may-apple, I did not raise one green tent without finding a flower beneath.

And now farewell, Niagara. I have seen thee, and I think all who come here must in some sort see thee; thou art not to be got rid of as easily as the stars. I will be here again beneath some flooding July moon and sun. Owing to the absence of light, I have seen the rainbow only two or three times by day; the lunar bow not at all. However, the imperial presence needs not its crown, though illustrated by it.

General Porter and Jack Downing were not unsuitable figures here. The former heroically planted the bridges by which we cross to Goat Island and the wake-robin-crowned genius has punished his temerity with deafness, which must, I think, have come upon him when he sank the first stone in the rapids. Jack seemed an acute and entertaining representative of Jonathan, come to look at his great water-privilege. He told us all about the Americanisms of the spectacle; that is to say, the battles that have been fought here. It seems strange that men could fight in such a place; but no temple can still the personal griefs and strifes in the breasts of its visitors.

No less strange is the fact that, in this neighborhood, an eagle should be chained for a plaything. When a child, I used often to stand at a window from which I could see an eagle chained in the balcony of a museum. The people used to poke at it with sticks, and my childish heart would swell with indignation as I saw their insults and the mien with which they were borne by the monarch-bird. Its eye was dull and its plumage soiled and shabby, yet in its form and attitude all the king was visible, though sorrowful and dethroned. I never saw another of the family till when passing through the Notch of the White Mountains, at that moment glowing before us in all the panoply of sunset, the driver shouted, "Look there!" and following with our eyes his upward-pointing finger, we saw, soaring slow in majestic poise above the highest summit, the bird of Jove. It was a glorious sight, yet I know not that I felt more on seeing the bird in all its natural freedom and royalty than when, imprisoned and insulted, he had filled my early thoughts with the Byronic "silent rages" of misanthropy.

Now again I saw him a captive, and addressed by the vulgar with the language they seem to find most appropriate to such occasions—that of thrusts and blows. Silently, his head averted, he ignored their existence, as Plotinus or Sophocles might that of a modern reviewer. Probably he listened to the voice of the cataract, and felt that congenial powers flowed free, and was consoled, though his own wing was broken.

The story of the Recluse of Niagara interested me a little. It is wonderful that men do not oftener attach their lives to localities of great beauty— that, when once deeply penetrated, they will let themselves so easily be borne away by the general stream of things, to live anywhere and anyhow. But there is something ludicrous in being the hermit of a showplace, unlike St. Francis in his mountain-bed, where none but the stars and rising sun ever saw him.

There is also a "guide to the falls," who wears his title labeled on his hat; otherwise, indeed, one might as soon think of asking for a gentleman usher to point out the moon. Yet why should we wonder at such, when we have Commentaries on Shakespeare and Harmonies of the Gospels?

And now you have the little all I have to write. Can it interest you? To one who has enjoyed the full life of any scene, of any hour, what thoughts can be recorded about it seem like the commas and semicolons in the paragraph—mere stops. Yet I suppose it is not so to the absent. At least, I have read things written about Niagara, music, and the like, that interested *me*. Once I was moved by Mr. Greenwood's remark that he could not realize this marvel till, opening his eyes the next morning after he had seen it, his doubt as to the possibility of its being still there taught him what he had experienced. I remember this now with pleasure, though, or because, it is exactly the opposite to what I myself felt. For all greatness affects different minds, each in "its own particular kind," and the variations of testimony mark the truth of feeling.*

---

* "Somewhat avails, in one regard, the mere sight of beauty without the union of feeling therewith. Carried away in memory, it hangs there in the lonely hall as a pic-

I will here add a brief narrative of the experience of another, as being much better than anything I could write, because more simple and individual.

"Now that I have left this 'Earth-wonder,' and the emotions it excited are past, it seems not so much like profanation to analyze my feelings, to recall minutely and accurately the effect of this manifestation of the Eternal. But one should go to such a scene prepared to yield entirely to its influences, to forget one's little self and one's little mind. To see a miserable worm creep to the brink of this falling world of waters, and watch the trembling of its own petty bosom, and fancy that this is made alone to act upon him excites—derision? No—pity."

As I rode up to the neighborhood of the falls, a solemn awe imperceptibly stole over me, and the deep sound of the ever-hurrying rapids prepared my mind for the lofty emotions to be experienced. When I reached the hotel, I felt a strange indifference about seeing the aspiration of my life's hopes. I lounged about the rooms, read the stage-bills upon the walls, looked over the register, and, finding the name of an acquaintance, sent to see if he was still there. What this hesitation arose from, I know not; perhaps it was a feeling of my unworthiness to enter this temple which nature has erected to its God.

At last, slowly and thoughtfully I walked down to the bridge leading to Goat Island, and when I stood upon this frail support and saw a quarter of a mile of tumbling, rushing rapids and heard their everlasting roar, my emotions overpowered me, a choking sensation rose to my throat, a thrill rushed through my veins, "my blood ran rippling to my fingers' ends." This was the climax of the effect which the falls produced upon me—neither the American nor the British fall moved me as did these rapids. For the magnificence, the sublimity of the latter, I was prepared by descriptions and by paintings. When I arrived in sight of them I merely felt, "Ah, yes! here is the fall, just as I have seen it in a picture." When I arrived at the Terrapin Bridge, I expected to be overwhelmed, to retire trembling from this giddy eminence, and gaze with unlimited wonder and awe upon the

ture, and may some time do its message. I trust it may be so in my case, for I *saw* every object far more clearly than if I had been moved and filled with the presence, and my recollections are equally distinct and vivid." Extracted from *Manuscript Notes* of this Journey left by Margaret Fuller.—A. B. F.

immense mass rolling on and on; but somehow or other I thought only of comparing the effect on my mind with what I had read and heard. I looked for a short time, and then with almost a feeling of disappointment turned to go to the other points of view, to see if I was not mistaken in not feeling any surpassing emotion at this sight. But from the foot of Biddle's Stairs and the middle of the river and from below the Table Rock, it was still "barren, barren all."

Provoked with my stupidity in feeling most moved in the wrong place, I turned away to the hotel, determined to set off for Buffalo that afternoon. But the stage did not go, and after nightfall, as there was a splendid moon, I went down to the bridge and leaned over the parapet where the boiling rapids came down in their might. It was grand and it was also gorgeous; the yellow rays of the moon made the broken waves appear like auburn tresses twining around the black rocks. But they did not inspire me as before. I felt a foreboding of a mightier emotion to rise up and swallow all others, and I passed on to the Terrapin Bridge. Everything was changed, the misty apparition had taken off its many-colored crown which it had worn by day, and a bow of silvery white spanned its summit. The moonlight gave a poetical indefiniteness to the distant parts of the waters, and while the rapids were glancing in her beams, the river below the falls was black as night, save where the reflection of the sky gave it the appearance of a shield of blued steel. No gaping tourists loitered, eying with their glasses or sketching on cards the hoary locks of the ancient river-god. All tended to harmonize with the natural grandeur of the scene. I gazed long. I saw how here mutability and unchangeableness were united. I surveyed the conspiring waters rushing against the rocky ledge to overthrow it at one mad plunge till, like toppling ambition, o'erleaping themselves, they fall on t'other side, expanding into foam ere they reach the deep channel where they creep submissively away.

Then arose in my breast a genuine admiration, and a humble adoration of the Being who was the architect of this and of all. Happy were the first discoverers of Niagara, those who could come unawares upon this view and upon that, whose feelings were entirely their own. With what gusto does Father Hennepin describe "this great downfall of water," "this vast and prodigious cadence of water, which falls down after a surprising and astonishing manner, insomuch that the universe does not afford its parallel. 'Tis true Italy and Swedeland boast of some such things, but we may well say that they be sorry patterns when compared with this of which we do now speak."

Chapter II

THE LAKES—CHICAGO—GENEVA—A THUNDERSTORM—PAPAW GROVE

SCENE: *Steamboat about to leave Buffalo. Baggage coming on board—passengers bustling for their berths—little boys persecuting everybody with their newspapers and pamphlets. J., S., and M. huddled up in a forlorn corner, behind a large trunk. A heavy rain falling.*

M. Water, water everywhere. After Niagara one would like a dry strip of existence. And at any rate it is quite enough for me to have it underfoot without having it overhead in this way.

J. Ah, do not abuse the gentle element. It is hardly possible to have too much of it, and indeed if I were obliged to choose amid the four, it would be the one in which I could bear confinement best.

S. You would make a pretty Undine, to be sure!

J. Nay, I only offered myself as a Triton, a boisterous Triton of the sounding shell. You, M., I suppose, would be a salamander, rather.

M. No! that is too equivocal a position, whether in modern mythology or Hoffmann's tales. I should choose to be a gnome.

J. That choice savors of the pride that apes humility.

M. By no means; the gnomes are the most important of all the elemental tribes. Is it not they who make the money?

J. And are accordingly a dark, mean, scoffing——

M. You talk as if you had always lived in that wild, unprofitable element you are so fond of, where all things glitter and nothing is gold; all show and no substance. My people work in the secret, and their works praise them in the open light; they remain in the dark because only there such marvels could be bred. You call them mean. They do not spend their energies on their own growth or their own play, but to feed the veins of

Mother Earth with permanent splendors, very different from what she shows on the surface.

Think of passing a life, not merely in heaping together, but *making* gold. Of all dreams, that of the alchemist is the most poetical, for he looked at the finest symbol. "Gold," says one of our friends, "is the hidden light of the earth, it crowns the mineral, as wine the vegetable order, being the last expression of vital energy."

J. Have you paid for your passage?

M. Yes! and in gold, not in shells or pebbles.

J. No really wise gnome would scoff at the water, the beautiful water. "The spirit of man is like the water."

S. And like the air and fire, no less.

J. Yes, but not like the earth, this low-minded creature's chosen dwelling.

M. The earth is spirit made fruitful—life. And its heartbeats are told in gold and wine.

J. Oh! it is shocking to hear such sentiments in these times. I thought that Bacchic energy of yours was long since repressed.

M. No! I have only learnt to mix water with my wine, and stamp upon my gold the heads of kings, or the hieroglyphics of worship. But since I have learnt to mix with water, let's hear what you have to say in praise of your favorite.

J. From water Venus was born, what more would you have? It is the mother of Beauty, the girdle of earth, and the marriage of nations.

S. Without any of that high-flown poetry, it is enough, I think, that it is the great artist, turning all objects that approach it to picture.

J. True, no object that touches it, whether it be the cart that plows the wave for seaweed, or the boat or plank that rides upon it, but is brought at once from the demesne of coarse utilities into that of picture. All trades, all callings, become picturesque by the waterside or on the water. The soil, the slovenliness, is washed out of every calling by its touch. All river-craft, sea-craft, are picturesque, are poetical. Their very slang is poetry.

M. The reasons for that are complex.

J. The reason is that there can be no plodding, groping words and motions on my water as there are on your earth. There is no time, no chance for them where all moves so rapidly, though so smoothly; everything connected with water must be like itself, forcible but clear. That is why sea-slang is so poetical; there is a word for everything and every act, and a thing and an act for every word. Seamen must speak quick and bold, but also with utmost precision. They cannot reef and brace other than in a Homeric dialect—therefore— (*Steamboat bell rings.*) But I must say a quick good-by.

M. What, going, going back to earth after all this talk upon the other side? Well, that is nowise Homeric, but truly modern.

J. is borne off without time for any reply, but a laugh—at himself, of course.

S. and M. retire to their staterooms to forget the wet, the chill, and steamboat smell, in their just-bought new world of novels.

Next day, when we stopped at Cleveland, the storm was just clearing up; ascending the bluff, we had one of the finest views of the lake that could have been wished. The varying depths of these lakes give to their surface a great variety of coloring, and beneath this wild sky and changeful light, the waters presented a kaleidoscopic variety of hues, rich but mournful. I admire these bluffs of red, crumbling earth. Here land and water meet under very different auspices from those of the rock-bound coast to which I have been accustomed. There they meet tenderly to challenge and proudly to refuse, though not in fact repel. But here they meet to mingle, are always rushing together, and changing places; a new creation takes place beneath the eye.

The weather grew gradually clearer, but not bright; yet we could see the shore and appreciate the extent of these noble waters.

Coming up the river St. Clair, we saw Indians for the first time. They were camped out on the bank. It was twilight, and their blanketed forms, in listless groups or stealing along the bank with a lounge and a stride so different in its wildness from the rudeness of the white settler, gave me the first feeling that I really approached the West.

The people on the boat were almost all New Englanders seeking their fortunes. They had brought with them their habits of calculation, their cautious manners, their love of polemics. It grieved me to hear these immigrants, who were to be the fathers of a new race, all, from the old man down to the little girl, talking not of what they should do, but of what they should get in the new scene. It was to them a prospect, not of the unfolding nobler energies, but of more ease and larger accumulation. It wearied me, too, to hear Trinity and Unity discussed in the poor, narrow, doctrinal way on these free waters; but that will soon cease; there is not time for this clash of opinions in the West, where the clash of material interests is so noisy. They will need the spirit of religion more than ever to guide them, but will find less time than before for its doctrine. This change was to me, who am tired of the war of words on these subjects and believe it only sows the wind to reap the whirlwind, refreshing, but I argue nothing from it; there is nothing real in the freedom of thought at the West—it is from the position of men's lives, not the state of their minds. So soon as they have time, unless they grow better meanwhile, they will cavil and criticize, and judge other men by their own standard, and outrage the law of love every way, just as they do with us.

We reached Mackinaw the evening of the third day, but to my great disappointment it was too late and too rainy to go ashore. The beauty of the island, though seen under the most unfavorable circumstances, did not disappoint my expectations.* But I shall see it to more purpose on my return.

As the day has passed dully, a cold rain preventing us from keeping out in the air, my thoughts have been dwelling on a story told when we were off Detroit this morning by a fellow-passenger, whose moral beauty touched me profoundly.

"Some years ago," said Mrs. L., "my father and mother stopped to dine at Detroit. A short time before dinner my father met in the hall Captain P., a friend of his youthful days. He had loved P. extremely, as did many who knew him, and had not been surprised to hear of the distinction and popular esteem which his wide knowledge, talents, and noble temper commanded,

---

* "Mackinaw, that long desired sight, was dimly discerned under a thick fog, yet it soothed and cheered me. All looked mellow there; man seemed to have worked in harmony with Nature instead of rudely invading her, as in most Western towns. It seemed possible, on that spot, to lead a life of serenity and cheerfulness. Some richly dressed Indians came down to show themselves. Their dresses were of blue broadcloth, with splendid leggings and knee-ties. On their heads were crimson scarfs adorned with beads and falling on one shoulder; their hair long and looking cleanly. Near were one or two wild figures clad in the common white blankets."—*Manuscript Notes.* —A. B. F.

as he went onward in the world. P. was every way fitted to succeed; his aims were high, but not too high for his powers, suggested by an instinct of his own capacities, not by an ideal standard drawn from culture. Though steadfast in his course, it was not to overrun others; his wise self-possession was no less for them than himself. He was thoroughly the gentleman, gentle because manly, and was a striking instance that, where there is strength for sincere courtesy, there is no need of other adaptation to the character of others, to make one's way freely and gracefully through the crowd.

"My father was delighted to see him, and after a short parley in the hall, 'We will dine together,' he cried, 'then we shall have time to tell all our stories.'

"P. hesitated a moment, then said, 'My wife is with me.'

"'And mine with me,' said my father; 'that's well; they, too, will have an opportunity of getting acquainted, and can entertain one another, if they get tired of our college stories.'

"P. acquiesced with a grave bow, and shortly after they all met in the dining-room. My father was much surprised at the appearance of Mrs. P. He had heard that his friend married abroad, but nothing further, and he was not prepared to see the calm, dignified P. with a woman on his arm, still handsome indeed, but whose coarse and imperious expression showed as low habits of mind as her exaggerated dress and gesture did of education. Nor could there be a greater contrast to my mother, who, though understanding her claims and place with the certainty of a lady, was soft and retiring in an uncommon degree.

"However, there was no time to wonder or fancy; they sat down, and P. engaged in conversation, without much vivacity but with his usual ease. The first quarter of an hour passed well enough. But soon it was observable that Mrs. P. was drinking glass after glass of wine, to an extent few gentlemen did even then, and soon that she was actually excited by it. Before this, her manner had been brusque, if not contemptuous, toward her new acquaintance; now it became, toward my mother especially, quite rude. Presently she took up some slight remark made by my mother, which, though it did not naturally mean anything of the sort, could be twisted into some reflection upon England, and made it a handle first of vulgar sarcasm, and then, upon my mother's defending herself with some surprise and gentle dignity, hurled upon her a volley of abuse beyond billingsgate.

"My mother, confounded by scenes and ideas presented to her mind equally new and painful, sat trembling; she knew not what to do; tears rushed into her eyes. My father, no less distressed, yet unwilling to outrage the feelings of his friend by doing or saying what his indignation prompted, turned an appealing look on P.

"Never, as he often said, was the painful expression of that sight effaced from his mind. It haunted his dreams and disturbed his waking thoughts. P. sat with his head bent forward, and his eyes cast down, pale but calm, with a fixed expression not merely of patient woe but of patient shame, which it would not have been thought possible for that noble countenance to wear. 'Yet,' said my father, 'it became him. At other times he was handsome, but then beautiful, though of a beauty saddened and abashed. For a spiritual light borrowed from the worldly perfection of his mien that illustration by contrast, which the penitence of the Magdalen does from the glowing earthliness of her charms.'

"Seeing that he preserved silence, while Mrs. P. grew still more exasperated, my father rose and led his wife to her own room. Half an hour had passed, in painful and wondering surmises, when a gentle knock was heard at the door, and P. entered equipped for a journey. 'We are just going,' he said, and holding out his hand, but without looking at them, 'Forgive.'

"They each took his hand, and silently pressed it; then he went without a word more.

"Some time passed, and they heard now and then of P., as he passed from one army station to another with his uncongenial companion, who became, it was said, constantly more degraded. Whoever mentioned having seen them wondered at the chance which had yoked him to such a woman, but yet more at the silent fortitude with which he bore it. Many blamed him for enduring it, apparently without efforts to check her; others answered that he had probably made such at an earlier period, and finding them unavailing, had resigned himself to despair, and was too delicate to meet the scandal that, with such resistance as such a woman could offer, must attend a formal separation.

"But my father, who was not in such haste to come to conclusions and substitute some plausible explanation for the truth, found something in the look of P. at that trying moment to which none of these explanations offered a key. There was in it, he felt, a fortitude, but not the fortitude of the hero; a religious submission above the penitent, if not enkindled with the enthusiasm of the martyr.

"I have said that my father was not one of those who are ready to substitute specious explanations for truth, and those who are thus abstinent rarely lay their hand on a thread without making it a clew. Such a man, like the dexterous weaver, lets not one color go till he finds that which matches it in the pattern—he keeps on weaving but chooses his shades; and my father found at last what he wanted to make out the pattern for himself. He met a lady who had been intimate with both himself and P. in early days, and finding she had seen the latter abroad, asked if she knew the circumstances of the marriage.

" 'The circumstances of the act which sealed the misery of our friend, I know,' she said, 'though as much in the dark as anyone about the motives that led to it.

" 'We were quite intimate with P. in London, and he was our most delightful companion. He was then in the full flower of the varied accomplishments which set off his fine manners and dignified character, joined, towards those he loved, with a certain soft willingness which gives the desirable chivalry to a man. None was more clear of choice where his personal affections were not touched, but where they were, it cost him pain to say no, on the slightest occasion. I have thought this must have had some connection with the mystery of his misfortunes.

" 'One day he called on me, and without any preface asked if I would be present next day at his marriage. I was so surprised, and so unpleasantly surprised, that I did not at first answer a word. We had been on terms so familiar that I thought I knew all about him, yet had never dreamed of his having an attachment; and though I had never inquired on the subject, yet this reserve where perfect openness had been supposed, and really on my side existed, seemed to me a kind of treachery. Then it is never pleasant to know that a heart on which we have some claim is to be given to another. We cannot tell how it will affect our own relations with a person; it may strengthen or it may swallow up other affections; the crisis is hazardous, and our first thought on such an occasion is too often for ourselves—

at least mine was. Seeing me silent, he repeated his question. "To whom," said I, "are you to be married?" "That," he replied, "I cannot tell you." He was a moment silent, then continued with an impassive look of cold self-possession that affected me with strange sadness: "The name of the person you will hear, of course, at the time, but more I cannot tell you. I need, however, the presence not only of legal but of respectable and friendly witnesses. I have hoped you and your husband would do me this kindness. Will you?" Something in his manner made it impossible to refuse. I answered before I knew I was going to speak, "We will," and he left me.

" 'I will not weary you with telling how I harassed myself and my husband, who was, however, scarce less interested, with doubts and conjectures. Suffice it that next morning P. came and took us in a carriage to a distant church. We had just entered the porch when a cart, such as fruit and vegetables are brought to market in, drove up, containing an elderly woman and a young girl. P. assisted them to alight, and advanced with the girl to the altar.

" 'The girl was neatly dressed and quite handsome, yet something in her expression displeased me the moment I looked upon her. Meanwhile the ceremony was going on, and at its close P. introduced us to the bride, and we all went to the door. "Good-by, Fanny," said the elderly woman. The new-made Mrs. P. replied without any token of affection or emotion. The woman got into the cart and drove away.

" 'From that time I saw but little of P. or his wife. I took our mutual friends to see her, and they were civil to her for his sake. Curiosity was very much excited, but entirely baffled; no one, of course, dared speak to P. on the subject, and no other means could be found of solving the riddle.

" 'He treated his wife with grave and kind politeness, but it was always obvious that they had nothing in common between them. Her manners and tastes were not at that time gross, but her character showed itself hard and material. She was fond of riding, and spent much time so. Her style in this, and in dress, seemed the opposite of P.'s; but he indulged all her wishes, while for himself he plunged into his own pursuits.

" 'For a time he seemed, if not happy, not positively unhappy; but after a few years Mrs. P. fell into the habit of drinking, and then such scenes as you witnessed grew frequent. I have often heard of them, and always that

P. sat as you describe him, his head bowed down and perfectly silent all through, whatever might be done or whoever be present, and always his aspect has inspired such sympathy that no person has questioned him or resented her insults, but merely got out of the way as soon as possible.'

" 'Hard and long penance,' said my father, after some minutes' musing, 'for an hour of passion, probably for his only error.'

" 'Is that your explanation?' said the lady. 'Oh, improbable! P. might err, but not be led beyond himself.'

"I know that his cool, gray eye and calm complexion seemed to say so, but a different story is told by the lip that could tremble, and showed what flashes might pierce those deep blue heavens; and when these over-intellectual beings do swerve aside, it is to fall down a precipice, for their narrow path lies over such. But he was not one to sin without making a brave atonement, and that it had become a holy one was written on that downcast brow."

The fourth day on these waters, the weather was milder and brighter, so that we could now see them to some purpose. At night the moon was clear, and for the first time from the upper deck I saw one of the great steamboats come majestically up. It was glowing with lights, looking many-eyed and sagacious; in its heavy motion it seemed a dowager queen, and this motion, with its solemn pulse and determined sweep, becomes these smooth waters, especially at night, as much as the dip of the sail-ship the long billows of the ocean.

But it was not so soon that I learned to appreciate the lake scenery; it was only after a daily and careless familiarity that I entered into its beauty, for Nature always refuses to be seen by being stared at. Like Bonaparte, she discharges her face of all expression when she catches the eye of impertinent curiosity fixed on her. But he who has gone to sleep in childish ease on her lap, or leaned an aching brow upon her breast, seeking there comfort with full trust as from a mother, will see all a mother's beauty in the look she bends upon him. Later I felt that I had really seen these regions, and shall speak of them again.

In the afternoon we went on shore at the Manitou Islands, where the boat stops to wood. No one lives here except woodcutters for the steamboats. I had thought of such a position, from its mixture of profound solitude with service to the great world, as possessing an ideal beauty. I think so still, even after seeing the woodcutters and their slovenly huts.

In times of slower growth man did not enter a situation without a certain preparation or adaptedness to it. He drew from it, if not to the poetical extent at least in some proportion, its moral and its meaning. The woodcutter did not cut down so many trees a day that the Hamadryads had not time to make their plaints heard; the shepherd tended his sheep, and did no jobs or chores the while; the idyl had a chance to grow up, and modulate his oaten pipe. But now the poet must be at the whole expense of the poetry in describing one of these positions; the worker is a true Midas to the gold he makes. The poet must describe as the painter sketches Irish peasant girls and Danish fishwives, adding the beauty and leaving out the dirt.

I come to the West prepared for the distaste I must experience at its mushroom growth. I know that where "go ahead" is the only motto, the village cannot grow into the gentle proportions that successive lives and the gradations of experience involuntarily give. In older countries the house of the son grew from that of the father, as naturally as new joints on a bough, and the cathedral crowned the whole as naturally as the leafy summit the tree. This cannot be here. The march of peaceful is scarce less wanton than that of warlike invasion. The old landmarks are broken down, and the land for a season bears none, except of the rudeness of conquest and the needs of the day, whose bivouac-fires blacken the sweetest forest glades. I have come prepared to see all this, to dislike it, but not with stupid narrowness to distrust or defame. On the contrary, while I will not be so obliging as to confound ugliness with beauty, discord with harmony, and laud and be contented with all I meet, when it conflicts with my best desires and tastes, I trust by reverent faith to woo the mighty meaning of the scene, perhaps to foresee the law by which a new order, a new poetry, is to be evoked from this chaos, and with a curiosity as ardent but not so selfish as that of Macbeth, to call up the apparitions of future kings from the strange ingredients of the witch's caldron. Thus I will not grieve that all the noble trees are gone already from this island to feed this caldron, but believe it will have Medea's virtue and reproduce them in the form of new intellectual growths, since centuries cannot again adorn the land with such as have been removed.

On this most beautiful beach of smooth white pebbles, interspersed with agates and carnelians for those who know how to find them, we stepped, not like the Indian with some humble offering which, if no better than an arrow-head or a little parched corn, would, he judged, please the Manitou who looks only at the spirit in which it is offered. Our visit was so far for a religious purpose that one of our party went to inquire the fate of some Unitarian tracts left among the woodcutters a year or two before. But the old Manitou, though daunted like his children by the approach of the fire-ships, which he probably considered demons of a new dynasty, he had suffered his woods to be felled to feed their pride, had been less patient of an encroachment which did not to him seem so authorized by the law of the strongest, and had scattered those leaves as carelessly as the others of that year.

But S. and I, like other emigrants, went not to give but to get, to rifle the wood of flowers for the service of the fire-ship. We returned with a rich booty, among which was the *Uva-ursi,* whose leaves the Indians smoke with the *Kinnikinnik,* and which had then just put forth its highly finished little blossoms, as pretty as those of the blueberry.

Passing along still farther, I thought it would be well if the crowds assembled to stare from the various landings were still confined to the *Kinnikinnik,* for almost all had tobacco written on their faces, their cheeks rounded with plugs, their eyes dull with its fumes. We reached Chicago on the evening of the sixth day, having been out five days and a half, a rather longer passage than usual at a favorable season of the year.

Chicago, June 20

There can be no two places in the world more completely thoroughfares than this place and Buffalo. They are the two correspondent valves that open and shut all the time, as the life-blood rushes from east to west and back again from west to east.

Since it is their office thus to be the doors and let in and out, it would be unfair to expect from them much character of their own. To make the best provisions for the transmission of produce is their office, and the people who live there are such as are suited for this—active, complaisant, inventive, business people. There are no provisions for the student or idler; to know what the place can give, you should be at work with the rest; the mere traveler will not find it profitable to loiter there as I did.

Since circumstances made it necessary for me so to do, I read all the books I could find about the new region, which now began to become real to me. Especially I read all the books about the Indians—a paltry collection truly, yet which furnished material for many thoughts. The most narrow-minded and awkward recital still bears some lineaments of the great features of this nature, and the races of men that illustrated them.

Catlin's book is far the best. I was afterwards assured by those acquainted with the regions he describes, that he is not to be depended on for the accuracy of his facts, and indeed it is obvious without the aid of such assertions that he sometimes yields to the temptation of making out a story. They admitted, however, what from my feelings I was sure of, that he is true to the spirit of the scene, and that a far better view can be got from him than from any source at present existing, of the Indian tribes of the Far West and of the country where their inheritance lay.

Murray's *Travels* I read, and was charmed by their accuracy and clear, broad tone. He is the only Englishman that seems to have traversed these regions as man simply, not as John Bull. He deserves to belong to an aristocracy, for he showed his title to it more when left without a guide in the wilderness than he can at the court of Victoria. He has himself no poetic force at description, but it is easy to make images from his hints. Yet we believe the Indian cannot be looked at truly except by a poetic eye. The Pawnees no doubt are such as he describes them, filthy in their habits and treacherous in their character, but some would have seen, and seen truly, more beauty and dignity than he does with all his manliness and fairness of mind. However, his one fine old man is enough to redeem the rest, and is perhaps the relic of a better day, a Phocion among the Pawnees.

Schoolcraft's *Algic Researches* is a valuable book, though a worse use could hardly have been made of such fine material. Had the mythological or hunting stories of the Indians been written down exactly as they were received from the lips of the narrators, the collection could not have been surpassed in interest, both for the wild charm they carry with them and the light they throw on a peculiar modification of life and mind. As it is, though the incidents have an air of originality and pertinence to the occasion that gives us confidence that they have not been altered, the phraseology in which they were expressed has been entirely set aside, and the flimsy graces common to the style of annuals and souvenirs substituted for the Spartan brevity and sinewy grasp of Indian speech. We can just guess what might have been there, as we can detect the fine proportions of the brave whom the bad taste of some white patron has arranged in frockcoat, hat, and pantaloons.

The few stories Mrs. Jameson wrote out, though to these also a sentimental air has been given, offend much less in that way than is common in this book. What would we not give for a completely faithful version of some among them! Yet with all these drawbacks we cannot doubt from internal evidence that they truly ascribe to the Indian a delicacy of sentiment and of fancy that justifies Cooper in such inventions as his Uncas. It is a white man's view of a savage hero, who would be far finer in his natural proportions; still, through a masquerade figure, it implies the truth.

Irving's books I also read, some for the first, some for the second time, with increased interest now that I was to meet such people as he received his materials from. Though the books are pleasing from their grace and luminous arrangement, yet with the exception of the *Tour to the Prairies* they have a stereotype, secondhand air. They lack the breath, the glow, the charming minute traits of living presence. His scenery is only fit to be glanced at from dioramic distance; his Indians are academic figures only. He would have made the best of pictures, if he could have used his own eyes for studies and sketches; as it is, his success is wonderful but inadequate.

McKenney's *Tour to the Lakes* is the dullest of books, yet faithful and quiet, and gives some facts not to be met with everywhere.

I also read a collection of Indian anecdotes and speeches, the worst compiled and arranged book possible, yet not without clues of some value. All these books I read in anticipation of a canoe-voyage on Lake Superior as far as the Pictured Rocks, and though I was afterwards compelled to give up this project, they aided me in judging of what I subsequently saw and heard of the Indians.

In Chicago I first saw the beautiful prairie-flowers. They were in their glory the first ten days we were there:

The golden and the flame-like flowers.

The flame-like flower I was taught afterwards by an Indian girl to call *Wickapee;* and she told me, too, that its splendors had a useful side, for it was used by the Indians as a remedy for an illness to which they were subject.

Beside these brilliant flowers, which gemmed and gilt the grass in a sunny afternoon's drive near the blue lake between the low oak wood and the narrow beach, stimulated, whether sensuously by the optic nerve un-used to so much gold and crimson with such tender green, or symbolically through some meaning dimly seen in the flowers, I enjoyed a sort of fairy-land exultation never felt before, and the first drive amid the flowers gave me anticipation of the beauty of the prairies.

At first the prairie seemed to speak of the very desolation of dullness. After sweeping over the vast monotony of the lakes to come to this monotony of land, with all around a limitless horizon—to walk, and walk, and run, but never climb, oh! it was too dreary for any but a Hollander to bear. How the eye greeted the approach of a sail or the smoke of a steamboat; it seemed that anything so animated must come from a better land, where mountains gave religion to the scene.

The only thing I liked at first to do was to trace with slow and unexpect-ing step the narrow margin of the lake. Sometimes a heavy swell gave it expression; at others, only its varied coloring, which I found more admirable every day and which gave it an air of mirage instead of the vastness of ocean. Then there was a grandeur in the feeling that I might continue that walk, if I had any seven-leagued mode of conveyance to save fatigue, for hundreds of miles without an obstacle and without a change.

But after I had ridden out and seen the flowers, and observed the sun-set with that calmness seen only in the prairies, and the cattle winding slowly to their homes in the "island groves"—most peaceful of sights—I began to love because I began to know the scene, and shrank no longer from "the encircling vastness."

It is always thus with the new form of life; we must learn to look at it by its own standard. At first, no doubt, my accustomed eye kept saying, if the mind did not, "What! no distant mountains? What! no valleys?" But after a while I would ascend the roof of the house where we lived and pass many hours, needing no sight but the moon reigning in the heavens or starlight falling upon the lake, till all the lights were out in the island grove of men beneath my feet, and felt nearer heaven that there was nothing but this lovely, still reception on the earth; no towering mountains, no deep tree-shadows, nothing but plain earth and water bathed in light.

Sunset, as seen from that place, presented most generally low-lying, flaky clouds of the softest serenity.

One night a star "shot madly from its sphere," and it had a fair chance to be seen, but that serenity could not be astonished.

Yes! it was a peculiar beauty, that of those sunsets and moonlights on the levels of Chicago, which Chamonix or the Trossachs could not make me forget.*

Notwithstanding all the attractions I thus found out by degrees on the flat shores of the lake, I was delighted when I found myself really on my way into the country for an excursion of two or three weeks. We set forth in a strong wagon, almost as large and with the look of those used elsewhere for transporting caravans of wild beasts, loaded with everything we might want, in case nobody would give it to us—for buying and selling were no longer to be counted on—with a pair of strong horses, able and willing to force their way through mud-holes and amid stumps, and a guide equally admirable as marshal and companion, who knew by heart the country and its history, both natural and artificial, and whose clear hunter's eye needed neither road nor goal to guide it to all the spots where beauty best loves to dwell.

Add to this the finest weather, and such country as I had never seen even in my dreams, although these dreams had been haunted by wishes for just such a one, and you may judge whether years of dullness might not by

---

* "From the prairie near Chicago had I seen, some days before, the sun set with that calmness observed only on the prairies. I know not what it says, but something quite different from sunset at sea. There is no motion except of waving grasses—the cattle move slowly homeward in the distance. That *home!* where is it? It seems as if there was no home, and no need of one, and there is room enough to wander on forever."—*Manuscript Notes.*—A. B. F.

these bright days be redeemed, and a sweetness be shed over all thoughts of the West.

The first day brought us through woods rich in the moccasin flower and lupine, and plains whose soft expanse was continually touched with expression by the slow moving clouds which:

> Sweep over with their shadows, and beneath
> The surface rolls and fluctuates to the eye;
> Dark hollows seem to glide along and chase
> The sunny ridges,

to the banks of the Fox River, a sweet and graceful stream. We reached Geneva just in time to escape being drenched by a violent thundershower, whose rise and disappearance threw expression into all the features of the scene.

Geneva reminds me of a New England village, as indeed there and in the neighborhood are many New Englanders of an excellent stamp, generous, intelligent, discreet, and seeking to win from life its true values. Such are much wanted, and seem like points of light among the swarms of settlers, whose aims are sordid, whose habits thoughtless and slovenly.*

With great pleasure we heard, with his attentive and affectionate congregation, the Unitarian clergyman Mr. Conant, and afterward visited him in his house, where almost everything bore traces of his own handiwork or that of his father. He is just such a teacher as it wanted in this region, familiar enough with the habits of those he addresses to come home to their experience and their wants; earnest and enlightened enough to draw the important inferences from the life of every day.†

---

* "We passed a portion of one day with Mr. and Mrs. ——, young, healthy, and, thank Heaven, *gay* people. In the general dullness that broods over this land where so little genius flows, and care, business, and fashionable frivolity are equally dull, unspeakable is the relief of some flashes of vivacity, some sparkles of wit. Of course it is hard enough for those most natively disposed that way to strike fire. I would willingly be the tinder to promote the cheering blaze."—*Manuscript Notes.*—A. B. F.

† "Let any who think men do not need or want the church, hear these people talk about it as if it were the only indispensable thing, and see what I saw in Chicago. An elderly lady from Philadelphia, who had been visiting her sons in the West, arrived there about one o'clock on a hot Sunday noon. She rang the bell and requested a room immediately, as she wanted to get ready for afternoon service. Some delay occurring, she expressed great regret, as she had ridden all night for the sake of attending church. She went to church, neither having dined nor taken any repose after her journey."— *Manuscript Notes.*—A. B. F.

A day or two we remained here, and passed some happy hours in the woods that fringe the stream, where the gentlemen found a rich booty of fish.

Next day, traveling along the river's banks was an uninterrupted pleasure. We closed our drive in the afternoon at the house of an English gentleman who has gratified, as few men do, the common wish to pass the evening of an active day amid the quiet influences of country life. He showed us a bookcase filled with books about this country; these he had collected for years, and become so familiar with the localities that, on coming here at last, he sought and found at once the very spot he wanted, and where he is as content as he hoped to be, thus realizing Wordsworth's description of the wise man who "sees what he foresaw."

A wood surrounds the house, through which paths are cut in every direction. It is for this new country a large and handsome dwelling; but round it are its barns and farmyard, with cattle and poultry. These, however, in the framework of wood have a very picturesque and pleasing effect. There is that mixture of culture and rudeness in the aspect of things which gives a feeling of freedom, not of confusion.

I wish it were possible to give some idea of this scene as viewed by the earliest freshness of dewy dawn. This habitation of man seemed like a nest in the grass, so thoroughly were the buildings and all the objects of human care harmonized with what was natural. The tall trees bent and whispered all around, as if to hail with sheltering love the men who had come to dwell among them.

The young ladies were musicians, and spoke French fluently, having been educated in a convent. Here in the prairie they had learned to take care of the milk-room, and kill the rattlesnakes that assailed their poultry-yard. Beneath the shade of heavy curtains you looked out from the high and large windows to see Norwegian peasants at work in their national dress. In the wood grew not only the flowers I had before seen, and wealth of tall, wild roses, but the splendid blue spiderwort, that ornament of our gardens. Beautiful children strayed there, who were soon to leave these civilized regions for some really wild and Western place, a post in the buffalo country. Their no less beautiful mother was of Welsh descent, and the eldest child bore the name of Gwynthleon. Perhaps there she will meet some young descendants of Madoc to be her friends; at any rate her looks may retain that sweet, wild beauty that is soon made to vanish from eyes which look too much on shops and streets and the vulgarities of city "parties."

Next day we crossed the river. We ladies crossed on a little footbridge, from which we could look down the stream and see the wagon pass over at the ford. A black thundercloud was coming up; the sky and waters heavy with expectation. The motion of the wagon with its white cover and the laboring horses gave just the due interest to the picture, because it seemed as if they would not have time to cross before the storm came on. However, they did get across, and we were a mile or two on our way before the violent shower obliged us to take refuge in a solitary house upon the prairie. In this country it is as pleasant to stop as to go on, to lose your way as to find it, for the variety in the population gives you a chance for fresh entertainment in every hut, and the luxuriant beauty makes every path attractive. In this house we found a family "quite above the common," but I grieve to say not above false pride, for the father, ashamed of being caught barefoot, told us a story of a man, one of the richest men, he said, in one of the Eastern cities, who went barefoot from choice and taste.

Near the door grew a Provence rose, then in blossom. Other families we saw had brought with them and planted the locust. It was pleasant to see their old home loves, brought into connection with their new splendors. Wherever there were traces of this tenderness of feeling, only too rare among Americans, other things bore signs also of prosperity and intelligence, as if the ordering mind of man had some idea of home beyond a mere shelter beneath which to eat and sleep.

No heaven need wear a lovelier aspect than earth did this afternoon after the clearing up of the shower. We traversed the blooming plain, unmarked by any road, only the friendly track of wheels which bent, not broke, the grass. Our stages were not from town to town, but from grove to grove. These groves first floated like blue islands in the distance. As we drew nearer, they seemed fair parks, and the little log-houses on the edge with their curling smokes harmonized beautifully with them.

One of these groves, Ross's Grove, we reached just at sunset. It was of the noblest trees I saw during this journey, for generally the trees were not

large or lofty, but only of fair proportions. Here they were large enough
to form with their clear stems pillars for grand cathedral aisles. There was
space enough for crimson light to stream through upon the floor of water
which the shower had left. As we slowly plashed through, I thought I
was never in a better place for vespers.

That night we rested, or rather tarried, at a grove some miles beyond,
and there partook of the miseries so often jocosely portrayed of bedcham-
bers for twelve, a milk dish for universal handbasin, and expectations that
you would use and lend your "hankercher" for a towel. But this was the
only night, thanks to the hospitality of private families, that we passed
thus; and it was well that we had this bit of experience, else might we
have pronounced all Trollopean records of the kind to be inventions of
pure malice.

With us was a young lady who showed herself to have been bathed in the
Britannic fluid wittily described by a late French writer, by the impossibility
she experienced of accommodating herself to the indecorums of the scene.
We ladies were to sleep in the barroom, from which its drinking visitors
could be ejected only at a late hour. The outer door had no fastening
to prevent their return. However, our host kindly requested we would
call him if they did, as he had "conquered them for us" and would do
so again. We had also rather hard couches (mine was the supper-table);
but we Yankees, born to rove, were altogether too much fatigued to stand
upon trifles, and slept as sweetly as we would in the "bigly bower" of any
baroness. But I think England sat up all night, wrapped in her blanket-
shawl, and with a neat lace cap upon her head—so that she would have
looked perfectly the lady, if anyone had come in—shuddering and listening. I know that she was very ill next day in requital. She watched, as her
parent country watches the seas, that nobody may do wrong in any case,
and deserved to have met some interruption, she was so well prepared.
However, there was none, other than from the nearness of some twenty
sets of powerful lungs, which would not leave the night to a deathly stillness. In this house we had, if not good beds, yet good tea, good bread, and
wild strawberries, and were entertained with most free communications of
opinion and history from our hosts. Neither shall any of us have a right
to say again that we cannot find any who may be willing to hear all we

may have to say. "A's fish that comes to the net," should be painted on the sign at Papaw Grove.

Chapter III

In the afternoon of this day we reached the Rock River, in whose neighborhood we proposed to make some stay, and crossed at Dixon's Ferry.

This beautiful stream flows full and wide over a bed of rocks, traversing a distance of near two hundred miles, to reach the Mississippi. Great part of the country along its banks is the finest region of Illinois, and the scene of some of the latest romance of Indian warfare. To these beautiful regions Black Hawk returned with his band "to pass the summer," when he drew upon himself the warfare in which he was finally vanquished. No wonder he could not resist the longing, unwise though its indulgence might be, to return in summer to this home of beauty.

Of Illinois in general it has often been remarked that it bears the character of country which has been inhabited by a nation skilled like the English in all the ornamental arts of life, especially in landscape-gardening. The villas and castles seem to have been burnt, the enclosures taken down, but the velvet lawns, the flower-gardens, the stately parks, scattered at graceful intervals by the decorous hand of art, the frequent deer, and the peaceful herd of cattle that make picture of the plain, all suggest more of the masterly mind of man than the prodigal but careless motherly love of Nature. Especially is this true of the Rock River country. The river flows sometimes through these parks and lawns, then betwixt high bluffs, whose grassy ridges are covered with fine trees or broken with crumbling stone that easily assumes the forms of buttress, arch, and clustered columns. Along the face of such crumbling rocks, swallows' nests are clustered thick as cities, and eagles and deer do not disdain their summits. One morning, out in the boat along the base of these rocks, it was amusing, and affecting too, to see these swallows put their heads out to look at us. There was something very hospitable about it, as if man had never shown himself a tyrant near them. What a morning that was! Every sight is worth twice as much by the early morning light. We borrow something of the spirit of the hour to look upon them.

The first place where we stopped was one of singular beauty, a beauty of soft, luxuriant wildness. It was on the bend of the river, a place chosen by an Irish gentleman whose absenteeship seems of the wisest kind, since, for a sum which would have been but a drop of water to the thirsty fever of his native land, he commands a residence which has all that is desirable in its independence, its beautiful retirement, and means of benefit to others.

His park, his deer-chase, he found already prepared; he had only to make an avenue through it. This brought us to the house by a drive which in the heat of noon seemed long, though afterwards in the cool of morning and evening delightful. This is for that part of the world a large and commodious dwelling. Near it stands the log-cabin where its master lived while it was building, a very ornamental accessory.

In front of the house was a lawn adorned by the most graceful trees. A few of these had been taken out to give a full view of the river, gliding through banks such as I have described. On this bend the bank is high and bold, so from the house or the lawn the view was very rich and commanding. But if you descended a ravine at the side to the water's edge, you found there a long walk on the narrow shore, with a wall above of the richest hanging wood in which they said the deer lay hid. I never saw one, but often fancied that I heard them rustling at daybreak by these bright clear waters, stretching out in such smiling promise where no sound broke the deep and blissful seclusion, unless now and then this rustling or the splash of some fish a little gayer than the others; it seemed not necessary to have any better heaven or fuller expression of love and freedom than in the mood of Nature here.

Then leaving the bank, you would walk far and yet farther through long, grassy paths, full of the most brilliant, also the most delicate flowers. The brilliant are more common on the prairie, but both kinds loved this place.

Amid the grass of the lawn, with a profusion of wild strawberries, we greeted also a familiar love, the Scottish harebell, the gentlest and most touching form of the flower world.

The master of the house was absent, but with a kindness beyond thanks had offered us a resting-place there. Here we were taken care of by a deputy, who would for his youth have been assigned the place of a page in former times, but in the young West, it seems, he was old enough for a steward. Whatever be called his function, he did the honors of the place so much in harmony with it as to leave the guests free to imagine themselves in Elysium. And the three days passed here were days of unalloyed, spotless happiness.

There was a peculiar charm in coming here where the choice of location, and the unobtrusive good taste of all the arrangements, showed such intelligent appreciation of the spirit of the scene, after seeing so many dwellings of the new settlers which showed plainly that they had no thought beyond satisfying the grossest material wants. Sometimes they looked attractive, these little brown houses, the natural architecture of the country, in the edge of the timber. But almost always when you came near, the slovenliness of the dwelling and the rude way in which objects around it were treated, when so little care would have presented a charming whole, were very repulsive. Seeing the traces of the Indians, who chose the most beautiful sites for their dwellings and whose habits do not break in on that aspect of Nature under which they were born, we feel as if they were the rightful lords of a beauty they forbore to deform. But most of these settlers do not see it at all; it breathes, it speaks in vain to those who are rushing into its sphere. Their progress is Gothic not Roman, and their mode of cultivation will in the course of twenty, perhaps ten years, obliterate the natural expression of the country.

This is inevitable, fatal; we must not complain, but look forward to a good result. Still in traveling through this country, I could not but be struck with the force of a symbol. Wherever the hog comes, the rattlesnake disappears; the omnivorous traveler, safe in its stupidity, willingly and easily makes a meal of the most dangerous of reptiles and one which the Indian looks on with a mystic awe. Even so the white settler pursues the Indian and is victor in the chase. But I shall say more upon the subject by and by.

While we were here, we had one grand thunderstorm which added new glory to the scene.

One beautiful feature was the return of the pigeons every afternoon to their home. At this time they would come sweeping across the lawn, positively in clouds, and with a swiftness and softness of winged motion more beautiful than anything of the kind I ever knew. Had I been a musician such as Mendelssohn, I felt that I could have improvised a music quite peculiar from the sound they made, which should have indicated all the beauty over which their wings bore them. I will here insert a few lines left at this house on parting, which feebly indicate some of the features.

THE WESTERN EDEN

Familiar to the childish mind were tales
  Of rock-girt isles amid a desert sea,
Where unexpected stretch the flowery vales
  To soothe the shipwrecked sailor's misery.
Fainting, he lay upon a sandy shore,
And fancied that all hope of life was o'er;
But let him patient climb the frowning wall,
Within, the orange glows beneath the palm-tree tall,
And all that Eden boasted waits his call.

Almost these tales seem realized today,
When the long dullness of the sultry way,
Where "independent" settlers' careless cheer
Made us indeed feel we were "strangers" here,
Is cheered by sudden sight of this fair spot,
On which "improvement" yet has made no blot,
But Nature all-astonished stands, to find
Her plan protected by the human mind.

Blest be the kindly genius of the scene;
  The river, bending in unbroken grace,
The stately thickets, with their pathways green,
  Fair, lonely trees, each in its fittest place;
Those thickets haunted by the deer and fawn;
Those cloudlike flights of birds across the lawn!
The gentlest breezes here delight to blow,
And sun and shower and star are emulous to deck the show.

Wondering, as Crusoe, we survey the land;
Happier than Crusoe we, a friendly band.
Blest be the hand that reared this friendly home,
The heart and mind of him to whom we owe
Hours of pure peace such as few mortals know;

May he find such, should he be led to roam—
Be tended by such ministering sprites—
Enjoy such gaily childish days, such hopeful nights!
And yet, amid the goods to mortals given,
To give those goods again is most like heaven.

Hazelwood, Rock River, June 30, 1843

The only really rustic feature was of the many coops of poultry near the house, which I understood it to be one of the chief pleasures of the master to feed.

Leaving this place, we proceeded a day's journey along the beautiful stream to a little town named Oregon. We called at a cabin from whose door looked out one of those faces which, once seen, are never forgotten; young, yet touched with many traces of feeling not only possible but endured; spirited, too, like the gleam of a finely tempered blade. It was a face that suggested a history and many histories, but whose scene would have been in courts and camps. At this moment their circles are dull for want of that life which is waning unexcited in this solitary recess.

The master of the house proposed to show us a "short cut," by which we might to especial advantage pursue our journey. This proved to be almost perpendicularly down a hill studded with young trees and stumps. From these he proposed, with a hospitality of service worthy an Oriental, to free our wheels whenever they should get entangled, also to be himself the drag to prevent our too rapid descent. Such generosity deserved trust; however, we women could not be persuaded to render it. We got out and admired from afar the process. Left by our guide and prop, we found ourselves in a wide field, where by playful quips and turns an endless "creek" seemed to divert itself with our attempts to cross it. Failing in this, the next best was to whirl down a steep bank, which feat our charioteer performed with an air not unlike that of Rhesus, had he but been as suitably furnished with chariot and steeds!

At last, after wasting some two or three hours on the "short cut," we got out by following an Indian trail—Black Hawk's! How fair the scene through which it led! How could they let themselves be conquered, with such a country to fight for?

Afterwards in the wide prairie we saw a lively picture of nonchalance (to speak in the fashion of dear Ireland). There in the wide sunny field, with neither tree nor umbrella above his head, sat a peddler with his pack, waiting apparently for customers. He was not disappointed. We bought what hold in regard to the human world as unmarked, as mysterious, and as important an existence as the infusoria to the natural, to wit, pins. This incident would have delighted those modern sages who, in imitation of the sitting philosophers of ancient Ind, prefer silence to speech, waiting to going, and scornfully smile, in answer to the motions of earnest life:

> Of itself will nothing come,
> That ye must still be seeking?

However, it seemed to me today, as formerly on these sublime occasions, obvious that nothing would come unless something would go; now if we had been as sublimely still as the peddler, his pins would have tarried in the pack, and his pockets sustained an aching void of pence.

Passing through one of the fine park-like woods, almost clear from underbrush and carpeted with thick grasses and flowers, we met (for it was Sunday) a little congregation just returning from their service, which had been performed in a rude house in its midst. It had a sweet and peaceful air, as if such words and thoughts were very dear to them. The parents had with them all their little children; but we saw no old people; that charm was wanting which exists in such scenes in older settlements, of seeing the silver bent in reverence beside the flaxen head.

At Oregon, the beauty of the scene was of even a more sumptuous character than at our former "stopping-place." Here swelled the river in its boldest course, interspersed by halcyon isles on which Nature had lavished all her prodigality in tree, vine, and flower, banked by noble bluffs three hundred feet high, their sharp ridges as exquisitely definite as the edge of a shell; their summits adorned with those same beautiful trees, and with buttresses of rich rock, crested with old hemlocks, which wore a touching and antique grace amid the softer and more luxuriant vegetation. Lofty natural mounds rose amidst the rest, with the same lovely and sweeping outline, showing everywhere the plastic power of water—water, mother of beauty—which by its sweet and eager flow had left such lineaments as human genius never dreamed of.

Not far from the river was a high crag called the Pine Rock, which looks out, as our guide observed, like a helmet above the brow of the country. It seems as if the water left here and there a vestige of forms and materials that preceded its course, just to set off its new and richer designs.

The aspect of this country was to me enchanting beyond any I have ever seen from its fullness of expression, its bold and impassioned sweetness. Here the flood of emotion has passed over and marked everywhere its course by a smile. The fragments of rock touch it with a wildness and liberality which give just the needed relief. I should never be tired here, though I have elsewhere seen country of more secret and alluring charms, better calculated to stimulate and suggest. Here the eye and heart are filled.

How happy the Indians must have been here! It is not long since they were driven away, and the ground, above and below, is full of their traces:

The earth is full of men.

You have only to turn up the sod to find arrowheads and Indian pottery. On an island belonging to our host and nearly opposite his house, they loved to stay, and no doubt enjoyed its lavish beauty as much as the myriad wild pigeons that now haunt its flower-filled shades. Here are still the marks of their tomahawks, the troughs in which they prepared their corn, their caches.

A little way down the river is the site of an ancient Indian village with its regularly arranged mounds. As usual, they had chosen with the finest taste. When we went there, it was one of those soft shadowy afternoons when Nature seems ready to weep not from grief but from an overfull heart. Two prattling, lovely little girls and an African boy, with glittering eye and ready grin, made our party gay; but all were still as we entered the little inlet and trod those flowery paths. They may blacken Indian life as they will, talk of its dirt, its brutality; I will ever believe that the men who chose that dwelling-place were able to feel emotions of noble happiness as they returned to it, and so were the women that received them. Neither were the children sad or dull who lived so familiarly with the deer and the birds, and swam that clear wave in the shadow of the Seven Sisters. The whole scene suggested to me a Greek splendor, a Greek sweetness, and I can believe that an Indian brave, accustomed to ramble in such paths and be bathed by such sunbeams, might be mistaken for Apollo, as Apollo was for him by West. Two of the boldest bluffs are called the Deer's Walk (not because deer do *not* walk there) and the Eagle's Nest. The latter I visited one glorious morning; it was that of the fourth of July, and certainly I think I had never felt so happy that I was born in America. Woe to all country folks that never saw this spot, never swept an enraptured gaze over the prospect that stretched beneath. I do believe Rome and Florence are suburbs compared to this capital of Nature's art.

The bluff was decked with great bunches of a scarlet variety of the milkweed, like cut coral, and all starred with a mysterious-looking dark flower, whose cup rose lonely on a tall stem. This had for two or three days disputed the ground with the lupine and phlox. My companions disliked, I liked it.

Here I thought of, or rather saw, what the Greek expresses under the form of Jove's darling, Ganymede, and the following stanzas took form.

GANYMEDE TO HIS EAGLE

SUGGESTED BY A WORK OF THORWALDSEN'S

Composed on the height called the Eagle's Nest, Oregon,
Rock River, July 4, 1843

Upon the rocky mountain stood the boy,
   A goblet of pure water in his hand;
His face and form spoke him one made for joy,
   A willing servant to sweet love's command,
But a strange pain was written on his brow,
   And thrilled throughout his silver accents now.

"My bird," he cries, "my destined brother friend,
   O whither fleets today thy wayward flight?
Hast thou forgotten that I here attend,
   From the full noon until this sad twilight?
A hundred times, at least, from the clear spring,
   Since the full noon o'er hill and valley glowed,
I've filled the vase which our Olympian king
   Upon my care for thy sole use bestowed;
That, at the moment when thou shouldst descend,
A pure refreshment might thy thirst attend.

"Hast thou forgotten earth, forgotten me,
   Thy fellow-bondsman in a royal cause,
Who, from the sadness of infinity,

Only with thee can know that peaceful pause
In which we catch the flowing strain of love,
Which binds our dim fates to the throne of Jove?

"Before I saw thee, I was like the May,
   Longing for summer that must mar its bloom,
Or like the morning star that calls the day,
   Whose glories to its promise are the tomb;
And as the eager fountain rises higher
   To throw itself more strongly back to earth,
Still, as more sweet and full rose my desire,
   More fondly it reverted to its birth,
For what the rosebud seeks tells not the rose,
The meaning that the boy foretold the man cannot disclose.

"I was all Spring, for in my being dwelt
   Eternal youth, where flowers are the fruit;
Full feeling was the thought of what was felt,
   Its music was the meaning of the lute;
But heaven and earth such life will still deny,
For earth, divorced from heaven, still asks the question *Why?*

"Upon the highest mountains my young feet
   Ached, that no pinions from their lightness grew,
My starlike eyes the stars would fondly greet,
   Yet win no greeting from the circling blue;
Fair, self-subsistent each in its own sphere,
   They had no care that there was none for me;
Alike to them that I was far or near,
   Alike to them time and eternity.

"But from the violet of lower air
   Sometimes an answer to my wishing came;
Those lightning-births my nature seemed to share,
   They told the secrets of its fiery frame,
The sudden messengers of hate and love,
The thunderbolts that arm the hand of Jove,
And strike sometimes the sacred spire, and strike the sacred grove.

"Come in a moment, in a moment gone,
They answered me, then left me still more lone;
They told me that the thought which ruled the world
As yet no sail upon its course had furled,
That the creation was but just begun,
New leaves still leaving from the primal one,
But spoke not of the goal to which *my* rapid wheels would run.

"Still, still my eyes, though tearfully, I strained
To the far future which my heart contained,
And no dull doubt my proper hope profaned.

"At last, O bliss! thy living form I spied,
　　Then a mere speck upon a distant sky;
Yet my keen glance discerned its noble pride,
　　And the full answer of that sun-filled eye;
I knew it was the wing that must upbear
My earthlier form into the realms of air.

"Thou knowest how we gained that beauteous height,
Where dwells the monarch of the sons of light;
Thou knowest he declared us two to be
The chosen servants of his ministry,
Thou as his messenger, a sacred sign
Of conquest, or, with omen more benign,
To give its due weight to the righteous cause,
To express the verdict of Olympian laws.

"And I to wait upon the lonely spring,
　　Which slakes the thirst of bards to whom 'tis given
The destined dues of hopes divine to sing,
　　And weave the needed chain to bind to heaven.
Only from such could be obtained a draught
For him who in his early home from Jove's own cup has quaffed.

"To wait, to wait, but not to wait too long,
Till heavy grows the burden of a song;
O bird! too long hast thou been gone today,
My feet are weary of their frequent way,
The spell that opes the spring my tongue no more can say.

"If soon thou com'st not, night will fall around,
My head with a sad slumber will be bound,
And the pure draught will be spilt upon the ground.

"Remember that I am not yet divine,
Long years of service to the fatal Nine
Are yet to make a Delphian vigor mine.

"O, make them not too hard, thou bird of Jove!
Answer the stripling's hope, confirm his love,
Receive the service in which he delights,
And bear him often to the serene heights,
Where hands that were so prompt in serving thee
Shall be allowed the highest ministry,
And Rapture live with bright Fidelity."

The afternoon was spent in a very different manner. The family whose guests we were possessed a gay and graceful hospitality that gave zest to each moment. They possessed that rare politeness which, while fertile in pleasant expedients to vary the enjoyment of a friend, leaves him perfectly free the moment he wishes to be so. With such hosts pleasure may be combined with repose. They lived on the bank opposite the town, and as their house was full, we slept in the town and passed three days with them, passing to and fro morning and evening in their boats. To one of these, called the Fairy, in which a sweet little daughter of the house moved about lighter than any Scotch Ellen ever sung, I should indite a poem, if I had not been guilty of rhyme on this very page. At morning this boating was very pleasant; at evening, I confess, I was generally too tired with the excitements of the day to think it so.

The house—a double log-cabin—was to my eye the model of a Western villa. Nature had laid out before it grounds which could not be improved. Within, female taste had veiled every rudeness, availed itself of every sylvan grace.

In this charming abode what laughter, what sweet thoughts, what pleasing fancies did we not enjoy! May such never desert those who reared it, and made us so kindly welcome to all its pleasures!

Fragments of city life were dexterously crumbled into the dish prepared for general entertainment. Ice cream followed the dinner, which was drawn by the gentlemen from the river, and music and fireworks wound up the evening of days spent on the Eagle's Nest. Now they had prepared a little fleet to pass over to the Fourth of July celebration, which some queer drumming and fifing from the opposite bank had announced to be "on hand."

We found the free and independent citizens there collected beneath the trees, among whom many a round Irish visage dimpled at the usual puffs of "Ameriky."

The orator was a New Englander, and the speech smacked loudly of Boston, but was received with much applause and followed by a plentiful dinner provided by and for the Sovereign People, to which *Hail Columbia* served as grace.

Returning, the gay flotilla cheered the little flag which the children had raised from a log-cabin, prettier than any president ever saw, and drank the health of our country and all mankind with a clear conscience.

Dance and song wound up the day. I know not when the mere local habitation has seemed to me to afford so fair a chance of happiness as this. To a person of unspoiled tastes the beauty alone would afford stimulus enough. But with it would be naturally associated all kinds of wild sports, experiments, and the studies of natural history. In these regards, the poet, the sportsman, the naturalist would alike rejoice in this wide range of untouched loveliness.

Then with a very little money a ducal estate may be purchased, and by a very little more and moderate labor a family be maintained upon it with raiment, food, and shelter. The luxurious and minute comforts of a city life are not yet to be had without effort disproportionate to their value. But where there is so great a counterpoise, cannot these be given up once for all? If the houses are imperfectly built, they can afford immense fires and plenty of covering; if they are small, who cares—with such fields to roam in?—in winter, it may be borne; in summer, is of no consequence. With plenty of fish and game and wheat, can they not dispense with a baker to bring "muffins hot" every morning to the door for their breakfast?

A man need not here take a small slice from the landscape, and fence it in from the obtrusions of an uncongenial neighbor, and there cut down his fancies to miniature improvements which a chicken could run over in ten minutes. He may have water and wood and land enough to dread no incursions on his prospect from some chance vandal that may enter his neighborhood. He need not painfully economize and manage how he may use it all; he can afford to leave some of it wild and to carry out his own plans without obliterating those of Nature.

Here whole families might live together, if they would. The sons might return from their pilgrimages to settle near the parent hearth; the daughters might find room near their mother. Those painful separations, which already desecrate and desolate the Atlantic coast, are not enforced here by the stern need of seeking bread; and where they are voluntary, it is no matter. To me, too used to the feelings which haunt a society of struggling men, it was delightful to look upon a scene where Nature still wore her motherly smile and seemed to promise room, not only for those favored or cursed with the qualities best adapting for the strifes of competition, but for the delicate, the thoughtful, even the indolent or eccentric. She did not say, fight or starve; nor even, work or cease to exist; but merely showing that the apple was a finer fruit than the wild crab, gave both room to grow in the garden.

A pleasant society is formed of the families who live along the banks of this stream upon farms. They are from various parts of the world, and have much to communicate to one another. Many have cultivated minds and refined manners, all a varied experience, while they have in common the interests of a new country and a new life. They must traverse some space to get at one another, but the journey is through scenes that make it a separate pleasure. They must bear inconveniences to stay in one another's houses; but these to the well-disposed are only a source of amusement and adventure.

The great drawback upon the lives of these settlers at present is the unfitness of the women for their new lot. It has generally been the choice of the men, and the women follow as women will, doing their best for affection's sake but too often in heart-sickness and weariness. Besides, it frequently not being a choice or conviction of their own minds that it is best to be here, their part is the hardest and they are least fitted for it. The men can find assistance in field labor, and recreation with the gun and fishing-rod. Their bodily strength is greater, and enables them to bear and enjoy both these forms of life.

The women can rarely find any aid in domestic labor. All its various and careful tasks must often be performed, sick or well, by the mother and daughters to whom a city education has imparted neither the strength nor skill now demanded.

The wives of the poorer settlers, having more hard work to do than before, very frequently become slatterns; but the ladies, accustomed to a refined neatness, feel that they cannot degrade themselves by its absence and struggle under every disadvantage to keep up the necessary routine of small arrangements.

With all these disadvantages for work, their resources for pleasure are fewer. When they can leave the housework, they have not learned to ride, to drive, to row alone. Their culture has too generally been that given to women to make them the "ornaments of society." They can dance but not draw; talk French, but know nothing of the language of flowers; neither in childhood were allowed to cultivate them, lest they should tan their complexions. Accustomed to the pavement of Broadway, they dare not tread the wildwood paths for fear of rattlesnakes!

Seeing much of this joylessness and inaptitude, both of body and mind, for a lot which would be full of blessings for those prepared for it, we could not but look with deep interest on the little girls, and hope they would grow up with the strength of body, dexterity, simple tastes, and resources that would fit them to enjoy and refine the Western farmer's life.

But they have a great deal to war with in the habits of thought acquired by their mothers from their own early life. Everywhere the fatal spirit of imitation, of reference to European standards, penetrates and threatens to blight whatever of original growth might adorn the soil.

If the little girls grow up strong, resolute, able to exert their faculties, their mothers mourn over their want of fashionable delicacy. Are they gay, enterprising, ready to fly about in the various ways that teach them so much, these ladies lament that "they cannot go to school, where they might learn to be quiet." They lament the want of "education" for their daughters, as if the thousand needs which call out their young energies, and the language of Nature around, yielded no education.

Their grand ambition for their children is to send them to school in some Eastern city, the measure most likely to make them useless and unhappy at home. I earnestly hope that erelong the existence of good schools near themselves, planned by persons of sufficient thought to meet the wants of the place and time, instead of copying New York or Boston, will correct this mania. Instruction the children want to enable them to profit by the great natural advantages of their position; but methods copied from the education of some English Lady Augusta are as ill suited to the daughter of an Illinois farmer as satin shoes to climb the Indian mounds. An elegance she would diffuse around her, if her mind were opened to appreciate elegance; it might be of a kind new, original, enchanting, as different from that of the city belle as that of the prairie torch-flower from the shopworn article that touches the cheek of that lady within her bonnet.

To a girl really skilled to make home beautiful and comfortable, with bodily strength to enjoy plenty of exercise, the woods, the streams, a few studies, music, and the sincere and familiar intercourse far more easily to be met with here than elsewhere, would afford happiness enough. Her eyes would not grow dim nor her cheeks sunken in the absence of parties, morning visits, and milliners' shops.

As to music, I wish I could see in such places the guitar rather than the piano, and good vocal more than instrumental music.

The piano many carry with them, because it is the fashionable instrument in the Eastern cities. Even there it is so merely from the habit of imitating Europe, for not one in a thousand is willing to give the labor requisite to insure any valuable use of the instrument.

But out here where the ladies have so much less leisure, it is still less desirable. Add to this, they never know how to tune their own instruments, and as persons seldom visit them who can do so, these pianos are constantly out of tune and would spoil the ear of one who began by having any.

The guitar, or some portable instrument which requires less practice and could be kept in tune by themselves, would be far more desirable for most of these ladies. It would give all they want as a household companion to fill up the gaps of life with a pleasant stimulus or solace, and be sufficient accompaniment to the voice in social meetings.

Singing in parts is the most delightful family amusement, and those who are constantly together can learn to sing in perfect accord. All the practice it needs, after some good elementary instruction, is such as meetings by summer twilight and evening firelight naturally suggest. And as music is a universal language, we cannot but think a fine Italian duet would be as much at home in the log-cabin as one of Mrs. Gore's novels.

The 6th of July we left this beautiful place. It was one of those rich days of bright sunlight, varied by the purple shadows of large, sweeping clouds. Many a backward look we cast, and left the heart behind.

Our journey today was no less delightful than before, still all new, boundless, limitless. Kinmont says that limits are sacred; that the Greeks were in the right to worship a god of limits. I say that what is limitless is alone divine, that there was neither wall nor road in Eden, that those who walked there lost and found their way just as we did, and that all the gain from the Fall was that we had a wagon to ride in. I do not think, either, that even the horses doubted whether this last was any advantage.

Everywhere the rattlesnake-weed grows in profusion. The antidote survives the bane. Soon the coarser plantain, the "white man's footstep," shall take its place.

We saw also the compass-plant, and the Western tea-plant. Of some of the brightest flowers an Indian girl afterward told me the medicinal virtues. I doubt not those students of the soil knew a use to every fair emblem, on which we could only look to admire its hues and shape.

After noon we were ferried by a girl (unfortunately not of the most picturesque appearance) across the Kishwaukie, the most graceful of streams, and on whose bosom rested many full-blown water-lilies—twice as large as any of ours. I was told that *en revanche* they were scentless, but I still regret that I could not get at one of them to try. Query, did the lilied fragrance which, in the miraculous times, accompanied visions of saints and angels, proceed from water- or garden-lilies?

Kishwaukie is according to tradition the scene of a famous battle, and its many grassy mounds contain the bones of the valiant. On these waved thickly the mysterious purple flower of which I have spoken before. I think it springs from the blood of the Indians, as the hyacinth did from that of Apollo's darling.

The ladies of our host's family at Oregon, when they first went there after all the pains and plagues of building and settling, found their first pastime in opening one of these mounds, in which they found, I think, three of the departed seated in the Indian fashion.

One of these same ladies, as she was making bread one winter morning, saw from the window a deer directly before the house. She ran out with her hands covered with dough, calling the others, and they caught him bodily before he had time to escape.

Here (at Kishwaukie) we received a visit from a ragged and barefooted, but bright-eyed gentleman, who seemed to be the intellectual loafer, the walking Will's coffee-house of the place. He told us many charming snake-stories; among others, of himself having seen seventeen young ones re-enter the mother snake on the approach of a visitor.

This night we reached Belvidere, a flourishing town in Boone County, where was the tomb, now despoiled, of Big Thunder. In this later day we felt happy to find a really good hotel.

From this place by two days of very leisurely and devious journeying we reached Chicago, and thus ended a journey which one at least of the party might have wished unending.

I have not been particularly anxious to give the geography of the scene, inasmuch as it seemed to me no route or series of stations, but a garden interspersed with cottages, groves, and flowery lawns, through which a stately river ran. I had no guidebook, kept no diary, do not know how many miles we traveled each day or how many in all. What I got from the journey was the poetic impression of the country at large; it is all I have aimed to communicate.

The narrative might have been made much more interesting, as life was at the time, by many piquant anecdotes and tales drawn from private life. But here courtesy restrains the pen, for I know those who received the stranger with such frank kindness would feel ill requited by its becoming the means of fixing many spyglasses, even though the scrutiny might be one of admiring interest, upon their private homes.

For many of these anecdotes, too, I was indebted to a friend whose property they more lawfully are. This friend was one of those rare beings who are equally at home in nature and with man. He knew a tale of all that ran and swam and flew or only grew, possessing that extensive familiarity with things which shows equal sweetness of sympathy and playful penetration. Most refreshing to me was his unstudied lore, the unwritten poetry which common life presents to a strong and gentle mind. It was a great contrast to the subtleties of analysis, the philosophic strainings of which I had seen too much. But I will not attempt to transplant it. May it profit others as it did me in the region where it was born, where it belongs.

The evening of our return to Chicago, the sunset was of a splendor and calmness beyond any we saw at the West. The twilight that succeeded was equally beautiful; soft, pathetic, but just so calm. When afterwards I learned this was the evening of Allston's death, it seemed to me as if this glorious pageant was not without connection with that event; at least, it inspired similar emotions—a heavenly gate closing a path adorned with shows well worthy Paradise.

FAREWELL TO ROCK RIVER VALLEY

Farewell, ye soft and sumptuous solitudes!
Ye fairy distances, ye lordly woods,
Haunted by paths like those that Poussin knew,
When after his all gazers' eyes he drew;
I go—and if I never more may steep
An eager heart in your enchantments deep,
Yet ever to itself that heart may say,
Be not exacting; thou hast lived one day—
Hast looked on that which matches with thy mood,
Impassioned sweetness of full being's flood,
Where nothing checked the bold yet gentle wave,
Where naught repelled the lavish love that gave.
A tender blessing lingers o'er the scene,
Like some young mother's thought, fond, yet serene,
And through its life new-born our lives have been.
Once more farewell—a sad, a sweet farewell;
And if I never must behold you more,
In other worlds I will not cease to tell
The rosary I here have numbered o'er;
And bright-haired Hope will lend a gladdened ear,
And Love will free him from the grasp of Fear,
And Gorgon critics, while the tale they hear,
Shall dew their stony glances with a tear,
If I but catch one echo from your spell—
And so farewell—a grateful, sad farewell!

Chapter IV

A SHORT CHAPTER—CHICAGO AGAIN—MORRIS BIRKBECK

Chicago had become interesting to me now that I knew it as the portal to so fair a scene. I had become interested in the land, in the people, and looked sorrowfully on the lake on which I must soon embark, to leave behind what I had just begun to enjoy.

Now was the time to see the lake. The July moon was near its full, and night after night it rose in a cloudless sky above this majestic sea. The heat was excessive, so that there was no enjoyment of life except in the night; but then the air was of that delicious temperature worthy of orange-groves. However, they were not wanted—nothing was, as that full light fell on the faintly rippling waters which then seemed boundless.

The most picturesque objects to be seen from Chicago on the inland side were the lines of Hoosier wagons. These rude farmers, the large first product of the soil, travel leisurely along, sleeping in their wagons by night, eating only what they bring with them. In the town they observe the same plan, and trouble no luxurious hotel for board and lodging. Here they look like foreign peasantry, and contrast well with the many Germans, Dutch, and Irish. In the country it is very pretty to see them prepared to "camp out" at night, their horses taken out of harness, and they lounging under the trees, enjoying the evening meal.

On the lakeside it is fine to see the great boats come panting in from their rapid and marvelous journey. Especially at night the motion of their lights is very majestic.

When the favorite boats, the "Great Western" and "Illinois," are going out, the town is thronged with people from the South and farther West, to go in them. These moonlight nights I would hear the French rippling and fluttering familiarly amid the rude ups and downs of the Hoosier dialect.

At the hotel table were daily to be seen new faces, and new stories to be learned. And anyone who has a large acquaintance may be pretty sure of meeting some of them here in the course of a few days.

At Chicago I read again *Philip van Artevelde,* and certain passages in it will always be in my mind associated with the deep sound of the lake as heard in the night. I used to read a short time at night, and then open the blind to look out. The moon would be full upon the lake, and the calm breath, pure light, and the deep voice harmonized well with the thought of the Flemish hero. When will this country have such a man? It is what she needs; no thin Idealist, no coarse Realist, but a man whose eye reads the heavens while his feet step firmly on the ground and his hands are strong and dexterous for the use of human implements. A man religious, virtuous, and sagacious; a man of universal sympathies, but self-possessed; a man who knows the region of emotion, though he is not its slave; a man to whom this world is no mere spectacle or fleeting shadow, but a great solemn game to be played with good heed, for its stakes are of eternal value, yet who, if his own play be true, heeds not what he loses by the falsehood of others; a man who hives from the past, yet knows that its honey can but moderately avail him; whose comprehensive eye scans the present, neither infatuated by its golden lures nor chilled by its many ventures; who possesses prescience, as the wise man must, but not so far as to be driven mad today by the gift which discerns tomorrow— when there is such a man for America, the thought which urges her on will be expressed.

Now that I am about to leave Illinois, feelings of regret and admiration come over me, as in parting with a friend whom we have not had the good sense to prize and study while hours of association, never perhaps to return, were granted. I have fixed my attention almost exclusively on the picturesque beauty of this region; it was so new, so inspiring. But I ought to have been more interested in the housekeeping of this magnificent State, in the education she is giving her children, in their prospects.

Illinois is at present a byword of reproach among the nations, for the careless, prodigal course by which in early youth she has endangered her honor. But you cannot look about you there without seeing that there are resources abundant to retrieve, and soon to retrieve, far greater errors, if they are only directed with wisdom.

Would that the simple maxim, that honesty is the best policy, might be laid to heart; that a sense of the true aim of life might elevate the tone of politics and trade till public and private honor became identical; that the Western man, in that crowded and exciting life which develops his faculties so fully for today, might not forget that better part which could not be taken from him; that the Western woman might take that interest and acquire that light for the education of the children, for which she alone has leisure!

This is indeed the great problem of the place and time. If the next generation be well prepared for their work, ambitious of good and skillful to achieve it, the children of the present settlers may be leaven enough for the mass constantly increasing by immigration. And how much is this needed, where those rude foreigners can so little understand the best interests of the land they seek for bread and shelter! It would be a happiness to aid in this good work, and interweave the white and golden threads into the fate of Illinois. It would be a work worthy the devotion of any mind.

In the little that I saw was a large proportion of intelligence, activity, and kind feeling; but if there was much serious laying to heart of the true purposes of life, it did not appear in the tone of conversation.

Having before me the *Illinois Guidebook,* I find there mentioned as a "visionary" one of the men I should think of as able to be a truly valuable settler in a new and great country—Morris Birkbeck of England. Since my return, I have read his journey to, and letters from, Illinois. I see nothing promised there that will not surely belong to the man who knows how to seek for it.

Mr. Birkbeck was an enlightened philanthropist, the rather that he did not wish to sacrifice himself to his fellow-men, but to benefit them with all he had and was and wished. He thought all the creatures of a divine love ought to be happy and ought to be good, and that his own soul and his own life were not less precious than those of others; indeed that to keep these healthy was his only means of a healthy influence.

But his aims were altogether generous. Freedom, the liberty of law, not license; not indolence, work for himself and children and all men, but under genial and poetic influences—these were his aims. How different from those of the new settlers in general! And into his mind so long ago shone steadily the two thoughts, now so prevalent in thinking and aspiring minds, of "Resist not evil," and "Every man his own priest, and the heart the only true church."

He has lost credit for sagacity from accidental circumstances. It does not appear that his position was ill chosen, or his means disproportioned to his ends, had he been sustained by funds from England as he had a right to expect. But through the profligacy of a near relative, commissioned to collect these dues, he was disappointed of them, and his paper protested and credit destroyed in our cities before he became aware of his danger.

Still, though more slowly and with more difficulty, he might have succeeded in his designs. The English farmer might have made the English settlement a model for good methods and good aims to all that region, had not death prematurely cut short his plans.

I have wished to say these few words because the veneration with which I have been inspired for his character by those who knew him well makes me impatient of this careless blame being passed from mouth to mouth and book to book. Success is no test of a man's endeavor, and Illinois will yet, I hope, regard this man, who knew so well what *ought* to be, as one of her true patriarchs, the Abraham of a promised land.

He was one too much before his time to be soon valued; but the time is growing up to him, and will understand his mild philanthropy and clear, large views.

I subjoin the account of his death given me by a friend, as expressing in fair picture the character of the man.

"Mr. Birkbeck was returning from the seat of government, whither he had been on public business, and was accompanied by his son Bradford, a youth of sixteen or eighteen. It was necessary to cross a ford, which was rendered difficult by the swelling of the stream. Mr. B.'s horse was unwilling to plunge into the water, so his son offered to go first, and he followed. Bradford's horse had just gained footing on the opposite shore, when he looked back and perceived his father was dismounted, struggling in the water, and carried down by the current.

"Mr. Birkbeck could not swim; Bradford could; so he dismounted, and plunged into the stream to save his father. He got him before he sank, held him up above water, and told him to take hold of his collar, and he would swim ashore with him. Mr. B. did so, and Bradford exerted all his strength to stem the current and reach the shore at a point where they could land; but encumbered by his own clothing and his father's weight, he made no progress; when Mr. B. perceived this, he, with his characteristic calmness and resolution, gave up his hold of his son, and, motioning to him to save himself, resigned himself to his fate. His son reached the shore, but was too much overwhelmed by his loss to leave it. He was found by some travelers, many hours after, seated on the margin of the stream, with his face in his hands, stupefied with grief.

"The body was found, and on the countenance was the sweetest smile; and Bradford said, 'Just so he smiled upon me when he let go and pushed me away from him.'"

Many men can choose the right and best on a great occasion, but not many can, with such ready and serene decision, lay aside even life, when that is right and best. This little narrative touched my imagination in very early youth, and often has come up in lonely vision that face, serenely smiling above the current which bore him away to another realm of being.

Chapter V

THOUGHTS AND SCENES IN WISCONSIN—SOCIETY IN MILWAUKIE—INDIAN ANECDOTE—SEERESS OF PREVORST—MILWAUKIE

A Territory, not yet a State; * still nearer the acorn than we were.

It was very pleasant coming up. These large and elegant boats are so well arranged that every excursion may be a party of pleasure. There are many fair shows to see on the lake and its shores, almost always new and agreeable persons on board, pretty children playing about, ladies singing (and if not very well, there is room to keep out of the way). You may see a great deal here of Life in the London sense, if you know a few people; or if you do not, and have the tact to look about you without seeming to stare.

We came to Milwaukie, where we were to pass a fortnight or more.

This place is most beautifully situated. A little river with romantic banks passes up through the town. The bank of the lake is here a bold bluff, eighty feet in height. From its summit is enjoyed a noble outlook on the lake. A little narrow path winds along the edge of the lake below. I liked this walk much—above me this high wall of rich earth, garlanded on its crest with trees, the long ripples of the lake coming up to my feet. Here standing in the shadow, I could appreciate better its magnificent changes of color which are the chief beauties of the lake-waters; but these are indescribable.

It was fine to ascend into the lighthouse above this bluff, and thence

---

* Wisconsin was not admitted into the Union as a State till 1847, after this volume was written.—A. B. F.

watch the thunderclouds which so frequently rose over the lake, or the great boats coming in. Approaching the Milwaukie pier, they made a bend and seemed to do obeisance in the heavy style of some dowager duchess entering a circle she wishes to treat with especial respect.

These boats come in and out every day, and still afford a cause for general excitement. The people swarm down to greet them, to receive and send away their packages and letters. To me they seemed such mighty messengers, to give by their noble motion such an idea of the power and fullness of life, that they were worthy to carry dispatches from king to king. It must be very pleasant for those who have an active share in carrying on the affairs of this great and growing world to see them approach, and pleasant to such as have dearly loved friends at the next station. To those who have neither business nor friends, it sometimes gives a desolating sense of insignificance.

The town promises to be sometime a fine one, as it is so well situated; and they have good building material—a yellow brick very pleasing to the eye. It seems to grow before you, and has indeed but just emerged from the thickets of oak and wild-roses. A few steps will take you into the thickets, and certainly I never saw so many wild-roses, or of so beautiful a red. Of such a color were the first red ones the world ever saw when, says the legend, Venus flying to the assistance of Adonis, the rosebushes kept catching her to make her stay, and the drops of blood the thorns drew from her feet, as she tore herself away, fell on the white roses and turned them this beautiful red.

One day, walking along the river's bank in search of a waterfall to be seen from one ravine, we heard tones from a band of music, and saw a gay troop shooting at a mark on the opposite bank. Between every shot the band played; the effect was very pretty.

On this walk we found two of the oldest and most gnarled hemlocks that ever afforded study for a painter. They were the only ones we saw; they seemed the veterans of a former race.

At Milwaukie, as at Chicago, are many pleasant people drawn together from all parts of the world. A resident here would find great piquancy in the associations—those he met having such dissimilar histories and topics. And several persons I saw, evidently transplanted from the most refined circles to be met in this country. There are lures enough in the West for people of all kinds—the enthusiast and the cunning man; the naturalist, and the lover who needs to be rich for the sake of her he loves.

The torrent of immigration swells very strongly towards this place. During the fine weather, the poor refugees arrive daily, in their national dresses, all travel-soiled and worn. The night they pass in rude shanties in a particular quarter of the town, then walk off into the country—the mothers carrying their infants, the fathers leading the little children by the hand, seeking a home where their hands may maintain them.

One morning we set off in their track, and traveled a day's journey into this country—fair, yet not in that part which I saw comparable in my eyes to the Rock River region. Rich fields, proper for grain, alternate with oak openings, as they are called; bold, various, and beautiful were the features of the scene, but I saw not those majestic sweeps, those boundless distances, those heavenly fields; it was not the same world.

Neither did we travel in the same delightful manner. We were now in a nice carriage, which must not go off the road for fear of breakage, with a regular coachman whose chief care was not to tire his horses, and who had no taste for entering fields in pursuit of wild-flowers, or tempting some strange wood-path in search of whatever might befall. It was pleasant, but almost as tame as New England.

But charming indeed was the place where we stopped. It was in the vicinity of a chain of lakes, and on the bank of the loveliest little stream, called the Bark River, which flowed in rapid amber brightness through fields and dells and stately knolls of most poetic beauty.

The little log-cabin where we slept, with its flower-garden in front, disturbed the scene no more than a stray lock on the fair cheek. The hospitality of that house I may well call princely; it was the boundless hospitality of the heart which, if it has no Aladdin's lamp to create a palace for the guest, does him still higher service by the freedom of its bounty to the very last drop of its powers.

Sweet were the sunsets seen in the valley of this stream, though here and, I grieve to say, no less near the Rock River, the fiend, who has every liberty to tempt the happy in this world, appeared in the shape of mosquitoes and allowed us no bodily to enjoy our mental peace.

One day we ladies gave, under the guidance of our host, to visiting all the beauties of the adjacent lakes—Nomabbin, Silver, and Pine Lakes. On the shore of Nomabbin had formerly been one of the finest Indian villages. Our host said that once, as he was lying there beneath the bank, he saw a tall Indian standing at gaze on the knoll. He lay a long time, curious to see how long the figure would maintain its statue-like absorption. But at last his patience yielded, and in moving he made a slight noise. The Indian saw him, gave a wild, snorting sound of indignation and pain, and strode away.

What feelings must consume their hearts at such moments! I scarcely see how they can forbear to shoot the white man where he stands.

But the power of fate is with the white man, and the Indian feels it. This same gentleman told of his traveling through the wilderness with an Indian guide. He had with him a bottle of spirit which he meant to give him in small quantities, but the Indian, once excited, wanted the whole at once. "I would not," said Mr. ——, "give it him, for I thought, if he got really drunk, there was an end to his services as a guide. But he persisted, and at last tried to take it from me. I was not armed; he was, and twice as strong as I. But I knew an Indian could not resist the look of a white man, and I fixed my eye steadily on his. He bore it for a moment, then his eye fell; he let go the bottle. I took his gun and threw it to a distance. After a few moments' pause, I told him to go and fetch it, and left it in his hands. From that moment he was quite obedient, even servile, all the rest of the way."

This gentleman, though in other respects of most kindly and liberal heart, showed the aversion that the white man soon learns to feel for the Indian on whom he encroaches—the aversion of the injurer for him he has degraded. After telling the anecdote of his seeing the Indian gazing at the seat of his former home,

A thing for human feelings the most trying,

and which, one would think, would have awakened soft compassion—almost remorse—in the present owner of that fair hill, which contained for the exile the bones of his dead, the ashes of his hopes, he observed: "They cannot be prevented from straggling back here to their old haunts.

I wish they could. They ought not to be permitted to drive away *our* game."
Our game—just heavens!

The same gentleman showed on a slight occasion the true spirit of a sportsman, or perhaps I might say of Man, when engaged in any kind of chase. Showing us some antlers, he said: "This one belonged to a majestic creature. But this other was the beauty. I had been lying a long time at watch, when at last I heard them come crackling along. I lifted my head cautiously as they burst through the trees. The first was a magnificent fellow; but then I saw coming one, the prettiest, the most graceful I ever beheld—there was something so soft and beseeching in its look. I chose him at once, took aim, and shot him dead. You see the antlers are not very large; it was young, but the prettiest creature!"

In the course of this morning's drive, we visited the gentlemen on their fishing party. They hailed us gaily, and rowed ashore to show us what fine booty they had. No disappointment there, no dull work.

On the beautiful point of land from which we first saw them lived a contented woman, the only one I heard of out there. She was English, and said she had seen so much suffering in her own country that the hardships of this seemed as nothing to her. But the others—even our sweet and gentle hostess—found their labors disproportioned to their strength, if not to their patience; and, while their husbands and brothers enjoyed the country in hunting or fishing, they found themselves confined to a comfortless and laborious indoor life. But it need not be so, long.

This afternoon, driving about on the banks of these lakes, we found the scene all of one kind of loveliness; wide, graceful woods, and then these fine sheets of water, with fine points of land jutting out boldly into them. It was lovely, but not striking or peculiar.

All woods suggest pictures. The European forest, with its long glades and green, sunny dells, naturally suggested the figures of armed knight on his proud steed, or maiden, decked in gold and pearl, pricking along them on a snow-white palfrey; the green dells, of weary palmer sleeping there beside the spring with his head upon his wallet. Our minds, familiar with such figures, people with them the New England woods, wherever the sunlight falls down a longer than usual cart-track, wherever a cleared spot has lain still enough for the trees to look friendly, with their exposed sides cultivated by the light, and the grass to look velvet warm and be embroidered with flowers. These Western woods suggest a different kind of ballad. The Indian legends have often an air of the wildest solitude, as has the one Mr. Lowell has put into verse in his late volume. But I did not see those wild woods; only such as suggest to me little romances of love and sorrow, like this:

GUNHILDA

A maiden sat beneath the tree,
Tear-bedewed her pale cheeks be,
And she sigheth heavily.

From forth the wood into the light
A hunter strides, with carol light,
And a glance so bold and bright.

He careless stopped and eyed the maid;
"Why weepest thou?" he gently said;
"I love thee well; be not afraid."

He takes her hand, and leads her on;
She should have waited there alone,
For he was not her chosen one.

He leans her head upon his breast,
She knew 'twas not her home of rest,
But ah! she had been sore distrest.

The sacred stars looked sadly down;
The parting moon appeared to frown,
To see thus dimmed the diamond crown.

Then from the thicket starts a deer,
The huntsman, seizing on his spear,
Cries, "Maiden, wait thou for me here."

She sees him vanish into night,
She starts from sleep in deep affright,
For it was not her own true knight.

Though but in dream Gunhilda failed,
Though but a fancied ill assailed,
Though she but fancied fault bewailed—

Yet thought of day makes dream of night:
She is not worthy of the knight,
The inmost altar burns not bright.

If loneliness thou canst not bear,
Cannot the dragon's venom dare,
Of the pure meed thou shouldst despair.

Now sadder that lone maiden sighs,
Far bitterer tears profane her eyes,
Crushed in the dust her heart's flower lies.

On the bank of Silver Lake we saw an Indian encampment. A shower threatened us, but we resolved to try if we could not visit it before it came on. We crossed a wide field on foot, and found the Indians amid the trees on a shelving bank; just as we reached them, the rain began to fall in torrents, with frequent thunderclaps, and we had to take refuge in their lodges. These were very small, being for temporary use, and we crowded the occupants much, among whom were several sick on the damp ground or with only a ragged mat between them and it. But they showed all the gentle courtesy which marks their demeanor towards the stranger who stands in any need; though it was obvious that the visit, which inconvenienced them, could only have been caused by the most impertinent curiosity, they made us as comfortable as their extreme poverty permitted. They seemed to think we would not like to touch them; a sick girl in the lodge where I was persisted in moving so as to give me the dry place; a woman with the sweet melancholy eye of the race kept off the children and wet dogs from even the hem of my garment.

Without, their fires smoldered and black kettles, hung over them on sticks, smoked and seethed in the rain. An old, theatrical-looking Indian stood with arms folded, looking up to the heavens, from which the rain dashed and the thunder reverberated; his air was French-Roman; that is, more Romanesque than Roman. The Indian ponies, much excited, kept careering through the wood around the encampment, and now and then, halting suddenly, would thrust in their intelligent though amazed faces, as if to ask their masters when this awful pother would cease, and then after a moment rush and trample off again.

At last we got away, well wetted, but with a picturesque scene for memory. At a house where we stopped to get dry, they told us that this wandering band (of Pottawattamies), who had returned on a visit, either from homesickness or need of relief, were extremely destitute. The women had been there to see if they could barter for food their headbands, with which they club their hair behind into a form not unlike a Grecian knot. They seemed, indeed, to have neither food, utensils, clothes, nor bedding; nothing but the ground, the sky, and their own strength. Little wonder if they drove off the game!

Part of the same band I had seen in Milwaukie, on a begging dance. The effect of this was wild and grotesque. They wore much paint and feather headdresses. "Indians without paint are poor coots," said a gentleman who had been a great deal with and really liked them; and I like the effect of the paint on them; it reminds of the gay fantasies of nature. With them in Milwaukie was a chief, the finest Indian figure I saw, more than six feet in height, erect, and of a sullen but grand gait and gesture. He wore a deep-red blanket, which fell in large folds from his shoulders to his feet, did not join in the dance, but slowly strode about through the streets, a fine sight, not a French-Roman but a real Roman. He looked unhappy, but listlessly unhappy, as if he felt it was of no use to strive or resist.

While in the neighborhood of these lakes, we visited also a foreign settlement of great interest. Here were minds, it seemed, to "comprehend the trust" of their new life; and, if they can only stand true to them, will derive and bestow great benefits therefrom.

But sad and sickening to the enthusiast who comes to these shores, hoping the tranquil enjoyment of intellectual blessings and the pure happiness of mutual love, must be a part of the scene that he encounters at first. He has escaped from the heartlessness of courts, to encounter the vulgarity of the mob; he has secured solitude, but it is a lonely, a deserted solitude. Amid the abundance of nature, he cannot, from petty but insuperable obstacles, procure for a long time comforts or a home.

But let him come sufficiently armed with patience to learn the new spells which the new dragons require (and this can only be done on the spot) he will not finally be disappointed of the promised treasure; the mob will resolve itself into men, yet crude, but of good dispositions and capable of good character; the solitude will become sufficiently enlivened, and home grow up at last from the rich sod.

In this transition state we found one of these homes. As we approached, it seemed the very Eden which earth might still afford to a pair willing to give up the hackneyed pleasures of the world for a better and more intimate communion with one another and with beauty: the wild road led through wide, beautiful woods to the wilder and more beautiful shores of the finest lake we saw. On its waters, glittering in the morning sun, a few Indians were paddling to and fro in their light canoes. On one of those fair knolls I have so often mentioned stood the cottage, beneath trees which stooped as if they yet felt brotherhood with its rooftree. Flowers waved, birds fluttered round, all had the sweetness of a happy seclusion; all invited to cry to those who inhabited it, All hail, ye happy ones!

But on entrance to those evidently rich in personal beauty, talents, love, and courage, the aspect of things was rather sad. Sickness had been with them, death, care, and labor; these had not yet blighted them, but had turned their gay smiles grave. It seemed that hope and joy had given place to resolution. How much, too, was there in them, worthless in this place, which would have been so valuable elsewhere! Refined graces, cultivated powers, shine in vain before field-laborers, as laborers are in this present world; you might as well cultivate heliotropes to present to an ox. Oxen and heliotropes are both good, but not for one another.

With them were some of the old means of enjoyment, the books, the pencil, the guitar; but where the washtub and the ax are so constantly in requisition, there is not much time and pliancy of hand for these.

In the inner room, the master of the house was seated; he had been sitting there long, for he had injured his foot on shipboard, and his farming had to be done by proxy. His beautiful young wife was his only attendant and nurse, as well as a farm housekeeper. How well she performed hard and unaccustomed duties, the objects of her care showed; everything that belonged to the house was rude, but neatly arranged. The invalid, confined to an uneasy wooden chair—they had not been able to induce anyone to bring them an easy-chair from the town—looked as neat and elegant as if he had been dressed by the valet of a duke. He was of Northern blood, with clear, full blue eyes, calm features, a tempering of the soldier, scholar, and man of the world in his aspect. Either various intercourses had given him that thoroughbred look never seen in Americans, or it was inherited from a race who had known all these disciplines. He formed a great but pleasing contrast to his wife, whose glowing complexion and dark yellow eye bespoke an origin in some climate more familiar with the sun. He looked as if he could sit there a great while patiently and live on his own mind, biding his time; she, as if she could bear anything for affection's sake, but would feel the weight of each moment as it passed.

Seeing the album full of drawings and verses, which bespoke the circle of elegant and affectionate intercourse they had left behind, we could not but see that the young wife sometimes must need a sister, the husband a companion, and both must often miss that electricity which sparkles from the chain of congenial minds.

For mankind, a position is desirable in some degree proportioned to education. Mr. Birkbeck was bred a farmer, but these were nurslings of the court and city; they may persevere, for an affectionate courage shone in their eyes, and if so, become true lords of the soil and informing geniuses to those around; then perhaps they will feel that they have not paid too dear for the tormented independence of the new settler's life. But generally damask roses will not thrive in the wood, and a ruder growth, if healthy and pure, we wish rather to see there.

I feel about these foreigners very differently from what I do about Americans. American men and women are inexcusable if they do not bring up children so as to be fit for vicissitudes; the meaning of our star is that here all men being free and equal, every man should be fitted for freedom and an independence by his own resources wherever the changeful wave of our mighty stream may take him. But the star of Europe brought a different horoscope, and to mix destinies breaks the thread of both. The Arabian horse will not plow well, nor can the plow-horse be rode to play the jereed. Yet a man is a man wherever he goes, and something precious cannot fail to be gained by one who knows how to abide by a resolution of any kind, and pay the cost without a murmur.

Returning, the fine carriage at last fulfilled its threat of breaking down. We took refuge in a farmhouse. Here was a pleasant scene—a rich and beautiful estate, several happy families, who had removed together and formed a natural community, ready to help and enliven one another. They were farmers at home in Western New York, and both men and women knew how to work. Yet even here the women did not like the change, but they were willing, "as it might be best for the young folks." Their hospitality was great: the houseful of women and pretty children seemed all of one mind.

Returning to Milwaukie much fatigued, I entertained myself for a day or two with reading. The book I had brought with me was in strong contrast with the life around me. Very strange was this vision of an exalted and sensitive existence, which seemed to invade the next sphere, in contrast with the spontaneous, instinctive life, so healthy and so near the ground I had been surveying. This was the German book entitled: *The Seeress of Prevorst: Revelations concerning the Inward Life of Man, and the Projection of a World of Spirits into Ours, communicated by Justinus Kerner.*

This book, published in Germany some twelve years since, and which called forth there plenteous dews of admiration, as plenteous hailstorms of jeers and scorns, I never saw mentioned in any English publication till some year or two since. Then a playful but not sarcastic account of it in the *Dublin Magazine* so far excited my curiosity that I procured the book, intending to read it so soon as I should have some leisure days, such as this journey has afforded.

Dr. Kerner, its author, is a man of distinction in his native land, both as a physician and a thinker, though always on the side of reverence, marvel, and mysticism. He was known to me only through two or three little poems of his in Catholic legends, which I much admired for the fine sense they showed of the beauty of symbols.

He here gives a biography, mental and physical, of one of the most remarkable cases of high nervous excitement that the age so interested in such yet affords, with all its phenomena of clairvoyance and susceptibility of magnetic influences. As to my own mental position on these subjects, it may be briefly expressed by a dialogue between several persons who honor me with a portion of friendly confidence and criticism, and myself, personified as *Free Hope*. The others may be styled *Old Church, Good Sense,* and *Self-Poise.*

DIALOGUE

Good Sense. I wonder you can take any interest in such observations or experiments. Don't you see how almost impossible it is to make them with any exactness, how entirely impossible to know anything about them unless made by yourself, when the least leaven of credulity, excited fancy, to say nothing of willing or careless imposture, spoils the whole loaf? Besides, allowing the possibility of some clear glimpses into a higher state of being, what do we want of it now? All around us lies what we neither understand nor use. Our capacities, our instincts for this our present sphere are but half developed. Let us confine ourselves to that till the lesson be learned; let us be completely natural, before we trouble ourselves with the super-natural. I never see any of these things but I long to get away and lie under a green tree and let the wind blow on me. There is marvel and charm enough in that for me.

Free Hope. And for me also. Nothing is truer than the Wordsworthian creed, on which Carlyle lays such stress, that we need only look on the miracle of every day, to sate ourselves with thought and admiration every day. But how are our faculties sharpened to do it? Precisely by apprehending the infinite results of every day.

Who sees the meaning of the flower uprooted in the plowed field? The plowman who does not look beyond its boundaries and does not raise his eyes from the ground? No—but the poet who sees that field in its relations with the universe, and looks oftener to the sky than on the ground. Only the dreamer shall understand realities, though in truth his dreaming must be not out of proportion to his waking!

The mind, roused powerfully by this existence, stretches of itself into what the French sage calls the "aromal state." From the hope thus gleaned it forms the hypothesis under whose banner it collects its facts.

Long before these slight attempts were made to establish as a science what is at present called animal magnetism, always in fact, men were occupied more or less with this vital principle—principle of flux and in-flux—dynamic of our mental mechanics—human phase of electricity. Poetic observation was pure; there was no quackery in its free course, as there is so often in this willful tampering with the hidden springs of life, for it is tampering unless done in a patient spirit and with severe truth; yet it may be by the rude or greedy miners some good ore is unearthed. And some there are who work in the true temper, patient and accurate in trial, not rushing to conclusions, feeling there is a mystery, not eager to call it by name till they can know it as a reality: such may learn, such may teach.

Subject to the sudden revelations, the breaks in habitual existence, caused by the aspect of death, the touch of love, the flood of music, I never lived that I remember what you call a common natural day. All my days are touched by the supernatural, for I feel the pressure of hidden causes and the presence, sometimes the communion, of unseen powers. It needs not that I should ask the clairvoyant whether "a spirit-world projects into ours." As to the specific evidence, I would not tarnish my mind by hasty reception. The mind is not, I know, a highway but a temple, and its doors should not be carelessly left open. Yet it were sin, if indolence or coldness excluded what had a claim to enter; and I doubt whether in the eyes of pure intelligence an ill-grounded hasty rejection be not a greater sign of weakness than an ill-grounded and hasty faith.

I will quote as my best plea the saying of a man old in years but not in heart, and whose long life has been distinguished by that clear adaptation of means to ends which gives the credit of practical wisdom. He wrote to his child, "I have lived too long, and seen too much, to be *in*credulous." Noble the thought, no less so its frank expression instead of saws of caution, mean advices, and other modern instances. Such was the romance of Socrates when he bade his disciple "sacrifice a cock to Aesculapius."

Old Church. You are always so quick-witted and voluble, Free Hope, you don't get time to see how often you err, and even perhaps sin and blaspheme. The Author of all has intended to confine our knowledge within certain boundaries, has given us a short span of time for a certain probation, for which our faculties are adapted. By wild speculation and intemperate curiosity we violate His will, and incur dangerous, perhaps fatal consequences. We waste our powers, and becoming morbid and visionary, are unfitted to obey positive precepts, and perform positive duties.

Free Hope. I do not see how it is possible to go further beyond the results of a limited human experience than those do who pretend to settle the origin and nature of sin, the final destiny of souls, and the whole plan of the Causal Spirit with regard to them. I think those who take your view have not examined themselves, and do not know the ground on which they stand.

I acknowledge no limit set up by man's opinion as to the capacities of man. "Care is taken," I see it, "that the trees grow not up into heaven"; but to me it seems the more vigorously they aspire, the better. Only let it be a vigorous, not a partial or sickly aspiration. Let not the tree forget its root.

So long as the child insists on knowing where its dead parent is, so long as bright eyes weep at mysterious pressures, too heavy for the life, so long as that impulse is constantly arising which made the Roman emperor address his soul in a strain of such touching softness, vanishing from the thought as the column of smoke from the eye, I know of no inquiry which the impulse of man suggests that is forbidden to the resolution of man to pursue. In every inquiry, unless sustained by a pure and reverent spirit, he gropes in the dark or falls headlong.

Self-Poise. All this may be very true, but what is the use of all this straining? Far-sought is dear-bought. When we know that all is in each, and that the ordinary contains the extraordinary, why should we play the baby and insist upon having the moon for a toy when a tin dish will do as well? Our deep ignorance is a chasm that we can only fill up by degrees, but the commonest rubbish will help us as well as shred silk. The god Brahma while on earth was set to fill up a valley, but he had only a basket given him in which to fetch earth for this purpose; so is it with us all. No leaps, no starts will avail us; by patient crystallization alone the equal temper of wisdom is attainable. Sit at home, and the spirit-world will look in at your window with moonlit eyes; run out to find it, and rainbow and golden cup will have vanished, and left you the beggarly child you were. The better part of wisdom is a sublime prudence, a pure and patient truth that will receive nothing it is not sure it can permanently lay to heart. Of our study, there should be in proportion two thirds of rejection to one of acceptance. And amid the manifold infatuations and illusions of this world of emotion, a being capable of clear intelligence can do no better service than to hold himself upright, avoid nonsense, and do what chores lie in his way, acknowledging every moment that primal truth which no fact exhibits, nor if pressed by too warm a hope will even indicate. I think indeed it is part of our lesson to give a formal consent to what is farcical, and to pick up our living and our virtue amid what is so ridiculous, hardly deigning a smile, and certainly not vexed. The work is done through all, if not by everyone.

Free Hope. Thou art greatly wise, my friend, and ever respected by me, yet I find not in your theory or your scope room enough for the lyric inspirations or the mysterious whispers of life. To me it seems that it is madder never to abandon one's self than often to be infatuated; better to be wounded, a captive and a slave, than always to walk in armor. As to magnetism, that is only a matter of fancy. You sometimes need just such a field in which to wander vagrant, and if it bear a higher name, yet it may be that in last result the trance of Pythagoras might be classed with the more infantine transports of the Seeress of Prevorst.

What is done interests me more than what is thought and supposed. Every fact is impure, but every fact contains in it the juices of life. Every fact is a clod, from which may grow an amaranth or a palm.

Climb you the snowy peaks whence come the streams, where the atmosphere is rare, where you can see the sky nearer, from which you can get a commanding view of the landscape? I see great disadvantages as well as advantages in this dignified position. I had rather walk myself through all kinds of places, even at the risk of being robbed in the forest, half drowned at the ford, and covered with dust in the street.

I would beat with the living heart of the world, and understand all the moods, even the fancies or fantasies, of nature. I dare to trust to the interpreting spirit to bring me out all right at last—establish truth through error.

Whether this be the best way is of no consequence, if it be the one individual character points out.

> For one like me, it would be vain
> From glittering heights the eyes to strain;
> I the truth can only know,
> Tested by life's most fiery glow.
> Seeds of thought will never thrive,
> Till dews of love shall bid them live.

Let me stand in my age with all its waters flowing round me. If they sometimes subdue, they must finally upbear me, for I seek the universal —and that must be the best.

The Spirit, no doubt, leads in every movement of my time: if I seek the how, I shall find it, as well as if I busied myself more with the why.

Whatever is, is right, if only men are steadily bent to make it so by comprehending and fulfilling its design.

May not I have an office, too, in my hospitality and ready sympathy? If I sometimes entertain guests who cannot pay with gold coin, with "fair rose nobles," that is better than to lose the chance of entertaining angels unawares.

You, my three friends, are held in heart-honor by me. You especially, Good Sense, because where you do not go yourself, you do not object to another's going, if he will. You are really liberal. You, Old Church, are of use by keeping unforgot the effigies of old religion, and reviving the tone of pure Spenserian sentiment, which this time is apt to stifle in its childish haste. But you are very faulty in censuring and wishing to limit others by your own standard. You, Self-Poise, fill a priestly office. Could but a larger intelligence of the vocations of others, and a tender sympathy with their individual natures, be added, had you more of love, or more of apprehensive genius (for either would give you the needed expansion and delicacy), you would command my entire reverence. As it is, I must at times deny and oppose you, and so must others, for you tend, by your influence, to exclude us from our full, free life. We must be content when you censure, and rejoiced when you approve; always admonished to good by your whole being, and sometimes by your judgment.

Do not blame me that I have written so much suggested by the German seeress, while you were looking for news of the West. Here on the pier, I see disembarking the Germans, the Norwegians, the Swedes, the Swiss. Who knows how much of old legendary lore, of modern wonder, they have already planted amid the Wisconsin forests? Soon their tales of the origin of things, and the Providence which rules them, will be so mingled with those of the Indian that the very oak-tree will not know them apart—will not know whether itself be a Runic, a Druid, or a Winnebago oak.

Some seeds of all growths that have ever been known in this world might no doubt already be found in these Western wilds, if we had the power to call them to life.

I saw in the newspaper that the American Tract Society boasted of their agent's having exchanged at a Western cabin door tracts for the *Devil on*

Two Sticks, and then burnt that more entertaining than edifying volume. No wonder, though, they study it there. Could one but have the gift of reading the dreams dreamed by men of such various birth, various history, various mind, it would afford much more extensive amusement than did the chambers of one Spanish city!

Could I but have flown at night through such mental experiences, instead of being shut up in my little bedroom at the Milwaukie boarding-house, this chapter would have been worth reading. As it is, let us hasten to a close.

Had I been rich in money, I might have built a house or set up in business during my fortnight's stay at Milwaukie, matters move on there at so rapid a rate. But being only rich in curiosity, I was obliged to walk the streets and pick up what I could in casual intercourse. When I left the street indeed and walked on the bluffs or sat beside the lake in their shadow, my mind was rich in dreams congenial to the scene, sometime to be realized, though not by me.

A boat was left keel up, half on the sand, half in the water, swaying with each swell of the lake. It gave a picturesque grace to that part of the shore, as the only image of inaction—only object of a pensive character to be seen. Near this I sat, to dream my dreams and watch the colors of the lake, changing hourly, till the sun sank. These hours yielded impulses, wove webs, such as life will not again afford.

Returning to the boarding-house, which was also a boarding-school, we were sure to be greeted by gay laughter.

This school was conducted by two girls of nineteen and seventeen years; their pupils were nearly as old as themselves. The relation seemed very pleasant between them; the only superiority—that of superior knowledge —was sufficient to maintain authority—all the authority that was needed to keep daily life in good order.

In the West people are not respected merely because they are old in years; people there have not time to keep up appearances in that way; when persons cease to have a real advantage in wisdom, knowledge, or enterprise, they must stand back, and let those who are oldest in character "go ahead," however few years they may count. There are no banks of established respectability in which to bury the talent there; no napkin of precedent in which to wrap it. What cannot be made to pass current is not esteemed coin of the realm.

To the windows of this house where the daughter of a famous "Indian fighter," i.e., fighter against the Indians, was learning French and the piano, came wild, tawny figures offering for sale their baskets of berries. The boys now instead of brandishing the tomahawk tame their hands to pick raspberries.

Here the evenings were much lightened by the gay chat of one of the party, who with the excellent practical sense of mature experience, and the kindest heart, united a naïveté and innocence such as I never saw in any other who had walked so long life's tangled path. Like a child she was everywhere at home, and like a child received and bestowed entertainment from all places, all persons. I thanked her for making me laugh, as did the sick and poor, whom she was sure to find out in her briefest sojourn in any place, for more substantial aid. Happy are those who never grieve, and so often aid and enliven their fellow-men!

This scene, however, I was not sorry to exchange for the much celebrated beauties of the island of Mackinaw.

Chapter VI

MACKINAW—INDIANS—INDIAN WOMEN—EVERETT'S RECEPTION OF CHIEFS—
UNFITNESS OF INDIAN MISSIONARIES—OUR DUTIES TOWARD THIS RACE

Late at night we reached this island of Mackinaw, so famous for its beauty, and to which I proposed a visit of some length. It was the last week in August, at which time a large representation from the Chippewa and Ottawa tribes are here to receive their annual payments from the American government. As their habits make traveling easy and inexpensive to them, neither being obliged to wait for steamboats nor write to see whether hotels are full, they come hither by thousands, and those thousands in families, secure of accommodation on the beach and food from the lake, to make a long holiday out of the occasion. There were near two thousand encamped on the island already, and more arriving every day.

As our boat came in, the captain had some rockets let off. This greatly excited the Indians, and their yells and wild cries resounded along the shore. Except for the momentary flash of the rockets, it was perfectly dark, and my sensations as I walked with a stranger to a strange hotel through the midst of these shrieking savages, and heard the pants and snorts of the departing steamer which carried away all my companions, were somewhat of the dismal sort; though it was pleasant, too, in the way that everything strange is; everything that breaks in upon the routine that so easily incrusts us.

I had reason to expect a room to myself at the hotel but found none, and was obliged to take up my rest in the common parlor and eating-room, a circumstance which insured my being an early riser.

With the first rosy streak, I was out among my Indian neighbors, whose lodges honeycombed the beautiful beach that curved away in long, fair outline on either side the house. They were already on the alert, the children creeping out from beneath the blanket door of the lodge, the women pounding corn in their rude mortars, the young men playing on their pipes. I had been much amused, when the strain proper to the Winnebago courting flute was played to me on another instrument, at anyone fancying it a melody; but now when I heard the notes in their true tone and time, I thought it not unworthy comparison, in its graceful sequence and the light flourish at the close, with the sweetest bird-song; and this, like the bird-song, is only practiced to allure a mate. The Indian, become a citizen and a husband, no more thinks of playing the flute than one of the "settled-down" members of our society would of choosing the "purple light of love" as dyestuff for a surtout.

Mackinaw has been fully described by able pens, and I can only add my tribute to the exceeding beauty of the spot and its position. It is charming to be on an island so small that you can sail round it in an afternoon, yet large enough to admit of long, secluded walks through its gentle groves. You can go round it in your boat; or on foot you can tread its narrow beach, resting at times beneath the lofty walls of stone, richly wooded, which rise from it in various architectural forms. In this stone, caves are continually forming from the action of the atmosphere; one of these is quite deep, and a rocky fragment left at its mouth, wreathed with little creeping plants, looks as you sit within like a ruined pillar.

The arched rock surprised me, much as I had heard of it, from the perfection of the arch. It is perfect, whether you look up through it from the lake or down through it to the transparent waters. We both ascended and descended—no very easy matter—the steep and crumbling path, and rested at the summit beneath the trees and at the foot upon the cool, mossy stones beside the lapsing wave. Nature has carefully decorated all this architecture with shrubs that take root within the crevices and small creeping vines. These natural ruins may vie for beautiful effect with the remains of European grandeur, and have besides a charm as of a playful mood in Nature.

The sugar-loaf rock is a fragment in the same kind as the pine rock we saw in Illinois. It has the same air of a helmet, as seen from an eminence at the side which you descend by a long and steep path. The rock itself may be ascended by the bold and agile: halfway up is a niche to which those who are neither can climb by a ladder. A very handsome young officer and lady who were with us did so, and then facing round, stood there side by side looking in the niche, if not like saints or angels wrought by pious hands in stone, as romantically, if not as holily, worthy the gazer's eye.

The woods which adorn the central ridge of the island are very full in foliage, and in August showed the tender green and pliant leaf of June elsewhere. They are rich in beautiful mosses and the wild raspberry.

From Fort Holmes, the old fort, we had the most commanding view of the lake and straits, opposite shores, and fair islets. Mackinaw itself is best seen from the water. Its peculiar shape is supposed to have been the origin of its name, Michilimackinac, which means the Great Turtle. One person whom I saw wished to establish another etymology, which he fancied to be more refined; but I doubt not this is the true one, both because the shape might suggest such a name, and the existence of an island of such form in this commanding position would seem a significant fact to the Indians. For Henry gives the details of peculiar worship paid to the Great Turtle, and the oracles received from this extraordinary Apollo of the Indian Delphos.

It is crowned most picturesquely by the white fort with its gay flag. From this, on one side, stretches the town. How pleasing a sight, after the raw, crude, staring assemblage of houses everywhere else to be met in this country, is an old French town mellow in its coloring, and with the harmonious effect of a slow growth which assimilates naturally with objects round it! The people in its streets, Indian, French, half-breeds, and others, walked with a leisure step as of those who live a life of taste and inclination, rather than of the hard press of business as in American towns elsewhere.

On the other side, along the fair, curving beach below the white houses scattered on the declivity, clustered the Indian lodges, with their amber-brown matting, so soft and bright of hue in the late afternoon sun. The first afternoon I was there, looking down from a near height, I felt that I never wished to see a more fascinating picture. It was an hour of the deepest serenity; bright blue and gold with rich shadows. Every moment the sunlight fell more mellow. The Indians were grouped and scattered among the lodges; the women preparing food in the kettle or frying-pan over the many small fires; the children, half naked, wild as little goblins, were playing both in and out of the water. Here and there lounged a young girl with a baby at her back, whose bright eyes glanced as if born into a world of courage and of joy, instead of ignominious servitude and slow decay. Some girls were cutting wood a little way from me, talking and laughing in the low musical tone so charming in the Indian women. Many bark canoes were upturned upon the beach and by that light of almost the same amber as the lodges; others coming in, their square sails set, and with almost arrowy speed, though heavily laden with dusky forms and all the apparatus of their household. Here and there a sailboat glided by, with a different but scarce less pleasing motion.

It was a scene of ideal loveliness, and these wild forms adorned it, as looking so at home in it. All seemed happy and they were happy that day, for they had no firewater to madden them, as it was Sunday and the shops were shut.

From my window at the boarding-house my eye was constantly attracted by these picturesque groups. I was never tired of seeing the canoes come in and the new arrivals set up their temporary dwellings. The women ran to set up the tent-poles and spread the mats on the ground. The men brought the chests, kettles, &c.; the mats were then laid on the outside, the cedar-boughs strewed on the ground, the blanket hung up for a door, and all was completed in less than twenty minutes. Then they began to prepare the night meal and to learn of their neighbors the news of the day.

The habit of preparing food out of doors gave all the gypsy charm and variety to their conduct. Continually I wanted Sir Walter Scott to have been there. If such romantic sketches were suggested to him by the sight of a few gypsies, not a group near one of these fires but would have furnished him material for a separate canvas. I was so taken up with the spirit of the scene that I could not follow out the stories suggested by these weather-beaten, sullen, but eloquent figures.

They talked a great deal and with much variety of gesture, so that I often had a good guess at the meaning of their discourse. I saw that whatever the Indian may be among the whites, he is anything but taciturn with his own people; and he often would declaim or narrate at length. Indeed it is obvious, if only from the fables taken from their stores by Mr. Schoolcraft, that these tribes possess great power that way.

I liked very much to walk or sit among them. With the women I held much communication by signs. They are almost invariably coarse and ugly with the exception of their eyes, with a peculiarly awkward gait and forms bent by burdens. This gait, so different from the steady and noble step of the men, marks the inferior position they occupy. I had heard much eloquent contradiction of this. Mrs. Schoolcraft had maintained to a friend that they were in fact as nearly on a par with their husbands as the white woman with hers. "Although," said she, "on account of inevitable causes, the Indian woman is subjected to many hardships of a peculiar nature, yet her position, compared with that of the man, is higher and freer than that of the white woman. Why will people look only on one side? They either exalt the red man into a demigod, or degrade him into a beast. They say that he compels his wife to do all the drudgery, while he does nothing but hunt and amuse himself; forgetting that upon his activity and power of endurance as a hunter depends the support of his family; that this is labor of the most fatiguing kind, and that it is absolutely necessary that he should keep his frame unbent by burdens and unworn by toil, that he may be able to obtain the means of subsistence. I have witnessed scenes of conjugal and parental love in the Indian's wigwam, from which I have often, often thought the educated white man, proud of his superior civilization, might learn a useful lesson. When he returns from hunting worn out with fatigue, having tasted nothing since dawn, his wife, if she is a good wife, will take off his moccasins and replace them with dry ones, and will prepare his game for their repast, while his children will climb upon him, and he will caress them with all the tenderness of a woman; and in the evening the Indian wigwam is the scene of the purest domestic pleasures. The father will relate for the amusement of the wife and for the instruction of the children all the events of the day's hunt, while they will treasure up every word that falls, and thus learn the theory of the art whose practice is to be the occupation of their lives."

Mrs. Grant speaks thus of the position of woman amid the Mohawk Indians:

"Lady Mary Montagu says that the court of Vienna was the paradise of old women, and that there is no other place in the world where a woman past fifty excites the least interest. Had her travels extended to the interior of North America, she would have seen another instance of this inversion of the common mode of thinking. Here a woman never was of consequence till she had a son old enough to fight the battles of his country. From that date she held a superior rank in society; was allowed to live at ease, and even called to consultations on national affairs. In savage and warlike countries the reign of beauty is very short, and its influence comparatively limited. The girls in childhood had a very pleasing appearance; but excepting their fine hair, eyes, and teeth, every external grace was soon banished by perpetual drudgery, carrying burdens too heavy to be borne, and other slavish employments, considered beneath the dignity of the men. These walked before, erect and graceful, decked with ornaments which set off to advantage the symmetry of their well-formed persons, while the poor women followed, meanly attired, bent under the weight of the children and the utensils, which they carried everywhere with them, and disfigured and degraded by ceaseless toils. They were very early married, for a Mohawk had no other servant but his wife; and whenever he commenced hunter, it was requisite he should have someone to carry his load, cook his kettle, make his moccasins, and above all produce the young warriors who were to succeed him in the honors of the chase and of the tomahawk. Wherever man is a mere hunter, woman is a mere slave. It is domestic intercourse that softens man and elevates woman; and of that there can be but little, where the employments and amusements are not in common. The ancient Caledonians honored the fair; but then it is to be observed, they were fair huntresses, and moved in the light of their beauty to the hill of roes; and the culinary toils were entirely left to the rougher sex. When the young warrior made his appearance, it softened the cares of his mother, who well knew that when he grew up every deficiency in tenderness to his wife would be made up in superabundant duty and affection to her. If it were possible to carry filial veneration to excess, it was done here; for all other charities were absorbed in it. I wonder this system of depressing the sex in their early years, to exalt them when all their juvenile attractions are flown and when mind alone can distinguish them, has not occurred to our modern reformers. The Mohawks took good care not to admit their women to share their prerogatives, till they approved themselves good wives and mothers."

The observations of women upon the position of woman are always more valuable than those of men; but of these two, Mrs. Grant's seem much nearer the truth than Mrs. Schoolcraft's because, though her opportunities for observation did not bring her so close, she looked more at both sides to find the truth.

Carver, in his travels among the Winnebagos, describes two queens, one nominally so like Queen Victoria, the other invested with a genuine royalty springing from her own conduct.

In the great town of the Winnebagos, he found a queen presiding over the tribe instead of a sachem. He adds that in some tribes the descent is given to the female line in preference to the male, that is, a sister's son will succeed to the authority rather than a brother's son. The position of this Winnebago queen reminded me forcibly of Queen Victoria's.

"She sat in the council, but only asked a few questions or gave some trifling directions in matters relative to the state, for women are never allowed to sit in their councils except they happen to be invested with the supreme authority, and then it is not customary for them to make any formal speeches, as the chiefs do. She was a very ancient woman, small in stature and not much distinguished by her dress from several young women that attended her. These, her attendants, seemed greatly pleased whenever I showed any tokens of respect to their queen, especially when I saluted her, which I frequently did to acquire her favor."

The other was a woman who, being taken captive, found means to kill her captor and make her escape; and the tribe were so struck with admiration at the courage and calmness she displayed on the occasion as to make her chieftainess in her own right.

Notwithstanding the homage paid to women and the consequence allowed them in some cases, it is impossible to look upon the Indian women without feeling that they *do* occupy a lower place than women among the nations of European civilization. The habits of drudgery expressed in their form and gesture, the soft and wild but melancholy expression of their eye, reminded me of the tribe mentioned by Mackenzie, where the women destroy their female children whenever they have a good opportunity; and of the eloquent reproaches addressed by the Paraguay woman to her mother that she had not in the same way saved her from the anguish and weariness of her lot.

More weariness than anguish, no doubt, falls to the lot of most of these women. They inherit submission, and the minds of the generality accommodate themselves more or less to any posture. Perhaps they suffer less than their white sisters, who have more aspiration and refinement with little power of self-sustenance. But their place is certainly lower and their share of the human inheritance less.

Their decorum and delicacy are striking and show that, when these are native to the mind, no habits of life make any difference. Their whole gesture is timid, yet self-possessed. They used to crowd round me to inspect little things I had to show them, but never press near; on the contrary, would reprove and keep off the children. Anything they took from my hand was held with care, then shut or folded, and returned with an air of ladylike precision. They would not stare, however curious they might be, but cast sidelong glances.

A locket that I wore was an object of untiring interest; they seemed to regard it as a talisman. My little sunshade was still more fascinating to them; apparently they had never before seen one. For an umbrella they entertained profound regard, probably looking upon it as the most luxurious superfluity a person can possess and therefore a badge of great wealth. I used to see an old squaw, whose sullied skin and coarse, tanned locks told that she had braved sun and storm without a doubt or care for sixty years at least, sitting gravely at the door of her lodge with an old green umbrella over her head, happy for hours together in the dignified shade. For her happiness pomp came not, as it so often does, too late; she received it with grateful enjoyment.

One day as I was seated on one of the canoes, a woman came and sat beside me, with her baby in its cradle set up at her feet. She asked me by a gesture to let her take my sunshade, and then to show her how to open it. Then she put it into her baby's hand and held it over its head, looking at me the while with a sweet, mischievous laugh, as much as to say, "You carry a thing that is only fit for a baby." Her pantomime was very pretty. She, like the other women, had a glance, and shy, sweet expression in the eye; the men have a steady gaze.

That noblest and loveliest of modern *preux,* Lord Edward Fitzgerald, who came through Buffalo to Detroit and Mackinaw with Brant and was adopted into the Bear tribe by the name of Eghnidal, was struck in the same way by the delicacy of manners in women. He says: "Notwithstanding the life they lead, which would make most women rough and masculine, they are as soft, meek, and modest as the best brought up girls in England. Somewhat coquettish, too! Imagine the manners of Mimi in a poor *squaw* that has been carrying packs in the woods all her life."

McKenney mentions that the young wife during the short bloom of her beauty is an object of homage and tenderness to her husband. One Indian woman, the Flying Pigeon, a beautiful and excellent person of whom he gives some particulars, is an instance of the power uncommon characters will always exert of breaking down the barriers custom has erected round them. She captivated by her charms, and inspired her husband and son with reverence for her character. The simple praise with which the husband indicates the religion, the judgment, and the generosity he saw in her, are as satisfying as Count Zinzendorf's more labored eulogium on his "noble consort." The conduct of her son when, many years after her death, he saw her picture at Washington is unspeakably affecting. Catlin gives anecdotes of the grief of a chief for the loss of a daughter, and the princely gifts he offers

in exchange for her portrait, worthy not merely of European but of Trou-
badour sentiment. It is also evident that, as Mrs. Schoolcraft says, the women
have great power at home. It can never be otherwise, men being dependent
upon them for the comfort of their lives. Just so among ourselves, wives
who are neither esteemed nor loved by their husbands have great power
over their conduct by the friction of every day, and over the formation of
their opinions by the daily opportunities so close a relation affords of per-
verting testimony and instilling doubts. But these sentiments should not
come in brief flashes, but burn as a steady flame; then there would be more
women worthy to inspire them. This power is good for nothing, unless the
woman be wise to use it aright. Has the Indian, has the white woman, as
noble a feeling of life and its uses, as religious a self-respect, as worthy a field
of thought and action, as man? If not, the white woman, the Indian woman,
occupies a position inferior to that of man. It is not so much a question of
power as of privilege.

The men of these subjugated tribes, now accustomed to drunkenness and
every way degraded, bear but a faint impress of the lost grandeur of the
race. They are no longer strong, tall, or finely proportioned. Yet as you see
them stealing along a height or striding boldly forward, they remind you
of what *was* majestic in the red man.

On the shores of Lake Superior, it is said, if you visit them at home, you
may still see a remnant of the noble blood. The Pillagers (*Pilleurs*), a band
celebrated by the old travelers, are still existent there.

> Still some, "the eagles of their tribe," may rush.

I have spoken of the hatred felt by the white man for the Indian: with
white women it seems to amount to disgust, to loathing. How I could endure the dirt, the peculiar smell of the Indians and their dwellings was a
great marvel in the eyes of my lady acquaintance; indeed I wonder why
they did not quite give me up, as they certainly looked on me with great
distaste for it. "Get you gone, you Indian dog," was the felt, if not the
breathed, expression towards the hapless owners of the soil—all their claims,
all their sorrows quite forgot in abhorrence of their dirt, their tawny skins,
and the vices the whites have taught them.

A person who had seen them during the great part of a life expressed his prejudices to me with such violence that I was no longer surprised that the Indian children threw sticks at him as he passed. A lady said: "Do what you will for them, they will be ungrateful. The savage cannot be washed out of them. Bring up an Indian child, and see if you can attach it to you." The next moment she expressed, in the presence of one of those children whom she was bringing up, loathing at the odor left by one of her people, and one of the most respected, as he passed through the room. When the child is grown she will be considered basely ungrateful not to love the lady, as she certainly will not; and this will be cited as an instance of the impossibility of attaching the Indian.

Whether the Indian could, by any efforts of love and intelligence from the white man, have been civilized and made a valuable ingredient in the new state, I will not say; but this we are sure of—the French Catholics at least did not harm them or disturb their minds merely to corrupt them. The French they loved. But the stern Presbyterian with his dogmas and his taskwork, the city circle and the college with their niggard concessions and unfeeling stare, have never tried the experiment. It has not been tried. Our people and our government have sinned alike against the first-born of the soil, and if they are the fated agents of a new era, they have done nothing—have invoked no god to keep them sinless while they do the hest of fate.

Worst of all is it when they invoke the holy power only to mask their iniquity; when the felon trader, who all the week has been besotting and degrading the Indian with rum mixed with red pepper and damaged tobacco, kneels with him on Sunday before a common altar to tell the rosary which recalls the thought of Him crucified for love of suffering men, and to listen to sermons in praise of "purity"!!

"My savage friends," cries the old, fat priest, "you must, above all things, aim at *purity.*"

Oh! my heart swelled when I saw them in a Christian church. Better their own dog-feasts and bloody rites than such mockery of that other faith.

"The dog," said an Indian, "was once a spirit; he has fallen for his sin, and was given by the Great Spirit in this shape to man as his most intelligent companion. Therefore we sacrifice it in highest honor to our friends in this world—to our protecting geniuses in another."

There was religion in that thought. The white man sacrifices his own brother and to Mammon, yet he turns in loathing from the dog-feast.

"You say," said the Indian of the South to the missionary, "that Christianity is pleasing to God. How can that be? Those men at Savannah are Christians."

Yes, slavedrivers and Indian traders are called Christians, and the Indian is to be deemed less like the Son of Mary than they! Wonderful is the deceit of man's heart!

I have not, on seeing something of them in their own haunts, found reason to change the sentiments expressed in the following lines when a deputation of the Sacs and Foxes visited Boston in 1837, and were by one person at least received in a dignified and courteous manner.

GOVERNOR EVERETT RECEIVING THE INDIAN CHIEFS

NOVEMBER 1837

> Who says that Poesy is on the wane,
> And that the Muses tune their lyres in vain?
> 'Mid all the treasures of romantic story,
> When thought was fresh and fancy in her glory,
> Has ever Art found out a richer theme,
> More dark a shadow, or more soft a gleam,
> Than fall upon the scene, sketched carelessly,
> In the newspaper column of today?
>
> American romance is somewhat stale.
> Talk of the hatchet, and the faces pale,
> Wampum and calumets and forests dreary,
> Once so attractive, now begins to weary.
> Uncas and Magawisca please us still,
> Unreal, yet idealized with skill;
> But every poetaster, scribbling witling,
> From the majestic oak his stylus whittling,
> Has helped to tire us, and to make us fear
> The monotone in which so much we hear
> Of "stoics of the wood," and "men without a tear."
>
> Yet Nature, ever buoyant, ever young,
> If let alone, will sing as erst she sung;
> The course of circumstance gives back again
> The Picturesque erewhile pursued in vain;

Shows us the fount of Romance is not wasted—
The lights and shades of contrast not exhausted.

Shorn of his strength, the Samson now must sue
  For fragments from the feast his fathers gave;
The Indian dare not claim what is his due,
  But as a boon his heritage must crave;
His stately form shall soon be seen no more
Through all his father's land, the Atlantic shore;
Beneath the sun, to *us* so kind, *they* melt,
More heavily each day our rule is felt.
The tale is old—we do as mortals must:
Might makes right here, but God and Time are just.

Though near the drama hastens to its close,
On this last scene awhile your eyes repose;
The polished Greek and Scythian meet again,
The ancient life is lived by modern men;
The savage through our busy cities walks,
He in his untouched grandeur silent stalks.
Unmoved by all our gaieties and shows,
Wonder nor shame can touch him as he goes;
He gazes on the marvels we have wrought,
But knows the models from whence all was brought;
In God's first temples he has stood so oft,
And listened to the natural organ-loft,
Has watched the eagle's flight, the muttering thunder heard,
Art cannot move him to a wondering word.
Perhaps he sees that all this luxury
Brings less food to the mind than to the eye;
Perhaps a simple sentiment has brought
More to him than your arts had ever taught.
What are the petty triumphs *Art* has given,
To eyes familiar with the naked heaven?

All has been seen—dock, railroad, and canal,
Fort, market, bridge, college, and arsenal,
Asylum, hospital, and cotton-mill,
The theater, the lighthouse, and the jail.
The Braves each novelty, reflecting, saw,
And now and then growled out the earnest *"Yaw."*
And now the time is come, 'tis understood,
When, having seen and thought so much, a *talk* may do some good.

A well-dressed mob have thronged the sight to greet,
And motley figures throng the spacious street;

Majestical and calm through all they stride,
Wearing the blanket with a monarch's pride;
The gazers stare and shrug, but can't deny
Their noble forms and blameless symmetry.
If the Great Spirit their *morale* has slighted,
And wigwam smoke their mental culture blighted,
Yet the *physique,* at least, perfection reaches,
In wilds where neither Combe nor Spurzheim teaches;
Where whispering trees invite man to the chase,
And bounding deer allure him to the race.

Would thou hadst seen it! That dark, stately band,
Whose ancestors enjoyed all this fair land,
Whence they, by force or fraud, were made to flee,
Are brought, the white man's victory to see.
Can kind emotions in their proud hearts glow,
As through these realms, now decked by Art, they go?
The church, the school, the railroad, and the mart—
Can these a pleasure to their minds impart?
All once was theirs—earth, ocean, forest, sky—
How can they joy in what now meets the eye?
Not yet Religion has unlocked the soul,
Nor Each has learned to glory in the Whole!

Must they not think, so strange and sad their lot,
That they by the Great Spirit are forgot?
From the far border to which they are driven,
They might look up in trust to the clear heaven;
But *here*—what tales doth every object tell
Where Massasoit sleeps, where Philip fell!

We take our turn, and the Philosopher
Sees through the clouds a hand which cannot err.
An unimproving race, with all their graces
And all their vices, must resign their places;
And Human Culture rolls its onward flood
Over the broad plains steeped in Indian blood.
Such thoughts steady our faith; yet there will rise
Some natural tears into the calmest eyes—
Which gaze where forest princes haughty go,
Made for a gaping crowd a raree-show.

But *this* a scene seems where, in courtesy,
The pale face with the forest prince could vie,
For one presided, who, for tact and grace,

In any age had held an honored place—
In Beauty's own dear day had shone a polished Phidian vase!

Oft have I listened to his accents bland,
    And owned the magic of his silvery voice,
In all the graces which life's arts demand,
    Delighted by the justness of his choice.
Not his the stream of lavish, fervid thought—
The rhetoric by passion's magic wrought;
Not his the massive style, the lion port,
Which with the granite class of mind assort;
But, in a range of excellence his own,
With all the charms to soft persuasion known,
Amid our busy people we admire him—"elegant and lone."

He scarce needs words: so exquisite the skill
Which modulates the tones to do his will,
That the mere sound enough would charm the ear,
And lap in its Elysium all who hear.
The intellectual paleness of his cheek,
    The heavy eyelids and slow, tranquil smile,
The well-cut lips from which the graces speak,
    Fit him alike to win or to beguile;
Then those words so well chosen, fit, though few,
Their linked sweetness as our thoughts pursue,
We deem them spoken pearls, or radiant diamond dew.

And never yet did I admire the power
    Which makes so lustrous every threadbare theme—
Which won for Lafayette one other hour,
    And e'en on July Fourth could cast a gleam—
As now, when I behold him play the host,
With all the dignity which red men boast—
With all the courtesy the whites have lost;
Assume the very hue of savage mind,
Yet in rude accents show the thought refined;
Assume the naïveté of infant age,
And in such prattle seem still more a sage;
The golden mean with tact unerring seized,
A courtly critic shone, a simple savage pleased.
The stoic of the woods his skill confessed,
As all the father answered in his breast;
To the sure mark the silver arrow sped,
The "man without a tear" a tear has shed;
And thou hadst wept, hadst thou been there, to see

How true one sentiment must ever be,
In court or camp, the city or the wild—
To rouse the father's heart, you need but name his child.

The speech of Governor Everett on that occasion was admirable; as I think, the happiest attempt ever made to meet the Indian in his own way and catch the tone of his mind. It was said in the newspapers that Keokuck did actually shed tears when addressed as a father. If he did not with his eyes, he well might in his heart.

Not often have they been addressed with such intelligence and tact. The few who have not approached them with sordid rapacity, but from love to them as men having souls to be redeemed, have most frequently been persons intellectually too narrow, too straitly bound in sects or opinions to throw themselves into the character or position of the Indians, or impart to them anything they can make available. The Christ shown them by these missionaries is to them but a new and more powerful Manitou; the signs of the new religion but the fetishes that have aided the conquerors.

Here I will copy some remarks made by a discerning observer, on the methods used by the missionaries, and their natural results:

"Mr. ——— and myself had a very interesting conversation upon the subject of the Indians, their character, capabilities, &c. After ten years' experience among them, he was forced to acknowledge that the results of the missionary efforts had produced nothing calculated to encourage. He thought that there was an intrinsic disability in them to rise above or go beyond the sphere in which they had so long moved. He said that even those Indians who had been converted, and who had adopted the habits of civilization, were very little improved in their real character; they were as selfish, as deceitful, and as indolent as those who were still heathens. They had repaid the kindnesses of the missionaries with the basest ingratitude, killing their cattle and swine and robbing them of their harvests, which they wantonly destroyed. He had abandoned the idea of effecting any general good to the Indians. He had conscientious scruples as to promoting an enterprise so hopeless as that of missions among the Indians by sending accounts to the East that might induce philanthropic individuals to contribute to their support. In fact the whole experience of his intercourse with them seemed to have convinced him of the irremediable degradation of the race. Their fortitude under suffering he considered the result of physical and mental insensibility; their courage, a mere animal excitement, which they found it necessary to inflame before daring to meet a foe. They have no constancy of purpose; and are in fact but little superior to the brutes in point of moral development. It is not astonishing that one looking upon the Indian character from Mr. ——'s point of view should entertain such sentiments. The object of his intercourse with them was to make them apprehend the mysteries of a theology which, to the most enlightened, is an abstruse, metaphysical study; and it is not singular they should prefer their pagan superstitions, which address themselves more directly to the senses. Failing in the attempt to Christianize before civilizing them, he inferred that in the intrinsic degradation of their faculties the obstacle was to be found."

Thus the missionary vainly attempts by once or twice holding up the cross to turn deer and tigers into lambs; vainly attempts to convince the red man that a heavenly mandate takes from him his broad lands. He bows his head, but does not at heart acquiesce. He cannot. It is not true; and if it were, the descent of blood through the same channels for centuries has formed habits of thought not so easily to be disturbed.

Amalgamation would afford the only true and profound means of civilization. But nature seems like all else to declare that this race is fated to perish. Those of mixed blood fade early, and are not generally a fine race. They lose what is best in either type, rather than enhance the value of each, by mingling. There are exceptions—one or two such I know of—but this, it is said, is the general rule.

A traveler observes that the white settlers who live in the woods soon become sallow, lanky, and dejected; the atmosphere of the trees does not agree with Caucasian lungs; and it is perhaps in part an instinct of this which causes the hatred of the new settlers towards trees. The Indian breathed the atmosphere of the forests freely; he loved their shade. As they are effaced from the land, he flees too; a part of the same manifestation, which cannot linger behind its proper era.

The Chippewas have lately petitioned the State of Michigan that they may be admitted as citizens; but this would be vain, unless they could be admitted as brothers to the heart of the white man. And while the latter feels that conviction of superiority which enabled our Wisconsin friend to throw away the gun and send the Indian to fetch it, he needs to be very good, and very wise not to abuse his position. But the white man as yet is a half-tamed pirate, and avails himself as much as ever of the maxim "Might makes right." All that civilization does for the generality is to cover up this with a veil of subtle evasions and chicane, and here and there to rouse the individual mind to appeal to Heaven against it.

I have no hope of liberalizing the missionary, of humanizing the sharks of trade, of infusing the conscientious drop into the flinty bosom of policy, of saving the Indian from immediate degradation and speedy death. The whole sermon may be preached from the text "Needs be that offenses must come, yet woe unto them by whom they come." Yet ere they depart I wish there might be some masterly attempt to reproduce in art or literature what is proper to them—a kind of beauty and grandeur which few of the everyday crowd have hearts to feel, yet which ought to leave in the world its monuments to inspire the thought of genius through all ages. Nothing in this kind has been done masterly; since it was Clevenger's ambition, 'tis pity he had not opportunity to try fully his powers. We hope some other mind may be bent upon it, ere too late. At present the only lively impress of their passage through the world is to be found in such books as Catlin's, and some stories told by the old travelers.

Let me here give another brief tale of the power exerted by the white man over the savage in a trying case; but in this case it was righteous, was moral power.

"We were looking over McKenney's *Tour to the Lakes,* and, on observing the picture of Key-way-no-wut, or the Going Cloud, Mr. B. observed, 'Ah, that is the fellow I came near having a fight with'; and he detailed at length the circumstances. This Indian was a very desperate character, and of whom all the Leech Lake band stood in fear. He would shoot down any Indian who offended him, without the least hesitation, and had become quite the bully of that part of the tribe. The trader at Leech Lake warned Mr. B. to beware of him, and said that he once, when he (the trader) refused to give up to him his stock of wild-rice, went and got his gun and tomahawk, and shook the tomahawk over his head, saying, 'Now, give me your wild-rice.' The trader complied with his exaction, but not so did Mr. B. in the adventure which I am about to relate. Key-way-no-wut came frequently to him with furs, wishing him to give for them cotton-cloth, sugar, flour, &c. Mr. B. explained to him that he could not trade for furs, as he was sent there as a teacher and that it would be like putting his hand into the fire to do so, as the traders would inform against him and he would be sent out of the country. At the same time, he *gave* him the articles which he wished. Key-way-no-wut found this a very convenient way of getting what he wanted, and followed up this sort of game, until at last it became insupportable. One day the Indian brought a very large otter-skin, and said, 'I want to get for this ten pounds of sugar, and some flour and cloth,' adding, 'I am not like other Indians, *I* want to pay for what I get.' Mr. B. found that he must either be robbed of all he had by submitting to these exactions, or take a stand at once. He thought, however, he would try to avoid a scrape, and told his customer he had not so much sugar to spare. 'Give me, then,' said he, 'what you can spare'; and Mr. B., thinking to make him back out, told him he would give him five pounds of sugar for his skin. 'Take it,' said the Indian. He left the skin, telling Mr. B. to take good care of it. Mr. B. took it at once to the trader's store and related the circumstance, congratulating himself that he had got rid of the Indian's exactions. But in about a month Key-way-no-wut appeared, bringing some dirty Indian sugar, and said, 'I have brought back the sugar that I borrowed of you, and I want my otter-skin back.' Mr. B. told him, 'I *bought* an otter-skin of you, but if you will return the other articles you have got for it, perhaps I can get it for you.' 'Where is the skin?' said he very quickly. 'What have you done with it?' Mr. B. replied it was in the trader's store, where he (the Indian) could not get it. At this information he was furious, laid his hands on his knife and tomahawk, and commanded Mr. B. to bring it at once. Mr. B. found this was the crisis, where he must take a stand or be 'rode over rough-shod' by this man. His wife, who was present, was much alarmed and begged he would get the skin for the Indian, but he told her that 'either he or the Indian would soon be master of his house, and if she was afraid to see it decided which was to be so, she had better retire.' He turned to Key-way-no-wut, and addressed him in a stern voice as follows: 'I will *not* give you the skin. How often have you come to my house, and I have shared with you what I had. I gave you tobacco when you were well and medicine when you were sick, and you never went away from my wigwam with your hands empty. And this is the way you return my treatment to you. I had thought you were a man and a chief, but you are not, you are nothing but an old woman. Leave this house, and never enter it again.' Mr. B. said he expected the Indian would attempt his life when he said this, but that he had placed himself in a position so that he could defend himself, and looked straight into the Indian's eye, and like other wild beasts, he quailed before the glance of mental and moral courage. He calmed down at once, and soon began to make apologies. Mr. B. then told him kindly but firmly that, if he wished to walk in the same path with him, he must walk as straight as the crack on the floor before them; adding that he would not walk with anybody who would jostle him by walking so crooked as he had done. He was perfectly tamed, and Mr. B. said he never had any more trouble with him."

The conviction here livingly enforced of the superiority on the side of the white man was thus expressed by the Indian orator at Mackinaw while we were there. After the customary compliments about sun, dew, &c., "This," said he, "is the difference between the white and the red man; the white man looks to the future and paves the way for posterity. The red man never thought of this." This is a statement uncommonly refined for an Indian; but one of the gentlemen present, who understood the Chippewa, vouched for it as a literal rendering of his phrases; and he did indeed touch the vital point of difference. But the Indian, if he understands, cannot make use of his intelligence. The fate of his people is against it, and Pontiac and Philip have no more chance than Julian in the times of old.

The Indian is steady to that simple creed which forms the basis of all his mythology; that there is a God and a life beyond this; a right and wrong which each man can see, betwixt which each man should choose; that good brings with it its reward, and vice its punishment. His moral code, if not as refined as that of civilized nations, is clear and noble in the stress laid upon truth and fidelity. And all unprejudiced observers bear testimony that the Indians, until broken from their old anchorage by intercourse with the whites—who offer them instead a religion of which they furnish neither interpretation nor example—were singularly virtuous, if virtue be allowed to consist in a man's acting up to his own ideas of right.

My friend who joined me at Mackinaw happened on the homeward journey to see a little Chinese girl, who had been sent over by one of the missionaries, and observed that in features, complexion, and gesture, she was a counterpart to the little Indian girls she had just seen playing about on the lake shore.

The parentage of these tribes is still an interesting subject of speculation, though if they be not created for this region, they have become so assimilated to it as to retain little trace of any other. To me it seems most probable that a peculiar race was bestowed on each region, as the lion on one latitude and the white bear on another. As man has two natures—one like that of the plants and animals, adapted to the uses and enjoyments of this planet, another which presages and demands a higher sphere—he is constantly breaking bounds, in proportion as the mental gets the better of the mere instinctive existence. As yet, he loses in harmony of being what he gains in height and extension; the civilized man is a larger mind but a more imperfect nature than the savage.

We hope there will be a national institute containing all the remains of the Indians, all that has been preserved by official intercourse at Washington, Catlin's collection, and a picture-gallery as complete as can be made, with a collection of skulls from all parts of the country. To this should be joined the scanty library that exists on the subject.

A little pamphlet giving an account of the massacre at Chicago has lately been published, which I wish much I had seen while there, as it would have imparted an interest to spots otherwise barren. It is written with animation and in an excellent style, telling just what we want to hear and no more. The traits given of Indian generosity are as characteristic as those of Indian cruelty. A lady who was saved by a friendly chief holding her under the waters of the lake at the moment the balls endangered her, received also in the heat of the conflict a reviving draught from a squaw who saw she was exhausted; and as she lay down, a mat was hung up between her and the scene of butchery, so that she was protected from the sight, though she could not be from sounds full of horror.

I have not wished to write sentimentally about the Indians, however moved by the thought of their wrongs and speedy extinction. I know that the Europeans who took possession of this country felt themselves justified by their superior civilization and religious ideas. Had they been truly civilized or Christianized, the conflicts which sprang from the collision of the two races might have been avoided; but this cannot be expected in movements made by masses of men. The mass has never yet been humanized, though the age may develop a human thought. Since those conflicts and differences did arise, the hatred which sprang from terror and suffering on the European side has naturally warped the whites still further from justice.

The Indian brandishing the scalps of his wife and friends, drinking their blood, and eating their hearts, is by him viewed as a fiend, though at a distant day he will no doubt be considered as having acted the Roman or Carthaginian part of heroic and patriotic self-defense, according to the standard of right and motives prescribed by his religious faith and education. Looked at by his own standard, he is virtuous when he most injures his enemy, and the white, if he be really the superior in enlargement of thought, ought to cast aside his inherited prejudices enough to see this, to look on him in pity and brotherly good will, and do all he can to mitigate the doom of those who survive his past injuries.

In McKenney's book is proposed a project for organizing the Indians under a patriarchal government; but it does not look feasible, even on paper. Could their own intelligent men be left to act unimpeded in their behalf, they would do far better for them than the white thinker with all his general knowledge. But we dare not hope the designs of such will not always be frustrated by barbarous selfishness, as they were in Georgia. *There* was a chance of seeing what might have been done, now lost forever.

Yet let every man look to himself how far this blood shall be required at his hands. Let the missionary, instead of preaching to the Indian, preach to the trader who ruins him of the dreadful account which will be demanded of the followers of Cain, in a sphere where the accents of purity and love come on the ear more decisively than in ours. Let every legislator take the subject to heart, and if he cannot undo the effects of past sin, try for that clear view and right sense that may save us from sinning still more deeply. And let every man and every woman in their private dealings with the subjugated race, avoid all share in embittering by insult or unfeeling prejudice the captivity of Israel.

Chapter VII

SAULT STE MARIE—ST. JOSEPH'S ISLAND—THE LAND OF MUSIC—RAPIDS—
HOMEWARD—GENERAL HULL—THE BOOK TO THE READER

Nine days I passed alone at Mackinaw, except for occasional visits from kind and agreeable residents at the fort and Mr. and Mrs. A. Mr. A., long engaged in the fur-trade, is gratefully remembered by many travelers. From Mrs. A. also I received kind attentions, paid in the vivacious and graceful manner of her nation.

The society at the boarding-house entertained, being of a kind entirely new to me. There were many traders from the remote stations such as La Pointe, Arbre Croche—men who had become half wild and wholly rude by living in the wild; but good-humored, observing, and with a store of knowledge to impart of the kind proper to their place.

There were two little girls here that were pleasant companions for me. One gay, frank, impetuous, but sweet and winning. She was an American, fair and with bright brown hair. The other, a little French Canadian, used to join me in my walks, silently take my hand, and sit at my feet when I stopped in beautiful places. She seemed to understand without a word; and I never shall forget her little figure, with its light but pensive motion, and her delicate, grave features with the pale, clear complexion and soft eye. She was motherless, and much left alone by her father and brothers, who were boatmen. The two little girls were as pretty representatives of Allegro and Penseroso as one would wish to see.

I had been wishing that a boat would come in to take me to the Sault Ste Marie, and several times started to the window at night in hopes that the pant and dusky-red light crossing the waters belonged to such a one; but they were always boats for Chicago or Buffalo, till on the 28th of August Allegro, who shared my plans and wishes, rushed in to tell me that the "General Scott" had come; and in this little steamer accordingly I set off the next morning.

I was the only lady, and attended in the cabin by a Dutch girl and an Indian woman. They both spoke English fluently and entertained me much by accounts of their different experiences.

The Dutch girl told me of a dance among the common people at Amsterdam called the shepherd's dance. The two leaders are dressed as shepherd and shepherdess; they invent to the music all kinds of movements descriptive of things that may happen in the field, and the rest are obliged to follow. I have never heard of any dance which gave such free play to the fancy as this. French dances merely describe the polite movements of society; Spanish and Neapolitan, love; the beautiful mazurkas, &c., are warlike or expressive of wild scenery. But in this one is great room both for fun and fancy.

The Indian was married when young by her parents to a man she did not love. He became dissipated, and did not maintain her. She left him, taking with her their child, for whom and herself she earns a subsistence by going as chambermaid in these boats. Now and then, she said, her husband called on her and asked if he might live with her again; but she always answered no. Here she was far freer than she would have been in civilized life. I was pleased by the nonchalance of this woman, and the perfectly national manner she had preserved after so many years of contact with all kinds of people.

The two women, when I left the boat, made me presents of Indian work such as travelers value, and the manner of the two was characteristic of their different nations. The Indian brought me hers when I was alone, looked bashfully down when she gave it, and made an almost sentimental little speech. The Dutch girl brought hers in public, and bridling her short chin with a self-complacent air, observed she had *bought* it for me. But the feeling of affectionate regard was the same in the minds of both.

Island after island we passed, all fairly shaped and clustering in a friendly way, but with little variety of vegetation. In the afternoon the weather became foggy, and we could not proceed after dark. That was as dull an evening as ever fell.

The next morning the fog still lay heavy, but the captain took me out in his boat on an exploring expedition, and we found the remains of the old English fort on Point St. Joseph. All around was so wholly unmarked by anything but stress of wind and weather, the shores of these islands and their woods so like one another, wild and lonely but nowhere rich and majestic, that there was some charm in the remains of the garden, the remains even of chimneys and a pier. They gave feature to the scene.

Here I gathered many flowers, but they were the same as at Mackinaw.

The captain, though he had been on this trip hundreds of times, had never seen this spot, and never would but for this fog and his desire to entertain me. He presented a striking instance of how men for the sake of getting a living forget to live. It is just the same in the most romantic as the most dull and vulgar places. Men get the harness on so fast that they can never shake it off, unless they guard against this danger from the very first. In Chicago how many men live who never find time to see the prairies, or learn anything unconnected with the business of the day, or about the country they are living in!

So this captain, a man of strong sense and good eyesight, rarely found time to go off the track or look about him on it. He lamented, too, that there had been no call which induced him to develop his powers of expression, so that he might communicate what he had seen for the enjoyment or instruction of others.

This is a common fault among the active men, the truly living, who could tell what life is. It should not be so. Literature should not be left to the mere *literati;* eloquence to the mere orator; every Caesar should be able to write his own commentary. We want a more equal, more thorough, more harmonious development, and there is nothing to hinder the men of this country from it except their own supineness or sordid views.

When the weather did clear, our course up the river was delightful. Long stretched before us the island of St. Joseph, with its fair woods of sugar maple. A gentleman on board, who belongs to the fort at the Sault, said their pastime was to come in the season of making sugar, and pass some time on this island—the days at work and the evening in dancing and other amusements. Work of this kind done in the open air, where everything is temporary and every utensil prepared on the spot, gives life a truly festive air. At such times, there is labor and no care—energy with gaiety, gaiety of the heart.

I think with the same pleasure of the Italian vintage, the Scotch harvest home with its evening dance in the barn, the Russian cabbage feast even, and our huskings and hop-gatherings. The hop-gatherings, where the groups of men and girls are pulling down and filling baskets with the gay festoons, present as graceful pictures as the Italian vintage.

How pleasant is the course along a new river, the sight of new shores— like a life, would but life flow as fast and upbear us with as full a stream. I hoped we should come in sight of the rapids by daylight; but the beautiful sunset was quite gone, and only a young moon trembling over the scene when we came within hearing of them.

I sat up long to hear them merely. It was a thoughtful hour. These two days, the 29th and 30th of August, are memorable in my life; the latter is the birthday of a near friend. I pass them alone, approaching Lake Superior; but I shall not enter into that truly wild and free region; shall not have the canoe voyage, whose daily adventure, with the camping out at night beneath the stars, would have given an interlude of such value to my existence. I shall not see the Pictured Rocks, their chapels and urns. It did not depend on me; it never has, whether such things shall be done or not.

My friends! May they see and do and be more; especially those who have before them a greater number of birthdays, and a more healthy and unfettered existence!

I should like to hear some notes of earthly music tonight. By the faint moonshine I can hardly see the banks; how they look I have no guess, except that there are trees and now and then a light lets me know there are homes with their various interests. I should like to hear some strains of the flute from beneath those trees, just to break the sound of the rapids.

THE LAND OF MUSIC

When no gentle eyebeam charms;
No fond hope the bosom warms;
Of thinking the lone mind is tired—
Naught seems bright to be desired.

Music, be thy sails unfurled;
Bear me to thy better world;
O'er a cold and weltering sea,
Blow thy breezes warm and free.

By sad sighs they ne'er were chilled,
By skeptic spell were never stilled.

> Take me to that far-off shore,
> Where lovers meet to part no more.
> There doubt and fear and sin are o'er;
> The star of love shall set no more.

With the first light of dawn I was up and out, and then was glad I had not seen all the night before, it came upon me with such power in its dewy freshness. Oh, they are beautiful indeed, these rapids! The grace is so much more obvious than the power. I went up through the old Chippewa burying-ground to their head, and sat down on a large stone to look. A little way off was one of the home-lodges, unlike in shape to the temporary ones at Mackinaw, but these have been described by Mrs. Jameson. Women, too, I saw coming home from the woods, stooping under great loads of cedar-boughs that were strapped upon their backs. But in many European countries women carry great loads, even of wood, upon their backs. I used to hear the girls singing and laughing as they were cutting down boughs at Mackinaw; this part of their employment, though laborious, gives them the pleasure of being a great deal in the free woods.

I had ordered a canoe to take me down the rapids, and presently I saw it coming, with the two Indian canoe-men in pink calico shirts moving it about with their long poles with a grace and dexterity worthy fairyland. Now and then they cast the scoop-net—all looked just as I had fancied, only far prettier.

When they came to me, they spread a mat in the middle of the canoe; I sat down, and in less than four minutes we had descended the rapids, a distance of more than three quarters of a mile. I was somewhat disappointed in this being no more of an exploit than I found it. Having heard such expressions used as of "darting" or "shooting down" these rapids, I had fancied there was a wall of rock somewhere, where descent would somehow be accomplished and that there would come some one gasp of terror and delight, some sensation entirely new to me; but I found myself in smooth water before I had time to feel anything but the buoyant pleasure of being carried so lightly through this surf amid the breakers. Now and then the Indians spoke to one another in a vehement jabber, which, however, had no tone that expressed other than pleasant excitement. It is no doubt an act of wonderful dexterity to steer amid these jagged rocks, when one rude touch would tear a hole in the birch canoe; but these men are evidently so used to doing it and so adroit that the silliest person could not feel afraid. I should like to have come down twenty times that I might have had leisure to realize the pleasure. But the fog which had detained us on the way shortened the boat's stay at the Sault, and I wanted my time to walk about.

While coming down the rapids, the Indians caught a whitefish for my breakfast; and certainly it was the best of breakfasts. The whitefish I found quite another thing caught on the spot and cooked immediately from what I had found it at Chicago or Mackinaw. Before, I had had the bad taste to prefer the trout despite the solemn and eloquent remonstrances of the *habitués,* to whom the superiority of whitefish seemed a cardinal point of faith.

I am here reminded that I have omitted that indispensable part of a traveling journal, the account of what we found to eat. I cannot hope to make up by one bold stroke all my omissions of daily record; but that I may show myself not destitute of the common feelings of humanity, I will observe that he whose affections turn in summer towards vegetables should not come to this region till the subject of diet be better understood; that of fruit, too, there is little yet, even at the best hotel tables; that the prairie chickens require no praise from me, and that the trout and whitefish are worthy of the transparency of the lake waters.

In this brief mention I by no means intend to give myself an air of superiority to the subject. If a dinner in the Illinois woods, on dry bread and drier meat with water from the stream that flowed hard by, pleased me best of all, yet at one time when living at a house where nothing was prepared for the table fit to touch, and even the bread could not be partaken of without a headache in consequence, I learnt to understand and sympathize with the anxious tone in which fathers of families, about to take their innocent children into some scene of wild beauty, ask first of all, "Is there a good table?" I shall ask just so in future. Only those whom the Powers have furnished with small traveling cases of ambrosia can take exercise all day, and be happy without even bread morning or night.

Our voyage back was all pleasure. It was the fairest day. I saw the river, the islands, the clouds to the greatest advantage.

On board was an old man, an Illinois farmer, whom I found a most agreeable companion. He had just been with his son and eleven other young men on an exploring expedition to the shores of Lake Superior. He was the only old man of the party, but he had enjoyed most of any the journey. He had been the counselor and playmate, too, of the young ones. He was one of those parents—why so rare?—who understand and live a new life in that of their children, instead of wasting time and young happiness in trying to make them conform to an object and standard of their own. The character and history of each child may be a new and poetic experience to the parent, if he will let it. Our farmer was domestic, judicious, solid; the son, inventive, enterprising, superficial, full of follies, full of resources, always liable to failure, sure to rise above it. The father conformed to and learnt from a character he could not change, and won the sweet from the bitter.

His account of his life at home and of his late adventures among the Indians was very amusing, but I want talent to write it down, and I have not heard the slang of these people intimately enough. There is a good book about Indiana, called the *New Purchase,* written by a person who knows the people of the country well enough to describe them in their own way. It is not witty but penetrating, valuable for its practical wisdom and good-humored fun.

There were many sportsman stories told, too, by those from Illinois and Wisconsin. I do not retain any of these well enough, nor any that I heard earlier, to write them down, though they always interested me from bringing wild natural scenes before the mind. It is pleasant for the sportsman to be in countries so alive with game; yet it is so plentiful that one would think shooting pigeons or grouse would seem more like slaughter than the excitement of skill to a good sportsman. Hunting the deer is full of adventure, and needs only a Scrope to describe it to invest the Western woods with *historic* associations.

How pleasant it was to sit and hear rough men tell pieces out of their own common lives, in place of the frippery talk of some fine circle with its conventional sentiment and timid, secondhand criticism. Free blew the wind, and boldly flowed the stream, named for Mary mother mild.

A fine thundershower came on in the afternoon. It cleared at sunset just as we came in sight of beautiful Mackinaw, over which a rainbow bent in promise of peace.

I have always wondered in reading travels at the childish joy travelers felt at meeting people they knew, and their sense of loneliness when they did not, in places where there was everything new to occupy the attention. So childish, I thought, always to be longing for the new in the old, and the old in the new. Yet just such sadness I felt when I looked on the island glittering in the sunset, canopied by the rainbow, and thought no friend would welcome me there; just such childish joy I felt to see unexpectedly on the landing the face of one whom I called friend.

The remaining two or three days were delightfully spent in walking or boating or sitting at the window to see the Indians go. This was not quite so pleasant as their coming in, though accomplished with the same rapidity; a family not taking half an hour to prepare for departure, and the departing canoe a beautiful object. But they left behind on all the shore the blemishes of their stay—old rags, dried boughs, fragments of food, the marks of their fires. Nature likes to cover up and gloss over spots and scars, but it would take her some time to restore that beach to the state it was in before they came.

S. and I had a mind for a canoe excursion, and we asked one of the traders to engage us two good Indians, that would not only take us out but be sure and bring us back, as we could not hold converse with them. Two others offered their aid besides the chief's son, a fine-looking youth of about sixteen, richly dressed in blue broadcloth, scarlet sash and leggins, with a scarf of brighter red than the rest tied around his head, its ends falling gracefully on one shoulder. They thought it apparently fine amusement to be attending two white women; they carried us into the path of the steamboat which was going out, and paddled with all their force—rather too fast, indeed, for there was something of a swell on the lake and they sometimes threw water into the canoe. However, it flew over the waves, light as a seagull. They would say, "Pull away," and "Ver' warm," and after these words would laugh gaily. They enjoyed the hour, I believe, as much as we.

The house where we lived belonged to the widow of a French trader, an Indian by birth, and wearing the dress of her country. She spoke French fluently, and was very ladylike in her manners. She is a great character among them. They were all the time coming to pay her homage or to get her aid and advice; for she is, I am told, a shrewd woman of business. My companion carried about her sketchbook with her, and the Indians were interested when they saw her using her pencil, though less so than about the sunshade. This lady of the tribe wanted to borrow the sketches of the beach with its lodges and wild groups "to show to the *savages,*" she said.

Of the practical ability of the Indian women, a good specimen is given by McKenney in an amusing story of one who went to Washington, and acted her part there in the "first circles" with a tact and sustained dissimulation worthy of Cagliostro. She seemed to have a thorough love of intrigue for its own sake, and much dramatic talent. Like the chiefs of her nation, when on an expedition among the foe whether for revenge or profit, no impulses of vanity or wayside seductions had power to turn her aside from carrying out her plan as she had originally projected it.

Although I have little to tell, I feel that I have learnt a great deal of the Indians from observing them even in this broken and degraded condition. There is a language of eye and motion which cannot be put into words, and which teaches what words never can. I feel acquainted with the soul of this race; I read its nobler thought in their defaced figures. There *was* a greatness, unique and precious, which he who does not feel will never duly appreciate the majesty of nature in this American continent.

I have mentioned that the Indian orator who addressed the agents on this occasion said the difference between the white man and the red man is this: "The white man no sooner came here than he thought of preparing the way for his posterity; the red man never thought of this." I was assured this was exactly his phrase; and it defines the true difference. We get the better because we do

Look before and after.

But, from the same cause, we

Pine for what is not.

The red man when happy was thoroughly happy; when good, was simply good. He needed the medal to let him know that he *was* good.

These evenings we were happy looking over the old-fashioned garden, over the beach, over the waters and pretty island opposite beneath the growing moon. We did not stay to see it full at Mackinaw; at two o'clock one

night or rather morning, the "Great Western" came snorting in and we must go; and Mackinaw and all the Northwest summer is now to me no more than picture and dream:

A dream within a dream.

These last days at Mackinaw have been pleasanter than the "lonesome" nine, for I have recovered the companion with whom I set out from the East—one who sees all, prizes all, enjoys much, interrupts never.

At Detroit we stopped for half a day. This place is famous in our history, and the unjust anger at its surrender is still expressed by almost everyone who passes there. I had always shared the common feeling on this subject; for the indignation at a disgrace to our arms that seemed so unnecessary has been handed down from father to child, and few of us have taken the pains to ascertain where the blame lay. But now upon the spot, having read all the testimony, I felt convinced that it should rest solely with the government, which by neglecting to sustain General Hull, as he had a right to expect they would, compelled him to take this step or sacrifice many lives, and of the defenseless inhabitants, not of soldiers, to the cruelty of a savage foe for the sake of his reputation.

I am a woman and unlearned in such affairs; but to a person with common sense and good eyesight it is clear, when viewing the location, that under the circumstances he had no prospect of successful defense, and that to attempt it would have been an act of vanity, not valor.

I feel that I am not biased in this judgment by my personal relations, for I have always heard both sides, and though my feelings had been moved by the picture of the old man sitting down in the midst of his children to a retired and despoiled old age, after a life of honor and happy intercourse with the public, yet tranquil, always secure that justice must be done at last, I supposed like others that he deceived himself, and deserved to pay the penalty for failure to the responsibility he had undertaken. Now on the spot I change and believe the country at large must erelong change from this opinion. And I wish to add my testimony, however trifling its weight, before it be drowned in the voice of general assent, that I may do some justice to the feelings which possess me here and now.

A noble boat, the "Wisconsin," was to be launched this afternoon; the whole town was out in many-colored array, the band playing. Our boat swept round to a good position, and all was ready but the "Wisconsin," which could not be made to stir. This was quite a disappointment. It would have been an imposing sight.

In the boat many signs admonished that we were floating eastward. A shabbily dressed phrenologist laid his hand on every head which would bend with half-conceited, half-sheepish expression to the trial of his skill. Knots of people gathered here and there to discuss points of theology. A bereaved lover was seeking religious consolation in Butler's *Analogy,* which he had purchased for that purpose. However, he did not turn over many pages before his attention was drawn aside by the gay glances of certain damsels that came on board at Detroit, and though Butler might afterward be seen sticking from his pocket, it had not weight to impede him from many a feat of lightness and liveliness. I doubt if it went with him from the boat. Some there were, even, discussing the doctrines of Fourier. It seemed a pity they were not going to rather than from the rich and free country where it would be so much easier than with us to try the great experiment of voluntary association, and show beyond a doubt that "an ounce of prevention is worth a pound of cure," a maxim of the "wisdom of nations" which has proved of little practical efficacy as yet.

Better to stop before landing at Buffalo, while I have yet the advantage over some of my readers.

THE BOOK TO THE READER

WHO OPENS, AS AMERICAN READERS OFTEN DO, AT THE END

> To see your cousin in her country home,
> If at the time of blackberries you come,
> "Welcome, my friends," she cries with ready glee,
> "The fruit is ripened, and the paths are free.
> But, madam, you will tear that handsome gown;
> The little boy be sure to tumble down;
> And in the thickets where they ripen best,
> The matted ivy, too, its bower has drest.
> And then the thorns your hands are sure to rend,
> Unless with heavy gloves you will defend;
> Amid most thorns the sweetest roses blow,
> Amid most thorns the sweetest berries grow."

If undeterred you to the fields must go,
　You tear your dresses and you scratch your hands;
But in the places where the berries grow,
　A sweeter fruit the ready sense commands,
Of wild, gay feelings, fancies springing sweet—
Of birdlike pleasures, fluttering and fleet.

Another year, you cannot go yourself,
　To win the berries from the thickets wild,
And housewife skill, instead, has filled the shelf
　With blackberry jam, "by best receipts compiled—
Not made with country sugar, for too strong
The flavors that to maple-juice belong;
But foreign sugar, nicely mixed 'to suit
The taste,' spoils not the fragrance of the fruit."

" 'Tis pretty good," half-tasting, you reply,
"I scarce should know it from fresh blackberry.
But the best pleasure such a fruit can yield
Is to be gathered in the open field;
If only as an article of food,
Cherry or crabapple is quite as good;
And for occasions of festivity,
West India sweetmeats you had better buy."

Thus, such a dish of homely sweets as these
In neither way may chance the taste to please.

Yet try a little with the evening-bread;
Bring a good needle for the spool of thread;
Take fact with fiction, silver with the lead,
And at the mint you can get gold instead;
In fine, read me, even as you would be read.

PART II

Woman in the Nineteenth Century

Prefatory Note

This is Margaret Fuller's best-known and perhaps most important work. One of the famous books of the period, it found an audience both on the American frontier and in Europe, and is a landmark in the history of feminism. It paved the way philosophically for the Seneca Falls Convention in 1848 and the woman's rights movement of later years. The book, with its forthright attack on the conventions and taboos of the polite society of the day, was its author's farewell to the little world of Boston and Cambridge, which had done as much to hamper as to help her development. The thread of feminist thought runs through all Margaret Fuller's works: she was always struggling against the fetters which her sex imposed upon her in her day. Illustration of this preoccupation will be found in *Summer on the Lakes, Things and Thoughts in Europe,* and her letters. Many of the essays she contributed to the *Tribune* are devoted to feminist topics.

Woman was revised and expanded, during a vacation at Fishkill on the Hudson in the fall of 1844, from an earlier version which had appeared in the *Dial* for July 1843 under the title of "The Great Lawsuit." It was published in February 1845 by Greeley & McElrath of New York, and created considerable stir. As Greeley wrote to Rufus W. Griswold, one of the critical pontiffs of the day, "It is not elegantly written, but every line talks." Commenting on its independence and unmitigated radicalism, Poe observed: *"Woman in the Nineteenth Century* is a book which few women in the country could have written, and no woman in the country would have published, with the exception of Miss Fuller." It established its author as a serious writer in a larger world than that of Boston; when its author went to London a year and a half later, she wrote home: "I have been recd here with a warmth that surprized me; it is chiefly to *Woman in the 19th* that I am indebted for this; that little volume has been read & prized by many."

Soon after finishing the book, Margaret Fuller wrote an interesting letter about it to her close friend William Henry Channing, which will be found on page 567.

The text here given is from Arthur B. Fuller's reprint, *Woman in the*

Nineteenth Century and Kindred Papers relating to the Sphere, Condition, and Duties of Woman (Boston: John P. Jewett and Co., 1855). It is unfortunate that only in this instance did Arthur Fuller see fit "to publish . . . without alteration, as most just to her views and the reader." Since the work is abundantly provided with literary illustrations, the appendices have been omitted. They consist of extracts from Apuleius, Petrarch, Lockhart, Spinoza, W. E. Channing, Stirling, Sue, Alcott(?), Mrs. Grant, the author's own early notes on Euripides and Sophocles, and Milton.

Woman in the Nineteenth Century

The following essay is a reproduction, modified and expanded, of an article published in the *Dial,* Boston, July 1843, under the title of "The Great Lawsuit —Man *versus* Men; Woman *versus* Women."

This article excited a good deal of sympathy and still more interest. It is in compliance with wishes expressed from many quarters that it is prepared for publication in its present form.

Objections having been made to the former title as not sufficiently easy to be understood, the present has been substituted as expressive of the main purpose of the essay; though by myself the other is preferred, partly for the reason others do not like it—that is, that it requires some thought to see what it means, and might thus prepare the reader to meet me on my own ground. Besides it offers a larger scope, and is in that way more just to my desire. I meant by that title to intimate the fact that while it is the destiny of Man in the course of the ages to ascertain and fulfill the law of his being, so that his life shall be seen as a whole to be that of an angel or messenger, the action of prejudices and passions which attend in the day the growth of the individual is continually obstructing the holy work that is to make the earth a part of heaven. By Man I mean both man and woman; these are the two halves of one thought. I lay no especial stress on the welfare of either. I believe that the development of the one cannot be effected without that of the other. My highest wish is that this truth should be distinctly and rationally apprehended, and the conditions of life and freedom recognized as the same for the daughters and the sons of time; twin exponents of a divine thought.

I solicit a sincere and patient attention from those who open the following pages at all. I solicit of women that they will lay it to heart to ascertain what is for them the liberty of law. It is for this and not for any, the largest, extension of partial privileges that I seek. I ask them, if interested by these suggestions, to search their own experience and intuitions for better, and fill up with fit materials the trenches that hedge them in. From men I ask a noble and earnest attention to anything that can be offered on this great and still obscure subject, such as I have met from many with whom I stand in private relations.

And may truth, unpolluted by prejudice, vanity, or selfishness, be granted daily more and more as the due of inheritance and only valuable conquest for us all!

November 1844

Frailty, thy name is WOMAN.

The Earth waits for her Queen.

The connection between these quotations may not be obvious but it is strict. Yet would any contradict us, if we made them applicable to the other side and began also,

> Frailty, thy name is MAN.
>
> The Earth waits for its King?

Yet Man, if not yet fully installed in his powers, has given much earnest of his claims. Frail he is indeed—how frail, how impure! Yet often has the vein of gold displayed itself amid the baser ores, and Man has appeared before us in princely promise worthy of his future.

If oftentimes we see the prodigal son feeding on the husks in the fair field no more his own, anon we raise the eyelids, heavy from bitter tears, to behold in him the radiant apparition of genius and love, demanding not less than the all of goodness, power, and beauty. We see that in him the largest claim finds a due foundation. That claim is for no partial sway, no exclusive possession. He cannot be satisfied with any one gift of life, any one department of knowledge or telescopic peep at the heavens. He feels himself called to understand and aid Nature, that she may through his intelligence be raised and interpreted; to be a student of and servant to the universe-spirit; and king of his planet, that as an angelic minister he may bring it into conscious harmony with the law of that spirit.

In clear, triumphant moments many times has rung through the spheres the prophecy of his jubilee; and those moments, though past in time, have been translated into eternity by thought; the bright signs they left hang in the heavens as single stars or constellations and already a thickly sown radiance consoles the wanderer in the darkest night. Other heroes since Hercules have fulfilled the zodiac of beneficent labors, and then given up

their mortal part to the fire without a murmur; while no God dared deny
that they should have their reward,

> Siquis tamen, Hercule, siquis
> Forte Deo doliturus erit, data præmia nollet,
> Sed meruise dari sciet, invitus que probabit,
> Assensere Dei.

Sages and lawgivers have bent their whole nature to the search for truth,
and thought themselves happy if they could buy, with the sacrifice of all
temporal ease and pleasure, one seed for the future Eden. Poets and priests
have strung the lyre with the heartstrings, poured out their best blood upon
the altar, which, reared anew from age to age, shall at last sustain the flame
pure enough to rise to highest heaven. Shall we not name with as deep a
benediction those who, if not so immediately or so consciously in connection with the eternal truth, yet led and fashioned by a divine instinct serve
no less to develop and interpret the open secret of love passing into life,
energy creating for the purpose of happiness; the artist whose hand, drawn
by a pre-existent harmony to a certain medium, molds it to forms of life
more highly and completely organized than are seen elsewhere, and by
carrying out the intention of Nature reveals her meaning to those who are
not yet wise enough to divine it; the philosopher who listens steadily for
laws and causes, and from those obvious infers those yet unknown; the historian who in faith that all events must have their reason and their aim
records them, and thus fills archives from which the youth of prophets may
be fed; the man of science dissecting the statements, testing the facts, and
demonstrating order, even where he cannot its purpose?

Lives, too, which bear none of these names have yielded tones of no less
significance. The candlestick set in a low place has given light as faithfully
where it was needed as that upon the hill. In close alleys, in dismal nooks,
the Word has been read as distinctly as when shown by angels to holy men
in the dark prison. Those who till a spot of earth scarcely larger than is
wanted for a grave have deserved that the sun should shine upon its sod
till violets answer.

So great has been from time to time the promise, that in all ages men
have said the gods themselves came down to dwell with them; that the
All-Creating wandered on the earth to taste in a limited nature the sweet-

ness of virtue; that the All-Sustaining incarnated himself to guard in space and time the destinies of this world; that heavenly genius dwelt among the shepherds to sing to them and teach them how to sing. Indeed,

Der stets den Hirten gnädig sich bewies.

"He has constantly shown himself favorable to shepherds."

And the dwellers in green pastures and natural students of the stars were selected to hail first among men the holy child, whose life and death were to present the type of excellence which has sustained the heart of so large a portion of mankind in these later generations.

Such marks have been made by the footsteps of *man* (still, alas, to be spoken of as the *ideal* man) wherever he has passed through the wilderness of *men,* and whenever the pygmies stepped in one of those, they felt dilate within the breast somewhat that promised nobler stature and purer blood. They were impelled to forsake their evil ways of decrepit skepticism and covetousness of corruptible possessions. Convictions flowed in upon them. They, too, raised the cry: God is living now, today; and all beings are brothers, for they are his children. Simple words enough, yet which only angelic natures can use or hear in their full, free sense.

These were the triumphant moments; but soon the lower nature took its turn, and the era of a truly human life was postponed.

Thus is Man still a stranger in his inheritance, still a pleader, still a pilgrim. Yet his happiness is secure in the end. And now no more a glimmering consciousness but assurance begins to be felt and spoken, that the highest ideal Man can form of his own powers is that which he is destined to attain. Whatever the soul knows how to seek, it cannot fail to obtain. This is the Law and the Prophets. Knock and it shall be opened; seek and ye shall find. It is demonstrated; it is a maxim. Man no longer paints his proper nature in some form, and says, 'Prometheus had it; it is God-like"; but "Man must have it; it is human." However disputed by many, however ignorantly used or falsified by those who do receive it, the fact of a universal, unceasing revelation has been too clearly stated in words to be lost sight of in thought; and sermons preached from the text, "Be ye perfect," are the only sermons of a pervasive and deep-searching influence.

But among those who meditate upon this text there is a great difference of view as to the way in which perfection shall be sought.

"Through the intellect," say some. "Gather from every growth of life its seed of thought; look behind every symbol for its law; if thou canst *see* clearly, the rest will follow."

"Through the life," say others. "Do the best thou knowest today. Shrink not from frequent error in this gradual, fragmentary state. Follow thy light for as much as it will show thee; be faithful as far as thou canst, in hope that faith presently will lead to sight. Help others without blaming their need of thy help. Love much, and be forgiven."

"It needs not intellect, needs not experience," says a third. "If you took the true way, your destiny would be accomplished in a purer and more natural order. You would not learn through facts of thought or action, but express through them the certainties of wisdom. In quietness yield thy soul to the causal soul. Do not disturb thy apprenticeship by premature effort; neither check the tide of instruction by methods of thy own. Be still; seek not, but wait in obedience. Thy commission will be given."

Could we indeed say what we want, could we give a description of the child that is lost, he would be found. As soon as the soul can affirm clearly that a certain demonstration is wanted, it is at hand. When the Jewish prophet described the Lamb as the expression of what was required by the coming era, the time drew nigh. But we say not, see not as yet clearly what we would. Those who call for a more triumphant expression of love, a love that cannot be crucified, show not a perfect sense of what has already been given. Love has already been expressed that made all things new, that gave the worm its place and ministry as well as the eagle; a love to which it was alike to descend into the depths of hell, or to sit at the right hand of the Father.

Yet no doubt a new manifestation is at hand, a new hour in the day of Man. We cannot expect to see any one sample of completed being, when the mass of men still lie engaged in the sod, or use the freedom of their limbs only with wolfish energy. The tree cannot come to flower till its root be free from the cankering worm, and its whole growth open to air and light. While any one is base, none can be entirely free and noble. Yet something new shall presently be shown of the life of man, for hearts crave, if minds do not know how to ask it.

Among the strains of prophecy, the following by an earnest mind of a foreign land, written some thirty years ago, is not yet outgrown; and it has the merit of being a positive appeal from the heart, instead of a critical declaration what Man should *not* do.

"The ministry of Man implies that he must be filled from the divine fountains which are being engendered through all eternity, so that at the mere name of his master he may be able to cast all his enemies into the abyss; that he may deliver all parts of nature from the barriers that imprison them; that he may purge the terrestrial atmosphere from the poisons that infect it; that he may preserve the bodies of men from the corrupt influences that surround and the maladies that afflict them; still more, that he may keep their souls pure from the malignant insinuations which pollute and the gloomy images that obscure them; that he may restore its serenity to the Word, which false words of men fill with mourning and sadness; that he may satisfy the desires of the angels, who await from him the development of the marvels of nature; that in fine his world may be filled with God, as eternity is." *

Another attempt we will give, by an obscure observer of our own day and country, to draw some lines of the desired image. It was suggested by seeing the design of Crawford's *Orpheus,* and connecting with the circumstance of the American in his garret at Rome making choice of this subject, that of Americans here at home showing such ambition to represent the character by calling their prose and verse "Orphic sayings," "Orphics." We wish we could add that they have shown that musical apprehension of the progress of Nature through her ascending gradations which entitled them so to do, but their attempts are frigid though sometimes grand; in their strain we are not warmed by the fire which fertilized the soil of Greece.

Orpheus was a lawgiver by theocratic commission. He understood Nature, and made her forms move to his music. He told her secrets in the form of hymns, Nature as seen in the mind of God. His soul went forth toward all beings, yet could remain sternly faithful to a chosen type of excellence. Seeking what he loved, he feared not death nor hell; neither

---

* St. Martin.

could any shape of dread daunt his faith in the power of the celestial harmony that filled his soul.

It seemed significant of the state of things in this country that the sculptor should have represented the seer at the moment when he was obliged with his hand to shade his eyes.

> Each Orpheus must to the depths descend;
>   For only thus the Poet can be wise;
> Must make the sad Persephone his friend,
>   And buried love to second life arise;
> Again his love must lose through too much love,
>   Must lose his life by living life too true,
> For what he sought below is passed above,
>   Already done is all that he would do;
> Must tune all being with his single lyre,
>   Must melt all rocks free from their primal pain,
> Must search all nature with his one soul's fire,
>   Must bind anew all forms in heavenly chain.
> If he already sees what he must do,
> Well may he shade his eyes from the far-shining view.

A better comment could not be made on what is required to perfect Man, and place him in that superior position for which he was designed, than by the interpretation of Bacon upon the legends of the Siren coast. "When the wise Ulysses passed," says he, "he caused his mariners to stop their ears with wax, knowing there was in them no power to resist the lure of that voluptuous song. But he, the much experienced man, who wished to be experienced in all, and use all to the service of wisdom, desired to hear the song that he might understand its meaning. Yet, distrusting his own power to be firm in his better purpose, he caused himself to be bound to the mast, that he might be kept secure against his own weakness. But Orpheus passed unfettered, so absorbed in singing hymns to the gods that he could not even hear those sounds of degrading enchantment."

Meanwhile not a few believe, and men themselves have expressed the opinion, that the time is come when Eurydice is to call for an Orpheus rather than Orpheus for Eurydice; that the idea of Man, however imperfectly brought out, has been far more so than that of Woman; that she, the other half of the same thought, the other chamber of the heart of life, needs now take her turn in the full pulsation, and that improvement in the daughters will best aid in the reformation of the sons of this age.

It should be remarked that as the principle of liberty is better understood, and more nobly interpreted, a broader protest is made in behalf of Woman. As men become aware that few men have had a fair chance, they are inclined to say that no women have had a fair chance. The French Revolution, that strangely disguised angel, bore witness in favor of Woman, but interpreted her claims no less ignorantly than those of Man. Its idea of happiness did not rise beyond outward enjoyment, unobstructed by the tyranny of others. The title it gave was *citoyen, citoyenne;* and it is not unimportant to Woman that even this species of equality was awarded her. Before, she could be condemned to perish on the scaffold for treason, not as a citizen but as a subject. The right with which this title then invested a human being was that of bloodshed and license. The Goddess of Liberty was impure. As we read the poem addressed to her not long since by Béranger, we can scarcely refrain from tears as painful as the tears of blood that flowed when "such crimes were committed in her name." Yes! Man, born to purify and animate the unintelligent and the cold, can in his madness degrade and pollute no less the fair and the chaste. Yet truth was prophesied in the ravings of that hideous fever caused by long ignorance and abuse. Europe is conning a valued lesson from the bloodstained page. The same tendencies further unfolded will bear good fruit in this country.

Yet by men in this country, as by the Jews when Moses was leading them to the promised land, everything has been done that inherited depravity could do to hinder the promise of Heaven from its fulfillment. The cross, here as elsewhere, has been planted only to be blasphemed by cruelty and fraud. The name of the Prince of Peace has been profaned by all kinds of injustice toward the Gentile whom he said he came to save. But I need not speak of what has been done toward the Red Man, the Black Man. Those deeds are the scoff of the world; and they have been accompanied by such pious words that the gentlest would not dare to intercede with, "Father, forgive them, for they know not what they do."

Here as elsewhere the gain of creation consists always in the growth of individual minds, which live and aspire as flowers bloom and birds sing in the midst of morasses; and in the continual development of that thought, the thought of human destiny, which is given to eternity adequately to express, and which ages of failure only seemingly impede. Only seemingly; and whatever seems to the contrary, this country is as surely destined to elucidate a great moral law as Europe was to promote the mental culture of Man.

Though the national independence be blurred by the servility of individuals; though freedom and equality have been proclaimed only to leave room for a monstrous display of slavedealing and slavekeeping; though the free American so often feels himself free, like the Roman, only to pamper his appetites and his indolence through the misery of his fellow-beings; still it is not in vain that the verbal statement has been made, "All men are born free and equal." There it stands, a golden certainty wherewith to encourage the good, to shame the bad. The New World may be called clearly to perceive that it incurs the utmost penalty if it reject or oppress the sorrowful brother. And if men are deaf, the angels hear. But men cannot be deaf. It is inevitable that an external freedom, an independence of the encroachments of other men such as has been achieved for the nation, should be so also for every member of it. That which has once been clearly conceived in the intelligence cannot fail sooner or later to be acted out. It has become a law as irrevocable as that of the Medes in their ancient dominion; men will privately sin against it, but the law, as expressed by a leading mind of the age,*

> *Tutti fatti a sembianza d'un Solo,*
> *Figli tutti d'un solo riscatto,*
> *In qual'ora, in qual parte del suolo*
> *Trascorriamo quest' aura vital,*
> *Siam fratelli, siam stretti ad un patto:*
> *Maladetto colui che lo infrange,*
> *Che s'innalza sul fiacco che piange*
> *Che contrista uno spirito immortal.*

> (All made in the likeness of the One,
>   All children of one ransom,
> In whatever hour, in whatever part of the soil,
>   We draw this vital air,
> We are brothers; we must be bound by one compact;
>   Accursed he who infringes it,

---

* Manzoni.

Who raises himself upon the weak who weep,
Who saddens an immortal spirit.)

This law cannot fail of universal recognition. Accursed be he who willingly saddens an immortal spirit—doomed to infamy in later, wiser ages, doomed in future stages of his own being to deadly penance only short of death. Accursed be he who sins in ignorance, if that ignorance be caused by sloth.

We sicken no less at the pomp than the strife of words. We feel that never were lungs so puffed with the wind of declamation on moral and religious subjects as now. We are tempted to implore these "word-heroes," these word-Catos, word-Christs, to beware of cant * above all things; to remember that hypocrisy is the most hopeless as well as the meanest of crimes, and that those must surely be polluted by it who do not reserve a part of their morality and religion for private use. Landor says that he cannot have a great deal of mind who cannot afford to let the larger part of it lie fallow; and what is true of genius is not less so of virtue. The tongue is a valuable member, but should appropriate but a small part of the vital juices that are needful all over the body. We feel that the mind may "grow black and rancid in the smoke" even "of altars." We start up from the harangue to go into our closet and shut the door. There inquires the spirit, "Is this rhetoric the bloom of healthy blood, or a false pigment artfully laid on?" And yet again we know where is so much smoke, must be some fire; with so much talk about virtue and freedom, must be mingled some desire for them; that it cannot be in vain that such have become the common topics of conversation among men rather than schemes for tyranny and plunder, that the very newspapers see it best to proclaim themselves "Pilgrims," "Puritans," "Heralds of Holiness." The king that maintains so costly a retinue cannot be a mere boast or Barabbas fiction. We have waited here long in the dust, we are tired and hungry, but the triumphal procession must appear at last.

Of all its banners, none has been more steadily upheld, and under none

---

* Dr. Johnson's one piece of advice should be written on every door: "Clear your mind of cant." But Byron, to whom it was so acceptable, in clearing away the noxious vine shook down the building. Sterling's emendation is worthy of honor:

Realize your cant, not cast it off.

have more valor and willingness for real sacrifices been shown, than that of the champions of the enslaved African. And this band it is which, partly from a natural following out of principles, partly because many women have been prominent in that cause, makes just now the warmest appeal in behalf of Woman.

Though there has been a growing liberality on this subject, yet society at large is not so prepared for the demands of this party, but that its members are and will be for some time coldly regarded as the Jacobins of their day.

"Is it not enough," cries the irritated trader, "that you have done all you could to break up the national union and thus destroy the prosperity of our country, but now you must be trying to break up family union, to take my wife away from the cradle and the kitchen-hearth to vote at polls and preach from a pulpit? Of course, if she does such things, she cannot attend to those of her own sphere. She is happy enough as she is. She has more leisure than I have—every means of improvement, every indulgence."

"Have you asked her whether she was satisfied with these *indulgences?*"

"No, but I know she is. She is too amiable to desire what would make me unhappy, and too judicious to wish to step beyond the sphere of her sex. I will never consent to have our peace disturbed by any such discussions."

" 'Consent—you?' It is not consent from you that is in question—it is assent from your wife."

"Am not I the head of my house?"

"You are not the head of your wife. God has given her a mind of her own."

"I am the head, and she the heart."

"God grant you play true to one another, then! I suppose I am to be grateful that you did not say she was only the hand. If the head represses no natural pulse of the heart, there can be no question as to your giving your consent. Both will be of one accord, and there needs but to present any question to get a full and true answer. There is no need of precaution, of indulgence, or consent. But our doubt is whether the heart *does* consent with the head, or only obeys its decrees with a passiveness that precludes the exercise of its natural powers, or a repugnance that turns sweet qualities to bitter, or a doubt that lays waste the fair occasions of life. It is to ascertain the truth that we propose some liberating measures."

Thus vaguely are these questions proposed and discussed at present. But their being proposed at all implies much thought and suggests more. Many women are considering within themselves what they need that they have not, and what they can have if they find they need it. Many men are considering whether women are capable of being and having more than they are and have, *and* whether, if so, it will be best to consent to improvement in their condition.

This morning, I open the Boston *Daily Mail,* and find in its "poet's corner" a translation of Schiller's "Dignity of Woman." In the advertisement of a book on America, I see in the table of contents this sequence, "Republican Institutions. American Slavery. American Ladies."

I open the *Deutsche Schnellpost,* published in New York, and find at the head of a column, *Juden- und Frauen-emanzipation in Ungarn* ("Emancipation of Jews and Women in Hungary").

The past year has seen action in the Rhode Island legislature to secure married women rights over their own property, where men showed that a very little examination of the subject could teach them much; an article in the *Democratic Review* on the same subject more largely considered, written by a woman impelled, it is said, by glaring wrong to a distinguished friend, having shown the defects in the existing laws and the state of opinion from which they spring; and an answer from the revered old man, J. Q. Adams, in some respects the Phocion of his time, to an address made him by some ladies. To this last I shall again advert in another place.

These symptoms of the times have come under my view quite accidentally: one who seeks may each month or week collect more.

The numerous party, whose opinions are already labeled and adjusted too much to their mind to admit of any new light, strive by lectures on some model woman of bridelike beauty and gentleness, by writing and lending little treatises intended to mark out with precision the limits of Woman's sphere and Woman's mission, to prevent other than the rightful shepherd from climbing the wall, or the flock from using any chance to go astray.

Without enrolling ourselves at once on either side, let us look upon the subject from the best point of view which today offers; no better, it is to be feared, than a high house-top. A high hilltop or at least a cathedral-spire would be desirable.

It may well be an Anti-Slavery party that pleads for Woman, if we consider merely that she does not hold property on equal terms with men; so that if a husband dies without making a will, the wife, instead of taking at once his place as head of the family, inherits only a part of his fortune, often brought him by herself, as if she were a child or ward only, not an equal partner.

We will not speak of the innumerable instances in which profligate and idle men live upon the earnings of industrious wives; or if the wives leave them and take with them the children to perform the double duty of mother and father, follow from place to place and threaten to rob them of the children, if deprived of the rights of a husband as they call them, planting themselves in their poor lodgings, frightening them into paying tribute by taking from them the children, running into debt at the expense of these otherwise so overtasked helots. Such instances count up by scores within my own memory. I have seen the husband who had stained himself by a long course of low vice, till his wife was wearied from her heroic forgiveness by finding that his treachery made it useless, and that if she would provide bread for herself and her children, she must be separate from his ill fame—I have known this man come to install himself in the chamber of a woman who loathed him, and say she should never take food without his company. I have known these men steal their children, whom they knew they had no means to maintain, take them into dissolute company, expose them to bodily danger, to frighten the poor woman to whom, it seems, the fact that she alone had borne the pangs of their birth and nourished their infancy does not give an equal right to them. I do believe that this mode of kidnaping—and it is frequent enough in all classes of society—will be by the next age viewed as it is by Heaven now, and that the man who avails himself of the shelter of men's laws to steal from a mother her own children, or arrogate any superior right in them, save that of superior virtue, will bear the stigma he deserves in common with him who steals grown men from their motherland, their hopes, and their homes.

I said we will not speak of this now; yet I *have* spoken, for the subject makes me feel too much. I could give instances that would startle the most vulgar and callous; but I will not, for the public opinion of their own sex is already against such men, and where cases of extreme tyranny are made known, there is private action in the wife's favor. But she ought not to need this, nor, I think, can she long. Men must soon see that as on their own ground Woman is the weaker party, she ought to have legal protection which would make such oppression impossible. But I would not deal with "atrocious instances" except in the way of illustration, neither demand from men a partial redress in some one matter, but go to the root of the whole. If principles could be established, particulars would adjust themselves aright. Ascertain the true destiny of Woman; give her legitimate hopes, and a standard within herself; marriage and all other relations would by degrees be harmonized with these.

But to return to the historical progress of this matter. Knowing that there exists in the minds of men a tone of feeling toward women as toward slaves, such as is expressed in the common phrase, "Tell that to women and children"; that the infinite soul can only work through them in already ascertained limits; that the gift of reason, Man's highest prerogative, is allotted to them in much lower degree; that they must be kept from mischief and melancholy by being constantly engaged in active labor, which is to be furnished and directed by those better able to think, &c., &c.—we need not multiply instances, for who can review the experience of last week without recalling words which imply, whether in jest or earnest, these views or views like these—knowing this, can we wonder that many reformers think that measures are not likely to be taken in behalf of women, unless their wishes could be publicly represented by women?

"That can never be necessary," cry the other side. "All men are privately influenced by women; each has his wife, sister, or female friends, and is too much biased by these relations to fail of representing their interests; and if this is not enough, let them propose and enforce their wishes with the pen. The beauty of home would be destroyed, the delicacy of the sex be violated, the dignity of halls of legislation degraded by an attempt to introduce them there. Such duties are inconsistent with those of a mother"; and then we have ludicrous pictures of ladies in hysterics at the polls, and senate chambers filled with cradles.

But if in reply we admit as truth that Woman seems destined by nature rather for the inner circle, we must add that the arrangements of civilized life have not been as yet such as to secure it to her. Her circle, if the duller, is not the quieter. If kept from "excitement," she is not from drudgery. Not only the Indian squaw carries the burdens of the camp, but the favorites of Louis XIV accompany him in his journeys, and the washerwoman stands at her tub and carries home her work at all seasons and in all states of health. Those who think the physical circumstances of Woman would make a part in the affairs of national government unsuitable are by no means those who think it impossible for Negresses to endure field work even during pregnancy, or for seamstresses to go through their killing labors.

As to the use of the pen, there was quite as much opposition to Woman's possessing herself of that help to free agency as there is now to her seizing on the rostrum or the desk; and she is likely to draw, from a permission to plead her cause that way, opposite inferences to what might be wished by those who now grant it.

As to the possibility of her filling with grace and dignity any such position, we should think those who had seen the great actresses and heard the Quaker preachers of modern times would not doubt that Woman can express publicly the fullness of thought and creation without losing any of the peculiar beauty of her sex. What can pollute and tarnish is to act thus from any motive except that something needs to be said or done. Woman could take part in the processions, the songs, the dances of old religion; no one fancied her delicacy was impaired by appearing in public for such a cause.

As to her home, she is not likely to leave it more than she now does for balls, theaters, meetings for promoting missions, revival meetings, and others to which she flies in hope of an animation for her existence commensurate with what she sees enjoyed by men. Governors of ladies' fairs are no less engrossed by such a charge than the governor of a state by his; presidents of Washingtonian societies no less away from home than presidents of conventions. If men look straitly to it, they will find that unless their lives are domestic, those of the women will not be. A house is no home unless it contain food and fire for the mind as well as for the body. The female Greek of our day is as much in the street as the male to cry, "What news?" We doubt not it was the same in Athens of old. The women, shut out from the market-place, made up for it at the religious festivals. For human beings are not so constituted that they can live without expansion. If they do not get it in one way, they must in another or perish.

As to men's representing women fairly at present, while we hear from men who owe to their wives not only all that is comfortable or graceful but all that is wise in the arrangement of their lives the frequent remark, "You cannot reason with a woman"—when from those of delicacy, nobleness, and poetic culture falls the contemptuous phrase "women and children," and that in no light sally of the hour, but in works intended to give a permanent statement of the best experiences—when not one man in the million, shall I say? no, not in the hundred million, can rise above the belief that Woman was made *for Man*—when such traits as these are daily forced upon the attention, can we feel that Man will always do justice to the interests of Woman? Can we think that he takes a sufficiently discerning and religious view of her office and destiny *ever* to do her justice, except when prompted by sentiment—accidentally or transiently, that is, for the sentiment will vary according to the relations in which he is placed? The lover, the poet, the artist are likely to view her nobly. The father and the philosopher have some chance of liberality; the man of the world, the legislator for expediency none.

Under these circumstances, without attaching importance in themselves to the changes demanded by the champions of Woman, we hail them as signs of the times. We would have every arbitrary barrier thrown down. We would have every path laid open to Woman as freely as to Man. Were this done and a slight temporary fermentation allowed to subside, we should see crystallizations more pure and of more various beauty. We believe the divine energy would pervade nature to a degree unknown in the history of former ages, and that no discordant collision but a ravishing harmony of the spheres would ensue.

Yet then and only then will mankind be ripe for this, when inward and outward freedom for Woman as much as for Man shall be acknowledged as a *right,* not yielded as a concession. As the friend of the Negro assumes that one man cannot by right hold another in bondage, so should the friend of Woman assume that Man cannot by right lay even well-meant restrictions on Woman. If the Negro be a soul, if the woman be a soul, appareled in flesh, to one Master only are they accountable. There is but one law for souls, and if there is to be an interpreter of it, he must come not as man or son of man, but as son of God.

Were thought and feeling once so far elevated that Man should esteem himself the brother and friend, but nowise the lord and tutor, of Woman— were he really bound with her in equal worship—arrangements as to function and employment would be of no consequence. What Woman needs is not as a woman to act or rule, but as a nature to grow, as an intellect to discern, as a soul to live freely and unimpeded to unfold such powers as were given her when we left our common home. If fewer talents were given her, yet if allowed the free and full employment of these, so that she may render back to the giver his own with usury, she will not complain; nay, I dare to say she will bless and rejoice in her earthly birthplace, her earthly lot. Let us consider what obstructions impede this good era, and what signs give reason to hope that it draws near.

I was talking on this subject with Miranda, a woman, who, if any in the world could, might speak without heat and bitterness of the position of her sex. Her father was a man who cherished no sentimental reverence for Woman, but a firm belief in the equality of the sexes. She was his eldest child, and came to him at an age when he needed a companion. From the time she could speak and go alone, he addressed her not as a plaything but as a living mind. Among the few verses he ever wrote was a copy addressed to this child, when the first locks were cut from her head; and the reverence expressed on this occasion for that cherished head, he never belied. It was to him the temple of immortal intellect. He respected his child, however, too much to be an indulgent parent. He called on her for clear judgment, for courage, for honor and fidelity; in short, for such virtues as he knew. In so far as he possessed the keys to the wonders of this universe, he allowed free use of them to her, and by the incentive of a high expectation he forbade, so far as possible, that she should let the privilege lie idle.

Thus this child was early led to feel herself a child of the spirit. She took her place easily not only in the world of organized being, but in the world of mind. A dignified sense of self-dependence was given as all her portion, and she found it a sure anchor. Herself securely anchored, her relations

with others were established with equal security. She was fortunate in a
total absence of those charms which might have drawn to her bewildering
flatteries, and in a strong electric nature which repelled those who did not
belong to her and attracted those who did. With men and women her relations were noble—affectionate without passion, intellectual without coldness. The world was free to her, and she lived freely in it. Outward adversity came and inward conflict, but that faith and self-respect had early
been awakened which must always lead at last to an outward serenity and
an inward peace.

Of Miranda I had always thought as an example, that the restraints upon
the sex were insuperable only to those who think them so, or who noisily
strive to break them. She had taken a course of her own, and no man stood
in her way. Many of her acts had been unusual, but excited no uproar. Few
helped but none checked her; and the many men who knew her mind and
her life showed to her confidence as to a brother, gentleness as to a sister. And
not only refined, but very coarse men approved and aided one in whom they
saw resolution and clearness of design. Her mind was often the leading
one, always effective.

When I talked with her upon these matters and had said very much
what I have written, she smilingly replied: "And yet we must admit that
I have been fortunate, and this should not be. My good father's early trust
gave the first bias, and the rest followed of course. It is true that I have had
less outward aid in after years than most women; but that is of little consequence. Religion was early awakened in my soul—a sense that what the
soul is capable to ask it must attain, and that though I might be aided and
instructed by others, I must depend on myself as the only constant friend.
This self-dependence, which was honored in me, is deprecated as a fault
in most women. They are taught to learn their rule from without, not to
unfold it from within.

"This is the fault of Man, who is still vain, and wishes to be more important to Woman than by right he should be."

"Men have not shown this disposition toward you," I said.

"No, because the position I early was enabled to take was one of self-
reliance. And were all women as sure of their wants as I was, the result
would be the same. But they are so overloaded with precepts by guardians

who think that nothing is so much to be dreaded for a woman as originality of thought or character, that their minds are impeded by doubts till they lose their chance of fair, free proportions. The difficulty is to get them to the point from which they shall naturally develop self-respect and learn self-help.

"Once I thought that men would help to forward this state of things more than I do now. I saw so many of them wretched in the connections they had formed in weakness and vanity. They seemed so glad to esteem women whenever they could.

" 'The soft arms of affection,' said one of the most discerning spirits, 'will not suffice for me, unless on them I see the steel bracelets of strength.'

"But early I perceived that men never in any extreme of despair wished to be women. On the contrary, they were ever ready to taunt one another at any sign of weakness with,

> Art thou not like the women, who—

The passage ends various ways, according to the occasion and rhetoric of the speaker. When they admired any woman, they were inclined to speak of her as 'above her sex.' Silently I observed this, and feared it argued a rooted skepticism which for ages had been fastening on the heart and which only an age of miracles could eradicate. Ever I have been treated with great sincerity; and I look upon it as a signal instance of this, that an intimate friend of the other sex said in a fervent moment that I 'deserved in some star to be a man.' He was much surprised when I disclosed my view of my position and hopes, when I declared my faith that the feminine side, the side of love, of beauty, of holiness, was now to have its full chance, and that if either were better, it was better now to be a woman; for even the slightest achievement of good was furthering an especial work of our time. He smiled incredulously. 'She makes the best she can of it,' thought he. 'Let Jews believe the pride of Jewry, but I am of the better sort, and know better.'

"Another used as highest praise in speaking of a character in literature, the words 'a manly woman.'

"So in the noble passage of Ben Jonson:

I meant the day-star should not brighter ride,
 Nor shed like influence from its lucent seat;
I meant she should be courteous, facile, sweet,
 Free from that solemn vice of greatness, pride;
I meant each softest virtue there should meet,
 Fit in that softer bosom to abide,
Only a learned and a *manly* soul
 I purposed her, that should with even powers
The rock, the spindle, and the shears control
 Of destiny, and spin her own free hours."

"Methinks," said I, "you are too fastidious in objecting to this. Jonson in using the word 'manly' only meant to heighten the picture of this, the true, the intelligent fate with one of the deeper colors."

"And yet," said she, "so invariable is the use of this word when a heroic quality is to be described, and I feel so sure that persistence and courage are the most womanly no less than the most manly qualities, that I would exchange these words for others of a larger sense, at the risk of marring the fine tissue of the verse. Read, 'A heavenward and instructed soul,' and I should be satisfied. Let it not be said, wherever there is energy or creative genius, 'She has a masculine mind.' "

This by no means argues a willing want of generosity toward Woman. Man is as generous toward her as he knows how to be.

Wherever she has herself arisen in national or private history and nobly shone forth in any form of excellence, men have received her not only willingly, but with triumph. Their encomiums, indeed, are always in some sense mortifying; they show too much surprise. "Can this be you?" he cries to the transfigured Cinderella; "well, I should never have thought it, but I am very glad. We will tell everyone that you have '*surpassed your sex.*' "

In everyday life, the feelings of the many are stained with vanity. Each wishes to be lord in a little world, to be superior at least over one; and he does not feel strong enough to retain a lifelong ascendancy over a strong nature. Only a Theseus could conquer before he wed the Amazonian queen. Hercules wished rather to rest with Dejanira, and received the poisoned robe as a fit guerdon. The tale should be interpreted to all those who seek repose with the weak.

But not only is Man vain and fond of power, but the same want of development, which thus affects him morally, prevents his intellectually discerning the destiny of Woman. The boy wants no woman, but only a girl to play ball with him and mark his pocket handkerchief.

Thus, in Schiller's "Dignity of Woman," beautiful as the poem is, there is no "grave and perfect man," but only a great boy to be softened and restrained by the influence of girls. Poets—the elder brothers of their race—have usually seen further; but what can you expect of everyday men, if Schiller was not more prophetic as to what women must be? Even with Richter, one foremost thought about a wife was that she would "cook him something good." But as this is a delicate subject, and we are in constant danger of being accused of slighting what are called "the functions," let me say in behalf of Miranda and myself that we have high respect for those who "cook something good," who create and preserve fair order in houses and prepare therein the shining raiment for worthy inmates, worthy guests. Only these "functions" must not be a drudgery or enforced necessity, but a part of life. Let Ulysses drive the beeves home, while Penelope there piles up the fragrant loaves; they are both well employed if these be done in thought and love, willingly. But Penelope is no more meant for a baker or weaver solely, than Ulysses for a cattle-herd.

The sexes should not only correspond to and appreciate, but prophesy to one another. In individual instances this happens. Two persons love in one another the future good which they aid one another to unfold. This is imperfectly or rarely done in the general life. Man has gone but little way; now he is waiting to see whether Woman can keep step with him, but instead of calling out like a good brother, "You can do it, if you only think so," or impersonally, "Anyone can do what he tries to do"; he often discourages with schoolboy brag: "Girls can't do that; girls can't play ball." But let anyone defy their taunts, break through and be brave and secure, they rend the air with shouts.

This fluctuation was obvious in a narrative I have lately seen, the story of the life of Countess Emily Plater, the heroine of the last revolution in Poland. The dignity, the purity, the concentrated resolve, the calm deep enthusiasm, which yet could when occasion called sparkle up a holy, an indignant fire, make of this young maiden the figure I want for my frontispiece. Her portrait is to be seen in the book, a gentle shadow of her soul. Short was the career. Like the Maid of Orleans, she only did enough to verify her credentials, and then passed from a scene on which she was probably a premature apparition.

When the young girl joined the army where the report of her exploits had preceded her, she was received in a manner that marks the usual state of feeling. Some of the officers were disappointed at her quiet manners; that she had not the air and tone of a stage-heroine. They thought she could not have acted heroically unless in buskins; had no idea that such deeds only showed the habit of her mind. Others talked of the delicacy of her sex, advised her to withdraw from perils and dangers, and had no comprehension of the feelings within her breast that made this impossible. The gentle irony of her reply to these self-constituted tutors (not one of whom showed himself her equal in conduct or reason) is as good as her indignant reproof at a later period to the general whose perfidy ruined all.

But though to the mass of these men she was an embarrassment and a puzzle, the nobler sort viewed her with a tender enthusiasm worthy of her. "Her name," said her biographer, "is known throughout Europe. I paint her character that she may be as widely loved."

With pride he shows her freedom from all personal affections; that though tender and gentle in an uncommon degree, there was no room for a private love in her consecrated life. She inspired those who knew her with a simple energy of feeling like her own. "We have seen," they felt, "a woman worthy the name, capable of all sweet affections, capable of stern virtue."

It is a fact worthy of remark that all these revolutions in favor of liberty have produced female champions that share the same traits, but Emily alone has found a biographer. Only a near friend could have performed for her this task, for the flower was reared in feminine seclusion, and the few and simple traits of her history before her appearance in the field could only have been known to the domestic circle. Her biographer has gathered them up with a brotherly devotion.

No, Man is not willingly ungenerous. He wants faith and love because he is not yet himself an elevated being. He cries with sneering skepticism,

"Give us a sign." But if the sign appears, his eyes glisten and he offers not merely approval but homage.

The severe nation which taught that the happiness of the race was forfeited through the fault of a Woman, and showed its thought of what sort of regard Man owed her by making him accuse her on the first question to his God—who gave her to the patriarch as a handmaid, and by the Mosaical law bound her to allegiance like a serf—even they greeted with solemn rapture all great and holy women as heroines, prophetesses, judges in Israel; and if they made Eve listen to the serpent, gave Mary as a bride to the Holy Spirit. In other nations it has been the same down to our day. To the Woman who could conquer a triumph was awarded. And not only those whose strength was recommended to the heart by association with goodness and beauty, but those who were bad, if they were steadfast and strong, had their claims allowed. In any age a Semiramis, an Elizabeth of England, a Catherine of Russia makes her place good, whether in a large or small circle. How has a little wit, a little genius, been celebrated in a Woman! What an intellectual triumph was that of the lonely Aspasia, and how heartily acknowledged! She, indeed, met a Pericles. But what annalist, the rudest of men, the most plebeian of husbands, will spare from his page one of the few anecdotes of Roman women—Sappho! Héloïse! The names are of threadbare celebrity. Indeed, they were not more suitably met in their own time than the Countess Colonel Plater on her first joining the army. They had much to mourn, and their great impulses did not find due scope. But with time enough, space enough, their kindred appear on the scene. Across the ages forms lean, trying to touch the hem of their retreating robes. The youth here by my side cannot be weary of the fragments from the life of Sappho. He will not believe they are not addressed to himself, or that he to whom they were addressed could be ungrateful. A recluse of high powers devotes himself to understand and explain the thought of Heloïse; he asserts her vast superiority in soul and genius to her master; he curses the fate that casts his lot in another age than hers. He could have understood her; he would have been to her a friend, such as Abélard never could. And this one Woman he could have loved and reverenced, and she, alas, lay cold in her grave hundreds of years ago. His sorrow is truly pathetic. These responses that come too late to give joy are as tragic as anything we know, and yet the tears of later ages glitter as they fall on Tasso's prison bars. And we know how elevating to the captive is the security that somewhere an intelligence must answer to his.

The Man habitually most narrow towards Woman will be flushed as by the worst assault on Christianity, if you say it has made no improvement in her condition. Indeed those most opposed to new acts in her favor, are jealous of the reputation of those which have been done.

We will not speak of the enthusiasm excited by actresses, *improvisatrici,* female singers—for here mingles the charm of beauty and grace—but female authors, even learned women if not insufferably ugly and slovenly, from the Italian professor's daughter who taught behind the curtain down to Mrs. Carter and Madame Dacier, are sure of an admiring audience, and what is far better, chance to use what they have learned and to learn more, if they can once get a platform on which to stand.

But how to get this platform or how to make it of reasonably easy access is the difficulty. Plants of great vigor will almost always struggle into blossom despite impediments. But there should be encouragement and a free genial atmosphere for those of more timid sort, fair play for each in its own kind. Some are like the little delicate flowers which love to hide in the dripping mosses by the sides of mountain torrents or in the shade of tall trees. But others require an open field, a rich and loosened soil, or they never show their proper hues.

It may be said that Man does not have his fair play either; his energies are repressed and distorted by the interposition of artificial obstacles. Aye, but he himself has put them there; they have grown out of his own imperfections. If there *is* a misfortune in Woman's lot, it is in obstacles being interposed by men which do *not* mark her state; and if they express her past ignorance, do not her present needs. As every Man is of Woman born, she has slow but sure means of redress; yet the sooner a general justness of thought makes smooth the path, the better.

Man is of Woman born, and her face bends over him in infancy with an expression he can never quite forget. Eminent men have delighted to pay tribute to this image, and it is a hackneyed observation that most men of genius boast some remarkable development in the mother. The rudest tar brushes off a tear with his coat-sleeve at the hallowed name. The other day I met a decrepit old man of seventy on a journey who challenged the stage company to guess where he was going. They guessed aright, "To see your mother." "Yes," said he, "she is ninety-two, but has good eyesight still, they say. I have not seen her these forty years, and I thought I could not die in peace without." I should have liked his picture painted as a companion-piece to that of a boisterous little boy, whom I saw attempt to declaim at a school exhibition:

> O that those lips had language! Life has passed
> With me but roughly since I heard thee last.

He got but very little way before sudden tears shamed him from the stage.

Some gleams of the same expression which shone down upon his infancy angelically pure and benign, visit Man again with hopes of pure love, of a holy marriage. Or if not before, in the eyes of the mother of his child they again are seen, and dim fancies pass before his mind that Woman may not have been born for him alone, but have come from heaven a commissioned soul, a messenger of truth and love; that she can only make for him a home in which he may lawfully repose, in so far as she is

> True to the kindred points of Heaven and home.

In gleams, in dim fancies, this thought visits the mind of common men. It is soon obscured by the mists of sensuality, the dust of routine, and he thinks it was only some meteor or *ignis fatuus* that shone. But as a Rosicrucian lamp it burns unwearied, though condemned to the solitude of tombs; and to its permanent life, as to every truth, each age has in some form borne witness. For the truths which visit the minds of careless men only in fitful gleams, shine with radiant clearness into those of the poet, the priest, and the artist.

Whatever may have been the domestic manners of the ancients, the idea of Woman was nobly manifested in their mythologies and poems, where she appears as Sita in the "Ramayana," a form of tender purity; as the Egyptian Isis, of divine wisdom never yet surpassed. In Egypt, too, the

Sphinx, walking the earth with lion tread, looked out upon its marvels in the calm, inscrutable beauty of a virgin's face, and the Greek could only add wings to the great emblem. In Greece Ceres and Proserpine, significantly termed the "great goddesses," were seen seated side by side. They needed not to rise for any worshiper or any change; they were prepared for all things, as those initiated to their mysteries knew. More obvious is the meaning of these three forms, the Diana, Minerva, and Vesta. Unlike in the expression of their beauty, but alike in this—that each was self-sufficing. Other forms were only accessories and illustrations, none the complement to one like these. Another might indeed be the companion, and the Apollo and Diana set off one another's beauty. Of the Vesta it is to be observed that not only deep-eyed, deep-discerning Greece, but ruder Rome, who represents the only form of good man (the always busy warrior) that could be indifferent to Woman, confided the permanence of its glory to a tutelary goddess, and her wisest legislator spoke of meditation as a nymph.

Perhaps in Rome the neglect of Woman was a reaction on the manners of Etruria, where the priestess-queen, warrior-queen, would seem to have been so usual a character.

An instance of the noble Roman marriage, where the stern and calm nobleness of the nation was common to both, we see in the historic page through the little that is told us of Brutus and Portia. Shakespeare has seized on the relation in its native lineaments, harmonizing the particular with the universal; and while it is conjugal love and no other, making it unlike the same relation as seen in *Cymbeline* or *Othello,* even as one star differeth from another in glory.

> By that great vow
> Which did incorporate and make us one,
> Unfold to me, yourself, your other half,
> Why you are heavy. . . .
> . . . Dwell I but in the suburbs
> Of your good pleasure? If it be no more,
> Portia is Brutus' harlot, not his wife.

Mark the sad majesty of his tone in answer. Who would not have lent a lifelong credence to that voice of honor?

> You are my true and honorable wife;
> As dear to me as are the ruddy drops
> That visit this sad heart.

It is the same voice that tells the moral of his life in the last words:

> Countrymen,
> My heart doth joy, that, yet in all my life,
> I found no man but he was true to me.

It was not wonderful that it should be so.

Shakespeare, however, was not content to let Portia rest her plea for confidence on the essential nature of the marriage bond:

> I grant I am a woman; but withal,
> A woman that lord Brutus took to wife.
> I grant I am a woman; but withal,
> A woman well reputed—Cato's daughter.
> Think you I am *no stronger than my sex,*
> Being so fathered and so husbanded?

And afterward in the very scene where Brutus is suffering under that "insupportable and touching loss," the death of his wife, Cassius pleads:

> Have you not love enough to bear with me,
> When that rash humor which my mother gave me
> Makes me forgetful?
> *Brutus:* Yes, Cassius, and henceforth,
> When you are over-earnest with your Brutus,
> He'll think your mother chides, and leaves you so.

As indeed it was a frequent belief among the ancients, as with our Indians, that the *body* was inherited from the mother, the *soul* from the father. As in that noble passage of Ovid already quoted where Jupiter, as his divine synod are looking down on the funeral pyre of Hercules, thus triumphs:

> *Nec nisi* materna *Vulcanum parte potentem,*
> *Sentiet. Aeternum est, a me quod traxit, et expers*
> *Atque immune necis, nullaque domabile flamma*
> *Idque ego defunctum terra cœlestibus oris*
> *Accipiam, cunctisque meum lætabile factum*
> *Dis fore confido.*

(The part alone of gross *maternal* frame
Fire shall devour; while that from me he drew
Shall live immortal and its force renew;
That, when he's dead, I'll raise to realms above;
Let all the powers the righteous act approve.)

It is indeed a god speaking of his union with an earthly Woman, but it expresses the common Roman thought as to marriage—the same which permitted a man to lend his wife to a friend as if she were a chattel.

She dwelt but in the suburbs of his good pleasure.

Yet the same city, as I have said, leaned on the worship of Vesta the Preserver, and in later times was devoted to that of Isis. In Sparta thought, in this respect as in all others, was expressed in the characters of real life, and the women of Sparta were as much Spartans as the men. The *citoyen, citoyenne* of France was here actualized. Was not the calm equality they enjoyed as honorable as the devotion of chivalry? They intelligently shared the ideal life of their nation.

Like the men they felt

Honor gone, all's gone:
Better never have been born.

They were the true friends of men. The Spartan surely would not think that he received only his body from his mother. The sage, had he lived in that community, could not have thought the souls of "vain and foppish men will be degraded after death to the forms of women; and if they do not then make great efforts to retrieve themselves, will become birds."

(By the way, it is very expressive of the hard intellectuality of the merely *mannish* mind to speak thus of birds, chosen always by the *feminine* poet as the symbols of his fairest thoughts.)

We are told of the Greek nations in general that Woman occupied there an infinitely lower place than Man. It is difficult to believe this when we see such range and dignity of thought on the subject in the mythologies, and find the poets producing such ideals as Cassandra, Iphigenia, Antigone, Macaria; where Sibylline priestesses told the oracle of the highest god, and he could not be content to reign with a court of fewer than nine muses. Even Victory wore a female form.

But whatever were the facts of daily life, I cannot complain of the age and nation which represents its thought by such a symbol as I see before me at this moment. It is a zodiac of the busts of gods and goddesses, arranged in pairs. The circle breathes the music of a heavenly order. Male and female heads are distinct in expression, but equal in beauty, strength, and calmness. Each male head is that of a brother and a king—each female of a sister and a queen. Could the thought thus expressed be lived out, there would be nothing more to be desired. There would be unison in variety, congeniality in difference.

Coming nearer our own time, we find religion and poetry no less true in their revelations. The rude man, just disengaged from the sod, the Adam, accuses Woman to his God and records her disgrace to their posterity. He is not ashamed to write that he could be drawn from heaven by one beneath him—one made, he says, from but a small part of himself. But in the same nation educated by time, instructed by a succession of prophets, we find Woman in as high a position as she has ever occupied. No figure that has ever arisen to greet our eyes has been received with more fervent reverence than that of the Madonna. Heine calls her the *Dame du Comptoir* of the Catholic church, and this jeer well expresses a serious truth.

And not only this holy and significant image was worshiped by the pilgrim and the favorite subject of the artist, but it exercised an immediate influence on the destiny of the sex. The empresses who embraced the cross converted sons and husbands. Whole calendars of female saints, heroic dames of chivalry binding the emblem of faith on the heart of the best-beloved, and wasting the bloom of youth in separation and loneliness for the sake of duties they thought it religion to assume, with innumerable forms of poesy trace their lineage to this one. Nor, however imperfect may be the action in our day of the faith thus expressed, and though we can scarcely think it nearer this ideal than that of India or Greece was near their ideal, is it in vain that the truth has been recognized that Woman is not only a part of Man, bone of his bone and flesh of his flesh, born that men might not be lonely—but that women are in themselves possessors of and possessed by immortal souls. This truth undoubtedly received a greater outward stability from the belief of the church that the earthly parent of the Saviour of souls was a woman.

The "Assumption of the Virgin," as painted by sublime artists, as also Petrarch's "Hymn to the Madonna," cannot have spoken to the world wholly without result, yet oftentimes those who had ears heard not.

See upon the nations the influence of this powerful example. In Spain look only at the ballads. Woman in these is "very Woman"; she is the betrothed, the bride, the spouse of Man; there is on her no hue of the philosopher, the heroine, the *savante,* but she looks great and noble. Why? Because she is also through her deep devotion the betrothed of Heaven. Her upturned eyes have drawn down the light that casts a radiance round her. See only such a ballad as that of "Lady Teresa's Bridal," where the Infanta given to the Moorish bridegroom calls down the vengeance of Heaven on his unhallowed passion, and thinks it not too much to expiate by a life in the cloister the involuntary stain upon her princely youth. It was this constant sense of claims above those of earthly love or happiness that made the Spanish lady who shared this spirit a guerdon to be won by toils and blood and constant purity, rather than a chattel to be bought for pleasure and service.

Germany did not need to *learn* a high view of Woman; it was inborn in that race. Woman was to the Teuton warrior his priestess, his friend, his sister—in truth a wife. And the Christian statues of noble pairs, as they lie above their graves in stone, expressing the meaning of all the bygone pilgrimage by hands folded in mutual prayer, yield not a nobler sense of the place and powers of Woman than belonged to the *altvater* day. The holy love of Christ which summoned them also to choose "the better part— that which could not be taken from them," refined and hallowed in this nation a native faith; thus showing that it was not the warlike spirit alone that left the Latins so barbarous in this respect.

But the Germans, taking so kindly to this thought, did it the more justice. The idea of Woman in their literature is expressed both to a greater height and depth than elsewhere.

I will give as instances the themes of three ballads:

One is upon a knight who had always the name of the Virgin on his lips. This protected him all his life through in various and beautiful modes both from sin and other dangers; and when he died, a plant sprang from his grave, which so gently whispered the Ave Maria that none could pass it by with an unpurified heart.

Another is one of the legends of the famous Drachenfels. A maiden, one of the earliest converts to Christianity, was carried by the enraged populace to this dread haunt of the "dragon's fabled brood" to be their prey. She was left alone but undismayed, for she knew in whom she trusted. So when the dragons came rushing towards her, she showed them a crucifix and they crouched reverently at her feet. Next day the people came, and seeing these wonders, were all turned to the faith which exalts the lowly.

The third I have in mind is another of the Rhine legends. A youth is sitting with the maid he loves on the shore of an isle, her fairy kingdom, then perfumed by the blossoming grapevines which draped its bowers. They are happy; all blossoms with them, and life promises its richest wine. A boat approaches on the tide; it pauses at their feet. It brings perhaps some joyous message, fresh dew for their flowers, fresh light on the wave. No, it is the usual check on such great happiness. The father of the count departs for the crusade; will his son join him, or remain to rule their domain and wed her he loves? Neither of the affianced pair hesitates a moment. "I must go with my father"—"Thou must go with thy father." It was one thought, one word. "I will be here again," he said, "when these blossoms have turned to purple grapes." "I hope so," she sighed, while the prophetic sense said no.

And there she waited, and the grapes ripened and were gathered into the vintage, and he came not. Year after year passed thus, and no tidings; yet still she waited.

He meanwhile was in a Moslem prison. Long he languished there without hope, till at last his patron saint appeared in vision and announced his release, but only on condition of his joining the monastic order for the service of the saint.

And so his release was effected, and a safe voyage home given. And once more he sets sail upon the Rhine. The maiden, still watching beneath the vines, sees at last the object of all this patient love approach—approach, but not to touch the strand to which she with outstretched arms has rushed. He dares not trust himself to land, but in low heartbroken tones tells her of Heaven's will; and that he in obedience to his vow is now on his way to a convent on the riverbank, there to pass the rest of his earthly life in the service of the shrine. And then he turns his boat and floats away from her and hope of any happiness in this world, but urged as he believes by the breath of Heaven.

The maiden stands appalled, but she dares not murmur and cannot hesitate long. She also bids them prepare her boat. She follows her lost love to the convent gate, requests an interview with the abbot, and devotes her Elysian isle, where vines had ripened their ruby fruit in vain for her, to the service of the monastery where her love was to serve. Then passing over to the nunnery opposite, she takes the veil, and meets her betrothed at the altar and for a lifelong union, if not the one they had hoped in earlier years.

Is not this sorrowful story of a lofty beauty? Does it not show a sufficiently high view of Woman, of Marriage? This is commonly the chivalric, still more the German view.

Yet wherever there was a balance in the mind of Man of sentiment with intellect, such a result was sure. The Greek Xenophon has not only painted us a sweet picture of the domestic Woman, in his *Economics,* but in the *Cyropedia* has given in the picture of Panthea a view of Woman which no German picture can surpass, whether lonely and quiet with veiled lids, the temple of a vestal loveliness, or with eyes flashing and hair flowing to the free wind, cheering on the hero to fight for his God, his country, or whatever name his duty might bear at the time. This picture I shall copy by and by. Yet Xenophon grew up in the same age with him who makes Iphigenia say to Achilles:

Better a thousand women should perish than one man cease to see the light.

This was the vulgar Greek sentiment. Xenophon, aiming at the ideal Man, caught glimpses of the ideal Woman also. From the figure of a Cyrus the Pantheas stand not afar. They do not in thought; they would not in life.

I could swell the catalogue of instances far beyond the reader's patience. But enough have been brought forward to show that though there has been great disparity betwixt the nations as between individuals in their culture on this point, yet the idea of Woman has always cast some rays and often been forcibly represented.

Far less has Woman to complain that she has not had her share of power. This, in all ranks of society except the lowest, has been hers to the extent that vanity would crave, far beyond what wisdom would accept. In the very lowest, where Man pressed by poverty sees in Woman only the partner of toils and cares, and cannot hope, scarcely has an idea of, a comfortable home, he often maltreats her and is less influenced by her. In all ranks those who are gentle and uncomplaining, too candid to intrigue, too delicate to encroach, suffer much. They suffer long and are kind; verily they have their reward. But wherever Man is sufficiently raised above extreme poverty or brutal stupidity to care for the comforts of the fireside or the bloom and ornament of life, Woman has always power enough if she choose to exert it, and is usually disposed to do so in proportion to her ignorance and childish vanity. Unacquainted with the importance of life and its purposes, trained to a selfish coquetry and love of petty power, she does not look beyond the pleasure of making herself felt at the moment, and governments are shaken and commerce broken up to gratify the pique of a female favorite. The English shopkeeper's wife does not vote, but it is for her interest that the politician canvasses by the coarsest flattery. France suffers no woman on her throne, but her proud nobles kiss the dust at the feet of Pompadour and du Barry; for such flare in the lighted foreground where a Roland would modestly aid in the closet. Spain (that same Spain which sang of Ximena and the Lady Teresa) shuts up her women in the care of duennas and allows them no book but the breviary; but the ruin follows only the more surely from the worthless favorite of a worthless queen. Relying on mean precautions, men indeed cry peace, peace, where there is no peace.

It is not the transient breath of poetic incense that women want; each can receive that from a lover. It is not lifelong sway; it needs but to become a coquette, a shrew, or a good cook to be sure of that. It is not money nor notoriety nor the badges of authority which men have appropriated to themselves. If demands made in their behalf lay stress on any of these particulars, those who make them have not searched deeply into the need. The want is for that which at once includes these and precludes them;

which would not be forbidden power, lest there be temptation to steal and misuse it; which would not have the mind perverted by flattery from a worthiness of esteem; it is for that which is the birthright of every being capable of receiving it—the freedom, the religious, the intelligent freedom of the universe to use its means, to learn its secret as far as Nature has enabled them, with God alone for their guide and their judge.

Ye cannot believe it, men; but the only reason why women ever assume what is more appropriate to you, is because you prevent them from finding out what is fit for themselves. Were they free, were they wise fully to develop the strength and beauty of Woman; they would never wish to be men or manlike. The well-instructed moon flies not from her orbit to seize on the glories of her partner. No, for she knows that one law rules, one heaven contains, one universe replies to them alike. It is with women as with the slave:

> *Vor dem Sklaven, wenn er die Kette bricht,*
> *Vor dem freien Menschen erzittert nicht.*

("Tremble not before the free man, but before the slave who has chains to break.")

In slavery, acknowledged slavery, women are on a par with men. Each is a worktool, an article of property—no more! In perfect freedom, such as is painted in Olympus, in Swedenborg's angelic state, in the heaven where there is no marrying nor giving in marriage, each is a purified intelligence, an enfranchised soul—no less.

> *Jene himmlische Gestalten*
> *Sie fragen nicht nach Mann und Weib,*
> *Und keine kleider, keine Falten*
> *Umgeben den verklarten Leib.*

The child who sang this was a prophetic form expressive of the longing for a state of perfect freedom, pure love. She could not remain here, but was translated to another air. And it may be that the air of this earth will never be so tempered that such can bear it long. But while they stay, they must bear testimony to the truth they are constituted to demand.

That an era approaches which shall approximate nearer to such a temper than any has yet done, there are many tokens; indeed so many that only a few of the most prominent can here be enumerated.

The reigns of Elizabeth of England and Isabella of Castile foreboded this era. They expressed the beginning of the new state while they forwarded its progress. These were strong characters and in harmony with the wants of their time. One showed that this strength did not unfit a woman for the duties of a wife and a mother; the other, that it could enable her to live and die alone, a wide energetic life, a courageous death. Elizabeth is certainly no pleasing example. In rising above the weakness, she did not lay aside the foibles ascribed to her sex; but her strength must be respected now as it was in her own time.

Mary Stuart and Elizabeth seem types, molded by the spirit of the time and placed upon an elevated platform, to show to the coming ages Woman such as the conduct and wishes of Man in general is likely to make her. The first shows Woman lovely even to allurement; quick in apprehension and weak in judgment; with grace and dignity of sentiment, but no principle; credulous and indiscreet, yet artful; capable of sudden greatness or of crime, but not of a steadfast wisdom, nor self-restraining virtue. The second reveals Woman half-emancipated and jealous of her freedom, such as she has figured before or since in many a combative attitude; mannish, not equally manly; strong and prudent more than great or wise; able to control vanity, and the wish to rule through coquetry and passion, but not to resign these dear deceits from the very foundation, as unworthy a being capable of truth and nobleness. Elizabeth, taught by adversity, put on her virtues as armor, more than produced them in a natural order from her soul. The time and her position called on her to act the wise sovereign and she was proud that she could do so, but her tastes and inclinations would have led her to act the weak woman. She was without magnanimity of any kind.

We may accept as an omen for ourselves that it was Isabella who furnished Columbus with the means of coming hither. This land must pay back its debt to Woman, without whose aid it would not have been brought into alliance with the civilized world.

A graceful and meaning figure is that introduced to us by Mr. Prescott in the *Conquest of Mexico* in the Indian girl Marina, who accompanied

Cortez and was his interpreter in all the various difficulties of his career. She stood at his side on the walls of the besieged palace to plead with her enraged countrymen. By her name he was known in New Spain, and after the conquest her gentle intercession was often of avail to the conquered. The poem of the future may be read in some features of the story of "Malinche."

The influence of Elizabeth on literature was real, though by sympathy with its finer productions she was no more entitled to give name to an era than Queen Anne. It was simply that the fact of having a female sovereign on the throne affected the course of a writer's thoughts. In this sense, the presence of a woman on the throne always makes its mark. Life is lived before the eyes of men, by which their imaginations are stimulated as to the possibilities of Woman. "We will die for our king, Maria Theresa," cry the wild warriors, clashing their swords; and the sounds vibrate through the poems of that generation. The range of female character in Spenser alone might content us for one period. Britomart and Belphoebe have as much room on the canvas as Florimel; and where this is the case, the haughtiest Amazon will not murmur that Una should be felt to be the fairest type.

Unlike as was the English queen to a fairy queen, we may yet conceive that it was the image of *a* queen before the poet's mind that called up this splendid court of women. Shakespeare's range is also great; but he has left out the heroic characters such as the Macaria of Greece, the Britomart of Spenser. Ford and Massinger have in this respect soared to a higher flight of feeling than he. It was the holy and heroic Woman they most loved, and if they could not paint an Imogen, a Desdemona, a Rosalind, yet in those of a stronger mold they showed a higher ideal, though with so much less poetic power to embody it, than we see in Portia or Isabella. The simple truth of Cordelia, indeed, is of this sort. The beauty of Cordelia is neither male nor female; it is the beauty of virtue.

The ideal of love and marriage rose high in the mind of all the Christian nations who were capable of grave and deep feeling. We may take as examples of its English aspect the lines,

> I could not love thee, dear, so much,
> Loved I not honor more.

Or the address of the Commonwealth's man to his wife, as she looked out from the Tower window to see him, for the last time, on his way to the scaffold. He stood up in the cart, waved his hat, and cried, "To Heaven, my love, to Heaven, and leave you in the storm!"

Such was the love of faith and honor—a love which stopped like Colonel Hutchinson's "on this side idolatry" because it was religious. The meeting of two such souls Donne describes as giving birth to an "abler soul."

Lord Herbert wrote to his love,

> Were not our souls immortal made,
> Our equal loves can make them such.

In the *Broken Heart* of Ford, Penthea, a character which engages my admiration even more deeply than the famous one of Calanthe, is made to present to the mind the most beautiful picture of what these relations should be in their purity. Her life cannot sustain the violation of what she so clearly feels.

Shakespeare, too, saw that in true love, as in fire, the utmost ardor is coincident with the utmost purity. It is a true lover that exclaims in the agony of Othello,

> If thou art false, O then Heaven mocks itself!

The son, framed like Hamlet to appreciate truth in all the beauty of relations, sinks into deep melancholy when he finds his natural expectations disappointed. He has no other. She to whom he gave the name, disgraces from his heart's shrine all the sex.

> Frailty, thy name is Woman.

It is because a Hamlet could find cause to say so, that I have put the line whose stigma has never been removed at the head of my work. But as a lover, surely Hamlet would not have so far mistaken as to have finished with such a conviction. He would have felt the faith of Othello, and that faith could not in his more dispassionate mind have been disturbed by calumny.

In Spain this thought is arrayed in a sublimity which belongs to the somber and passionate genius of the nation. Calderon's Justina resists all the temptation of the demon, and raises her lover with her above the sweet lures of mere temporal happiness. Their marriage is vowed at the stake; their souls are liberated together by the martyr flame into "a purer state of sensation and existence."

In Italy the great poets wove into their lives an ideal love which answered to the highest wants. It included those of the intellect and the affections, for it was a love of spirit for spirit. It was not ascetic or super-human, but interpreting all things, gave their proper beauty to details of the common life, the common day. The poet spoke of his love, not as a flower to place in his bosom or hold carelessly in his hand, but as a light toward which he must find wings to fly or a "stair to heaven." He delighted to speak of her not only as the bride of his heart, but the mother of his soul; for he saw that in cases where the right direction had been taken, the greater delicacy of her frame and stillness of her life left her more open than is Man to spiritual influx. So he did not look upon her as betwixt him and earth to serve his temporal needs, but rather betwixt him and heaven to purify his affections and lead him to wisdom through love. He sought in her not so much the Eve as the Madonna.

In these minds the thought which gleams through all the legends of chivalry shines in broad intellectual effulgence, not to be misinterpreted; and their thought is reverenced by the world, though it lies far from the practice of the world as yet—so far that it seems as though a gulf of death yawned between.

Even with such men the practice was often widely different from the mental faith. I say mental; for if the heart were thoroughly alive with it, the practice could not be dissonant. Lord Herbert's was a marriage of convention, made for him at fifteen; he was not discontented with it, but looked only to the advantages it brought of perpetuating his family on the basis of a great fortune. He paid in act what he considered a dutiful attention to the bond; his thoughts traveled elsewhere; and while forming a high ideal of the companionship of minds in marriage, he seems never to have doubted that its realization must be postponed to some other state of being. Dante, almost immediately after the death of Beatrice, married a lady chosen for him by his friends, and Boccaccio, in describing the miseries that attended in this case,

The form of an union where union is none,

speaks as if these were inevitable to the connection, and as if the scholar and poet, especially, could expect nothing but misery and obstruction in a domestic partnership with Woman.

Centuries have passed since, but civilized Europe is still in a transition state about marriage; not only in practice but in thought. It is idle to speak with contempt of the nations where polygamy is an institution or seraglios a custom, while practices far more debasing haunt, well-nigh fill, every city and every town, and so far as union of one with one is believed to be the only pure form of marriage, a great majority of societies and individuals are still doubtful whether the earthly bond must be a meeting of souls, or only supposes a contract of convenience and utility. Were Woman established in the rights of an immortal being, this could not be. She would not in some countries be given away by her father, with scarcely more respect for her feelings than is shown by the Indian chief who sells his daughter for a horse, and beats her if she runs away from her new home. Nor in societies where her choice is left free, would she be perverted by the current of opinion that seizes her, into the belief that she must marry, if it be only to find a protector and a home of her own. Neither would Man, if he thought the connection of permanent importance, form it so lightly. He would not deem it a trifle that he was to enter into the closest relations with another soul, which, if not eternal in themselves, must eternally affect his growth. Neither did he believe Woman capable of friendship, would he by rash haste lose the chance of finding a friend in the person who might probably live half a century by his side. Did love to his mind stretch forth into infinity, he would not miss his chance of its revelations, that he might the sooner rest from his weariness by a bright fireside, and secure a sweet and graceful attendant "devoted to him alone." Were he a step higher, he would not carelessly enter into a relation where he might not be able to do the duty of a friend, as well as a protector from external ill, to the other party, and have a being in his power pining for sympathy, intelligence, and aid that he could not give.

What deep communion, what real intercourse is implied in sharing the joys and cares of parentage, when any degree of equality is admitted between the parties! It is true that in a majority of instances the man looks upon his wife as an adopted child, and places her to the other children in the relation of nurse or governess rather than that of parent. Her influence with them is sure; but she misses the education which should enlighten that influence, by being thus treated. It is the order of nature that children should complete the education, moral and mental, of parents by making them think what is needed for the best culture of human beings, and conquer all faults and impulses that interfere with their giving this to these dear objects who represent the world to them. Father and mother should assist one another to learn what is required for this sublime priesthood of Nature. But for this a religious recognition of equality is required.

Where this thought of equality begins to diffuse itself, it is shown in four ways.

First: The household partnership. In our country the woman looks for a "smart but kind" husband; the man for a "capable, sweet-tempered" wife. The man furnishes the house; the woman regulates it. Their relation is one of mutual esteem, mutual dependence. Their talk is of business; their affection shows itself by practical kindness. They know that life goes more smoothly and cheerfully to each for the other's aid; they are grateful and content. The wife praises her husband as a "good provider"; the husband, in return, compliments her as a "capital housekeeper." This relation is good so far as it goes.

Next comes a closer tie, which takes the form either of mutual idolatry or of intellectual companionship. The first, we suppose, is to no one a pleasing subject of contemplation. The parties weaken and narrow one another; they lock the gate against all the glories of the universe that they may live in a cell together. To themselves they seem the only wise; to all others steeped in infatuation; the gods smile as they look forward to the crisis of cure; to men, the woman seems an unlovely siren; to women, the man an effeminate boy.

The other form, of intellectual companionship, has become more and more frequent. Men engaged in public life, literary men, and artists have often found in their wives companions and confidantes in thought no less than in feeling. And as the intellectual development of Woman has spread wider and risen higher, they have not unfrequently shared the same employment; as in the case of Roland and his wife, who were friends in the household and in the nation's councils, read, regulated home affairs, or prepared public documents together indifferently. It is very pleasant, in letters begun by Roland and finished by his wife, to see the harmony of mind and the difference of nature; one thought but various ways of treating it.

This is one of the best instances of a marriage of friendship. It was only friendship, whose basis was esteem; probably neither party knew love except by name. Roland was a good man, worthy to esteem and be esteemed; his wife as deserving of admiration as able to do without it.

Madame Roland is the fairest specimen we yet have of her class; as clear to discern her aim, as valiant to pursue it as Spenser's Britomart; austerely set apart from all that did not belong to her whether as Woman or as mind. She is an antetype of a class to which the coming time will afford a field—the Spartan matron brought by the culture of the age of books to intellectual consciousness and expansion. Self-sufficingness, strength, and clear-sightedness were in her combined with a power of deep and calm affection. She, too, would have given a son or husband the device for his shield: "Return with it or upon it"; and this not because she loved little, but much. The page of her life is one of unsullied dignity. Her appeal to posterity is one against the injustice of those who committed such crimes in the name of Liberty. She makes it in behalf of herself and her husband. I would put beside it on the shelf a little volume, containing a similar appeal from the verdict of contemporaries to that of mankind made by Godwin in behalf of his wife, the celebrated, the by most men detested Mary Wollstonecraft. In his view it was an appeal from the injustice of those who did such wrong in the name of virtue. Were this little book interesting for no other cause, it would be so for the generous affection evinced under the peculiar circumstances. This man had courage to love and honor this woman in the face of the world's sentence and of all that was repulsive in her own past history. He believed he saw of what soul she was, and that the impulses she had struggled to act out were noble, though the opinions to which they had led might not be thoroughly weighed. He loved her, and he defended her for the meaning and tendency of her inner life. It was a good fact.

Mary Wollstonecraft, like Madame Dudevant (commonly known as George Sand) in our day, was a woman whose existence better proved the need of some new interpretation of Woman's Rights than anything she wrote. Such beings as these, rich in genius, of most tender sympathies, capable of high virtue and a chastened harmony, ought not to find themselves by birth in a place so narrow that in breaking bonds they become outlaws. Were there as much room in the world for such as in Spenser's poem for Britomart, they would not run their heads so wildly against the walls, but prize their shelter rather. They find their way at last to light and air, but the world will not take off the brand it has set upon them. The champion of the Rights of Woman found in Godwin one who would plead that cause like a brother. He who delineated with such purity of traits the form of Woman in the Marguerite of whom the weak St. Leon could never learn to be worthy—a pearl indeed whose price was above rubies—was not false in life to the faith by which he had hallowed his romance. He acted as he wrote, like a brother. This form of appeal rarely fails to touch the basest man: "Are you acting toward other women in the way you would have men act toward your sister?" George Sand smokes, wears male attire, wishes to be addressed as *"Mon frère"*—perhaps if she found those who were as brothers indeed, she would not care whether she were brother or sister. We rejoice to see that she, who expresses such a painful contempt for men in most of her works as shows she must have known great wrong from them, depicts in *La Roche Mauprat* a man raised by the workings of love from the depths of savage sensualism to a moral and intellectual life. It was love for a pure object, for a steadfast woman, one of those who the Italian said could make the "stair to heaven."

This author, beginning like the many in assault upon bad institutions, and external ills, yet deepening the experience through comparative freedom, sees at last that the only efficient remedy must come from individual character. These bad institutions indeed, it may always be replied, prevent individuals from forming good character, therefore we must remove them. Agreed; yet keep steadily the higher aim in view. Could you clear away all the bad forms of society, it is vain unless the individual begin to be ready for better. There must be a parallel movement in these two branches of life. And all the rules left by Moses availed less to further the best life than the living example of one Messiah.

Still the mind of the age struggles confusedly with these problems, better discerning as yet the ill it can no longer bear than the good by which it may supersede it. But women like Sand will speak now and cannot be silenced; their characters and their eloquence alike foretell an era when such as they shall easier learn to lead true lives. But though such forebode, not such shall be parents of it. Those who would reform the world must show that they do not speak in the heat of wild impulse; their lives must be unstained by passionate error; they must be severe lawgivers to themselves. They must be religious students of the divine purpose with regard to man, if they would not confound the fancies of a day with the requisitions of eternal good. Their liberty must be the liberty of law and knowledge. But as to the transgressions against custom which have caused such outcry against those of noble intention, it may be observed that the resolve of Héloïse to be only the mistress of Abélard, was that of one who saw in practice around her the contract of marriage made the seal of degradation. Shelley feared not to be fettered unless so to be was to be false. Wherever abuses are seen, the timid will suffer; the bold will protest. But society has a right to outlaw them till she has revised her law; and this she must be taught to do by one who speaks with authority, not in anger or haste.

If Godwin's choice of the calumniated authoress of the *Rights of Woman* for his honored wife be a sign of a new era, no less so is an article to which I have alluded some pages back, published five or six years ago in one of the English reviews, where the writer in doing full justice to Héloïse, shows his bitter regret that she lives not now to love him, who might have known better how to prize her love than did the egotistical Abélard.

These marriages, these characters, with all their imperfections express an onward tendency. They speak of aspiration of soul, of energy of mind, seeking clearness and freedom. Of a like promise are the tracts lately published by Goodwyn Barmby (the European pariah, as he calls himself) and his wife Catharine. Whatever we may think of their measures, we see in them wedlock; the two minds are wed by the only contract that can permanently avail, that of a common faith and a common purpose.

We might mention instances nearer home of minds, partners in work and in life, sharing together on equal terms public and private interests, and which wear not on any side the aspect of offense shown by those last-named: persons who steer straight onward, yet in our comparatively free life have not been obliged to run their heads against any wall. But the principles which guide them might under petrified and oppressive institutions have made them warlike, paradoxical, and in some sense pariahs. The phenomena are different, the law is the same in all these cases. Men and women have been obliged to build up their house anew from the very foundation. If they found stone ready in the quarry, they took it peaceably; otherwise they alarmed the country by pulling down old towers to get materials.

These are all instances of marriage as intellectual companionship. The parties meet mind to mind, and a mutual trust is produced which can buckler them against a million. They work together for a common purpose, and in all these instances with the same implement—the pen. The pen and the writing-desk furnish forth as naturally the retirement of Woman as of Man.

A pleasing expression in this kind is afforded by the union in the names of the Howitts. William and Mary Howitt we heard named together for years, supposing them to be brother and sister; the equality of labors and reputation even so was auspicious; more so, now we find them man and wife. In his late work on Germany, Howitt mentions his wife with pride as one among the constellation of distinguished Englishwomen, and in a graceful, simple manner. And still we contemplate with pleasure the partnership in literature and affection between the Howitts—the congenial pursuits and productions—the pedestrian tours wherein the married pair showed that marriage on a wide enough basis does not destroy the "inexhaustible" entertainment which lovers find in one another's company.

In naming these instances I do not mean to imply that community of employment is essential to the union of husband and wife, more than to the union of friends. Harmony exists in difference no less than in likeness, if only the same keynote govern both parts. Woman the poem, Man the poet! Woman the heart, Man the head! Such divisions are only important when they are never to be transcended. If nature is never bound down nor the voice of inspiration stifled, that is enough. We are pleased that women should write and speak, if they feel need of it from having something to tell; but silence for ages would be no misfortune, if that silence be from divine command and not from Man's tradition.

While Goetz Von Berlichingen rides to battle, his wife is busy in the kitchen; but difference of occupation does not prevent that community of inward life, that perfect esteem, with which he says,

> Whom God loves, to him gives he such a wife.

Manzoni thus dedicates his *Adelchi:*
"To his beloved and venerated wife, Enrichetta Luigia Blondel, who with conjugal affection and maternal wisdom has preserved a virgin mind, the author dedicates this *Adelchi,* grieving that he could not by a more splendid and more durable monument honor the dear name and the memory of so many virtues."

The relation could not be fairer nor more equal if she, too, had written poems. Yet the position of the parties might have been the reverse as well; the Woman might have sung the deeds, given voice to the life of the Man, and beauty would have been the result; as we see in pictures of Arcadia the nymph singing to the shepherds, or the shepherd with his pipe alluring the nymphs; either makes a good picture. The sounding lyre requires not muscular strength, but energy of soul to animate the hand which would control it. Nature seems to delight in varying the arrangements, as if to show that she will be fettered by no rule; and we must admit the same varieties that she admits.

The fourth and highest grade of marriage union is the religious, which may be expressed as pilgrimage toward a common shrine. This includes the others: home sympathies and household wisdom, for these pilgrims must know how to assist each other along the dusty way; intellectual communion, for how sad it would be on such a journey to have a companion to whom you could not communicate your thoughts and aspirations as they sprang to life; who would have no feeling for the prospects that open more and more glorious as we advance; who would never see the flowers that may be gathered by the most industrious traveler! It must include all these.

Such a fellow-pilgrim Count Zinzendorf seems to have found in his countess, of whom he thus writes:

"Twenty-five years' experience has shown me that just the helpmeet whom I have is the only one that could suit my vocation. Who else could have so carried through my family affairs? Who lived so spotlessly before the world? Who so wisely aided me in my rejection of a dry morality? Who so clearly set aside the Pharisaism which as years passed threatened to creep in among us? Who so deeply discerned as to the spirits of delusion which sought to bewilder us? Who would have governed my whole economy so wisely, richly, and hospitably when circumstances commanded? Who have taken indifferently the part of servant or mistress, without on the one side affecting an especial spirituality; on the other, being sullied by any worldly pride? Who, in a community where all ranks are eager to be on a level, would from wise and real causes have known how to maintain inward and outward distinctions? Who without a murmur have seen her husband encounter such dangers by land and sea? Who undertaken with him and *sustained* such astonishing pilgrimages? Who amid such difficulties would have always held up her head and supported me? Who found such vast sums of money, and acquitted them on her own credit? And finally, who of all human beings could so well understand and interpret to others my inner and outer being as this one of such nobleness in her way of thinking, such great intellectual capacity, and so free from the theological perplexities that enveloped me!"

Let anyone peruse with all intentness the lineaments of this portrait, and see if the husband had not reason with this air of solemn rapture and conviction to challenge comparison? We are reminded of the majestic cadence of the line whose feet step in the just proportion of Humanity,

Daughter of God and Man, accomplished Eve!

An observer * adds this testimony:

"We may in many marriages regard it as the best arrangement, if the man has so much advantage over his wife that she can, without much thought of her own, be led and directed by him as by a father. But it was not so with the count and his consort. She was not made to be a copy;

---

* Spangenberg.

she was an original; and while she loved and honored him, she thought for herself on all subjects, with so much intelligence that he could and did look on her as a sister and friend also."

Compare with this refined specimen of a religiously civilized life the following imperfect sketch of a North American Indian, and we shall see that the same causes will always produce the same results. The Flying Pigeon (Ratchewaine) was the wife of a barbarous chief, who had six others; but she was his only true wife because the only one of a strong and pure character, and having this, inspired a veneration as like as the mind of the man permitted to that inspired by the Countess Zinzendorf. She died when her son was only four years old, yet left on his mind a feeling of reverent love worthy the thought of Christian chivalry. Grown to manhood, he shed tears on seeing her portrait.

THE FLYING PIGEON

"Ratchewaine was chaste, mild, gentle in her disposition, kind, generous, and devoted to her husband. A harsh word was never known to proceed from her mouth; nor was she ever known to be in a passion. Mahaskah used to say of her after her death that her hand was shut when those who did not want came into her presence; but when the really poor came in it was like a strainer full of holes, letting all she held in it pass through. In the exercise of generous feeling she was uniform. It was not indebted for its exercise to whim nor caprice nor partiality. No matter of what nation the applicant for her bounty was, or whether at war or peace with her nation; if he were hungry, she fed him; if naked, she clothed him; and if houseless, she gave him shelter. The continued exercise of this generous feeling kept her poor. And she has been known to give away her last blanket—all the honey that was in the lodge, the last bladder of bear's oil, and the last piece of dried meat.

"She was scrupulously exact in the observance of all the religious rites which her faith imposed upon her. Her conscience is represented to have been extremely tender. She often feared that her acts were displeasing to the Great Spirit, when she would blacken her face and retire to some lone place and fast and pray."

To these traits should be added, but for want of room, anecdotes which

show the quick decision and vivacity of her mind. Her face was in harmony
with this combination. Her brow is as ideal and the eyes and lids as devout and modest as the Italian picture of the Madonna, while the lower
part of the face has the simplicity and childish strength of the Indian race.
Her picture presents the finest specimen of Indian beauty we have ever
seen. Such a Woman is the sister and friend of all beings, as the worthy
Man is their brother and helper.

With like pleasure we survey the pairs wedded on the eve of missionary
effort. They, indeed, are fellow-pilgrims on the well-made road, and
whether or no they accomplish all they hope for the sad Hindu or the
nearer savage, we feel that in the burning waste their love is like to be
a healing dew, in the forlorn jungle a tent of solace to one another. They
meet as children of one Father to read together one book of instruction.

We must insert in this connection the most beautiful picture presented
by ancient literature of wedded love under this noble form.

It is from the romance in which Xenophon, the chivalrous Greek, presents his ideal of what human nature should be.

The generals of Cyrus had taken captive a princess, a woman of unequaled beauty, and hastened to present her to the prince as that part of
the spoil he would think most worthy of his acceptance. Cyrus visits the
lady, and is filled with immediate admiration by the modesty and majesty
with which she receives him. He finds her name is Panthea, and that she
is the wife of Abradatus, a young king whom she entirely loves. He protects her as a sister in his camp till he can restore her to her husband.

After the first transports of joy at this reunion, the heart of Panthea is
bent on showing her love and gratitude to her magnanimous and delicate
protector. And as she has nothing so precious to give as the aid of Abradatus, that is what she most wishes to offer. Her husband is of one soul
with her in this as in all things.

The description of her grief and self-destruction after the death which
ensued upon this devotion I have seen quoted, but never that of their
parting when she sends him forth to battle. I shall copy both. If they have
been read by any of my readers, they may be so again with profit in
this connection, for never were the heroism of a true Woman and the

purity of love in a true marriage painted in colors more delicate and more lively.

"The chariot of Abradatus that had four perches and eight horses was completely adorned for him; and when he was going to put on his linen corslet, which was a sort of armor used by those of his country, Panthea brought him a golden helmet and arm-pieces, broad bracelets for his wrists, a purple habit that reached down to his feet, and hung in folds at the bottom, and a crest dyed of a violet color. These things she had made, unknown to her husband and by taking the measure of his armor. He wondered when he saw them, and inquired thus of Panthea: 'And have you made me these arms, woman, by destroying your own ornaments?' 'No, by Jove!' said Panthea, 'not what is the most valuable of them; for it is you, if you appear to others to be what I think you, that will be my greatest ornament.' And saying that, she put on him the armor, and though she endeavored to conceal it, the tears poured down her cheeks. When Abradatus, who was before a man of fine appearance, was set out in those arms, he appeared the most beautiful and noble of all, especially being likewise so by nature. Then taking the reins from the driver, he was just preparing to mount the chariot, when Panthea, after she had desired all that were there to retire, thus said:

" 'O Abradatus! If ever there was a woman who had a greater regard to her husband than to her own soul, I believe you know that I am such a one; what need I therefore speak of things in particular, for I reckon that my actions have convinced you more than any words I can now use. And yet, though I stand thus affected toward you as you know I do, I swear by this friendship of mine and yours that I certainly would rather choose to be put underground jointly with you, approving yourself a brave man, than to live with you in disgrace and shame; so much do I think you and myself worthy of the noblest things. Then I think that we both lie under great obligations to Cyrus that, when I was a captive and chosen out for himself, he thought fit to treat me neither as a slave nor indeed as a woman of mean account, but he took and kept me for you as if I were his brother's wife. Besides when Araspes who was my guard went away from him, I promised him that if he would allow me to send for you, you would come to him, and approve yourself a much better and more faithful friend than Araspes.'

"Thus she spoke; and Abradatus, being struck with admiration at her discourse, laying his hand gently on her head and lifting up his eyes to heaven, made this prayer: 'Do thou, O greatest Jove, grant me to appear a husband worthy of Panthea, and a friend worthy of Cyrus who has done us so much honor!'

"Having said this, he mounted the chariot by the door of the driver's seat; and after he had got up, when the driver shut the door, Panthea who had now no other way to salute him kissed the seat of the chariot. The chariot then moved, and she, unknown to him, followed, till Abradatus turning about and seeing her said: 'Take courage, Panthea! Fare you happily and well, and now go your ways.' On this her women and servants carried her to her conveyance, and laying her down, concealed her by throwing the covering of a tent over her. The people, though Abradatus and his chariot made a noble spectacle, were not able to look at him till Panthea was gone."

After the battle:

"Cyrus calling to some of his servants, 'Tell me,' said he, 'has anyone seen Abradatus? For I admire that he now does not appear.' One replied, 'My sovereign, it is because he is not living, but died in the battle as he broke in with his chariot on the Egyptians. All the rest, except his particular companions, they say, turned off when they saw the Egyptians' compact body. His wife is now said to have taken up his dead body, to have placed it in the carriage that she herself was conveyed in, and to have brought it hither to some place on the river Pactolus, and her servants are digging a grave on a certain elevation. They say that his wife, after setting him out with all the ornaments she has, is sitting on the ground with his head on her knees.' Cyrus, hearing this, gave himself a blow on the thigh, mounted his horse at a leap, and taking with him a thousand horse, rode away to this scene of affliction; but gave orders to Gadatas and Gobryas to take with them all the rich ornaments proper for a friend and an excellent man deceased, and to follow after him; and whoever had herds of cattle with him, he ordered them to take both oxen and horses and sheep in good number, and to bring them away to the place where by inquiry they should find him to be, that he might sacrifice these to Abradatus.

"As soon as he saw the woman sitting on the ground, and the dead body there lying, he shed tears at the afflicting sight and said: 'Alas, thou brave and faithful soul, hast thou left us, and art thou gone?' At the same time he took him by the right hand, and the hand of the deceased came away, for it had been cut off with a sword by the Egyptians. He, at the sight of this, became yet much more concerned than before. The woman shrieked out in a lamentable manner, and taking the hand from Cyrus, kissed it, fitted it to its proper place again as well she could, and said: 'The rest, Cyrus, is in the same condition, but what need you see it? And I know that I was not one of the least concerned in these his sufferings, and perhaps, you were not less so; for I, fool that I was, frequently exhorted him to behave in such a manner as to appear a friend to you worthy of notice; and I know he never thought of what he himself should suffer, but of what he should do to please you. He is dead, therefore,' said she, 'without reproach, and I who urged him on sit here alive.' Cyrus, shedding tears for some time in silence, then spoke: 'He has died, woman, the noblest death; for he has died victorious! Do you adorn him with these things that I furnish you with.' (Gobryas and Gadatas were then come up, and had brought rich ornaments in great abundance with them.) 'Then,' said he, 'be assured that he shall not want respect and honor in all other things; but over and above, multitudes shall concur in raising him a monument that shall be worthy of us, and all the sacrifices shall be made him that are proper to be made in honor of a brave man. You shall not be left destitute, but for the sake of your modesty and every other virtue I will pay you all other honors, as well as place those about you who will conduct you wherever you please. Do you but make it known to me where it is that you desire to be conveyed to.' And Panthea replied: 'Be confident, Cyrus, I will not conceal from you to whom it is that I desire to go.'

"He, having said this, went away with great pity for her that she should have lost such a husband, and for the man that he should have left such a wife behind him, never to see her more. Panthea then gave orders for her servants to retire, 'Till such time,' said she, 'as I shall have lamented my husband as I please.' Her nurse she bid to stay, and gave orders that when she was dead, she would wrap her and her husband up in one mantle together. The nurse, after having repeatedly begged her not to do this and meeting with no success, but observing her to grow angry, sat herself down, breaking out into tears. She, being beforehand provided with a sword, killed herself, and laying her head down on her husband's breast, she died. The nurse set up a lamentable cry, and covered them both as Panthea had directed.

"Cyrus, as soon as he was informed of what the woman had done, being struck with it, went to help her if he could. The servants, three in number, seeing what had been done, drew their swords and killed themselves as they stood at the place where she had ordered them. And the monument is now said to have been raised by continuing the mound onto the servants; and on a pillar above, they say, the names of the man and woman were written in Syriac letters.

"Below were three pillars, and they were inscribed thus, 'Of the servants.' Cyrus, when he came to this melancholy scene, was struck with admiration of the woman, and, having lamented over her, went away. He took care, as was proper, that all the funeral rites should be paid them in the noblest manner, and the monument, they say, was raised up to a very great size."

These be the ancients, who so many assert had no idea of the dignity of Woman or of marriage. Such love Xenophon could paint as subsisting between those who after death "would see one another never more." Thousands of years have passed since, and with the reception of the Cross, the nations assume the belief that those who part thus may meet again and forever, if spiritually fitted to one another as Abradatus and Panthea were, and yet do we see such marriages among them? If at all, how often?

I must quote two more short passages from Xenophon, for he is a writer who pleases me well.

Cyrus, receiving the Armenians whom he had conquered:

" 'Tigranes,' said he, 'at what rate would you purchase the regaining of your wife?' Now Tigranes happened to be *but lately married,* and had a very great love for his wife." (That clause perhaps sounds *modern.*)

" 'Cyrus,' said he, 'I would ransom her at the expense of my life.'

" 'Take then your own to yourself,' said he. . . .

"When they came home, one talked of Cyrus' wisdom, another of his patience and resolution, another of his mildness. One spoke of his beauty and smallness of his person, and on that Tigranes asked his wife, 'And do you, Armenian dame, think Cyrus handsome?' 'Truly,' said she, 'I did not look at him.' 'At whom then *did* you look?' said Tigranes. 'At him who said that to save me from servitude he would ransom me at the expense of his own life.' "

From the *Banquet:*

"Socrates, who observed her with pleasure, said, 'This young girl has confirmed me in the opinion I have had for a long time that the female sex are nothing inferior to ours, excepting only in strength of body, or perhaps in steadiness of judgment.' "

In the *Economics,* the manner in which the husband gives counsel to his young wife presents the model of politeness and refinement. Xenophon is thoroughly the gentleman, gentle in breeding and in soul. All the men he describes are so, while the shades of manner are distinctly marked. There is the serene dignity of Socrates, with gleams of playfulness thrown across its cool, religious shades, the princely mildness of Cyrus, and the more domestic elegance of the husband in the *Economics.*

There is no way that men sin more against refinement, as well as discretion, than in their conduct toward their wives. Let them look at the men of Xenophon. Such would know how to give counsel, for they would know how to receive it. They would feel that the most intimate relations claimed most, not least, of refined courtesy. They would not suppose that confidence justified carelessness, nor the reality of affection want of delicacy in the expression of it.

Such men would be too wise to hide their affairs from the wife, and then expect her to act as if she knew them. They would know that if she is expected to face calamity with courage, she must be instructed and trusted in prosperity, or if they had failed in wise confidence such as the husband shows in the *Economics,* they would be ashamed of anger or querulous surprise at the results that naturally follow,

Such men would not be exposed to the bad influence of bad wives; for all wives, bad or good, loved or unloved, inevitably influence their husbands from the power their position not merely gives but necessitates, of coloring evidence and infusing feelings in hours when the—patient, shall I call him?—is off his guard. Those who understand the wife's mind, and think it worth while to respect her springs of action, know better where they are. But to the bad or thoughtless man, who lives carelessly and irreverently so near another mind, the wrong he does daily back upon himself recoils. A Cyrus, an Abradatus, knows where he stands.

But to return to the thread of my subject.

Another sign of the times is furnished by the triumphs of Female Authorship. These have been great and are constantly increasing. Women have taken possession of so many provinces for which men had pronounced them unfit, that though these still declare there are some inaccessible to them, it is difficult to say just *where* they must stop.

The shining names of famous women have cast light upon the path of the sex, and many obstructions have been removed. When a Montagu could learn better than her brother and use her lore afterward to such purpose as an observer, it seemed amiss to hinder women from preparing themselves to see, or from seeing all they could when prepared. Since Somerville has achieved so much, will any young girl be prevented from seeking a knowledge of the physical sciences if she wishes it? De Staël's name was not so clear of offense; she could not forget the Woman in the thought; while she was instructing you as a mind, she wished to be admired as a Woman; sentimental tears often dimmed the eagle glance. Her intellect, too, with all its splendor, trained in a drawing-room, fed on flattery, was tainted and flawed; yet its beams make the obscurest schoolhouse in New England warmer and lighter to the little rugged girls who are gathered together on its wooden bench. They may never through life hear her name, but she is not the less their benefactress.

The influence has been such that the aim certainly is now, in arranging school instruction for girls, to give them as fair a field as boys. As yet, indeed, these arrangements are made with little judgment or reflection; just as the tutors of Lady Jane Grey and other distinguished women of her time taught them Latin and Greek, because they knew nothing else themselves, so now the improvement in the education of girls is to be made by giving them young men as teachers, who only teach what has been taught themselves at college, while methods and topics need revision for these new subjects, which could better be made by those who had experienced the same wants. Women are often at the head of these institutions; but they have as yet seldom been thinking women, capable of organizing a new whole for the wants of the time, and choosing persons to officiate in the departments. And when some portion of instruction of a good sort is got from the school, the far greater proportion which is infused from the general atmosphere of society contradicts its purport. Yet books and a little elementary instruction are not furnished in vain. Women are better aware how great and rich the universe is, not so easily blinded by narrowness or partial views of a home circle. "Her mother did so before her" is no longer a sufficient excuse. Indeed it was never received as an excuse to mitigate the severity of censure, but was adduced as a reason, rather, why there should be no effort made for reformation.

Whether much or little has been done, or will be done—whether women will add to the talent of narration the power of systematizing—whether they will carve marble as well as draw and paint—is not important. But that it should be acknowledged that they have intellect which needs developing—that they should not be considered complete if beings of affection and habit alone—is important.

Yet even this acknowledgment, rather conquered by Woman than proffered by Man, has been sullied by the usual selfishness. Too much is said of women being better educated that they may become better companions and mothers *for men*. They should be fit for such companionship, and we have mentioned with satisfaction instances where it has been established. Earth knows no fairer, holier relation than that of a mother. It is one which rightly understood must both promote and require the highest attainments. But a being of infinite scope must not be treated with an exclusive view to any one relation. Give the soul free course, let the organization both of body and mind be freely developed, and the being will be fit for any and every relation to which it may be called. The intellect, no more than the sense of hearing, is to be cultivated merely that Woman may be a more valuable companion to Man, but because the Power who gave a power by its mere existence signifies that it must be brought out toward perfection.

In this regard of self-dependence, and a greater simplicity and fullness of being, we must hail as a preliminary the increase of the class contemptuously designated as "old maids."

We cannot wonder at the aversion with which old bachelors and old maids have been regarded. Marriage is the natural means of forming a sphere, of taking root in the earth; it requires more strength to do this without such an opening; very many have failed, and their imperfections have been in everyone's way. They have been more partial, more harsh, more officious and impertinent than those compelled by severer friction to render themselves endurable. Those who have a more full experience of the instincts have a distrust as to whether the unmarried can be thoroughly human and humane, such as is hinted in the saying, "Old maids' and bachelors' children are well cared for," which derides at once their ignorance and their presumption.

Yet the business of society has become so complex that it could now scarcely be carried on without the presence of these despised auxiliaries; and detachments from the army of aunts and uncles are wanted to stop gaps in every hedge. They rove about, mental and moral Ishmaelites, pitching their tents amid the fixed and ornamented homes of men.

In a striking variety of forms, genius of late, both at home and abroad, has paid its tribute to the character of the aunt and the uncle, recognizing in these personages the spiritual parents who have supplied defects in the treatment of the busy or careless actual parents.

They also gain a wider, if not so deep experience. Those who are not intimately and permanently linked with others are thrown upon themselves; and if they do not there find peace and incessant life, there is none to flatter them that they are not very poor and very mean.

A position which so constantly admonishes may be of inestimable benefit. The person may gain, undistracted by other relationships, a closer communion with the one. Such a use is made of it by saints and sibyls. Or she may be one of the lay sisters of charity, a canoness bound by an inward vow—or the useful drudge of all men, the Martha, much sought, little prized—or the intellectual interpreter of the varied life she sees; the Urania of a half-formed world's twilight.

Or she may combine all these. Not "needing to care that she may please a husband," a frail and limited being, her thoughts may turn to the center, and she may, by steadfast contemplation entering into the secret of truth and love, use it for the good of all men instead of a chosen few, and interpret through it all the forms of life. It is possible, perhaps, to be at once a priestly servant and a loving muse.

Saints and geniuses have often chosen a lonely position, in the faith that if, undisturbed by the pressure of near ties, they would give themselves up to the inspiring spirit, it would enable them to understand and reproduce life better than actual experience could.

How many "old maids" take this high stand we cannot say: it is an unhappy fact that too many who have come before the eye are gossips rather, and not always good-natured gossips. But if these abuse, and none make the best of their vocation, yet it has not failed to produce some good results. It has been seen by others, if not by themselves, that beings, likely to be left alone, need to be fortified and furnished within themselves; and education and thought have tended more and more to regard these beings as related to absolute Being, as well as to others. It has been seen that as the breaking of no bond ought to destroy a man, so ought the missing of none to hinder him from growing. And thus a circumstance of the time which springs rather from its luxury than its purity, has helped to place women on the true platform.

Perhaps the next generation, looking deeper into this matter, will find that contempt is put upon old maids or old women at all, merely because they do not use the elixir which would keep them always young. Under its influence, a gem brightens yearly which is only seen to more advantage through the fissures Time makes in the casket. No one thinks of Michelangelo's "Persican Sibyl" or St. Theresa or Tasso's Leonora or the Greek Electra as an old maid, more than of Michelangelo or Canova as old bachelors, though all had reached the period in life's course appointed to take that degree.

See a common woman at forty; scarcely has she the remains of beauty, of any soft poetic grace which gave her attraction as Woman, which kindled the hearts of those who looked on her to sparkling thoughts, or diffused round her a roseate air of gentle love. See her who was indeed a lovely girl in the coarse, full-blown dahlia flower of what is commonly matron-beauty, "fat, fair, and forty," showily dressed, and with manners as broad and full as her frill or satin cloak. People observe, "How well she is pre-served!" "She is a fine woman still," they say. This woman, whether as a duchess in diamonds or one of our city dames in mosaics, charms the poet's heart no more, and would look much out of place kneeling before the Madonna. She "does well the honors of her house"—"leads society"—is in short always spoken and thought of upholstery-wise.

Or see that careworn face from which every soft line is blotted—those faded eyes from which lonely tears have driven the flashes of fancy, the mild white beam of a tender enthusiasm. This woman is not so ornamental to a tea party; yet she would please better in picture. Yet surely she, no more than the other, looks as a human being should at the end of forty years. Forty years! Have they bound those brows with no garland? Shed in the lamp no drop of ambrosial oil?

Not so looked the Iphigenia in Aulis. Her forty years had seen her in anguish, in sacrifice, in utter loneliness. But those pains were borne for her father and her country; the sacrifice she had made pure for herself and those around her. Wandering alone at night in the vestal solitude of her imprisoning grove, she has looked up through its "living summits" to the stars, which shed down into her aspect their own lofty melody. At forty she would not misbecome the marble.

Not so looks the Persica. She is withered; she is faded; the drapery that enfolds her has in its dignity an angularity, too, that tells of age, of sorrow, of a stern resignation to the *must*. But her eye, that torch of the soul, is un-tamed, and in the intensity of her reading we see a soul invincibly young in faith and hope. Her age is her charm, for it is the night of the past that gives this beacon-fire leave to shine. Wither more and more, black Chrysalid, thou dost but give the winged beauty time to mature its splendors!

Not so looked Vittoria Colonna after her life of a great hope and of true conjugal fidelity. She had been not merely a bride but a wife, and each hour had helped to plume the noble bird. A coronet of pearls will not shame her brow; it is white and ample, a worthy altar for love and thought.

Even among the North American Indians, a race of men as completely engaged in mere instinctive life as almost any in the world, and where each chief, keeping many wives as useful servants, of course looks with no kind eye on celibacy in Woman, it was excused in the following instance mentioned by Mrs. Jameson. A woman dreamt in youth that she was betrothed to the Sun. She built her a wigwam apart, filled it with emblems of her alliance and means of an independent life. There she passed her days, sustained by her own exertions and true to her supposed engagement.

In any tribe, we believe, a woman who lived as if she was betrothed to the Sun would be tolerated, and the rays which made her youth blossom sweetly would crown her with a halo in age.

There is on this subject a nobler view than heretofore, if not the noblest, and improvement here must coincide with that in the view taken of marriage. "We must have units before we can have union," says one of the ripe thinkers of the times.

If larger intellectual resources begin to be deemed needful to Woman, still more is a spiritual dignity in her, or even the mere assumption of it, looked upon with respect. Joanna Southcote and Mother Anne Lee are sure of a band of disciples; Ecstatica, Dolorosa, of enraptured believers who will visit them in their lowly huts, and wait for days to revere them in their trances. The foreign noble traverses land and sea to hear a few words from the lips of the lowly peasant girl whom he believes especially visited by the Most High. Very beautiful in this way was the influence of the invalid of St. Petersburg, as described by De Maistre.

Mysticism, which may be defined as the brooding soul of the world, cannot fail of its oracular promise as to Woman. "The mothers," "the mother of all things," are expressions of thought which lead the mind towards this side of universal growth. Whenever a mystical whisper was heard from Behmen down to St. Simon, sprang up the thought that, if it be true as the legend says that Humanity withers through a fault committed by and a curse laid upon Woman, through her pure child or influence shall the new Adam, the redemption, arise. Innocence is to be replaced by virtue, dependence by a willing submission in the heart of the Virgin-Mother of the new race.

The spiritual tendency is toward the elevation of Woman, but the intellectual by itself is not so. Plato sometimes seems penetrated by that high idea of love which considers Man and Woman as the twofold expression of one thought. This the angel of Swedenborg, the angel of the coming age, cannot surpass but only explain more fully. But then again Plato, the man of intellect, treats Woman in the *Republic* as property, and in the *Timæus* says that Man, if he misuse the privileges of one life, shall be degraded into the form of Woman; and then, if he do not redeem himself, into that of a bird. This, as I said above, expresses most happily how antipoetical is this state of mind. For the poet contemplating the world of things selects various birds as the symbols of his most gracious and ethereal thoughts, just as he calls upon his genius as muse rather than as God. But the intellect, cold, is ever more masculine than feminine; warmed by emotion, it rushes toward mother-earth, and puts on the forms of beauty.

The electrical, the magnetic element in Woman has not been fairly brought out at any period. Everything might be expected from it; she has far more of it than Man. This is commonly expressed by saying that her intuitions are more rapid and more correct. You will often see men of high intellect absolutely stupid in regard to the atmospheric changes, the fine invisible links which connect the forms of life around them, while common women, if pure and modest so that a vulgar self do not overshadow the mental eye, will seize and delineate these with unerring discrimination.

Women who combine this organization with creative genius are very commonly unhappy at present. They see too much to act in conformity with those around them, and their quick impulses seem folly to those who do not discern the motives. This is a usual effect of the apparition of genius whether in Man or Woman, but is more frequent with regard to the latter, because a harmony, an obvious order and self-restraining decorum, is most expected from her.

Then women of genius, even more than men, are likely to be enslaved by an impassioned sensibility. The world repels them more rudely, and they are of weaker bodily frame.

Those who seem overladen with electricity frighten those around them. "When she merely enters the room, I am what the French call *hérissé*," said a man of petty feelings and worldly character of such a woman, whose depth of eye and powerful motion announced the conductor of the mysterious fluid.

Woe to such a woman who finds herself linked to such a man in bonds too close! It is the cruelest of errors. He will detest her with all the bitterness of wounded self-love. He will take the whole prejudice of manhood upon himself, and to the utmost of his power imprison and torture her by its imperious rigors.

Yet allow room enough, and the electric fluid will be found to invigorate and embellish, not destroy life. Such women are the great actresses, the songsters. Such traits we read in a late searching, though too French, analysis of the character of Mademoiselle Rachel by a modern La Rochefoucauld. The Greeks thus represent the muses; they have not the golden serenity of Apollo; they are *overflowed* with thought; there is something tragic in their air. Such are the Sibyls of Guercino; the eye is overfull of expression, dilated and lustrous; it seems to have drawn the whole being into it.

Sickness is the frequent result of this overcharged existence. To this region, however misunderstood or interpreted with presumptuous carelessness, belong the phenomena of magnetism, or mesmerism as it is now often called, where the trance of the Ecstatica purports to be produced by the agency of one human being on another, instead of as in her case direct from the spirit.

The worldling has his sneer at this as at the services of religion. "The churches can always be filled with women"—"Show me a man in one of your magnetic states, and I will believe."

Women are, indeed, the easy victims both of priestcraft and self-delusion; but this would not be, if the intellect was developed in proportion to the other powers. They would then have a regulator and be more in equipoise, yet must retain the same nervous susceptibility while their physical structure is such as it is.

It is with just that hope that we welcome everything that tends to strengthen the fiber and develop the nature on more sides. When the intellect and affections are in harmony; when intellectual consciousness is calm and deep; inspiration will not be confounded with fancy. Then,

> . . . she who advances
> With rapturous, lyrical glances,
> Singing the song of the earth, singing
> Its hymn to the Gods,

will not be pitied as a madwoman nor shrunk from as unnatural.

The Greeks, who saw everything in forms which we are trying to ascertain as law and classify as cause, embodied all this in the form of Cassandra. Cassandra was only unfortunate in receiving her gift too soon. The remarks, however, that the world still makes in such cases are well expressed by the Greek dramatist.

In the Trojan dames there are fine touches of nature with regard to Cassandra. Hecuba shows that mixture of shame and reverence that prosaic kindred always do toward the inspired child, the poet, the elected sufferer for the race.

When the herald announces that Cassandra is chosen to be the mistress of Agamemnon, Hecuba answers with indignation, betraying the pride and faith she involuntarily felt in this daughter.

> *Hec.* The maiden of Phoebus, to whom the golden-haired
> Gave as a privilege a virgin life!
> *Tal.* Love of the inspired maiden hath pierced him.
> *Hec.* Then cast away, my child, the sacred keys, and from thy person
> The consecrated garlands which thou wearest.

Yet, when, a moment after, Cassandra appears, singing wildly her inspired song, Hecuba calls her, "My *frantic* child."

Yet how graceful she is in her tragic *raptus,* the chorus shows.

> *Chorus.* How sweetly at thy house's ills thou smil'st,
> Chanting what, haply, thou wilt not show true.

If Hecuba dares not trust her highest instinct about her daughter, still less can the vulgar mind of the herald Talthybius, a man not without feeling but with no princely, no poetic blood, abide the wild, prophetic mood which insults all his prejudices.

> *Tal.* The venerable, and that accounted wise,
> Is nothing better than that of no repute;
> For the greatest king of all the Greeks,
> The dear son of Atreus, is possessed with the love

Of this madwoman. I indeed am poor;
Yet I would not receive her to my bed.

The royal Agamemnon could see the beauty of Cassandra; *he* was not afraid of her prophetic gifts.

The best topic for a chapter on this subject in the present day would be the history of the Seeress of Prevorst, the best observed subject of magnetism in our present times, and who, like her ancestresses of Delphos, was roused to ecstasy or frenzy by the touch of the laurel.

I observe in her case, and in one known to me here, that what might have been a gradual and gentle disclosure of remarkable powers was broken and jarred into disease by an unsuitable marriage. Both these persons were unfortunate in not understanding what was involved in this relation, but acted ignorantly as their friends desired. They thought that this was the inevitable destiny of Woman. But when engaged in the false position, it was impossible for them to endure its dissonances, as those of less delicate perceptions can; and the fine flow of life was checked and sullied. They grew sick, but even so learned and disclosed more than those in health are wont to do.

In such cases worldlings sneer; but reverent men learn wondrous news either from the person observed or by thoughts caused in themselves by the observation. Fénelon learns from Guyon, Kerner from his Seeress, what we fain would know. But to appreciate such disclosures one must be a child; and here the phrase "women and children" may perhaps be interpreted aright, that only little children shall enter into the kingdom of heaven.

All these motions of the time, tides that betoken a waxing moon, overflow upon our land. The world at large is readier to let Woman learn and manifest the capacities of her nature than it ever was before, and here is a less encumbered field and freer air than anywhere else. And it ought to be so; we ought to pay for Isabella's jewels.

The names of nations are feminine—Religion, Virtue, and Victory are feminine. To those who have a superstition as to outward reigns, it is not without significance that the name of the queen of our motherland should at this crisis be Victoria—Victoria the First. Perhaps to us it may be given to disclose the era thus outwardly presaged.

Another Isabella, too, at this time ascends the throne. Might she open a new world to her sex! But probably these poor little women are least of any educated to serve as examples or inspirers for the rest. The Spanish queen is younger; we know of her that she sprained her foot the other day dancing in her private apartments; of Victoria, that she reads aloud in a distinct voice and agreeable manner her addresses to Parliament on certain solemn days, and yearly that she presents to the nation some new prop of royalty. These ladies have very likely been trained more completely to the puppet life than any other. The queens who have been queens indeed were trained by adverse circumstances to know the world around them and their own powers.

It is moving, while amusing, to read of the Scottish peasant measuring the print left by the queen's foot as she walks, and priding himself on its beauty. It is so natural to wish to find what is fair and precious in high places—so astonishing to find the Bourbon a glutton or the Guelph a dullard or gossip.

In our own country women are in many respects better situated than men. Good books are allowed, with more time to read them. They are not so early forced into the bustle of life, nor so weighed down by demands for outward success. The perpetual changes incident to our society make the blood circulate freely through the body politic, and if not favorable at present to the grace and bloom of life, they are so to activity, resource, and would be to reflection, but for a low materialist tendency from which the women are generally exempt in themselves, though its existence among the men has a tendency to repress their impulses and make them doubt their instincts, thus often paralyzing their action during the best years.

But they have time to think, and no traditions chain them and few conventionalities, compared with what must be met in other nations. There is no reason why they should not discover that the secrets of nature are open, the revelations of the spirit waiting for whoever will seek them. When the mind is once awakened to this consciousness, it will not be restrained by the habits of the past, but fly to seek the seeds of a heavenly future.

Their employments are more favorable to meditation than those of men. Woman is not addressed religiously here more than elsewhere. She is told that she should be worthy to be the mother of a Washington or the companion of some good man. But in many, many instances, she has already learned that all bribes have the same flaw; that truth and good are to be sought solely for their own sakes. And already an ideal sweetness floats over many forms, shines in many eyes.

Already deep questions are put by young girls on the great theme: What shall I do to enter upon the eternal life?

Men are very courteous to them. They praise them often, check them seldom. There is chivalry in the feeling toward the "ladies," which gives them the best seats in the stage-coach, frequent admission not only to lectures of all sorts but to courts of justice, halls of legislature, reform conventions. The newspaper editor "would be better pleased that the Lady's Book should be filled up exclusively by ladies. It would then indeed be a true gem, worthy to be presented by young men to the mistress of their affections." Can gallantry go further?

In this country is venerated, wherever seen, the character which Goethe spoke of as an Ideal, which he saw actualized in his friend and patroness, the Grand Duchess Amelia: "The excellent woman is she who, if the husband dies, can be a father to the children." And this, if read aright, tells a great deal.

Women who speak in public, if they have a moral power such as has been felt from Angelina Grimké and Abby Kelly—that is, if they speak for conscience' sake, to serve a cause which they hold sacred—invariably subdue the prejudices of their hearers and excite an interest proportionate to the aversion with which it had been the purpose to regard them.

A passage in a private letter so happily illustrates this, that it must be inserted here.

Abby Kelly in the Town House of ———

"The scene was not unheroic—to see that woman, true to humanity and her own nature, a center of rude eyes and tongues, even gentlemen feeling licensed to make part of a species of mob around a female out of her sphere. As she took her seat in the desk amid the great noise, and in the throng full, like a wave, of something to ensue, I saw her humanity in a gentleness and unpretension, tenderly open to the sphere around her, and had she not been supported by the power of the will of genuineness and principle, she would have failed. It led her to prayer, which, in Woman especially, is childlike; sensibility and will going to the side of God and looking up to him; and humanity was poured out in aspiration.

"She acted like a gentle hero with her mild decision and womanly calmness. All heroism is mild and quiet and gentle, for it is life and possession; and combativeness and firmness show a want of actualness. She is as earnest, fresh, and simple as when she first entered the crusade. I think she did much good, more than the men in her place could do, for Woman feels more as being and reproducing—this brings the subject more into home relations. Men speak through and mostly from intellect, and this addresses itself to that in others which is combative."

Not easily shall we find elsewhere or before this time any written observations on the same subject so delicate and profound.

The late Dr. Channing, whose enlarged and tender and religious nature shared every onward impulse of his time, though his thoughts followed his wishes with a deliberative caution which belonged to his habits and temperament, was greatly interested in these expectations for women. His own treatment of them was absolutely and thoroughly religious. He regarded them as souls, each of which had a destiny of its own, incalculable to other minds, and whose leading it must follow, guided by the light of a private conscience. He had sentiment, delicacy, kindness, taste; but they were all pervaded and ruled by this one thought, that all beings had souls and must vindicate their own inheritance. Thus all beings were treated by him with an equal and sweet though solemn courtesy. The young and unknown, the woman and the child, all felt themselves regarded with an infinite expectation from which there was no reaction to vulgar prejudice. He demanded of all he met, to use his favorite phrase, "great truths."

His memory, every way dear and reverend, is by many especially cherished for this intercourse of unbroken respect.

At one time, when the progress of Harriet Martineau through this country, Angelina Grimké's appearance in public, and the visit of Mrs. Jameson had turned his thoughts to this subject, he expressed high hopes as to what the coming era would bring to Woman. He had been much pleased with the dignified courage of Mrs. Jameson in taking up the defense of her sex in a way from which women usually shrink because, if they express themselves on such subjects with sufficient force and clearness to do any good, they are exposed to assaults whose vulgarity makes them painful. In intercourse with such a woman, he had shared her indignation at the base injustice, in many respects and in many regions, done to the sex; and been led to think of it far more than ever before. He seemed to think that he might some time write upon the subject. That his aid is withdrawn from the cause is a subject of great regret; for on this question as on others he would have known how to sum up the evidence, and take, in the noblest spirit, middle ground. He always furnished a platform on which opposing parties could stand and look at one another under the influence of his mildness and enlightened candor.

Two younger thinkers, men both, have uttered noble prophecies auspicious for Woman. Kinmont, all whose thoughts tended towards the establishment of the reign of love and peace, thought that the inevitable means of this would be an increased predominance given to the idea of Woman. Had he lived longer to see the growth of the Peace Party, the reforms in life and medical practice which seek to substitute water for wine and drugs, pulse for animal food, he would have been confirmed in his view of the way in which the desired changes are to be effected.

In this connection I must mention Shelley, who like all men of genius shared the feminine development, and unlike many knew it. His life was one of the first pulse beats in the present reform-growth. He, too, abhorred blood and heat, and by his system and his song tended to reinstate a plant-like gentleness in the development of energy. In harmony with this, his ideas of marriage were lofty, and of course no less so of Woman, her nature, and destiny.

For Woman, if by a sympathy as to outward condition she is led to aid the enfranchisement of the slave, must be no less so by inward tendency to favor measures which promise to bring the world more thoroughly and deeply into harmony with her nature. When the lamb takes place of the lion as the emblem of nations, both women and men will be as children of one spirit, perpetual learners of the word and doers thereof, not hearers only.

A writer in the New York *Pathfinder,* in two articles headed "Femality," has uttered a still more pregnant word than any we have named. He views Woman truly from the soul and not from society, and the depth and leading of his thoughts are proportionably remarkable. He views the feminine nature as a harmonizer of the vehement elements, and this has often been hinted elsewhere; but what he expresses most forcibly is the lyrical, the inspiring and inspired apprehensiveness of her being.

This view being identical with what I have before attempted to indicate, as to her superior susceptibility to magnetic or electric influence, I will now try to express myself more fully.

There are two aspects of Woman's nature, represented by the ancients as Muse and Minerva. It is the former to which the writer in the *Pathfinder* looks. It is the latter which Wordsworth has in mind when he says,

> With a placid brow,
> Which woman ne'er should forfeit, keep thy vow.

The especial genius of Woman I believe to be electrical in movement, intuitive in function, spiritual in tendency. She excels not so easily in classification or recreation, as in an instinctive seizure of causes, and a simple breathing out of what she receives that has the singleness of life, rather than the selecting and energizing of art.

More native is it to her to be the living model of the artist than to set apart from herself any one form in objective reality; more native to inspire and receive the poem than to create it. In so far as soul is in her completely developed, all soul is the same; but in so far as it is modified in her as Woman, it flows, it breathes, it sings, rather than deposits soil or finishes work; and that which is especially feminine flushes in blossom the face of earth, and pervades like air and water all this seeming solid globe, daily renewing and purifying its life. Such may be the especially feminine element spoken of as Femality. But it is no more the order of nature that it should be incarnated pure in any form, than that the masculine energy should exist unmingled with it in any form.

Male and female represent the two sides of the great radical dualism. But in fact they are perpetually passing into one another. Fluid hardens to solid, solid rushes to fluid. There is no wholly masculine man, no purely feminine woman.

History jeers at the attempts of physiologists to bind great original laws by the forms which flow from them. They make a rule; they say from observation what can and cannot be. In vain! Nature provides exceptions to every rule. She sends women to battle, and sets Hercules spinning; she enables women to bear immense burdens, cold, and frost; she enables the man who feels maternal love to nourish his infant like a mother. Of late she plays still gayer pranks. Not only she deprives organizations but organs of a necessary end. She enables people to read with the top of the head and see with the pit of the stomach. Presently she will make a female Newton and a male siren.

Man partakes of the feminine in the Apollo; Woman of the masculine as Minerva.

What I mean by the Muse is that unimpeded clearness of the intuitive powers, which a perfectly truthful adherence to every admonition of the higher instincts would bring to a finely organized human being. It may appear as prophecy or as poesy. It enabled Cassandra to foresee the results of actions passing round her; the Seeress to behold the true character of the person through the mask of his customary life. (Sometimes she saw a feminine form behind the man, sometimes the reverse.) It enabled the daughter of Linnaeus to see the soul of the flower exhaling from the flower.* It gave a man, but a poet-man, the power of which he thus speaks: "Often in my contemplation of nature, radiant intimations and as it were sheaves of light appear before me as to the facts of cosmogony, in which my mind has perhaps taken especial part." He wisely adds, "But it is necessary with earnestness to verify the knowledge we gain by these flashes of light." And none should forget this. Sight must be verified by light before it can deserve the honors of piety and genius. Yet sight comes first, and of this sight of the world of causes, this approximation to the region of primitive motions, women I hold to be especially capable. Even without equal freedom with the other sex, they have already shown themselves so; and should these faculties have free play, I believe they will open new, deeper, and purer sources of joyous inspiration than have as yet refreshed the earth.

Let us be wise, and not impede the soul. Let her work as she will. Let us have one creative energy, one incessant revelation. Let it take what form

---

* The daughter of Linnaeus states that while looking steadfastly at the red lily, she saw its spirit hovering above it as a red flame. It is true this, like many fair spirit-stories, may be explained away as an optical illusion, but its poetic beauty and meaning would even then make it valuable as an illustration of the spiritual fact.

it will, and let us not bind it by the past to man or woman, black or white. Jove sprang from Rhea, Pallas from Jove. So let it be.

If it has been the tendency of these remarks to call Woman rather to the Minerva side—if I, unlike the more generous writer, have spoken from society no less than the soul—let it be pardoned! It is love that has caused this—love for many incarcerated souls that might be freed could the idea of religious self-dependence be established in them, could the weakening habit of dependence on others be broken up.

Proclus teaches that every life has in its sphere a totality or wholeness of the animating powers of the other spheres, having only as its own characteristic a predominance of some one power. Thus Jupiter comprises within himself the other twelve powers, which stand thus: the first triad is *demiurgic* or *fabricative,* that is, Jupiter, Neptune, Vulcan; the second, *defensive,* Vesta, Minerva, Mars; the third, *vivific,* Ceres, Juno, Diana; and the fourth, *elevating* and *harmonic,* Mercury, Venus, Apollo. In the sphere of Jupiter, energy is predominant—with Venus, beauty; but each comprehends and apprehends all the others.

When the same community of life and consciousness of mind begin among men, humanity will have positively and finally subjugated its brute elements and Titanic childhood; criticism will have perished; arbitrary limits and ignorant censure be impossible; all will have entered upon the liberty of law and the harmony of common growth.

Then Apollo will sing to his lyre what Vulcan forges on the anvil, and the Muse weave anew the tapestries of Minerva.

It is therefore only in the present crisis that the preference is given to Minerva. The power of continence must establish the legitimacy of freedom, the power of self-poise the perfection of motion.

Every relation, every gradation of nature is incalculably precious, but only to the soul which is poised upon itself and to whom no loss, no change, can bring dull discord, for it is in harmony with the central soul.

If any individual live too much in relations, so that he becomes a stranger to the resources of his own nature, he falls after a while into a distraction, or imbecility, from which he can only be cured by a time of isolation which gives the renovating fountains time to rise up. With a society it is the same. Many minds, deprived of the traditionary or instinctive means of passing a cheerful existence, must find help in self-impulse or perish. It is therefore that, while any elevation in the view of union is to be hailed with joy, we shall not decline celibacy as the great fact of the time. It is one from which no vow, no arrangement can at present save a thinking mind. For now the rowers are pausing on their oars; they wait a change before they can pull together. All tends to illustrate the thought of a wise contemporary. Union is only possible to those who are units. To be fit for relations in time, souls, whether of Man or Woman, must be able to do without them in the spirit.

It is therefore that I would have Woman lay aside all thought, such as she habitually cherishes, of being taught and led by men. I would have her, like the Indian girl, dedicate herself to the Sun, the Sun of Truth, and go nowhere if his beams did not make clear the path. I would have her free from compromise, from complaisance, from helplessness, because I would have her good enough and strong enough to love one and all beings, from the fullness, not the poverty of being.

Men as at present instructed will not help this work, because they also are under the slavery of habit. I have seen with delight their poetic impulses. A sister is the fairest ideal, and how nobly Wordsworth and even Byron have written of a sister!

There is no sweeter sight than to see a father with his little daughter. Very vulgar men become refined to the eye when leading a little girl by the hand. At that moment, the right relation between the sexes seems established, and you feel as if the man would aid in the noblest purpose, if you ask him in behalf of his little daughter. Once, two fine figures stood before me thus. The father of very intellectual aspect, his falcon eye softened by affection as he looked down on his fair child; she the image of himself, only more graceful and brilliant in expression. I was reminded of Southey's Kehama; when, lo, the dream was rudely broken! They were talking of education, and he said:

"I shall not have Maria brought too forward. If she knows too much, she will never find a husband; superior women hardly ever can."

"Surely," said his wife with a blush, "you wish Maria to be as good and wise as she can, whether it will help her to marriage or not."

"No," he persisted, "I want her to have a sphere and a home, and someone to protect her when I am gone."

It was a trifling incident, but made a deep impression. I felt that the holiest relations fail to instruct the unprepared and perverted mind. If this man indeed could have looked at it on the other side, he was the last that would have been willing to have been taken himself for the home and protection he could give, but would have been much more likely to repeat the tale of Alcibiades with his phials.

But men do *not* look at both sides, and women must leave off asking them and being influenced by them, but retire within themselves, and explore the groundwork of life till they find their peculiar secret. Then, when they come forth again, renovated and baptized, they will know how to turn all dross to gold, and will be rich and free though they live in a hut, tranquil if in a crowd. Then their sweet singing shall not be from passionate impulse, but the lyrical overflow of a divine rapture, and a new music shall be evolved from this many-chorded world.

Grant her, then, for a while the armor and the javelin. Let her put from her the press of other minds, and meditate in virgin loneliness. The same idea shall reappear in due time as Muse, or Ceres, the all-kindly, patient Earth Spirit.

Among the throng of symptoms which denote the present tendency to a crisis in the life of Woman—which resembles the change from girlhood, with its beautiful instincts but unharmonized thoughts, its blind pupilage and restless seeking, to self-possessed, wise, and graceful womanhood—I have attempted to select a few.

One of prominent interest is the unison upon the subject of three male minds, which for width of culture, power of self-concentration, and dignity of aim take rank as the prophets of the coming age, while their histories and labors are rooted in the past.

Swedenborg came, he tells us, to interpret the past revelation and unfold a new. He announces the New Church that is to prepare the way for the New Jerusalem, a city built of precious stones hardened and purified by secret processes in the veins of earth through the ages.

Swedenborg approximated to that harmony between the scientific and poetic lives of mind, which we hope from the perfected man. The links that bind together the realms of nature, the mysteries that accompany her births and growths, were unusually plain to him. He seems a man to whom insight was given at a period when the mental frame was sufficiently matured to retain and express its gifts.

His views of Woman are in the main satisfactory. In some details we may object to them, as in all his system there are still remains of what is arbitrary and seemingly groundless—fancies that show the marks of old habits, and a nature as yet not thoroughly leavened with the spiritual leaven. At least so it seems to me now. I speak reverently, for I find such reason to venerate Swedenborg from an imperfect knowledge of his mind that I feel one more perfect might explain to me much that does not now secure my sympathy.

His idea of Woman is sufficiently large and noble to interpose no obstacle to her progress. His idea of marriage is consequently sufficient. Man and Woman share an angelic ministry; the union is of one with one, permanent and pure.

As the New Church extends its ranks, the needs of Woman must be more considered.

Quakerism also establishes Woman on a sufficient equality with Man. But though the original thought of Quakerism is pure, its scope is too narrow, and its influence, having established a certain amount of good and made clear some truth, must by degrees be merged in one of wider range.* The mind of Swedenborg appeals to the various nature of Man, and allows room for aesthetic culture and the free expression of energy.

As apostle of the new order, of the social fabric that is to rise from love and supersede the old that was based on strife, Charles Fourier comes next, expressing in an outward order many facts of which Swedenborg saw the secret springs. The mind of Fourier, though grand and clear, was in some respects superficial. He was a stranger to the highest experiences. His eye was fixed on the outward more than the inward needs of Man. Yet he too was a seer of the divine order in its musical expression, if not in its poetic soul. He has filled one department of instruction for the new era, and the harmony in action and freedom for individual growth, he hopes, shall exist;

---

* In worship at stated periods, in daily expression whether by word or deed, the Quakers have placed Woman on the same platform with Man. Can anyone assert that they have reason to repent this?

and if the methods he proposes should not prove the true ones, yet his fair propositions shall give many hints and make room for the inspiration needed for such.

He, too, places Woman on an entire equality with Man, and wishes to give to one as to the other that independence which must result from intellectual and practical development.

Those who will consult him for no other reason might do so to see how the energies of Woman may be made available in the pecuniary way. The object of Fourier was to give her the needed means of self-help, that she might dignify and unfold her life for her own happiness and that of society. The many who now see their daughters liable to destitution or vice to escape from it, may be interested to examine the means, if they have not yet soul enough to appreciate the ends he proposes.

On the opposite side of the advancing army leads the great apostle of individual culture, Goethe. Swedenborg makes organization and union the necessary results of solitary thought. Fourier, whose nature was above all constructive, looked to them too exclusively. Better institutions, he thought, will make better men. Goethe expressed in every way the other side. If one man could present better forms, the rest could not use them till ripe for them.

Fourier says, as the institutions, so the men! All follies are excusable and natural under bad institutions.

Goethe thinks, as the man, so the institutions! There is no excuse for ignorance and folly. A man can grow in any place, if he will.

Aye! But, Goethe, bad institutions are prison-walls and impure air that make him stupid, so that he does not will.

And thou, Fourier, do not expect to change mankind at once, or even "in three generations," by arrangement of groups and series or flourish of trumpets for attractive industry. If these attempts are made by unready men, they will fail.

Yet we prize the theory of Fourier no less than the profound suggestion of Goethe. Both are educating the age to a clearer consciousness of what Man needs, what Man can be; and better life must ensue.

Goethe proceeding on his own track, elevating the human being in the most imperfect states of society by continual efforts at self-culture, takes as good care of women as of men. His mother, the bold, gay Frau Aja, with such playful freedom of nature; the wise and gentle maiden, known in his youth, over whose sickly solitude the "Holy Ghost brooded as a dove"; his sister, the intellectual woman *par excellence;* the Duchess Amelia; Lili, who combined the character of the woman of the world with the lyrical sweetness of the shepherdess, on whose chaste and noble breast flowers and gems were equally at home; all these had supplied abundant suggestions to his mind, as to the wants and the possible excellences of Woman. And from his poetic soul grew up forms new and more admirable than life has yet produced, for whom his clear eye marked out paths in the future.

In *Faust* Margaret represents the redeeming power, which at present upholds Woman while waiting for a better day. The lovely little girl, pure in instinct, ignorant in mind, is misled and profaned by man abusing her confidence.* To the Mater Dolorosa she appeals for aid. It is given to the soul, if not against outward sorrow; and the maiden, enlightened by her sufferings, refusing to receive temporal salvation by the aid of an evil power, obtains the eternal in its stead.

In the second part, the intellectual man, after all his manifold strivings, owes to the interposition of her whom he had betrayed *his* salvation. She intercedes, this time, herself a glorified spirit, with the Mater Gloriosa.

Leonora, too, is Woman as we see her now, pure, thoughtful, refined by much acquaintance with grief.

Iphigenia he speaks of in his journals as his "daughter," and she is the daughter † whom a man will wish, even if he has chosen his wife from very mean motives. She is the virgin, steadfast soul to whom falsehood is more dreadful than any other death.

But it is to *Wilhelm Meister's Apprenticeship* and *Wandering Years* that I would especially refer, as these volumes contain the sum of the Sage's

---

* As Faust says, her only fault was a "kindly delusion" *("ein guter Wahn").*

† Goethe was as false to his ideas in practice as Lord Herbert. And his punishment was the just and usual one of connections formed beneath the standard of right from the impulses of the baser self. Iphigenia was the worthy daughter of his mind; but the son, child of his degrading connection in actual life, corresponded with that connection. This son, on whom Goethe vainly lavished so much thought and care, was like his mother, and like Goethe's attachment for his mother. "This young man," says a late well-informed writer (M. Henri Blaze), "Wieland with good reason called the son of the servant, *der Sohn der Magd.* He inherited from his father only his name and his *physique."*

observations during a long life as to what Man should do, under present circumstances, to obtain mastery over outward through an initiation into inward life and severe discipline of faculty.

As Wilhelm advances into the upward path, he becomes acquainted with better forms of Woman by knowing how to seek and how to prize them when found. For the weak and immature man will often admire a superior woman, but he will not be able to abide by a feeling which is too severe a tax on his habitual existence. But with Wilhelm the gradation is natural, and expresses ascent in the scale of being. At first he finds charm in Mariana and Philina, very common forms of feminine character, not without redeeming traits no less than charms, but without wisdom or purity. Soon he is attended by Mignon, the finest expression ever yet given to what I have called the lyrical element in Woman. She is a child, but too full-grown for this man; he loves but cannot follow her; yet is the association not without an enduring influence. Poesy has been domesticated in his life; and though he strives to bind down her heavenward impulse as art or apothegm, these are only the tents beneath which he may sojourn for a while, but which may be easily struck and carried on limitless wanderings.

Advancing into the region of thought, he encounters a wise philanthropy in Natalia (instructed, let us observe, by an *uncle*); practical judgment and the outward economy of life in Theresa; pure devotion in the Fair Saint.

Further and last, he comes to the house of Macaria, the soul of a star; that is, a pure and perfected intelligence embodied in feminine form, and the center of a world whose members revolve harmoniously around her. She instructs him in the archives of a rich human history, and introduces him to the contemplation of the heavens.

From the hours passed by the side of Mariana to these with Macaria, is a wide distance for human feet to traverse. Nor has Wilhelm traveled so far, seen and suffered so much, in vain. He now begins to study how he may aid the next generation; he sees objects in harmonious arrangement, and from his observations deduces precepts by which to guide his course as a teacher and a master, "help-full, comfort-full."

In all these expressions of Woman, the aim of Goethe is satisfactory to me. He aims at a pure self-subsistence, and a free development of any powers with which they may be gifted by nature as much for them as for men. They are units, addressed as souls. Accordingly the meeting between Man and Woman, as represented by him, is equal and noble; and if he does not depict marriage, he makes it possible.

In the Macaria, bound with the heavenly bodies in fixed revolutions, the center of all relations, herself unrelated, he expresses the Minerva side of feminine nature. It was not by chance that Goethe gave her this name. Macaria, the daughter of Hercules, who offered herself as a victim for the good of her country, was canonized by the Greeks and worshiped as the Goddess of true Felicity. Goethe has embodied this Felicity as the Serenity that arises from Wisdom, a Wisdom such as the Jewish wise man venerated, alike instructed in the designs of heaven and the methods necessary to carry them into effect upon earth.

Mignon is the electrical, inspired, lyrical nature. And wherever it appears we echo in our aspirations that of the child,

> So let me seem until I be:
> Take not the *white robe* away.
>
> .   .   .   .
>
> Though I lived without care and toil,
> Yet felt I sharp pain enough:
> Make me again forever young.

All these women, though we see them in relations, we can think of as unrelated. They all are very individual, yet seem nowhere restrained. They satisfy for the present, yet arouse an infinite expectation.

The economist Theresa, the benevolent Natalia, the Fair Saint have chosen a path, but their thoughts are not narrowed to it. The functions of life to them are not ends but suggestions.

Thus to them all things are important, because none is necessary. Their different characters have fair play, and each is beautiful in its minute indications, for nothing is enforced or conventional; but everything, however slight, grows from the essential life of the being.

Mignon and Theresa wear male attire when they like, and it is graceful for them to do so, while Macaria is confined to her armchair behind the green curtain, and the Fair Saint could not bear a speck of dust on her robe.

All things are in their places in this little world because all is natural and free, just as "there is room for everything out of doors." Yet all is rounded in by natural harmony, which will always arise where Truth and Love are sought in the light of Freedom.

Goethe's book bodes an era of freedom like its own of "extraordinary, generous seeking" and new revelations. New individualities shall be developed in the actual world, which shall advance upon it as gently as the figures come out upon his canvas.

I have indicated on this point the coincidence between his hopes and those of Fourier, though his are directed by an infinitely higher and deeper knowledge of human nature. But for our present purpose it is sufficient to show how surely these different paths have conducted to the same end two earnest thinkers. In some other place I wish to point out similar coincidences between Goethe's model school and the plans of Fourier, which may cast light upon the page of prophecy.

Many women have observed that the time drew nigh for a better care of the sex, and have thrown out hints that may be useful. Among these may be mentioned:

Miss Edgeworth, who although restrained by the habits of her age and country and belonging more to the eighteenth than the nineteenth century, has done excellently as far as she goes. She had a horror of sentimentalism and of the love of notoriety, and saw how likely women in the early stages of culture were to aim at these. Therefore she bent her efforts to recommending domestic life. But the methods she recommends are such as will fit a character for any position to which it may be called. She taught a contempt of falsehood, no less in its most graceful than in its meanest apparitions; the cultivation of a clear, independent judgment and adherence to its dictates; habits of various and liberal study and employment, and a capacity for friendship. Her standard of character is the same for both sexes—truth, honor, enlightened benevolence, and aspiration after knowledge. Of poetry she knows nothing, and her religion consists in honor and loyalty to obligations once assumed—in short in "the great idea of duty which holds us upright." Her whole tendency is practical.

Mrs. Jameson is a sentimentalist and therefore suits us ill in some respects, but she is full of talent, has a just and refined perception of the beautiful, and a genuine courage when she finds it necessary. She does not appear to have thought out thoroughly the subject on which we are engaged, and her opinions, expressed as opinions, are sometimes inconsistent with one another. But from the refined perception of character, admirable suggestions are given in her *Women of Shakspeare* and *Loves of the Poets*.

But that for which I most respect her is the decision with which she speaks on a subject which refined women are usually afraid to approach, for fear of the insult and scurrile jest they may encounter; but on which she neither can nor will restrain the indignation of a full heart. I refer to the degradation of a large portion of women into the sold and polluted slaves of men, and the daring with which the legislator and man of the world lifts his head beneath the heavens and says, "This must be; it cannot be helped; it is a necessary accompaniment of *civilization*."

So speaks the *citizen*. Man born of Woman, the father of daughters, declares that he will and must buy the comforts and commercial advantages of his London, Vienna, Paris, New York, by conniving at the moral death, the damnation so far as the action of society can insure it, of thousands of women for each splendid metropolis.

O men! I speak not to you. It is true that your wickedness (for you must not deny that at least nine thousand out of the ten fall through the vanity you have systematically flattered, or the promises you have treacherously broken); yes, it is true that your wickedness is its own punishment. Your forms degraded and your eyes clouded by secret sin; natural harmony broken and fineness of perception destroyed in your mental and bodily organization; God and love shut out from your hearts by the foul visitants you have permitted there; incapable of pure marriage; incapable of pure parentage; incapable of worship; O wretched men, your sin is its own punishment! You have lost the world in losing yourselves. Who ruins another has admitted the worm to the root of his own tree, and the fuller ye fill the cup of evil, the deeper must be your own bitter draft. But I speak not to you—you need to teach and warn one another. And more than one voice rises in earnestness. And all that *women* say to the heart that has once chosen the evil path is considered prudery or ignorance or perhaps a feebleness of nature which exempts from similar temptations.

But to you women, American women, a few words may not be addressed in vain. One here and there may listen.

You know how it was in the Oriental clime. One man, if wealth permitted, had several wives and many handmaidens. The chastity and equality of genuine marriage, with the "thousand decencies that flow" from its communion, the precious virtues that gradually may be matured within its enclosure, were unknown.

But this man did not wrong according to his light. What he did, he might publish to God and Man; it was not a wicked secret that hid in vile lurking-places and dens, like the banquets of beasts of prey. Those women were not lost, not polluted in their own eyes nor those of others. If they were not in a state of knowledge and virtue, they were at least in one of comparative innocence.

You know how it was with the natives of this continent. A chief had many wives whom he maintained and who did his household work; those women were but servants, still they enjoyed the respect of others and their own. They lived together in peace. They knew that a sin against what was in their nation esteemed virtue would be as strictly punished in Man as in Woman.

Now pass to the countries where marriage is between one and one. I will not speak of the pagan nations, but come to those which own the Christian rule. We all know what that enjoins; there is a standard to appeal to.

See now not the mass of the people, for we all know that it is a proverb and a bitter jest to speak of the "downtrodden million." We know that down to our own time a principle never had so fair a chance to pervade the mass of the people, but that we must solicit its illustration from select examples.

Take the Paladin, take the Poet. Did *they* believe purity more impossible to Man than to Woman? Did they wish Woman to believe that Man was less amenable to higher motives—that pure aspirations would not guard him against bad passions—that honorable employments and temperate habits would not keep him free from slavery to the body? Oh, no! Love was to them a part of heaven, and they could not even wish to receive its happiness unless assured of being worthy of it. Its highest happiness to them was that it made them wish to be worthy. They courted probation.

They wished not the title of knight till the banner had been upheld in the heats of battle amid the rout of cowards.

I ask of you, young girls—I do not mean *you* whose heart is that of an old coxcomb, though your locks have not yet lost their sunny tinge. Not of you whose whole character is tainted with vanity inherited or taught, who have early learned the love of coquettish excitement and whose eyes rove restlessly in search of a "conquest" or a "beau"; you who are ashamed *not* to be seen by others as the mark of the most contemptuous flattery or injurious desire. To such I do not speak. But to thee, maiden, who if not so fair, art yet of that unpolluted nature which Milton saw when he dreamed of Comus and the Paradise. Thou child of an unprofaned wedlock, brought up amid the teachings of the woods and fields, kept fancy-free by useful employment and a free flight into the heaven of thought, loving to please only those whom thou wouldst not be ashamed to love; I ask of thee, whose cheek has not forgotten its blush nor thy heart its larklike hopes, if he whom thou mayest hope the Father will send thee as the companion of life's toils and joys, is not to thy thought pure? Is not manliness to thy thought purity, *not* lawlessness? Can his lips speak falsely? Can he do in secret what he could not avow to the mother that bore him? Oh, say, dost thou not look for a heart free, open as thine own, all whose thoughts may be avowed, incapable of wronging the innocent or still further degrading the fallen—a man in short in whom brute nature is entirely subject to the impulses of his better self?

Yes! It was thus that thou didst hope; for I have many, many times seen the image of a future life, of a destined spouse, painted on the tablets of a virgin heart.

It might be that she was not true to these hopes. She was taken into what is called the "world," froth and scum as it mostly is on the social caldron. There, she saw fair Woman carried in the waltz close to the heart of a being who appeared to her a Satyr. Being warned by a male friend that he was in fact of that class and not fit for such familiar nearness to a chaste being, the advised replied that "women should know nothing about such things." She saw one fairer given in wedlock to a man of the same class. "Papa and mamma said that 'all men were faulty at some time in their lives; they had a great many temptations.' Frederick would be so happy at home; he would not want to do wrong." She turned to the married women; they, O ten-fold horror, laughed at her supposing "men were like women." Sometimes I say she was not true, and either sadly accommodated herself to "Woman's lot" or acquired a taste for satyr society, like some of the Nymphs and all the Bacchanals of old. But to those who could not and would not accept a mess of pottage or a Circe cup in lieu of their birthright, and to these others who have yet their choice to make, I say, courage! I have some words of cheer for you. A man, himself of unbroken purity, reported to me the words of a foreign artist that the "world would never be better till men subjected themselves to the same laws they had imposed on women"; that artist, he added, was true to the thought. The same was true of Canova, the same of Beethoven. "Like each other demigod, they kept themselves free from stain"; and Michelangelo, looking over here from the loneliness of his century, might meet some eyes that need not shun his glance.

In private life, I am assured by men who are not so sustained and oc-cupied by the worship of pure beauty, a similar consecration is possible, is practiced; many men feel that no temptation can be too strong for the will of man, if he invokes the aid of the Spirit instead of seeking extenuation from the brute alliances of his nature. In short what the child fancies is really true, though almost the whole world declares it a lie. Man is a child of God; and if he seeks His guidance to keep the heart with diligence, it will be so given that all the issues of life may be pure. Life will then be a temple.

> The temple round
> Spread green the pleasant ground;
> The fair colonnade
> Be of pure marble pillars made;
> Strong to sustain the roof,
> Time and tempest proof;
> Yet amidst which the lightest breeze
> Can play as it please;
> The audience hall
> Be free to all
> Who revere
> The power worshiped here,
> Sole guide of youth,
> Unswerving Truth.
> In the inmost shrine

Stands the image divine,
Only seen
By those whose deeds have worthy been—
Priestlike clean.
Those who initiated are
Declare,
As the hours
Usher in varying hopes and powers;
It changes its face,
It changes its age,
Now a young, beaming grace,
Now Nestorian sage:
But to the pure in heart,
This shape of primal art
In age is fair,
In youth seems wise,
Beyond compare,
Above surprise;
What it teaches native seems,
Its new lore our ancient dreams;
Incense rises from the ground;
Music flows around;
Firm rest the feet below, clear gaze the eyes above,
When Truth, to point the way through life, assumes the wand of Love;
But if she cast aside the robe of green,
Winter's silver sheen,
White, pure as light,
Makes gentle shroud as worthy weed as bridal robe had been.*

We are now in a transition state, and but few steps have yet been taken. From polygamy Europe passed to the marriage *de convenance*. This was scarcely an improvement. An attempt was then made to substitute genuine marriage (the mutual choice of souls inducing a permanent union), as yet baffled on every side by the haste, the ignorance, or the impurity of Man.

Where Man assumes a high principle to which he is not yet ripened, it will happen for a long time that the few will be nobler than before; the

---

* As described by the historian:

The temple of Juno is like what the character of Woman should be.
Columns! Graceful decorums, attractive yet sheltering.
Porch! Noble, inviting aspect of the life.
Kaos! Receives the worshipers. See here the statue of the Divinity.
Ophistodomos! Sanctuary where the most precious possessions were kept safe from the hand of the spoiler and the eye of the world.

many, worse. Thus now. In the country of Sidney and Milton, the metropolis is a den of wickedness and a sty of sensuality; in the country of Lady Russell, the custom of English peeresses of selling their daughters to the highest bidder, is made the theme and jest of fashionable novels by unthinking children who would stare at the idea of sending them to a Turkish slavedealer, though the circumstances of the bargain are there less degrading as the will and thoughts of the person sold are not so degraded by it, and it is not done in defiance of an acknowledged law of right in the land and the age.

I must here add that I do not believe there ever was put upon record more depravation of Man and more despicable frivolity of thought and aim in Woman, than in the novels which purport to give the picture of English fashionable life, which are read with such favor in our drawing-rooms and give the tone to the manners of some circles. Compared with the cold, hardhearted folly there described, crime is hopeful; for it at least shows some power remaining in the mental constitution.

To return—attention has been awakened among men to the stains of celibacy and the profanations of marriage. They begin to write about it and lecture about it. It is the tendency now to endeavor to help the erring by showing them the physical law. This is wise and excellent; but forget not the better half. Cold bathing and exercise will not suffice to keep a life pure, without an inward baptism and noble, exhilarating employment for the thoughts and the passions. Early marriages are desirable, but if (and the world is now so out of joint that there are a hundred thousand chances to one against it) a man does not early or at all find the person to whom he can be united in the marriage of souls, will you give him in the marriage *de convenance?* Or if not married, can you find no way for him to lead a virtuous and happy life? Think of it well, ye who think yourselves better than pagans, for many of *them* knew this sure way.*

---

* The Persian sacred books, the *Desatir,* describe the great and holy prince Ky Khosrou as being an "angel, and the son of an angel," one to whom the Supreme says: "Thou art not absent from before me for one twinkling of an eye. I am never out of thy heart. And I am contained in nothing but in thy heart, and in a heart like thy heart. And I am nearer unto thee than thou art to thyself." This prince had in his Golden Seraglio three ladies of surpassing beauty, and all four in this royal monastery passed their lives, and left the world as virgins.

The Persian people had no skepticism when the history of such a mind was narrated.

To you, women of America, it is more especially my business to address myself on this subject, and my advice may be classed under three heads:

Clear your souls from the taint of vanity.

Do not rejoice in conquests, either that your power to allure may be seen by other women, or for the pleasure of rousing passionate feelings that gratify your love of excitement.

It must happen no doubt that frank and generous women will excite love they do not reciprocate, but in nine cases out of ten, the woman has half consciously done much to excite. In this case she shall not be held guiltless, either as to the unhappiness or injury of the lover. Pure love inspired by a worthy object must ennoble and bless, whether mutual or not; but that which is excited by coquettish attraction of any grade of refinement, must cause bitterness and doubt as to the reality of human goodness, so soon as the flush of passion is over. And that you may avoid all taste for these false pleasures,

> Steep the soul
> In one pure love, and it will last thee long.

The love of truth, the love of excellence, whether you clothe them in the person of a special object or not, will have power to save you from following Duessa, and lead you in the green glades where Una's feet have trod.

It was on this one subject that a venerable champion of good, the last representative of the spirit which sanctified the Revolution and gave our country such a sunlight of hope in the eyes of the nations, the same who lately in Boston offered anew to the young men the pledge taken by the young men of his day, offered also his counsel on being addressed by the principal of a girl's school, thus:

REPLY OF MR. ADAMS

Mr. Adams was so deeply affected by the address of Miss Foster, as to be for some time inaudible. When heard, he spoke as follows:

"This is the first instance in which a lady has thus addressed me personally; and I trust that all the ladies present will be able sufficiently to enter into my feelings to know that I am more affected by this honor than by any other I could have received.

"You have been pleased, madam, to allude to the character of my father, and the history of my family, and their services to the country. It is indeed true that, from the existence of the republic as an independent nation, my father and myself have been in the public service of the country, almost without interruption. I came into the world, as a person having personal responsibilities, with the Declaration of Independence which constituted us a nation. I was a child at that time, and had then perhaps the greatest of blessings that can be bestowed on man—a mother who was anxious and capable to form her children to be what they ought to be. From that mother I derived whatever instruction—religious especially and moral—has pervaded a long life; I will not say perfectly and as it ought to be; but I will say, because it is justice only to the memory of her whom I revere, that if in the course of my life there has been any imperfection or deviation from what she taught me, the fault is mine and not hers.

"With such a mother and such other relations with the sex, of sister, wife, and daughter, it has been the perpetual instruction of my life to love and revere the female sex. And in order to carry that sentiment of love and reverence to its highest degree of perfection, I know of nothing that exists in human society better adapted to produce that result than institutions of the character that I have now the honor to address.

"I have been taught, as I have said, through the course of my life to love and to revere the female sex; but I have been taught, also—and that lesson has perhaps impressed itself on my mind even more strongly, it may be, than the other—I have been taught not to flatter them. It is not unusual in the intercourse of Man with the other sex—and especially for young men—to think that the way to win the hearts of ladies is by flattery. To love and to revere the sex is what I think the duty of Man; but *not to flatter them;* and this I would say to the young ladies here—and if they and others present will allow me, with all the authority which nearly fourscore years may have with those who have not yet attained one score —I would say to them what I have no doubt they say to themselves and are taught here, not to take the flattery of men as proof of perfection.

"I am now however, I fear, assuming too much of a character that does not exactly belong to me. I therefore conclude by assuring you, madam, that your reception of me has affected me, as you perceive, more than I can express in words; and that I shall offer my best prayers till my latest hour to the Creator of us all, that this institution especially, and all others of a similar kind designed to form the female mind to wisdom and virtue, may prosper to the end of time."

It will be interesting to add here the character of Mr. Adams' mother, as drawn by her husband, the first John Adams, in a family letter * written just before his death.

"I have reserved for the last the life of Lady Russell. This I have not yet read, because I read it more than forty years ago. On this hangs a tale which you ought to know and communicate it to your children. I bought the *Life and Letters of Lady Russell* in the year 1775, and sent it to your grandmother, with an express intent and desire that she should consider it a mirror in which to contemplate herself; for at that time I thought it extremely probable, from the daring and dangerous career I was determined to run, that she would one day find herself in the situation of Lady Russell, her husband without a head. This lady was more beautiful than Lady Russell, had a brighter genius, more information, a more refined taste, and at least her equal in the virtues of the heart; equal fortitude and firmness of character, equal resignation to the will of Heaven, equal in all the virtues and graces of the Christian life. Like Lady Russell, she never by word or look discouraged me from running all hazards for the salvation of my country's liberties; she was willing to share with me, and that her children should share with us both, in all the dangerous consequences we had to hazard."

Will a woman who loves flattery or an aimless excitement, who wastes the flower of her mind on transitory sentiments, ever be loved with a love like that, when fifty years' trial has entitled to the privileges of "the golden marriage"?

Such was the love of the iron-handed warrior for her, not his handmaid, but his helpmeet:

"Whom God loves, to him gives he such a wife."

I find the whole of what I want in this relation in the two epithets by which Milton makes Adam address *his* wife.

In the intercourse of every day he begins:

---

* *Journal and Correspondence of Miss Adams,* Vol. I, p. 246.

> Daughter of God and man, *accomplished* Eve.

In a moment of stronger feeling,

> Daughter of God and man, IMMORTAL Eve.

What majesty in the cadence of the line; what dignity, what reverence in the attitude both of giver and receiver!

The woman who permits in her life the alloy of vanity; the woman who lives upon flattery coarse or fine, shall never be thus addressed. She is *not* immortal so far as her will is concerned, and every woman who does so creates miasma, whose spread is indefinite. The hand which casts into the waters of life a stone of offense knows not how far the circles thus caused may spread their agitations.

A little while since I was at one of the most fashionable places of public resort. I saw there many women, dressed without regard to the season or the demands of the place in apery, or as it looked in mockery, of European fashions. I saw their eyes restlessly courting attention. I saw the way in which it was paid; the style of devotion, almost an open sneer, which it pleased those ladies to receive from men whose expression marked their own low position in the moral and intellectual world. Those women went to their pillows with their heads full of folly, their hearts of jealousy or gratified vanity; those men, with the low opinion they already entertained of Woman confirmed. These were American *ladies;* that is, they were of that class who have wealth and leisure to make full use of the day and confer benefits on others. They were of that class whom the possession of external advantages makes of pernicious example to many, if these advantages be misused.

Soon after I met a circle of women stamped by society as among the most degraded of their sex. "How," it was asked of them, "did you come here?" for by the society that I saw in the former place they were shut up in a prison. The causes were not difficult to trace: love of dress, love of flattery, love of excitement. They had not dresses like the other ladies, so they stole them; they could not pay for flattery by distinctions and the dower of a worldly marriage, so they paid by the profanation of their persons. In excitement, more and more madly sought from day to day, they drowned the voice of conscience.

Now I ask you, my sisters, if the women at the fashionable house be not answerable for those women being in the prison?

As to position in the world of souls, we may suppose the women of the prison stood fairest, both because they had misused less light, and because loneliness and sorrow had brought some of them to feel the need of better life, nearer truth and good. This was no merit in them, being an effect of circumstance, but it was hopeful. But you, my friends (and some of you I have already met), consecrate yourselves without waiting for reproof, in free love and unbroken energy, to win and to diffuse a better life. Offer beauty, talents, riches on the altar; thus shall ye keep spotless your own hearts and be visibly or invisibly the angels to others.

I would urge upon those women who have not yet considered this subject to do so. Do not forget the unfortunates who dare not cross your guarded way. If it does not suit you to act with those who have organized measures of reform, then hold not yourself excused from acting in private. Seek out these degraded women, give them tender sympathy, counsel, employment. Take the place of mothers, such as might have saved them originally.

If you can do little for those already under the ban of the world—and the best-considered efforts have often failed from a want of strength in those unhappy ones to bear up against the sting of shame and the prejudices of the world, which makes them seek oblivion again in their old excitements—you will at least leave a sense of love and justice in their hearts that will prevent their becoming utterly embittered and corrupt. And you may learn the means of prevention for those yet uninjured. These will be found in a diffusion of mental culture, simple tastes, best taught by your example, a genuine self-respect, and above all, what the influence of Man tends to hide from Woman, the love and fear of a divine, in preference to a human tribunal.

But suppose you save many who would have lost their bodily innocence (for as to mental, the loss of that is incalculably more general) through mere vanity and folly; there still remain many, the prey and spoil of the brute passions of Man; for the stories frequent in our newspapers outshame antiquity and vie with the horrors of war.

As to this, it must be considered that as the vanity and proneness to seduction of the imprisoned women represented a general degradation in their sex, so do these acts a still more general and worse in the male. Where so many are weak, it is natural there should be many lost; where legislators admit that ten thousand prostitutes are a fair proportion to one city, and husbands tell their wives that it is folly to expect chastity from men, it is inevitable that there should be many monsters of vice.

I must in this place mention with respect and gratitude the conduct of Mrs. Child in the case of Amelia Norman. The action and speech of this lady was of straightforward nobleness, undeterred by custom or cavil from duty toward an injured sister. She showed the case and the arguments the counsel against the prisoner had the assurance to use in their true light to the public. She put the case on the only ground of religion and equity. She was successful in arresting the attention of many who had before shrugged their shoulders, and let sin pass as necessarily a part of the company of men. They begin to ask whether virtue is not possible, perhaps necessary, to Man as well as to Woman. They begin to fear that the perdition of a woman must involve that of a man. This is a crisis. The results of this case will be important.

In this connection I must mention Eugene Sue, the French novelist, several of whose works have been lately translated among us, as having the true spirit of reform as to women. Like every other French writer, he is still tainted with the transmissions of the old regime. Still, falsehood may be permitted for the sake of advancing truth, evil as the way to good. Even George Sand, who would trample on every graceful decorum and every human law for the sake of a sincere life, does not see that she violates it by making her heroines able to tell falsehoods in a good cause. These French writers need ever to be confronted by the clear perception of the English and German mind that the only good man, consequently the only good reformer, is he

> Who bases good on good alone, and owes
> To virtue every triumph that he knows.

Still Sue has the heart of a reformer, and especially towards women; he sees what they need and what causes are injuring them. From the histories of Fleur de Marie and La Louve, from the lovely and independent character of Rigolette, from the distortion given to Matilda's mind by the present views of marriage, and from the truly noble and immortal character of the "humpbacked Seamstress" in the *Wandering Jew,* may be gathered much that shall elucidate doubt and direct inquiry on this subject. In reform, as in philosophy, the French are the interpreters to the civilized world. Their own attainments are not great, but they make clear the past and break down barriers to the future.

Observe that the good man of Sue is as pure as Sir Charles Grandison.

Apropos to Sir Charles. Women are accustomed to be told by men that the reform is to come *from them.* "You," say the men, "must frown upon vice; you must decline the attentions of the corrupt; you must not submit to the will of your husband when it seems to you unworthy, but give the laws in marriage and redeem it from its present sensual and mental pollutions."

This seems to us hard. Men have indeed been for more than a hundred years rating women for countenancing vice. But at the same time they have carefully hid from them its nature, so that the preference often shown by women for bad men arises rather from a confused idea that they are bold and adventurous, acquainted with regions which women are forbidden to explore, and the curiosity that ensues, than a corrupt heart in the woman. As to marriage, it has been inculcated on women for centuries that men have not only stronger passions than they, but of a sort that it would be shameful for them to share or even understand; that therefore they must "confide in their husbands," that is, submit implicitly to their will; that the least appearance of coldness or withdrawal, from whatever cause, in the wife is wicked because liable to turn her husband's thoughts to illicit indulgence; for a man is so constituted that he must indulge his passions or die!

Accordingly a great part of women look upon men as a kind of wild beasts, but "suppose they are all alike"; the unmarried are assured by the married that "if they knew men as they do," that is, by being married to them, "they would not expect continence or self-government from them."

I might accumulate illustrations on this theme, drawn from acquaintance with the histories of women, which would startle and grieve all thinking men, but I forbear. Let Sir Charles Grandison preach to his own sex; or if none there be who feels himself able to speak with authority from a life unspotted in will or deed, let those who are convinced of the practicability and need of a pure life, as the foreign artist was, advise the others and warn them by their own example, if need be.

The following passage from a female writer on female affairs expresses a prevalent way of thinking on this subject:

"It may be that a young woman, exempt from all motives of vanity, determines to take for a husband a man who does not inspire her with a very decided inclination. Imperious circumstances, the evident interest of her family, or the danger of suffering celibacy may explain such a resolution. If however she were to endeavor to surmount a personal repugnance, we should look upon this as *injudicious*. Such a rebellion of nature marks the limit that the influence of parents or the self-sacrifice of the young girl should never pass. *We shall be told that this repugnance is an affair of the imagination.* It may be so; but imagination is a power which it is temerity to brave; and its antipathy is more difficult to conquer than its preference." *

Among ourselves the exhibition of such a repugnance from a woman who had been given in marriage "by advice of friends," was treated by an eminent physician as sufficient proof of insanity. If he had said sufficient cause for it, he would have been nearer right.

It has been suggested by men who were pained by seeing bad men admitted freely to the society of modest women—thereby encouraged to vice by impunity and corrupting the atmosphere of homes—that there should be a senate of the matrons in each city and town, who should decide what candidates were fit for admission to their houses and the society of their daughters.†

Such a plan might have excellent results; but it argues a moral dignity and decision which does not yet exist and needs to be induced by knowledge and reflection. It has been the tone to keep women ignorant on these subjects, or when they were not, to command that they should seem so. "It is indelicate," says the father or husband, "to inquire into the private character of such a one. It is sufficient that I do not think him unfit to visit

---

* Madame Necker de Saussure.
† See Goethe's *Tasso*. "A synod of good women should decide"—if the golden age is to be restored.

you." And so this man, who would not tolerate these pages in his house, "unfit for family reading" because they speak plainly, introduces there a man whose shame is written on his brow as well as the open secret of the whole town, and presently, if *respectable* still and rich enough, gives him his daughter to wife. The mother affects ignorance, "supposing he is no worse than most men." The daughter *is* ignorant; something in the mind of the new spouse seems strange to her, but she supposes it is "woman's lot" not to be perfectly happy in her affections; she has always heard "men could not understand women," so she weeps alone or takes to dress and the duties of the house. The husband of course makes no avowal, and dreams of no redemption.

"In the heart of every young woman," says the female writer above quoted, addressing herself to the husband, "depend upon it, there is a fund of exalted ideas; she conceals, represses, without succeeding in smothering them. *So long as these ideas in your wife are directed to* you, *they are no doubt innocent,* but take care that they be not accompanied with *too much* pain. In other respects also, spare her delicacy. Let all the antecedent parts of your life, if there are such which would give her pain, be concealed from her; *her happiness and her respect for you would suffer from this misplaced confidence.* Allow her to retain that flower of purity, *which should distinguish her in your eyes from every other woman.*" We should think so truly under this canon. Such a man must esteem purity an exotic that could only be preserved by the greatest care. Of the degree of mental intimacy possible in such a marriage, let everyone judge for himself!

On this subject, let every woman who has once begun to think examine herself; see whether she does not suppose virtue possible and necessary to Man, and whether she would not desire for her son a virtue which aimed at a fitness for a divine life and involved, if not asceticism, that degree of power over the lower self which shall "not exterminate the passions, but keep them chained at the feet of reason." The passions, like fire, are a bad master; but confine them to the hearth and the altar, and they give life to the social economy and make each sacrifice meet for heaven.

When many women have thought upon this subject, some will be fit for the senate, and one such senate in operation would affect the morals of the civilized world.

At present I look to the young. As preparatory to the senate, I should like to see a society of novices such as the world has never yet seen, bound by no oath, wearing no badge. In place of an oath, they should have a religious faith in the capacity of Man for virtue; instead of a badge, should wear in the heart a firm resolve not to stop short of the destiny promised him as a son of God. Their service should be action and conservatism, not of old habits but of a better nature, enlightened by hopes that daily grow brighter.

If sin was to remain in the world, it should not be by their connivance at its stay or one moment's concession to its claims.

They should succor the oppressed, and pay to the upright the reverence due in hero-worship by seeking to emulate them. They would not denounce the willingly bad, but they could not be with them, for the two classes could not breathe the same atmosphere.

They would heed no detention from the timeserving, the worldly, and the timid.

They could love no pleasures that were not innocent and capable of good fruit.

I saw in a foreign paper the title now given to a party abroad, *"los Exaltados."* Such would be the title now given these children by the world: *los Exaltados, las Exaltadas;* but the world would not sneer always, for from them would issue a virtue by which it would at last be exalted too.

I have in my eye a youth and a maiden whom I look to as the nucleus of such a class. They are both in early youth; both as yet uncontaminated, both aspiring without rashness, both thoughtful, both capable of deep affection, both of strong nature and sweet feelings, both capable of large mental development. They reside in different regions of earth, but their place in the soul is the same. To them I look as perhaps the harbingers and leaders of a new era, for never yet have I known minds so truly virgin, without narrowness or ignorance.

When men call upon women to redeem them, they mean such maidens. But such are not easily formed under the present influences of society. As there are more such young men to help give a different tone, there will be more such maidens.

The English novelist Disraeli has in his novel of *The Young Duke* made a man of the most depraved stock be redeemed by a woman who despises him when he has only the brilliant mask of fortune and beauty to cover the poverty of his heart and brain, but knows how to encourage him when he enters on a better course. But this woman was educated by a father who valued character in women.

Still there will come now and then one who will, as I hope of my young Exaltada, be example and instruction for the rest. It was not the opinion of Woman current among Jewish men that formed the character of the mother of Jesus.

Since the sliding and backsliding men of the world, no less than the mystics, declare that as through Woman Man was lost, so through Woman must Man be redeemed, the time must be at hand. When she knows herself indeed as "accomplished," still more as "immortal Eve," this may be.

As an immortal she may also know and inspire immortal love, a happiness not to be dreamed of under the circumstances advised in the last quotation. Where love is based on concealment, it must of course disappear when the soul enters the scene of clear vision!

And without this hope how worthless every plan, every bond, every power!

"The giants," said the Scandinavian saga, "had induced Loki (the spirit that hovers between good and ill) to steal for them Iduna (goddess of immortality) and her apples of pure gold. He lured her out by promising to show on a marvelous tree he had discovered apples beautiful as her own, if she would only take them with her for a comparison. Thus having lured her beyond the heavenly domain, she was seized and carried away captive by the powers of misrule.

"As now the gods could not find their friend Iduna, they were confused with grief; indeed, they began visibly to grow old and gray. Discords arose, and love grew cold. Indeed Odur, spouse of the goddess of love and beauty, wandered away and returned no more. At last, however, the gods discovering the treachery of Loki, obliged him to win back Iduna from the prison in which she sat mourning. He changed himself into a falcon and brought her back as a swallow, fiercely pursued by the Giant King in the form of an eagle. So she strives to return among us, light and small as a swallow. We must welcome her form as the speck on the sky that assures the glad blue of summer. Yet one swallow does not make a summer. Let us solicit them in flights and flocks!"

Returning from the future to the present, let us see what forms Iduna takes as she moves along the declivity of centuries to the valley where the lily flower may concentrate all its fragrance.

It would seem as if this time were not very near to one fresh from books, such as I have of late been—no, *not* reading, but sighing over. A crowd of books having been sent me since my friends knew me to be engaged in this way, on Woman's "Sphere," Woman's "Mission," and Woman's "Destiny," I believe that almost all that is extant of formal precept has come under my eye. Among these I read with refreshment a little one called *The Whole Duty of Woman,* "indited by a noble lady at the request of a noble lord," and which has this much of nobleness that the view it takes is a religious one. It aims to fit Woman for heaven; the main bent of most of the others is to fit her to please, or at least not to disturb, a husband.

Among these I select as a favorable specimen the book I have already quoted, *The Study * of the Life of Woman* by Madame Necker de Saussure of Geneva, translated from the French. This book was published at Philadelphia, and has been read with much favor here. Madame Necker is the cousin of Madame de Staël, and has taken from her works the motto prefixed to this:

"Cette vie n'a quelque prix que si elle sert à l'education morale de notre cœur."

Madame Necker is by nature capable of entire consistency in the application of this motto, and therefore the qualifications she makes in the instructions given to her own sex show forcibly the weight which still paralyzes and distorts the energies of that sex.

The book is rich in passages marked by feeling and good suggestions; but taken in the whole, the impression it leaves is this:

Woman is and *shall remain* inferior to Man and subject to his will, and in endeavoring to aid her we must anxiously avoid anything that can be mis-

---

* This title seems to be incorrectly translated from the French. I have not seen the original.—A. B. F.

construed into expression of the contrary opinion, else the men will be alarmed and combine to defeat our efforts.

The present is a good time for these efforts, for men are less occupied about women than formerly. Let us then seize upon the occasion, and do what we can to make our lot tolerable. But we must sedulously avoid encroaching on the territory of Man. If we study natural history, our observations may be made useful by some male naturalist; if we draw well, we may make our services acceptable to the artists. But our names must not be known; and to bring these labors to any result, we must take some man for our head and be his hands.

The lot of Woman is sad. She is constituted to expect and need a happiness that cannot exist on earth. She must stifle such aspirations within her secret heart, and fit herself as well as she can for a life of resignations and consolations.

She will be very lonely while living with her husband. She must not expect to open her heart to him fully, or that after marriage he will be capable of the refined service of love. The man is not born for the woman, only the woman for the man. "Men cannot understand the hearts of women." The life of Woman must be outwardly a well-intentioned, cheerful dissimulation of her real life.

Naturally the feelings of the mother at the birth of a female child resemble those of the Paraguay woman described by Southey as lamenting in such heart-breaking tones that her mother did not kill her the hour she was born—"her mother, who knew what the life of a woman must be"— or of those women seen at the north by Sir A. Mackenzie, who performed this pious duty towards female infants whenever they had an opportunity.

"After the first delight the young mother experiences feelings a little different, according as the birth of a son or a daughter has been announced.

"Is it a son? A sort of glory swells at this thought the heart of the mother; she seems to feel that she is entitled to gratitude. She has given a citizen, a defender to her country; to her husband an heir of his name; to herself a protector. And yet the contrast of all these fine titles with this being so humble soon strikes her. At the aspect of this frail treasure, opposite feelings agitate her heart; she seems to recognize in him *a nature superior to her own,* but subjected to a low condition, and she honors a future greatness in the object of extreme compassion. Somewhat of that respect and adoration for a feeble child of which some fine pictures offer the expression in the features of the happy Mary, seem reproduced with the young mother who has given birth to a son.

"Is it a daughter? There is usually a slight degree of regret; so deeply rooted is the idea of the superiority of Man in happiness and dignity; and yet as she looks upon this child, she is more and more *softened* towards it. A deep sympathy—a sentiment of identity with this delicate being—takes possession of her; an extreme pity for so much weakness, a more pressing need of prayer stirs her heart. Whatever sorrows she may have felt, she dreads for her daughter; but she will guide her to become much wiser, much better than herself. And then the gaiety, the frivolity of the young woman have their turn. This little creature is a flower to cultivate, a doll to decorate."

Similar sadness at the birth of a daughter I have heard mothers express not unfrequently.

As to this living so entirely for men, I should think when it was proposed to women they would feel, at least, some spark of the old spirit of races allied to our own. "If he is to be my bridegroom and *lord,*" cries Brunhilda,* "he must first be able to pass through fire and water." "I will serve at the banquet," says the Valkyrie, "but only him who in the trial of deadly combat has shown himself a hero."

If women are to be bondmaids, let it be to men superior to women in fortitude, in aspiration, in moral power, in refined sense of beauty! You who give yourselves "to be supported" or because "one must love something," are they who make the lot of the sex such that mothers are sad when daughters are born.

It marks the state of feeling on this subject that it was mentioned as a bitter censure on a woman who had influence over those younger than herself—"She makes those girls want to see heroes!"

"And will that hurt them?"

"Certainly; how *can* you ask? They will find none, and so they will never be married."

"*Get* married" is the usual phrase, and the one that correctly indicates

---

* See the *Nibelungenlied.*

the thought; but the speakers on this occasion were persons too outwardly refined to use it. They were ashamed of the word but not of the thing. Madame Necker, however, sees good possible in celibacy.

Indeed I know not how the subject could be better illustrated than by separating the wheat from the chaff in Madame Necker's book; place them in two heaps, and then summon the reader to choose; giving him first a nearsighted glass to examine the two—it might be a Christian, an astronomical, or an artistic glass—any kind of good glass to obviate acquired defects in the eye. I would lay any wager on the result.

But time permits not here a prolonged analysis. I have given the clues for fault-finding.

As a specimen of the good take the following passage, on the phenomena of what I have spoken of as the lyrical or electric element in Woman.

"Women have been seen to show themselves poets in the most pathetic pantomimic scenes where all the passions were depicted full of beauty; and these poets used a language unknown to themselves, and the performance once over, their inspiration was a forgotten dream. Without doubt there is an interior development to beings so gifted; but their sole mode of communication with us is their talent. They are in all besides the inhabitants of another planet."

Similar observations have been made by those who have seen the women at Irish wakes or the funeral ceremonies of modern Greece or Brittany, at times when excitement gave the impulse to genius; but apparently, without a thought that these rare powers belonged to no other planet, but were a high development of the growth of this, and might by wise and reverent treatment be made to inform and embellish the scenes of every day. But when Woman has her fair chance she will do so, and the poem of the hour will vie with that of the ages.

I come now with satisfaction to my own country and to a writer, a female writer, whom I have selected as the clearest, wisest, and kindliest who has as yet used pen here on these subjects. This is Miss Sedgwick.

Miss Sedgwick, though she inclines to the private path and wishes that by the cultivation of character might should vindicate right, sets limits nowhere, and her objects and inducements are pure. They are the free and careful cultivation of the powers that have been given, with an aim at moral and intellectual perfection. Her speech is moderate and sane, but never palsied by fear or skeptical caution.

Herself a fine example of the independent and beneficent existence that intellect and character can give to Woman no less than Man, if she know how to seek and prize it—also that the intellect need not absorb or weaken, but rather will refine and invigorate the affections—the teachings of her practical good sense come with great force, and cannot fail to avail much. Every way her writings please me, both as to the means and the ends. I am pleased at the stress she lays on observance of the physical laws, because the true reason is given. Only in a strong and clean body can the soul do its message fitly.

She shows the meaning of the respect paid to personal neatness, both in the indispensable form of cleanliness and of that love of order and arrangement that must issue from a true harmony of feeling.

The praises of cold water seem to me an excellent sign in the age. They denote a tendency to the true life. We are now to have as a remedy for ills not orvietan or opium or any quack medicine, but plenty of air and water, with due attention to warmth and freedom in dress and simplicity of diet.

Every day we observe signs that the natural feelings on these subjects are about to be reinstated, and the body to claim care as the abode and organ of the soul; not as the tool of servile labor, or the object of voluptuous indulgence.

A poor woman who had passed through the lowest grades of ignominy seemed to think she had never been wholly lost, "for," said she, "I would always have good underclothes"; and indeed who could doubt that this denoted the remains of private self-respect in the mind?

A woman of excellent sense said, "It might seem childish, but to her one of the most favorable signs of the times was that the ladies had been persuaded to give up corsets."

Yes, let us give up all artificial means of distortion. Let life be healthy, pure, all of a piece. Miss Sedgwick, in teaching that domestics must have the means of bathing as much as their mistresses, and time, too, to bathe, has symbolized one of the most important of human rights.

Another interesting sign of the time is the influence exercised by two women, Miss Martineau and Miss Barrett, from their sick-rooms. The lamp of life which if it had been fed only by the affections, dependent on precarious human relations, would scarce have been able to maintain a feeble glare in the lonely prison, now shines far and wide over the nations, cheering fellow-sufferers and hallowing the joy of the healthful.

These persons need not health or youth or the charms of personal presence to make their thoughts available. A few more such, and "old woman" shall not be the synonym for imbecility, nor "old maid" a term of contempt, nor Woman be spoken of as a reed shaken by the wind.

It is time indeed that men and women both should cease to grow old in any other way than as the tree does, full of grace and honor. The hair of the artist turns white, but his eye shines clearer than ever, and we feel that age brings him maturity, not decay. So would it be with all, were the springs of immortal refreshment but unsealed within the soul; then like these women they would see from the lonely chamber window the glories of the universe; or shut in darkness, be visited by angels.

I now touch on my own place and day, and as I write events are occurring that threaten the fair fabric approached by so long an avenue. Week before last, the Gentile was requested to aid the Jew to return to Palestine; for the millennium, the reign of the Son of Mary was near. Just now at high and solemn Mass thanks were returned to the Virgin for having delivered O'Connell from unjust imprisonment in requital of his having consecrated to her the league formed in behalf of liberty on Tara's Hill. But last week brought news which threatens that a cause identical with the enfranchisement of Jews, Irish, women, aye, and of Americans in general too, is in danger, for the choice of the people threatens to rivet the chains of slavery and the leprosy of sin permanently on this nation through the annexation of Texas!

Ah, if this should take place, who will dare again to feel the throb of heavenly hope as to the destiny of this country? The noble thought that gave unity to all our knowledge, harmony to all our designs—the thought that the progress of history had brought on the era, the tissue of prophecies pointed out the spot where humanity was at last to have a fair chance to know itself, and all men be born free and equal for the eagle's flight— flutters as if about to leave the breast which, deprived of it, will have no more a nation, no more a home on earth.

Women of my country—Exaltadas, if such there be—women of English, old English nobleness, who understand the courage of Boadicea, the sacrifice of Godiva, the power of Queen Emma to tread the red-hot iron unharmed—women who share the nature of Mrs. Hutchinson, Lady Russell, and the mothers of our own revolution—have you nothing to do with this? You see the men, how they are willing to sell shamelessly the happiness of countless generations of fellow-creatures, the honor of their country, and their immortal souls for a money market and political power. Do you not feel within you that which can reprove them, which can check, which can convince them? You would not speak in vain; whether each in her own home or banded in unison.

Tell these men that you will not accept the glittering baubles, spacious dwellings, and plentiful service they mean to offer you through these means. Tell them that the heart of Woman demands nobleness and honor in Man, and that if they have not purity, have not mercy, they are no longer fathers, lovers, husbands, sons of yours.

This cause is your own for, as I have before said, there is a reason why the foes of African Slavery seek more freedom for women; but put it not upon that ground, but on the ground of right.

If you have a power, it is a moral power. The films of interest are not so close around you as around the men. If you will but think, you cannot fail to wish to save the country from this disgrace. Let not slip the occasion, but do something to lift off the curse incurred by Eve.

You have heard the women engaged in the Abolition movement accused of boldness, because they lifted the voice in public and lifted the latch of the stranger. But were these acts, whether performed judiciously or no, *so* bold as to dare before God and Man to partake the fruits of such offense as this?

You hear much of the modesty of your sex. Preserve it by filling the mind with noble desires that shall ward off the corruptions of vanity and idleness. A profligate woman who left her accustomed haunts and took service in a New York boarding-house said she "had never heard talk so vile at the Five Points as from the ladies at the boarding-house." And why? Because they were idle; because having nothing worthy to engage them, they dwelt with unnatural curiosity on the ill they dared not go to see.

It will not so much injure your modesty to have your name by the unthinking coupled with idle blame, as to have upon your soul the weight of not trying to save a whole race of women from the scorn that is put upon *their* modesty.

Think of this well, I entreat, I conjure you, before it is too late. It is my belief that something effectual might be done by women, if they would only consider the subject, and enter upon it in the true spirit—a spirit gentle but firm, and which feared the offense of none, save One who is of purer eyes than to behold iniquity.

And now I have designated in outline, if not in fullness, the stream which is ever flowing from the heights of my thought.

In the earlier tract I was told I did not make my meaning sufficiently clear. In this I have consequently tried to illustrate it in various ways, and may have been guilty of much repetition. Yet as I am anxious to leave no room for doubt, I shall venture to retrace once more the scope of my design in points, as was done in old-fashioned sermons.

Man is a being of twofold relations, to nature beneath and intelligences above him. The earth is his school, if not his birthplace; God his object; life and thought his means of interpreting nature and aspiring to God.

Only a fraction of this purpose is accomplished in the life of any one man. Its entire accomplishment is to be hoped only from the sum of the lives of men, or Man considered as a whole.

As this whole has one soul and one body, any injury or obstruction to a part or to the meanest member affects the whole. Man can never be perfectly happy or virtuous till all men are so.

To address Man wisely, you must not forget that his life is partly animal, subject to the same laws with Nature.

But you cannot address him wisely unless you consider him still more as soul, and appreciate the conditions and destiny of soul.

The growth of Man is twofold, masculine and feminine.

So far as these two methods can be distinguished, they are so as

Energy and Harmony;

Power and Beauty;

Intellect and Love;

or by some such rude classification; for we have not language primitive and pure enough to express such ideas with precision.

These two sides are supposed to be expressed in Man and Woman, that is, as the more and the less, for the faculties have not been given pure to either, but only in preponderance. There are also exceptions in great number, such as men of far more beauty than power, and the reverse. But as a general rule it seems to have been the intention to give a preponderance on the one side that is called masculine, and on the other, one that is called feminine.

There cannot be a doubt that if these two developments were in perfect harmony, they would correspond to and fulfill one another, like hemispheres or the tenor and bass in music.

But there is no perfect harmony in human nature; and the two parts answer one another only now and then; or if there be a persistent consonance, it can only be traced at long intervals, instead of discoursing an obvious melody.

What is the cause of this?

Man in the order of time was developed first; as energy comes before harmony; power before beauty.

Woman was therefore under his care as an elder. He might have been her guardian and teacher.

But as human nature goes not straight forward, but by excessive action and then reaction in an undulated course, he misunderstood and abused his advantages, and became her temporal master instead of her spiritual sire.

On himself came the punishment. He educated Woman more as a servant than a daughter, and found himself a king without a queen.

The children of this unequal union showed unequal natures, and more and more men seemed sons of the handmaid rather than princess.

At last there were so many Ishmaelites that the rest grew frightened and indignant. They laid the blame on Hagar, and drove her forth into the wilderness.

But there were none the fewer Ishmaelites for that.

At last men became a little wiser, and saw that the infant Moses was in every case saved by the pure instincts of Woman's breast. For as too much adversity is better for the moral nature than too much prosperity,

Woman in this respect dwindled less than Man, though in other respects still a child in leading-strings.

So Man did her more and more justice, and grew more and more kind.

But yet—his habits and his will corrupted by the past—he did not clearly see that Woman was half himself; that her interests were identical with his; and that by the law of their common being he could never reach his true proportions while she remained in any wise shorn of hers.

And so it has gone on to our day; both ideas developing, but more slowly than they would under a clearer recognition of truth and justice, which would have permitted the sexes their due influence on one another and mutual improvement from more dignified relations.

Wherever there was pure love, the natural influences were for the time restored.

Wherever the poet or artist gave free course to his genius, he saw the truth and expressed it in worthy forms, for these men especially share and need the feminine principle. The divine birds need to be brooded into life and song by mothers.

Wherever religion (I mean the thirst for truth and good, not the love of sect and dogma) had its course, the original design was apprehended in its simplicity, and the dove presaged sweetly from Dodona's oak.

I have aimed to show that no age was left entirely without a witness of the equality of the sexes in function, duty, and hope.

Also that when there was unwillingness or ignorance which prevented this being acted upon, women had not the less power for their want of light and noble freedom. But it was power which hurt alike them and those against whom they made use of the arms of the servile—cunning, blandishment, and unreasonable emotion.

That now the time has come when a clearer vision and better action are possible—when Man and Woman may regard one another as brother and sister, the pillars of one porch, the priests of one worship.

I have believed and intimated that this hope would receive an ampler fruition than ever before in our own land.

And it will do so if this land carry out the principles from which sprang our national life.

I believe that at present women are the best helpers of one another.

Let them think, let them act, till they know what they need.

We only ask of men to remove arbitrary barriers. Some would like to do more. But I believe it needs that Woman show herself in her native dignity to teach them how to aid her; their minds are so encumbered by tradition.

When Lord Edward Fitzgerald traveled with the Indians, his manly heart obliged him at once to take the packs from the squaws and carry them. But we do not read that the red men followed his example, though they are ready enough to carry the pack of the white woman, because she seems to them a superior being.

Let Woman appear in the mild majesty of Ceres, and rudest churls will be willing to learn from her.

You ask: what use will she make of liberty, when she has so long been sustained and restrained?

I answer: in the first place this will not be suddenly given. I read yesterday a debate of this year on the subject of enlarging women's rights over property. It was a leaf from the classbook that is preparing for the needed instruction. The men learned visibly as they spoke. The champions of Woman saw the fallacy of arguments on the opposite side, and were startled by their own convictions. With their wives at home, and the readers of the paper, it was the same. And so the stream flows on; thought urging action, and action leading to the evolution of still better thought.

But were this freedom to come suddenly, I have no fear of the consequences. Individuals might commit excesses, but there is not only in the sex a reverence for decorums and limits inherited and enhanced from generation to generation, which many years of other life could not efface, but a native love in Woman, as Woman, of proportion, of "the simple art of not too much"—a Greek moderation which would create immediately a restraining party, the natural legislators and instructors of the rest, and would gradually establish such rules as are needed to guard without impeding life.

The Graces would lead the choral dance, and teach the rest to regulate their steps to the measure of beauty.

But if you ask me what offices they may fill, I reply—any. I do not care what case you put; let them be sea-captains, if you will. I do not doubt there are women well fitted for such an office, and if so, I should be as glad to see them in it as to welcome the maid of Saragossa or the maid of Missolonghi or the Suliote heroine or Emily Plater.

I think women need especially at this juncture a much greater range of occupation than they have, to rouse their latent powers. A party of travelers lately visited a lonely hut on a mountain. There they found an old woman, who told them she and her husband had lived there forty years. "Why," they said, "did you choose so barren a spot?" She did not know; *"it was the man's notion."*

And during forty years she had been content to act, without knowing why, upon the "man's notion." I would not have it so.

In families that I know, some little girls like to saw wood, others to use carpenters' tools. Where these tastes are indulged, cheerfulness and good-humor are promoted. Where they are forbidden, because "such things are not proper for girls," they grow sullen and mischievous.

Fourier had observed these wants of women, as no one can fail to do who watches the desires of little girls or knows the ennui that haunts grown women, except where they make to themselves a serene little world by art of some kind. He therefore, in proposing a great variety of employments in manufactures or the care of plants and animals, allows for one third of women as likely to have a taste for masculine pursuits, one third of men for feminine.

Who does not observe the immediate glow and serenity that is diffused over the life of women before restless or fretful by engaging in gardening, building, or the lowest department of art? Here is something that is not routine, something that draws forth life towards the infinite.

I have no doubt, however, that a large proportion of women would give themselves to the same employments as now, because there are circumstances that must lead them. Mothers will delight to make the nest soft and warm. Nature would take care of that; no need to clip the wings of any bird that wants to soar and sing, or finds in itself the strength of pinion for a migratory flight unusual to its kind. The difference would be that *all* need not be constrained to employments for which *some* are unfit.

I have urged upon the sex self-subsistence in its two forms of self-reliance and self-impulse, because I believe them to be the needed means of the present juncture.

I have urged on Woman independence of Man, not that I do not think the sexes mutually needed by one another, but because in Woman this fact has led to an excessive devotion which has cooled love, degraded marriage, and prevented either sex from being what it should be to itself or the other.

I wish Woman to live *first* for God's sake. Then she will not make an imperfect man her god, and thus sink to idolatry. Then she will not take what is not fit for her from a sense of weakness and poverty. Then if she finds what she needs in Man embodied, she will know how to love and be worthy of being loved.

By being more a soul she will not be less Woman, for nature is perfected through spirit.

Now there is no woman, only an overgrown child.

That her hand may be given with dignity, she must be able to stand alone. I wish to see men and women capable of such relations as are depicted by Landor in his *Pericles and Aspasia,* where grace is the natural garb of strength, and the affections are calm, because deep. The softness is that of a firm tissue, as when

> The gods approve
> The depth, but not the tumult of the soul,
> A fervent, not ungovernable love.

A profound thinker has said, "No married woman can represent the female world, for she belongs to her husband. The idea of Woman must be represented by a virgin."

But that is the very fault of marriage and of the present relation between the sexes, that the woman *does* belong to the man instead of forming a whole with him. Were it otherwise, there would be no such limitation to the thought.

Woman, self-centered, would never be absorbed by any relation; it would be only an experience to her as to man. It is a vulgar error that love, *a* love, to Woman is her whole existence; she also is born for Truth and Love in their universal energy. Would she but assume her inheritance,

Mary would not be the only virgin mother. Not Manzoni alone would celebrate in his wife the virgin mind with the maternal wisdom and conjugal affections. The soul is ever young, ever virgin.

And will not she soon appear? The woman who shall vindicate their birthright for all women; who shall teach them what to claim, and how to use what they obtain? Shall not her name be for her era Victoria, for her country and life Virginia? Yet predictions are rash; she herself must teach us to give her the fitting name.

An idea not unknown to ancient times has of late been revived, that in the metamorphoses of life the soul assumes the form first of Man, then of Woman, and takes the chances and reaps the benefits of either lot. Why then, say some, lay such emphasis on the rights or needs of Woman? What she wins not as Woman will come to her as Man.

That makes no difference. It is not Woman, but the law of right, the law of growth that speaks in us and demands the perfection of each being in its kind—apple as apple, Woman as Woman. Without adopting your theory, I know that I, a daughter, live through the life of Man; but what concerns me now is that my life be a beautiful, powerful, in a word, a complete life in its kind. Had I but one more moment to live I must wish the same.

Suppose at the end of your cycle, your great world-year, all will be completed whether I exert myself or not (and the supposition is *false*— but suppose it true), am I to be indifferent about it? Not so! I must beat my own pulse true in the heart of the world; for *that* is virtue, excellence, health.

Thou, Lord of Day, didst leave us tonight so calmly glorious, not dismayed that cold winter is coming, not postponing thy beneficence to the fruitful summer! Thou didst smile on thy day's work when it was done, and adorn thy down-going as thy up-rising, for thou art loyal, and it is thy nature to give life, if thou canst, and shine at all events!

I stand in the sunny noon of life. Objects no longer glitter in the dews of morning, neither are yet softened by the shadows of evening. Every spot is seen, every chasm revealed. Climbing the dusty hill, some fair effigies that once stood for symbols of human destiny have been broken; those I still have with me show defects in this broad light. Yet enough is left, even by experience, to point distinctly to the glories of that destiny; faint but not to be mistaken streaks of the future day. I can say with the bard,

> Though many have suffered shipwreck, still beat noble hearts.

Always the soul says to us all, cherish your best hopes as a faith, and abide by them in action. Such shall be the effectual fervent means to their fulfillment:

> For the Power to whom we bow
> Has given its pledge that, if not now,
> They of pure and steadfast mind,
> By faith exalted, truth refined,
> *Shall* hear all music loud and clear,
> Whose first notes they ventured here.
> Then fear not thou to wind the horn,
> Though elf and gnome thy courage scorn;
> Ask for the castle's King and Queen;
> Though rabble rout may rush between,
> Beat thee senseless to the ground,
> In the dark beset thee round;
> Persist to ask, and it will come;
> Seek not for rest in humbler home;
> So shalt thou see, what few have seen,
> The palace home of King and Queen.

November 15, 1844

PART III

Criticism

Prefatory Note

Margaret Fuller was first and last a critic. It is one of the many ironies of her fate that she should be remembered as a feminist and forgotten as a critic. The great majority of her writings were critical in nature, yet only one of the five volumes she published during her life, *Papers on Literature and Art,* is devoted to her criticism. As she says in her preface, "In the original plan for publishing a selection from my essays in different kinds which have appeared in periodicals, I had aimed at more completeness of arrangement than has been attained in these two volumes. . . . I find, indeed, that the matter which I had supposed could be comprised in two of these numbers would fill six or eight. Had I been earlier aware of this, I should have made a different selection, and one which would do more justice to the range and variety of subjects which have been before my mind during the ten years that, in the intervals allowed me by other engagements, I have written for the public." Writing from London of the book's kindly reception there, she laments that "a false impression has been given here of the range and scope of my efforts." In the two posthumous volumes edited by Arthur B. Fuller the false impression was not corrected, for the editor was more intent upon establishing "a true appreciation of the beauty of her soul" than her reputation as a critic. This editorial bias led to some curious selections and omissions.

Margaret Fuller had probably as adequate a training for critical writing as any practitioner before 1850. Schooled by her father from the age of six in the Greek and Roman classics, nurtured by much reading on her own in English, French, German, and Italian literature, accustomed by the habit of years to recording on paper her impressions of everything she read and saw, she deserved her reputation as a paragon of erudition. She had a genius for classification, penetration, independence of judgment, and a talent for frank speaking. She lacked Poe's facility of expression, but her verdicts are more reliable than his.

The selection made here from her criticism has been designed to reveal her critical theories, the literary influences which helped to shape her intellectual growth, her creative ability, her functions as the interpreter of Continental literature to an America which was just becoming aware that there were other literatures than English and as the herald of an American literature which had outgrown its imitative period and was beginning to be original. Her art criticism has been left unrepresented, in agreement with Emerson's verdict that her taste in this field was "more idiosyncratic than universal; she mistook the emotions that were roused in her by art for those the artist intended." Illustrations of this tendency will be found in the selections from her *Things and Thoughts in Europe*.

Most of Margaret Fuller's criticism was written for the *Western Messenger,* the *Dial,* and the New York *Daily Tribune.* For one to whom writing was always difficult, "the little library, quite large enough to exhaust the patience of the collector, if not of the reader," which she produced during her twenty months as literary critic for the *Tribune* is a remarkable achievement. A bibliography of her periodic writings will be found on pages 593–598.

Criticism

I

A SHORT ESSAY ON CRITICS *

An essay on criticism were a serious matter; for though this age be emphatically critical, the writer would still find it necessary to investigate the laws of criticism as a science to settle its conditions as an art. Essays entitled critical are epistles addressed to the public, through which the mind of the recluse relieves itself of its impressions. Of these the only law is, "Speak the best word that is in thee." Or they are regular articles got up to order by the literary hack writer for the literary mart, and the only law is to make them plausible. There is not yet deliberate recognition of a standard of criticism, though we hope the always strengthening league of the republic of letters must erelong settle laws on which its amphictyonic council may act. Meanwhile let us not venture to write on criticism, but by classifying the critics imply our hopes and thereby our thoughts.

First there are the subjective class (to make use of a convenient term introduced by our German benefactors). These are persons to whom writing is no sacred, no reverend employment. They are not driven to consider, not forced upon investigation by the fact that they are deliberately giving their thoughts an independent existence, and that it may live to others when dead to them. They know no agonies of conscientious research, no timidities of self-respect. They see no ideal beyond the present hour, which makes its mood an uncertain tenure. How things affect them now they know; let the future, let the whole take care of itself. They state their impressions as they rise of other men's spoken, written, or acted thoughts. They never dream of going out of themselves to seek the motive, to trace the law of another nature. They never dream that there are statures which cannot be measured from their point of view. They love, they like, or they hate; the book is detestable, immoral, absurd, or admirable, noble, of a most approved scope—these statements they

---

* First published in the *Dial,* Vol. I, No. 1. Reprinted in *Papers on Literature and Art.*

make with authority, as those who bear the evangel of pure taste and accurate judgment, and need be tried before no human synod. To them it seems that their present position commands the universe.

Thus the essays on the works of others which are called criticisms are often in fact mere records of impressions. To judge of their value you must know where the man was brought up, under what influences—his nation, his church, his family, even. He himself has never attempted to estimate the value of these circumstances, and find a law or raise a standard above all circumstances, permanent against all influence. He is content to be the creature of his place, and to represent it by his spoken and written word. He takes the same ground with a savage who does not hesitate to say of the product of a civilization on which he could not stand, "It is bad" or "It is good."

The value of such comments is merely reflex. They characterize the critic. They give an idea of certain influences on a certain act of men in a certain time or place. Their absolute, essential value is nothing. The long review, the eloquent article by the man of the nineteenth century, are of no value by themselves considered, but only as samples of their kind. The writers were content to tell what they felt, to praise or to denounce without needing to convince us or themselves. They sought not the divine truths of philosophy, and she proffers them not if unsought.

Then there are the apprehensive. These can go out of themselves and enter fully into a foreign existence. They breathe its life; they live in its law; they tell what it meant, and why it so expressed its meaning. They reproduce the work of which they speak, and make it better known to us in so far as two statements are better than one. There are beautiful specimens in this kind. They are pleasing to us as bearing witness of the genial sympathies of nature. They have the ready grace of love with somewhat of the dignity of disinterested friendship. They sometimes give more pleasure than the original production of which they treat, as melodies will sometimes ring sweetlier in the echo. Besides, there is a peculiar pleasure in a true response; it is the assurance of equipoise in the universe. These, if not true critics, come nearer the standard than the subjective class, and the value of their work is ideal as well as historical.

Then there are the comprehensive, who must also be apprehensive.

They enter into the nature of another being and judge his work by its own law. But having done so, having ascertained his design and the degree of his success in fulfilling it, thus measuring his judgment, his energy, and skill, they do also know how to put that aim in its place and how to estimate its relations. And this only the critic can do who perceives the analogies of the universe, and how they are regulated by an absolute, invariable principle. He can see how far that work expresses this principle, as well as how far it is excellent in its details. Sustained by a principle such as can be girt within no rule, no formula, he can walk around the work, he can stand above it, he can uplift it, and try its weight. Finally he is worthy to judge it.

Critics are poets cut down, says someone by way of jeer; but in truth they are men with the poetical temperament to apprehend, with the philosophical tendency to investigate. The maker is divine; the critic sees this divine, but brings it down to humanity by the analytic process. The critic is the historian who records the order of creation. In vain for the maker who knows without learning it, but not in vain for the mind of his race.

The critic is beneath the maker, but is his needed friend. What tongue could speak but to an intelligent ear, and every noble work demands its critic. The richer the work, the more severe should be its critic; the larger its scope, the more comprehensive must be his power of scrutiny. The critic is not a base caviler, but the younger brother of genius. Next to invention is the power of interpreting invention; next to beauty the power of appreciating beauty.

And of making others appreciate it; for the universe is a scale of infinite gradation, and below the very highest every step is explanation down to the lowest. Religion in the two modulations of poetry and music descends through an infinity of waves to the lowest abysses of human nature. Nature is the literature and art of the divine mind; human literature and art the criticism on that; and they too find their criticism within their own sphere.

The critic then should be not merely a poet, not merely a philosopher, not merely an observer, but tempered of all three. If he criticize the poem, he must want nothing of what constitutes the poet except the power of creating forms and speaking in music. He must have as good an eye and as fine a sense; but if he had as fine an organ for expression also, he would make the poem instead of judging it. He must be inspired by the philosopher's spirit of inquiry and need of generalization, but he must not be constrained by the hard-cemented masonry of method to which philosophers are prone. And he must have the organic acuteness of the observer, with a love of ideal perfection which forbids him to be content with mere beauty of details in the work or the comment upon the work.

There are persons who maintain that there is no legitimate criticism except the reproductive; that we have only to say what the work is or is to us, never what it is not. But the moment we look for a principle, we feel the need of a criterion, of a standard; and then we say what the work is *not,* as well as what it *is;* and this is as healthy though not as grateful and gracious an operation of the mind as the other. We do not seek to degrade but to classify an object by stating what it is not. We detach the part from the whole lest it stand between us and the whole. When we have ascertained in what degree it manifests the whole, we may safely restore it to its place and love or admire it there ever after.

The use of criticism in periodical writing is to sift, not to stamp a work. Yet should they not be "sieves and drainers for the use of luxurious readers," but for the use of earnest inquirers, giving voice and being to their objections as well as stimulus to their sympathies. But the critic must not be an infallible adviser to his reader. He must not tell him what books are not worth reading or what must be thought of them when read, but what he read in them. Woe to that coterie where some critic sits despotic, intrenched behind the infallible "We." Woe to that oracle who has infused such soft sleepiness, such a gentle dullness into his atmosphere that when he opes his lips no dog will bark. It is this attempt at dictatorship in the reviewers, and the indolent acquiescence of their readers, that has brought them into disrepute. With such fairness did they make out their statements, with such dignity did they utter their verdicts that the poor reader grew all too submissive. He learned his lesson with such docility that the greater part of what will be said at any public or private meeting can be foretold by anyone who has read the leading periodical works for twenty years back. Scholars sneer at and would fain dispense with them altogether; and the public, grown lazy and helpless by this constant use of props and stays, can now scarce brace itself even to get through a magazine article, but reads in the daily paper laid beside the breakfast plate a short notice of the last number of the long established and popular review, and thereupon passes its judgment and is content.

Then the partisan spirit of many of these journals has made it unsafe to rely upon them as guidebooks and expurgatory indexes. They could not be content merely to stimulate and suggest thought; they have at last become powerless to supersede it.

From these causes and causes like these, the journals have lost much of their influence. There is a languid feeling about them, an inclination to suspect the justice of their verdicts, the value of their criticisms. But their golden age cannot be quite past. They afford too convenient a vehicle for the transmission of knowledge; they are too natural a feature of our time to have done all their work yet. Surely they may be redeemed from their abuses, they may be turned to their true uses. But how?

It were easy to say what they should *not* do. They should not have an object to carry or a cause to advocate, which obliges them either to reject all writings which wear the distinctive traits of individual life or to file away what does not suit them, till the essay, made true to their design, is made false to the mind of the writer. An external consistency is thus produced at the expense of all salient thought, all genuine emotion of life, in short, and all living influence. Their purpose may be of value, but by such means was no valuable purpose ever furthered long. There are those who have with the best intention pursued this system of trimming and adaptation, and thought it well and best to

Deceive their country for their country's good.

But their country cannot long be so governed. It misses the pure, the full tone of truth; it perceives that the voice is modulated to coax, to persuade, and it turns from the judicious man of the world, calculating the effect to be produced by each of his smooth sentences, to some earnest voice which is uttering thoughts, crude, rash, ill-arranged it may be, but true to one human breast and uttered in full faith that the God of Truth will guide them aright.

And here it seems to me has been the greatest mistake in the conduct of these journals. A smooth monotony has been attained, a uniformity of tone, so that from the title of a journal you can infer the tenor of all its chapters. But nature is ever various, ever new, and so should be her daughters, art and literature. We do not want merely a polite response to what we thought before, but by the freshness of thought in other minds to have new thought awakened in our own. We do not want stores of information only, but to be roused to digest these into knowledge. Able and experienced men write for us, and we would know what they think, as they think it not for us but for themselves. We would live with them rather than be taught by them how to live: we would catch the contagion of their mental activity rather than have them direct us how to regulate our own. In books, in reviews, in the senate, in the pulpit we wish to meet thinking men, not schoolmasters or pleaders. We wish that they should do full justice to their own view, but also that they should be frank with us, and, if now our superiors, treat us as if we might sometime rise to be their equals. It is this true manliness, this firmness in his own position, and this power of appreciating the position of others that alone can make the critic our companion and friend. We would converse with him, secure that he will tell us all his thought and speak as man to man. But if he adapts his work to us, if he stifles what is distinctively his, if he shows himself either arrogant or mean, or above all if he wants faith in the healthy action of free thought and the safety of pure motive, we will not talk with him, for we cannot confide in him. We will go to the critic who trusts genius and trusts us, who knows that all good writing must be spontaneous, and who will write out the bill of fare for the public as he read it for himself—

> Forgetting vulgar rules, with spirit free
> To judge each author by his own intent,
> Nor think one standard for all minds is meant.

Such a one will not disturb us with personalities, with sectarian prejudices, or an undue vehemence in favor of petty plans or temporary objects. Neither will he disgust us by smooth obsequious flatteries and an inexpressive, lifeless gentleness. He will be free and make us free from the mechanical and distorting influences we hear complained of on every side. He will teach us to love wisely what we before loved well, for he knows the difference between censoriousness and discernment, infatuation and reverence; and while delighting in the genial melodies of Pan, can perceive, should Apollo bring his lyre into audience, that there may be strains more divine than those of his native groves.

THREE CLASSES OF LITERATURE *

The office of literature is twofold. It preserves through ages the flowers of life which came to perfect bloom in minds of genius. What bloomed but for a day in the highest epochs of thought or of love becomes an amaranth if translated into literature. A small part of literature has a permanent value.

But the office of the larger part is temporary, as affording the means of interpreting contemporary minds to each other on a larger scale than actual conversation in words or deeds furnishes. And the requisites for success in this class are very different from, in some respects opposite to, those for the other.

Excellence in this kind is not to be held lightly. It is no small matter to live a full life in the day; it is what those who live for the ages rarely do. Those who are most geniuses are very commonly least men, and take the total growth of a man, we may well doubt whether an equable expansion of harmonious growth of the nature is to be sacrificed to a partial though exquisite result. What is said fully and pertinently now does its office and cheers the heart of the world, though it may not pass to posterity with the name of the speaker. We confess our partiality for those noble men who lived too full and vigorous a life to have time to set apart portions of it—those men whose soul was in their eyes, and whose tongue or pen did justice to the occasion as it came. The mistletoe is a sacred plant, but we must have oaks before mistletoes. It is well that we have both, when he who fulfills the life of the day has such a superfluity besides as to scatter its seed through a wide future. But let the oaks grow first, though their fruit be no larger than the acorn. The common and daily purposes of literature are the most important. It cannot and will not dispense with the prophecies of genius, but the healthy discharge of its functions must not be disparaged to exalt these.

Thus whatever is truly said and forcibly said is valuable in literature as in life, though its pretensions be not the highest as to originality of

* From "English Writers Little Known Here," New York *Daily Tribune,* March 4, 1845.

thought or form. Individuality is sufficient, for every fact is worth knowing and stating. Only we must not dwell too long on what is temporary, nor give to what is but relatively good, absolute praise.

There is a class of writers, midway between geniuses and men of merely healthy energy, who are very valuable also. They are audience to the genius, interpreter to the multitude, cultivated friends for those who need such.

The writers of this class do not enjoy extensive fame. They are not poets nor merely active men; they may be called in distinction gentlemen and scholars. They have not perhaps the deep glow of experience that makes the universal heart thrill at their slight magnetic tokens; they have not the magician's wand to evoke from the realm of shadows forms that in life they have never seen.

Yet they are delightful private companions. We are not their lovers nor their worshipers, but their familiar friendship we prize. We would introduce them to others that they may find and be found by their own. They need to be thus introduced, for they do not command fame, nor make the earth shake with their tread so that all may know where to find them.

3

TRANSLATOR'S PREFACE TO
ECKERMANN'S CONVERSATIONS WITH GOETHE *

This book cannot fail to interest all who are desirous to understand the character and opinions of Goethe or the state of literary society in Germany. The high opinion which Goethe entertained of Eckermann's fidelity, judgment, and comprehension of himself is sufficiently proved by his appointing him editor of his posthumous works. The light in which this book is regarded by the distinguished circle of which Goethe was the glory may be seen by a reference to the first volume of Mrs. Jameson's late work, *Winter Studies and Summer Rambles in Canada.*

It is obviously a most faithful record. Perhaps there is no instance in which one mind has been able to give out what it received from another, so little colored by its own substance. It is true that the simple reverence and thorough subordination to the mind of Goethe, which make Eckermann so transparent a medium, prevent his being of any value as an interpreter. Never was satellite more completely in harmony with his ruling orb. He is merely the sounding-board to the various notes played by the master's hand; and what we find here is to all intents and purposes not conversations but monologue. A finer book might be made by selections from Goethe's miscellanies; but here some subjects are brought forward on which he never wrote. The journal form gives an ease and life to the discussion, and what is wanting in fullness and beauty is made up to us by the pleasure we always take in the unpremeditated flow of thought, and in seeing what topics come up naturally with such a person as Goethe.

An imperial genius must have not only willing subjects but good instruments. Eckermann has all the merit of an intelligent minister and a discreet secretary. He is ruled and modeled, but not blinded by Goethe. When we look at the interesting sketch of his youthful struggles and see what obligations he owed to Goethe, as well before as after their personal acquaintance, we cannot blame him for his boundless gratitude

---

* From *Conversations with Goethe in the Last Years of His Life,* translated from the German of Eckermann by S. M. Fuller. Boston: Hilliard, Gray and Co., 1839.

to the sun which chased away so many clouds from his sky. He seems indeed led onward to be the foster child and ready helper of this great man, and could not so well have filled this place if he had kept sufficiently aloof to satisfy our pride. I say *our* pride because we are jealous for minds which we see in this state of subordination. We feel it too dangerous to what is most valuable in character; and rare as independence is, we cannot but ask it from all who live in the light of genius.

Still our feeling towards Eckermann is not only kindly but respectful. He is not ridiculous like Boswell, for no vanity or littleness sullies his sincere enthusiasm. In these sober and enlightened days, we rebel against man-worship, even though it be hero-worship. But how could this person so rich in natural gifts, so surrounded by what was bright, beautiful, and courtly, and at so high a point of culture, fail to be overpowering to an obscure youth whose abilities he had been the chief means of unfolding? It could not be otherwise than that Eckermann should sit at his feet and live on his bounty. Enough for the disciple to know how to use what he received with thoughtful gratitude. That Goethe also knew how to receive is evident from his correspondences with Zelter, Schiller, and Meyer —relations which show him in a better light than this with Eckermann because the parties were on more equal terms.

Those letters or the substance of them will sometime be published here. Meanwhile the book before us has merits which they do not possess. It paints Goethe to us as he was in the midst of his family and in most careless or weary hours. Under such circumstances whatever may be thought of his views (and they are often still less suited to our public than to that of Germany), his courteous grace, his calm wisdom and reliance on the harmony of his faith with his nature, must be felt by the unprejudiced reader to be beautiful and rare.

And here it may not be amiss to give some intimation (more my present limits do not permit) of the grounds on which Goethe is to myself an object of peculiar interest and constant study.

I hear him much assailed by those among us who know him, some few in his own language but most from translations of *Wilhelm Meister* and *Faust*. These, his two great works in which he proposed to himself the enigma of life and solved it after his own fashion, were naturally enough selected in preference to others for translating. This was for all but the translators unfortunate, because these two, above all others, require a knowledge of the circumstances and character from which they rose, to ascertain their scope and tendency.

It is sneeringly said, "Those persons who are so fanatical for German literature always say, if you object to any of their idols, that you are not capable of appreciating them." And it is truly though oftentimes too impatiently said. The great movement in German literature is too recent to be duly estimated even by those most interested to examine it. The waves have scarcely yet ebbed from this new continent, and those who are visiting its shores see so much that is new and beautiful that of their many obligations to the phenomenon the chief is as yet that of the feeling of fresh creative life at work there. No wonder that they feel vexed at those who declare from an occasional peep through a spyglass that they see no new wonders for geology; that they can botanize all the flowers, and find nothing worthy of fresh attempts at classification; and that there are no birds except a few sea-gulls. Would these hasty critics but recollect how long it was before similar movements in Italy, Spain, France, and England found their proper place in the thoughts of other nations, they would not think fifty years' investigation too much for fifty years' growth, and would no longer provoke the ire of those who are lighting their tapers at the German torch. Meanwhile it is silly to be in a pet always; and disdainful answers have been recognized as useless since Solomon's time or earlier. What could have been the reason they were not set aside while that wise prince lived, once for all?

The objections usually made, though not without a foundation in truth, are such as would answer themselves on a more thorough acquaintance with the subject. In France and England there has seemed an approximation of late to juster views. Yet in a recent number of *Blackwood's Magazine* has appeared an article as ignorant (and that is a strong word) as anything that has ever been written about Goethe.

The objections, so far as I know them, may be resolved into these classes—

He is not a Christian;

He is not an idealist;

He is not a democrat;

He is not Schiller.

If by Christian be meant the subordination of the intellectual to the spiritual, I shall not deny that with Goethe the reverse was the case. He sought always for unity; but the want with him was chiefly one of the intellect. A creative activity was his law. He was far from insensible to spiritual beauty in the human character. He has embodied it in its finest forms; but he merely put it in what seemed to him its place as the keystone of the social arch, and paints neither that nor any other state with partiality. Such was his creed as a writer. "I paint," he seems to say, "what I have seen; choose from it or take it all, as you will or can." In his love of form Goethe was a Greek; constitutionally and by the habit of his life averse to the worship of sorrow. His God was rather the creative and uplifting than the paternal spirit; his religion, that all his powers must be unfolded; his faith, "that nature could not dispense with immortality." In the most trying occasions of his life he referred to "the great idea of duty which alone can hold us upright." Renunciation, the power of sacrificing the temporary for the permanent, is a leading idea in one of his great works, *Wilhelm Meister*. The thought of the Catholic Dante is repeated in his other great work, *Faust,* where Margaret by her innocence of heart and the resolute aversion to the powers of darkness which her mind in its most shattered state does not forget, redeems not only her own soul, but that of her erring lover. The virgin Ottilia, who immolates herself to avoid the possibility of spotting her thoughts with passion, gives to that much abused book *Die Wahlverwandtschaften* the pathetic moral of the pictures of the Magdalen. His two highest characters, Natalia and Macaria, are representations of beneficence and heavenly wisdom. Iphigenia by her steadfast truth hallows all about her and disarms the powers of hell. Such traits as these may be accumulated; yet it remains not the less true that Goethe was not what is called a spiritual writer. Those who cannot draw the moral for themselves had best leave his books alone; they require the power as life does. This advantage only does he give or intend to give you, of looking at life brought into a compass convenient to your eye by a great observer and artist, and at times when you can look uninterrupted by action, undisturbed by passion.

He was not an idealist; that is to say, he thought not so much of what might be as what is. He did not seek to alter or exalt Nature, but merely to select from her rich stores. Here indeed, even as an artist, he would always have stopped short of the highest excellence if he had not at times been inspired beyond his knowledge and his will. Had his views been different, his peculiar powers of minute, searching, and extended observation would have been much injured; as instead of looking at objects with the single aim of ascertaining their properties, he would have examined them only to gain from them what most favored his plans. I am well satisfied that "he went the way that God and Nature called him."

He was an aristocrat. And in the present day hostility arises instinctively against one who does not believe in the people and whose tastes are in favor of a fixed external gradation. My sympathies are with the great onward movement now obvious throughout the civilized world; my hope is that we may make a fair experiment whether men can be educated to rule themselves and communities be trusted to choose their own rulers. This is, it seems, the present tendency of the ages; and had I influence, I would not put a straw in the way. Yet a minority is needed to keep these liberals in check and make them pause upon their measures long enough to know what they are doing; for as yet the caldron of liberty has shown a constant disposition to overboil. The artist and literary man is naturally thrown into this body by his need of repose and a firm ground to work in his proper way. Certainly Goethe by nature belonged on that side; and no one who can understand the structure of his mind, instead of judging him by his outward relations, will impute to him unworthy motives or think he could, being what he was, hold other opinions. And is not this all which is important? The gates that keep out the water while the ship is building have their place also, as well as the ship itself or the wind which fills the sails. To be sincere, consistent, and intelligent in what one believes is what is important; a higher power takes care of the rest.

In reply to those who object to him that he is not Schiller, it may be remarked that Shakespeare was not Milton, nor Ariosto Tasso. It was indeed unnecessary that there should be two Schillers, one being sufficient to represent a certain class of thoughts and opinions. It would be well if the admirers of Schiller would learn from him to admire and profit by his friend and coadjutor, as he himself did.

Schiller was wise enough to judge each nature by its own law, great enough to understand greatness of an order different from his own. He was too well aware of the value of the more beautiful existences to quarrel with the rose for not being a lily, the eagle for not being a swan.

I am not fanatical as to the benefits to be derived from the study of German literature. I suppose indeed that there lie the life and learning of the century, and that he who does not go to those sources can have no just notion of the workings of the spirit in the European world these last fifty years or more; but my tastes are often displeased by German writers, even by Goethe—of German writers the most English and Greek. To cultivate the tastes we must go to another school; but I wish that we could learn from the Germans habits of more liberal criticism, and leave this way of judging from comparison or personal predilections. If we must draw parallels, we ought to be sure that we are capable of a love for all greatness as fervent as that of Plutarch's time. Perhaps it may be answered that the comparison between Goethe and Schiller began in Germany; it did so, but arose there from circumstances with which we have nothing to do. Generally the wise German criticizes with the positive degree and is well aware of the danger in using the comparative.

For the rest no one who has a higher aim in reading German books than mere amusement; no one who knows what it is to become acquainted with a literature as literature, in its history of mutual influences, diverse yet harmonious tendencies, can leave aside either Schiller or Goethe; but far, far least the latter. It would be leaving Augustus Caesar out of the history of Rome because he was not Brutus.

Having now confessed to what Goethe is not, I would indicate as briefly as possible what to me he is.

Most valuable as a means of balancing the judgment and suggesting thought from his antagonism to the spirit of the age. He prefers the perfecting of the few to the slight improvement of the many. He believes more in man than men, effort than success, thought than action, nature than providence. He does not insist on my believing with him. I would go up often into this fortress, and look from its battlements to see how goes the fight below. I need not fear to be detained. He knows himself too well to ask anything of another except to know him.

As one of the finest lyric poets of modern times. Bards are also prophets; and woe be to those who refuse to hear the singer, to tender him the golden cup of homage. Their punishment is in their fault.

As the best writer of the German language, who has availed himself of all its advantages of richness and flexibility and added to them a degree of lightness, grace, clearness, and precision beyond any other writer of his time; who has more than any other tended to correct the fantastic, cumbrous, centipede style indigenous to Germany.

As a critic on art and literature, not to be surpassed in independence, fairness, powers of sympathy, and largeness of view.

As almost the finest observer of his time of human nature, and almost as much so of external nature. He has great delicacy of penetration, and a better tact at selecting objects than almost any who has looked at the time of which I am a child. Could I omit to study this eighty years' journal of my parent's life, traced from so commanding a position by so sure a hand, and one informed by so keen and cultivated an eye? Where else shall we find so large a mirror or one with so finely decorated a frame?

As a mind which has known how to reconcile individuality of character with universality of thought; a mind which, whatever be its faults, ruled and relied on itself alone; a nature which knew its law and revolved on its proper axis, unrepenting, never bustling, always active, never stagnant, always calm.

A distinguished critic speaks of Goethe as the conqueror of his century. I believe I do not take so admiring a view of the character of Goethe as this, his only competent English critic. I refer to Mr. Carlyle. But so far as attaining the object he himself proposed, a choice of aim, a "wise limitation," and unwearied constancy in the use of means; so far as leaving behind the limbo of self-questioning uncertainty in which most who would fain think as well as act are wading, and bringing his life into an uninterrupted harmony with his thought, he did indeed conquer. He knew both what he sought and how to seek it—a great matter!

I am not a blind admirer of Goethe. I have felt what others feel, and seen what others see. I too have been disturbed by his aversion to pain and isolation of the heart. I also have looked in vain for the holy and heroic elements. Nor do I believe that any degree of objectivity is inconsistent with a partiality for what is noblest in individual characters. Shakespeare is a proof to the contrary. As a critic he does not treat subjects masterfully. He does not give you at once a central point, and make you feel the root of the matter; but you must read his essays as aggregates of thoughts, rather clustering round than unfolding the subject. In his later years he lost his architectural vigor; and his works are built up like the piles in Piranesi's *Visions* of galleries and balconies connected only by cobweb ladders. Many of his works I feel to be fragmentary and inadequate. I am even disposed to deny him the honors most generally awarded him—those of the artist. I think he had the artist's eye and the artist's hand, but not the artist's love of structure.

But I will stop here, and wait until the time when I shall have room to substantiate my changes. I flatter myself I have now found fault enough to prove me a worthy critic after the usual fashion. Mostly I prefer leveling upward, in the way recommended by Goethe in speaking of the merchants he met while traveling.

While it is so undesirable that any man should receive what he has not examined, a far more frequent danger is that of flippant irreverence. Not all that the heavens contain is obvious to the unassisted eye of the careless spectator. Few men are great; almost as few able to appreciate greatness. The critics have written little upon the *Iliad* in all these ages which Alexander would have thought worth keeping with it in his golden box. Nor Shakespeare nor Dante nor Calderon has as yet found a sufficient critic, though Coleridge and the Schlegels have lived since they did. The greatness of Goethe his nation has felt for more than half a century; the world is beginning to feel it, but time may not yet have ripened his critic; especially as the grand historical standpoint is the only one from which a comprehensive view could be taken of him.

Meanwhile it is safer to take off the hat and shout *Vivat!* to the conqueror who may become a permanent sovereign than to throw stones and mud from the gutter. The star shines, and that it is with no borrowed light his foes are his voucher. And every planet is a portent to the world; but whether for good or ill, only he can know who has science for many calculations. Not he who runs can read these books, or any books of any worth. I am content to describe him in the terms Hamlet thought sufficiently honorable to him he honored most:

> He was a man, *take him for all in all,*
> We shall not look upon his like again.

As such worth our study—and more to us than elder great men, because of our own day and busied most with those questions which lie nearest us.

With regard to the manner in which the task of translation has been performed, I have been under some disadvantages which should be briefly mentioned. I thought the book would be an easy one to translate, as for a book of tabletalk so much the greater liberty would be allowed and so much less care demanded than for a classical work or one of science. But the wide range of topics and the use of coterie "technics" have made it more difficult and less fit for the amusement of leisure hours than was expected. Some of these "technics" I have used as they stood, such as "motiv," "grandiose," and "apprehensive," the last-named of which I do not understand; the first, Mrs. Jameson has explained in a note to the *Winter Studies.* Generally my acquaintance with Goethe's works on the same subjects makes me confident that I have the thought.

Then I was unexpectedly obliged by ill-health to dictate a considerable part of it. I was not accustomed to this way of getting thoughts put upon paper, and do not feel as well satisfied with these pages as with those written by my own hand. I have, however, looked them over so carefully that I think there can be no inaccuracies of consequence.

But besides—it being found that the two German volumes would not by any means make two, yet were too much for one of the present series— it seemed necessary in some way to compress or curtail the book. For this purpose passages have been omitted relating to Goethe's theory of colors. These contain accounts of experiments made by Eckermann, and remarks of Goethe's suggested by them. As the *Farbenlehre* is scarcely known here, I thought these would not now be interesting, and that if the work to which they refer should by and by be translated, they might to better advantage be inserted in an appendix. And I was glad to dispense with them because I have no clear understanding of the subject, and could not have been secure of doing them justice.

I have also omitted Eckermann's meager record of his visit to Italy, some discussions about a novel of Goethe's not yet translated, which would scarcely be intelligible to those who have not read it, and occasionally other passages which seemed to me expletive or so local as to be uninteresting. I have also frequently condensed Eckermann's remarks and sometimes, though more rarely, those of his patron.

I am aware that there is a just prejudice against paraphrastic or mutilated translations, and that in this delicate process I have laid myself open to much blame. But I have done it with such care that I feel confident the substance of the work and its essential features will be found here, and hope if so that any who may be acquainted with the original, and regret omissions, will excuse them. These two rules have been observed—not to omit even such details as snuffing the candles and walking to the stove (given by the good Eckermann with that truly German minuteness which many years ago so provoked the wit of Mr. Jeffrey) when they seem needed to finish out the picture, either of German manners or Goethe's relations to his friends or household. Neither has anything been omitted which would cast either light or shade on his character. I am sure that nothing has been softened or extenuated, and believe that Goethe's manners, temper, and opinions wear here the same aspect that they do in the original.

I have a confidence that the translation is in the truest sense faithful, and trust that those who find the form living and symmetrical will not be inclined severely to censure some change in the cut or make of the garment in which it is arrayed.

Jamaica Plain, May 23, 1839

4

GOETHE *

* First published in the *Dial*, Vol. II, No. 1.

Nemo contra Deum nisi Deus ipse.

Wer Grosses will muss sich zusammen raffen;
In der Beschränkung zeigt sich erst der Meister,
Und der Gesetz nur kann uns Freiheit geben.†

The first of these mottoes is that prefixed by Goethe to the last books of *Dichtung und Wahrheit*. These books record the hour of turning tide in his life, the time when he was called on for a choice at the "Parting of the Ways." From these months which gave the sun of his youth, the crisis of his manhood, date the birth of *Egmont* and of *Faust* too, though the latter was not published so early. They saw the rise and decline of his love for Lili, apparently the truest love he ever knew. That he was not himself dissatisfied with the results to which the decisions of this era led him we may infer from his choice of a motto and from the calm beauty with which he has invested the record.

The Parting of the Ways! The way he took led to court-favor, wealth, celebrity, and an independence of celebrity. It led to large performance and a wonderful economical management of intellect. It led Faust, the Seeker, from the heights of his own mind to the trodden ways of the world. There indeed he did not lose sight of the mountains, but he never breathed their keen air again.

After this period we find in him rather a wide and deep wisdom than the inspiration of genius. His faith, that all *must* issue well, wants the sweetness of piety, and the God he manifests to us is one of law or necessity rather than of intelligent love. As this God makes because he must, so Goethe, his instrument, observes and recreates because he must, observing with minutest fidelity the outward exposition of Nature; never blinded by a sham or detained by a fear, he yet makes us feel that he wants insight to her sacred secret. The calmest of writers does not give us repose because it is too difficult to find his center. Those flamelike

---

† "He who would do great things must quickly draw together his forces. The master can only show himself such through limitation, and the law alone can give us freedom."

natures which he undervalues give us more peace and hope through their restless aspirations than he with his hearth-enclosed fires of steady fulfillment. For true as it is that God is everywhere, we must not only see him but see him acknowledged. Through the consciousness of man "shall not Nature interpret God?" We wander in diversity and, with each new turning of the path, long anew to be referred to the One.

Of Goethe, as of other natures where the intellect is too much developed in proportion to the moral nature, it is difficult to speak without seeming narrow, blind, and impertinent. For such men *see* all that others *live,* and if you feel a want of a faculty in them, it is hard to say they have it not, lest next moment they puzzle you by giving some indication of it. Yet they are not, nay, *know* not; they only discern. The difference is that between sight and life, prescience and being, wisdom and love. Thus with Goethe. Naturally of a deep mind and shallow heart, he felt the sway of the affections enough to appreciate their workings in other men, but never enough to receive their inmost regenerating influence.

How this might have been had he ever once abandoned himself entirely to a sentiment, it is impossible to say. But the education of his youth seconded rather than balanced his natural tendency. His father was a gentlemanly martinet: dull, sour, well-informed, and of great ambition as to externals. His influence on the son was wholly artificial. He was always turning his powerful mind from side to side in search of information, for the attainment of what are called accomplishments. The mother was a delightful person in her way: open, genial, playful, full of lively talent, but without earnestness of soul. She was one of those charming but not noble persons who take the day and the man as they find them, seeing the best that is there already, but never making the better grow in its stead. His sister, though of graver kind, was social and intellectual, not religious or tender. The mortifying repulse of his early love checked the few pale buds of faith and tenderness that his heart put forth. His friends were friends of the intellect merely; altogether he seemed led by destiny to the place he was to fill.

Pardon him, world, that he was too worldly. Do not wonder, heart, that he was so heartless. Believe, soul, that one so true as far as he went must yet be initiated into the deeper mysteries of soul. Perhaps even now he sees that we must accept limitations only to transcend them; work in processes only to detect the organizing power which supersedes them; and that sphinxes of fifty-five volumes might well be cast into the abyss before the single word that solves them all.

Now when I think of Goethe, I seem to see his soul, all the variegated plumes of knowledge, artistic form, *und so weiter,* burnt from it by the fires of divine love, wingless, motionless, unable to hide from itself in any subterfuge of labor, saying again and again the simple words which he would never distinctly say on earth—God beyond Nature—faith beyond sight—the Seeker nobler than the *Meister*.

For this mastery that Goethe prizes seems to consist rather in the skillful use of means than in the clear manifestation of ends. His Master indeed makes acknowledgment of a divine order, but the temporal uses are always uppermost in the mind of the reader. But of this, more at large in reference to his works.

Apart from this want felt in his works, there is a littleness in his aspect as a character. Why waste his time in Weimar court entertainments? His duties as minister were not unworthy of him, though it would have been perhaps finer if he had not spent so large a portion of that prime of intellectual life, from five and twenty to forty, upon them.

But granted that the exercise these gave his faculties, the various lore they brought, and the good they did to the community, made them worth his doing—why that perpetual dangling after the royal family? Why all that verse-making for the albums of serene highnesses, and those pretty poetical entertainments for the young princesses, and that cold setting himself apart from his true peers, the real sovereigns of Weimar—Herder, Wieland, and the others? The excuse must be found in circumstances of his time and temperament, which made the character of man of the world and man of affairs more attractive to him than the children of nature can conceive it to be in the eyes of one who is capable of being a consecrated bard.

The man of genius feels that literature has become too much a craft by itself. No man should live by or for his pen. Writing is worthless except as the record of life; and no great man ever was satisfied thus to express all his being. His book should be only an indication of himself.

The obelisk should point to a scene of conquest. In the present state of division of labor, the literary man finds himself condemned to be nothing else. Does he write a good book? It is not received as evidence of his ability to live and act, but rather the reverse. Men do not offer him the care of embassies, as an earlier age did to Petrarch; they would be surprised if he left his study to go forth to battle like Cervantes. We have the swordsman and statesman and penman, but it is not considered that the same mind which can rule the destiny of a poem may as well that of an army or an empire.* Yet surely it should be so. The scientific man may need seclusion from the common affairs of life, for he has his materials before him; but the man of letters must seek them in life, and he who cannot act will but imperfectly appreciate action.

The literary man is impatient at being set apart. He feels that monks and troubadours, though in a similar position, were brought into more healthy connection with man and nature than he who is supposed to look at them merely to write them down. So he rebels; and Sir Walter Scott is prouder of being a good sheriff and farmer than of his reputation as the Great Unknown. Byron piques himself on his skill in shooting and swimming. Sir H. Davy and Schlegel would be admired as dandies, and Goethe, who had received an order from a publisher "for a dozen more dramas in the same style as *Götz von Berlichingen*," and though (in sadder sooth) he had already *Faust* in his head asking to be written out, thought it no degradation to become premier in the little Duchy of Weimar.

"Straws show which way the wind blows," and a comment may be drawn from the popular novels where the literary man is obliged to wash off the ink in a violet bath, attest his courage in the duel, and hide his idealism beneath the vulgar nonchalance and coxcombry of the man of fashion.

If this tendency of his time had some influence in making Goethe find pleasure in tangible power and decided relations with society, there were other causes which worked deeper. The growth of genius in its relations to men around must always be attended with daily pain. The enchanted eye turns from the far-off star it has detected to the shortsighted bystander, and the seer is mocked for pretending to see what others cannot. The large and

---

* Except in "la belle France."—M. F.

generalizing mind infers the whole from a single circumstance, and is reproved by all around for its presumptuous judgment. Its Ithuriel temper pierces shams, creeds, covenants, and chases the phantoms which others embrace, till the lovers of the false Florimels hurl the true knight to the ground. Little men are indignant that Hercules, yet an infant, declares he has strangled the serpent; they demand a proof; they send him out into scenes of labor to bring thence the voucher that his father is a god. What the ancients meant to express by Apollo's continual disappointment in his loves is felt daily in the youth of genius. The sympathy he seeks flies his touch, the objects of his affection sneer at his sublime credulity, his self-reliance is arrogance, his farsightedness infatuation, and his ready detection of fallacy fickleness and inconsistency. Such is the youth of genius, before the soul has given that sign of itself which an unbelieving generation cannot controvert. Even then he is little benefited by the transformation of the mockers into worshipers. For the soul seeks not adorers but peers; not blind worship but intelligent sympathy. The best consolation even then is that which Goethe puts into the mouth of Tasso: "To me gave a God to tell what I suffer." In *Tasso* Goethe has described the position of the poetical mind in its prose relations with equal depth and fullness. We see what he felt must be the result of entire abandonment to the highest nature. We see why he valued himself on being able to understand the Alphonsos, and meet as an equal the Antonios of everyday life.

But, you say, there is no likeness between Goethe and Tasso. Never believe it; such pictures are not painted from observation merely. That deep coloring which fills them with light and life is given by dipping the brush in one's own lifeblood. Goethe had not from nature that character of self-reliance and self-control in which he so long appeared to the world. It was wholly acquired, and so highly valued because he was conscious of the opposite tendency. He was by nature as impetuous though not as tender as Tasso, and the disadvantage at which this constantly placed him was keenly felt by a mind made to appreciate the subtlest harmonies in all relations. Therefore was it that when he at last cast anchor, he was so reluctant again to trust himself to wave and breeze.

I have before spoken of the antagonistic influences under which he was educated. He was driven from the severity of study into the world and then again drawn back many times in the course of his crowded youth. Both the world and the study he used with unceasing ardor, but not with the sweetness of a peaceful hope. Most of the traits which are considered to mark his character at a later period were wanting to him in youth. He was very social, and continually perturbed by his social sympathies. He was deficient both in outward self-possession and mental self-trust. "I was always," he says, "either *too volatile or too infatuated,* so that those who looked kindly on me did by no means always honor me with their esteem." He wrote much and with great freedom. The pen came naturally to his hand, but he had no confidence in the merit of what he wrote, and persons much inferior to Merck and Herder might have induced him to throw aside as worthless what it had given him sincere pleasure to compose. It was hard for him to isolate himself, to console himself, and though his mind was always busy with important thoughts, they did not free him from the pressure of other minds. His youth was as sympathetic and impetuous as any on record.

The effect of all this outward pressure on the poet is recorded in *Werther* —a production that he afterward undervalued, and to which he even felt positive aversion. It was natural that this should be. In the calm air of the cultivated plain he attained, the remembrance of the miasma of sentimentality was odious to him. Yet sentimentality is but sentiment diseased, which to be cured must be patiently observed by the wise physician; so are the morbid desire and despair of Werther, the sickness of a soul aspiring to a purer, freer state, but mistaking the way.

The best or the worst occasion in man's life is precisely that misused in Werther, when he longs for more love, more freedom, and a larger development of genius than the limitations of this terrene sphere permit. Sad is it indeed if persisting to grasp too much at once, he lose all as Werther did. He must accept limitation, must consent to do his work in time, must let his affections be baffled by the barriers of convention. Tantalus-like, he makes this world a Tartarus, or, like Hercules, rises in fires to heaven, according as he knows how to interpret his lot. But he must only use, not adopt it. The boundaries of the man must never be confounded with the destiny of the soul. If he does not decline his destiny as Werther did, it is his honor to have felt its unfitness for his eternal scope. He was born for wings; he is held to walk in leading-strings; nothing lower than faith must make him resigned, and only in hope should he find content—a hope not of some slight improvement in his own condition or that of other men, but a hope justified by the divine justice which is bound in due time to satisfy every want of his nature.

Schiller's great command is, "Keep true to the dream of thy youth." The great problem is how to make the dream real, through the exercise of the waking will.

This was not exactly the problem Goethe tried to solve. To *do* somewhat became too important, as is indicated both by the second motto to this essay and by his maxim, "It is not the knowledge of what *might be* but what *is*, that forms us."

Werther, like his early essays now republished from the Frankfort *Journal*, is characterized by a fervid eloquence of Italian glow, which betrays a part of his character almost lost sight of in the quiet transparency of his later productions, and may give us some idea of the mental conflicts through which he passed to manhood.

The acting out the mystery into life, the calmness of survey, and the passionateness of feeling, above all the ironical baffling at the end, and want of point to a tale got up with such an eye to effect as he goes along, mark well the man that was to be. Even so did he demand in *Werther;* even so resolutely open the door in the first part of *Faust;* even so seem to play with himself and his contemporaries in the second part of *Faust* and *Wilhelm Meister*.

Yet was he deeply earnest in his play, not for men but for himself. To himself as a part of nature it was important to grow, to lift his head to the light. In nature he had all confidence; for man as a part of nature, infinite hope; but in him as an individual will, seemingly not much trust at the earliest age.

The history of his intimacies marks his course; they were entered into with passionate eagerness, but always ended in an observation of the intellect, and he left them on his road, as the snake leaves his skin. The first man he met of sufficient force to command a large share of his attention was Herder, and the benefit of this intercourse was critical not genial. Of the good Lavater he soon perceived the weakness. Merck, again, commanded his respect; but the force of Merck also was cold.

But in the Grand Duke of Weimar he seems to have met a character strong enough to exercise a decisive influence upon his own. Goethe was not so politic and worldly that a little man could ever have become his Maecenas. In the Duchess Amelia and her son he found that practical sagacity, large knowledge of things as they are, active force, and genial feeling which he had never before seen combined.

The wise mind of the Duchess gave the first impulse to the noble course of Weimar. But that her son should have availed himself of the foundation she laid is praise enough, in a world where there is such a rebound from parental influence that it generally seems that the child makes use of the directions given by the parent only to avoid the prescribed path. The Duke availed himself of guidance, though with a perfect independence in action. The Duchess had the unusual wisdom to know the right time for giving up the reins, and thus maintained her authority as far as the weight of her character was calculated to give it.

Of her Goethe was thinking when he wrote, "The admirable woman is she who, if the husband dies, can be a father to the children."

The Duke seems to have been one of those characters which are best known by the impression their personal presence makes on us, resembling an elemental and pervasive force rather than wearing the features of an individuality. Goethe describes him as *"Dämonische,"* that is, gifted with an instinctive, spontaneous force which at once, without calculation or foresight, chooses the right means to an end. As these beings do not calculate, so is their influence incalculable. Their repose has as much influence over other beings as their action, even as the thundercloud lying black and distant in the summer sky is not less imposing than when it bursts and gives forth its quick lightnings. Such men were Mirabeau and Swift. They had also distinct talents, but their influence was from a perception in the minds of men of this spontaneous energy in their natures. Sometimes, though rarely, we see such a man in an obscure position; circumstances have not led him to a large sphere; he may not have expressed in words a single thought worth recording; but by his eye and voice he rules all around him.

He stands upon his feet with a firmness and calm security which make other men seem to halt and totter in their gait. In his deep eye is seen an infinite comprehension, an infinite reserve of power. No accent of his sonorous voice is lost on any ear within hearing; and when he speaks, men hate or fear perhaps the disturbing power they feel, but never dream of disobeying. But hear Goethe himself:

"The boy believed in nature, in the animate and inanimate, the intelligent and unconscious, to discover somewhat which manifested itself only through contradiction, and therefore could not be comprehended by any conception, much less defined by a word. It was not divine, for it seemed without reason; not human, because without understanding; not devilish, because it worked to good; not angelic, because it often betrayed a petulant love of mischief. It was like chance in that it proved no sequence; it suggested the thought of Providence, because it indicated connection. To this all our limitations seem penetrable; it seemed to play at will with all the elements of our being; it compressed time and dilated space. Only in the impossible did it seem to delight, and to cast the possible aside with disdain.

"This existence which seemed to mingle with others, sometimes to separate, sometimes to unite, I called the *Dämonische,* after the example of the ancients, and others who have observed somewhat similar."—*Dichtung und Wahrheit.*

"The *Dämonische* is that which cannot be explained by reason or understanding; it lies not in my nature, but I am subject to it.

"Napoleon was a being of this class, and in so high a degree that scarce anyone is to be compared with him. Also our late Grand Duke was such a nature, full of unlimited power of action and unrest, so that his own dominion was too little for him, and the greatest would have been too little. Demoniac beings of this sort the Greeks reckoned among their demigods."—*Eckermann's Conversations with Goethe.*

This great force of will, this instinctive directness of action, gave the Duke an immediate ascendancy over Goethe which no other person had ever possessed. It was by no means mere sycophancy that made him give up the next ten years, in the prime of his manhood, to accompanying the Grand Duke in his revels, or aiding him in his schemes of practical utility, or to contriving elegant amusements for the ladies of the court. It was a real admiration for the character of the genial man of the world and its environment.

Whoever is turned from his natural path may, if he will, gain in largeness and depth what he loses in simple beauty; and so it was with Goethe. Faust became a wiser if not a nobler being. Werther, who must die because life was not wide enough and rich enough in love for him, ends as the Meister of the *Wanderjahre,* well content to be one never inadequate to the occasion, "help-full, comfort-full."

A great change was during these years perceptible to his friends in the character of Goethe. From being always "either too volatile or infatuated," he retreated into a self-collected state which seemed at first even icy to those around him. No longer he darted about him the lightnings of his genius, but sat Jove-like and calm, with the thunderbolts grasped in his hand and the eagle gathered to his feet. His freakish wit was subdued into a calm and even cold irony; his multiplied relations no longer permitted him to abandon himself to any; the minister and courtier could not expatiate in the free regions of invention and bring upon paper the signs of his higher life, without subjecting himself to an artificial process of isolation. Obliged to economy of time and means, he made of his intimates not objects of devout tenderness, of disinterested care, but the crammers and feeders of his intellect. The world was to him an arena or a studio, but not a temple.

"Ye cannot serve God and Mammon."

Had Goethe entered upon practical life from the dictate of his spirit, which bade him not be a mere author but a living, loving man, then had all been well. But he must also be a man of the world, and nothing can be more unfavorable to true manhood than this ambition. The citizen, the hero, the general, the poet, all these are in true relations; but what is called being a man of the world is to truckle to it, not truly to serve it.

Thus fettered in false relations, detained from retirement upon the center of his being, yet so relieved from the early pressure of his great thoughts as to pity more pious souls for being restless seekers, no wonder that he wrote:

"Es ist dafür gesorgt dass die Bäume nicht in den Himmel wachsen."

("Care is taken that the trees grow not up into the heavens.") Aye, Goethe, but in proportion to their force of aspiration is their height.

Yet never let him be confounded with those who sell all their birthright. He became blind to the more generous virtues, the nobler impulses, but ever in self-respect was busy to develop his nature. He was kind, industrious, wise, gentlemanly if not manly. If his genius lost sight of the highest aim, he is the best instructor in the use of means; ceasing to be a prophet poet, he was still a poetic artist. From this time forward he seems a listener to nature, but not himself the highest product of nature—a priest to the soul of nature. His works grow out of life, but are not instinct with the peculiar life of human resolve as are Shakespeare's or Dante's.

Faust contains the great idea of his life, as indeed there is but one great poetic idea possible to man—the progress of a soul through the various forms of existence.

All his other works, whatever their miraculous beauty of execution, are mere chapters to this poem, illustrative of particular points. *Faust,* had it been completed in the spirit in which it was begun, would have been the *Divina Commedia* of its age.

But nothing can better show the difference of result between a stern and earnest life and one of partial accommodation than a comparison between the "Paradiso" and that of the second part of *Faust.* In both a soul gradually educated and led back to God is received at last not through merit but grace. But oh, the difference between the grandly humble reliance of old Catholicism, and the loophole redemption of modern sagacity! Dante was a *man,* of vehement passions, many prejudices, bitter as much as sweet. His knowledge was scanty, his sphere of observation narrow, the objects of his active life petty, compared with those of Goethe. But constantly retiring to his deepest self, clearsighted to the limitations of man but no less so to the illimitable energy of the soul, the sharpest details in his work convey a larger sense, as his strongest and steadiest flights only direct the eye to heavens yet beyond.

Yet perhaps he had not so hard a battle to wage as this other great poet. The fiercest passions are not so dangerous foes to the soul as the cold skepticism of the understanding. The Jewish demon assailed the man of Uz with physical ills; the Lucifer of the Middle Ages tempted his passions; but the Mephistopheles of the eighteenth century bade the finite strive to compass the infinite, and the intellect attempt to solve all the problems of the soul.

This path Faust had taken: it is that of modern necromancy. Not willing to grow into God by the steady worship of a life, men would enforce his presence by a spell; not willing to learn his existence by the slow processes of their own, they strive to bind it in a word that they may wear it about the neck as a talisman.

Faust, bent upon reaching the center of the universe through the intellect alone, naturally, after a length of trial which has prevented the harmonious unfolding of his nature, falls into despair. He has striven for one object, and that object eludes him. Returning upon himself, he finds large tracts of his nature lying waste and cheerless. He is too noble for apathy, too wise for vulgar content with the animal enjoyments of life. Yet the thirst he has been so many years increasing is not to be borne. Give me, he cries, but a drop of water to cool my burning tongue! Yet in casting himself with a wild recklessness upon the impulses of his nature yet untried, there is a disbelief that anything short of the All can satisfy the immortal spirit. His first attempt was noble though mistaken, and under the saving influence of it he makes the compact whose condition cheats the fiend at last.

> *Kannst du mich schmeichelnd je belügen*
> *Dass ich mir selbst gefallen mag,*
> *Kannst du mich mit Genuss betrügen:*
> *Das sey für mich der letzte Tag.*
>
> *Werd ich zum Augenblicke sagen:*
> *Verweile doch! du bist so schön!*
> *Dann magst du mich in Fesseln schlagen,*
> *Dann will ich gern zu Grunde gehen.*
>
> (Canst thou by falsehood or by flattery
> Make me one moment with myself at peace,
> Cheat me into tranquillity? Come then
> And welcome, life's last day.
> Make me but to the moment say,
> O fly not yet, thou art so fair,
> Then let me perish, etc.)

But this condition is never fulfilled. Faust cannot be content with sensuality, with the charlatanry of ambition, nor with riches. His heart never becomes callous, nor his moral and intellectual perceptions obtuse. He is saved at last.

With the progress of an individual soul is shadowed forth that of the soul of the age; beginning in intellectual skepticism; sinking into license; cheating itself with dreams of perfect bliss, to be at once attained by means no surer than a spurious paper currency; longing itself back from conflict between the spirit and the flesh, induced by Christianity, to the Greek era with its harmonious development of body and mind; striving to re-embody the loved phantom of classical beauty in the heroism of the Middle Ages; flying from the Byronic despair of those who die because they cannot soar without wings, to schemes of practical utility, however narrow—redeemed at last through mercy alone.

The second part of *Faust* is full of meaning, resplendent with beauty; but it is rather an appendix to the first part than a fulfillment of its promise. The world, remembering the powerful stamp of individual feeling, universal indeed in its application but individual in its life, which had conquered all its scruples in the first part, was vexed to find instead of the man Faust, the spirit of the age—discontented with the shadowy manifestation of truths it longed to embrace, and above all disappointed that the author no longer met us face to face, or riveted the ear by his deep tones of grief and resolve.

When the world shall have got rid of the still overpowering influence of the first part, it will be seen that the fundamental idea is never lost sight of in the second. The change is that Goethe, though the same thinker, is no longer the same person.

The continuation of *Faust* in the practical sense of the education of a man is to be found in *Wilhelm Meister*. Here we see the change by strongest contrast. The mainspring of action is no longer the impassioned and noble seeker, but a disciple of circumstance, whose most marked characteristic is a *taste* for virtue and knowledge. Wilhelm certainly prefers these conditions of existence to their opposites, but there is nothing so decided in his character as to prevent his turning a clear eye on every part of that variegated world-scene which the writer wished to place before us.

To see all till he knows all sufficiently to put objects into their relations, then to concentrate his powers and use his knowledge under recognized conditions—such is the progress of man from apprentice to master.

'Tis pity that the volumes of the *Wanderjahre* have not been translated entire, as well as those of the *Lehrjahre*, for many who have read only the latter fancy that Wilhelm becomes a master in that work. Far from it; he has but just become conscious of the higher powers that have ceaselessly been weaving his fate. Far from being as yet a Master, he but now begins to be a Knower. In the *Wanderjahre* we find him gradually learning the duties of citizenship, and hardening into manhood, by applying what he has learned for himself to the education of his child. He converses on equal terms with the wise and beneficent; he is no longer duped and played with for his good, but met directly mind to mind.

Wilhelm is a master when he can command his actions, yet keep his mind always open to new means of knowledge; when he has looked at various ways of living, various forms of religion and of character, till he has learned to be tolerant of all, discerning of good in all; when the astronomer imparts to his equal ear his highest thoughts, and the poor cottager seeks his aid as a patron and counselor.

To be capable of all duties, limited by none, with an open eye, a skillful and ready hand, an assured step, a mind deep, calm, foreseeing without anxiety, hopeful without the aid of illusion—such is the ripe state of manhood. This attained, the great soul should still seek and labor, but strive and battle never more.

The reason for Goethe's choosing so negative a character as Wilhelm and leading him through scenes of vulgarity and low vice would be obvious enough to a person of any depth of thought, even if he himself had not announced it. He thus obtained room to paint life as it really is, and bring forward those slides in the magic lantern which are always known to exist, though they may not be spoken of to ears polite.

Wilhelm cannot abide in tradition nor do as his fathers did before him, merely for the sake of money or a standing in society. The stage, here an emblem of the ideal life as it gleams before unpracticed eyes, offers, he fancies, opportunity for a life of thought as distinguished from one of routine. Here, no longer the simple citizen but Man, all Men, he will rightly take upon himself the different aspects of life, till, poetwise, he shall have learned them all.

No doubt the attraction of the stage to young persons of a vulgar character is merely the brilliancy of its trappings; but to Wilhelm, as to Goethe, it was this poetic freedom and daily suggestion which seemed likely to offer such an agreeable studio in the greenroom.

But the ideal must be rooted in the real, else the poet's life degenerates into buffoonery or vice. Wilhelm finds the characters formed by this would-be ideal existence more despicable than those which grew up on the track, dusty and bustling and dull as it had seemed, of common life. He is prepared by disappointment for a higher ambition.

In the house of the Count he finds genuine elegance, genuine sentiment, but not sustained by wisdom or a devotion to important objects. This love, this life, is also inadequate.

Now with Teresa he sees the blessings of domestic peace. He sees a mind sufficient for itself, finding employment and education in the perfect economy of a little world. The lesson is pertinent to the state of mind in which his former experiences have left him, as indeed our deepest lore is won from reaction. But a sudden change of scene introduces him to the society of the sage and learned uncle, the sage and beneficent Natalia. Here he finds the same virtues as with Teresa, and enlightened by a larger wisdom.

A friend of mine says that his ideal of a friend is a worthy aunt, one who has the tenderness without the blindness of a mother, and takes the same charge of the child's mind as the mother of its body. I don't know but this may have a foundation in truth, though if so aunt-ism, like other grand professions, has sadly degenerated. At any rate Goethe seems to be possessed with a similar feeling. The Count de Thorane, a man of powerful character who made a deep impression on his childhood, was, he says, "reverenced by me as an uncle." And the ideal wise man of this common-life epic stands before us as "The Uncle."

After seeing the working of just views in the establishment of the uncle, learning piety from the confessions of a beautiful soul and religious beneficence from the beautiful life of Natalia, Wilhelm is deemed worthy of admission to the society of the Illuminati, that is, those who have pierced the secret of life, and know what it is to be and to do.

Here he finds the scroll of his life "drawn with large, sharp strokes," that is, these truly wise read his character for him, and "mind and destiny are but two names for one idea."

He now knows enough to enter on the *Wanderjahre*.

Goethe always represents the highest principle in the feminine form. Woman is the Minerva, man the Mars. As in the *Faust* the purity of Gretchen, resisting the demon always, even after all her faults, is announced to have saved her soul to heaven; and in the second part she appears not only redeemed herself, but by her innocence and forgiving tenderness hallowed to redeem the being who had injured her.

So in the *Meister* these women hover around the narrative, each embodying the spirit of the scene. The frail Philina, graceful though contemptible, represents the degradation incident to an attempt at leading an exclusively poetic life. Mignon—gift divine as ever the muse bestowed on the passionate heart of man, with her soft mysterious inspiration, her pining for perpetual youth—represents the high desire that leads to this mistake, as Aurelia, the desire for excitement; Teresa, practical wisdom, gentle tranquillity, which seem most desirable after the Aurelia glare. Of the beautiful soul and Natalia we have already spoken. The former embodies what was suggested to Goethe by the most spiritual person he knew in youth—Mademoiselle von Klettenberg, over whom, as he said, in her invalid loneliness the Holy Ghost brooded like a dove.

Entering on the *Wanderjahre,* Wilhelm becomes acquainted with another woman who seems the complement of all the former, and represents the idea which is to guide and mold him in the realization of all the past experience. This person, long before we see her, is announced in various ways as a ruling power. She is the last hope in cases of difficulty and, though an invalid and living in absolute retirement, is consulted by her connections and acquaintance as an unerring judge in all their affairs.

All things tend towards her as a center; she knows all, governs all, but never goes forth from herself.

Wilhelm at last visits her. He finds her infirm in body, but equal to all she has to do. Charity and counsel to men who need her are her business, astronomy her pleasure.

After a while Wilhelm ascertains from the Astronomer, her companion, what he had before suspected, that she really belongs to the solar system and only appears on earth to give men a feeling of the planetary harmony. From her youth up, says the Astronomer, till she knew me, though all recognized in her an unfolding of the highest moral and intellectual qualities, she was supposed to be sick at her times of clear vision. When her thoughts were not in the heavens, she returned and acted in obedience to them on earth; she was then said to be well.

When the Astronomer had observed her long enough, he confirmed her inward consciousness of a separate existence and peculiar union with the heavenly bodies.

Her picture is painted with many delicate traits, and a gradual preparation leads the reader to acknowledge the truth; but even in the slight indication here given, who does not recognize thee, divine Philosophy, sure as the planetary orbits and inexhaustible as the fountain of light, crowning the faithful Seeker at last with the privilege to possess his own soul?

In all that is said of Macaria * we recognize that no thought is too religious for the mind of Goethe. It was indeed so; you can deny him nothing, but only feel that his works are not instinct and glowing with the central fire, and after catching a glimpse of the highest truth, are forced again to find him too much afraid of losing sight of the limitations of nature to overflow you or himself with the creative spirit.

While the apparition of the celestial Macaria seems to announce the ultimate destiny of the soul of man, the practical application of all Wilhelm has thus painfully acquired is not of pure Delphian strain. Goethe draws, as he passes, a dart from the quiver of Phoebus, but ends as Aesculapius or Mercury. Wilhelm at the school of the Three Reverences thinks out what can be done for man in his temporal relations. He learns to practice moderation and even painful renunciation. The book ends, simply indicating what the course of his life will be, by making him perform an act of kindness with good judgment and at the right moment.

Surely the simple soberness of Goethe should please at least those who style themselves pre-eminently people of common sense.

The following remarks are by the celebrated Rahel von Ense, whose discernment as to his works was highly prized by Goethe.

"*Don Quixote* and *Wilhelm Meister*

"Embrace one another, Cervantes and Goethe!

"Both, using their own clear eyes, vindicated human nature. They saw the champions through their errors and follies, looking down into the deep-

---

* The name of Macaria is one of noblest association. It is that of the daughter of Hercules, who devoted herself a voluntary sacrifice for her country. She was adored by the Greeks as the true Felicity.

est soul, seeing there the true form. *Respectable* people call the Don as well as Meister a fool, wandering hither and thither, transacting no business of real life, bringing nothing to pass, scarce even knowing what he ought to think on any subject, very unfit for the hero of a romance. Yet has our sage known how to paint the good and honest mind in perpetual toil and conflict with the world, as it is embodied; never sharing one moment the impure confusion; always striving to find fault with and improve itself, always so innocent as to see others far better than they are and generally preferring them to itself, learning from all, indulging all except the manifestly base; the more you understand, the more you respect and love this character. Cervantes has painted the knight, Goethe the culture of the entire man—both their own time."

But those who demand from him a lifelong continuance of the early ardor of Faust, who wish to see throughout his works not only such manifold beauty and subtle wisdom but the clear assurance of divinity, the pure white light of Macaria, wish that he had not so variously unfolded his nature, and concentrated it more. They would see him slaying the serpent with the divine wrath of Apollo, rather than taming it to his service like Aesculapius. They wish that he had never gone to Weimar, had never become a universal connoisseur and dilettante in science and courtier as "graceful as a born nobleman," but had endured the burden of life with the suffering crowd and deepened his nature in loneliness and privation, till Faust had conquered rather than cheated the devil, and the music of heavenly faith superseded the grave and mild eloquence of human wisdom.

The expansive genius which moved so gracefully in its self-imposed fetters is constantly surprising us by its content with a choice low in so far as it was not the highest of which the mind was capable. The secret may be found in the second motto of this slight essay:

"He who would do great things must quickly draw together his forces. The master can only show himself such through limitation, and the law alone can give us freedom."

But there is a higher spiritual law always ready to supersede the temporal laws at the call of the human soul. The soul that is too content with usual limitations will never call forth this unusual manifestation.

If there be a tide in the affairs of men which must be taken at the right moment to lead on to fortune, it is the same with inward as with outward life. He who in the crisis hour of youth has stopped short of himself, is not likely to find again what he has missed in one life, for there are a great number of blanks to a prize in each lottery.

But the pang we feel that "those who are so much are not more," seems to promise new spheres, new ages, new crises to enable these beings to complete their circle.

Perhaps Goethe is even now sensible that he should not have stopped at Weimar as his home, but made it one station on the way to Paradise; not stopped at humanity, but regarded it as symbolical of the divine, and given to others to feel more distinctly the center of the universe, as well as the harmony in its parts. It is great to be an Artist, a Master, greater still to be a Seeker till the Man has found all himself.

What Goethe meant by self-collection was a collection of means for work, rather than to divine the deepest truths of being. Thus are these truths always indicated, never declared; and the religious hope awakened by his subtle discernment of the workings of nature never gratified, except through the intellect.

He whose prayer is only work will not leave his treasure in the secret shrine.

One is ashamed when finding any fault with one like Goethe, who is so great. It seems the only criticism should be to do all he omitted to do, and that none who cannot is entitled to say a word. Let that one speak who was all Goethe was not—noble, true, virtuous, but neither wise nor subtle in his generation, a divine ministrant, a baffled man, ruled and imposed on by the pygmies whom he spurned, a heroic artist, a democrat to the tune of Burns:

> The rank is but the guinea's stamp;
> The man's the gowd for a' that.

Hear Beethoven speak of Goethe on an occasion which brought out the two characters in strong contrast:

"Kings and princes can indeed make professors and privy councilors, and hang upon them titles; but great men they cannot make; souls that rise above the mud of the world, these they must let be made by other means than theirs, and should therefore show them respect. When two such as I and Goethe come together, then must great lords observe what is esteemed great by one of us. Coming home yesterday we met the whole imperial family. We saw them coming, and Goethe left me and insisted on standing to one side; let me say what I would, I could not make him come on one step. I pressed my hat upon my head, buttoned my surtout, and passed on through the thickest crowd. Princes and parasites made way; the Arch-duke Rudolph took off his hat; the Empress greeted me first. Their high-nesses KNOW ME. I was well amused to see the crowd pass by Goethe. At the side stood he, hat in hand, low bowed in reverence till all had gone by. Then I scolded him well; I gave no pardon, but reproached him with all his sins, most of all those towards you, dearest Bettina; we had just been talking of you." *

If Beethoven appears in this scene somewhat arrogant and bearish, yet how noble his extreme compared with the opposite! Goethe's friendship with the Grand Duke we respect, for Karl August was a strong man. But we regret to see at the command of any and all members of the ducal family and their connections, who had nothing but rank to recommend them, his time and thoughts, of which he was so chary to private friends. Beethoven could not endure to teach the Archduke Rudolph, who had the soul duly to revere his genius, because he felt it to be *Hofdienst,* court service. He received with perfect nonchalance the homage of the sover-eigns of Europe. Only the Empress of Russia and the Archduke Karl, whom he esteemed as individuals, had power to gratify him by their attentions. Compare with Goethe's obsequious pleasure at being able grace-fully to compliment such high personages, Beethoven's conduct with re-gard to the famous *Heroic Symphony.* This was composed at the sugges-tion of Bernadotte while Napoleon was still in his first glory. He was then the hero of Beethoven's imagination, who hoped from him the liberation of Europe. With delight the great artist expressed in his eternal harmonies the progress of the hero's soul. The symphony was finished, and even dedicated to Bonaparte, when the news came of his declaring himself Emperor of the French. The first act of the indignant artist was to tear

---

* Extract from a letter of Beethoven to Bettina Brentano, Töplitz, 1812.

off his dedication and trample it under foot; nor could he endure again even the mention of Napoleon until the time of his fall.

Admit that Goethe had a natural taste for the trappings of rank and wealth, from which the musician was quite free, yet we cannot doubt that both saw through these externals to man as a nature; there can be no doubt on whose side was the simple greatness, the noble truth. We pardon thee, Goethe—but thee, Beethoven, we revere, for thou hast maintained the worship of the manly, the permanent, the true!

The clear perception which was in Goethe's better nature of the beauty of that steadfastness, of that singleness and simple melody of soul, which he too much sacrificed to become the "many-sided One," is shown most distinctly in his two surpassingly beautiful works, the *Elective Affinities* and *Iphigenia*.

Not *Werther,* not the *Nouvelle Héloïse,* have been assailed with such a storm of indignation as the first-named of these works on the score of gross immorality.

The reason probably is the subject, any discussion of the validity of the marriage vow making society tremble to its foundation; and secondly the cold manner in which it is done. All that is in the book would be bearable to most minds if the writer had had less the air of a spectator, and had larded his work here and there with ejaculations of horror and surprise.

These declarations of sentiment on the part of the author seem to be required by the majority of readers, in order to gain an interpretation of his purpose, as sixthly, seventhly, and eighthly were in an old-fashioned sermon to rouse the audience to a perception of the method made use of by the preacher.

But it has always seemed to me that those who need not such helps to their discriminating faculties, but read a work so thoroughly as to apprehend its whole scope and tendency, rather than hear what the author says it means, will regard the *Elective Affinities* as a work especially what is called moral in its outward effect, and religious even to piety in its spirit. The mental aberrations of the consorts from their plighted faith, though in the one case never indulged, and though in the other no veil of sophistry is cast over the weakness of passion, but all that is felt expressed with the openness of one who desires to legitimate what he feels, are punished by terrible griefs and a fatal catastrophe. Ottilia, that being of exquisite purity, with intellect and character so harmonized in feminine beauty as they never before were found in any portrait of woman painted by the hand of man, perishes on finding she has been breathed on by unhallowed passion, and led to err even by her ignorant wishes against what is held sacred. The only personage whom we do not pity is Edward, for he is the only one who stifles the voice of conscience.

There is indeed a sadness, as of an irresistible fatality, brooding over the whole. It seems as if only a ray of angelic truth could have enabled these men to walk wisely in this twilight, at first so soft and alluring, then deepening into blind horror.

But if no such ray came to prevent their earthly errors, it seems to point heavenward in the saintly sweetness of Ottilia. Her nature, too fair for vice, too finely wrought even for error, comes lonely, intense, and pale, like the evening star on the cold wintry night. It tells of other worlds where the meaning of such strange passages as this must be read to those faithful and pure like her, victims perishing in the green garlands of a spotless youth to atone for the unworthiness of others.

An unspeakable pathos is felt from the minutest trait of this character, and deepens with every new study of it. Not even in Shakespeare have I so felt the organizing power of genius. Through dead words I find the least gestures of this person stamping themselves on my memory, betraying to the heart the secret of her life which she herself, like all these divine beings, knew not. I feel myself familiarized with all beings of her order. I see not only what she was but what she might have been, and live with her in yet untrodden realms.

Here is the glorious privilege of a form known only in the world of genius. There is on it no stain of usage or calculation to dull our sense of its immeasurable life. What in our daily walk mid common faces and common places fleets across us at moments from glances of the eye or tones of the voice is felt from the whole being of one of these children of genius.

This precious gem is set in a ring complete in its enamel. I cannot hope to express my sense of the beauty of this book as a work of art. I would not attempt it if I had elsewhere met any testimony to the same. The perfect picture, always before the mind, of the château, the moss hut, the park, the garden, the lake, with its boat and the landing beneath the platan trees; the gradual manner in which both localities and persons grow upon us, more living than life, inasmuch as we are unconsciously kept at our best temperature by the atmosphere of genius, and thereby more delicate in our perceptions than amid our customary fogs; the gentle unfolding of the central thought as a flower in the morning sun; then the conclusion rising like a cloud, first soft and white but darkening as it comes, till with a sudden wind it bursts above our heads; the ease with which we everywhere find points of view all different, yet all bearing on the same circle, for though we feel every hour new worlds, still before our eye lie the same objects, new yet the same, unchangeable yet always changing their aspects as we proceed, till at last we find we ourselves have traversed the circle, and know all we overlooked at first—these things are worthy of our highest admiration.

For myself, I never felt so completely that very thing which genius should always make us feel—that I was in its circle, and could not get out till its spell was done and its last spirit permitted to depart. I was not carried away, instructed, delighted more than by other works, but I was *there,* living there, whether as the platan tree or the architect or any other observing part of the scene. The personages live too intensely to let us live in them; they draw around themselves circles within the circle; we can only see them close, not be themselves.

Others, it would seem, on closing the book exclaim, "What an immoral book!" I well remember my own thought, "It is a work of art!" At last I understood that world within a world, that ripest fruit of human nature, which is called art. With each perusal of the book my surprise and delight at this wonderful fulfillment of design grew. I understood why Goethe was well content to be called artist, and his works, works of art, rather than revelations. At this moment, remembering what I then felt, I am inclined to class all my negations just written on this paper as stuff, and to look upon myself for thinking them with as much contempt as Mr. Carlyle or Mrs. Austin or Mrs. Jameson might do, to say nothing of the German Goetheans.

Yet that they were not without foundation I feel again when I turn to the *Iphigenia*—a work beyond the possibility of negation; a work where a religious meaning not only pierces but enfolds the whole; a work as admirable in art, still higher in significance, more single in expression.

There is an English translation (I know not how good) of Goethe's *Iphigenia*. But as it may not be generally known, I will give a sketch of the drama. Iphigenia, saved at the moment of the sacrifice made by Agamemnon in behalf of the Greeks by the goddess and transferred to the temple at Tauris, appears alone in the consecrated grove. Many years have passed since she was severed from the home of such a tragic fate, the palace of Mycenae. Troy had fallen, Agamemnon been murdered, Orestes had grown up to avenge his death. All these events were unknown to the exiled Iphigenia. The priestess of Diana in a barbarous land, she had passed the years in the duties of the sanctuary and in acts of beneficence. She had acquired great power over the mind of Thoas, King of Tauris, and used it to protect strangers, whom it had previously been the custom of the country to sacrifice to the goddess.

She salutes us with a soliloquy, of which I give a rude translation:

> Beneath your shade, living summits
> Of this ancient, holy, thick-leaved grove,
> As in the silent sanctuary of the Goddess,
> Still I walk with those same shuddering feelings,
> As when I trod these walks for the first time.
> My spirit cannot accustom itself to these places;
> Many years now has kept me here concealed
> A higher will, to which I am submissive;
> Yet ever am I, as at first, the stranger;
> For ah! the sea divides me from my beloved ones,
> And on the shore whole days I stand,
> Seeking with my soul the land of the Greeks,
> And to my sighs brings the rushing wave only
> Its hollow tones in answer.
> Woe to him who, far from parents and brothers and sisters,
> Drags on a lonely life. Grief consumes
> The nearest happiness away from his lips;
> His thoughts crowd downwards—
> Seeking the hall of his fathers, where the Sun
> First opened heaven to him, and kindred-born
> In their first plays knit daily firmer and firmer
> The bond from heart to heart—I question not the Gods,
> Only the lot of woman is one of sorrow;

In the house and in the war man rules,
Knows how to help himself in foreign lands,
Possessions gladden and victory crowns him,
And an honorable death stands ready to end his days.
Within what narrow limits is bounded the luck of woman!
To obey a rude husband even is duty and comfort; how sad
When instead a hostile fate drives her out of her sphere!
So holds me Thoas, indeed a noble man, fast
In solemn, sacred, but slavish bonds.
O, with shame I confess that with secret reluctance
I serve thee, Goddess, thee, my deliverer.
   My life should freely have been dedicate to thee,
But I have always been hoping in thee, O Diana,
Who didst take in thy soft arms me, the rejected daughter
Of the greatest king! Yes, daughter of Zeus,
I thought if thou gavest such anguish to him, the high hero,
The godlike Agamemnon;
Since he brought his dearest, a victim, to thy altar,
That, when he should return crowned with glory from Ilium,
At the same time thou wouldst give to his arms his other treasures,
His spouse, Electra, and the princely son;
Me also, thou wouldst restore to mine own,
Saving a second time me, whom from death thou didst save,
From this worse death—the life of exile here.

These are the words and thoughts; but how give an idea of the sweet simplicity of expression in the original, where every word has the grace and softness of a flower petal?

She is interrupted by a messenger from the king, who prepares her for a visit from himself of a sort she has dreaded. Thoas, who has always loved her, now left childless by the calamities of war, can no longer resist his desire to reanimate by her presence his desert house. He begins by urging her to tell him the story of her race, which she does in a way that makes us feel as if that most famous tragedy had never before found a voice, so simple, so fresh in its naïveté is the recital.

Thoas urges his suit undismayed by the fate that hangs over the race of Tantalus.

THOAS

Was it the same Tantalus,
Whom Jupiter called to his council and banquets,

In whose talk so deeply experienced, full of various learning,
The Gods delighted as in the speech of oracles?

IPHIGENIA

It is the same, but the Gods should not
Converse with men, as with their equals.
The mortal race is much too weak
Not to turn giddy on unaccustomed heights.
He was not ignoble, neither a traitor,
But for a servant too great, and as a companion
Of the great Thunderer only a man. So was
His fault also that of a man, its penalty
Severe, and poets sing—Presumption
And faithlessness cast him down from the throne of Jove,
Into the anguish of ancient Tartarus;
Ah, and all his race bore their hate.

THOAS

Bore it the blame of the ancestor, or its own?

IPHIGENIA

Truly the vehement breast and powerful life of the Titan
Were the assured inheritance of son and grandchild;
But the Gods bound their brows with a brazen band,
Moderation, counsel, wisdom, and patience
Were hid from their wild, gloomy glance,
Each desire grew to fury,
And limitless ranged their passionate thoughts.

Iphigenia refuses with gentle firmness to give to gratitude what was not due. Thoas leaves her in anger, and to make her feel it, orders that the old barbarous custom be renewed and two strangers just arrived be immolated at Diana's altar.

Iphigenia, though distressed, is not shaken by this piece of tyranny. She trusts her heavenly protectress will find some way for her to save these unfortunates without violating her truth.

The strangers are Orestes and Pylades, sent thither by the oracle of Apollo, who bade them go to Tauris and bring back "The Sister"; thus shall the heaven-ordained parricide of Orestes be expiated, and the Furies cease to pursue him.

The Sister they interpret to be Dian, Apollo's sister; but Iphigenia, sister to Orestes, is really meant.

The next act contains scenes of most delicate workmanship, first between the light-hearted Pylades, full of worldly resources and ready tenderness, and the suffering Orestes, of far nobler, indeed heroic nature, but less fit for the day and more for the ages. In the first scene the characters of both are brought out with great skill, and the nature of the bond between "the butterfly and the dark flower" distinctly shown in few words.

The next scene is between Iphigenia and Pylades. Pylades, though he truly answers the questions of the priestess about the fate of Troy and the house of Agamemnon, does not hesitate to conceal from her who Orestes really is, and manufactures a tissue of useless falsehoods with the same readiness that the wise Ulysses showed in exercising his ingenuity on similar occasions.

It is said, I know not how truly, that the modern Greeks are Ulyssean in this respect, never telling straightforward truth when deceit will answer the purpose; and if they tell any truth, practicing the economy of the King of Ithaca in always reserving a part for their own use. The character which this denotes is admirably hit off with few strokes in Pylades, the fair side of whom Iphigenia thus paints in a later scene:

> Bless, ye Gods, our Pylades,
> And whatever he may undertake;
> He is the arm of the youth in battle,
> The light-giving eye of the aged man in the council.
> For his soul is still; it preserves
> The holy possession of Repose unexhausted,
> And from its depths still reaches
> Help and advice to those tossed to and fro.

Iphigenia leaves him in sudden agitation when informed of the death of Agamemnon. Returning, she finds in his place Orestes, whom she had not before seen, and draws from him by her artless questions the sequel to this terrible drama wrought by his hand. After he has concluded his narrative, in the deep tones of cold anguish, she cries:

> Immortals, you who through your bright days
> Live in bliss, throned on clouds ever renewed,
> Only for this have you all these years

Kept me separate from men, and so near yourselves,
Given me the childlike employment to cherish the fires on your altars,
That my soul might, in like pious clearness,
Be ever aspiring towards your abodes,
That only later and deeper I might feel
The anguish and horror that have darkened my house.
                              O Stranger,
Speak to me of the unhappy one, tell me of Orestes.

ORESTES

             Oh, might I speak of his death!
Vehement flew up from the reeking blood
His mother's soul!
And called to the ancient daughters of Night,
Let not the parricide escape;
Pursue that man of crime; he is yours!
They obey, their hollow eyes
Darting about with vulture eagerness;
They stir themselves in their black dens,
From corners their companions
Doubt and Remorse steal out to join them:
Before them roll the mists of Acheron;
In its cloudy volumes rolls
The eternal contemplation of the irrevocable.
Permitted now in their love of ruin they tread
The beautiful fields of a God-planted earth,
From which they had long been banished by an early curse,
Their swift feet follow the fugitive,
They pause never except to gather more power to dismay.

IPHIGENIA

Unhappy man, thou art in like manner tortured,
And feelest truly what he, the poor fugitive, suffers!

ORESTES

What sayest thou? What meanest by "like manner"?

IPHIGENIA

Thee, too, the weight of a fratricide crushes to earth; the tale
I had from thy younger brother.

ORESTES

I cannot suffer that thou, great soul,
Shouldst be deceived by a false tale;

A web of lies let stranger weave for stranger
Subtle with many thoughts, accustomed to craft,
Guarding his feet against a trap.
                              But between us
Be Truth—
I am Orestes—and this guilty head
Bent downward to the grave seeks death;
In any shape were he welcome.
Whoever thou art, I wish thou mightst be saved,
Thou and my friend; for myself I wish it not.
Thou seemst against thy will here to remain;
Invent a way to fly and leave me here.

Like all pure productions of genius this may be injured by the slightest
change, and I dare not flatter myself that the English words give an idea
of the heroic dignity expressed in the cadence of the original, by the words:

Zwischen uns
Sey Wahrheit!
Ich bin Orest!

where the Greek seems to fold his robe around him in the full strength
of classic manhood, prepared for worst and best, not like a cold stoic but
a hero who can feel all, know all, and endure all. The name of two syllables
in the German is much more forcible for the pause than the three-syllable
Orestes.

Between us
Be Truth,

is fine to my ear, on which our word truth also pauses with a large dignity.

The scenes go on more and more full of breathing beauty. The lovely
joy of Iphigenia, the meditative softness with which the religiously educated mind perpetually draws the inference from the most agitating events,
inpress us more and more. At last the hour of trial comes. She is to keep
off Thoas by a cunningly devised tale, while her brother and Pylades con-
trive their escape. Orestes has received to his heart the sister long lost,
divinely restored, and in the embrace the curse falls from him, he is well,
and Pylades more than happy. The ship waits to carry her to the palace
home she is to free from a century's weight of pollution; and already the
blue heavens of her adored Greece gleam before her fancy.

But, oh, the step before all this can be obtained—to deceive Thoas, a savage and a tyrant indeed, but long her protector—in his barbarous fashion, her benefactor! How can she buy life, happiness, or even the safety of those dear ones at such a price?

Woe,

O Woe upon the lie! It frees not the breast,
Like the true-spoken word; it comforts not, but tortures
Him who devised it, and returns,
An arrow once let fly, God-repelled, back,
On the bosom of the Archer!

O, must I then resign the silent hope
Which gave a beauty to my loneliness?
Must the curse dwell forever, and our race
Never be raised to life by a new blessing?
All things decay, the fairest bliss is transient,
The powers most full of life grow faint at last;
And shall a curse alone boast an incessant life?

Then have I idly hoped that here kept pure,
So strangely severed from my kindred's lot,
I was designed to come at the right moment,
And with pure hand and heart to expiate
The many sins that stain my native home.
To lie, to steal the sacred image!
Olympians, let not these vulture talons
Seize on the tender breast. O, save me,
And save your image in my soul!

Within my ears resounds the ancient lay—
I had forgotten it, and would so gladly—
The lay of the Parcae, which they awful sung;
As Tantalus fell from his golden seat
They suffered with the noble friend. Wrathful
Was their heart, and fearful was the song.
In our childhood the nurse was wont to sing it
To me, and my brother and sister. I marked it well.

Then follows the sublime song of the Parcae, well known through translations.

But Iphigenia is not a victim of fate, for she listens steadfastly to the god in her breast. Her lips are incapable of subterfuge. She obeys her own heart, tells all to the king, calls up his better nature, wins, hallows, and purifies all around her, till the heaven-prepared way is cleared by the obedient child of heaven, and the great trespass of Tantalus canceled by a woman's reliance on the voice of her innocent soul.

If it be not possible to enhance the beauty with which such ideal figures as the Iphigenia and the Antigone appeared to the Greek mind, yet Goethe has unfolded a part of the life of this being, unknown elsewhere in the records of literature. The character of the priestess, the full beauty of virgin womanhood, solitary but tender, wise and innocent, sensitive and self-collected, sweet as spring, dignified as becomes the chosen servant of God, each gesture and word of deep and delicate significance—where else is such a picture to be found?

It was not the courtier, nor the man of the world, nor the connoisseur, nor the friend of Mephistopheles, nor Wilhelm the Master, nor Egmont the generous, free liver, that saw Iphigenia in the world of spirits, but Goethe in his first-born glory; Goethe, the poet; Goethe, designed to be the brightest star in a new constellation. Let us not in surveying his works and life abide with him too much in the suburbs and outskirts of himself. Let us enter into his higher tendency, thank him for such angels as Iphigenia, whose simple truth mocks at all his wise *Beschränkungen,* and hope the hour when girt about with many such, he will confess, contrary to his opinion given in his latest days, that it *is* well worth while to live seventy years, if only to find that they are nothing in the sight of God.

5

THE TWO HERBERTS *

The following sketch is meant merely to mark some prominent features in the minds of the two Herberts, under a form less elaborate and more reverent than that of criticism.

A mind of penetrating and creative power could not find a better subject for a masterly picture. The two figures stand as representatives of natural religion and of that of the Son of Man, of the life of the philosophical man of the world and the secluded, contemplative though beneficent existence.

The present slight effort is not made with a view to the great and dramatic results so possible to the plan. It is intended chiefly as a setting to the Latin poems of Lord Herbert, which are known to few—a year ago, seemingly, were so to none in this part of the world. The only desire in translating them has been to do so literally, as any paraphrase or addition of words impairs their profound meaning. It is hoped that even in their present repulsive garb without rhyme or rhythm, stripped too of the majestic Roman mantle, the greatness of the thoughts and the large lines of spiritual experience will attract readers, who will not find time misspent in reading them many times.

George Herbert's heavenly strain is better though far from generally known.

There has been no attempt really to represent these persons speaking their own dialect or in their own individual manners. The writer loves too well to hope to imitate the sprightly, fresh, and varied style of Lord Herbert or the quaintness and keen sweets of his brother's. Neither have accessories been given, such as might easily have been taken from their works. But the thoughts imputed to them they might have spoken, only in better and more concise terms, and the facts are facts. So let this be gently received with the rest of the modern tapestries. We can no longer weave them of the precious materials princes once furnished, but we can give, in our way, some notion of the original design.

---

* From *Papers on Literature and Art,* 1846.

It was an afternoon of one of the longest summer days. The sun had showered down his amplest bounties, the earth put on her richest garment to receive them. The clear heavens seemed to open themselves to the desire of mortals; the day had been long enough and bright enough to satisfy an immortal.

In a green lane leading from the town of Salisbury in England, the noble stranger was reclining beneath a tree. His eye was bent in the direction of the town, as if upon some figure approaching or receding; but its inward turned expression showed that he was in fact no longer looking, but lost in thought.

"Happiness!" thus said his musing mind. "It would seem at such hours and in such places as if it not merely hovered over the earth, a poetic presence to animate our pulses and give us courage for what must be, but sometimes alighted. Such fullness of expression pervades these fields, these trees, that it excites not rapture but a blissful sense of peace. Yet even were this permanent in the secluded lot, would I accept it in exchange for the bitter sweet of a wider, freer life? I could not if I would; yet methinks I would not if I could. But here comes George; I will argue the point with him."

He rose from his seat and went forward to meet his brother, who at this moment entered the lane.

The two forms were faithful expressions of their several lives. There was a family likeness between them, for they shared in that beauty of the noble English blood of which in these days few types remain: the Norman tempered by the Saxon, the fire of conquest by integrity and a self-contained, inflexible habit of mind. In the times of the Sydneys and Russells, the English body was a strong and nobly proportioned vase, in which shone a steady and powerful if not brilliant light.

The chains of convention, an external life grown out of proportion with that of the heart and mind, have destroyed for the most part this dignified beauty. There is no longer in fact an aristocracy in England, because the saplings are too puny to represent the old oak. But that it once existed and did stand for what is best in that nation, any collection of portraits from the sixteenth century will show.

The two men who now met had character enough to exhibit in their persons not only the stock from which they sprang, but what was special in themselves harmonized with it. There were ten years betwixt them, but the younger verged on middle age; and permanent habits as well as tendencies of character were stamped upon their persons.

Lord Edward Herbert was one of the handsomest men of his day, of a beauty alike stately, chivalric, and intellectual. His person and features were cultivated by all the disciplines of a time when courtly graces were not insignificant because a monarch mind informed the court, nor warlike customs rude or mechanical, for individual nature had free play in the field except as restrained by the laws of courtesy and honor. The steel glove became his hand, and the spur his heel; neither can we fancy him out of his place, for any place he would have made his own. But all this grace and dignity of the man of the world was in him subordinated to that of the man, for in his eye and in the brooding sense of all his countenance was felt the life of one who, while he deemed that his present honor lay in playing well the part assigned him by destiny, never forgot that it was but a part, and fed steadily his forces on that within that passes show.

It has been said with a deep wisdom that the figure we most need to see before us now is not that of a saint, martyr, sage, poet, artist, preacher, or any other whose vocation leads to a seclusion and partial use of faculty, but a "spiritual man of the world," able to comprehend all things, exclusively dedicated to none. Of this idea we need a new expression peculiarly adapted to our time; but in the past it will be difficult to find one more adequate than the life and person of Lord Herbert.

George Herbert, like his elder brother, was tall, erect, and with the noble air of one sprung from a race whose spirit has never been broken or bartered; but his thin form contrasted with the full development which generous living, various exercise, and habits of enjoyment had given his brother. Nor had his features that range and depth of expression which tell of many-colored experiences and passions undergone or vanquished. The depth, for there was depth, was of feeling rather than experience. A penetrating sweetness beamed from him on the observer, who was rather raised and softened in himself than drawn to think of the being who infused this heavenly fire into his veins. Like the violet, the strong and subtle odor of his mind was arrayed at its source with such an air of meekness that the receiver blessed rather the liberal winds of heaven than any earthborn flower for the gift.

Raphael has lifted the transfigured Savior only a little way from the ground; but in the forms and expression of the feet you see that though they may walk there again, they would tread far more naturally a more delicate element. This buoyant lightness, which by seeking seems to tread the air, is indicated by the text: "Beautiful upon the mountains are the feet of those who come with glad tidings." And such thoughts were suggested by the gait and gesture of George Herbert, especially as he approached you. Through the faces of most men, even of geniuses, the soul shines as through a mask or at best a crystal; we look behind a shield for the heart. But with those of seraphic nature or so filled with spirit that translation may be near, it seems to hover before or around, announcing or enfolding them like a luminous atmosphere. Such a one advances like a vision, and the eye must steady itself before a spiritual light, to recognize him as a reality.

Some such emotion was felt by Lord Herbert as he looked on his brother, who for a moment or two approached without observing him, but absorbed and radiant in his own happy thoughts. They had not met for long, and it seemed that George had grown from an uncertain boy, often blushing and shrinking either from himself or others, into an angelic clearness such as the noble seeker had not elsewhere found.

But when he was seen, the embrace was eager and affectionate as that of the brother and the child.

"Let us not return at once," said Lord Herbert. "I had already waited for you long, and have seen all the beauties of the parsonage and church."

"Not many, I think, in the eyes of such a critic," said George, as they seated themselves in the spot his brother had before chosen for the extent and loveliness of prospect.

"Enough to make me envious of you, if I had not early seen enough to be envious of none. Indeed I know not if such a feeling can gain admittance to your little paradise, for I never heard such love and reverence expressed as by your people for you."

George looked upon his brother with a pleased and open sweetness. Lord

Herbert continued, with a little hesitation: "To tell the truth, I wondered a little at the boundless affection they declared. Our mother has long and often told me of your pure and beneficent life, and I know what you have done for this place and people, but as I remember, you were of a choleric temper."

"And am so still!"

"Well, and do you not sometimes by flashes of that lose all you may have gained?"

"It does not often now," he replied, "find open way. My Master has been very good to me in suggestions of restraining prayer, which come into my mind at the hour of temptation."

Lord H. Why do you not say rather that your own discerning and maturer mind will show you more and more the folly and wrong of such outbreaks?

George H. Because that would not be saying all that I think. At such times I feel a higher power interposed, as much as I see that yonder tree is distinct from myself. Shall I repeat to you some poor verses in which I have told by means of various likenesses, in an imperfect fashion, how it is with me in this matter?

Lord H. Do so! I shall hear them gladly; for I, like you, though with less time and learning to perfect it, love the deliberate composition of the closet, and believe we can better understand one another by thoughts expressed so, than in the more glowing but hasty words of the moment.

George H.

> Prayer—the church's banquet; angel's age;
>   God's breath in man returning to his birth;
> The soul in paraphrase; heart in pilgrimage;
>   The Christian plummet, sounding heaven and earth.
>
> Engine against th' Almighty; sinner's tower;
>   Reversed thunder; Christ's side-piercing spear;
> The six-days' world transposing in an hour;
>   A kind of tune, which all things hear and fear.
>
> Softness, and peace, and joy, and love, and bliss;
>   Exalted manna; gladness of the best;
> Heaven in ordinary; man well drest;
>   The milky way; the bird of paradise;

Church bells beyond the stars heard; the soul's blood;
The land of spices; something understood.

Lord H. (*who has listened attentively, after a moment's thought*) There
is something in the spirit of your lines which pleases me, and in general
I know not that I should differ; yet you have expressed yourself nearest
to mine own knowledge and feeling where you have left more room to
consider our prayers as aspirations rather than the gifts of grace; as—

"Heart in pilgrimage";
"A kind of tune, which all things hear and fear."
"Something understood."

In your likenesses you sometimes appear to quibble in a way unworthy
the subject.

George H. It is the nature of some minds, brother, to play with what
they love best. Yours is of a grander and severer cast; it can only grasp
and survey steadily what interests it. My walk is different, and I have
always admired you in yours without expecting to keep pace with you.

Lord H. I hear your sweet words with the more pleasure, George, that
I had supposed you were now too much of the churchman to value the
fruits of my thought.

George H. God forbid that I should ever cease to reverence the mind
that was to my own so truly that of an elder brother! I do lament that you
will not accept the banner of my Master, and drink at what I have found
the fountain of pure wisdom. But as I would not blot from the book of
life and prophets and priests that came before Him, nor those antique
sages who knew all

That Reason hath from Nature borrowed,
Or of itself, like a good housewife spun,
In laws and policy: what the stars conspire:
What willing Nature speaks; what, freed by fire:
Both th' old discoveries, and the new found seas:
The stock and surplus, cause and history;

as I cannot resign and disparage these because they have not what I conceive to be the pearl of all knowledge, how could I you?

Lord H. You speak wisely, George, and, let me add, religiously. Were
all churchmen as tolerant, I had never assailed the basis of their belief. Did

they not insist and urge upon us their way as the one only way, not for them alone but for all, none would wish to put stumbling-blocks before their feet.

George H. Nay, my brother, do not misunderstand me. None more than I can think there is but one way to arrive finally at truth.

Lord H. I do not misunderstand you; but feeling that you are one who accepts what you do from love of the best and not from fear of the worst, I am as much inclined to tolerate your conclusions as you to tolerate mine.

George H. I do not consider yours as conclusions, but only as steps to such. The progress of the mind should be from natural to revealed religion, as there must be a sky for the sun to give light through its expanse.

Lord H. The sky is—nothing!

George H. Except room for a sun, and such there is in you. Of your own need of such, did you not give convincing proof, when you prayed for a revelation to direct whether you should publish a book against revelation? *

Lord H. You borrow that objection from the crowd, George, but I wonder you have not looked into the matter more deeply. Is there anything inconsistent with disbelief in a partial plan of salvation for the nations,

---

* The following narration, published by Lord Herbert in his life, has often been made use of by his opponents. It should be respected as an evidence of his integrity, being like the rest of his memoir a specimen of absolute truth and frankness towards himself and all other beings:

Having many conscientious doubts whether or no to publish his book, *De Veritate* (which was against revealed religion, on the ground that it was improbable that Heaven should deal partially with men, revealing its will to one race and nation, not to another), "Being thus doubtful in my chamber, one fair day in the summer, my casement being opened to the south, the sun shining clear and no wind stirring, I took my book, *De Veritate,* in my hand, and kneeling on my knees, devoutly said these words: O thou eternal God, author of the light which now shines upon me, and giver of all inward illuminations, I do beseech thee, of thy infinite goodness, to pardon a greater request than a sinner ought to make. I am not satisfied enough whether I shall publish this book, *De Veritate.* If it be for thy glory, I beseech thee give me some sign from heaven; if not, I shall suppress it.—I had no sooner spoken these words, but a loud, though yet gentle noise came from the heavens (for it was like nothing on earth) which did so comfort and cheer me, that I took my petition as granted, and that I had the sign I demanded, whereupon, also, I resolved to print my book. This, how strange soever it may seem, I protest before the Eternal God, is true; neither am I any way superstitiously deceived herein, since I did not only clearly hear the noise, but in the serenest sky that ever I saw, being without all cloud, did, to my thinking, see the place from whence it came."

Lord Orford observes, with his natural sneer, "How could a man who doubted of *partial,* believe *individual revelation?*"

which by its necessarily limited working excludes the majority of men up to our day, with belief that each individual soul, wherever born, however nurtured, may receive immediate response, in an earnest hour from the source of truth?

George H. But you believed the customary order of nature to be deranged in your behalf. What miraculous record does more?

Lord H. It was at the expense of none other. A spirit asked, a spirit answered, and its voice was thunder; but in this there was nothing special, nothing partial wrought in my behalf, more than if I had arrived at the same conclusion by a process of reasoning.

George H. I cannot but think that if your mind were allowed by the nature of your life its free force to search, it would survey the subject in a different way, and draw inferences more legitimate from a comparison of its own experience with the gospel.

Lord H. My brother does not think the mind is free to act in courts and camps. To me it seems that the mind takes its own course everywhere, and that if men cannot have outward, they can always mental seclusion. None is so profoundly lonely, none so in need of constant self-support as he who, living in the crowd, thinks an inch aside from or in advance of it. The hermitage of such an one is still and cold; its silence unbroken to a degree of which these beautiful and fragrant solitudes give no hint. These sunny sights and sounds, promoting reverie rather than thought, are scarce more favorable to a great advance in the intellect than the distractions of the busy street. Besides we need the assaults of other minds to quicken our powers, so easily hushed to sleep, and call it peace. The mind takes a bias too easily, and does not examine whether from tradition or a native growth intended by the heavens.

George H. But you are no common man. You shine, you charm, you win, and the world presses too eagerly on you to leave many hours for meditation.

Lord H. It is a common error to believe that the most prosperous men love the world best. It may be hardest for them to leave it, because they have been made effeminate and slothful by want of that exercise which difficulty brings. But this is not the case with me; for while the common boons of life's game have been too easily attained to hold high value in my eyes, the goal which my secret mind from earliest infancy prescribed has been high enough to task all my energies. Every year has helped to make that and that alone of value in my eyes; and did I believe that life in scenes like this would lead me to it more speedily than in my accustomed broader way, I would seek it tomorrow—nay, today. But is it worthy of a man to make him a cell in which alone he can worship? Give me rather the always open temple of the universe! To me it seems that the only course for a man is that pointed out by birth and fortune. Let him take that and pursue it with clear eyes and head erect, secure that it must point at last to those truths which are central to us wherever we stand; and if my road leading through the busy crowd of men, amid the clang and bustle of conflicting interests and passions, detain me longer than would the still path through the groves, the chosen haunt of contemplation, yet I incline to think that progress so, though slower, is surer. Owing no safety, no clearness to my position, but so far as it is attained to mine own effort, encountering what temptations, doubts, and lures may beset a man, what I do possess is more surely mine and less a prey to contingencies. It is a well-tempered wine that has been carried over many seas and escaped many shipwrecks.

George H. I can the less gainsay you, my lord and brother, that your course would have been mine could I have chosen.

Lord H. Yes; I remember thy verse:

> Whereas my birth and spirits rather took
> The way that takes the town;
> Thou didst betray me to a lingering book,
> And wrap me in a gown.

It was not my fault, George, that it so chanced.

George H. I have long learnt to feel that it noway chanced; that thus and no other was it well for me. But how I view these matters you are or may be well aware through a little book I have writ. Of you I would fain learn more than can be shown me by the display of your skill in controversy in your printed works, or the rumors of your feats at arms or success with the circles of fair ladies which reach even this quiet nook. Rather let us in this hour of intimate converse, such as we have not had for years and may not have again, draw near in what is nearest; and do you, my dear lord, vouchsafe your friend and brother some clear tokens as to that goal you say has from childhood been mentally prescribed you, and the way you have taken to gain it.

Lord H. I will do this willingly, and the rather that I have with me a leaf in which I have lately recorded what appeared to me in glimpse or flash in my young years, and now shines upon my life with steady ray. I brought it with some thought that I might impart it to you, which confidence I have not shown to any yet; though if as I purpose some memoir of my life and times should fall from my pen, these poems may be interwoven there as cause and comment for all I felt and knew and was. The first contains my thought of the beginning and progress of life:

(From the Latin of Lord Herbert)

LIFE

First, the life stirred within the genial seed,
Seeking its properties, whence plastic power
Was born. Chaos, with lively juice pervading,
External form in its recess restraining,
While the conspiring causes might accede,
And full creation safely be essayed.

Next, movement was in the maternal field;
Fermenting spirit puts on tender limbs,
And, earnest, now prepares, of wondrous fabric,
The powers of sense, a dwelling not too mean for mind contriving
That, sliding from its heaven, it may put on
These faculties, and, prophesying future fate,
Correct the slothful weight (of matter) nor uselessly be manifested.

A third stage, now, scene truly great contains
The solemn feast of heaven, the theatre of earth,
Kindred and species, varied forms of things
Are here discerned—and, from its own impulse,
It is permitted to the soul to circle,
Hither and thither rove, that it may see
Laws and eternal covenants of its world,
And stars returning in assiduous course,
The causes and the bonds of life to learn,
And from afar foresee the highest will.
How he to admirable harmony
Tempers the various motions of the world,

And Father, Lord, Guardian, and Builder-up,
And Deity on every side is styled.
Next, from this knowledge the fourth stage proceeds:
Cleansing away its stains, mind daily grows more pure,
Enriched with various learning, strong in virtue,
Extends its powers, and breathes sublimer air:
A secret spur is felt within the inmost heart,
That he who will, may emerge from this perishable state,
And a happier is sought
By ambitious rites, consecrations, religious worship,
And a new hope succeeds, conscious of a better fate,
Clinging to things above, expanding through all the heavens,
And the Divine descends to meet a holy love,
And unequivocal token is given of celestial life.
That, as a good servant, I shall receive my reward;
Or, if worthy, enter as a son, into the goods of my father,
God himself is my surety. When I shall put off this life,
Confident in a better, free in my own will,
He himself is my surety, that a fifth, yet higher state shall ensue,
And a sixth, and all, in fine, that my heart shall know how to ask.

CONJECTURES CONCERNING THE HEAVENLY LIFE

Purified in my whole genius, I congratulate myself
Secure of fate, while neither am I downcast by any terrors,
Nor store up secret griefs in my heart,
But pass my days cheerfully in the midst of mishaps,
Despite the evils which engird the earth,
Seeking the way above the stars with ardent virtue.
I have received, beforehand, the first fruits of heavenly life—
I now seek the later, sustained by divine love,
Through which, conquering at once the scoffs of a gloomy destiny,
I leave the barbarous company of a frantic age,
Breathing out for the last time the infernal air—breathing in the supernal,
I enfold myself wholly in these sacred flames,
And, sustained by them, ascend the highest dome,
And far and wide survey the wonders of a new sphere,
And see well-known spirits, now beautiful in their proper light,
And the choirs of the higher powers, and blessed beings
With whom I desire to mingle fires and sacred bonds—
Passing from joy to joy the heaven of all,
What has been given to ourselves, or sanctioned by a common vow.
God, in the meantime, accumulating his rewards,
May at once increase our honour and illustrate his own love.
Nor heavens shall be wanting to heavens, nor numberless ages to life,

Nor new joys to these ages, such as an
Eternity shall not diminish, nor the infinite bring to an end.
Nor, more than all, shall the fair favour of the Divine be wanting—
Constantly increasing these joys, varied in admirable modes,
And making each state yield only to one yet happier,
And what we never even knew how to hope, is given to us—
Nor is aught kept back except what only the One can conceive,
And what in their own nature are by far most perfect
In us, at least, appear embellished,
Since the sleeping minds which heaven prepares from the beginning—
Only our labour and industry can vivify,
Polishing them with learning and with morals,
That they may return all fair, bearing back a dowry to heaven,
When, by use of our free will, we put to rout those ills
Which heaven has neither dispelled, nor will hereafter dispel.
Thus through us is magnified the glory of God,
And our glory, too, shall resound throughout the heavens,
And what are the due rewards of virtue, finally
Must render the Father himself more happy than his wont.
Whence still more ample grace shall be showered upon us,
Each and all yielding to our prayer,
For, if *liberty* be dear, it is permitted
To roam through the loveliest regions obvious to innumerable heavens,
And gather, as we pass, the delights of each,
If *fixed contemplation* be chosen rather in the mind,
All the mysteries of the high regions shall be laid open to us,
And the joy will be to know the methods of God—
Then it may be permitted to act upon earth, to have a care
Of the weal of men, and to bestow just laws.
If we are more delighted with celestial *love,*
We are dissolved into flames which glide about and excite one another
Mutually, embraced in sacred ardours,
Spring upwards, enfolded together in firmest bonds,
In parts and wholes, mingling by turns,
And the ardour of the Divine kindles (in them) still new ardours,
It will make us happy to praise God, while he commands us,
The angelic choir, singing together with sweet modulation,
Sounds through heaven, publishing our joys,
And beauteous spectacles are put forth, hour by hour,
And, as it were, the whole fabric of heaven becomes a theatre,
Till the divine energy pervades the whole sweep of the world,
And chisels out from it new forms,
Adorned with new faculties, of larger powers.
Our forms, too, may then be renewed—

Assume new forms and senses, till our
Joys again rise up consummate.
If trusting thus, I shall have put off this mortal weed,
Why may not then still greater things be disclosed?

George H. (*who during his brother's reading has listened with head bowed down, leaned on his arm, looks up after a few moments' silence*) Pardon, my lord, if I have not fit words to answer you. The flood of your thought has swept over me like music, and like that, for the time at least, it fills and satisfies. I am conscious of many feelings which are not touched upon there—of the depths of love and sorrow made known to men through One whom you as yet know not. But of these I will not speak now, except to ask, borne on this strong pinion, have you never faltered till you felt the need of a friend? Strong in this clear vision, have you never sighed for a more homefelt assurance to your faith? Steady in your demand of what the soul requires, have you never known fear lest you want purity to receive the boon if granted?

Lord H. I do not count those weak moments, George; they are not my true life.

George H. It suffices that you know them, for in time I doubt not that every conviction which a human being needs to be reconciled to the Parent of all, will be granted to a nature so ample, so open, and so aspiring. Let me answer in a strain which bespeaks my heart as truly, if not as nobly as yours answers to your great mind—

> My joy, my life, my crown!
> My heart was meaning all the day
> Somewhat it fain would say;
> And still it runneth, muttering, up and down,
> With only this—*my joy, my life, my crown.*
>
> Yet slight not these few words;
> If truly said, they may take part
> Among the best in art.
> The fineness which a hymn or psalm affords,
> Is, when the soul unto the lines accords.
>
> He who craves all the mind
> And all the soul, and strength and time;
> If the words only rhyme,

Justly complains, that somewhat is behind
To make his verse or write a hymn in kind.

Whereas, if the heart be moved,
Although the verse be somewhat scant,
God doth supply the want—
As when the heart says, sighing to be approved,
"Oh, could I love!" and stops; God writeth, *loved*.

Lord H. I cannot say to you truly that my mind replies to this, although I discern a beauty in it. You will say I lack humility to understand yours.

George H. I will say nothing, but leave you to time and the care of a greater than I. We have exchanged our verse, let us now change our subject too, and walk homeward; for I trust you this night intend to make my roof happy in your presence, and the sun is sinking.

Lord H. Yes, you know I am there to be introduced to my new sister, whom I hope to love and win from her a sisterly regard in turn.

George H. You, none can fail to regard; and for her, even as you love me, you must her, for we are one.

Lord H. (*smiling*) Indeed; two years wed, and say that.

George H. Will your lordship doubt it? From your muse I took my first lesson.

With a look, it seem'd denied
All earthly powers but hers, yet so
As if to her breath he did owe
This borrow'd life, he thus replied—

And shall our love, so far beyond
That low and dying appetite,
And which so chaste desires unite,
Not hold in an eternal bond?

O no, belov'd! I am most sure
Those virtuous habits we acquire,
As being with the soul entire,
Must with it evermore endure.

Else should our souls in vain elect;
And vainer yet were heaven's laws
When to an everlasting cause
They gave a perishing effect.

Lord H. (*sighing*) You recall a happy season when my thoughts were as delicate of hue and of as heavenly a perfume as the flowers of May.

George H. Have those flowers borne no fruit?

Lord H. My experience of the world and men had made me believe that they did not indeed bloom in vain, but that the fruit would be ripened in some future sphere of our existence. What my own marriage was you know—a family arrangement made for me in my childhood. Such obligations as such a marriage could imply, I have fulfilled, and it has not failed to bring me some benefits of goodwill and esteem, and far more in the happiness of being a parent. But my observation of the ties formed by those whose choice was left free has not taught me that a higher happiness than mine was the destined portion of men. They are too immature to form permanent relations; all that they do seems experiment, and mostly fails for the present. Thus I had postponed all hopes except of fleeting joys or ideal pictures. Will you tell me that you are possessed already of so much more?

George H. I am indeed united in a bond whose reality I cannot doubt with one whose thoughts, affections, and objects every way correspond with mine, and in whose life I see a purpose so pure that if we are ever separated, the fault must be mine. I believe God in his exceeding grace gave us to one another, for we met almost at a glance, without doubt before, jar or repentance after, the vow which bound our lives together.

Lord H. Then there is indeed one circumstance of your lot I could wish to share with you. (*After some moments' silence on both sides*) They told me at the house that, with all your engagements, you go twice a week to Salisbury. How is that? How can you leave your business and your happy home so much and often?

George H. I go to hear the music, the great solemn church music. This is at once the luxury and the necessity of my life. I know not how it is with others, but with me there is a frequent drooping of the wings, a smoldering of the inward fires, a languor, almost a loathing of corporeal existence. Of this visible diurnal sphere I am by turns the master, the interpreter, and the victim; an ever-burning lamp to warm again the embers of the altar; a skiff that cannot be becalmed, to bear me again on the ocean of hope; an elixir that fills the dullest fiber with ethereal energy; such music is to me. It stands in relation to speech, even to the speech of poets, as the angelic choir who in their subtler being may inform the space around us, unseen but felt, do to men, even to prophetic men. It answers to the soul's presage, and in its fluent life embodies all I yet know how to desire. As all the thoughts and hopes of human souls are blended by the organ to a stream of prayer and praise, I tune at it my separate breast, and return to my little home cheered and ready for my day's work, as the lark does to her nest after her morning visit to the sun.

Lord H. The ancients held that the spheres made music to those who had risen into a state which enabled them to hear it. Pythagoras, who prepared different kinds of melody to guide and expand the differing natures of his pupils, needed himself to hear none on instruments made by human art, for the universal harmony which comprehends all these was audible to him. Man feels in all his higher moments the need of traversing a subtler element, of a winged existence. Artists have recognized wings as the symbol of the state next above ours; but they have not been able so to attach them to the forms of gods and angels as to make them agree with the anatomy of the human frame. Perhaps music gives this instruction, and supplies the deficiency. Although I see that I do not feel it as habitually or as profoundly as you do, I have experienced such impressions from it.

George H. That is truly what I mean. It introduces me into that winged nature, and not as by way of supplement but of inevitable transition. All that has budded in me, bursts into bloom under this influence. As I sit in our noble cathedral, in itself one of the holiest thoughts ever embodied by the power of man, the great tides of song come rushing through its aisles; they pervade all the space and my soul within it, perfuming me like incense, bearing me on like the wind, and on and on to regions of unutterable joy and freedom and certainty. As their triumph rises, I rise with them and learn to comprehend by living them, till at last a calm rapture seizes me and holds me poised. The same life you have attained in your description of the celestial choirs. It is the music of the soul when centered in the will of God, thrilled by the love, expanded by the energy with which it is fulfilled through all the ranges of active life. From such hours I return through these green lanes to hear the same tones from the slightest flower, to long for a life of purity and praise, such as is manifested by the flowers.

At this moment they reached the door, and there paused to look back. George Herbert bent upon the scene a half-abstracted look, yet which had a celestial tearfulness in it, a pensiveness beyond joy. His brother looked on *him*, and beneath that fading twilight it seemed to him a farewell look. It was so. Soon George Herbert soared into the purer state, for which his soul had long been ready, though not impatient.

The brothers met no more; but they had enjoyed together one hour of true friendship, when mind drew near to mind by the light of faith, and heart mingled with heart in the atmosphere of Divine love. It was a great boon to be granted two mortals.

6

CARLYLE'S *CROMWELL* *

A long expectation is awarded at last by the appearance of this book. We cannot wonder that it should have been long, when Mr. Carlyle shows us what a world of ill-arranged and almost worthless materials he has had to wade through before achieving any possibility of order and harmony for his narrative.

The method he has chosen of letting the letters and speeches of Cromwell tell the story when possible, only himself doing what is needful to throw light where it is most wanted and fill up gaps, is an excellent one. Mr. Carlyle indeed is a most peremptory showman, and with each slide of his magic lantern informs us not only of what is necessary to enable us to understand it, but how we must look at it, under peril of being ranked as Imbeciles, Canting Skeptics, disgusting Rose-Water Philanthropists, and the like. And aware of his power of tacking a nickname or ludicrous picture to anyone who refuses to obey, we might perhaps feel ourselves, if in his neighborhood, under such constraint and fear of deadly laughter as to lose the benefit of having under our eye to form our judgment upon the same materials on which he formed his.

But the ocean separates us and the showman had his own audience of despised victims or scarce less despised pupils, and we need not fear to be handed down to posterity as "a little gentleman in a gray coat" "shrieking" unutterable "imbecilities" or with the like damnatory affixes, when we profess that having read the book and read the letters and speeches thus far, we cannot submit to the showman's explanation of the lantern, but must more than ever stick to the old "Philistine," "Dilettante," "Imbecile," and what-not view of the character of Cromwell.

We all know that to Mr. Carlyle greatness is well-nigh synonymous with virtue, and that he has shown himself a firm believer in Providence by receiving the men of destiny as always entitled to reverence. Sometimes a great success has followed the portraits painted by him in the light of such faith, as with Mohammed for instance. The natural autocrat is his delight,

---

* From the New York *Daily Tribune*, December 19, 1845.

and in such pictures as that of the Monk in *Past and Present,* where the geniuses of artist and subject coincide, the result is no less delightful for us.

But Mr. Carlyle reminds us of the man in a certain parish who had always looked up to one of its squires as a secure and blameless idol, and one day in church, when the minister asked "all who felt in concern for their souls to rise," looked to the idol and seeing him retain his seat (asleep perchance!) sat still also. One of his friends asking him afterward how he could refuse to answer such an appeal, he replied, he thought it safest to stay with the Squire.

Mr. Carlyle's squires are all Heaven's justices of peace or war (usually the latter); they are beings of true energy and genius, and so far as he describes them, "genuine men." But in doubtful cases where the doubt is between them and principles, he will insist that the men must be in the right. On such occasions he favors us with such doctrines as the following, which we confess we had the weakness to read with "sibylline execration" and extreme disgust.

Speaking of Cromwell's course in Ireland:

"Oliver's proceedings here have been the theme of much loud criticism, sibylline execration; into which it is not our plan to enter at present. We shall give these Fifteen Letters of his in a mass, and without any commentary whatever. To those who think that a land overrun with Sanguinary Quacks can be healed by sprinkling it with rose-water, these Letters must be very horrible. Terrible Surgery this; but *is* it Surgery and Judgment, or atrocious Murder merely? This is a question which should be asked: and answered. Oliver Cromwell did believe in God's Judgments; and did not believe in the rose-water plan of Surgery;—which, in fact, is this Editor's case too! Every idle lie and piece of empty bluster this Editor hears, he too, like Oliver, has to shudder at it; has to think: 'Thou, idle bluster, not true, thou also art shutting men's minds against the God's Fact; thou wilt issue as a cleft crown to some poor man some day; thou also wilt have to take shelter in bogs whither cavalry cannot follow!'— But in Oliver's time, as I say, there was still belief in the Judgments of God, in Oliver's time, there was yet no distracted jargon of 'abolishing Capital Punishments,' of Jean-Jacques Philanthropy, and universal rose-water in this world still so full of sin. Men's notion was, not for abolishing punishments, but for making laws just: God the Maker's Laws, they considered, had not yet got the Punishment abolished from them! Men had a notion that the difference between Good and Evil was still considerable;—equal to the difference between Heaven and Hell. It was a true notion. Which all men yet saw, and felt, in all fibers of their existence, to be true. Only in late decadent generations, fast hastening toward radical change or final perdition, can such indiscriminate mashing-up of Good and Evil into one universal patent-treacle, and most unmedical electuary, of Rousseau Sentimentalism, universal Pardon and Benevolence with dinner and drink and one cheer more, take effect in our Earth. Electuary very poisonous, as sweet as it is, and very nauseous; of which Oliver, happier than we, had not yet heard the slightest intimation even in dreams.

"The reader of these Letters, who has swept all that very ominous twaddle out of his head and heart, and still looks with a recognizing eye on the ways of the Supreme Powers with this world, will find here, in the rude Practical state, a Phenomenon which he will account noteworthy. An armed Soldier, solemnly conscious to himself that he is the Soldier of God the Just—a consciousness which it well beseems all soldiers and all men to have always;—armed Soldier, terrible as Death, relentless as Doom; doing God's Judgments on the Enemies of God! It is a Phenomenon not of joyful nature; no, but of awful, to be looked at with pious terror and awe. Not a Phenomenon which you are called to recognize with bright smiles, and fall in love with at sight:—thou, art thou worthy to love such a thing; worthy to do other than hate it, and shriek over it? Darest thou wed the Heaven's lightning, then; and say to it, Godlike One? Is thy own life beautiful and terrible to thee; steeped in the eternal depths, in the eternal splendors? Thou also, art thou in thy sphere the minister of God's Justice; feeling that thou art here to do it, and to see it done, at thy soul's peril? Thou wilt then judge Oliver with increasing clearness; otherwise, with increasing darkness, misjudge him.

"In fact, Oliver's dialect is rude and obsolete; the phrases of Oliver, to him solemn on the perilous battle-field as voices of God, have become to us most mournful when spouted as frothy cant from Exeter Hall. The reader has, all along, to make steady allowance for that. And on the whole, clear recognition will be difficult for him. To a poor slumberous Canting

Age, mumbling to itself everywhere, Peace, Peace, where there is no Peace —such a Phenomenon as Oliver, in Ireland or elsewhere, is not the most recognizable in all its meanings. But it waits there for recognition: and can wait an age or two. The Memory of Oliver Cromwell, as I count, has a good many centuries in it yet; and Ages of very varied complexion to apply to, before all end. My reader, in this passage and others, shall make of it what he can.

"But certainly, at lowest, here is a set of Military Dispatches of the most unexampled nature! Most rough, unkempt, shaggy as the Numidian lion. A style rugged as crags; coarse, drossy; yet with a meaning in it, an energy, a depth; pouring on like a fire-torrent; perennial fire of it visible athwart all dresses and defacements; not uninteresting to see! This man has come into distracted Ireland with a God's Truth in the heart of him, though an unexpected one; the first such man they have seen for a great while indeed. He carries Acts of Parliament, Laws of Earth and Heaven, in one hand; drawn sword in the other. He addresses the bewildered Irish populations, the black ravening coil of sanguinary blustering individuals at Tredah and elsewhere: 'Sanguinary blustering individuals, whose word is grown worthless as the barking of dogs; whose very thought is false, representing no fact but the contrary of fact—behold, I am come to speak and to do the truth among you. Here are acts of Parliament, methods of regulation and veracity, emblems the nearest we poor Puritans could make them of God's Law-Book, to which it is and shall be our perpetual effort to make them correspond nearer and nearer. Obey them, help us to perfect them, be peaceable and true under them, it shall be well with you. Refuse to obey them, I will not let you continue living! As articulate speaking veracious orderly men, not as a blustering murderous kennel of dogs run rabid, shall you continue in this Earth. Choose!'—They chose to disbelieve him; could not understand that he, more than the others, meant any truth or justice to them. They rejected his summons and terms at Tredah: he stormed the place; and according to his promise, put every man of the Garrison to death. His own soldiers are forbidden to plunder, by paper Proclamation; and in ropes of authentic hemp they are hanged when they do it. To Wexford Garrison the like terms as at Tredah; and, failing these, the like storm. Here is a man whose word represents a thing! Not bluster this, and false jargon scattering itself to the winds; what this man speaks out of him comes to pass as a fact; speech with this man is accurately prophetic of deed. This is the first King's face poor Ireland ever saw; the first Friend's face, *little as it recognizes him*—poor Ireland!"

The whole doctrine of which glowing morceau of eloquence lies in this trait of the revered Oliver: "Not bluster this, and false jargon scattering itself to the winds; what this man speaks out of him comes to pass as a fact; speech with this man is accurately prophetic of deed."

Yes, Cromwell had force and sagacity to get that done which he had resolved to get done, and this is the whole truth about your admiration, Mr. Carlyle. Accordingly at Drogheda quoth Cromwell:

"I believe we put to sword the whole number of the defendants. . . . Indeed, being in the heat of action, I forbade them to spare any that were in arms in the Town, and I think that night they put to the sword about 2,000 men, divers of the officers and soldiers being fled over the Bridge into the other part of the Town; and where about 100 of them possessed St. Peter's Church Steeple, etc. These, being summoned to yield to mercy, refused. Whereupon I ordered the Steeple of St. Peter's Church to be fired, when one of them was heard to say in the midst of the flames: God, confound me; I burn, I burn.

"I am persuaded that this is a righteous judgement of God upon these barbarous wretches who have imbrued their hands in so much innocent blood; and that it will tend to prevent the effusion of blood for the future. Which are the satisfactory grounds to such actions, which otherwise cannot but work remorse and regret. . . . This hath been an exceeding great mercy."

Certainly one not of the rose-water or treacle kind. Mr. Carlyle says such measures "cut to the heart of the war" and brought peace. Was there *then* no crying of "Peace, Peace," when there was no peace? Ask the Irish peasantry why they mark that period with the solemn phrase of Cromwell's Curse.

For ourselves, though aware of the mistakes and errors in particulars that must occur, we believe the summing up of a man's character in the verdict of his time is likely to be correct. We believe that Cromwell was a "curse" as much as a blessing in these acts of his. We believe him ruthless, ambitious, half a hypocrite (few men have courage or want of soul to bear being wholly so), and we think it is rather too bad to rave at us in our time for canting, and then hold up the Prince of Canters for our reverence in his "dimly seen nobleness." Dimly indeed, despite the rhetoric and satire of Mr. Carlyle!

In previous instances where Mr. Carlyle has acted out his predeterminations as to the study of a character, we have seen circumstances favor him at least sometimes. There were fine moments, fine lights upon the character that he would seize upon. But here the facts look just as they always have. He indeed ascertains that the Cromwell family were not mere brewers or plebeians but "substantial gentry," and that there is not the least ground for the common notion that Cromwell lived at any time a dissolute life. But with the exception of these emendations, still the history looks as of old. We see a man of strong and of wise mind, educated by the pressure of great occasions to station of command; we see him wearing the religious garb which was the custom of the times, and even preaching to himself as well as to others—for well can we imagine that his courage and his pride would have fallen without keeping up the illusion; but we never see Heaven answering his invocations in any way that can interfere with the rise of his fortunes or the accomplishment of his plans. To ourselves the tone of these religious holdings-forth is of stuff sufficiently expressive; they all ring hollow; we have never read anything of the sort more repulsive to us than the letter to Mr. Hammond, which Mr. Carlyle thinks such a noble contrast to the impiety of the present time. Indeed we cannot recover from our surprise at Mr. Carlyle's liking these letters; his predetermination must have been strong indeed. Again, we see Cromwell ruling with the strong arm and carrying the spirit of monarchy to an excess which no Stuart could surpass. Cromwell indeed is wise, and the king he had punished with death is foolish; Charles is faithless, and Cromwell crafty; we see no other difference. Cromwell does not in power abide by the principles that led him to it; and we can't help—so rose-water imbecile are we—admiring those who do: one Lafayette for instance—poor chevalier so despised by Mr. Carlyle—for abiding by his principles, though impracticable, more than Louis

Philippe, who laid them aside so far as necessary "to secure peace to the kingdom"; and to us it looks black for one who kills kings to grow to be more kingly than a king.

The death of Charles I was a boon to the world, for it marked the dawn of a new era, when kings in common with other men are to be held accountable by God and mankind for what they do. Many who took part in this act, which *did* require a courage and faith almost unparalleled, were no doubt moved by the noblest sense of duty. We doubt not this had its share in the bosom councils of Cromwell. But we cannot sympathize with the apparent satisfaction of Mr. Carlyle in seeing him engaged, two days after the execution, in marriage treaty for his son. This seems more ruthlessness than calmness. One who devoted so many days to public fasting and prayer on less occasions might well make solemn pause on this. Mr. Carlyle thinks much of some pleasant domestic letters from Cromwell. What brigand, what pirate fails to have some such soft and light feelings?

In short we have not time to say all we think, but we stick to the received notions of Old Noll, with his great red nose, hard heart, long head, and crafty ambiguities. Nobody ever doubted his great abilities and force of will, neither doubt we that he was made an "instrument" just as he professeth. But as to looking on him through Mr. Carlyle's glasses we shall not be sneered or stormed into it unless he has other proof to offer than is shown yet. And we resent the violence he offers both to our prejudice and our perceptions. If he has become interested in Oliver or any other pet hyena by studying his habits, is that any reason we should admit him to our Pantheon? No, our imbecility shall keep fast the door against anything short . of proofs that in the hyena a god is incarnated. Mr. Carlyle declares that he sees it, but we really cannot. The hyena is surely not out of the kingdom of God, but as to being the finest emblem of what is divine—no, no!

In short, we can sympathize with the words of John Maidstone:

"He [Cromwell] was a strong man in the dark perils of war; in the high places of the field, hope shone in him like a pillar of fire, when it had gone out in the others."

A poetic and sufficient account of the secret of his power.

But Mr. Carlyle goes on to gild the refined gold thus:

"A genuine King among men, Mr. Maidstone? The divinest sight this world sees, when it is privileged to see such, and not be sickened with the unholy apery of such."

We know you do with all your soul love kings and heroes, Mr. Carlyle, but we are not sure you would always know the Sauls from the Davids. We fear if you had the disposal of the holy oil, you would be tempted to pour it on the head of him who is taller by the head than all his brethren, without sufficient care as to purity of inward testimony.

Such is the impression left on us by the book thus far as to the view of its hero, but as to what such a history should be and especially how that of Cromwell is to be treated, the reader will like to see what Mr. Carlyle says:

"Histories are *as* perfect as the Historian is wise, and is gifted with an eye and a soul! For the leafy blossoming Present Time springs from the whole Past, remembered and unrememberable, so confusedly as we say:—and truly the Art of History, the grand difference between a Dryasdust and a sacred Poet, is very much even this:—To distinguish well what does still reach to the surface, and is alive and frondent for us; and what reaches no longer to the surface, but molders safe underground, never to send forth leaves or fruit for mankind any more: of the former we shall rejoice to hear; to hear of the latter will be an affliction to us; of the latter only Pedants and Dullards, and disastrous *male*factors to the world, will find good to speak. By wise memory and by wise oblivion; it lies all there!—Without oblivion, there is no remembrance possible. When both oblivion and memory are wise, when the general soul of man is clear, melodious, true, there may come a modern *Iliad* as memorial of the Past; when both are foolish, and the general soul is overclouded with confusions, with unveracities and discords, there is a 'Rushworthian chaos.' . . .

"Ours is a very small enterprise, but seemingly a useful one; preparatory perhaps to greater and more useful, on this same matter:—The collecting of the *Letters and Speeches of Oliver Cromwell,* and presenting them in natural sequence, with the still possible elucidation, to ingenuous readers. This is a thing that can be done; and after some reflection, it has appeared worth doing. No great thing; one other dull Book added to the thousand, dull every one of them, which have been issued on this subject! But situated as we are, new Dullness is unhappily inevitable; readers do not reascend out of some deep confusions without some trouble as they climb.

"These authentic utterances of the man Oliver himself—I have gathered them from far and near; fished them up from the foul Lethean quagmires where they lay buried; I have washed, or endeavored to wash, them clean from foreign stupidities (such a job of back-washing as I do not long to repeat); and the world shall now see them in their own shape. Working for long years in those unspeakable Historic Provinces, of which the reader has already had account, it becomes more and more apparent to one, That this man Oliver Cromwell was, as the popular fancy represents him, the soul of the Puritan Revolt, without whom it had never been a revolt transcendently memorable, and an Epoch in the World's History, that in fact he, more than is common in such cases, does deserve to give his name to the Period in question, and have the Puritan Revolt considered as a *Cromwelliad,* which issue is already very visible for it. And then farther, altogether contrary to the popular fancy, it becomes apparent that this Oliver was not a man of falsehoods, but a man of truths; whose words do carry a meaning with them, and above all others of that time, are worth considering. His words,—and still more his *silences,* and unconscious instincts, when you have spelt and lovingly deciphered these also out of his words,—will in several ways reward the study of an earnest man. An earnest man, I apprehend, may gather from these words of Oliver's, were there even no other evidence, that the character of Oliver and of the Affairs he worked in is much the reverse of that mad jumble of 'hypocrisies,' etc., etc., which at present passes current as such."

For the rest this book is of course entertaining, witty, dramatic, picturesque; all traits that are piquant, many that have profound interest are brought out better than new. The letters and speeches are put into readable state and this alone is a great benefit. They are a relief after Mr. Carlyle's high-seasoned writing, and this again is a relief after their longwinded dimnesses. Most of the heroic anecdotes had been used up before, but they lose nothing in the hands of Carlyle, and pictures of the scenes, such as of Naseby fight for instance, it was left to him to give. We have passed over the hackneyed ground attended by a torch-bearer who has given a new animation to the procession of events, and cast a ruddy glow on many a striking physiognomy. That any truth of high value has been brought to light, we do not perceive; certainly nothing has been added to our own sense of the greatness of the times, nor any new view presented that we can adopt as to the position and character of the agents.

We close with only one of Cromwell's letters that we really like. Here his religious words and his temper seem quite sincere, for the occasion was one that touched him really and nearly:

To my loving Brother, Colonel Valentine Walton: These:

Leaguer before York, 5th July, 1644.

Dear Sir:—It's our duty to sympathize in all mercies; and to praise the Lord together in chastisements or trials, so that we may sorrow together.

Truly England and the Church of God hath had a great favor from the Lord, in the great Victory given unto us, such as the like never was since this War began. It had all the evidence of an absolute Victory obtained by the Lord's blessing upon the Godly Party principally. We never charged but we routed the enemy. The Left Wing, which I commanded, being our own horse, saving a few Scots in our rear, beat all the Prince's horse.—God made them as stubble to our swords. We charged their regiments of foot with our horse, and routed all we charged. The particulars I cannot relate now; but I believe, of twenty thousand the Prince hath not four thousand left. Give glory, all the glory, to God.—

Sir, God hath taken away your eldest Son by a cannon-shot. It brake his leg. We were necessitated to have it cut off, whereof he died.

Sir, you know my own trials this way *: but the Lord supported me with this, That the Lord took him into the happiness we all pant for and live for. There is your precious child, full of glory, never to know sin or sorrow any more. He was a gallant young man, exceedingly gracious. God give you His comfort. Before his death he was so full of comfort that to Frank Russel and myself he could not express it, "It was so great above his pain." This he said to us. Indeed it was admirable. A little after, he said, One thing lay upon his spirit. I asked him, What that was? he told me it was, That God had not suffered him to be any more the executioner of His enemies. At his fall, his horse being killed with the bullet, and as I am informed, three horses more, I am told he bid them, Open to the right and left, that he might see the rogues run. Truly he was exceedingly beloved in the Army, of all that knew him— But few knew him; for he was a precious young man, fit for God. You have cause to bless the Lord. He is a glorious Saint in Heaven; wherein you ought exceedingly to rejoice. Let this drink up your sorrow; seeing these are not feigned words to comfort you, but the thing is so real and undoubted a truth. You may do all things by the strength of Christ. Seek that, and you shall easily bear your

---

* I conclude the poor Boy Oliver has already fallen in these Wars,—none of us knows where, though his Father well knew.

trial. Let this public mercy to the Church of God make you to forget your private sorrow. The Lord be your strength: so prays

Your truly faithful and loving Brother,
OLIVER CROMWELL

And add this noble passage in which Carlyle speaks of the morbid affection of Cromwell's mind:

"In those years it must be that Dr. Simcott, Physician in Huntingdon, had to do with Oliver's hypochondriac maladies. He told Sir Philip Warwick, unluckily specifying no date, or none that has survived, 'he had often been sent for at midnight'; Mr. Cromwell for many years was very 'splenetic' (spleen-struck), often thought he was just about to die, and also 'had fancies about the Town Cross.' Brief intimation; of which the reflective reader may make a great deal. Samuel Johnson too had hypochondrias; all great souls are apt to have,—and to be in thick darkness generally till the eternal ways and the celestial guiding-stars disclose themselves, and the vague Abyss of Life knit itself up into Firmaments for them. Temptations in the wilderness, Choices of Hercules, and the like, in succinct or loose form are appointed for every man that will assert a soul in himself and be a man. Let Oliver take comfort in his dark sorrows and melancholies. The quantity of sorrow he has, does it not mean withal the quantity of sympathy he has, the quantity of faculty and victory he shall yet have? 'Our sorrow is the inverted image of our nobleness.' The depth of our despair measures what capability, and height of claim we have, to hope. Black smoke as of Tophet filling all your universe, it can yet by true heart-energy become *flame,* and brilliancy of Heaven. Courage!"

Were the flame but a pure as well as a bright flame! Sometimes we know the black phantoms change to white angel forms; the vulture is metamorphosed into a dove. Was it so in this instance? Unlike Mr. Carlyle, we are willing to let each reader judge for himself, but perhaps we should not be so generous if we had studied ourselves sick in wading through all that mass of papers, and had nothing to defend us against the bitterness of biliousness except a growing enthusiasm about our hero.

7

FRENCH NOVELISTS OF THE DAY *

This thirteenth number of the *Wandering Jew,* just published by Winchester, has delivered us from our anxieties as to the objects of Jesuit persecution, though by a *coup de main* clumsier than is usual even with Sue. Now we have matters arranged for a few months more of contest with the Society of Jesus, but we think our author must depend for interest during the last volume no longer on the conduct of the plot, but on the portraiture of characters.

It is cheering to know how great is the influence such a writer as Sue exerts, from his energy of feeling on some objects of moral interest. It is true that he has also much talent and a various experience of life; but writers who far surpass him here, as we think Balzac does, wanting this heart of faith, have no influence except merely on the tastes of their readers.

We hear much lamentation among good people at the introduction of so many French novels among us, corrupting, they say, our youth by pictures of decrepit vice and prurient crime such as would never otherwise be dreamed of here, and corrupting it the more that such knowledge is so precocious—for the same reason that a boy may be more deeply injured by initiation into wickedness than a man, for he is not only robbed of his virtue, but prevented from developing the strength that might restore it. But it is useless to bewail what is the inevitable result of the movement of our time. Europe must pour her corruptions no less than her riches on our shores, both in the form of books and of living men. She cannot if she would check the tide which bears them hitherward; no defenses are possible on our vast extent of shore that would preclude their ingress. We have exulted in premature and hasty growth; we must brace ourselves to bear the evils that ensue. Our only hope lies in rousing in our own community a soul of goodness, a wise aspiration, that shall give us strength to assimilate this unwholesome food to better substance, or cast off its contaminations. A mighty sea of life swells within our nation, and if there be salt enough, foreign bodies shall not have power to breed infection there.

We have had some opportunity to observe that the worst works offered

---

* From the New York *Daily Tribune,* February 1, 1845.

are rejected. On the steamboats we have seen translations of vile books, bought by those who did not know from the names of their authors what to expect, torn after a cursory glance at their contents and scattered to the winds. Not even the all but all-powerful desire to get one's money's worth, since it had once been paid, could contend against the blush of shame that rose on the cheek of the reader.

It would be desirable for our people to know something of these writers and of the position they occupy abroad; for the nature of their circulation, rather than its extent, might be the guide both to translator and buyer. The object of the first is generally money—of the last, amusement. But the merest mercenary might prefer to pass his time in translating a good book, and our imitation of Europe does not yet go so far that the American milliner can be depended on to copy anything from the Parisian grisette except her cap.

One of the most unexceptionable and attractive writers of modern France is de Vigny. His life has been passed in the army, but many years of peace have given him time for literary culture, while his acquaintance with the traditions of the army from the days of its dramatic achievements under Bonaparte supplies the finest materials both for narrative and reflection. His tales are written with infinite grace, refined sensibility, and a dignified view. His treatment of a subject shows that closeness of grasp and clearness of sight which are rarely attained by one who is not at home in active as well as thoughtful life. He has much penetration too, and has touched some of the most delicate springs of human action. His works have been written in hours of leisure; this has diminished their number but given him many advantages over the thousands of professional writers that fill the coffee-house of Paris by day and its garrets by night. We wish he were more read here in the original; with him would be found good French and the manners, thoughts, and feelings of a cosmopolite gentleman. We have seen, with pleasure, one or two of his tales translated into the pages of the *Democratic Review*.

But the three who have been and will be most read here, as they occupy the first rank in their own country, are Balzac, George Sand, and Eugene Sue.

Balzac has been a very fruitful writer, and as he is fond of juggler's tricks of every description and holds nothing earnest or sacred, he is vain of the wonderful celerity with which some of his works, and those quite as good as any, have been written. They seem to have been conceived, composed, and written down with that degree of speed with which it is possible to lay pen to paper. Indeed we think he cannot be surpassed in the ready and sustained command of his resources. His aim at unsurpassed quickness and fidelity of eye, both as to the disposition of external objects and the symptoms of human passion, combined with a strong memory, have filled his mind with materials, and we doubt not that if his thoughts could be put into writing with the swiftness of thought, he would give us one of his novels every week in the year.

Here end our praises of Balzac; what he is as a man in daily life, we know not. He must originally have had a heart, or he could not read so well the hearts of others; perhaps there are still private ties that touch him. But as a writer, never was the modern Mephistopheles, "the spirit that denieth," more worthily represented than by Balzac.

He combines the spirit of the man of science with that of the amateur collector. He delights to analyze, to classify; there is no anomaly too monstrous, no specimen too revolting, to ensure his ardent but passionless scrutiny. But then he has taste and judgment to know what is fair, rare, and exquisite. He takes up such an object carefully and puts it in a good light. But he has no hatred for what is loathsome, no contempt for what is bare, no love for what is lovely, no faith in what is noble. To him there is no virtue and no vice; men and women are more or less finely organized; noble and tender conduct is more agreeable than the reverse because it argues better health; that is all.

Nor is this from an intellectual calmness, nor from an unusual power of analyzing motives and penetrating delusions merely; neither is it mere indifference. There is a touch of the demon also in Balzac; the cold but gaily familiar demon, and the smile of the amateur yields easily to a sneer, as he delights to show you on what foul juices the fair flower was fed. He is a thorough and willing materialist. The trance of religion is congestion of the brain; the joy of the poet the thrilling of the blood in the rapture of sense; and every good not only rises from but hastens back into the jaws of death and nothingness: a rainbow arch above a pestilential chaos!

Thus Balzac with all his force and fullness of talent never rises one moment into the region of genius. For genius is in its nature positive and creative, and cannot exist where there is no heart to believe in realities. Neither can he have a permanent influence on a nature which is not thoroughly corrupt. He might for a while stagger an ingenuous mind which had not yet thought for itself. But this could not last. His unbelief makes his thought too shallow. He has not that power which a mind only in part sophisticated may retain where the heart still beats warmly, though it sometimes beats amiss. Write, paint, argue as you will, where there is a sound spot in any human being, he cannot be made to believe that this present bodily frame is more than a temporary condition of his being, though one to which he may have become shamefully enslaved by fault of inheritance, education, or his own carelessness.

Taken in his own way, we know no modern tragedies more powerful than Balzac's *Eugenie Grandet, Sweet Pea, Search after the Absolute, Father Goriot.* See there goodness, aspiration, the loveliest instincts, stifled, strangled by fate in the form of our own brute nature. The fate of the ancient Prometheus was happiness to that of those who must pay for ever having believed there was divine fire in Heaven by agonies of despair and conscious degradation unknown to those who began by believing man to be the most richly endowed of brutes—no more!

Balzac is admirable in his description of look, tone, gesture. He has a keen sense of whatever is peculiar to the individual. Nothing in modern literature surpasses the death scene of Father Goriot, the Parisian Lear, in the almost immortal life with which the parental instincts are displayed. And with equal precision and delicacy of shading he will paint the by-plays in the manners of some young girl.

Seraphita is merely a specimen of his great powers of intellectual transposition. Amid his delight at the botanical riches of the new and elevated region in which he is traveling, we catch, if only by echo, the hem and chuckle of the French materialist.

No more of him!—We leave him to his suicidal work.

An entirely opposite character in every leading trait, yet bearing traces of the same influences, is the celebrated George Sand. It is probably known to a great proportion of readers that this writer is a woman who writes under the name of and frequently assumes the dress and manners of a man. It is also known that she has not only broken the marriage bond, and since that, formed other connections independent of the civil or ecclesiastical sanction, but that she first rose into notice through works which systematically assailed the present institution of marriage and the social bonds which are connected with it.

No facts are more adapted to startle every feeling of our community; but since the works of Sand are read here notwithstanding, and cannot fail to be so while they exert so important an influence abroad, it would be well they should be read intelligently as to the circumstances of their birth and their tendency.

George Sand we esteem to be a person of strong passions, but of original nobleness and a love of right sufficient to guide them all to the service of worthy aims. But she fell upon evil times. She was given in marriage according to the fashion of the old regime; she was taken from a convent where she had heard a great deal about the law of God and the example of Jesus, into a society where no vice was proscribed if it would wear the cloak of hypocrisy. She found herself impatient of deception and loudly called by passion: she yielded; but she could not do so as others did, sinning against what she owned to be the rule of right and the will of Heaven. She protested; she examined; she assailed. She "hacked into the roots of things," and the bold sound of her ax called around her every foe that finds a home amid the growth of civilization. Still she persisted. "If it be real," thought she, "it cannot be destroyed; as to what is false, the sooner it goes the better; and I for one had rather perish beneath its fall than wither in its shade."

Schiller puts into the mouth of Mary Stuart these words as her only plea: "The world knows the worst of me; and I may boast that though I have erred, I am better than my reputation." Sand may say the same. All is open, noble; the free descriptions, the sophistry of passion are at least redeemed by a desire for truth as strong as ever beat in any heart. To the weak or unthinking the reading of such books may not be desirable, for only those who take exercise as men can digest strong meat. But to anyone able to understand the position and circumstances, we believe this reading cannot fail of bringing good impulses, valuable suggestions, and it is quite free from that subtle miasma which taints so large a portion of French literature, not less since the Revolution than before. This we say to the foreign reader. To her own country Sand is a boon precious and prized both as a warning and a leader, for which none there can be ungrateful. She has dared to probe its festering wounds, and if they be not past all surgery, she is one who, most of any, helps toward a cure.

Would indeed the surgeon had come with quite clean hands! A woman of Sand's genius, as free, as bold, and pure from even the suspicion of error, might have filled an apostolic station among her people. Then with what force had come her cry, "If it be false, give it up; but if it be true, keep to it —one or the other!"

But we have read all we wish to say upon this subject, lately uttered just from the quarter we could wish. It is such a woman, so unblemished in character, so high in aim and pure in soul, that should address this other, as noble in nature but clouded by error and struggling with circumstances. It is such women that will do such justice. They are not afraid to look for virtue and reply to aspiration, among those who have *not* "dwelt in decencies for ever." It is a source of pride and happiness to read this address from the heart of Elizabeth Barrett:

TO GEORGE SAND

A Desire

Thou large-brained woman, and large-hearted man,
  Self-called George Sand! whose soul, amid the lions
  Of thy tumultuous senses moans defiance,
And answers roar for roar, as spirits can:
I would some mild miraculous thunder ran
  Above th' applauded circus, in appliance
  Of thine own nobler nature's strength and science,
Drawing two pinions, white as wings of swan,
From the strong shoulders, to amaze the place
  With holier light! that thou to woman's claim,
And man's, might join, beside, the angel's grace
  Of a pure genius sanctified from blame;
Thy child and maiden pressed to thine embrace,
  To kiss upon thy lips a stainless fame.

TO THE SAME

A Recognition

True genius, but true woman! dost deny
   Thy woman's nature with a manly scorn,
And break away the gauds and armlets worn
   By weaker women in captivity?
Ah, vain denial! that revolted cry
   Is sobbed in by a woman's voice forlorn:—
Thy woman's hair, my sister, all unshorn,
   Floats back disheveled strength in agony,
Disproving thy man's name, and while before
   The world thou burnest in a poet-fire,
We see thy woman-heart beat evermore
   Through the large flame. Beat purer, heart, and higher,
Till God unsex thee on the spirit shore:
   To which alone unsexing, purely aspire.

This last sonnet seems to have been written after seeing the picture of Sand which represents her in a man's dress, but with long loose hair and an eye whose mournful fire is impressive even in the caricature.

For some years Sand has quitted her post of assailant. She has seen that it is better to seek some form of life worthy to supersede the old than rudely to destroy it, heedless of the future. Her fire is bending towards philanthropic measures. She does appear to possess much of the constructive faculty, and though her writings command a great pecuniary compensation and have a wide sway, it is rather for their tendency than for their thought. She has reached no commanding point of view from which she may give orders to the advanced corps. She is still at work with others in the trench, though she works with more force than almost any.

In power indeed Sand bears the palm above any of the novelists. She is vigorous in conception, often great in the apprehension and the contrast of characters. She knows passion, as has been well hinted, at a white heat, when all the lower particles are remolded by its power. Her descriptive talent is very great, and her poetic feeling exquisite. She wants but little of being a poet, but that little is indispensable. Yet she keeps us always hovering on the borders of the enchanted fields. She has to a signal degree that power of exact transcript from her own mind of which almost all writers fail. There is no veil, no half-plastic integument between us and the thought. We vibrate perfectly with it.

This is her chief charm, and next to it is one in which we know no French writer that resembles her except Rousseau, though he indeed is vastly her superior in it. This is, of concentrated glow. Her nature glows beneath the words, like fire beneath the ashes, deep—deep!

Her best works are unequal; in many parts written hastily or carelessly or with flagging spirits. They all promise far more than they perform; the work is not done masterly; she has not reached that point where a writer sits at the helm of his own genius. Sometimes she plies the oar; sometimes she drifts. But what greatness she has is genuine; there is no tinsel of any kind, no drapery carefully adjusted or chosen gesture about her. May Heaven lead her at last to the full possession of her best self, in harmony with the higher laws of life!

We are not acquainted with all her works, but among those we know, mention *La Roche Mauprat, André, Jacques, Les Sept Cordes de la Lyre,* and *Les Maîtres Mosaïstes* as representing her higher inspirations, her sincerity in expression, and her dramatic powers. They are full of faults; still they also show her scope and aim with some fairness, which those readers who chance at first on such of her books as *Leone Leoni* may fail to find, or even such as *Simon* and *Spiridion,* though into the imperfect web of these are woven threads of pure gold. Such is the first impression made by the girl Fiamma as she appears before us, so noble, with the words *"E l'onore"*; such the thought in *Spiridion* of making the apparition the reward of virtue.

The work she is now publishing, *Consuelo,* with its sequel *Baroness de Rudolstadt,* exhibit her genius poised on a firmer pedestal, breathing a serener air. Still it is faulty in conduct and shows some obliquity of vision. She has not reached the interpreter's house yet. But when she does, she will have clues to guide many a pilgrim whom one less tried, less tempted than herself could not help on the way.

Eugene Sue is a writer of far inferior powers on the whole to Sand, though he possesses some brilliant talents that she wants. His aims and modes are more external than hers; he is not so deeply acquainted with his own nature or with that of any other person. Like her, he began life in a corrupt society

—struggled, doubted, half-despaired; erred apparently himself, and feared there was no virtue and no truth; but is conquering now.

We observe in a late notice of Sue that he began to write at quite mature age, at the suggestion of a friend. We should think it was so; that he was by nature intended for a practical man rather than a writer. He paints all his characters from the practical point of view.

As an observer, when free from exaggeration, he has as good an eye as Balzac, but he is far more rarely thus free, for in temperament he is unequal and sometimes muddy. But then he has the heart and faith that Balzac wants, yet is less enslaved by emotion than Sand; therefore he has made more impression on his time and place than either. We refer now to his later works; though his earlier show much talent, yet his progress both as a writer and thinker has been so considerable that those of the last few years entirely eclipse his earlier essays.

These latter works are the *Mysteries of Paris, Matilda,* and the *Wandering Jew* which is now in course of publication. In these he has begun and is continuing a crusade against the evils of a corrupt civilization which are inflicting such woes and wrongs upon his contemporaries.

Sue, however, does not merely assail, but would build up. His anatomy is not intended to injure the corpse, or like that of Balzac, to entertain the intellect merely. Earnestly he hopes to learn from it the remedies for disease and the conditions of health. Sue is a Socialist. He believes he sees the means by which the heart of mankind may be made to beat with one great hope, one love; and instinct with this thought, his tales of horror are not tragedies.

This is the secret of the deep interest he has awakened in this country: that he shares a hope which is, half unconsciously to herself, stirring all her veins. It is not so warmly outspoken as in other lands, both because no such pervasive ills as yet call loudly for redress, and because private conservation is here great in proportion to the absence of authorized despotism. We are not disposed to quarrel with this; it is well for the value of new thoughts to be tested by a good deal of resistance. Opposition, if it does not preclude free discussion, is of use in educating men to know what they want. Only by intelligent men, exercised by thought and tried in virtue, can such measures as Sue proposes be carried out; and when such associates present themselves in sufficient numbers, we have no fear but the cause of Association in its grander forms will have fair play in America.

As a writer Sue shows his want of a high kind of imagination by his unshrinking portraiture of physical horrors. We do not believe any man could look upon some things he describes and live. He is very powerful in his description of the workings of animal nature; especially when he speaks of them in animals merely, they have the simplicity of the lower kind with the more full expression of human nature. His pictures of women are of rare excellence, and it is observable that the more simple and pure the character is, the more justice he does to it. This shows that whatever his career may have been, his heart is uncontaminated. Men he does not describe so well, and fails entirely when he aims at one grand and simple enough for a great moral agent. His conceptions are strong, but in execution, he is too melodramatic. Just compare his *Wandering Jew* with that of Béranger. The latter is as diamond compared with charcoal. Then like all those writers who write in numbers that come out weekly or monthly, he abuses himself and his subject; he often must; the arrangement is false and mechanical.

The attitude of Sue is at this moment imposing, as he stands pen in hand —this his only weapon against an innumerable host of foes; the champion of poverty, innocence, and humanity against superstition, selfishness, and prejudice. When his works are forgotten, and for all their strong points and brilliant decorations they may erelong be forgotten, still the writer's name shall be held in imperishable honor as the teacher of the ignorant, the guardian of the weak, a true tribune for the people of his own time.

To sum up this imperfect account of their merits, I see de Vigny a retiring figure, the gentleman, the solitary thinker, but in his way the efficient foe of false honor and superstitious prejudice. Balzac is the heartless surgeon, probing the wounds and describing the delirium of suffering for the amusement of his students. Sand, a grand, fertile, aspiring, but in some measure distorted and irregular nature. Sue, a bold and glittering crusader, with endless ballads jingling in the silence of the night before the battle. They are much right and a good deal wrong; for instance, all, even Sand, who would lay down her life for the sake of truth, will let their virtuous characters practice stratagems, falsehood, and violence; in fact do evil for the sake of good. They still show this taint of the old regime, and no wonder! "La belle France" has worn rouge so long that the purest mountain air will not at once or soon restore the natural hues to her complexion. But they are fine figures, and all ruled by the onward spirit of the time. Led by that spirit, I see them moving on the troubled waters; they do not sink, and I trust they will find their way to the coasts where the new era will introduce new methods in a spirit of nobler activity, wiser patience, and holier faith than the world has yet seen.

Will Balzac also see that shore, or has he only broken away the bars that hindered others from setting sail? We do not know. When we read an expression of such lovely innocence as the letter of the little country maidens to their Parisian brother (in *Father Goriot*), we hope; but presently we see him sneering behind the mask, and we fear. Let Frenchmen speak to this. They know best what disadvantages a Frenchman suffers under, and whether it is possible Balzac be still alive except in his eyes. Those, we know, are well alive.

To read these or any foreign works fairly, the reader must understand the national circumstances under which they were written. To use them worthily, he must know how to interpret them for the use of the universe.

8

MODERN BRITISH POETS *

Poets—dwell on earth,
To clothe whate'er the soul admires and loves,
With language and with numbers.

—Akenside

Nine muses were enough for one Greece, and nine poets are enough for one country, even in the nineteenth century. And these nine are a "sacred nine," who if not quite equal to Shakespeare, Spenser, and Milton, are fairly initiated masters of the wand and spell; and whose least moving incantation should have silenced that blasphemer who dared to say in the pages of *Blackwood* that "all men, women, and children are poets, saving only—those who write verses."

First there is Campbell—a poet; simply a poet—no philosopher. His forte is strong conception, a style free and bold; occasionally a passage is ill-finished, but the lights and shades are so happily distributed, the touch so masterly and vigorous, with such tact at knowing where to stop, that we must *look for* the faults in order to *see* them. There is little if any originality of thought; no profound meaning; no esoteric charm, which you cannot make your own on a first reading; yet we have all probably read Campbell many times. It is his *manner* which we admire; and in him we enjoy what most minds enjoy most, not new thoughts, new feelings, but recognition of

What oft was thought, but ne'er so well expressed.

Thus in Campbell's best productions we are satisfied, not stimulated. "The Mariners of England" is just what it should be—for we find free, deep tones from the seaman's breast, chorded into harmony by an artist happy enough to feel nature—wise enough to follow nature. "Lochiel" is what it should be, a wild breezy symphony from the romantic Highlands. There are in fact flat lines and tame passages in "Lochiel," but I should never have discovered them, if I had not chanced to hear that noble composition recited by a dull schoolboy. The idealizing tendency in the reader, stimulated by the poet's real magnetic power, would prevent their being perceived in a solitary

---

* From *Papers on Literature and Art,* 1846.

312

perusal, and a *bright* schoolboy would have been sufficiently inspired by the general grandeur of the piece to have known how to sink such lines as:

> Welcome be Cumberland's steed to the shock,
> Let him dash his proud foam like a wave on the rock;

or:

> Draw, dotard, around thy old, wavering sight;

and a few other imperfections in favor of:

> Proud bird of the mountain, thy plume shall be torn,

and other striking passages.

As for the sweet tale of "Wyoming," the expression of the dying Gertrude's lips is not more "bland, more beautiful" than the music of the lay in which she is embalmed. It were difficult to read this poem, so holy in its purity and tenderness, so deliciously soft and soothing in its coloring, without feeling better and happier.

The feeling of Campbell towards women is refined and deep. To him they are not angels—not in the common sense heroines; but of a "perfect woman nobly planned" he has a better idea than most men or even poets. Witness one of his poems which has never received its meed of fame; I allude to "Theodric." Who can be insensible to the charms of Constance, the matron counterpart to Gertrude's girlhood?

> To know her well,
> Prolonged, exalted, bound enchantment's spell;
> For with affections warm, intense, refined,
> She mixed such calm and holy strength of mind,
> That, like Heaven's image in the smiling brook,
> Celestial peace was pictured in her look;
> Hers was the brow in trials unperplexed,
> That cheered the sad and tranquillized the vexed;
> She studied not the meanest to eclipse,
> And yet the wisest listened to her lips;
> She sang not, knew not Music's magic skill,
> But yet her voice had tones that swayed the will.
>
> .   .   .   .
>
> To paint that being to a grovelling mind
> Were like portraying pictures to the blind.

'Twas needful even infectiously to feel
Her temper's fond, and firm, and gladsome zeal,
To share existence with her, and to gain
Sparks from her love's electrifying chain,
Of that pure pride, which, lessening to her breast
Life's ills, gave all its joys a treble zest,
Before the mind completely understood
That mighty truth—how happy are the good!
Even when her light forsook him, it bequeathed
Ennobling sorrow; and her memory breathed
A sweetness that survived her living days,
As odorous scents outlast the censer's blaze.
Or if a trouble dimmed their golden joy,
'Twas outward dross and not infused alloy;
Their home knew but affection's look and speech,
A little Heaven beyond dissension's reach.
But midst her kindred there was strife and gall;
Save one congenial sister, they were all
Such foils to her bright intellect and grace,
As if she had engrossed the virtue of her race;
Her nature strove th' unnatural feuds to heal,
Her wisdom made the weak to her appeal;
And though the wounds she cured were soon unclosed,
Unwearied still her kindness interposed.

The stanzas addressed to John Kemble I have never heard admired to the
fullness of my feeling. Can anything be finer than this?

A majesty possessed
His transport's most impetuous tone;
And to each passion of his breast
The graces gave their zone.

or:

Who forgets that white discrowned head,
Those bursts of reason's half-extinguished glare,
Those tears upon Cordelia's bosom shed
In doubt more touching than despair,
If 'twas reality he felt?

or:

Fair as some classic dome,
Robust and richly graced,
Your Kemble's spirit was the home

Of genius and of taste.—
Taste like the silent dial's power,
    That, when supernal light is given,
Can measure inspiration's hour
    And tell its height in Heaven.
At once ennobled and correct,
    His mind surveyed the tragic page;
And what the actor could effect,
    The scholar could presage.

These stanzas are in Campbell's best style. Had he possessed as much lyric flow as force, his odes might have vied with those of Collins. But though soaring upward on a strong pinion, his flights are never prolonged, and in this province, which earnestness and justness of sentiment, simplicity of imagery, and a picturesque turn in expression seem to have marked out as his own, he is surpassed by Shelley, Coleridge, and Wordsworth from their greater power of continuous self-impulse.

I do not know where to class Campbell as a poet. What he has done seems to be by snatches, and his poems might have been published under the title of *Leisure Hours, or Recreations of a Great Man*. They seem like fragments not very heedfully stricken off from the bed of a rich quarry; for with all their individual finish, there is no trace of a fixed purpose to be discerned in them. They appear to be merely occasional effusions, like natural popular poetry; but as they are written by an accomplished man in these modern days of design and system, we are prompted to look for an aim, a pervading purpose. We shall not find it. Campbell has given us much delight; if he has not directly stimulated our thoughts, he has done so much to refine our tastes that we must respectfully tender the poetic garland.

And thou, Anacreon Moore, sweet warbler of Erin, what an ecstasy of sensation must thy poetic life have been! Certainly the dancing of the blood never before inspired so many verses. Moore's poetry is to literature what the compositions of Rossini are to music. It is the heyday of animal existence, embellished by a brilliant fancy and ardent though superficial affections. The giddy flush of youthful impulse empurples the most pensive strains of his patriotism, throbs in his most delicate touches of pathos, and is felt as much in "Tara's Halls" as in the description of the harem. His muse is light of step and free of air, yet not vulgarly free; she is not a little excited, but it is with quaffing the purest and most sparkling champagne. There is no temperance, no chastened harmony in her grief or in her joy. His melodies are metrically perfect; they absolutely set themselves to music, and talk of spring, and the most voluptuous breath of the blossom-laden western breeze, and the wildest notes of the just returning birds. For his poetic embodying of a particular stage of human existence and his scintillating wit, will Moore chiefly be remembered. He has been boon-companion and toastmaster to the youth of his day. This could not last. When he ceased to be young, and to warble his own verses, their fascination in a great measure disappeared. Many are now not more attractive than dead flowers in a close room. Anacreon cannot really charm when his hair is gray; there is a time for all things, and the gayest youth loves not the Epicurean old man. Yet he too is a poet; and his works will not be suffered to go out of print, though they are even now little read. Of course his reputation as a prose writer is another matter, and apart from our present purpose.

The poetry of Walter Scott has been superseded by his prose, yet it fills no unimportant niche in the literary history of the last half century, and may be read at least once in life with great pleasure. "Marmion," "The Lay of the Last Minstrel," etc., cannot indeed be companions of those sabbath hours of which the weariest, dreariest life need not be destitute, for their bearing is not upon the true life of man, his immortal life. Coleridge felt this so deeply that in a lately published work (*Letters, Conversations, &c., of S. T. Coleridge*) he is recorded to have said, "not twenty lines of Scott's poetry will ever reach posterity; it has relation to nothing." This is altogether too harsh, and proves that the philosopher is subject to narrowness and partial views, from his peculiar mode of looking at an object, equally with the mere man of taste. These poems are chiefly remarkable for presenting pictures of particular epochs, and, considered in that light, truly admirable. Much poetry has come down to us thus far, whose interest is almost exclusively of the same nature; in which at least moral conflict does not constitute the prominent interest.

To one who has read Scott's novels first, and looks in his poems for the same dramatic interest, the rich humor, the tragic force, the highly wrought yet flowing dialogue, and the countless minutiae in the finish of character, they must bring disappointment. For their excellence consists in graphic descriptions of architecture and natural scenery, a happy choice of subject, and effective grouping of slightly sketched characters, combined with steady march and great simplicity of narrative. Here and there sentiments are introduced, always just and gracefully worded, but without that delicacy of shading, fine and harmonious as Nature's workmanship in the roseleaf, which delights us in his prose works. It is indeed astonishing that he should lose so much by a constraint so lightly worn; for his facility of versification is wonderful, his numbers seem almost to have coined themselves, and you cannot detect anything like searching for a word to tag a verse withal. Yet certain it is, we receive no adequate idea of the exuberance and versatility of his genius, or his great knowledge of the human heart, from his poetry. His lore is there as profusely displayed, his good sense and tact as admirable as in his prose works; and if only on account of their fidelity of description, these poems are invaluable, and must always hold a place in English literature. They are interesting, too, as giving a more complete idea of the character and habits of one of our greatest and best men than his remarkable modesty would permit the public to obtain more directly. His modes of life, his personal feelings, are nowhere so detailed as in the epistles prefixed to the cantos of "Marmion." These bring us close to his side, and leading us with him through the rural and romantic scenes he loved, talk with us by the way of all the rich associations of which he was master. His dogs are with him; he surveys these dumb friends with the eye of a sportsman and a philosopher, and omits nothing in the description of them which could interest either. An old castle frowns upon the road; he bids its story live before you with all the animation of a drama and the fidelity of a chronicle. Are topics of the day introduced? He states his opinions with firmness and composure, expresses his admiration with energy, and where he dissents from those he addresses, does so with unaffected candor and cordial benignity. Good and great man! More and more imposing as nearer seen; thou art like that product of a superhuman intellect, that stately temple which rears its head in the clouds, yet must be studied through and through for months and years, to be appreciated in all its grandeur.

Nothing surprises me more in Scott's poetry than that a person of so strong imagination should see everything so in detail as he does. Nothing interferes with his faculty of observation. No minor part is sacrificed to give effect to the whole; no peculiar light cast on the picture: you only see through a wonderfully farseeing and accurately observing pair of eyes, and all this when he has so decided a taste for the picturesque. Take as a specimen the opening description in "Marmion."

THE CASTLE

Day set on Norham's castled steep,
And Tweed's fair river, broad and deep,
  And Cheviot's mountains lone;
The battled towers, the donjon keep,
The loophole grates, where captives weep,
The flanking walls that round it sweep,
  In yellow lustre shone;—
The warriors on the turrets high,
Moving athwart the evening sky,
  Seemed forms of giant height;
Their armor, as it caught the rays,
Flashed back again the western blaze,
  In lines of dazzling light.
St. George's banner, broad and gay,
Now faded, as the fading ray
  Less bright, and less, was flung;
The evening gale had scarce the power
To wave it on the donjon tower,
  So heavily it hung.
The scouts had parted on their search,
  The castle gates were barred,
Above the gloomy portal arch,
Timing his footsteps to a march,
  The warden kept his guard,
Low humming, as he passed along,
Some ancient border gathering song.

How picturesque, yet how minute! Not even Wordsworth, devoted as he is to nature, and to visible as well as invisible truth, can compare with Scott in fidelity of description. Not even Crabbe, that least imaginative of poets, can compare with him for accuracy of touch and truth of coloring. Scott's faculties being nicely balanced, never disturbed one another; we perceive this even more distinctly in his poetry than in his prose, perhaps because less excited while reading it.

I have said that Crabbe was the least imaginative of poets. He has *no* imagination in the commonly received sense of the term; there is nothing of creation in his works; nay, I dare affirm, in opposition to that refined critic, Sir James Mackintosh, that there was no touch of an idealizing tendency in his mind; yet he is a poet; he is so through his calm but deep and steady sympathy with all that is human; he is so by his distinguished power of observation; he is so by his graphic skill. No literature boasts an author more individual than Crabbe. He is unique. Moore described him well.

> Grand from the truth that reigns o'er all,
> The unshrinking truth that lets her light
> Through life's low, dark interior fall,
> Opening the whole severely bright.
> Yet softening, as she frowns along,
> O'er scenes which angels weep to see,
> Where truth herself half veils the wrong
> In pity of the misery.

I could never enter into the state of a mind which could support viewing life and human nature as Crabbe's did, softened by no cool shadow, gladdened by no rose-light. I wish Sir Walter Scott, when expressing his admiration for the poetry of Crabbe, had told us more distinctly the nature of the impressions he received from it. Sir Walter, while he observes with equal accuracy, is sure to detect something comic or something lovely, some pretty dalliance of light and shade in the "low, dark interior" of the most outwardly desolate hovel. Cowper saw the follies and vices of mankind as clearly, but his Christian love is an ever softly murmuring undercurrent, which relieves the rude sounds of the upper world. Crabbe in his view of the human mind may be compared with Cowper; or Scott, as the anatomist in his view of the human form, may be compared with the painter or sculptor. Unshrinking, he tears apart that glorious fabric which has been called the "crown of creation," he sees its beauty and its strength with calm approval, its weaknesses, its liability to disease, with stern pity or cold indignation. His nicely dissected or undraped virtues are scarcely more attractive than vices, and with profound knowledge of the passions, not one ray of passionate enthusiasm casts a glow over the dramatic recitative of his poems.

Crabbe has the true spirit of the man of science; he seeks truth alone, content to take all parts of God's creations as they are, if he may but get a distinct idea of the laws which govern them. He sees human nature as only a human being could see it, but he describes it like a spirit which has never known human longings; yet in no unfriendly temper—far from it; but with a strange bleak fidelity, unbiased either by impatience or tenderness.

The poor and humble owe him much, for he has made them known to the upper classes not as they ought to be, but as they really are; and in so doing, in distinctly portraying the evils of their condition, he has opened the way to amelioration. He is the poet of the lower classes, though probably rather valuable to them as an interpreter than agreeable as a household friend. They like something more stimulating; they would prefer gin or rum to lemonade. Indeed that class of readers rarely like to find themselves in print; they want something romantic, something which takes them out of their sphere; and high-sounding words such as they are not in the habit of using have peculiar charms for them. That is a high stage of culture in which simplicity is appreciated.

The same cold tints pervade Crabbe's descriptions of natural scenery. We can conceive that his eye was educated at the seaside. An east wind blows, his colors are sharp and decided, and the glitter which falls upon land and wave has no warmth.

It is difficult to do Crabbe justice, both because the subject is so large a one, and because tempted to discuss it rather in admiration than in love.

I turn to one whom I love still more than I admire; the gentle, the gifted, the ill-fated Shelley.

Let not prejudice deny him a place among the great ones of the day. The youth of Shelley was unfortunate. He committed many errors; what else could be expected from one so precocious? No one begins life so early who is not at some period forced to retrace his steps; and those precepts which are learned so happily from a mother's lips must be paid for by the heart's best blood when bought from the stern teacher, experience. Poor Shelley! Thou wert the warmest of philanthropists, yet doomed to live at variance with thy country and thy time. Full of the spirit of genuine Christianity, yet ranking thyself among unbelievers, because in early life thou hadst been bewildered by seeing it perverted; sinking beneath those precious gifts which should have made a world thine own, intoxicated with thy lyric enthusiasm and thick-coming fancies, adoring Nature as a goddess, yet misinterpreting her oracles, cut off from life just as thou wert beginning to read it aright; O most musical, most melancholy singer; who that has a soul to feel genius, a heart to grieve over misguided nobleness, can forbear watering the profuse blossoms of thy too early closed spring with tears of sympathy, of love, and (if we may dare it for one so superior in intellect) of pity?

Although the struggles of Shelley's mind destroyed that serenity of tone which is essential to the finest poetry, and his tenderness has not always that elevation of hope which should hallow it; although in no one of his productions is there sufficient unity of purpose and regulation of parts to entitle it to unlimited admiration, yet they all abound with passages of infinite beauty, and in two particulars he surpasses any poet of the day.

First in fertility of fancy. Here his riches, from want of arrangement, sometimes fail to give pleasure, yet we cannot but perceive that they are priceless riches. In this respect parts of his "Adonais," "Marianne's Dream," and "Medusa" are not to be excelled except in Shakespeare.

Second in sympathy with Nature. To her lightest tones his being gave an echo; truly she *spoke* to him, and it is this which gives unequaled melody to his versification; I say "unequaled," for I do not think either Moore or Coleridge can here vie with him, though each is in his way a master of the lyre. The rush, the flow, the delicacy of vibration in Shelley's verse can only be paralleled by the waterfall, the rivulet, the notes of the bird and of the insect world. This is a sort of excellence not frequently to be expected now, when men listen less zealously than of old to the mystic whispers of Nature; when little is understood that is not told in set phrases, and when even poets write more frequently in curtained and carpeted rooms than "among thickets of odoriferous blossoming trees and flowery glades," as Shelley did.

It were a "curious piece of work enough" to run a parallel between the skylark of Shelley and that of Wordsworth, and thus illustrate mental processes so similar in dissimilitude. The mood of mind, the ideas, are not unlike in the two. Hear Wordsworth:

> *Up with me, up with me, into the clouds, etc.*

> Lift me, guide me, till I find
> The spot which seems so to thy mind,
> I have walked through wildernesses dreary,
> And to-day my heart is weary,

Had I now the wings of a Fairy
Up to thee would I fly;
There is madness about thee, and joy divine
In that song of thine:

Joyous as morning, thou art laughing and scorning;
And though little troubled with sloth,
Drunken Lark, thou would'st be loth
To be such a traveller as I!
Happy, happy liver,
With a soul as strong as a mountain river,
Pouring out praise to the Almighty Giver,
Joy and jollity be with us both.

Hear Shelley:

Hail to thee, blithe spirit!
Bird thou never wert,
That from heaven or near it,
Pourest thy full heart
In *profuse strains of unpremeditated art.*

Higher still and higher,
From the earth thou springest,
Like a cloud of fire
The blue deep thou wingest,
And singing still dost soar, and soaring ever singest.

In the golden lightning
Of the sunken sun,
O'er which clouds are bright'ning,
Thou dost float and run
Like an unbodied joy, whose race is just begun.

The pale purple even
Melts around thy flight;
Like a star of heaven,
In the broad daylight,
Thou art unseen, but yet I hear thy shrill delight.

Keen as are the arrows
Of that silver sphere,
Whose intense lamp narrows
In the white dawn clear,
Until we hardly see, we feel that it is there.

All the earth and air
With thy voice is loud,

As, when night is bare,
From one lonely cloud
The moon rains out her beams, and heaven is overflowed.

What thou art we know not;
What is most like thee?
From rainbow clouds there flow not
Drops so bright to see,
As from thy presence showers a rain of melody.

Like a poet hidden
In the light of thought,
Singing hymns unbidden,
Till the world is wrought
To sympathy with hopes and fears it heeded not.

Like a high-born maiden
In a palace tower,
Soothing her love-laden
Soul in secret hour,
With music sweet as love which overflows her bower.

Like a glow-worm golden
In a dell of dew
Scattering unbeholden
Its aerial hue
Among the flowers and grass which screen it from the view:

Like a rose embowered
In its own green leaves,
By warm winds deflowered,
Till the scent it gives
Makes faint with too much sweet, those heavy-winged thieves.

Sound of vernal showers
On the twinkling grass,
Rain-awakened flowers,
All that ever was
Joyous, and clear, and fresh, thy music doth surpass.

Teach us, sprite or bird,
What sweet thoughts are thine:
I have never heard
Praise of love or wine
That panted forth a flood of rapture so divine.

Chorus hymeneal,
Or triumphant chaunt,

Matched with thine would be all
    But an empty vaunt—
A thing wherein we feel there is some hidden want.

What objects are the fountains
    Of thy happy strain?
What fields, or waves, or mountains?
    What shapes of sky or plain?
What love of thine own kind? what ignorance of pain?

With thy clear keen joyance
    Languor cannot be;
Shadow of annoyance
    Never came near thee:
Thou lovest; but ne'er knew love's sad satiety.

I do not like to omit a word of it; but it is taking too much room. Should we not say from the samples before us that Shelley, in melody and exuberance of fancy, was incalculably superior to Wordsworth? But mark their *inferences.*

Shelley:

Teach me half the gladness
    That thy brain must know,
Such harmonious madness
    From my lips would flow
The world should listen, then, as I am listening now.

Wordsworth:

What though my course be rugged and uneven,
To prickly moors and dusty ways confined,
Yet, hearing thee and others of thy kind
As full of gladness and as free of heaven,
I o'er the earth will go plodding on
By myself, cheerfully, till the day is done.

If Wordsworth have superiority, then it consists in greater maturity and dignity of sentiment.

While reading Shelley, we must surrender ourselves without reserve to the magnetic power of genius; we must not expect to be satisfied, but rest content with being stimulated. He alone who can resign his soul in unquestioning simplicity to the descant of the nightingale or the absorption of the seaside may hope to receive from the mind of a Shelley the suggestions which, to those who know how to receive, he can so liberally impart.

I cannot leave Shelley without quoting two or three stanzas, in which
he speaks of himself, and which are full of his peculiar beauties and peculiar
faults:

> A frail form,
> A phantom among men, companionless,
> As the last cloud of an expiring storm,
> Whose thunder is its knell; he, as I guess,
> Had gazed on Nature's naked loveliness
> Actaeon-like, and now he fled astray
> With feeble steps o'er the world's wilderness,
> And his own thoughts, along that rugged way,
> Pursued like raging hounds their father and their prey.
>
> A pard-like Spirit, beautiful and swift—
> A love in desolation masked; a power
> Girt round with weakness; it can scarce uplift
> The weight of the superincumbent hour;
> It is a dying lamp, a falling shower,
> A breaking billow; even whilst we speak
> Is it not broken? On the withering flower
> The killing sun smiles brightly; on a cheek
> The life can burn in blood, even while the heart may break.
>
> His head was bound with pansies overblown,
> And faded violets, white, and pied, and blue;
> And a light spear, topped with a cypress cone,
> Round whose rude shaft dark ivy-tresses grew
> Yet dripping with the forest's noon-day dew,
> Vibrated as the ever-beating heart
> Shook the weak hand that grasped it; of that crew
> He came the last, neglected and apart;
> A herd-abandoned deer, struck by the hunter's dart.

Shelley is no longer "neglected," but I believe his works have never been
republished in this country, and therefore these extracts may be new to most
readers.

Byron naturally takes place next his friend in our hall of imagery. Both
are noble poetic shapes, both mournful in their beauty. The radiant gentleness of Shelley's brow and eye delights us, but there are marks of suffering
on that delicate cheek and about that sweet mouth; while a sorrowful
indignation curls too strongly the lip, lightens too fiercely in the eye of
Byron.

The unfortunate Byron ("unfortunate" I call him, because "mind and destiny are but two names for one idea") has long been at rest; the adoration and the hatred of which he was the object are both dying out. His poems have done their work; a strong personal interest no longer gives them a factitious charm, and they are beginning to find their proper level. Their value is twofold—immortal and eternal, as records of thoughts and feelings which must be immortally and eternally interesting to the mind of individual man; historical, because they are the most complete chronicle of a particular set of impulses in the public mind.

How much of the first sort of value the poems of Byron possess, posterity must decide, and the verdict can only be ascertained by degrees; I for one should say not much. There are many beautiful pictures; infinite wit, but too local and temporary in its range to be greatly prized beyond his own time; little originality; but much vigor, both of thought and expression; with a deep, even a passionate love of the beautiful and grand. I have often thought in relation to him of Wordsworth's description of

> A youth to whom was given
> So much of Earth, so much of Heaven,
> And such impetuous blood.

> .   .   .   .   .   .

> Whatever in those climes he found,
> Irregular in sight or sound,
>   Did to his mind impart
> A kindred impulse, seemed allied
> To his own powers, and justified
>   The workings of his heart.

> Nor less to feed voluptuous thought,
> The beauteous forms of nature wrought,
>   Fair trees and lovely flowers;
> The breezes their own languor lent,
> The stars had feelings which they sent
>   Into those gorgeous bowers.

> And in his worst pursuits, I ween,
> That sometimes there did intervene
>   Pure hopes of high intent;
> For passions linked to forms so fair
> And stately, needs must have their share
>   Of noble sentiment.

It is worthy of remark that Byron's moral perversion never paralyzed or obscured his intellectual powers, though it might lower their aims. With regard to the plan and style of his works, he showed strong good sense and clear judgment. The man who indulged such narrowing egotism, such irrational scorn, would prune and polish without mercy the stanzas in which he uttered them; and this bewildered idealist was a very bigot in behoof of the commonsensical satirist, the almost peevish realist, Pope.

Historically these poems are valuable as records of that strange malady, that sickness of the soul, which has in our day cankered so visibly the rose of youth. It is common to speak of the Byronic mood as morbid, false, and foolish; it is the two former, and if it could be avoided, would most assuredly be the latter also. But how can it always be avoided? Like as a fever rages in the blood before we are aware, even so creeps upon the soul this disease, offspring of a moral malaria, an influence impalpable till we feel its results within ourselves. Since skillful physicians are not always at hand, would it not be better to purify the atmosphere than to rail at the patient? Those who have passed through this process seem to have wondrous little pity for those who are still struggling with its horrors, and very little care to aid them. Yet if it be disease, does it not claim pity, and would it not be well to try some other remedy than hard knocks for its cure? What though these sick youths do mourn and lament somewhat wearisomely, and we feel vexed on bright May mornings to have them try to persuade us that this beautiful green earth, with all its flowers and birdnotes, is no better than a vast hospital? Consider, it is a relief to the delirious to rave audibly, and few like Professor Teufelsdröckh have strength to keep a whole satanic school in the soul from spouting aloud. What says the benign Uhland?

> If our first lays too piteous have been,
>   And you have feared our tears would never cease,
> If we too gloomily life's prose have seen,
>   Nor suffered Man nor Mouse to dwell in peace,
> Yet pardon us for our youth's sake. The vine
> Must weep from her crushed grapes the generous wine;
> Not without pain the precious beverage flows;
> Thus joy and power may yet spring from the woes
> Which have so wearied every long-tasked ear; etc.

There is no getting rid of the epidemic of the season, however annoying and useless it may seem. You cannot cough down an influenza; it will cough you down.

Why young people will just now profess themselves so very miserable, for no better reason than that assigned by the poet to some "inquiring friends,"

> Nought do I mourn I e'er possessed,
> I grieve that I cannot be blessed;

I have here no room to explain. Enough that there has for some time prevailed a sickliness of feeling, whose highest watermark may be found in the writings of Byron. He is the "power man" (as the Germans call him, meaning perhaps the *power-loom!*) who has woven into one tissue all those myriad threads, tear-stained and dull gray, with which the malignant spiders of speculation had filled the machine shop of society, and by so doing has, though I admit unintentionally, conferred benefits upon us incalculable for a long time to come. He has lived through this experience for us, and shown us that the natural fruits of indulgence in such a temper are dissonance, cynicism, irritability, and all uncharitableness. Accordingly since his time the evil has lessened. With this warning before them, let the young examine that world, which seems at times so deformed by evils and endless contradictions,

> Control them and subdue, transmute, bereave
> Of their bad influence, and the good receive.

Grief loses half its charm when we find that others have endured the same to a higher degree, and lived through it. Nor do I believe that the misanthropy of Byron ever made a single misanthrope; that his skepticism, so uneasy and sorrowful beneath its thin mask of levity, ever made a single skeptic. I know those whom it has cured of their yet half-developed errors. I believe it has cured thousands.

As supplying materials for the history of opinion then, Byron's poems will be valuable. And as a poet, I believe posterity will assign him no obscure place, though he will probably be classed far beneath some who have exercised a less obvious or immediate influence on their own times; beneath the noble three of whom I am yet to speak, whose merits are immortal because their tendencies are towards immortality, and all whose influence must be a growing influence; beneath Southey, Coleridge, and Wordsworth.

Before proceeding to discuss these last, for which there is hardly room in the present paper, I would be allowed to conclude this division of my subject with a fine passage in which Shelley speaks of Byron. I wish to quote it, because it is of kindred strain with what Walter Scott and Rogers (in his "Italy") have written about their much abused compeer. It is well for us to see great men judging so gently, and excusing so generously, faults from which they themselves are entirely free; faults at which men of less genius, and less purity too, found it so easy and pleasant to rail. I quote it in preference to anything from Scott and Rogers, because I presume it to be less generally known.

In apostrophizing Venice, Shelley says:

> Perish! let there only be
> Floating o'er thy hearthless sea,
> As the garment of thy sky
> Clothes the world immortally,
> One remembrance more sublime
> Than the tattered pall of Time,
> Which scarce hides thy visage wan;
> That a tempest-cleaving swan
>   Of the songs of Albion,
> Driven from his ancestral streams
>   By the might of evil dreams,
> Found a nest in thee; and Ocean
> Welcomed him with such emotion
> That its joy grew his, and sprung
> From his lips like music flung
> O'er a mighty thunder-fit
> Chastening terror;—What though yet
>   Poesy's unfailing river,
> Which through Albion winds for ever
>   Lashing with melodious wave
>   Many a sacred poet's grave,
>   Mourn its latest nursling fled!
> What though thou, with all thy dead,
>   Scarce can for this fame repay
>   Aught thine own;—oh, rather say
>   Though thy sins and slaveries foul
>   Overcloud a sun-like soul!

> As the ghost of Homer clings
> Round Scamander's wasting springs;
> As divinest Shakespeare's might
> Fills Avon and the world with light;
> Like omniscient power, which he
> Imaged 'mid mortality:
> As the love from Petrarch's urn
> Yet amid yon hills doth burn,
> A quenchless lamp by which the heart
> Sees things unearthly; so thou art,
> Mighty spirit; so shall be
> The city that did refuge thee.

In earlier days the greatest poets addressed themselves more to the passions or heart-emotions of their fellow-men than to their thoughts or mind-emotions. The passions were then in their natural state and held their natural places in the character. They were not made sickly by a false refinement, or stimulated to a diseased and incessantly craving state. Men loved and hated to excess, perhaps; but there was nothing factitious in their love or hatred. The tone of poetry, even when employed on the most tragic subjects, might waken in the hearer's heart a chord of joy; for on such natural sorrow there was a healthful life, an energy which told of healing yet to come and the endless riches of love and hope.

How different is its tone in *Faust* and *Manfred;* how false to simple nature, yet how true to the time! As the mechanism of society has become more complex and must be regulated more by combined efforts, desire after individuality brings him who manifests it into a state of conflict with society. This is felt from a passion, whether it be love or ambition, which seeks to make its own world independent of trivial daily circumstances, and struggles long against the lessons of experience, which tell it that such singleness of effort and of possession cannot be consistent with that grand maxim of the day, *the greatest happiness of the greatest number.* Not until equally enlightened and humble, can the human being learn that individuality of character is not necessarily combined with individuality of possession, but depends alone on the zealous observance of truth. Few can be wise enough to realize with Schiller that "to be truly immortal one must live in the whole." The mind struggles long, before it can resolve on sacrificing anything of its impulsive nature to the requisitions of the time. And while it struggles it mourns, and these lamentations compose the popular poetry. Men do not now look in poetry for a serene world, amid whose vocal groves and green meads they may refresh themselves after the heat of action, and in paradisaical quiet listen to the tales of other days. No! dissatisfied and repressed, they want to be made to weep, because in so doing they feel themselves in some sense free.

All this conflict and apparently bootless fretting and wailing mark a transition-state—a state of gradual revolution in which men try all things, seeing what they hold fast, and feel that it is good. But there are some, the pilot-minds of the age, who cannot submit to pass all their lives in experimentalizing. They cannot consent to drift across the waves in the hope of finding *somewhere* a haven and a home; but seeing the blue sky over them, and believing that God's love is everywhere, try to make the best of that spot on which they have been placed, and not infrequently, by the aid of spiritual assistance more benign than that of Faust's Lemures, win from the raging billows large territories whose sands they can convert into Eden bowers, tenanted by lovely and majestic shapes.

Such are Southey, Coleridge, and Wordsworth. They could not be satisfied like Byron with embodying the peculiar wit or peculiar sufferings of the times; nor like Scott, with depicting an era which has said its say and produced its fruit; nor like Campbell, with occasionally giving a voice and a permanent being to some brilliant moment or fair scene. Not of nobler nature, not more richly endowed than Shelley, they were not doomed to misguided efforts and baffled strivings; much less could they like Moore consider poetry merely as the harmonious expression of transient sensations. To them poetry was, must be, the expression of what is eternal in man's nature through illustrations drawn from his temporal state; a representation in letters of fire on life's dark curtain of that which lies beyond; philosophy dressed in the robes of taste and imagination; the voice of Nature and of God, humanized by being echoed back from the understanding hearts of priests and seers! Of course this could not be the popular poetry of the day. Being eminently the product of reflection and experience, it could only be appreciated by those who had thought and felt to some depth. I confess that it is not the best possible poetry, since so exclusively adapted to the meditative few. In Shakespeare or Homer there is for minds of every grade as much as they are competent to receive; the shallow or careless find there amusement; minds of a higher order, meaning which enlightens and beauty which enchants them.

This fault which I have admitted, this want of universality is not surprising, since it was necessary for those three poets to stand apart from the tide of opinion and disregard the popular tastes, in order to attain firmness, depth, or permanent beauty. And they being, as I have said, the pilot-minds of their time, their works enjoy a growing, though not a rapidly growing, popularity.

Coleridge in particular is now very much read, nor, notwithstanding his was but occasional homage to the shrine of poesy, was he the least valuable votary of the three, since if he has done least, if his works form a less perfect whole and are therefore less satisfactory than those of the other two, he is far more suggestive, more filled with the divine magnetism of intuition than they.

The muse of Southey is a beautiful statue of crystal in whose bosom burns an immortal flame. We hardly admire as they deserve the perfection of the finish and the elegance of the contours, because our attention is so fixed on the radiance which glows through them.

Thus Southey is remarkable for the fidelity and still more for the grace of his descriptions; for his elegant manner of expressing sentiments noble, delicate, and consistent in their tone; for his imagination, but more than all for his expansive and fervent piety.

In his fidelity of description there is nothing of the minute accuracy of Scott. Southey takes no pleasure in making little dots and marks; his style is free and bold, yet always true, sometimes elaborately true, to nature. Indeed if he has a fault, it is that he elaborates too much. He himself has said that poetry should be "thoroughly erudite, thoroughly animated, and thoroughly natural." His poetry cannot always boast of the two last essentials. Even in his most brilliant passages there is nothing of the heat of inspiration, nothing of that celestial fire which makes us feel that the author has by intensifying the action of his mind raised himself to communion with superior intelligences. It is where he is most calm that he is most beautiful; and accordingly, he is more excellent in the expression of sentiment than in narration. Scarce any writer presents to us a sentiment with such a tearful depth of expression; but though it is a tearful depth, those tears were shed long since, and faith and love have hallowed them. You nowhere are made to feel the bitterness, the vehemence of present emotion; but the phoenix born from passion is seen hovering over the ashes of what was once combined with it. Southey is particularly exquisite in painting those sentiments which arise from the parental and filial relation: whether the daughter looks back from her heavenly lover and the opening bowers of bliss, still tenderly solicitous for her father, whom she in the true language of woman's heart recommends to favor as

That wretched, persecuted, *poor good* man;

or the father, as in "Thalaba," shows a faith in the benignity and holiness of his lost daughter, which the lover, who had given up for her so high a destiny, wanted—or as in "Roderick," the miserable, sinful child wanders back to relieve himself from the load of pollution at the feet of a sainted mother; always—always he speaks from a full, a sanctified soul in tones of thrilling melody.

The imagination of Southey is marked by similar traits; there is no flash, no scintillation about it, but a steady light as of day itself. As specimens of his best manner, I would mention the last stage of Thalaba's journey to the Domdaniel Caves, and in the "Curse of Kehama," the sea-palace of Baly, "The Glendoveer," and "The Ship of Heaven." As Southey's poems are not very generally read, I will extract the two latter:

THE SHIP OF HEAVEN

The ship of heaven, instinct with thought displayed
Its living sail and glides along the sky,
    On either side, in wavy tide,
The clouds of morn along its path divide;
The winds that swept in wild career on high,
Before its presence check their charmed force;
The winds that, loitering, lagged along their course
Around the living bark enamored play,
Swell underneath the sail, and sing before its way.

That bark in shape was like the furrowed shell
Wherein the sea-nymphs to their parent king,
On festal days their duteous offerings bring;
Its hue? go watch the last green light

Ere evening yields the western sky to night,
Or fix upon the sun thy strenuous sight
Till thou hast reached its orb of chrysolite.
  The sail, from end to end displayed,
  Bent, like a rainbow, o'er the maid;
    An angel's head with visual eye,
Through trackless space directs its chosen way;
    Nor aid of wing, nor foot nor fin,
Requires to voyage o'er the obedient sky.
Smooth as the swan when not a breeze at even
    Disturbs the surface of the silver stream,
Through air and sunshine sails the ship of heaven.

Southey professes to have borrowed the description of the Glendoveer
from an old and forgotten book. He has given the prose extract in a note
to the "Curse of Kehama," and I think no one can compare the two without feeling that the true alchemy has been at work there. His poetry is a
new and life-giving element to the very striking thoughts he borrowed.
Charcoal and diamonds are not more unlike in their effect upon the observer.

THE GLENDOVEER

Of human form divine was he,
The immortal youth of heaven who floated by,
  Even such as that divinest form shall be
In those blest stages of our mortal race,
        When no infirmity,
Low thought, nor base desire, nor wasting care
Deface the semblance of our heavenly sire—
    The wings of eagle or of cherubim
    Had seemed unworthy him;
Angelic power and dignity and grace
Were in his glorious pennons; from the neck
Down to the ankle reached their swelling web
Richer than robes of Tyrian dye, that deck
                Imperial majesty:
Their color, like the winter's moonless sky
When all the stars of midnight's canopy
Shine forth; or like the azure deep at noon,
Reflecting back to heaven a brighter blue,
Such was their tint when closed, but when outspread,
                The permeating light

Shed through their substance thin a varying hue;
 Now bright as when the rose,
Beauteous as fragrant, gives to scent and sight
A like delight, now like the juice that flows
 From Douro's generous vine,
Or ruby when with deepest red it glows;
Or as the morning clouds refulgent shine
When at forthcoming of the lord of day,
 The orient, like a shrine,
Kindles as it receives the rising ray,
 And heralding his way
Proclaims the presence of the power divine—
 Thus glorious were the wings
Of that celestial spirit, as he went
Disporting through his native element—
 Nor these alone
The gorgeous beauties that they gave to view;
Through the broad membrane branched a pliant bone,
 Spreading like fibres from their parent stem;
Its vines like interwoven silver shone;
 Or as the chaster hue
Of pearls that grace some sultan's diadem.
Now with slow stroke and strong, behold him smite
 The buoyant air, and now in gentler flight
On motionless wing expanded, shoot along.

All Southey's works are instinct and replete with the experiences of piety, from that fine picture of natural religion, Joan of Arc's confession of faith, to that as noble sermon as ever was preached upon Christianity, the penitence of Roderic the Goth. This last is the most original and elevated in its design of all Southey's poems. In "Thalaba" and "Joan of Arc" he had illustrated the power of faith; in "Madoc" contrasted religion under a pure and simple form with the hydra ugliness of superstition. In "Kehama" he has exhibited virtue struggling against the most dreadful inflictions with heavenly fortitude, and made manifest to us the angel-guards who love to wait on innocence and goodness. But in "Roderic" the design has even a higher scope, is more difficult of execution; and, so far as I know, unique. The temptations which beset a single soul have been a frequent subject, and one sure of sympathy if treated with any power. Breathlessly we watch the conflict, with heartfelt anguish mourn defeat, or with heart-expanding triumph hail a conquest. But where there *has* been defeat, to lead us back with the fallen one through the thorny and desolate paths of repentance to purification, to win not only our pity but our sympathy for one crushed and degraded by his own sin; and finally, through his faithful though secret efforts to redeem the past, secure to him, justly blighted and world-forsaken as he is, not only our sorrowing love, but our respect—*this* Southey alone has done, perhaps alone could do. As a scene of unrivaled excellence, both for its meaning and its manner, I would mention that of Florinda's return with Roderic (who is disguised as a monk, and whom she does not know) to her father; when after such a strife of heart-rending words and heart-broken tears, they, exhausted, seat themselves on the bank of the little stream, and watch together the quiet moon. Never has Christianity spoken in accents of more penetrating tenderness since the promise was given to them that be weary and heavy-laden.

Of Coleridge I shall say little. Few minds are capable of fathoming his by their own sympathies, and he has left us no adequate manifestation of himself as a poet by which to judge him. As for his dramas, I consider them complete failures, and more like visions than dramas. For a metaphysical mind like his to attempt that walk was scarcely more judicious than it would be for a blind man to essay painting the bay of Naples. Many of his smaller pieces are perfect in their way, indeed no writer could excel him in depicting a single mood of mind, as dejection for instance. Could Shakespeare have surpassed these lines?

> A grief without a pang, void, dark, and drear,
> A stifled, drowsy, unimpassioned grief,
> Which finds no natural outlet, no relief,
> In word, or sigh, or tear.
>   O Lady, in this wan and heartless mood,
> To other thoughts by yonder throstle wooed,
> All this long eve, so balmy and serene,
>   Have I been gazing on the western sky
> And its peculiar tint of yellow green:
>   And still I gaze—and with how blank an eye!
> And those thin clouds above, in flakes and bars,
> That give away their motion to the stars;
> Those stars, that glide behind them or between,
> Now sparkling, now bedimmed, but always seen;
> Yon crescent moon, as fixed as if it grew

In its own cloudless, starless lake of blue;
   I see them all, so excellently fair,
I see, not feel, how beautiful they are!
      My genial spirits fail,
      And what can these avail
To lift the smothering weight from off my breast?
    It were a vain endeavour,
      Though I should gaze for ever
On that green light that lingers in the West,
I may not hope from outward forms to win
   The passion and the life whose fountains are within.

Give Coleridge a canvas, and he will paint a single mood as if his colors were made of the mind's own atoms. Here he is very unlike Southey. There is nothing of the spectator about Coleridge; he is all life; not impassioned, not vehement, but searching, intellectual life, which seems "listening through the frame" to its own pulses.

I have little more to say at present except to express a great, though not fanatical veneration for Coleridge, and a conviction that the benefits conferred by him on this and future ages are as yet incalculable. Every mind will praise him for what it can best receive from him. He can suggest to an infinite degree; he can *in*form, but he cannot *re*form and renovate. To the unprepared he is nothing, to the prepared, everything. Of him may be said what he said of Nature,

      We receive but what we give,
    In kind though not in measure.

I was once requested by a very sensible and excellent personage to explain what is meant by "Christabel" and "The Ancient Mariner." I declined the task. I had not then seen Coleridge's answer to a question of similar tenor from Mrs. Barbauld, or I should have referred to that as an expression not altogether unintelligible of the discrepancy which must ever exist between those minds which are commonly styled *rational* (as the received definition of *common* sense is insensibility to *uncommon* sense) and that of Coleridge. As to myself, if I understand nothing beyond the execution of those "singularly wild and original poems," I could not tell my gratitude for the degree of refinement which taste has received from them. To those who cannot understand the voice of Nature or poetry unless it speak in apothegms and tag each story with a moral, I have nothing to say. My own greatest obligation to Coleridge I have already mentioned. It is for his suggestive power that I thank him.

Wordsworth! Beloved friend and venerated teacher; it is more easy and perhaps as profitable to speak of thee. It is less difficult to interpret thee, since no *acquired nature* but merely a theory severs thee from my mind.

Classification on such a subject is rarely satisfactory, yet I will attempt to define in that way the impressions produced by Wordsworth on myself. I esteem his characteristics to be—of spirit,

> Perfect simplicity,
> Perfect truth,
> Perfect love.

Of mind or talent,

> Calmness,
> Penetration,
> Power of Analysis.

Of manner,

> Energetic greatness,
> Pathetic tenderness,
> Mild, persuasive eloquence.

The time has gone by when groundlings could laugh with impunity at "Peter Bell" and the "Idiot Mother." Almost every line of Wordsworth has been quoted and requoted; every feeling echoed back, and every drop of that "cup of still and serious thought" drunk up by some "spirit profound"; enough to satisfy the giver.

Wordsworth is emphatically the friend and teacher of mature years. Youth, in whose bosom "the stately passions burn," is little disposed to drink with him from the

> urn
> Of lowly pleasure.

He has not an idealizing tendency, if by this be meant the desire of creating from materials supplied by our minds, and by the world in which they abide for a season, a new and more beautiful world. It is the aspiration of a noble nature animated by genius, it is allied with the resolve for self-perfection; and few without some of its influence can bring to blossom the bud of any virtue. It is fruitful in illusions, but those illusions have heavenly truth interwoven with their temporary errors. But the mind of Wordsworth, like that of the man of science, finds enough of beauty in the real present world. He delights in penetrating the designs of God rather than in sketching designs of his own. Generally speaking, minds in which the faculty of observation is so prominent have little enthusiasm, little dignity of sentiment. That is indeed an intellect of the first order which can see the great in the little, and dignify the petty operations of Nature by tracing through them her most sublime principles. Wordsworth scrutinizes man and nature with the exact and searching eye of a Cervantes, a Fielding, or a Richter, but without any love for that humorous wit which cannot obtain its needful food unaided by such scrutiny; while dissection merely for curiosity's sake is his horror. He has the delicacy of perception, the universality of feeling which distinguish Shakespeare and the three or four other poets of the first class, and might have taken rank with them had he been equally gifted with versatility of talent. Many might reply, "in wanting this last he wants the better half." To this I cannot agree. Talent, or facility in making use of thought, is dependent in a great measure on education and circumstance; while thought itself is immortal as the soul from which it radiates. Wherever we perceive a profound thought, however imperfectly expressed, we offer a higher homage than we can to commonplace thoughts, however beautiful, or if expressed with all that grace of art which it is often most easy for ordinary minds to acquire. There is a suggestive and stimulating power in original thought which cannot be gauged by the first sensation or temporary effect it produces. The circles grow wider and wider as the impulse is propagated through the deep waters of eternity. An exhibition of talent causes immediate delight; almost all of us can enjoy seeing a thing well done; not all of us can enjoy being roused to do and dare for ourselves. Yet when the mind *is* roused to penetrate the secret meaning of each human effort, a higher pleasure and a greater benefit may be derived from the rude but masterly sketch than from the elaborately finished miniature. In the former case our creative powers are taxed to supply what is wanting, while in the latter our tastes are refined by admiring what another has created. Now since I esteem Wordsworth as superior in originality and philosophic unity of thought to the other poets I have been discussing, I give him the highest place, though they may be superior to *him* either in melody, brilliancy of fancy, dramatic power, or general versatility of talent. Yet I do not place him on a par with those who combine those minor excellencies with originality and philosophic unity of thought. He is not a Shakespeare, but he is the greatest poet of the day; and this is more remarkable, as he is *par excellence* a didactic poet.

I have paid him the most flattering tribute in saying that there is not a line of his which has not been quoted and requoted. Men have found such a response to their lightest as well as their deepest feelings, such beautiful morality with such lucid philosophy, that every thinking mind has consciously or unconsciously appropriated something from Wordsworth. Those who have never read his poems have imbibed some part of their spirit from the public or private discourse of his happy pupils; and it is as yet impossible to estimate duly the effect which the balm of his meditations has had in allaying the fever of the public heart, as exhibited in the writings of Byron and Shelley.

But as I said before, he is not for youth: he is too tranquil. His early years were passed in listening to, his mature years in interpreting, the oracles of Nature; and though in pity and in love he sympathizes with the conflicts of life, it is not by mingling his tears with the sufferer's, but by the consolations of patient faith that he would heal their griefs.

The sonnet on tranquillity, to be found in the present little volume, exhibits him true to his old love and natural religion.

> Tranquillity! the solemn aim wert thou
> In heathen schools of philosophic lore;
> Heart-stricken by stern destiny of yore,
> The tragic muse thee served with thoughtful vow;
> And what of hope Elysium could allow
> Was fondly seized by Sculpture, to restore
> Peace to the mourner's soul; but he who wore
> The crown of thorns around his bleeding brow,
> Warmed our sad being with his glorious light;
> Then arts which still had drawn a softening grace
> From shadowy fountains of the Infinite,
> Communed with that idea face to face;

And move around it now as planets run,
Each in its orbit round the central sun.

The doctrine of tranquillity does not suit the impetuous blood of the young, yet some there are who, with pulses of temperate and even though warm and lively beat, are able to prize such poetry from their earliest days. One young person in particular I knew, very like his own description of

Those whose hearts every hour run wild,
But never yet did go astray;

who had read nothing but Wordsworth, and had by him been plentifully fed. I do not mean that she never skimmed novels nor dipped into periodicals; but she never, properly speaking, read, i.e., comprehended and reflected on any other book. But as all knowledge has been taught by Professor Jacotot from the *Telemachus* of Fénelon, so was she taught the secrets of the universe from Wordsworth's poems. He pointed out to her how

The primal duties shine aloft like stars,
The charities that soothe, and heal, and bless,
Are scattered at the feet of Man—like flowers.

He read her lectures about the daisy, the robin red-breast, and the waterfall. He taught her to study Nature and *feel* God's presence; to enjoy and prize human sympathies without needing the stimulus of human passions; to love beauty with a faith which enabled her to perceive it amid seeming ugliness, to hope goodness so as to create it. And she was a very pretty specimen of Wordsworthianism; so sincere, so simple, so animated and so equable, so hopeful and so calm. She was confiding as an infant, and so may remain till her latest day, for she has no touch of idolatry; and her trustfulness is not in any chosen person or persons, but in the goodness of God, who will always protect those who are true to themselves and sincere towards others.

But the young in general are idolaters. They will have their private chapels of ease in the great temple of nature; they will ornament according to fancy their favorite shrines; and all too frequently look with aversion or contempt upon all others. Till this ceases to be so, till they can feel the general beauty of design and live content to be immortal in the grand whole, they cannot really love Wordsworth; nor can to them the "simplest flower" bring "thoughts that lie too deep for tears." Happy his pupils; they are gentle, they are calm, and they must always be progressing in our knowledge; for to a mind which can sympathize with his, no hour, no scene can possibly be barren.

The contents of the lately published little volume * accord perfectly in essentials with those of the preceding four. The sonnets are like those he has previously written—equally unfinished as sonnets, equally full of meaning as poems. If it be the case with all his poems, that scarcely one forms a perfect whole by itself, but is valuable as a leaf out of his mind, it is peculiarly so with his sonnets. I presume he only makes use of this difficult mode of writing because it is a concise one for the expression of a single thought or a single mood. I know not that one of his sonnets is polished and wrought to a point, as this most artistical of all poems should be; but neither do I know one which does not contain something we would not willingly lose. As the beautiful sonnet which I shall give presently, whose import is so wide and yet so easily understood, contains in the motto what Messer Petrarca would have said in the two concluding lines.

> (Miss not the occasion; by the forelock take
>   That subtle power, the never-halting time,
> Lest a mere moment's putting off should make
>   Mischance almost as heavy as a crime)—
> Wait, prithee, wait! this answer Lesbia threw
>   Forth to her dove, and took no further heed;
> Her eyes were busy, while her fingers flew
>   Across the harp, with soul-engrossing speed;
> But from that bondage when her thoughts were freed,
> She rose, and toward the shut casement drew,
> Whence the poor, unregarded favourite, true
> To old affections, had been heard to plead
> With flapping wing for entrance—What a shriek
> Forced from that voice so lately tuned to a strain
> Of harmony!—a shriek of terror, pain,
> And self-reproach!—for from aloft a kite
> Pounced, and the dove, which from its ruthless beak
> She could not rescue, perished in her sight!

* *Yarrow Revisited, and Other Poems.*

Even the sonnet upon sonnets, so perfect in the details, is not perfect as a whole.

However, I am not so fastidious as some persons about the dress of a thought. These sonnets are so replete with sweetness and spirit that we can excuse their want of symmetry; and probably should not feel it, except from comparison with more highly finished works of the same kind. One more let me extract, which should be laid to heart:

> Desponding father! mark this altered bough
> So beautiful of late, with sunshine warmed,
> Or moist with dews; what more unsightly now,
> Its blossom shrivelled, and its fruit, if formed,
> Invisible! yet Spring her genial brow
> Knits not o'er that discolouring and decay
> As false to expectation. Nor fret thou
> At like unlovely process in the May
> Of human life; a stripling's graces blow,
> Fade and are shed, that from their timely fall
> (Misdeem it not a cankerous change) may grow
> Rich mellow bearings that for thanks shall call;
> In all men sinful is it to be slow
> To hope—in parents sinful above all.

"Yarrow Revisited" is a beautiful reverie. It ought to be read as such, for it has no determined aim. These are fine verses:

> And what for this frail world were all
>   That mortals do or suffer,
> Did no responsive harp, no pen,
>   Memorial tribute offer?
> Yea, what were mighty Nature's self?
>   Her features, could they win us,
> Unhelped by the poetic voice
>   That hourly speaks within us?
>
> Nor deem that localized romance
>   Plays false with our affections;
> Unsanctifies our tears—made sport
>   For fanciful dejections;
> Ah, no! the visions of the past
>   Sustain the heart in feeling
> Life as she is—our changeful life,
>   With friends and kindred dealing.

and this stanza,

> Eternal blessings on the Muse,
>   And her divine employment!
> The blameless Muse, who trains her sons
>   For hope and calm enjoyment;
> Albeit sickness, lingering yet,
>   Has o'er their pillow brooded;
> And care waylay their steps—a sprite
>   Not easily eluded.

reminds us of what Scott says in his farewell to the Harp of the North:

> Much have I owed thy strains, on life's long way,
>   Through secret woes the world has never known,
> When on the weary night dawned wearier day,
>   And bitter was the grief devoured alone,
> That I o'erlive such woes, Enchantress, is thine own.

"The Egyptian Maid" is distinguished by a soft visionary style of painting, and a stealthy alluring movement like the rippling of advancing waters which I do not remember elsewhere in Wordsworth's writings.

"The Armenian Lady's Love" is a fine ballad. The following verses are admirable for delicacy of sentiment and musical sweetness:

> Judge both fugitives with knowledge;
>   In those old romantic days
> Mighty were the soul's commandments
>   To support, restrain, or raise.
> Foes might hang upon their path, snakes rustle near,
> But nothing from their inward selves had they to fear.

> Thought infirm ne'er came between them,
>   Whether printing desert sands
> With accordant steps, or gathering
>   Forest fruit with social hands;
> Or whispering like two reeds that in the cold moonbeam
> Bend with the breeze their heads beside a crystal stream.

The "Evening Voluntaries" are very beautiful in manner, and full of suggestions. The second is worth extracting as a forcible exhibition of one of Wordsworth's leading opinions:

> Not in the lucid intervals of life
> That come but as a curse to party strife;

Not in some hour when pleasure with a sigh
Of languor, puts his rosy garland by;
Not in the breathing times of that poor slave
Who daily piles up wealth in Mammon's cave,
Is nature felt, or can be; nor do words
Which practised talent readily affords
Prove that her hands have touched responsive chords.
Nor has her gentle beauty power to move
With genuine rapture and with fervent love
The soul of genius, if he dares to take
Life's rule from passion craved for passion's sake;
Untaught that meekness is the cherished bent
Of all the truly great and all the innocent;
But who is innocent? By grace divine,
Not otherwise, O Nature! we are thine,
Through good and evil thine, or just degree
Of rational and manly sympathy,
To all that earth from pensive hearts is stealing,
And heaven is now to gladdened eyes revealing,
Add every charm the universe can show
Through every change its aspects undergo,
Care may be respited, but not repealed;
No perfect cure grows on that bounded field,
Vain is the pleasure, a false calm the peace,
If he through whom alone our conflicts cease,
Our virtuous hopes without relapse advance,
Come not to speed the soul's deliverance;
To the distempered intellect refuse
His gracious help, or give what we abuse.

But nothing in this volume better deserves attention than "Lines Suggested by a Portrait from the Pencil of F. Stone" and "Stanzas on the Power of Sound." The first for a refinement and justness of thought rarely surpassed, and the second for a lyric flow, a swelling inspiration, and a width of range which Wordsworth has never equaled except in the "Ode on the Intimations of Immortality," and the noble ode or rather hymn to duty. It should be read entire, and I shall not quote a line. By a singular naïveté the poet has prefixed to these stanzas a table of contents. This distrust of his reader seems to prove that he had risen above his usual level.

What more to the purpose can we say about Wordsworth, except—read him. Like his beloved Nature, to be known he must be loved. His thoughts may be transfused, but never adequately interpreted. Verily,

To paint *his* being to a grovelling mind,
Were like describing pictures to the blind.

But no one in whose bosom there yet lives a spark of nature or feeling need despair of some time sympathizing with him; since one of the most brilliantly factitious writers of the day, one I should have singled out as sevenfold shielded against his gentle influence, has paid him so feeling a tribute:

How must thy lone and lofty soul have gone
Exulting on its way, beyond the loud
Self-taunting mockery of the scoffers grown
Tethered and dulled to Nature, in the crowd!
Earth has no nobler, no more moral sight
Than a Great Poet, whom the world disowns,
But stills not, neither angers; from his height
As from a star, float forth his sphere-like tones;
He wits not whether the vexed herd may hear
The music wafted to the reverent ear;
And far man's wrath, or scorn, or heed above,
Smiles down the calm disdain of his majestic love!
[*From Stanzas addressed by Bulwer to Wordsworth.*]

Read him then in your leisure hours, and when you walk into the summer fields you shall find the sky more blue, the flowers more fair, the birds more musical, your minds more awake, and your hearts more tender for having held communion with him.

I have not troubled myself to point out the occasional affectations of Southey, the frequent obscurity of Coleridge, or the diffuseness of Wordsworth. I should fear to be treated like the critic mentioned in the story Addison quotes from Boccalini, whom Apollo rewarded for his labors by presenting him with a bushel of chaff from which all the wheat had been winnowed. For myself I think that where there is such beauty and strength, we can afford to be silent about slight defects; and that we refine our tastes more effectually by venerating the grand and lovely than by detecting the little and mean.

9

ITALY *

I

These three publications [*Autobiography of Alfieri, Memoirs of Cellini, Cary's Dante*] have come to hand during the last month—a cheering gleam upon the winter of our discontent, as we saw the flood of bad translations of worse books which swelled upon the country.

We love our country well. The many false deeds and low thoughts—the devotion to interest—the forgetfulness of principle—the indifference to high and noble sentiment—which have in so many ways darkened her history for some years back, have not made us despair of her yet fulfilling the great destiny whose promise rose like a star only some half a century ago upon the hopes of the world.

Should that start be forsaken by its angel, and those hopes set finally in shame, the church which we had built out of the ruins of the ancient time must fall to the ground. This church seemed a model of divine art. It contained a labyrinth which, when threaded by aid of the clue of faith, presented, reviewed from its center, the most admirable harmony and depth of meaning in its design, and comprised in its decorations all the symbols of permanent interest of which the mind of man has made use for the benefit of man. Such was to be the church, a church not made with hands, catholic, universal, all whose stones should be living stones, its officials the cherubim of love and knowledge, its worship wiser and purer action than has before been known to men. To such a church men do indeed constitute the state, and men indeed we hoped from the American church and state, men so truly human that they could not live while those made in their own likeness were bound down to the condition of brutes.

Should hopes be baffled, should such a church fall in the building, such a state find no realization except to the eye of the poet, God would still be in the world and surely guide each bird that can be patient on the wing to its home at last. But expectations so noble which find so broad a basis in the past, which link it so harmoniously with the future, cannot lightly be

---

* From the New York *Daily Tribune,* November 13 and 18, 1845.

abandoned. The same Power leads by a pillar of cloud as by a pillar of fire—the Power that deemed even Moses worthy only of a distant view of the Promised Land.

And to those who cherish such expectations, rational education, considered in various ways and bearings, must be the one great topic of interest, an enterprise in which the humblest service is precious and honorable to any who can inspire its soul. Our thoughts anticipate with eager foresight the race that may grow up from this amalgamation of all races of the world which our situation induces. It was the pride and greatness of ancient nations to keep their blood unmixed, but it must be ours to be willing to mingle, to accept in a generous spirit what each clime and race has to offer us.

It is indeed the case that much diseased substance is offered to form this new body, and if there be not in ourselves a nucleus, a heart of force and purity to assimilate these strange and various materials into a very high form of organic life, they must needs induce one distorted, corrupt, and degraded beyond the example of other times and places. There will be no medium about it. Our grand scene of action demands grandeur and purity of action; declining these, one must suffer from so base failure in proportion to the success that should have been.

It would be the worthiest occupation of mind to ascertain the conditions propitious for this meeting of the nations in their new home, and to provide preventions for obvious dangers that attend it. It would be occupation for which the broadest and deepest knowledge of human nature in its mental, moral, and bodily relations, the noblest freedom from prejudice, with the finest discrimination as to differences and relations, directed and enlightened by a prophetic sense as to what Man is designed by God to become, would all be needed to fit the thinker. Yet some portion of these qualities or of some of those qualities, if accompanied by earnestness and aspiration, may enable him to offer useful suggestions. The mass of ignorance and selfishness is such that no grain of leaven must be despised.

And as the men of all countries come hither to find a home and become parts of a new life, so do the books of all countries gravitate towards the new center. Copious infusions from all quarters mingle daily with the new thought which is to grow into American mind and develop American literature.

As every ship brings us foreign teachers, a knowledge of living contemporary tongues must in the course of fifty years become the commonest attainment. There exists no doubt in the minds of those who can judge that the German, French, Italian, Spanish, and Portuguese tongues might by familiar instruction and *an intelligent method* be taught with perfect ease during the years of childhood, so that the child would have as distinct a sense of their several natures and nearly as much expertness in their use as in his own. The higher uses of such knowledge can of course be expected only in a more advanced state of the faculties, but it is a pity that the acquaintance with the medium of thought should be deferred to a period when the mind is sufficiently grown to bend its chief attention on the thoughts themselves. Much of the most precious part of short human lives is now wasted from an ignorance of what might easily be done for children, and without taking from them the time they need for common life, play, and bodily growth more than at present.

Meanwhile English begins to vie with German and French literature in the number, though not in the goodness of the translations from other languages. The indefatigable Germans can translate and do other things too, so that geniuses often there apply themselves to the work as an amusement; even the all-employed Goethe has translated one of the books before us (*Memoirs of Cellini*). But in English we know but of one, Coleridge's *Wallenstein,* where the reader will feel the electric current undiminished by the medium through which it comes to him. And then the profligate abuse of the power of translation has been unparalleled, whether in the choice of books or the carelessness in disguising those that were good in a hideous mask. No falsehood can be worse than this of deforming the expression of a great man's thoughts, of corrupting that form which he has watched and toiled and suffered to make beautiful and true. We know no falsehood that should call a more painful blush to the cheek of one engaged in it. We rejoice to see from Wiley & Putnam's advertisement that attention has been drawn to this subject, and that they are anxious to offer none but good and well-translated books for general reading.

We have no narrowness in our view of the contents of such books. We are not afraid of new standards and new examples. Only give enough of them, variety enough, and from well-intentioned, generous minds. America can choose what she wants, if she has sufficient range of choice, and if there is any real reason, any deep root in the tastes and opinions she holds at present, she will not lightly yield them. Only give her what is good of its kind. Her hope is not in ignorance but in knowledge. We are indeed very fond of range, and that if there is check, there should be countercheck; and in this view we are delighted to see these great Italians domesticated here. We have had somewhat too much of the French and Germans of late. We value unchangeably our sparkling and rapid French friend; still more the searching, honest, and in highest sense visionary German genius. But there is not on earth and, we dare to say it, will not be again genius like that of Italy or that can compare with it in its own way. Italy and Greece were alike in this: those sunny skies ripened their fruits perfectly. The oil and honey of Greece and the wine of Italy not only suggest but satisfy. There we find fulfillment, elsewhere great achievement only.

O acute, cautious, calculating Yankee, O graceful, witty, hotblooded, flimsy Southron, and thou, man of the West, going too fast to pick up a thought or leave a flower upon thy path, look at these men with their great fiery passions, but will and intellect still greater and stronger; perfectly sincere, from a contempt of falsehood; if they had acted wrong they said and felt that they had and that it was base and hateful in them; sagacious, as children are, not from calculation but because the fine instincts of nature were unspoiled in them. I speak now of Alfieri and Cellini. Dante had all their instinctive greatness and deep-seated fire, with the reflective and creative faculties besides, to an extent of which they never dreamed.

He who reads these biographies may take them from several points of view; as pictures of manners, as sincere transcripts of the men and true times, they are not and could not be surpassed. That truth which Rousseau sought so painfully and vainly by self-brooding, subtle analysis, they attained without an effort. Why they felt they cared little, but what they felt they surely knew, and where a fly or worm has injured the peach, its passage is exactly marked, so that you are sure the rest is fair and sound. Both as physiological and physical histories, they are full of instruction. In Alfieri especially, the nervous disease generated in the frame by any uncongenial tension of the brain, the periodical crises in his health, the manner in which his accesses of passion came upon him, afford infinite suggestion to one who has an eye for the circumstances which fashion the destiny of man. Let the physician compare the furies of Alfieri with the silent rages of Byron, and give the mother and pedagogue the light in which they are now wholly wanting, how to treat such noble plants in the early stages of growth.—We think the "hated cap" would not be put a second time on the head so easily diseased.

The biography of Cellini, it is commonly said, is more interesting than any romance. It is a romance, with the character of the hero fully brought out. Cellini lived in all the fullness of inward vigor, all the variety of outward adventure, and passed through all the signs of the Zodiac in his circling course, occasionally raising a little vapor from the art magic. He was really the Orlando Furioso turned goldsmith, and Angelica and all the Peers of France joined in the show. However, he never lived deeply; he had not the time; the creative energy turned outward too easily; and took those forms that still enchant the mind of Europe. Alfieri was different in this. He was like the root of some splendid southern plant, engaged beneath a heap of rubbish. Above him was a glorious sky fit to develop his form and excite his colors, but he was compelled to a long and terrible struggle to get up where he could be free to receive its influence. Institutions, language, family, modes of education—all were unfit for him; and perhaps no man was ever called to such efforts, after he had reached manly age, to unmake and remake himself before he could become what his inward aspiration craved. All this deepened his nature, and it was deep. It is his great force of will and the compression of nature within its iron grasp, where nature was so powerful and impulsive, that constitutes the charm of his writings. It is the man Alfieri who moves, nay, overpowers us, and not his writings, which have no flow nor plastic beauty. But we feel the vital dynamics and imagine it all.

By us Americans, if really such we ever are to be, Alfieri should be held sacred as a godfather and holy light. He was a harbinger of what most gives this time its character and value. He was the friend of liberty, the friend of man, in the sense that Burns was—of the native nobleness of man.

Soiled and degraded men he hated. He was indeed a man of pitiless hatred as of boundless love, and he had bitter prejudices too, but they were from antipathies too strongly intertwined with his sympathies for any hand less powerful than that of death to rend them away.

But space does not permit to do any justice to such a life as Alfieri's. Let others read it not from their habitual but an eternal point of view, and they cannot mistake its purport. Some will be most touched by the storms of his youth, others by the exploits and conquests of his later years, but all will find him in the words of his friend Casella, "sculptured just as he was, lofty, strange, and extreme, not only in his natural characteristics, but in every work that did not seem to him unworthy of his generous affections. And where he went too far, it is easy to perceive his excesses always flowed from some praiseworthy sentiment."

Among a crowd of remarks suggested to the mind by reperusal of this book, to us a friend of many years' standing, we hastily note the following:

Alfieri knew how to be a friend, and had friends such as his masculine and uncompromising temper fitted him to endure and keep. He had even two or three of these noble friends. He was a perfect lover in delicacy of sentiment, in person, in devotion, in a desire for constancy, in a high ideal growing always higher, and he was at last happy in love. Many geniuses have spoken worthily of women in their works, but he speaks of woman as she wishes to be spoken of and declares that he met the desire of his soul realized in life. This, almost alone, is an instance where a great nature was permanently satisfied, and the claims of man and woman equally met, where one of the parties had the impatient fire of genius. His testimony on this subject is of so rare a sort we must copy it:

"My fourth and last passion, fortunately for me, showed itself by symptoms entirely different from the three first. In the former my intellect had little of the fires of passion, but now my heart and my genius were both equally kindled, and if my passion was less impetuous, it became more profound and lasting. Such was the flame which by degrees absorbed every affection and thought of my being, and it will never fade away except with my life. Two months satisfied me that I had now found the *true woman*, for instead of encountering in her, as in all common women, an obstacle to literary glory, a hindrance to useful occupations, and a damper to thought, she proved a high stimulus, a pure solace, and an alluring example to every beautiful work. Prizing a treasure so rare, I gave myself away to her irrevocably. And I certainly erred not. More than twelve years have passed, and while I am writing this chitchat, having reached that calm season when passion loses its blandishments, I cherish her dearer than ever, and I love her just in proportion as flow by her in the lapse of time these esteemed toll-gatherers of departing beauty. In her my soul is exalted, softened, and made better day by day, and I will dare to say and believe she has found in me support and consolation."

We have spoken of the peculiarities in Alfieri's physical condition. These naturally led him to seek solace in violent exercise, and as in the case of Beckford and Byron horses were his friends in the hour of danger. This sort of man is the modern Achilles, the "tamer of horses." In what degree the health of Alfieri was improved and his sympathies awakened by the society and care of these noble animals is very evident. Almost all persons, perhaps all that are in a natural state, need to stand in patriarchal relations with the animals most correspondent with their character. We have the highest respect for this instinct and belief in the good it brings; if understood it would be cherished, not ridiculed. But these subjects are boundless. We must postpone what we had to say of Dante to the next occasion.

II

Translating Dante is indeed a labor of love. It is one in which even a moderate degree of success is impossible. No great poet can be well translated. The form of his thought is inseparable from his thought. The births of his genius are perfect beings; body and soul are in such perfect harmony that you cannot at all alter one without veiling the other. The variation in cadence and modulation, even where the words are exactly rendered, takes, not only from the form of the thought but from the thought itself, its most delicate charm. Translations come to us as a message to the lover from the lady of his love, through the lips of a confidant or menial—we are obliged to imagine what was most vital in the original utterance.

These difficulties, always insuperable, are accumulated a hundredfold in the case of Dante, both by the extraordinary depth and subtlety of his thought and his no less extraordinary power of concentrating its expression till every verse is like a blade of thoroughly tempered steel. You might as well attempt to translate a glance of fire from the human eye into any other language—even music cannot do that.

We think then that the use of Cary's translation or any other can never be to diffuse a knowledge of Dante. This is not in its nature diffusible; he is one of those to whom others must draw near; he cannot be brought to them. He has no superficial charm to cheat the reader into a belief that he knows him, without entrance into the same sphere.

These translations can be of use only to the translators as a means of deliberate study of the original, or to others who are studying the original and wish to compare their own version of doubtful passages with that of an older disciple, highly qualified both by devotion and mental develop- ment for the study.

We must say a few words as to the pedantic folly with which this study has been prosecuted in this country and, we believe, in England. Not only the tragedies of Alfieri and the *Faust* of Goethe but the *Divine Comedy* of Dante—a work which it is not probable there are at any one time a hun- dred minds able to appreciate—are turned into schoolbooks for little girls who have just left their hoops and dolls, and boys whose highest ambition it is to ride a horse that will run away and brave the tutor in a college frolic.

This is done from the idea that in order to get acquainted with a foreign language the student must read books that have attained the dignity of classics, and also which are "hard." Hard indeed it must be for the Muses to see their lyres thus turned into gridirons for preparation of a schoolgirl's lunch; harder still for the younglings to be called to chew and digest thunderbolts in lieu of their natural bread and butter.

Are there not "classics" enough which would not suffer by being put to such uses? In Greek, Homer is a book for a boy; must you give him Plato because it is harder? Is there no choice among the Latins? Are all who wrote in the Latin tongue equally fit for the appreciation of sixteen Yankee years? In Italian have you not Tasso, Ariosto, and other writers who have really a great deal that the immature mind can enjoy, without choking them with the stern politics of Alfieri or piling upon a brain still soft the mountainous meanings of Dante. Indeed they are saved from suffering by the perfect ignorance of all meaning in which they leave these great authors, fancying to their lifelong misfortune that they have read them. I have been reminded by the remarks of my young friends on these subjects of the Irish peasant who, having been educated on a book prepared for his use, called *Reading Made Easy*, blesses through life the kindness that taught him his *"Radamadasy,"* and of the child who, hearing her father quote Horace, observed, *"she* thought Latin was even sillier than French."

No less pedantic is the style in which the grown-up (in stature at least) undertake to become acquainted with Dante. They get the best Italian dictionary, all the notes they can find—amounting in themselves to a library, for his countrymen have not been less exerted and benighted in their way of regarding him. Painfully they study through the book, seeking with anxious attention to know who Signor This is and who was the cousin of Signora That, and whether any real papal or anti-papal meaning was couched by Dante under the remark that such a one wore a greatcoat. A mind whose small chambers look yet smaller from being crowded with furniture from all parts of the world, bought by labor, not received from inheritance or won by love, asserts that he must understand Dante well, better than any other person probably, because he has studied him through in this way thirty or forty times. As well declare you have a better appreciation of Shakespeare than anyone else because you had identified the birthplace of Dame Quickly, or ascertained the churchyard where the ghost of the Royal Dane hid from the sight of that far more celestial spirit, his son.

O painstaking friends, shut your books, clear your minds from artificial nonsense, and feel that only by spirit can spirit be discerned. Dante, like each other great one, took the stuff that lay around him and wove it to a garment of light. It is not by raveling that you will best appreciate its tissue or design. It is not by studying out the petty strifes or external relations of his time that you can become acquainted with the thought of Dante. To him these things were only soil in which to plant himself—figures by which to dramatize and evolve his ideas. Would you learn him, go listen in the forest of human passions to all the terrible voices he heard with a tormented but never to be deafened ear; go down into the hells where each excess that mars the harmony of nature is punished by the sinner finding no food except from his own harvest; pass through the purgatories of speculation, of struggling hope and faith, never quite quenched but smoldering often and long beneath the ashes. Soar if thou canst, but if thou canst not, clear thine eye to see this great eagle soar into the higher region where forms arrange themselves for stellar dance and spheral melody, and thought with constantly accelerated motion raises itself in a spiral which can end only in the heart of the Supreme.

He who finds in himself no fitness to study Dante in this way should regard himself as in the position of a candidate for the ancient Mysteries when rejected as unfit for initiation. He should seek in other ways to purify, expand, and strengthen his being, and when he feels that he is nobler and stronger, return and try again whether he is "grown up to it," as the Germans say.

"The difficulty is in the thoughts," and this cannot be obviated by the most minute acquaintance with the history of the times. Comparison of one edition with another is of use as a guard against obstruction through mistake. Still more useful will be the method recommended by Mr. Cary of comparing the poet with himself; this belongs to the intellectual method, and is the way in which we study our intellectual friend.

The versions of Cary and Lyell will be found of use to the student, if he wants to compare his ideas with those of accomplished fellow-students. The poems in the London book [Lyell's *Lyrical Poems of Dante*] would aid much in a full appreciation of the *Comedy;* they ought to be read in the original, but copies are not easily to be met here, unless in the great libraries. The *Vita Nuova* is the noblest expression extant of the inward life of love, the best preface and comment to everything else that Dante did.

'Tis pity that the designs of Flaxman are so poorly reproduced in this American book. It would have been far better to have had it a little clearer, and thus better done. The designs of Flaxman were a really noble comment upon Dante, and might help to interpret him; we are sorry that those who can see only a few of them should see them so imperfectly. But in some, as in that upon the meeting with Farinata, the expression cannot be destroyed, while one line of the original remains. The "lost portrait" we do not like as preface to the *Divine Comedy*. To that belongs our accustomed object of reverence, the head of Dante, such as the Florentine women saw him when they thought his hair and head were still singed, his face dark and sublime, with what he had seen *below*.

Prefixed to the other book is a head "from a cast taken after death at Ravenna, A.D. 1321." It has the grandeur which death sometimes puts on: the fullness of past life is there, but made sacred in eternity. It is also the only front view of Dante we have seen. It is not unworthy to mark the point

> When vigor failed the towering fantasy:
> But yet the will rolled onward, like a wheel
> In even motion by the love impelled
> That moves the sun in Heaven and all the stars.

We ought to say in behalf of this publication that whosoever wants Cary's version will rejoice at last to possess it in so fair and legible guise, as we do.

Before leaving the Italians, we must mourn over the misprints of our homages to the great tragedian in Thursday's paper. Our MSS. being as illegible as if we were a great genius, we never complain of these errata, except when we are made to reverse our meaning on some vital point. We did not say that Alfieri was a perfect man in person, nor sundry other things that are there; but we do mourn at seeming to say of our friends, "Why they felt they care little, but what they felt they *scarcely* knew," when in fact we asserted, "what they felt they *surely* knew."

In the article on China we had made this assertion of the Chinese music: "Like their poetry, the music is of the narrowest monotony"; in place of which stands this assertion: "Like true poetry, the music is of the narrowest monotony." But we trust the most careless reader would not think the merely human mind capable of so original a remark, and will put this blasphemy to account of that little demon who has so much to answer for in the sufferings of poor writers before they can get their thoughts to the eyes of their fellow-creatures in print, that there seems scarcely a chance of his being redeemed as long as there is one in existence to accuse him.

10

AMERICAN LITERATURE *

Some thinkers may object to this essay, that we are about to write of that which has as yet no existence.

For it does not follow because many books are written by persons born in America that there exists an American literature. Books which imitate or represent the thoughts and life of Europe do not constitute an American literature. Before such can exist, an original idea must animate this nation and fresh currents of life must call into life fresh thoughts along its shores.

We have no sympathy with national vanity. We are not anxious to prove that there is as yet much American literature. Of those who think and write among us in the methods and of the thoughts of Europe, we are not impatient; if their minds are still best adapted to such food and such action. If their books express life of mind and character in graceful forms, they are good and we like them. We consider them as colonists and useful schoolmasters to our people in a transition state; which lasts rather longer than is occupied in passing bodily the ocean which separates the New from the Old World.

We have been accused of an undue attachment to foreign continental literature, and it is true that in childhood we had well nigh "forgotten our English" while constantly reading in other languages. Still what we loved in the literature of continental Europe was the range and force of ideal manifestation in forms of national and individual greatness. A model was before us in the great Latins of simple masculine minds seizing upon life with unbroken power. The stamp both of nationality and individuality was very strong upon them; their lives and thoughts stood out in clear and bold relief. The English character has the iron force of the Latins, but not the frankness and expansion. Like their fruits, they need a summer sky to give them more sweetness and a richer flavor. This does not apply to Shakespeare, who has all the fine side of English genius, with the rich coloring and more fluent life of the Catholic countries. Other poets of

* From *Papers on Literature and Art,* 1846.

358

England also are expansive more or less, and soar freely to seek the blue sky, but take it as a whole, there is in English literature, as in English character, a reminiscence of walls and ceilings, a tendency to the arbitrary and conventional that repels a mind trained in admiration of the antique spirit. It is only in later days that we are learning to prize the peculiar greatness which a thousand times outweighs this fault, and which has enabled English genius to go forth from its insular position and conquer such vast dominion in the realms both of matter and of mind.

Yet there is often between child and parent a reaction from excessive influence having been exerted, and such a one we have experienced in behalf of our country against England. We use her language and receive in torrents the influence of her thought, yet it is in many respects uncongenial and injurious to our constitution. What suits Great Britain, with her insular position and consequent need to concentrate and intensify her life, her limited monarchy and spirit of trade, does not suit a mixed race continually enriched with new blood from other stocks the most unlike that of our first descent, with ample field and verge enough to range in and leave every impulse free, and abundant opportunity to develop a genius wide and full as our rivers, flowery, luxuriant, and impassioned as our vast prairies, rooted in strength as the rocks on which the Puritan fathers landed.

That such a genius is to rise and work in this hemisphere we are confident; equally so that scarce the first faint streaks of that day's dawn are yet visible. It is sad for those that foresee, to know they may not live to share its glories, yet it is sweet, too, to know that every act and word uttered in the light of that foresight may tend to hasten or ennoble its fulfillment.

That day will not rise till the fusion of races among us is more complete. It will not rise till this nation shall attain sufficient moral and intellectual dignity to prize moral and intellectual no less highly than political freedom, not till the physical resources of the country being explored, all its regions studded with towns, broken by the plow, netted together by railways and telegraph lines, talent shall be left at leisure to turn its energies upon the higher department of man's existence. Nor then shall it be seen till from the leisurely and yearning soul of that riper time national ideas shall take birth, ideas craving to be clothed in a thousand fresh and original forms.

Without such ideas all attempts to construct a national literature must end in abortions like the monster of Frankenstein, things with forms and the instincts of forms, but soulless and therefore revolting. We cannot have expression till there is something to be expressed.

The symptoms of such a birth may be seen in a longing felt here and there for the sustenance of such ideas. At present it shows itself, where felt, in sympathy with the prevalent tone of society by attempts at external action, such as are classed under the head of social reform. But it needs to go deeper before we can have poets, needs to penetrate beneath the springs of action, to stir and remake the soil as by the action of fire.

Another symptom is the need felt by individuals of being even sternly sincere. This is the one great means by which alone progress can be essentially furthered. Truth is the nursing mother of genius. No man can be absolutely true to himself, eschewing cant, compromise, servile imitation, and complaisance, without becoming original, for there is in every creature a fountain of life which, if not choked back by stones and other dead rubbish, will create a fresh atmosphere and bring to life fresh beauty. And it is the same with the nation as with the individual man.

The best work we do for the future is by such truth. By use of that in whatever way, we harrow the soil and lay it open to the sun and air. The winds from all quarters of the globe bring seed enough, and there is nothing wanting but preparation of the soil and freedom in the atmosphere, for ripening of a new and golden harvest.

We are sad that we cannot be present at the gathering-in of this harvest. And yet we are joyous too, when we think that though our name may not be writ on the pillar of our country's fame, we can really do far more towards rearing it than those who come at a later period and to a seemingly fairer task. *Now,* the humblest effort, made in a noble spirit and with religious hope, cannot fail to be even infinitely useful. Whether we introduce some noble model from another time and clime to encourage aspiration in our own, or cheer into blossom the simplest wood-flower that ever rose from the earth, moved by the genuine impulse to grow, independent of the lures of money or celebrity; whether we speak boldly when fear or doubt keep others silent, or refuse to swell the popular cry upon an unworthy occasion, the spirit of truth, purely worshiped, shall turn our acts and forbearances alike to profit, informing them with oracles which the latest time shall bless.

Under present circumstances the amount of talent and labor given to writing ought to surprise us. Literature is in this dim and struggling state, and its pecuniary results exceedingly pitiful. From many well-known causes it is impossible for ninety-nine out of the hundred who wish to use the pen to ransom by its use the time they need. This state of things will have to be changed in some way. No man of genius writes for money; but it is essential to the free use of his powers that he should be able to disembarrass his life from care and perplexity. This is very difficult here; and the state of things gets worse and worse, as less and less is offered in pecuniary meed for works demanding great devotion of time and labor (to say nothing of the ether engaged) and the publisher, obliged to regard the transaction as a matter of business, demands of the author to give him only what will find an immediate market, for he cannot afford to take anything else. This will not do! When an immortal poet was secure only of a few copyists to circulate his works, there were princes and nobles to patronize literature and the arts. Here is only the public, and the public must learn how to cherish the nobler and rarer plants, and to plant the aloe, able to wait a hundred years for its bloom, or its garden will contain presently nothing but potatoes and pot-herbs. We shall have in the course of the next two or three years a convention of authors to inquire into the causes of this state of things and propose measures for its remedy. Some have already been thought of that look promising, but we shall not announce them till the time be ripe; that date is not distant, for the difficulties increase from day to day in consequence of the system of cheap publication on a great scale.

The ranks that led the way in the first half century of this republic were far better situated than we, in this respect. The country was not so deluged with the dingy page reprinted from Europe, and patriotic vanity was on the alert to answer the question, "Who reads an American book?" And many were the books written as worthy to be read as any out of the first class in England. They were, most of them, except in their subject matter, English books.

The list is large, and in making some cursory comments we do not wish to be understood as designating *all* who are worthy of notice, but only those who present themselves to our minds with some special claims. In history there has been nothing done to which the world at large has not been eager to award the full meed of its deserts. Mr. Prescott for instance has been greeted with as much warmth abroad as here. We are not disposed to under-value his industry and power of clear and elegant arrangement. The rich-ness and freshness of his materials is such that a sense of enchantment must be felt in their contemplation. We must regret, however, that they should have been first presented to the public by one who possesses nothing of the higher powers of the historian, great leading views or discernment as to the motives of action and the spirit of an era. Considering the splendor of the materials, the books are wonderfully tame, and everyone must feel that having once passed through them and got the sketch in the mind, there is nothing else to which it will recur. The absence of thought as to that great picture of Mexican life, with its heroisms, its terrible but deeply significant superstitions, its admirable civic refinement, seems to be quite unbroken.

Mr. Bancroft is a far more vivid writer; he has great resources and great command of them, and leading thoughts by whose aid he groups his facts. But we cannot speak fully of his historical works, which we have only read and referred to here and there.

In the department of ethics and philosophy we may inscribe two names as likely to live and be blessed and honored in the later time. These are the names of Channing and of Emerson.

Dr. Channing had several leading thoughts which corresponded with the wants of his time, and have made him in it a father of thought. His leading idea of the "dignity of human nature" is one of vast results, and the peculiar form in which he advocated it had a great work to do in this new world. The spiritual beauty of his writings is very great; they are all distinguished for sweetness, elevation, candor, and a severe devotion to truth. On great questions he took middle ground and sought a panoramic view; he wished also to stand high, yet never forgot what was above more than what was around and beneath him. He was not well acquainted with man on the impulsive and passionate side of his nature, so that his view of character was sometimes narrow, but it was always noble. He exercised an expansive and purifying power on the atmosphere, and stands a godfather at the baptism of this country.

The Sage of Concord has a very different mind, in everything except that he has the same disinterestedness and dignity of purpose, the same purity of spirit. He is a profound thinker. He is a man of ideas, and deals with causes rather than effects. His ideas are illustrated from a wide range of literary culture and refined observation, and embodied in a style whose melody and subtle fragrance enchant those who stand stupefied before the thoughts themselves, because their utmost depths do not enable them to sound his shallows. His influence does not yet extend over a wide space; he is too far beyond his place and his time to be felt at once or in full, but it searches deep, and yearly widens its circles. He is a harbinger of the better day. His beautiful elocution has been a great aid to him in opening the way for the reception of his written word.

In that large department of literature which includes descriptive sketches, whether of character or scenery, we are already rich. Irving, a genial and fair nature, just what he ought to be and would have been at any time of the world, has drawn the scenes amid which his youth was spent in their primitive lineaments, with all the charms of his graceful jocund humor. He has his niche and need never be deposed; it is not one that another could occupy.

The first enthusiasm about Cooper having subsided, we remember more his faults than his merits. His ready resentment and way of showing it in cases which it is the wont of gentlemen to pass by in silence or meet with a good-humored smile have caused unpleasant associations with his name, and his fellow-citizens, in danger of being tormented by suits for libel if they spoke freely of him, have ceased to speak of him at all. But neither these causes, nor the baldness of his plots, shallowness of thought, and poverty in the presentation of character, should make us forget the grandeur and originality of his sea-sketches, nor the redemption from oblivion of our forest-scenery, and the noble romance of the hunter-pioneer's life. Already, but for him, this fine page of life's romance would be almost forgotten. He has done much to redeem these irrevocable beauties from the corrosive acid of a semi-civilized invasion.*

---

* Since writing the above we have read some excellent remarks by Mr. W. G. Simms on the writings of Cooper. We think the reasons are given for the powerful interest excited by Hawkeye and the Pilot, with great discrimination and force.

"They both think and feel, with a highly individual nature, that has been taught, by constant contemplation, in scenes of solitude. The vast unbroken ranges of forest

Miss Sedgwick and others have portrayed with skill and feeling scenes and personages from the revolutionary time. Such have a permanent value in proportion as their subject is fleeting. The same charm attends the spirited delineations of Mrs. Kirkland, and that amusing book, *A New Purchase*. The features of Hoosier, Sucker, and Wolverine life are worth fixing; they are peculiar to the soil and indicate its hidden treasures; they have also that charm which simple life lived for its own sake always has, even in rude and all but brutal forms.

What shall we say of the poets? The list is scanty; amazingly so, for there is nothing in the causes that paralyze other kinds of literature that could affect lyrical and narrative poetry. Men's hearts beat, hope, and suffer always, and they must crave such means to vent them; yet of the myriad leaves garnished with smooth, stereotyped rhymes that issue yearly from our press, you will not find, one time in a million, a little piece written from any such impulse or with the least sincerity or sweetness of tone. They are written for the press in the spirit of imitation or vanity, the paltriest offspring of the human brain, for the heart disclaims, as the ear is shut against them. This is the kind of verse which is cherished by the magazines as a correspondent to the tawdry pictures of smiling milliners' dolls in the frontispiece. Like these they are only a fashion, a fashion based on no reality of love or beauty. The inducement to write them consists in a little money, or more frequently the charm of seeing an anonymous name printed at the top in capitals.

We must here in passing advert also to the style of story current in the

---

to its one lonely occupant press upon the mind with the same sort of solemnity which one feels condemned to a life of partial isolation upon the ocean. Both are permitted that degree of commerce with their fellow beings, which suffices to maintain in strength the sweet and sacred sources of their humanity. . . . The very isolation to which, in the most successful of his stories, Mr. Cooper subjects his favorite personages, is, alone, a proof of his strength and genius. While the ordinary writer, the man of mere talent, is compelled to look around him among masses for his material, he contents himself with one man, and flings him upon the wilderness. The picture, then, which follows, must be one of intense individuality. Out of this one man's nature, his moods and fortunes, he spins his story. The agencies and dependencies are few. With self-reliance which is only found in true genius, he goes forward into the wilderness, whether of land or ocean; and the vicissitudes of either region, acting upon the natural resources of one man's mind, furnish the whole material of his work-shop. This mode of performance is highly dramatic, and thus it is that his scout, his trapper, his hunter, his pilot, all live to our eyes and thoughts, the perfect ideals of moral individuality."—*Views and Reviews* by W. G. Simms.

magazines, flimsy beyond any texture that was ever spun or even dreamed of by the mind of man in any other age and country. They are said to be "written for the seamstresses," but we believe that every-way injured class could relish and digest better fare even at the end of long days of exhausting labor. There are exceptions to this censure; stories by Mrs. Child have been published in the magazines, and now and then good ones by Mrs. Stephens and others; but take them generally, they are calculated to do a positive injury to the public mind, acting as an opiate, and of an adulterated kind too.

But to return to the poets. At their head Mr. Bryant stands alone. His range is not great, nor his genius fertile. But his poetry is purely the language of his inmost nature, and the simple lovely garb in which his thoughts are arranged, a direct gift from the Muse. He has written nothing that is not excellent, and the atmosphere of his verse refreshes and composes the mind, like leaving the highway to enter some green lovely fragrant wood.

Halleck and Willis are poets of society. Though the former has written so little, yet that little is full of fire—elegant, witty, delicate in sentiment. It is an honor to the country that these occasional sparks struck off from the flint of commercial life should have kindled so much flame as they have. It is always a consolation to see one of them sparkle amid the rubbish of daily life. One of his poems has been published within the last year, written in fact long ago but new to most of us, and it enlivened the literary thoroughfare as a green wreath might some dusty, musty hall of legislation.

Willis has not the same terseness or condensed electricity. But he has grace, spirit, at times a winning pensiveness, and a lively though almost wholly sensuous delight in the beautiful.

Dana has written so little that he would hardly be seen in a more thickly garnished galaxy. But the masculine strength of feeling, the solemn tenderness and refined thought displayed in such pieces as the "Dying Raven" and the "Husband and Wife's Grave" have left a deep impression on the popular mind.

Longfellow is artificial and imitative. He borrows incessantly, and mixes what he borrows, so that it does not appear to the best advantage. He is very faulty in using broken or mixed metaphors. The ethical part of his writing has a hollow, secondhand sound. He has, however, elegance, a love of the beautiful, and a fancy for what is large and manly, if not a full sympathy with it. His verse breathes at times much sweetness; and if not allowed to supersede what is better, may promote a taste for good poetry. Though imitative, he is not mechanical.

We cannot say as much for Lowell, who, we must declare it, though to the grief of some friends and the disgust of more, is absolutely wanting in the true spirit and tone of poesy. His interest in the moral questions of the day has supplied the want of vitality in himself; his great facility at versification has enabled him to fill the ear with a copious stream of pleasant sound. But his verse is stereotyped; his thought sounds no depth; and posterity will not remember him.

R. W. Emerson, in melody, in subtle beauty of thought and expression, takes the highest rank upon this list. But his poems are mostly philosophical, which is not the truest kind of poetry. They want the simple force of nature and passion, and while they charm the ear and interest the mind, fail to wake far-off echoes in the heart. The imagery wears a symbolical air, and serves rather as illustration than to delight us by fresh and glowing forms of life.

We must here mention one whom the country has not yet learned to honor, perhaps never may, for he wants artistic skill to give complete form to his inspiration. This is William Ellery Channing, nephew and namesake of Dr. C., a volume of whose poems, published three or four years ago in Boston, remains unknown except to a few friends, nor if known would they probably excite sympathy, as those which have been published in the periodicals have failed to do so. Yet some of the purest tones of the lyre are his, the finest inspirations as to the feelings and passions of men, deep spiritual insight, and an entire originality in the use of his means. The frequently unfinished and obscure state of his poems, a passion for forcing words out of their usual meaning into one which they may appropriately bear, but which comes upon the reader with an unpleasing and puzzling surprise, may repel at first glance from many of these poems, but do not mar the following sublime description of the beings we want to rule, to redeem, to recreate this nation, and under whose reign alone can there be an American literature, for then only could we have life worth recording. The simple grandeur of this poem as a whole must be felt by everyone, while each line and thought will be found worthy of earnest contemplation and satisfaction after the most earnest life and thought.

> Hearts of Eternity! hearts of the deep!
> Proclaim from land to sea your mighty fate;
> How that for you no living comes too late;
> How ye cannot in Theban labyrinth creep;
> How ye great harvests from small surface reap;
> Shout, excellent band, in grand primeval strain,
> Like midnight winds that foam along the main,
> And do all things rather than pause to weep.
> A human heart knows naught of littleness,
> Suspects no man, compares with no man's ways,
> Hath in one hour most glorious length of days,
> A recompense, a joy, a loveliness;
> Like eaglet keen, shoots into azure far,
> And always dwelling nigh is the remotest star.

A series of poems called "Man in the Republic," by Cornelius Mathews, deserves a higher meed of sympathy than it has received. The thoughts and views are strong and noble, the exhibition of them imposing. In plastic power this writer is deficient. His prose works sin in exuberance, and need consolidating and chastening. We find fine things, but not so arranged as to be seen in the right places and by the best light. In his poems Mr. Mathews is unpardonably rough and rugged; the poetic substance finds no musical medium in which to flow. Yet there *is* poetic substance which makes full chords, if not a harmony. He holds a worthy sense of the vocation of the poet, and worthily expresses it thus:

> To strike or bear, to conquer or to yield
> Teach thou! O topmost crown of duty, teach,
> What fancy whispers to the listening ear,
> At hours when tongue nor taint of care impeach
> The fruitful calm of greatly silent hearts;
> When all the stars for happy thought are set,
> And, in the secret chambers of the soul,
> All blessed powers of joyful truth are met;
> Though calm and garlandless thou mayst appear,
> The world shall know thee for its crowned seer.

A considerable portion of the hope and energy of this country still turns towards the drama, that greatest achievement when wrought to perfection of human power. For ourselves, we believe the day of the regular drama to be past; and though we recognize the need of some kind of spectacle and dramatic representation to be absolutely coincident with an animated state of the public mind, we have thought that the opera, ballet, pantomime, and briefer, more elastic forms, like the *vaudeville* of the French theater or the *proverb* of the social party, would take the place of elaborate tragedy and comedy.

But those who find the theaters of this city well filled all the year round by an audience willing to sit out the heroisms of Rolla, and the sentimentalism and stale morality of such a piece as we were doomed to listen to while the Keans were here (*Town and Country* was its name), still think there is room for the regular drama, if genius should engage in its creation. Accordingly there have been in this country, as well as in England, many attempts to produce dramas suitable for action no less than for the closet. The actor Murdoch, about to devote himself with enthusiasm and hope to prop up a falling profession, is to bring out a series of plays written not merely *for* him, but because his devotion is likely to furnish fit occasion for their appearance. The first of these, *Witchcraft, a Tragedy,* brought out successfully upon the boards at Philadelphia, we have read, and it is a work of strong and majestic lineaments; a fine originality is shown in the conception by which the love of a son for a mother is made a sufficient *motiv* (as the Germans call the ruling impulse of a work) in the production of tragic interest; no less original is the attempt, and delightful the success, in making an aged woman a satisfactory heroine to the piece through the greatness of her soul, and the magnetic influence it exerts on all around her, till the ignorant and superstitious fancy that the sky darkens and the winds wait upon her as she walks on the lonely hillside near her hut to commune with the past and seek instruction from Heaven. The working of her character on the other agents of the piece is depicted with force and nobleness. The deep love of her son for her; the little tender, simple ways in which he shows it, having preserved the purity and poetic spirit of childhood by never having been weaned from his first love, a mother's love; the anguish of his soul when he too becomes infected with distrust, and cannot discriminate the natural magnetism of a strong nature from the spells and lures of sorcery; the final triumph of his faith; all offered the highest scope

to genius and the power of moral perception in the actor. There are highly
poetic intimations of those lowering days with their veiled skies, brassy
light, and sadly whispering winds, very common in Massachusetts, so
ominous and brooding seen from any point, but from the idea of witchcraft,
invested with an awful significance. We do not know, however, that this
could bring it beyond what it has appeared to our own sane mind, as if the
air was thick with spirits in an equivocal and surely sad condition, whether
of purgatory or downfall; and the air was vocal with all manner of dark
intimations. We are glad to see this mood of nature so fitly characterized.

The sweetness and naïveté with which the young girl is made to describe
the effects of love upon her, as supposing them to proceed from a spell,
are also original, and there is no other way in which this revelation could
have been induced that would not have injured the beauty of the character
and position. Her visionary sense of her lover as an ideal figure is of a high
order of poetry, and these facts have very seldom been brought out from
the cloisters of the mind into the light of open day.

The play is very deficient as regards rhythm; indeed we might say there
is no apparent reason why the lines should begin with capital letters. The
minor personages are mere caricatures, very coarsely drawn; all the power is
concentrated on the main characters and their emotions. So did not Shakespeare, does not ever the genuine dramatist, whose mind teems with "the
fullness of forms." As Raphael in his most crowded groups can put in no misplaced or imperfect foot or hand, neither neglect to invest the least important
figure of his backgrounds with every characteristic trait, nor spare the invention of the most beautiful *coiffure* and accessories for the humblest handmaid of his Madonnas, so doth the great artist always clothe the whole picture with full and breathing life, for it appears so before his mental eye.
But minds not perfectly artistic, yet of strong conceptions, subordinate the
rest to one or two leading figures, and the imperfectly represented life of
the others incloses them as in a frame.

In originality of conception and resting the main interest upon force of
character in a woman, this drama naturally leads us to revert to a work in
the department of narrative fiction, which on similar grounds comes to
us as a harbinger of the new era. This book is *Margaret, or the Real and Ideal,*
a work which has appeared within the past year; and, considering its origi-

nality and genuineness, has excited admiration and sympathy amazingly soon. Even some leading reviews of what Byron used to speak of as the "garrison" class (a class the most opposite imaginable to that of Garrison abolitionists) have discussed its pretensions and done homage to its merits. It is a work of great power and richness, a genuine disclosure of the life of mind and the history of character. Its descriptions of scenery and the common people, in the place and time it takes up, impart to it the highest value as a representative of transient existence which had a great deal of meaning. The beautiful simplicity of action upon and within the mind of Margaret, Heaven lying so clearly about her in the infancy of the hut of drunkards, the woods, the village, and their ignorant, simply human denizens; her unconscious growth to the stature of womanhood, the flow of life impelled by her, the spiritual intimations of her dreams; the prophecies of music in the character of Chilion; the naïve discussion of the leading reform movements of the day in their rudimental forms; the archness, the humor, the profound religious faith, make of this book an aviary from which doves shall go forth to discover and report of all the green spots of promise in the land. Of books like this, as good and still better, our new literature shall be full; and though one swallow does not make a summer, yet we greet in this one "Yankee novel" the sufficient earnest of riches that only need the skill of competent miners to be made current for the benefit of man.

Meanwhile the most important part of our literature, while the work of diffusion is still going on, lies in the journals which monthly, weekly, daily send their messages to every corner of this great land, and form at present the only efficient instrument for the general education of the people.

Among these, the magazines take the lowest rank. Their object is principally to cater for the amusement of vacant hours, and as there is not a great deal of wit and light talent in this country, they do not even this to much advantage. More wit, grace, and elegant trifling embellish the annals of literature in one day of France than in a year of America.

The reviews are more able. If they cannot compare on equal terms with those of France, England, and Germany, where if genius be rare, at least a vast amount of talent and culture is brought to bear upon all the departments of knowledge, they are yet very creditable to a new country where so large a portion of manly ability must be bent on making laws, making speeches, making railroads and canals. They are, however, much injured by a partisan spirit and the fear of censure from their own public. This last is always slow death to a journal; its natural and only safe position is to *lead;* if instead it bows to the will of the multitude, it will find the ostracism of democracy far more dangerous than the worst censure of a tyranny could be. It is not half so dangerous to a man to be immured in a dungeon alone with God and his own clear conscience as to walk the streets fearing the scrutiny of a thousand eyes, ready to veil with anxious care whatever may not suit the many-headed monster in its momentary mood. Gentleness is dignified but caution is debasing; only a noble fearlessness can give wings to the mind, with which to soar beyond the common ken and learn what may be of use to the crowd below. Writers have nothing to do but to love truth fervently, seek justice according to their ability, and then express what is in the mind; they have nothing to do with consequences, God will take care of those. The want of such noble courage, such faith in the power of truth and good desire, paralyzes mind greatly in this country. Publishers are afraid; authors are afraid; and if a worthy resistance is not made by religious souls, there is danger that all the light will soon be put under bushels, lest some wind should waft from it a spark that may kindle dangerous fire.

For want of such faith, and the catholic spirit that flows from it, we have no great leading review. The *North American* was once the best. While under the care of Edward Everett, himself a host in extensive knowledge, grace and adroitness in applying it, and the power of enforcing grave meanings by a light and flexible satire that tickled while it wounded, it boasted more force, more life, a finer scope of power. But now though still exhibiting ability and information upon special points, it is entirely deficient in great leadings and the *vivida vis,* but ambles and jogs at an old gentlemanly pace along a beaten path that leads to no important goal.

Several other journals have more life, energy, and directness than this, but there is none which occupies a truly great and commanding position, a beacon-light to all who sail that way. In order to do this, a journal must know how to cast aside all local and temporary considerations when new convictions command, and allow free range in its columns to all kinds of ability and all ways of viewing subjects. That would give it a life rich, bold, various.

The life of intellect is becoming more and more determined to the weekly and daily papers, whose light leaves fly so rapidly and profusely over the land. Speculations are afloat as to the influence of the electric telegraph upon their destiny, and it seems obvious that it should raise their character by taking from them in some measure the office of gathering and dispersing the news, and requiring of them rather to arrange and interpret it.

This mode of communication is susceptible of great excellence in the way of condensed essay, narrative, criticism, and is the natural receptacle for the lyrics of the day. That so few good ones deck the poet's corner, is because the indifference or unfitness of editors as to choosing and refusing makes this place at present undesirable to the poet. It might be otherwise.

The means which this organ affords of diffusing knowledge and sowing the seeds of thought where they may hardly fail of an infinite harvest, cannot be too highly prized by the discerning and benevolent. Minds of the first class are generally indisposed to this kind of writing; what must be done on the spur of the occasion and cast into the world so incomplete, as the hurried offspring of a day or hour's labor must generally be, cannot satisfy their judgment or do justice to their powers. But he who looks to the benefit of others and sees with what rapidity and ease instruction and thought are assimilated by men, when they come thus as it were on the wings of the wind, may be content, as an unhonored servant to the grand purposes of Destiny, to work in such a way at the Pantheon which the ages shall complete, on which his name may not be inscribed but which will breathe the life of his soul.

The confidence in uprightness of intent and the safety of truth is still more needed here than in the more elaborate kinds of writing, as meanings cannot be fully explained nor expressions revised. Newspaper-writing is next door to conversation, and should be conducted on the same principles. It has this advantage: we address not our neighbor, who forces us to remember his limitations and prejudices, but the ideal presence of human nature as we feel it ought to be and trust it will be. We address America rather than Americans.

A worthy account of the vocation and duties of the journalist is given by Cornelius Mathews. Editors generally could not do better than every New Year's Day to read and insert the following verses.

As shakes the canvas of a thousand ships,
   Struck by a heavy land-breeze, far at sea,
Ruffle the thousand broad sheets of the land,
   Filled with the people's breath of potency.

A thousand images the hour will take,
   From him who strikes, who rules, who speaks, who sings,
Many within the hour their grave to make,
   Many to live, far in the heart of things.

A dark-dyed spirit he, who coins the time,
   To virtue's wrong, in base disloyal lies,
Who makes the morning's breath, the evening's tide,
   The utterer of his blighting forgeries.

How beautiful who scatters, wide and free,
   The gold-bright seeds of loved and loving truth!
By whose perpetual hand, each day supplied,
   Leaps to new life the empire's heart of youth.

To know the instant and to speak it true,
   Its passing lights of joy, its dark, sad cloud,
To fix upon the unnumbered gazer's view,
   Is to thy ready hand's broad strength allowed.

There is an inwrought life in every hour,
   Fit to be chronicled at large and told.
'Tis thine to pluck to light its secret power,
   And on the air its many-colored heart unfold.

The angel that in sand-dropped minutes lives,
   Demands a message cautious as the ages,
Who stuns, with dusk-red words of hate his ear,
   That mighty power to boundless wrath enrages.

This feeling of the dignity of his office, honor and power in fulfilling it, are not common in the journalist, but where they exist, a mark has been left fully correspondent to the weight of the instrument. The few editors of this country who with mental ability and resource have combined strength of purpose and fairness of conduct, who have never merged the man and the gentleman in the partisan, who have been willing to have all sides fully heard while their convictions were clear on one, who have disdained groundless assaults or angry replies, and have valued what was sincere, characteristic, and free too much to bend to popular errors they felt able to correct, have been so highly prized that it is wonderful that more do not learn the use of this great opportunity. It will be learned yet; the resources of this organ of thought and instruction begin to be understood, and shall yet be brought out and used worthily.

We see we have omitted honored names in this essay. We have not spoken of Brown, as a novelist by far our first in point of genius and instruction as to the soul of things. Yet his works have fallen almost out of print. It is their dark deep gloom that prevents their being popular, for their very beauties are grave and sad. But we see that *Ormond* is being republished at this moment. The picture of Roman character, of the life and resources of a single noble creature, of Constantia alone, should make that book an object of reverence. All these novels should be republished; if not favorites, they should at least not be lost sight of, for there will always be some who find in such powers of mental analysis the only response to their desires.

We have not spoken of Hawthorne, the best writer of the day, in a similar range with Irving, only touching many more points and discerning far more deeply. But we have omitted many things in this slight sketch, for the subject even in this stage lies as a volume in our mind, and cannot be unrolled in completeness unless time and space were more abundant. Our object was to show that although by a thousand signs the existence is foreshown of those forces which are to animate an American literature, that faith, those hopes are not yet alive which shall usher it into a homogeneous or fully organized state of being. The future is glorious with certainties for those who do their duty in the present, and larklike, seeking the sun, challenge its eagles to an earthward flight, where their nests may be built in our mountains, and their young raise their cry of triumph unchecked by dullness in the echoes.

Since finishing the foregoing essay, the publication of some volumes by Hawthorne and Brown has led to notices in the *Tribune* which, with a review of Longfellow's poems, are subjoined to eke out the statements as to the merits of those authors.

HAWTHORNE

We have been seated here the last ten minutes, pen in hand, thinking what we can possibly say about this book * that will not be either superfluous or impertinent.

Superfluous, because the attractions of Hawthorne's writings cannot fail of one and the same effect on all persons who possess the common sympathies of men. To all who are still happy in some groundwork of unperverted Nature, the delicate, simple, human tenderness, unsought, unbought, and therefore precious morality, the tranquil elegance and playfulness, the humor which never breaks the impression of sweetness and dignity, do an inevitable message which requires no comment of the critic to make its meaning clear. Impertinent, because the influence of this mind, like that of some loveliest aspects of Nature, is to induce silence from a feeling of repose. We do not think of anything particularly worth saying about this that has been so fitly and pleasantly said.

Yet it seems *un*fit that we, in our office of chronicler of intellectual advents and apparitions, should omit to render open and audible honor to one whom we have long delighted to honor. It may be, too, that this slight notice of ours may awaken the attention of those distant or busy who might not otherwise search for the volume, which comes betimes in the leafy month of June.

So we will give a slight account of it, even if we cannot say much of value. Though Hawthorne has now a standard reputation, both for the qualities we have mentioned and the beauty of the style in which they are embodied, yet we believe he has not been very widely read. This is only because his works have not been published in the way to insure extensive circulation in this new hurrying world of ours. The immense extent of country over which the reading (still very small in proportion to the mere working) community is scattered, the rushing and pushing of our life at this electrical stage of development, leave no work a chance to be speedily and largely known that is not trumpeted and placarded. And odious as are the features of a forced and artificial circulation, it must be considered that it does no harm in the end. Bad books will not be read if they are bought

---

* *Mosses from an Old Manse.* By Nathaniel Hawthorne. In two parts. New York: Wiley and Putnam, 1846.

instead of good, while the good have an abiding life in the log-cabin settlements and Red River steamboat landings, to which they would in no other
way penetrate. Under the auspices of Wiley and Putnam, Hawthorne will
have a chance to collect all his own public about him, and that be felt as
a presence which before was only a rumor.

The volume before us shares the charms of Hawthorne's earlier tales;
the only difference being that his range of subjects is a little wider. There is
the same gentle and sincere companionship with Nature, the same delicate
but fearless scrutiny of the secrets of the heart, the same serene independence
of petty and artificial restrictions, whether on opinions or conduct, the
same familiar yet pensive sense of the spiritual or demoniacal influences that
haunt the palpable life and common walks of men, not by many apprehended except in results. We have here to regret that Hawthorne, at this
stage of his mind's life, lays no more decisive hand upon the apparition—
brings it no nearer than in former days. We had hoped that we should see,
no more as in a glass darkly, but face to face. Still, still brood over his page
the genius of reverie and the nonchalance of Nature, rather than the ardent
earnestness of the human soul which feels itself born not only to see and
disclose, but to understand and interpret such things. Hawthorne intimates
and suggests, but he does not lay bare the mysteries of our being.

The introduction to the *Mosses,* in which the old manse, its inhabitants
and visitants are portrayed, is written with even more than his usual charm
of placid grace and many strokes of his admirable good sense. Those who
are not, like ourselves, familiar with the scene and its denizens, will still
perceive how true that picture must be; those of us who are thus familiar
will best know how to prize the record of objects and influences unique
in our country and time.

"The Birth Mark" and "Rapaccini's Daughter" embody truths of profound importance in shapes of aerial elegance. In these, as here and there
in all these pieces, shines the loveliest ideal of love, and the beauty of
feminine purity (by which we mean no mere acts or abstinences, but perfect
single truth felt and done in gentleness) which is its root.

"The Celestial Railroad," for its wit, wisdom, and the graceful adroitness with which the natural and material objects are interwoven with the
allegories, has already won its meed of admiration. "Fire-Worship" is a most

charming essay for its domestic sweetness and thoughtful life. "Goodman
Brown" is one of those disclosures we have spoken of, of the secrets of the
breast. Who has not known such a trial that is capable indeed of sincere
aspiration toward that only good, that infinite essence, which men call God.
Who has not known the hour when even that best beloved image cherished
as the one precious symbol left in the range of human nature, believed to be
still pure gold when all the rest have turned to clay, shows in severe ordeal
the symptoms of alloy. O hour of anguish, when the old familiar faces
grow dark and dim in the lurid light—when the gods of the hearth, honored
in childhood, adored in youth, crumble and nothing, nothing is left which
the daily earthly feelings can embrace—can cherish with unbroken faith!
Yet some survive that trial more happily than young Goodman Brown.
They are those who have not sought it—have never of their own accord
walked forth with the tempter into the dim shades of doubt. "Mrs. Bull-
frog" is an excellent humorous picture of what is called to be "content at last
with substantial realities!!" The "Artist of the Beautiful" presents, in a form
that is indeed beautiful, the opposite view as to what *are* the substantial
realities of life. Let each man choose between them according to his kind.
Had Hawthorne written "Roger Malvin's Burial" alone, we should be pervaded with the sense of the poetry and religion of his soul.

As a critic, the style of Hawthorne, faithful to his mind, shows repose,
a great reserve of strength, a slow secure movement. Though a very refined, he is also a very clear writer, showing, as we said before, a placid grace,
and an indolent command of language.

And now, beside the full, calm yet romantic stream of his mind, we will
rest. It has refreshment for the weary, islets of fascination no less than dark
recesses and shadows for the imaginative, pure reflections for the pure of
heart and eye, and, like the Concord he so well describes, many exquisite
lilies for him who knows how to get at them.

CHARLES BROCKDEN BROWN *

We rejoice to see these reprints of Brown's novels, as we have long been
ashamed that one who ought to be the pride of the country, and who is in

---

* *Ormond; or, The Secret Witness. Wieland; or, The Transformation.* By Charles
Brockden Brown. Library of Standard Romance. W. Taylor and Co., 2 Astor House.

the higher qualities of the mind so far in advance of our other novelists, should have become almost inaccessible to the public.

It has been the custom to liken Brown to Godwin. But there was no imitation, no second-hand in the matter. They were congenial natures, and whichever had come first might have lent an impulse to the other. Either mind might have been conscious of the possession of that peculiar vein of ore without thinking of working it for the mint of the world, till the other, led by accident or overflow of feeling, showed him how easy it was to put the reveries of his solitary hours into words and upon paper for the benefit of his fellow-men.

> My mind to me a kingdom is.

Such a man as Brown or Godwin has a right to say that. It is no scanty turbid rill, requiring to be daily fed from a thousand others or from the clouds! Its plenteous source rushes from a high mountain between bulwarks of stone. Its course, even and full, keeps ever green its banks and affords the means of life and joy to a million gliding shapes that fill its deep waters and twinkle above its golden sands.

Life and joy! Yes, joy! These two have been called the dark masters because they disclose the twilight recesses of the human heart. Yet their gravest page is joy compared with the mixed, shallow, uncertain pleasures of vulgar minds. Joy, because they were all alive and fulfilled the purposes of being. No sham, no imitation, no convention deformed or veiled their native lineaments, checked the use of their natural force. All alive themselves, they understood that there is no joy without truth, no perception of joy without real life. Unlike most men, existence was to them not a tissue of words and seemings, but a substantial possession.

Born Hegelians without the pretensions of science, they sought God in their own consciousness and found him. The heart, because it saw itself so fearfully and wonderfully made, did not disown its Maker. With the highest idea of the dignity, power, and beauty of which human nature is capable, they had courage to see by what an oblique course it proceeds, yet never lose faith that it would reach its destined aim. Thus their darkest disclosures are not hobgoblin shows, but precious revelations.

Brown is great as ever human writer was in showing the self-sustaining force of which a lonely mind is capable. He takes one person, makes him brood like the bee and extract from the common life before him all its sweetness, its bitterness, and its nourishment.

We say makes *him,* but it increases our own interest in Brown that, a prophet in this respect of a better era, he has usually placed this thinking, royal mind in the body of a woman. This personage too is always feminine, both in her character and circumstances, but a conclusive proof that the term "feminine" is not a synonym for "weak." Constantia, Clara Wieland, have loving hearts, graceful and plastic natures, but they have also noble thinking minds, full of resource, constancy, courage. The Marguerite of Godwin no less is all refinement, and the purest tenderness, but she is also the soul of honor, capable of deep discernment and of acting in conformity with the inferences she draws. The man of Brown and Godwin has not eaten of the fruit of the tree of knowledge and been driven to sustain himself by sweat of his brow for nothing, but has learned the structure and laws of things, and become a being rational, benignant, various, and desirous of supplying the loss of innocence by the attainment of virtue. So his woman need not be quite so weak as Eve, the slave of feeling or of flattery: she also has learned to guide her helm amid the storm across the troubled waters.

The horrors which mysteriously beset these persons, and against which, so far as outward facts go, they often strive in vain, are but a representation of those powers permitted to work in the same way throughout the affairs of this world. Their demoniacal attributes only represent a morbid state of the intellect, gone to excess from want of balance with the other powers. There is an intellectual as well as a physical drunkenness, and which no less impels to crime. Carwin, urged on to use his ventriloquism till the presence of such a strange agent wakened the seeds of fanaticism in the breast of Wieland, is in a state no more foreign to nature than that of the wretch executed last week, who felt himself drawn as by a spell to murder his victim because he had thought of her money and the pleasures it might bring him, till the feeling possessed his brain that hurls the gamester to ruin. The victims of such agency are like the soldier of the Rio Grande who, both legs shot off and his lifeblood rushing out with every pulse, replied serenely to his pitying comrades that "he had now that for which the soldier enlisted." The end of the drama is not in this world, and the fiction which rounds off the whole to harmony and felicity before the curtain falls sins against truth and deludes the reader. The Nelsons of the human race are all the more exposed to the assaults of fate that they are decorated with the badges of well-earned glory. Who but feels as they fall in death or rise again to a mutilated existence, that the end is not yet? Who that thinks, but must feel that the recompense is where Brown places it, in the accumulation of mental treasure, in the severe assay by fire that leaves the gold pure to be used sometime—somewhere.

Brown, man of the brooding eye, the teeming brain, the deep and fervent heart, if thy country prize thee not and has almost lost thee out of sight, it is that her heart is made shallow and cold, her eye dim, by the pomp of circumstance, the love of gross outward gain. She cannot long continue thus, for it takes a great deal of soul to keep a huge body from disease and dissolution. As there is more soul thou wilt be more sought, and many will yet sit down with thy Constantia to the meal and water on which she sustained her full and thoughtful existence, who could not endure the ennui of aldermanic dinners, or find any relish in the imitation of French cookery. Today many will read the words, and some have a cup large enough to receive the spirit before it is lost in the sand on which their feet are planted.

Brown's high standard of the delights of intellectual communion and of friendship correspond with the fondest hopes of early days. But in the relations of real life at present there is rarely more than one of the parties ready for such intercourse as he describes. On the one side there will be dryness, want of perception or variety, a stupidity unable to appreciate life's richest boon when offered to its grasp; and the finer nature is doomed to retrace its steps, unhappy as those who having force to raise a spirit cannot retain or make it substantial, and stretch out their arms only to bring them back empty to the breast.

LONGFELLOW *

Poetry is not a superhuman or supernatural gift. It is on the contrary the fullest and therefore most completely natural expression of what is human. It is that of which the rudiments lie in every human breast, but developed

---

* *Poems*. By Henry Wadsworth Longfellow; with illustrations by D. Huntington. Philadelphia: Carey and Hart, Chestnut St. 1845.

to a more complete existence than the obstructions of daily life permit, clothed in an adequate form, domesticated in nature by the use of apt images, the perception of grand analogies, and set to the music of the spheres for the delight of all who have ears to hear. We have uttered these remarks which may to many of our readers seem truisms, for the sake of showing that our definition of poetry is large enough to include all kinds of excellence. It includes not only the great bards but the humblest minstrels. The great bards bring to light the more concealed treasures, gems which centuries have been employed in forming and which it is their office to reveal, polish, and set for the royal purposes of man; the wandering minstrel with his lighter but beautiful office calls the attention of men to the meaning of the flowers, which also is hidden from the careless eye, though they have grown and bloomed in full sight of all who chose to look. All the poets are the priests of Nature, though the greatest are also the prophets of the manhood of man. For when fully grown, the life of man must be all poetry; each of his thoughts will be a key to the treasures of the universe, each of his acts a revelation of beauty, his language will be music, and his habitual presence will overflow with more energy and inspire with a nobler rapture than do the fullest strains of lyric poetry now.

Meanwhile we need poets, men more awakened to the wonders of life and gifted more or less with a power to express what they see; and to all who possess in any degree those requisites we offer and we owe welcome and tribute, whether the place of their song be in the Pantheon, from which issue the grand decrees of immortal thought, or by the fireside where hearts need kindling and eyes need clarifying by occasional drops of nectar in their tea.

But this—this alone we claim, and can welcome none who cannot present this title to our hearing: that the vision be genuine, the expression spontaneous. No imposition upon our young fellow-citizens of pinchbeck for gold! They must have the true article and pay the due intellectual price, or they will wake from a lifelong dream of folly to find themselves beggars.

And never was a time when satirists were more needed to scourge from Parnassus the magpies who are devouring the food scattered there for the singing birds. There will always be a good deal of mock poetry in the market with the genuine; it grows up naturally as tares among the wheat, and while there is a fair proportion preserved, we abstain from severe weeding lest the two come up together; but when the tares have almost usurped the field, it is time to begin and see if the field cannot be freed from them and made ready for a new seed-time.

The rules of versification are now understood and used by those who have never entered into that soul from which meters grow as acorns from the oak, shapes as characteristic of the parent tree, containing in like manner germs of limitless life for the future. And as to the substance of these jingling rhymes and dragging, stumbling rhythms, we might tell of bombast or still worse an affected simplicity, sickly sentiment, or borrowed dignity; but it is sufficient to comprise all in this one censure. The writers did not write because they felt obliged to relieve themselves of the swelling thought within, but as an elegant exercise which may win them rank and reputation above the crowd. Their lamp is not lit by the sacred and inevitable lightning from above, but carefully fed by their own will to be seen of men.

There are very few now rhyming in England not obnoxious to this censure, still fewer in our America. For such no laurel blooms. May the friendly poppy soon crown them and grant us stillness to hear the silver tones of genuine music, for if such there be, they are at present almost stifled by these fifes and gongs.

Yet there is a middle class, composed of men of little original poetic power, but of much poetic taste and sensibility, whom we would not wish to have silenced. They do no harm, but much good (if only their minds are not confounded with those of a higher class) by educating in others the faculties dominant in themselves. In this class we place the writer at present before us.

We must confess to a coolness towards Mr. Longfellow, in consequence of the exaggerated praises that have been bestowed upon him. When we see a person of moderate powers receive honors which should be reserved for the highest, we feel somewhat like assailing him and taking from him the crown which should be reserved for grander brows. And yet this is perhaps ungenerous. It may be that the management of publishers, the hyperbole of paid or undiscerning reviewers, or some accidental cause which gives a temporary interest to productions beyond what they would permanently command, have raised such a one to a place as much above his wishes as his claims, and which he would rejoice with honorable modesty to vacate at the approach of one worthier. We the more readily believe this of Mr. Longfellow, as one so sensible to the beauties of other writers and so largely indebted to them *must* know his own comparative rank better than his readers have known it for him.

And yet so much adulation is dangerous. Mr. Longfellow, so lauded on all hands—now able to collect his poems which have circulated so widely in previous editions, and been paid for so handsomely by the handsomest annuals, in this beautiful volume, illustrated by one of the most distinguished of our younger artists—has found a flatterer in that very artist. The portrait which adorns this volume is not merely flattered or idealized, but there is an attempt at adorning it by expression thrown into the eyes with just that which the original does not possess, whether in face or mind. We have often seen faces whose usually coarse and heavy lineaments were harmonized at times into beauty by the light that rises from the soul into the eyes. The intention Nature had with regard to the face and its wearer, usually eclipsed beneath bad habits or a bad education, is then disclosed, and we see what hopes death has in store for that soul. But here the enthusiasm thrown into the eyes only makes the rest of the face look more weak, and the idea suggested is the anomalous one of a dandy Pindar.

Such is not the case with Mr. Longfellow himself. He is never a Pindar, though he is sometimes a dandy even in the clean and elegantly ornamented streets and trim gardens of his verse. But he is still more a man of cultivated taste, delicate though not deep feeling, and some though not much poetic force.

Mr. Longfellow has been accused of plagiarism. We have been surprised that anyone should have been anxious to fasten special charges of this kind upon him, when we had supposed it so obvious that the greater part of his mental stores were derived from the works of others. He has no style of his own growing out of his own experiences and observations of nature. Nature with him, whether human or external, is always seen through the windows of literature. There are in his poems sweet and tender passages descriptive of his personal feelings, but very few showing him as an observer at first hand of the passions within or the landscape without.

This want of the free breath of nature, this perpetual borrowing of imagery, this excessive because superficial culture which he has derived from an acquaintance with the elegant literature of many nations and men out of proportion to the experience of life within himself, prevent Mr. Longfellow's verses from ever being a true refreshment to ourselves. He says in one of his most graceful verses:

> From the cool cisterns of the midnight air
>   My spirit drank repose;
> The fountain of perpetual peace flows there,
>   From those deep cisterns flows.

Now this is just what we cannot get from Mr. Longfellow. No solitude of the mind reveals to us the deep cisterns.

Let us take, for example of what we do not like, one of his worst pieces, the "Prelude to the Voices of the Night"—

> Beneath some patriarchal tree
>   I lay upon the ground;
> His hoary arms uplifted be,
> And all the broad leaves over me
> Clapped their little hands in glee
>   With one continuous sound.

What an unpleasant mixture of images! Such never rose in a man's mind as he lay on the ground and looked up to the tree above him. The true poetry for this stanza would be to give us an image of what was in the writer's mind as he lay there and looked up. But this idea of the leaves clapping their little hands with glee is taken out of some book; or at any rate is a book thought and not one that came in the place, and jars entirely with what is said of the tree uplifting its hoary arms. Then take this other stanza from a man whose mind *should* have grown up in familiarity with the American *genius loci:*

> Therefore at Pentecost, which brings
>   The Spring clothed like a bride,
> When nestling buds unfold their wings,
> And bishop's caps have golden rings,
>   Musing upon many things,
>   I sought the woodlands wide.

Musing upon many things—aye! and upon many books too, or we should have nothing of Pentecost or bishop's caps with their golden rings. For ourselves, we have not the least idea what bishop's caps are—are they flowers—

or what? Truly the schoolmaster was abroad in the woodlands that day! As to the conceit of the wings of the buds, it is a false image, because one that cannot be carried out. Such will not be found in the poems of poets; with such the imagination is all compact, and their works are not dead mosaics with substance inserted merely because pretty, but living growths, homogeneous and satisfactory throughout.

Such instances could be adduced everywhere throughout the poems, depriving us of any clear pleasure from any one piece, and placing his poems beside such as those of Bryant in the same light as that of the prettiest *made* shell, beside those whose every line and hue tells a history of the action of winds and waves and the secrets of one class of organizations.

But do we therefore esteem Mr. Longfellow a willful or conscious plagiarist? By no means. It is his misfortune that other men's thoughts are so continually in his head as to overshadow his own. The order of fine development is for the mind the same as the body, to take in just so much food as will sustain it in its exercise and assimilate with its growth. If it is so assimilated—if it becomes a part of the skin, hair, and eyes of the man, it is his own, no matter whether he pick it up in the woods or borrow from the dish of a fellow-man or receive it in the form of manna direct from Heaven. "Do you ask the genius," said Goethe, "to give an account of what he has taken from others? As well demand of the hero an account of the beeves and loaves which have nourished him to such martial stature."

But Mr. Longfellow presents us not with a new product in which all the old varieties are melted into a fresh form, but rather with a tastefully arranged museum, between whose glass cases are interspersed neatly potted rose trees, geraniums, and hyacinths, grown by himself with aid of indoor heat. Still we must acquit him of being a willing or conscious plagiarist. Some objects in the collection are his own; as to the rest, he has the merit of appreciation and a rearrangement not always judicious, but the result of feeling on his part.

Such works as Mr. Longfellow's we consider injurious only if allowed to usurp the place of better things. The reason of his being overrated here is because through his works breathes the air of other lands, with whose products the public at large is but little acquainted. He will do his office, and a desirable one, of promoting a taste for the literature of these lands before his readers are aware of it. As a translator he shows the same qualities as in his own writings; what is forcible and compact he does not render adequately; grace and sentiment he appreciates and reproduces. Twenty years hence when he stands upon his own merits, he will rank as a writer of elegant if not always accurate taste, of great imitative power, and occasional felicity in an original way where his feelings are really stirred. He has touched no subject where he has not done somewhat that is pleasing, though also his poems are much marred by ambitious failings. As instances of his best manner we would mention "The Reaper and the Flowers," "Lines to the Planet Mars," "A Gleam of Sunshine," and "The Village Blacksmith." His two ballads are excellent imitations, yet in them is no spark of fire. In "Nuremberg" are charming passages. Indeed, the whole poem is one of the happiest specimens of Mr. L.'s poetic feeling, taste and tact in making up a rosary of topics and images. Thinking it may be less known than most of the poems we will quote it. The engraving which accompanies it, of the rich old architecture, is a fine gloss on its contents.

NUREMBERG

In the valley of the Pegnitz, where across broad meadow lands
Rise the blue Franconian mountains, Nuremberg, the ancient, stands.
Quaint old town of toil and traffic—quaint old town of art and song—
Memories haunt thy pointed gables, like the rooks that round them throng;
Memories of the Middle Ages, when the Emperors, rough and bold,
Had their dwelling in thy castle, time defying, centuries old;
And thy brave and thrifty burghers boasted in their uncouth rhyme,
That their great imperial city stretched its hand through every clime.
In the court-yard of the castle, bound with many an iron band,
Stands the mighty linden, planted by Queen Cunigunda's hand.
On the square the oriel window, where in old heroic days,
Sat the poet Melchior, singing Kaiser Maximilian's praise.
Everywhere I see around me rise the wondrous world of Art—
Fountains wrought with richest sculpture, standing in the common mart;
And above cathedral doorways, saints and bishops carved in stone,
By a former age commissioned as apostles to our own.
In the church of sainted Sebald sleeps enshrined his holy dust,
And in bronze the Twelve Apostles guard from age to age their trust;
In the church of sainted Lawrence stands a Pix of sculpture rare,
Like the foamy sheaf of fountains, rising through the painted air.
Here, when Art was still Religion, with a simple reverent heart,
Lived and labored Albert Dürer, the Evangelist of Art;

Hence in silence and in sorrow, toiling still with busy hand,
Like an emigrant he wandered, seeking for the Better Land.
Emigravit is the inscription on the tomb-stone where he lies;
Dead he is not, but departed, for the Artist never dies.
Fairer seems the ancient city, and the sunshine seems more fair,
That he once has trod its pavement—that he once has breathed its air!
Through those streets so broad and stately, these obscure and dismal lanes,
Walked of yore the Master-singers, chanting rude poetic strains.
From remote and sunless suburbs came they to the friendly guild,
Building nests in Fame's great temple, as in spouts the swallows build.
As the weaver plied the shuttle, wove he to the mystic rhyme,
And the smith his iron measures hammered to the anvil's chime;
Thanking God, whose boundless wisdom makes the flowers of poesy bloom
In the forge's dust and cinders—in the tissues of the loom.
Here Hans Sachs, the cobbler-poet, laureate of the gentle craft,
Wisest of the Twelve Wise Masters, in huge folios sang and laughed.
But his house is now an ale-house, with a nicely sanded floor,
And a garland in the window, and his face above the door;
Painted by some humble artist, as in Adam Paschman's song,
As the old man gray and dove-like, with his great beard white and long.
And at night the swarth mechanic comes to drown his cank and care,
Quaffing ale from pewter tankards in the master's antique chair.
Vanished is the ancient splendor, and before my dreamy eye
Wave these mingling shapes and figures, like a faded tapestry.
Not thy Councils, not thy Kaisers, win for thee the world's regard;
But thy painter, Albert Dürer, and Hans Sachs, thy cobbler bard.
Thus, oh, Nuremberg! a wanderer from a region far away,
As he paced thy streets and court-yards, sang in thought his careless lay;
Gathering from the pavement's crevice, as a flow'ret of the soil,
The nobility of labor, the long pedigree of toil.

This image of the thought gathered like a flower from the crevice of the pavement is truly natural and poetical.

Here is another image which came into the mind of the writer as he looked at the subject of his verse, and which pleases accordingly. It is from one of the new poems, addressed to Driving Cloud, "chief of the mighty Omahaws."

Wrapt in thy scarlet blanket I see thee stalk through the city's
Narrow and populous streets, as once by the margin of rivers
Stalked those birds unknown, that have left us only their foot-prints.
What, in a few short years, will remain of thy race but the foot-prints?

Here is another very graceful and natural simile:

> A feeling of sadness and longing,
> That is not akin to pain,
> And resembles sorrow only
> As the mist resembles rain.

Another:

> I will forget her! All dear recollections,
> Pressed in my heart like flowers within a book,
> Shall be torn out and scattered to the winds.

The drama from which this is taken is an elegant exercise of the pen, after the fashion of the best models. Plans, figures, all are academical. It is a faint reflex of the actions and passions of men, tame in the conduct and lifeless in the characters but not heavy, and containing good meditative passages.

And now farewell to the handsome book, with its Preciosos and Preciosas, its Vikings and knights, and cavaliers, its flowers of all climes, and wild flowers of none. We have not wished to depreciate these writings below their current value more than truth absolutely demands. We have not forgotten that if a man cannot himself sit at the feet of the Muse, it is much if he prizes those who may; it makes him a teacher to the people. Neither have we forgotten that Mr. Longfellow has a genuine respect for his pen, never writes carelessly, nor when he does not wish to, nor for money alone. Nor are we intolerant to those who prize hothouse bouquets beyond all the free beauty of nature; that helps the gardener and has its uses. But still let us not forget—*Excelsior!*

EMERSON'S ESSAYS *

At the distance of three years this volume follows the first series of essays, which have already made to themselves a circle of readers attentive, thoughtful, more and more intelligent, and this circle is a large one if we consider the circumstances of this country and of England also, at this time.

In England it would seem there are a larger number of persons waiting for an invitation to calm thought and sincere intercourse than among ourselves. Copies of Mr. Emerson's first-published little volume, called *Nature,* have there been sold by thousands in a short time, while one edition has needed seven years to get circulated here. Several of his orations and essays from the *Dial* have also been republished there, and met with a reverent and earnest response.

We suppose that while in England the want of such a voice is as great as here, a larger number are at leisure to recognize that want; a far larger number have set foot in the speculative region and have ears refined to appreciate these melodious accents.

Our people, heated by a partisan spirit, necessarily occupied in these first stages by bringing out the material resources of the land, not generally prepared by early training for the enjoyment of books that require attention and reflection, are still more injured by a large majority of writers and speakers who lend all their efforts to flatter corrupt tastes and mental indolence, instead of feeling it their prerogative and their duty to admonish the community of the danger and arouse it to nobler energy. The aim of the writer or lecturer is not to say the best he knows in as few and well-chosen words as he can, making it his first aim to do justice to the subject. Rather he seeks to beat out a thought as thin as possible, and to consider what the audience will be most willing to receive.

The result of such a course is inevitable. Literature and art must become daily more degraded; philosophy cannot exist. A man who has within his mind some spark of genius or a capacity for the exercises of talent should consider himself as endowed with a sacred commission. He is the natural

---

* From the New York *Daily Tribune,* December 7, 1844.

priest, the shepherd of the people. He must raise his mind as high as he can toward the heaven of truth, and try to draw up with him those less gifted by nature with ethereal lightness. If he does not so, but rather employs his powers to flatter them in their poverty, and to hinder aspiration by useless words and a mere seeming of activity, his sin is great: he is false to God and false to man.

Much of this sin indeed is done ignorantly. The idea that literature calls men to the genuine hierarchy is almost forgotten. One who finds himself able uses his pen as he might a trowel solely to procure himself bread, without having reflected on the position in which he thereby places himself.

Apart from the troop of mercenaries, there is one still larger of those who use their powers merely for local and temporary ends, aiming at no excellence other than may conduce to these. Among these, rank persons of honor and the best intentions, but they neglect the lasting for the transient, as a man neglects to furnish his mind that he may provide the better for the house in which his body is to dwell for a few years.

When these sins and errors are prevalent and threaten to become more so, how can we sufficiently prize and honor a mind which is quite pure from such? When as in the present case we find a man whose only aim is the discernment and interpretation of the spiritual laws by which we live and move and have our being, all whose objects are permanent, and whose every word stands for a fact?

If only as a representative of the claims of individual culture in a nation which tends to lay such stress on artificial organization and external results, Mr. Emerson would be invaluable here. History will inscribe his name as a father of the country, for he is one who pleads her cause against herself.

If New England may be regarded as a chief mental focus of the New World, and many symptoms seem to give her this place, as to other centers the characteristics of heart and lungs to the body politic; if we may believe, as the writer does believe, that what is to be acted out in the country at large is most frequently first indicated there, as all the phenomena of the nervous system in the fantasies of the brain, we may hail as an auspicious omen the influence Mr. Emerson has there obtained, which is deep-rooted, increasing, and over the younger portion of the community far greater than that of any other person.

His books are received there with a more ready intelligence than elsewhere, partly because his range of personal experiences and illustration applies to that region, partly because he has prepared the way for his books to be read by his great powers as a speaker.

The audience that waited for years upon the lectures, a part of which is incorporated into these volumes of essays, was never large, but it was select and it was constant. Among the hearers were some who, attracted by the beauty of character and manner, though they were willing to hear the speaker through, always went away discontented. They were accustomed to an artificial method whose scaffolding could easily be retraced, and desired an obvious sequence of logical inferences. They insisted there was nothing in what they had heard, because they could not give a clear account of its course and purport. They did not see that Pindar's odes might be very well arranged for their own purpose, and yet not bear translating into the methods of Mr. Locke.

Others were content to be benefited by a good influence without a strict analysis of its means. "My wife says it is about the elevation of human nature, and so it seems to me," was a fit reply to some of the critics. Many were satisfied to find themselves excited to congenial thought and nobler life, without an exact catalogue of the thoughts of the speaker.

Those who believed no truth could exist unless encased by the burrs of opinion went away utterly baffled. Sometimes they thought he was on their side, then presently would come something on the other. He really seemed to believe there were two sides to every subject, and even to intimate higher ground from which each might be seen to have an infinite number of sides or bearings, an impertinence not to be endured! The partisan heard but once and returned no more.

But some there were, simple souls, whose life had been perhaps without clear light yet still a search after truth for its own sake, who were able to receive what followed on the suggestion of a subject in a natural manner as a stream of thought. These recognized beneath the veil of words the still small voice of conscience, the vestal fires of lone religious hours, and the mild teachings of the summer woods.

The charm of the elocution too was great. His general manner was that of the reader, occasionally rising into direct address or invocation in passages where tenderness or majesty demanded more energy. At such times both eye and voice called on a remote future to give a worthy reply. A future which shall manifest more largely the universal soul as it was then to this soul. The tone of the voice was a grave body-tone, full and sweet rather than sonorous, yet flexible and haunted by many modulations, as even instruments of wood and brass seem to become after they have been long played on with skill and taste; how much more so the human voice! In the more expressive passages it uttered notes of silvery clearness, winning yet still more commanding. The words uttered in those tones floated awhile above us, then took root in the memory like winged seed.

In the union of an even rustic plainness with lyric inspirations, religious dignity with philosophic calmness, keen sagacity in details with boldness of view, we saw what brought to mind the early poets and legislators of Greece—men who taught their fellows to plow and avoid moral evil, sing hymns to the gods and watch the metamorphoses of nature. Here in civic Boston was such a man—one who could see man in his original grandeur and his original childishness, rooted in simple nature, raising to the heavens the brow and eyes of a poet.

And these lectures seemed not so much lectures as grave didactic poems, theogonies perhaps, adorned by odes when some Power was in question whom the poet had best learned to serve, and with eclogues wisely portraying in familiar tongue the duties of man to man and "harmless animals."

Such was the attitude in which the speaker appeared to that portion of the audience who have remained permanently attached to him. They value his words as the signets of reality; receive his influence as a help and incentive to a nobler discipline than the age in its general aspect appears to require; and do not fear to anticipate the verdict of posterity in claiming for him the honors of greatness and in some respects of a master.

In New England he thus formed for himself a class of readers who rejoice to study in his books what they already know by heart. For though the thought has become familiar, its beautiful garb is always fresh and bright in hue.

A similar circle of like-minded the books must and do form for themselves, though with a movement less directly powerful, as more distant from its source.

The essays have also been obnoxious to many charges. To that of obscurity, or want of perfect articulation. Of "Euphuism," as an excess of fancy in proportion to imagination, and an inclination at times to subtlety at the expense of strength, has been styled. The human heart complains of inadequacy, either in the nature or experience of the writer, to represent its full vocation and its deeper needs. Sometimes it speaks of this want as "underdevelopment" or a want of expansion which may yet be remedied; sometimes doubts whether "in this mansion there be either hall or portal to receive the loftier of the passions." Sometimes the soul is deified at the expense of nature, then again nature at that of man, and we are not quite sure that we can make a true harmony by balance of the statements. This writer has never written one good work, if such a work be one where the whole commands more attention than the parts, if such an one be produced only where, after an accumulation of materials, fire enough be applied to fuse the whole into one new substance. This second series is superior in this respect to the former, yet in no one essay is the main stress so obvious as to produce on the mind the harmonious effect of a noble river or tree in full leaf. Single passages and sentences engage our attention too much in proportion. These essays, it has been justly said, tire like a string of mosaics or a house built of medals. We miss what we expect in the work of the great poet or the great philosopher, the liberal air of all the zones: the glow, uniform yet various in tint, which is given to a body by free circulation of the heart's blood from the hour of birth. Here is undoubtedly the man of ideas, but we want the ideal man also; want the heart and genius of human life to interpret it, and here our satisfaction is not so perfect. We doubt this friend raised himself too early to the perpendicular and did not lie along the ground long enough to hear the secret whispers of our parent life. We could wish he might be thrown by conflicts on the lap of mother earth, to see if he would not rise again with added powers.

All this we may say, but it cannot excuse us from benefiting by the great gifts that have been given and assigning them their due place.

Some painters paint on a red ground. And this color may be supposed to represent the groundwork most immediately congenial to most men, as it is the color of blood and represents human vitality. The figures traced upon it are instinct with life in its fullness and depths.

But other painters paint on a gold ground. And a very different but no less natural, because also a celestial beauty, is given to their works who choose for their foundation the color of the sunbeam, which nature has preferred for her most precious product, and that which will best bear the test of purification, gold.

If another simile may be allowed, another no less apt is at hand. Wine is the most brilliant and intense expression of the powers of earth—it is her potable fire, her answer to the sun. It exhilarates, it inspires, but then it is liable to fever and intoxicate too the careless partaker.

Mead was the chosen drink of the northern gods. And this essence of the honey of the mountain bee was not thought unworthy to revive the souls of the valiant who had left their bodies on the fields of strife below.

Nectar should combine the virtues of the ruby wine, the golden mead, without their defects or dangers.

Two high claims our writer can vindicate on the attention of his contemporaries. One from his *sincerity*. You have his thought just as it found place in the life of his own soul. Thus, however near or relatively distant its approximation to absolute truth, its action on you cannot fail to be healthful. It is a part of the free air.

He belongs to that band of whom there may be found a few in every age, and who now in known human history may be counted by hundreds, who worship the one God only, the God of Truth. They worship not saints nor creeds nor churches nor relics nor idols in any form. The mind is kept open to truth, and life only valued as a tendency toward it. This must be illustrated by acts and words of love, purity, and intelligence. Such are the salt of the earth; let the minutest crystal of that salt be willingly by us held in solution.

The other is through that part of his life which, if sometimes obstructed or chilled by the critical intellect, is yet the prevalent and the main source of his power. It is that by which he imprisons his hearer only to free him again as a "liberating God" (to use his own words). But indeed let us use them altogether, for none other, ancient or modern, can worthily express how, making present to us the courses and destinies of nature, he invests himself with her serenity and animates us with her joy.

"Poetry was all written before time was, and whenever we are so finely organized that we can penetrate into that region where the air is music, we hear those primal warblings and attempt to write them down, but we lose ever and anon a word or a verse, and substitute something of our own, and thus mistreat the poem. The men of more delicate ear write down these cadences more faithfully, and these transcripts, though imperfect, become the songs of the nations.

"As the eyes of Lyncaeus were said to see through the earth, so the poet turns the world to glass, and shows us all things in their right series and procession. For through that better perception he stands one step nearer to things, and sees the flowing or metamorphosis; perceives that thought is multiform; that within the form of every creature is a force impelling it to ascend into a higher form; and following with his eyes the life, uses the forms which express that life, and so the speech flows with the flowing of nature."

Thus have we in a brief and unworthy manner indicated some views of these books. The only true criticism of these or any good books may be gained by making them the companions of our lives. Does every accession of knowledge or a juster sense of beauty make us prize them more? Then they are good indeed, and more immortal than mortal. Let that test be applied to these; essays which will lead to great and complete poems—somewhere.

12

POE'S TALES *

Mr. Poe's tales need no aid of newspaper comment to give them popularity; they have secured it. We are glad to see them given to the public in this neat form, so that thousands more may be entertained by them without injury to their eyesight.

No form of literary activity has so terribly degenerated among us as the tale. Now that everybody who wants a new hat or bonnet takes this way to earn one from the magazines or annuals, we are inundated with the very flimsiest fabrics ever spun by mortal brain. Almost every person of feeling or fancy could supply a few agreeable and natural narratives, but when instead of using their materials spontaneously they set to work with geography in hand to find unexplored nooks of wild scenery in which to locate their Indians or interesting farmers' daughters, or with some abridgment of history to hunt monarchs or heroes yet unused to become the subjects of their crude coloring, the sale-work produced is a sad affair indeed and "gluts the market" to the sorrow both of buyers and lookers-on.

In such a state of things the writings of Mr. Poe are a refreshment, for they are the fruit of genuine observations and experience, combined with an invention which is not "making up," as children call their way of contriving stories, but a penetration into the causes of things which leads to original but credible results. His narrative proceeds with vigor, his colors are applied with discrimination, and where the effects are fantastic they are not unmeaningly so.

The "Murders in the Rue Morgue" especially made a great impression upon those who did not know its author and were not familiar with his mode of treatment. Several of his stories make us wish he would enter the higher walk of the metaphysical novel and, taking a mind of the self-possessed and deeply marked sort that suits him, give us a deeper and longer acquaintance with its life and the springs of its life than is possible in the compass of these tales.

As Mr. Poe is a professed critic and of all the band the most unsparing

---

* From the New York *Daily Tribune*, July 11, 1845.

to others, we are surprised to find some inaccuracies in the use of words, such as these: "he had with him many books, but rarely *employed* them." —"His results have, in truth, the *whole air* of intuition."

The degree of skill shown in the management of revolting or terrible circumstances makes the pieces that have such subjects more interesting than the others. Even the failures are those of an intellect of strong fiber and well-chosen aim.

13

POE'S POEMS *

Mr. Poe throws down the gauntlet in his preface by what he says of the "paltry compensations or more paltry commendations of mankind." Some champion might be expected to start up from the "somewhat sizable" class embraced, or, more properly speaking, boxed on the ear by this defiance, who might try whether the sting of criticism was as indifferent to this knight of the pen as he professes its honey to be.

Were there such a champion, gifted with acumen to dissect and a swift glancing wit to enliven the operation, he could find no more legitimate subject, no fairer game than Mr. Poe, who has wielded the weapons of criticism without relenting, whether with the dagger he rent and tore the garment in which some favored Joseph had pranked himself, secure of honor in the sight of all men, or whether with uplifted tomahawk he rushed upon the new-born children of some helpless genius who had fancied and persuaded his friends to fancy that they were beautiful and worthy a long and honored life. A large band of these offended dignitaries and aggrieved parents must be on the watch for a volume of poems by Edgar A. Poe, ready to cut, rend, and slash in turn, and hoping to see his own Raven left alone to prey upon the slaughter of which it is the herald.

Such joust and tournament we look to see, and indeed have some stake in the matter so far as we have friends whose wrongs cry aloud for the avenger. Nevertheless, we could not take part in the melee, except to join the crowd of lookers-on in the cry, Heaven speed the right!

Early we read that fable of Apollo who rewarded the critic, who had painfully winnowed the wheat, with the chaff for his pains. We joined the gentle affirmative school, and have confidence that if we indulge ourselves chiefly with the appreciation of good qualities, Time will take care of the faults. For Time holds a strainer like that used in the diamond mines; have but patience and the water and gravel will all pass through and only the precious stones be left. Yet we are not blind to the uses of severe criticism, especially in a time and place so degraded by venial and indiscriminate

* From the New York *Daily Tribune*, November 26, 1845.

398

praise as the present. That unholy alliance, that shameless sham whose motto is "Caw me, And I'll caw thee," that system of mutual adulation and organized puff which was carried to such perfection in the time and may be seen drawn to the life in the correspondence of Miss Hannah More, is fully represented in our day and generation. We see that it meets a counter agency from the league of truth-tellers, few but each of them mighty as Fingal or any other hero of the sort. Let such tell the whole truth, as well as nothing but the truth, but let their sternness be in the spirit of love. Let them seek to understand the purpose and scope of an author, his capacity as well as fulfillments, and how his faults are made to grow by the same sunshine that acts upon his virtues, for this is the case with talents no less than with character. The rich field requires frequent and careful weeding; frequent lest the weeds exhaust the soil; careful lest the flowers and grain be pulled up along with the weeds.

Well, to return to Mr. Poe, we are not unwilling that cavil should do her worst on his book because both by act and word he has challenged it, but as this is no office for us, we shall merely indicate in our usual slight way what naturally and unsought has struck ourselves in the reading of these verses.

It has often been our case to share the mistake of Gil Blas with regard to the Archbishop. We have taken people at their word, and while rejoicing that women could bear neglect without feeling mean pique, and that authors, rising above self-love, could show candor about their works and magnanimously meet both justice and injustice, we have been rudely awakened from our dream, and found that Chanticleer who crowed so bravely showed himself at last but a dunghill fowl. Yet Heaven grant we never become too worldly wise to trust a generous word, and we surely are not so yet, for we believe Mr. Poe to be sincere when he says:

"In defense of my own taste, it is incumbent upon me to say that I think nothing in this volume of much value to the public or very creditable to myself. Events not to be controlled have prevented me from making at any time any serious effort in what under happier circumstances would have been the field of my choice."

We believe Mr. Poe to be sincere in this declaration; if he is, we respect him; if otherwise, we do not. Such things should never be said unless in hearty earnest. If in earnest, they are honorable pledges; if not, a pitiful fence and foil of vanity. Earnest or not, the words are thus far true: the productions in this volume indicate a power to do something far better. With the exception of "The Raven," which seems intended chiefly to show the writer's artistic skill, and is in its way a rare and finished specimen, they are all fragments—*fyttes* upon the lyre, almost all of which leave us something to desire or demand. This is not the case, however, with these lines:

TO ONE IN PARADISE

Thou wast all that to me, love,
    For which my soul did pine—
A green isle in the sea, love,
    A fountain and a shrine,
All wreathed with fairy fruits and flowers,
    And all the flowers were mine.

Ah, dream too bright to last!
    Ah, starry Hope! that didst arise
But to be overcast!
    A voice from out the Future cries,
"On! On!"—but o'er the Past
    (Dim gulf!) my spirit hovering lies
Mute, motionless, aghast!

For, alas! alas! with me
    The light of Life is o'er!
    No more—no more—no more—
(Such language holds the solemn sea
    To the sands upon the shore)
Shall bloom the thunder-blasted tree,
    Or the stricken eagle soar!

And all my days are trances,
    And all my nightly dreams
Are where thy dark eye glances,
    And where thy footstep gleams—
In what ethereal dances,
    By what eternal streams.

The poems breathe a passionate sadness, relieved sometimes by touches very lovely and tender:

Amid the earnest woes
That crowd around my earthly path
(Drear path, alas! where grows
Not even one lovely rose).

For her, the fair and debonair, that now so lowly lies,
The life upon her yellow hair, but not within her eyes—
The life still there, upon her hair—the death upon her eyes.

This kind of beauty is especially conspicuous, then rising into dignity, in the poem called "The Haunted Palace."

The imagination of this writer rarely expresses itself in pronounced forms, but rather in a sweep of images thronging and distant like a procession of moonlight clouds on the horizon, but like them characteristic and harmonious one with another according to their office.

The descriptive power is greatest when it takes a shape not unlike an incantation, as in the first part of "The Sleeper," where

I stand beneath the mystic moon,
An opiate vapor, dewy, dim,
Exhales from out a golden rim,
And, softly dripping, drop by drop,
Upon the quiet mountain top,
Steals drowsily and musically
Into the Universal valley.

Why "Universal"?—"resolve me that, Master Moth."

And farther on, "the lily *lolls* upon the wave."

This word "lolls," often made use of in these poems, presents a vulgar image to our thought; we know not how it is to that of others.

The lines which follow about the open window are highly poetical. So is the "Bridal Ballad" in its power of suggesting a whole tribe and train of thoughts and pictures by few and simple touches.

The poems written in youth, written indeed, we understand, in childhood before the author was ten years old, are a great psychological curiosity. Is it the delirium of a prematurely excited brain that causes such a rapture of words? What is to be gathered from seeing the future so fully anticipated in the germ? The passions are not unfrequently felt in their full shock, if not in their intensity, at eight or nine years old, but here they are reflected upon:

Sweet was their death—with them to die was rife
With the last ecstasy of satiate life.

The scenes from Politian are done with clear sharp strokes; the power
is rather metaphysical than dramatic. We must repeat what we have heretofore said, that we could wish to see Mr. Poe engaged in a metaphysical
romance. He needs a sustained flight and a fair range to show what his
powers really are. Let us have from him the analysis of the passions, with
their appropriate fates; let us have his speculations clarified; let him inter-
sperse dialogue or poems as the occasion prompts, and give us something
really good and strong, firmly wrought and fairly blazoned. Such would
be better employment than detecting literary larcenies not worth pointing
out if they exist. Such employment is quite unworthy of one who dares
vie with the Angel.

ISRAFEL

In Heaven a spirit doth dwell
  "Whose heartstrings are a lute";
None sing so wildly well
As the Angel Israfel,
And the giddy stars (so legends tell),
Ceasing their hymns, attend the spell
  Of his voice, all mute.

Tottering above
  In her highest noon
  The enamored Moon
Blushes with love,
  While, to listen, the red levin
  (With the rapid Pleiads, even,
  Which were seven)
  Pauses in Heaven.

And they say (the starry choir
  And the other listening things)
That Israfeli's fire
Is owing to that lyre
  By which he sits and sings—
The trembling living wire
  Of those unusual strings.

But the skies that Angel trod,
  Where deep thoughts are a duty—

Where's Love's a grown-up god—
   Where the Houri glances are
Imbued with all the beauty
   Which we worship in a star!

Therefore, thou art not wrong,
   Israfeli, who despisest
An unimpassioned song;
To thee the laurels belong,
   Best bard, because the wisest!
Merrily live, and long!

The ecstasies above
   With thy burning measures suit—
Thy grief, thy joy, thy hate, thy love,
   With the fervor of thy lute—
Well may the stars be mute!

Yes, Heaven is thine; but this
   Is a world of sweets and sours;
   Our flowers are merely—flowers,
And the shadow of thy perfect bliss
   Is the sunshine of ours.

If I could dwell
Where Israfel
   Hath dwelt, and he where I,
He might not sing so wildly well
   A mortal melody,
While a bolder note than this might swell
   From my lyre within the sky.

PART IV

Italy and the Roman Revolution

Prefatory Note

Margaret Fuller sailed for Europe on August 1, 1846, with her friends Marcus and Rebecca Spring and their young son Eddie. The Springs, who delighted in playing the role of fairy godmother, had invited Margaret to accompany them on a European tour, knowing that such a trip had been her most cherished dream for years. Horace Greeley took the loss of his literary critic with good grace and commissioned her to write foreign correspondence for the *Tribune*. This arrangement was eminently satisfactory to Margaret, as she was thus not left dependent upon the generosity of the Springs.

She wrote thirty-three letters from Europe for publication in the *Tribune*. The first was dated August 23, 1846, the last July 6, 1849. During the intervening period she traveled through England and Scotland, France, Switzerland, and Italy. In Italy, which she had thought of as her spiritual home since her Cambridge childhood, she found fulfillment emotionally and intellectually. Of her romance with the impoverished Marchese Ossoli, and of the child she bore him, there is naturally nothing in these letters written for publication, but the events of her personal life are responsible for the irregular intervals at which they were sent. The Roman Revolution was the greatest cause of a woman who could not exist without a cause to cherish, and the active part she took in the movement is reflected in the political preoccupations of the later letters, which contrast so strangely with the literary and artistic concerns of the earlier dispatches. Her progress to intellectual maturity is mirrored in the development from the "my trip abroad" manner to the highly professional propagandist technique of the last letters. If her lost history of the Roman Revolution was written with the same fire and force, the loss was indeed a great one. In any case, Margaret Fuller had an insight into the inner workings of the movement such as was vouchsafed to no other English-speaking person in Italy at that time. The letters afford a curious parallel to the foreign correspondence of our day; though the manner has changed in our less leisurely and more hard-boiled day, some of them might have been filed from Spain in 1938.

The original manuscripts are lost, and the text here given is drawn from that printed by Arthur B. Fuller when he collected these letters from the *Tribune* files in 1856. The indicated omissions are passages dealing with matters not directly connected with Italy and the Revolution.

Italy and the Roman Revolution

. . . .

The excessive beauty of Genoa is well known, and the impression upon the eye alone was correspondent with what I expected; but, alas, the weather was still so cold I could not realize that I had actually touched those shores to which I had looked forward all my life, where it seemed that the heart would expand and the whole nature be turned to delight. Seen by a cutting wind, the marble palaces, the gardens, the magnificent water-view of Genoa, failed to charm—"I *saw,* not *felt,* how beautiful they were." Only at Naples have I found *my* Italy, and here not till after a week's waiting—not till I began to believe that all I had heard in praise of the climate of Italy was fable, and that there is really no spring anywhere except in the imagination of poets. For the first week was an exact copy of the miseries of a New England spring; a bright sun came for an hour or two in the morning, just to coax you forth without your cloak, and then came up a villainous, horrible wind exactly like the worst east wind of Boston, breaking the heart, racking the brain, and turning hope and fancy to an irrevocable green and yellow hue in lieu of their native rose.

However, here at Naples I *have* at last found *my* Italy; I have passed through the Grotto of Pausilippo, visited Cuma, Baiae, and Capri, ascended Vesuvius, and found all familiar except the sense of enchantment, of sweet exhilaration, this scene conveys.

Behold how brightly breaks the morning!

and yet all new as if never yet described, for Nature here, most prolific and exuberant in her gifts, has touched them all with a charm unhackneyed, unhackneyable, which the boots of English dandies cannot trample out, nor the raptures of sentimental tourists daub or fade. Baiae had still a hid divinity for me, Vesuvius a fresh baptism of fire, and Sorrento—oh,

Sorrento was beyond picture, beyond poesy, for the greatest Artist had been at work there in a temper beyond the reach of human art.

Beyond this, reader, my old friend and valued acquaintance on other themes, I shall tell you nothing of Naples, for it is a thing apart in the journey of life, and if represented at all, should be so in a fairer form than offers itself at present. Now the actual life here is over, I am going to Rome, and expect to see that fane of thought the last day of this week.

At Genoa and Leghorn, I saw for the first time Italians in their homes. Very attractive I found them, charming women, refined men, eloquent and courteous. If the cold wind hid Italy, it could not the Italians. A little group of faces, each so full of character, dignity, and, what is so rare in an American face, the capacity for pure exalting passion, will live ever in my memory —the fulfillment of a hope!

.   .   .   .

LETTER XIV

Rome, May 1847

There is very little that I can like to write about Italy. Italy is beautiful, worthy to be loved and embraced, not talked about. Yet I remember well that when afar I liked to read what was written about her; now all thought of it is very tedious.

The traveler passing along the beaten track, vetturinoed from inn to inn, ciceroned from gallery to gallery, thrown through indolence, want of tact, or ignorance of the language too much into the society of his compatriots, sees the least possible of the country; fortunately it is impossible to avoid seeing a great deal. The great features of the part pursue and fill the eye.

Yet I find that it is quite out of the question to know Italy; to say anything of her that is full and sweet, so as to convey any idea of her spirit, without long residence, and residence in the districts untouched by the scorch and dust of foreign invasion (the invasion of the dilettanti I mean) and without an intimacy of feeling, an abandonment to the spirit of the place, impossible to most Americans. They retain too much of their English blood; and the traveling English as a class seem to me the most unseeing of all possible animals. There are exceptions; for instance, the perceptions and pictures of Browning seem as delicate and just, here on the spot, as they did at a distance; but take them as a class, they have the vulgar familiarity of Mrs. Trollope without her vivacity, the cockneyism of Dickens without his graphic power and love of the odd corners of human nature. I admired the English at home in their island; I admired their honor, truth, practical intelligence, persistent power. But they do not look well in Italy; they are not the figures for this landscape. I am indignant at the contempt they have presumed to express for the faults of our semi-barbarous state. What is the vulgarity expressed in our tobacco-chewing, and way of eating eggs, compared to that which elbows the Greek marbles, guidebook in hand—chatters and sneers through the *Miserere* of the Sistine Chapel, beneath the very glance of Michelangelo's "Sibyls"—praises St. Peter's as "nice"—talks of "managing" the Colosseum by moonlight—and snatches "bits" for a "sketch" from the sublime silence of the Campagna.

．　　　．　　　．　　　．　　　．　　　．　　　．

I have heard owls hoot in the Colosseum by moonlight, and they spoke more to the purpose than I ever heard any other voice upon that subject. I have seen all the pomps and shows of Holy Week in the church of St. Peter, and found them less imposing than a habitual acquaintance with the place, with processions of monks and nuns stealing in now and then, or the swell of vespers from some side-chapel. I have ascended the dome and seen thence Rome and its Campagna, its villas with their cypresses and pines serenely sad as is nothing else in the world, and the fountains of the Vatican garden gushing hard by. I have been in the Subterranean to see a poor little boy introduced, much to his surprise, to the bosom of the Church; and then I have seen by torchlight the stone popes where they lie on their tombs and the old mosaics and virgins with gilt caps. It is all rich and full—very impressive in its way. St. Peter's must be to each one a separate poem.

The ceremonies of the Church have been numerous and splendid during our stay here; and they borrow unusual interest from the love and expectation inspired by the present Pontiff. He is a man of noble and good aspect who, it is easy to see, has set his heart upon doing something solid for the benefit of man. But pensively, too, must one feel how hampered and inadequate are the means at his command to accomplish these ends. The Italians do not feel it, but deliver themselves with all the vivacity of their temperament to perpetual hurrahs, *vivas,* rockets, and torchlight processions. I often think how grave and sad must the Pope feel, as he sits alone and hears all this noise of expectation.

A week or two ago the Cardinal Secretary published a circular inviting the departments to measures which would give the people a sort of representative council. Nothing could seem more limited than this improvement, but it was a great measure for Rome. At night the Corso in which we live was illuminated, and many thousands passed through it in a torch-bearing procession. I saw them first assembled in the Piazza del Popolo, forming around its fountain a great circle of fire. Then as a river of fire they streamed slowly through the Corso on their way to the Quirinal to thank the Pope, upbearing a banner on which the edict was printed. The stream of fire advanced slowly, with a perpetual surgelike sound of voices; the torches flashed on the animated Italian faces. I have never seen anything finer. Ascending the Quirinal they made it a mount of light. Bengal fires were thrown up which cast their red and white light on the noble Greek figures of men and horses that reign over it. The Pope appeared on his balcony; the crowd shouted three *vivas;* he extended his arms; the crowd fell on their knees and received his benediction; he retired, and the torches were extinguished, and the multitude dispersed in an instant.

The same week came the natal day of Rome. A great dinner was given at the Baths of Titus in the open air. The company was on the grass in the area; the music at one end; boxes filled with the handsome Roman women occupied the other sides. It was a new thing here, this popular dinner, and the Romans greeted it in an intoxication of hope and pleasure. Sterbini, author of *The Vestal,* presided; many others, like him long time exiled and restored to their country by the present Pope, were at the tables. The Colosseum and triumphal arches were in sight; an effigy of the Roman wolf with her royal nursling was erected on high; the guests with shouts and music congratulated themselves on the possession in Pius IX of a new and nobler founder for another state. Among the speeches that of the Marquis d'Azeglio, a man of literary note in Italy and son-in-law of Manzoni, contained this passage (he was sketching the past history of Italy):

"The crown passed to the head of a German monarch; but he wore it not to the benefit, but the injury of Christianity—of the world. The Emperor Henry was a tyrant who wearied out the patience of God. God said to Rome, 'I give you the Emperor Henry'; and from these hills that surround us Hildebrand, Pope Gregory VII, raised his austere and potent voice to say to the Emperor, 'God did not give you Italy that you might destroy her,' and Italy, Germany, Europe saw her butcher prostrated at the feet of Gregory in penitence. Italy, Germany, Europe had then kindled in the heart the first spark of liberty."

The narrative of the dinner passed the censor, and was published: the Ambassador of Austria read it, and found with a modesty and candor truly admirable that this passage was meant to allude to his Emperor. He must take his passports, if such home thrusts are to be made. And so the paper was seized, and the account of the dinner only told from mouth to mouth, from those who had already read it. Also the idea of a dinner for the Pope's fete-day is abandoned, lest something too frank should again be said; and they tell me here with a laugh, "I fancy you have assisted at the first and last popular dinner." Thus we may see that the liberty of Rome does not yet advance with seven-league boots; and the new Romulus will need to be prepared for deeds at least as bold as his predecessor, if he is to open a new order of things.

I cannot well wind up my gossip on this subject better than by translating a passage from the program of the *Contemporaneo,* which represents the hope of Rome at this moment. It is conducted by men of well-known talent.

"The *Contemporaneo* [Contemporary] is a journal of progress, but tempered, as the good and wise think best, in conformity with the will of our best of princes and the wants and expectations of the public. . . .

"Through discussion it desires to prepare minds to receive reforms so soon and far as they are favored by the law of *opportunity.*

"Every attempt which is made contrary to this social law must fail. It is vain to hope for fruits from a tree out of season, and equally in vain to introduce the best measures into a country not prepared to receive them."

And so on. I intended to have translated in full the program, but time fails and the law of opportunity does not favor, as my "opportunity" leaves for London this afternoon. I have given enough to mark the purport of the whole. It will easily be seen that it was not from the platform assumed by the *Contemporaneo* that Lycurgus legislated or Socrates taught—that the Christian religion was propagated, or the Church was reformed by Luther. The opportunity that the martyrs found here in the Colosseum, from whose blood grew up this great tree of Papacy, was not of the kind waited for by these moderate progressives. Nevertheless, they may be good schoolmasters for Italy, and are not to be disdained in these piping times of peace.

More anon of old and new from Tuscany.

LETTER XVI

Rome, October 1847

.   .   .   .

The Austrian rule is always equally hated, and the time instead of melting away differences only makes them more glaring. The Austrian race have no faculties that can ever enable them to understand the Italian character; their policy, so well contrived to palsy and repress for a time, cannot kill, and there is always a force at work underneath which shall yet, and I think now before long, shake off the incubus. The Italian nobility have always kept the invader at a distance; they have not been at all seduced or corrupted by the lures of pleasure or power, but have shown a passive patriotism highly honorable to them. In the middle class ferments much thought, and there is a capacity for effort; in the present system it cannot show itself, but it is there; thought ferments, and will yet produce a wine that shall set the Lombard veins on fire when the time for action shall arrive. The lower classes of the population are in a dull state indeed. The censorship of the press prevents all easy natural ways of instructing them; there are no public meetings, no free access to them by more instructed and aspiring minds. The Austrian policy is to allow them a degree of material well-being, and though so much wealth is drained from the country for the service of the foreigners, yet enough must remain on these rich plains comfortably to feed and clothe the inhabitants. Yet the great moral influence of the Pope's action, though obstructed in their case, does reach and rouse them, and they too felt the thrill of indignation at the occupation of Ferrara. The base conduct of the police toward the people when at Milan some youths were resolute to sing the hymn in honor of Pius IX, when the feasts for the Archbishop afforded so legitimate an occasion, roused all the people to unwonted feeling. The nobles protested, and Austria had not courage to persist as usual. She could not sustain her police, who rushed upon a defenseless crowd that had no share in what excited their displeasure except by sympathy and, driving them like sheep, wounded them *in the backs.* Austria feels that there is now no sympathy for her in these matters; that it is not the interest of the world to sustain her. Her policy is indeed too thoroughly organized to change except by revolution; its scope is to serve, first, a reigning family instead of the people; second, with the people to seek a physical in preference to an intellectual good; and third, to prefer a seeming outward peace to an inward life. This policy may change its opposition from the tyrannical to the insidious; it can know no other change. Yet do I meet persons who call themselves Americans— miserable, thoughtless Esaus, unworthy their high birthright—who think that a mess of pottage can satisfy the wants of man, and that the Viennese listening to Strauss's waltzes, the Lombard peasant supping full of his polenta, is *happy enough.* Alas, I have the more reason to be ashamed of my countrymen that it is not among the poor, who have so much toil, that there is little time to think, but among those who are rich, who travel—in body that is, they do not travel in mind. Absorbed at home by the lust of gain, the love of show, abroad they see only the equipages, the fine clothes, the food—they have no heart for the idea, for the destiny of our own great nation: how can they feel the spirit that is struggling now in this and others of Europe?

But of the hopes of Italy I will write more fully in another letter, and state what I have seen, what felt, what thought. I went from Milan to Pavia, and saw its magnificent Certosa. I passed several hours in examining its riches, especially the sculptures of its façade, full of force and spirit. I then went to Florence by Parma and Bologna. In Parma, though ill, I went to see all the works of the masters. A wonderful beauty it is that informs them—not that which is the chosen food of my soul, yet a noble beauty, and which did its message to me also. Those works are failing; it will not be useless to describe them in a book. Besides these pictures, I saw nothing in Parma and Modena; these states are obliged to hold their breath while their poor ignorant sovereigns skulk in corners, hoping to hide from the coming storm. Of all this more in my next.

LETTER XVII

Rome, October 18, 1847

In the spring, when I came to Rome, the people were in the intoxication of joy at the first serious measures of reform taken by the Pope. I saw with pleasure their childlike joy and trust. With equal pleasure I saw the Pope, who has not in his expression the signs of intellectual greatness so much as of nobleness and tenderness of heart, of large and liberal sympathies. Heart had spoken to heart between the prince and the people; it was beautiful to see the immediate good influence exerted by human feeling and generous designs on the part of a ruler. He had wished to be a father, and the Italians with that readiness of genius that characterizes them entered at once into the relation; they, the Roman people, stigmatized by prejudice as so crafty and ferocious, showed themselves children eager to learn, quick to obey, happy to confide.

Still doubts were always present whether all this joy was not premature. The task undertaken by the Pope seemed to present insuperable difficulties. It is never easy to put new wine into old bottles, and our age is one where all things tend to a great crisis; not merely to revolution, but to radical reform. From the people themselves the help must come, and not from princes; in the new state of things there will be none but natural princes, great men. From the aspirations of the general heart, from the teachings of conscience in individuals, and not from an old ivy-covered church long since undermined, corroded by time and gnawed by vermin, the help must come. Rome, to resume her glory, must cease to be an ecclesiastical capital; must renounce all this gorgeous mummery, whose poetry, whose picture, charms no one more than myself, but whose meaning is all of the past, and finds no echo in the future. Although I sympathized warmly with the warm love of the people, the adulation of leading writers, who were so willing to take all from the hand of the prince, of the Church, as a gift and a bounty, instead of implying steadily that it was the right of the people, was very repulsive to me. The moderate party, like all who in a transition state manage affairs with a constant eye to prudence, lacks dignity always in its expositions; it is disagreeable and depressing to read them.

Passing into Tuscany, I found the liberty of the press just established, and a superior preparation to make use of it. The *Alba*, the *Patria*, were begun, and have been continued with equal judgment and spirit. Their aim is to educate the youth, to educate the lower people; they see that this is to be done by promoting thought fearlessly, yet urge temperance in action, while the time is yet so difficult and many of its signs dubious. They aim at breaking down those barriers between the different states of Italy, relics of a barbarous state of polity artificially kept up by the craft of her foes. While anxious not to break down what is really native to the Italian character—defenses and differences that give individual genius a chance to grow and the fruits of each region to ripen in their natural way —they aim at a harmony of spirit as to measures of education and for the affairs of business, without which Italy can never as one nation present a front strong enough to resist foreign robbery, and for want of which so much time and talent are wasted here, and internal development almost wholly checked.

There is in Tuscany a large corps of enlightened minds, well prepared to be the instructors, the elder brothers and guardians of the lower people, and whose hearts burn to fulfill that noble office. Before it had been almost impossible to them, for the reasons I have named in speaking of Lombardy; but during these last four months that the way has been opened by the freedom of the press and establishment of the National Guard—so valuable, first of all, as giving occasion for public meetings and free interchange of thought between the different classes—it is surprising how much light they have been able to diffuse.

A Bolognese to whom I observed, "How can you be so full of trust when all your hopes depend not on the recognition of principles and wants throughout the people, but on the life of one mortal man?" replied, "Ah, but you don't consider that his life gives us a chance to effect that recognition. If Pius IX be spared to us five years, it will be impossible for his successors ever to take a backward course. Our nation is of a genius so vivacious—we are unhappy but not stupid, we Italians—we can learn as much in two months as other nations in twenty years." This seemed to me no brag when I returned to Tuscany and saw the great development and diffusion of thought that had taken place during my brief absence. The Grand Duke, a well-intentioned though dull man, had dared to declare himself "an *Italian* prince," and the heart of Tuscany had bounded with hope. It is now deeply and justly felt that *the* curse of Italy is foreign intrusion; that if she could dispense with foreign aid and be free from foreign aggression, she would find the elements of salvation within herself. All her efforts tend that way, to re-establish the natural position of things; may Heaven grant them success! For myself I believe they will attain it. I see more reason for hope as I know more of the people. Their rash and baffled struggles have taught them prudence; they are wanted in the civilized world as a peculiar influence; their leaders are thinking men, their cause is righteous. I believe that Italy will revive to new life and probably a greater one, more truly rich and glorious than at either epoch of her former greatness.

During the period of my absence, the Austrians had entered Ferrara. It is well that they hazarded this step, for it showed them the difficulties in acting against a prince of the Church who is at the same time a friend to the people. The position was new, and they were probably surprised at the result—surprised at the firmness of the Pope, surprised at the indignation tempered by calm resolve on the part of the Italians. Louis Philippe's mean apostasy has this time turned to the advantage of freedom. He renounced the good understanding with England which it had been one of the leading features of his policy to maintain, in the hope of aggrandizing and enriching his family (not France, he did not care for France); he did not know that he was paving the way for Italian freedom. England now is led to play a part a little nearer her pretensions as the guardian of progress than she often comes, and the ghost of Lafayette looks down not unappeased to see the "Constitutional King" decried by the subjects he has cheated and lulled so craftily. The King of Sardinia is a worthless man in whom nobody puts any trust so far as regards his heart or honor; but the stress of things seems likely to keep him on the right side. The little sovereigns blustered at first, then ran away affrighted when they found there was really a spirit risen at last within the charmed circle—a spirit likely to defy, to transcend the spells of haggard premiers and imbecile monarchs.

I arrived in Florence unhappily too late for the great fete of the 12th of September, in honor of the grant of a National Guard. But I wept at the mere recital of the events of that day which, if it should lead to no important results, must still be hallowed forever in the memory of Italy, for the great and beautiful emotions that flooded the hearts of her children. The National Guard is hailed with no undue joy by Italians as the earnest of progress, the first step toward truly national institutions and a representation of the people. Gratitude has done its natural work in their hearts; it has made them better. Some days before the fete were passed in reconciling all strifes, composing all differences between cities, districts, and individuals. They wished to drop all petty, all local differences, to wash away all stains, to bathe and prepare for a new great covenant of brotherly love, where each should act for the good of all. On that day they all embraced in sign of this—strangers, foes, all exchanged the kiss of faith and love; they exchanged banners as a token that they would fight for, would animate one another. All was done in that beautiful poetic manner peculiar to this artist people; but it was the spirit so great and tender that melts my heart to think of. It was the spirit of true religion—such, my country, as welling freshly from some great hearts in thy early hours, won for thee all of value that thou canst call thy own, whose groundwork is the assertion, still sublime though thou hast not been true to it, that all men have equal rights and that these are *birth*rights, derived from God alone.

I rejoice to say that the Americans took their share on this occasion, and that Greenough—one of the few Americans living in Italy who take the pains to know whether it is alive or dead, who penetrate beyond the cheats of tradesmen and the cunning of a mob corrupted by centuries of slavery, to know the real mind, the vital blood, of Italy—took a leading part. I am sorry to say that a large portion of my countrymen here take the same slothful and prejudiced view as the English, and after many years' sojourn betray entire ignorance of Italian literature and Italian life, beyond what is attainable in a month's passage through the thoroughfares. However, they did show this time a becoming spirit, and erected the American eagle where its cry ought to be heard from afar—where a nation is striving for independent existence, and a government representing the people. Crawford here in Rome has had the just feeling to join the Guard, and it is a real sacrifice for an artist to spend time on the exercises; but it well becomes the sculptor of Orpheus—of him who had such faith, such music of divine thought that he made the stones move, turned the beasts from their accustomed haunts, and shamed hell itself into sympathy with the grief of love. I do not deny that such a spirit is wanted here in Italy; it is everywhere, if anything great, anything permanent is to be done. In reference to what I have said of many Americans in Italy, I will only add that they talk about the corrupt and degenerate state of Italy as they do about that of our slaves at home. They come ready trained to that mode of reasoning which affirms that because men are degraded by bad institutions they are not fit for better.

As to the English, some of them are full of generous, intelligent sympathy—indeed what is more solidly, more wisely good than the right sort of Englishman?—but others are like a gentleman I traveled with the other day, a man of intelligence and refinement too as to the details of life and outside culture, who observed that he did not see what the Italians wanted of a National Guard, unless to wear these little caps. He was a man who had passed five years in Italy, but always covered with that non-conductor called by a witty French writer the "Britannic fluid."

Very sweet to my ear was the continual hymn in the streets of Florence in honor of Pius IX. It is the Roman hymn, and none of the new ones written in Tuscany have been able to take its place. The people thank the Grand Duke when he does them good, but they know well from whose mind that good originates, and all their love is for the Pope. Time presses, or I would fain describe in detail the troop of laborers of the lower class marching home at night, keeping step as if they were in the National Guard, filling the air and cheering the melancholy moon by the patriotic hymns sung with the mellow tone and in the perfect time which belong

to Italians. I would describe the extempore concerts in the streets, the re-
joicings at the theaters where the addresses of liberal souls to the people
through that best vehicle, the drama, may now be heard. But I am tired;
what I have to write would fill volumes, and my letter must go. I will only
add some words upon the happy augury I draw from the wise docility of
the people. With what readiness they listened to wise counsel and the hopes
of the Pope that they would give no advantage to his enemies, at a time
when they were so fevered by the knowledge that conspiracy was at work
in their midst! That was a time of trial. On all these occasions of popular
excitement their conduct is like music, in such order and with such union
of the melody of feeling with discretion where to stop; but what is wonderful is that they acted in the same manner on that difficult occasion. The
influence of the Pope here is without bounds; he can always calm the
crowd at once. But in Tuscany where they have no such idol, they listened
in the same way on a very trying occasion. The first announcement of the
regulation for the Tuscan National Guard terribly disappointed the people;
they felt that the Grand Duke, after suffering them to demonstrate such
trust and joy on the feast of the 12th, did not really trust on his side; that
he meant to limit them all he could. They felt baffled, cheated; hence young
men in anger tore down at once the symbols of satisfaction and respect;
but the leading men went among the people, begged them to be calm and
wait till a deputation had seen the Grand Duke. The people, listening at
once to men who they were sure had at heart their best good, waited; the
Grand Duke became convinced, and all ended without disturbance. If they
continue to act thus, their hopes cannot be baffled. Certainly I for one do
not think that the present road will suffice to lead Italy to her goal. But
it *is* an onward, upward road, and the people learn as they advance. Now
they can seek and think fearless of prisons and bayonets, a healthy circulation of blood begins, and the heart frees itself from disease.

I earnestly hope for some expression of sympathy from my country
toward Italy. Take a good chance and do something; you have shown
much good feeling toward the Old World in its physical difficulties—you
ought to do still more in its spiritual endeavor. This cause is *ours* above
all others; we ought to show that we feel it to be so. At present there is
no likelihood of war, but in case of it I trust the United States would not

fail in some noble token of sympathy toward this country. The soul of our nation need not wait for its government; these things are better done by individuals. I believe some in the United States will pay attention to these words of mine, will feel that I am not a person to be kindled by a childish sentimental enthusiasm, but that I must be sure I have seen something of Italy before speaking as I do. I have been here only seven months, but my means of observation have been uncommon. I have been ardently desirous to judge fairly, and had no prejudices to prevent; besides I was not ignorant of the history and literature of Italy, and had some common ground on which to stand with its inhabitants and hear what they have to say. In many ways Italy is of kin to us; she is the country of Columbus, of Amerigo, of Cabot. It would please me much to see a cannon here, bought by the contributions of Americans, at whose head should stand the name of Cabot, to be used by the Guard for salutes on festive occasions, if they should be so happy as to have no more serious need. In Tuscany they are casting one to be called the "Gioberti," from a writer who has given a great impulse to the present movement. I should like the gift of America to be called the "Amerigo," the "Columbo," or the "Washington." Please think of this, some of my friends who still care for the eagle, the Fourth of July, and the old cries of hope and honor. See if there are any objections that I do not think of, and do something if it is well and brotherly. Ah, America, with all thy rich boons thou hast a heavy account to render for the talent given; see in every way that thou be not found wanting.

LETTER XVIII

This letter will reach the United States about the 1st of January; and it may not be impertinent to offer a few New Year's reflections. Every new year, indeed, confirms the old thoughts, but also presents them under some new aspects.

The American in Europe, if a thinking mind, can only become more American. In some respects it is a great pleasure to be here. Although we have an independent political existence, our position toward Europe as to literature and the arts is still that of a colony, and one feels the same joy here that is experienced by the colonist in returning to the parent home. What was but picture to us becomes reality; remote allusions and derivations trouble no more: we see the pattern of the stuff and understand the whole tapestry. There is a gradual clearing up on many points, and many baseless notions and crude fancies are dropped. Even the posthaste passage of the business American through the great cities, escorted by cheating couriers and ignorant *valets de place*, unable to hold intercourse with the natives of the country and passing all his leisure hours with his countrymen who know no more than himself, clears his mind of some mistakes —lifts some mists from his horizon.

There are three species. First, the servile American—a being utterly shallow, thoughtless, worthless. He comes abroad to spend his money and indulge his tastes. His object in Europe is to have fashionable clothes, good foreign cookery, to know some titled persons, and furnish himself with coffeehouse gossip, by retailing which among those less traveled and as uninformed as himself he can win importance at home. I look with unspeakable contempt on this class—a class which has all the thoughtlessness and partiality of the exclusive classes in Europe, without any of their refinement or the chivalric feeling which still sparkles among them here and there. However, though these willing serfs in a free age do some little hurt and cause some annoyance at present, they cannot continue long; our country is fated to a grand, independent existence, and, as its laws develop, these parasites of a bygone period must wither and drop away.

Then there is the conceited American, instinctively bristling and proud of—he knows not what. He does not see, not he, that the history of humanity for many centuries is likely to have produced results it requires some training, some devotion, to appreciate and profit by. With his great clumsy hands, only fitted to work on a steam engine, he seizes the old Cremona violin, makes it shriek with anguish in his grasp, and then declares he thought it was all humbug before he came and now he knows it; that there is not really any music in these old things; that the frogs in one of our swamps make much finer, for they are young and alive. To him the etiquettes of courts and camps, the ritual of the Church, seem simply silly —and no wonder, profoundly ignorant as he is of their origin and meaning.

Just so the legends which are the subjects of pictures, the profound myths which are represented in the antique marbles, amaze and revolt him; as indeed such things need to be judged of by another standard than that of the Connecticut Blue Laws. He criticizes severely pictures, feeling quite sure that his natural senses are better means of judgment than the rules of connoisseurs—not feeling that to see such objects mental vision as well as fleshly eyes are needed, and that something is aimed at in Art beyond the imitation of the commonest forms of Nature. This is Jonathan in the sprawling state, the booby truant, not yet aspiring enough to be a good school-boy. Yet in his folly there is meaning; add thought and culture to his independence and he will be a man of might: he is not a creature without hope, like the thick-skinned dandy of the class first specified.

The artists form a class by themselves. Yet among them, though seeking special aims by special means, may also be found the lineaments of these two classes, as well as of the third, of which I am now to speak.

This is that of the thinking American—a man who, recognizing the immense advantage of being born to a new world and on a virgin soil, yet does not wish one seed from the past to be lost. He is anxious to gather and carry back with him every plant that will bear a new climate and new culture. Some will dwindle; others will attain a bloom and stature unknown before. He wishes to gather them clean, free from noxious insects, and to give them a fair trial in his new world. And that he may know the conditions under which he may best place them in that new world, he does not neglect to study their history in this.

The history of our planet in some moments seems so painfully mean and little—such terrible bafflings and failures to compensate some brilliant successes—such a crushing of the mass of men beneath the feet of a few, and these too often the least worthy—such a small drop of honey to each cup of gall, and in many cases so mingled that it is never one moment in life purely tasted—above all so little achieved for humanity as a whole, such tides of war and pestilence intervening to blot out the traces of each triumph—that no wonder if the strongest soul sometimes pauses aghast; no wonder if the many indolently console themselves with gross joys and frivolous prizes. Yes, those men *are* worthy of admiration who can carry this cross faithfully through fifty years; it is a great while for all the agonies that beset a lover of good, a lover of men; it makes a soul worthy of a speedier ascent, a more productive ministry in the next sphere. Blessed are they who ever keep that portion of pure, generous love with which they began life! How blessed those who have deepened the fountains, and have enough to spare for the thirst of others! Some such there are; and feeling that with all the excuses for failure still only the sight of those who triumph gives a meaning to life or makes its pangs endurable, we must arise and follow.

Eighteen hundred years of this Christian culture in these European kingdoms, a great theme never lost sight of, a mighty idea, an adorable history to which the hearts of men invariably cling, yet are genuine results rare as grains of gold in the river's sandy bed! Where is the genuine democracy to which the rights of all men are holy? Where the childlike wisdom learning all through life more and more of the will of God? Where the aversion to falsehood in all its myriad disguises of cant, vanity, covetousness, so clear to be read in all the history of Jesus of Nazareth? Modern Europe is the sequel to that history, and see this hollow England with its monstrous wealth and cruel poverty, its conventional life, and low, practical aims! See this poor France, so full of talent, so adroit, yet so shallow and glossy still, which could not escape from a false position with all its baptism of blood! See that lost Poland, and this Italy bound down by treacherous hands in all the force of genius! See Russia with its brutal Czar and innumerable slaves! See Austria and its royalty that represents nothing, and its people who as people are and have nothing! If we consider the amount of truth that has really been spoken out in the world, and the love that has beat in private hearts—how genius has decked each springtime with such splendid flowers, conveying each one enough of instruction in its life of harmonious energy, and how continually, unquenchably the spark of faith has striven to burst into flame and light up the universe— the public failure seems amazing, seems monstrous.

Still Europe toils and struggles with her idea, and at this moment all things bode and declare a new outbreak of the fire to destroy old palaces of crime. May it fertilize also many vineyards! Here at this moment a successor of St. Peter, after the lapse of near two thousand years, is called "Utopian" by a part of this Europe, because he strives to get some food to the mouths of the *leaner* of his flock. A wonderful state of things, and which leaves as the best argument against despair that men do not, *cannot* despair amid such dark experiences. And thou, my country, wilt thou not be more true; does no greater success await thee? All things have so conspired to teach, to aid! A new world, a new chance, with oceans to wall in the new thought against interference from the old—treasures of all kinds, gold, silver, corn, marble, to provide for every physical need! A noble, constant, starlike soul, an Italian, led the way to thy shores, and in the first days the strong, the pure, those too brave, too sincere for the life of the old world, hastened to people them. A generous struggle then shook off what was foreign, and gave the nation a glorious start for a worthy goal. Men rocked the cradle of its hopes, great, firm, disinterested men who saw, who wrote as the basis of all that was to be done a statement of the rights, the *inborn* rights of men, which, if fully interpreted and acted upon, leaves nothing to be desired.

Yet, O Eagle, whose early flight showed this clear sight of the sun, how often dost thou near the ground, how show the vulture in these later days! Thou wert to be the advance-guard of humanity, the herald of all progress; how often hast thou betrayed this high commission! Fain would the tongue in clear, triumphant accents draw example from thy story, to encourage the hearts of those who almost faint and die beneath the old oppressions. But we must stammer and blush when we speak of many things. I take pride here that I can really say the liberty of the press works well, and that checks and balances are found naturally which suffice to its government. I can say that the minds of our people are alert, and that talent has a free chance to rise. This is much. But dare I further say that political ambition is not as darkly sullied as in other countries? Dare I say that men of most influence in political life are those who represent most virtue or even intellectual power? Is it easy to find names in that career of which I can speak with enthusiasm? Must I not confess to a boundless lust of gain in my country? Must I not concede the weakest vanity, which bristles and blusters at each foolish taunt of the foreign press, and admit that the men who make these undignified rejoinders seek and find popularity so? Can I help admitting that there is as yet no antidote cordially adopted which will defend even that great rich country against the evils that have grown out of the commercial system in the old world? Can I say our social laws are generally better, or show a nobler insight into the wants of man and woman? I do indeed say what I believe, that voluntary association for improvement in these particulars will be the grand means for my nation to grow, and give a nobler harmony to the coming age. But it is only of a small minority that I can say they as yet seriously take to heart these things; that they earnestly meditate on what is wanted for their country, for mankind—for our cause is indeed the cause of all mankind at present. Could we succeed, really succeed, combine a deep religious love with practical development, the achievements of genius with the happiness of the multitude, we might believe man had now reached a commanding point in his ascent, and would stumble and faint no more. Then there is this horrible cancer of slavery, and the wicked war that has grown out of it. How dare I speak of these things here? I listen to the same arguments against the emancipation of Italy that are used against the emancipation of our blacks; the same arguments in favor of the spoliation of Poland as for the conquest of Mexico. I find the cause of tyranny and wrong everywhere the same— and lo, my country the darkest offender because with the least excuse; forsworn to the high calling with which she was called; no champion of the rights of men, but a robber and a jailer; the scourge hid behind her banner; her eyes fixed not on the stars, but on the possessions of other men.

How it pleases me here to think of the Abolitionists! I could never endure to be with them at home, they were so tedious, often so narrow, always so rabid and exaggerated in their tone. But after all they had a high motive, something eternal in their desire and life; and if it was not the only thing worth thinking of, it was really something worth living and dying for to free a great nation from such a terrible blot, such a threatening plague. God strengthen them, and make them wise to achieve their purpose!

I please myself too with remembering some ardent souls among the American youth, who I trust will yet expand and help to give soul to the huge, overfed, too hastily grown-up body. May they be constant! "Were man but constant, he were perfect," it has been said; and it is true that he who could be constant to those moments in which he has been truly human, not brutal, not mechanical, is on the sure path to his perfection and to effectual service of the universe.

It is to the youth that hope addresses itself; to those who yet burn with aspiration, who are not hardened in their sins. But I dare not expect too much of them. I am not very old; yet of those who in life's morning I saw touched by the light of a high hope, many have seceded. Some have become voluptuaries; some, mere family men who think it quite life enough to win bread for half a dozen people and treat them decently; others are lost through indolence and vacillation. Yet some remain constant;

> I have witnessed many a shipwreck,
> Yet still beat noble hearts.

I have found many among the youth of England, of France, of Italy also full of high desire; but will they have courage and purity to fight the battle through in the sacred, the immortal band? Of some of them I believe it, and await the proof. If a few succeed amid the trial, we have not lived and loved in vain.

To these, the heart and hope of my country, a happy New Year! I do not know what I have written; I have merely yielded to my feelings in thinking of America; but something of true love must be in these lines. Receive them kindly, my friends; it is of itself some merit for printed words to be sincere.

LETTER XIX

Rome, December 17, 1847

This 17th day of December I rise to see the floods of sunlight blessing us, as they have almost every day since I returned to Rome—two months and more—with scarce three or four days of rainy weather. I still see the fresh roses and grapes each morning on my table, though both these I expect to give up at Christmas.

This autumn is "something like," as my countrymen say at home. Like *what,* they do not say; so I always supposed they meant like their ideal standard. Certainly this weather corresponds with mine; and I begin to believe the climate of Italy is really what it has been represented. Shivering here last spring in an air no better than the cruel east wind of Puritan Boston, I thought all the praises lavished on

Italia, O Italia!

would turn out to be figments of the brain; and that even Byron, usually accurate beyond the conception of plodding pedants, had deceived us when he says you have the happiness in Italy to

See the sun set, sure he'll rise tomorrow,

and not, according to a view which exercises a withering influence on the enthusiasm of youth in my native land, be forced to regard each pleasant day as a "weather-breeder."

How delightful too is the contrast between this time and the spring in another respect! Then I was here, like travelers in general, expecting to be driven away in a short time. Like others I went through the painful process of sight-seeing, so unnatural everywhere, so counter to the healthful methods and true life of the mind. You rise in the morning knowing there are a great number of objects worth knowing, which you may never have the chance to see again. You go every day in all moods, under all circumstances; feeling probably in seeing them the inadequacy of your preparation for understanding or duly receiving them. This consciousness would be most valuable if one had time to think and study, being the natural way in which the mind is lured to cure its defects; but you have no time; you are always wearied body and mind, confused, dissipated, sad. The objects are of commanding beauty or full of suggestion, but there is no quiet to let that beauty breathe its life into the soul; no time to follow up these suggestions, and plant for the proper harvest. Many persons run about Rome for nine days, and then go away; they might as well expect to appreciate the Venus by throwing a stone at it, as hope really to see Rome in this time. I stayed in Rome nine weeks, and came away unhappy as he who, having been taken in the visions of the night through some wondrous realm, wakes unable to recall anything but the hues and outlines of the pageant; the real knowledge, the recreative power induced by familiar love, the assimilation of its soul and substance—all the true value of such a revelation—is wanting; and he remains a poor Tantalus, hungrier than before he had tasted this spiritual food.

No, Rome is not a nine-days' wonder; and those who try to make it such lose the ideal Rome (if they ever had it) without gaining any notion of the real. To those who travel, as they do everything else, only because others do, I do not speak; they are nothing. Nobody counts in the estimate of the human race who has not a character.

For one, I now really live in Rome, and I begin to see and feel the real Rome. She reveals herself day by day; she tells me some of her life. Now I never go out to see a sight, but I walk every day; and here I cannot miss of some object of consummate interest to end a walk. In the evenings, which are long now, I am at leisure to follow up the inquiries suggested by the day.

As one becomes familiar, ancient and modern Rome, at first so painfully and discordantly jumbled together, are drawn apart to the mental vision. One sees where objects and limits anciently were; the superstructures vanish and you recognize the local habitation of so many thoughts. When this begins to happen, one feels first truly at ease in Rome. Then the old kings, the consuls and tribunes, the emperors drunk with blood and gold, the warriors of eagle sight and remorseless beak, return for us, and the togated procession finds room to sweep across the scene; the seven hills tower, the innumerable temples glitter, and the Via Sacra swarms with triumphal life once more.

Ah, how joyful to see once more *this* Rome, instead of the pitiful, peddling, Anglicized Rome first viewed in unutterable dismay from the *coupé* of the vettura—a Rome all full of taverns, lodging-houses, cheating chambermaids, vilest *valets de place*, and fleas! A Niobe of nations indeed! Ah, why, secretly the heart blasphemed, did the sun omit to kill her too, when all the glorious race which wore her crown fell beneath his ray? Thank Heaven it is possible to wash away all this dirt, and come at the marble yet.

Then the later papal Rome: it requires much acquaintance, much thought, much reference to books, for the child of Protestant republican America to see where belong the legends illustrated by rite and picture, the sense of all the rich tapestry, where it has a united and poetic meaning, where it is broken by some accident of history. For all these things—a senseless mass of juggleries to the uninformed eye—are really growths of the human spirit struggling to develop its life, and full of instruction for those who learn to understand them.

Then modern Rome—still ecclesiastical, still darkened and damp in the shadow of the Vatican, but where bright hopes gleam now amid the ashes! Never was a people who have had more to corrupt them—bloody tyranny and incubus of priestcraft; the invasions, first of Goths, then of trampling emperors and kings, then of sight-seeing foreigners—everything to turn them from a sincere, hopeful, fruitful life; and they are much corrupted, but still a fine race. I cannot look merely with a pictorial eye on the lounge of the Roman dandy, the bold Juno gait of the Roman *contadina*. I love them—dandies and all. I believe the natural expression of these fine forms will animate them yet. Certainly there never was a people that showed a better heart than they do in this day of love, of purely moral influence. It makes me very happy to be for once in a place ruled by a father's love, and where the pervasive glow of one good generous heart is felt in every pulse of every day.

I have seen the Pope several times since my return, and it is a real pleasure to see him in the thoroughfares, where his passage is always greeted as that of *the* living soul.

. . . .

Next day was the feast of the Milanese saint, whose life has been made known to some Americans by Manzoni, when speaking in his popular novel of the cousin of St. Carlo, Federigo Borromeo. The Pope came in state to the church of St. Carlo in the Corso. The show was magnificent; the church is not very large, and was almost filled with Papal court and guards in all their splendid harmonies of color. An Italian child was next me, a little girl of four or five years, whom her mother had brought to see the Pope. As in the intervals of gazing the child smiled and made signs to me, I nodded in return, and asked her name. "Virginia," said she, "and how is the Signora named?" "Margherita." "My name," she rejoined, "is Virginia Gentili." I laughed, but did not follow up the cunning, graceful lead—still I chatted and played with her now and then. At last she said to her mother, *"La Signora è molto cara"* ("The Signora is very dear," or to use the English equivalent, "a darling"); "show her my two sisters." So the mother, herself a fine-looking woman, introduced two handsome young ladies, and with the family I was in a moment pleasantly intimate for the hour.

Before me sat three young English ladies, the pretty daughters of a noble earl; their manners were a strange contrast to this Italian graciousness, best expressed by their constant use of the pronoun "that." "See that man!" (i.e., some high dignitary of the Church); "Look at that dress!" dropped constantly from their lips. Ah, without being a Catholic, one may well wish Rome was not dependent on English sight-seers who violate her ceremonies with acts that bespeak their thoughts full of wooden shoes and warming-pans. Can anything be more sadly expressive of times out of joint than the fact that Mrs. Trollope is a resident in Italy? Yes, she is fixed permanently in Florence, as I am told, pensioned at the rate of two thousand pounds a year to trail her slime over the fruit of Italy. She is here in Rome this winter and, after having violated the virgin beauty of America, will have for many a year her chance to sully the imperial matron of the civilized world. What must the English public be, if it wishes to pay two thousand pounds a year to get Italy Trollopified?

But to turn to a pleasanter subject. When the Pope entered, borne in his chair of state amid the pomp of his tiara and his white and gold robes, he looked to me thin, or as the Italians murmur anxiously at times, *consumato,* or wasted. But during the ceremony he seemed absorbed in his devotions, and at the end I think he had become exhilarated by thinking of St. Carlo, who was such another over the human race as himself, and his face wore a bright glow of faith. As he blessed the people, he raised his eyes to heaven, with a gesture quite natural: it was the spontaneous act of a soul which felt that moment more than usual its relation with things above it, and sure of support from a higher Power. I saw him to still greater advantage a little while after, when, riding on the Campagna with a young gentleman who had been ill, we met the Pope on foot taking exercise. He often quits his carriage at the gates and walks in this way. He walked rapidly, robed in a simple white drapery, two young priests in spotless purple on either side; they gave silver to the poor who knelt beside the way, while the beloved Father gave his benediction. My companion knelt; he is not a Catholic, but he felt that "this blessing would do him no harm." The Pope saw at once he was ill and gave him a mark of interest, with that expression of melting love, the true, the only charity, which assures all who look on him that, were his power equal to his will, no living thing would ever suffer more. This expression the artists try in vain to catch; all busts and engravings of him are caricatures; it is a magnetic sweetness, a lambent light that plays over his features, and of which only great genius or a soul tender as his own would form an adequate image.

The Italians have one term of praise peculiarly characteristic of their highly endowed nature. They say of such and such, *"Ha una fisionomia simpatica"*—"He has a sympathetic expression"—and this is praise enough. This may be pre-eminently said of that of Pius IX. *He* looks indeed as if nothing human could be foreign to him. Such alone are the genuine kings of men.

He has shown undoubted wisdom, clear-sightedness, bravery, and firmness; but it is, above all, his generous human heart that gives him his power over this people. His is a face to shame the selfish, redeem the skeptic, alarm the wicked, and cheer to new effort the weary and heavy-laden. What form the issues of his life may take is yet uncertain; in my belief they are such as he does not think of, but they cannot fail to be for good. For my part I shall always rejoice to have been here in his time. The working of his influence confirms my theories, and it is a positive treasure to me to have seen him. I have never been presented, not wishing to approach so real a presence in the path of mere etiquette; I am quite content to see him standing amid the crowd, while the band plays the music he has inspired:

Sons of Rome, awake!

Yes, awake, and let no police-officer put you again to sleep in prison, as has happened to those who were called by the *Marseillaise*.

Affairs look well. The King of Sardinia has at last, though with evident distrust and heartlessness, entered the upward path in a way that makes it difficult to return. The Duke of Modena, the most senseless of all these ancient gentlemen, after publishing a declaration which made him more ridiculous than would the bitterest pasquinade penned by another, that he would fight to the death against reform, finds himself obliged to lend an ear as to the league for the customs; and if he joins that, other measures follow of course. Austria trembles; and in fine cannot sustain the point of Ferrara. The King of Naples, after having shed much blood for which he has a terrible account to render (ah, how many sad fair romances are to tell already about the Calabrian difficulties!), still finds the spirit foment-ing in his people; he cannot put it down. The dragon's teeth are sown, and the Lazzaroni may be men yet! The Swiss affairs have taken the right direction, and good will ensue if other powers act with decent honesty and think of healing the wounds of Switzerland, rather than merely of tying her down so that she cannot annoy them.

Here in Rome the new Council is inaugurated, and elections have given tolerable satisfaction. Already struggles ended in other places begin to be renewed here, as to gaslights, introduction of machinery, &c. We shall see at the end of the winter how they have gone on. At any rate the wants of the people are in some measure represented; and already the conduct of those who have taken to themselves so large a portion of the loaves and fishes on the very platform supposed to be selected by Jesus for a general feeding of his sheep begins to be the subject of spoken as well as whispered animadversion. Torlonia is assailed in his bank, Campana amid his urns or his Monte di Pieti; but these assaults have yet to be verified.

On the day when the Council was to be inaugurated, great preparations were made by representatives of other parts of Italy and also of foreign nations friendly to the cause of progress. It was considered to represent the same fact as the feast of the 12th of September in Tuscany—the dawn of an epoch when the people shall find their wants and aspirations represented and guarded. The Americans showed a warm interest; the gentlemen subscribing to buy a flag, the United States having none before in Rome, and the ladies meeting to make it. The same distinguished individual indeed, who at Florence made a speech to prevent the "American eagle being taken out on so trifling an occasion," with similar perspicuity and superiority of view on the present occasion was anxious to prevent "rash demonstrations, which might embroil the United States with Austria"; but the rash youth here present rushed on, ignorant how to value his Nestorian prudence—fancying, hot-headed simpletons, that the cause of freedom was the cause of America, and her eagle at home wherever the sun shed a warmer ray and there was reason to hope a happier life for man. So they hurried to buy their silk, red, white, and blue, and inquired of recent arrivals how many states there are this winter in the Union, in order to making the proper number of stars. A magnificent spread-eagle was procured not without difficulty, as this, once the aerie of the king of birds, is now a rookery rather, full of black, ominous fowl, ready to eat the harvest sown by industrious hands. This eagle, having previously spread its wings over a piece of furniture where its back was sustained by the wall, was somewhat deficient in a part of its anatomy. But we flattered ourselves he should be held so high that no Roman eye, if disposed, could carp and criticize. When lo! just as the banner was ready to unfold its young glories in the home of Horace, Virgil, and Tacitus, an ordinance appeared prohibiting the display of any but the Roman ensign.

This ordinance was, it is said, caused by representations made to the Pope that the Oscurantists, ever on the watch to do mischief, meant to make this the occasion of disturbance—as it is their policy to seek to create irritation here; that the Neapolitan and Lombardo-Venetian flags would appear draped with black, and thus the signal be given for tumult. I cannot help thinking these fears were groundless; that the people, on their guard, would have indignantly crushed at once any of these malignant efforts. However that may be, no one can ever be really displeased with any measure of the Pope, knowing his excellent intentions. But the limitation of the festival deprived it of the noble character of the brotherhood of nations and an ideal aim, worn by that of Tuscany. The Romans, chilled and disappointed, greeted their Councilors with but little enthusiasm. The procession too was but a poor affair for Rome. Twenty-four carriages had been lent by the princes and nobles at the request of the city to convey the Councilors. I found something symbolical in this. Thus will they be obliged to furnish from their old grandeur the vehicles of the new ideas. Each deputy was followed by his target and banner. When the deputy for Ferrara passed, many garlands were thrown upon his carriage. There has been deep respect and sympathy felt for the citizens of Ferrara, they have conducted themselves so well under their late trying circumstances. They contained themselves, knowing that the least indiscretion would give a handle for aggression to the enemies of the good cause. But the daily occasions of irritation must have been innumerable, and they have shown much power of wise and dignified self-government.

After the procession passed, I attempted to go on foot from the Café Novo in the Corso to St. Peter's to see the decorations of the streets, but it was impossible. In that dense but most vivacious, various, and good-humored crowd, with all best will on their part to aid the foreigner, it was impossible to advance. So I saw only themselves; but that was a great pleasure. There is so much individuality of character here that it is a great entertainment to be in a crowd.

In the evening there was a ball given at the Argentina. Lord Minto was there; Prince Corsini, now Senator; the Torlonias in uniform of the Civic Guard—Princess Torlonia in a sash of their colors given her by the Civic Guard, which she waved often in answer to their greetings. But the beautiful show of the evening was the Trasteverini dancing the saltarello in their most brilliant costume. I saw them thus to much greater advantage than ever before. Several were nobly handsome and danced admirably; it was really like Pinelli.

The saltarello enchants me; in this is really the Italian wine, the Italian sun. The first time I saw it danced one night very unexpectedly near the Colosseum; it carried me quite beyond myself, so that I most unamiably insisted on staying while the friends in my company, not heated by enthusiasm like me, were shivering and perhaps catching cold from the damp night air. I fear they remember it against me; nevertheless I cherish the memory of the moments wickedly stolen at their expense, for it is only the first time seeing such a thing that you enjoy a peculiar delight. But since, I love to see and study it much.

The Pope in receiving the Councilors made a speech—such as the King of Prussia intrenched himself in on a similar occasion, only much better and shorter—implying that he meant only to improve, not to *reform,* and should keep things *in statu quo,* safe locked with the keys of St. Peter. This little speech was made no doubt more to reassure czars, emperors, and kings than from the promptings of the spirit. But the fact of its necessity, as well as the inferior freedom and spirit of the Roman journals to those of Tuscany, seems to say that the pontifical government, though from the accident of this one man's accession it has taken the initiative to better times, yet may not after a while from its very nature be able to keep in the vanguard.

A sad contrast to the feast of this day was presented by the same persons a fortnight after following the body of Silvani, one of the Councilors, who died suddenly. The Councilors, the different societies of Rome, a corps of *frati* bearing tapers, the Civic Guard with drums slowly beating, the same state carriages with their liveried attendants, all were slowly, sadly moving with torches and banners drooped along the Corso in the dark night. A single horseman with his long white plume and torch reversed governed the procession; it was the Prince Aldobrandini. The whole had that grand effect so easily given by this artist people, who seize instantly the natural poetry of an occasion and with unanimous tact hasten to represent it. More and much anon.

LETTER XXI

Rome, January 10, 1848

.   .   .   .

The influence of the Oscurantist foe has shown itself more and more plainly in Rome, during the last four or five weeks. A false miracle is devised: the Madonna del Popolo (who has her handsome house very near me) has cured a paralytic youth (who in fact was never diseased) and, appearing to him in a vision, takes occasion to criticize severely the measures of the Pope. Rumors of tumult in one quarter are circulated, to excite it in another. Inflammatory handbills are put up in the night. But the Romans thus far resist all intrigues of the foe to excite them to bad conduct.

On New Year's Day, however, success was near. The people as usual asked permission of the Governor to go to the Quirinal and receive the benediction of the Pope. This was denied, and not as it might truly have been because the Pope was unwell, but in the most ungracious, irritating manner possible by saying, "He is tired of these things: he is afraid of disturbance." Then the people being naturally excited and angry, the Governor sent word to the Pope that there was excitement, without letting him know why, and had the guards doubled on the posts. The most absurd rumors were circulated among the people that the cannon of St. Angelo were to be pointed on them, &c. But they, with that singular discretion which they show now, instead of rising as their enemies had hoped, went to ask counsel of their lately appointed Senator, Corsini. He went to the Pope, found him ill, entirely ignorant of what was going on, and much distressed when he heard it. He declared that the people should be satisfied, and since they had not been allowed to come to him, he would go to them. Accordingly the next day, though rainy and of a searching cold like that of a Scotch mist, we had all our windows thrown open and the red and yellow tapestries hung out. He passed through the principal parts of the city, the people throwing themselves on their knees and crying out, "O Holy Father, don't desert us; don't forget us; don't listen to our enemies!" The Pope wept often, and replied, "Fear nothing, my people, my heart is yours." At last, seeing how ill he was, they begged him to go in and he returned to the Quirinal; the present Tribune of the People as far as rule in the heart is concerned, Ciceronacchio, following his carriage. I shall give some account of this man in another letter.

For the moment the difficulties are healed, as they will be whenever the Pope directly shows himself to the people. Then his generous affectionate heart will always act, and act on them, dissipating the clouds which others have been toiling to darken.

In speaking of the intrigues of these emissaries of the power of darkness, I will mention that there is a report here that they are trying to get an Italian Consul for the United States, and one in the employment of the Jesuits. This rumor seems ridiculous; yet it is true that Dr. Beecher's panic about Catholic influence in the United States is not quite unfounded, and that there is considerable hope of establishing a new dominion there. I hope the United States will appoint no Italian, no Catholic to a consulship. The representative of the United States should be American; our national character and interests are peculiar and cannot be fitly represented by a foreigner, unless, like Mr. Ombrossi of Florence, he has passed part of his youth in the United States. It would indeed be well if our government paid attention to qualification for the office in the candidate, and not to pretensions founded on partisan service; appointing only men of probity who would not stain the national honor in the sight of Europe. It would be wise also not to select men entirely ignorant of foreign manners, customs, ways of thinking, or even of any language in which to communicate with foreign society, making the country ridiculous by all sorts of blunders; but 'twere pity if a sufficient number of Americans could not be found who are honest, have some knowledge of Europe and gentlemanly tact, and are able at least to speak French.

To return to the Pope, although the shadow that has fallen on his popularity is in a great measure the work of his enemies, yet there is real cause for it too. His conduct in deposing for a time one of the Censors, about the banners of the 15th of December, his speech to the Council the same day, his extreme displeasure at the sympathy of a few persons with the triumph of the Swiss Diet because it was a Protestant triumph, and above all his speech to the Consistory, so deplorably weak in thought and absolute in manner, show a man less strong against domestic than foreign foes, instigated by a generous humane heart to advance but fettered by the prejudices of education, and terribly afraid to be or seem to be less the Pope of Rome in becoming a reform prince, and father to the fatherless. I insert a passage of this speech, which seems to say that, whenever there shall be collision between the priest and the reformer, the priest shall triumph:

"Another subject there is which profoundly afflicts and harasses our mind. It is not certainly unknown to you, Venerable Brethren, that many enemies of Catholic truth have, in our times especially, directed their efforts by the desire to place certain monstrous offsprings of opinion on a par with the doctrine of Christ, or to blend them therewith, seeking to propagate more and more that impious system of *indifference* toward all religion whatever.

"And lately some have been found, dreadful to narrate, who have offered such an insult to our name and Apostolic dignity, as slanderously to represent us participators in their folly, and favorers of that most iniquitous system above named. These have been pleased to infer from the counsels (certainly not foreign to the sanctity of the Catholic religion) which, in certain affairs pertaining to the civil exercise of the Pontific sway, we had benignly embraced for the increase of public prosperity and good, and also from the pardon bestowed in clemency upon certain persons subject to that sway, in the very beginning of our Pontificate, that we had such benevolent sentiments toward every description of persons as to believe that not only the sons of the Church, but others also, remaining aliens from Catholic unity, are alike in the way of salvation, and may attain eternal life. Words are wanting to us, from horror, to repel this new and atrocious calumny against us. It is true that with intimate affection of heart we love all mankind, but not otherwise than in the charity of God and of our Lord Jesus Christ, who came to seek and to save that which had perished, who wisheth that all men should be saved and come to a knowledge of the truth, and who sent his disciples through the whole world to preach the Gospel to every creature, declaring that those who should believe and be baptized should be saved, but those who should not believe, should be condemned. Let those therefore who seek salvation come to the pillar and support of the Truth, which is the Church—let them come, that is, to the true Church of Christ, which possesses in its bishops and the supreme head of all, the Roman Pontiff, a never-interrupted succession of Apostolic authority, and which for nothing has ever been more zealous than to preach, and with all care preserve and defend, the doctrine announced as the mandate of Christ by his Apostles; which Church afterward increased, from the time of the Apostles, in the midst of every species of difficulties, and flourished throughout the whole world, radiant in the splendor of miracles, amplified by the blood of martyrs, ennobled by the virtues of confessors and virgins, corroborated by the testimony and most sapient writings of the fathers— as it still flourishes throughout all lands, refulgent in perfect unity of the sacraments, of faith, and of holy discipline. We who, though unworthy, preside in this supreme chair of the Apostle Peter, in which Christ our Lord placed the foundation of his Church, have at no time abstained from any cares or toils to bring, through the grace of Christ himself, those who are in ignorance and error to this sole way of truth and salvation. Let those, whoever they be, that are adverse, remember that heaven and earth shall pass away, but nothing can ever perish of the words of Christ, nor be changed in the doctrine which the Catholic Church received, to guard, defend, and publish, from him.

"Next to this we cannot but speak to you, Venerable Brethren, of the bitterness of sorrow by which we were affected, on seeing that a few days since, in this our fair city, the fortress and center of the Catholic religion, it proved possible to find some—very few indeed and well-nigh frantic men —who, laying aside the very sense of humanity, and to the extreme disgust and indignation of other citizens of this town, were not withheld by horror from triumphing openly and publicly over the most lamentable intestine war lately excited among the Helvetic people; which truly fatal war we sorrow over from the depths of our heart, as well considering the blood shed by that nation, the slaughter of brothers, the atrocious, daily recurring, and fatal discords, hatreds, and dissensions (which usually redound among nations in consequence especially of civil wars), as the detriment which we learn the Catholic religion has suffered, and fear it may yet suffer, in consequence of this, and, finally, the deplorable acts of sacrilege committed in the first conflict, which our soul shrinks from narrating."

It is probably on account of these fears of Pius IX lest he should be called a Protestant Pope that the Roman journals thus far, in translating the American address to the Pope, have not dared to add any comment.

But if the heart, the instincts, of this good man have been beyond his thinking powers, that only shows him the providential agent to work out aims beyond his ken. A wave has been set in motion, which cannot stop till it casts up its freight upon the shore, and if Pius IX does not suffer himself to be surrounded by dignitaries and see the signs of the times through the eyes of others—if he does not suffer the knowledge he had of general society as a simple prelate to become incrusted by the ignorance habitual to princes—he cannot fail long to be a most important agent in fashioning a new and better era for this beautiful injured land.

I will now give another document, which may be considered as representing the view of what is now passing taken by the democratic party called "Young Italy." Should it in any other way have reached the United States, yet it will not come amiss to have it translated for the *Tribune,* as many of your readers may not otherwise have a chance of seeing this noble document, one of the milestones in the march of thought. It is a letter to the Most High Pontiff, Pius IX, from Joseph Mazzini.

"London, 8th September 1847

"MOST HOLY FATHER—Permit an Italian who has studied your every step for some months back with much hopefulness to address to you, in the midst of the applauses often far too servile and unworthy of you, which resound near you, some free and profoundly sincere words. Take, to read them, some moments from your infinite cares. From a simple individual animated by holy intentions may come sometimes a great counsel; and I write to you with so much love, with so much emotion of my whole soul, with so much faith in the destiny of my country which may be revived by your means, that my thoughts ought to speak truth.

"And first it is needful, Most Holy Father, that I should say to you somewhat of myself. My name has probably reached your ears, but accompanied by all the calumnies, by all the errors, by all the foolish conjectures which the police by system and many men of my party through want of knowledge or poverty of intellect have heaped upon it. I am not a subverter, nor a communist, nor a man of blood, nor a hater, nor intolerant nor exclusive adorer of a system or of a form imagined by my mind. I adore God, and an idea which seems to me of God—Italy an angel of moral unity and of progressive civilization for the nations of Europe. Here and everywhere I have written the best I know how against the vices of materialism, of egotism, of reaction, and against the destructive tendencies which contaminate many of our party. If the people should rise in violent attack against the selfishness and bad government of their rulers, I, while rendering homage to the right of the people, shall be among the first to prevent the excesses and the vengeance which long slavery has prepared. I believe profoundly in a religious principle supreme above all social ordinances; in a divine order which we ought to seek to realize here on earth; in a law, in a providential design, which we all ought according to our powers to study and to promote. I believe in the inspiration of my immortal soul, in the teaching of humanity which shouts to me, through the deeds and words of all its saints, incessant progress for all through the work of all my brothers toward a common moral amelioration, toward the fulfillment of the Divine Law. And in the great history of humanity I have studied the history of Italy and have found there Rome twice directress of the world— first through the Emperors, later through the Popes. I have found there that every manifestation of Italian life has also been a manifestation of European life; and that always when Italy fell, the moral unity of Europe began to fall apart in analysis, in doubt, in anarchy. I believe in yet another manifestation of the Italian idea; and I believe that another European world ought to be revealed from the Eternal City that had the Capitol and has the Vatican. And this faith has not abandoned me ever through years, poverty, and griefs which God alone knows. In these few words lies all my being, all the secret of my life. I may err in the intellect, but the heart has always remained pure. I have never lied through fear or hope, and I speak to you as I should speak to God beyond the sepulcher.

"I believe you good. There is no man this day, I will not say in Italy but in all Europe, more powerful than you; you then have, Most Holy Father, vast duties. God measures these according to the means which he has granted to his creatures.

"Europe is in a tremendous crisis of doubts and desires. Through the work of time, accelerated by your predecessors of the hierarchy of the Church, faith is dead, Catholicism is lost in despotism; Protestantism is lost in anarchy. Look around you; you will find superstitious and hypocrites, but not believers. The intellect travels in a void. The bad adore calculation, physical good; the good pray and hope; nobody *believes*. Kings, governments, the ruling classes combat for a power usurped, illegitimate since it does not represent the worship of truth, nor disposition to sacrifice one's self for the good of all; the people combat because they suffer, because they would fain take their turn to enjoy; nobody fights for duty, nobody because the war against evil and falsehood is a holy war, the crusade of God. We have no more a heaven; hence we have no more a society.

"Do not deceive yourself, Most Holy Father; this is the present state of Europe.

"But humanity cannot exist without a heaven. The idea of society is only a consequence of the idea of religion. We shall have then, sooner or later, religion and heaven. We shall have these not in the kings and the privileged classes—their very condition excludes love, the soul of all religions—but in the people. The spirit from God descends on many gathered together in his name. The people have suffered for ages on the cross, and God will bless them with a faith.

"You can, Most Holy Father, hasten that moment. I will not tell you my individual opinions on the religious development which is to come; these are of little importance. But I will say to you that whatever be the destiny of the creeds now existing, you can put yourself at the head of this development. If God wills that such creeds should revive, you can make them revive; if God wills that they should be transformed, that, leaving the foot of the cross, dogma and worship should be purified by rising a step nearer God, the Father and Educator of the world, you can put yourself between the two epochs and guide the world to the conquest and the practice of religious truth, extirpating a hateful egotism, a barren negation.

"God preserve me from tempting you with ambition; that would be profanation. I call you, in the name of the power which God has granted you, and has not granted without a reason, to fulfill the good, the regenerating European work. I call you, after so many ages of doubt and corruption, to be apostle of Eternal Truth. I call you to make yourself the 'servant of all,' to sacrifice yourself if needful, so that 'the will of God may be done on the earth as it is in heaven'; to hold yourself ready to glorify God in victory, or to repeat with resignation, if you must fail, the words of Gregory VII: 'I die in exile, because I have loved justice and hated iniquity.'

"But for this, to fulfill the mission which God confides to you, two things are needful—to be a believer and to unify Italy. Without the first, you will fall in the middle of the way, abandoned by God and by men; without the second, you will not have the lever with which only you can effect great, holy, and durable things.

"Be a believer; abhor to be king, politician, statesman. Make no compromise with error; do not contaminate yourself with diplomacy, make no compact with fear, with expediency, with the false doctrines of a *legality* which is merely a falsehood invented when faith failed. Take no counsel except from God, from the inspirations of your own heart, and from the imperious necessity of rebuilding a temple to truth, to justice, to faith. Self-collected, in enthusiasm of love for humanity, and apart from every human regard, ask of God that he will teach you the way; then enter upon it with the faith of a conqueror on your brow, with the irrevocable decision of the martyr in your heart; look neither to the right hand nor the left, but straight before you, and up to heaven. Of every object that meets you on the way, ask of yourself: 'Is this just or unjust, true or false, law of man or law of God?' Proclaim aloud the result of your examination, and act accordingly. Do not say to yourself: 'If I speak and work in such a way, the princes of the earth will disagree; the ambassadors will present notes and protests!' What are the quarrels of selfishness in princes or their notes, before a syllable of the eternal Evangelists of God? They have had importance till now because, though phantoms, they had nothing to oppose them but phantoms; oppose to them the reality of a man who sees the Divine view, unknown to them, of human affairs, of an immortal soul conscious of a high mission, and these will vanish before you as vapors accumulated in darkness before the sun which rises in the east. Do not let yourself be affrighted by intrigues; the creature who fulfills a duty belongs not to men, but to God. God will protect you; God will spread around you such a halo of love that neither the perfidy of men irreparably lost, nor the suggestions of hell, can break through it. Give to the world a spectacle new, unique: you will have results new, not to be foreseen by human calculation. Announce an era; declare that humanity is sacred, and a daughter of God; that all who violate her rights to progress, to association, are on the way of error; that in God is the source of every government; that those who are best by intellect and heart, by genius and virtue, must be the guides of the people. Bless those who suffer and combat; blame, reprove those who cause suffering, without regard to the name they bear, the rank that invests them. The people will adore in you the best interpreter of the Divine design, and your conscience will give you rest, strength, and ineffable comfort.

"Unify Italy, your country. For this you have no need to work, but to bless Him who works through you and in your name. Gather round you those who best represent the national party. Do not beg alliances with princes. Continue to seek the alliance of our own people; say, 'The unity of Italy ought to be a fact of the nineteenth century,' and it will suffice; we shall work for you. Leave our pens free; leave free the circulation of ideas in what regards this point, vital for us, of the national unity. Treat the Austrian government, even when it no longer menaces your territory, with the reserve of one who knows that it governs by usurpation in Italy and elsewhere; combat it with words of a just man, wherever it contrives oppressions and violations of the rights of others out of Italy. Require, in the name of the God of Peace, the Jesuits allied with Austria in Switzerland to withdraw from that country, where their presence prepares an inevitable and speedy effusion of the blood of the citizens. Give a word of sympathy which shall become public to the first Pole of Galicia who comes into your presence. Show us in fine by some fact that you intend not only to improve the physical condition of your own few subjects, but that you embrace in your love the twenty-four millions of Italians, your brothers; that you believe them called by God to unite in family unity under one and the same compact; that you would bless the national banner wherever it should be raised by pure and uncontaminate hands; and leave the rest to us. We will cause to rise around you a nation over whose free and popular development you, living, shall preside. We will found a government unique in Europe, which shall destroy the absurd divorce between spiritual and temporal power, and in which you shall be chosen to represent the principle of which the men chosen by the nation will make the application. We shall know how to translate into a potent fact the instinct which palpitates through all Italy. We will excite for you active support among the nations of Europe; we will find you friends even in the ranks of Austria; we alone, because we alone have unity of design, believe in the truth of our principle, and have never betrayed it. Do not fear excesses from the people once entered upon this way; the people only commit excesses when left to their own impulses without any guide whom they respect. Do not pause before the idea of becoming a cause of war. War exists everywhere, open or latent, but near breaking out, inevitable; nor can human power prevent it. Nor do I, it must be said frankly, Most Holy Father, address to you these words because I doubt in the least of our destiny, or because I believe you the sole, the indispensable means of the enterprise. The unity of Italy is a work of God—a part of the design of Providence and of all, even of those who show themselves most satisfied with local improvements, and who, less sincere than I, wish to make them means of attaining their own aims. It will be fulfilled, with you or without you. But I address you because I believe you worthy to take the initiative in a work so vast; because your putting yourself at the head of it would much abridge the road and diminish the dangers, the injury, the blood; because with you the conflict would assume a religious aspect, and be freed from many dangers of reaction and civil errors; because there might be attained at once under your banner a political result and a vast moral result; because the revival of Italy under the aegis of a religious idea, of a standard not of rights but of duties, would leave behind all the revolutions of other countries, and place her immediately at the head of European progress; because it is in your power to cause that God and the people, terms too often fatally disjoined, should meet at once in beautiful and holy harmony to direct the fate of nations.

"If I could be near you, I would invoke from God power to convince you by gesture, by accent, by tears; now I can only confide to the paper the cold corpse, as it were, of my thought; nor can I ever have the certainty that you have read and meditated a moment what I write. But I feel an imperious necessity of fulfilling this duty toward Italy and you, and whatsoever you may think of it, I shall find myself more in peace with my conscience for having thus addressed you.

"Believe, Most Holy Father, in the feelings of veneration and of high hope which confesses for you your most devoted

"JOSEPH MAZZINI"

Whatever may be the impression of the reader as to the ideas and propositions contained in this document, I think he cannot fail to be struck with its simple nobleness, its fervent truth.

A thousand petty interruptions have prevented my completing this letter till, now the hour of closing the mail for the steamer is so near, I shall not have time to look over it, either to see what I have written or make slight corrections. However, I suppose it represents the feelings of the last few days, and shows that without having lost any of my confidence in the Italian movement, the office of the Pope in promoting it has shown narrower limits, and sooner than I had expected.

This does not at all weaken my personal feeling toward this excellent man, whose heart I have seen in his face and can never doubt. It was necessary to be a great thinker, a great genius to compete with the difficulties of his position. I never supposed he was that; I am only disappointed that his good heart has not carried him on a little farther. With regard to the reception of the American address, it is only the Roman press that is so timid; the private expressions of pleasure have been very warm; the Italians say, "The Americans are indeed our brothers." It remains to be seen when Pius IX receives it whether the man, the reforming prince, or the Pope is uppermost at that moment.

LETTER XXII

Rome, January 1848

.   .   .   .

The Pope is anxious to have at least well-intentioned men in places of power. Men of much ability, it would seem, are not to be had. His last prime minister was a man said to have energy, good dispositions, but no thinking power. The Cardinal Bofondi, whom he has taken now, is said to be a man of scarce any ability; there being few among the new Councilors the public can name as fitted for important trust. In consolation we must remember that the Chancellor Oxenstiern found nothing more worthy of remark to show his son than by how little wisdom the world could be governed. We must hope these men of straw will serve as thatch to keep out the rain, and not be exposed to the assaults of a devouring flame.

Yet that hour may not be distant. The disturbances of the 1st of January here were answered by similar excitements in Leghorn and Genoa, produced by the same hidden and malignant foe. At the same time the Austrian government in Milan organized an attempt to rouse the people to revolt, with a view to arrests, and other measures calculated to stifle the spirit of independence they know to be latent there. In this iniquitous attempt they murdered eight persons; yet the citizens, on their guard, refused them the desired means of ruin, and they were forced to retractions as impudently vile as their attempts had been. The Viceroy proclaimed that "he hoped the people would confide in him as he did in them"; and no doubt they will. At Leghorn and Genoa the wiles of the foe were baffled by the wisdom of the popular leaders, as I trust they always will be; but it is needful daily to expect these nets laid in the path of the unwary.

Sicily is in full insurrection; and it is reported Naples, but this is not sure.

There was a report day before yesterday that the poor stupid king was already here, and had taken cheap chambers at the Hotel d'Allemagne, as indeed it is said he has always a turn for economy, when he cannot live at the expense of his suffering people. Day before yesterday, every carriage that the people saw with a stupid-looking man in it they did not know, they looked to see if it was not the royal runaway. But it was their wish was father to that thought, and it has not as yet taken body as fact. In like manner they report this week the death of Prince Metternich; but I believe it is not sure he is dead yet, only dying. With him passes one great embodiment of ill to Europe. As for Louis Philippe, he seems reserved to give the world daily more signal proofs of his base apostasy to the cause that placed him on the throne, and that heartless selfishness of which his face alone bears witness to anyone that has a mind to read it. How the French nation could look upon that face, while yet flushed with the hopes of the Three Days, and put him on the throne as representative of those hopes, I cannot conceive. There is a story current in Italy, that he is really the child of a man first a barber, afterwards a police-officer, and was substituted at nurse for the true heir of Orleans; and the vulgarity of form in his body of limbs, power of endurance, greed of gain, and hard cunning intellect, so unlike all traits of the weak but more "genteel" Bourbon race, might well lend plausibility to such a fable.

. . . .

January 22, 2 o'clock, p.m.

. . . .

This morning came the details of infamous attempts by the Austrian police to exasperate the students of Pavia. The way is to send persons to smoke cigars in forbidden places, who insult those who are obliged to tell them to desist. These traps seem particularly shocking when laid for fiery and sensitive young men. They succeeded: the students were lured into combat, and a number left dead and wounded on both sides. The University is shut up; the inhabitants of Pavia and Milan have put on mourning; even at the theater they wear it. The Milanese will not walk in that quarter where the blood of their fellow-citizens has been so wantonly shed. They have demanded a legal investigation of the conduct of the officials.

At Piacenza similar attempts have been made to excite the Italians, by smoking in their faces, and crying, "Long live the Emperor!" It is a worthy homage to pay to the Austrian crown—this offering of cigars and blood.

O this offense is rank; it smells to Heaven.

This morning authentic news is received from Naples. The King, when assured by his own brother that Sicily was in a state of irresistible revolt and that even the women quelled the troops—showering on them stones, furniture, boiling oil, and such means of warfare as the household may easily furnish to a thoughtful matron—had first a stroke of apoplexy, from which the loss of a good deal of bad blood relieved him. His mind apparently having become clearer thereby, he has offered his subjects an amnesty and terms of reform, which it is hoped will arrive before his troops have begun to bombard the cities in obedience to earlier orders.

Comes also today the news that the French Chamber of Peers propose an Address to the King, echoing back all the falsehoods of his speech, including those upon reform and the enormous one that "the peace of Europe is now assured"; but that some members have worthily opposed this address and spoken truth in an honorable manner.

Also that the infamous sacrifice of the poor little queen of Spain puts on more tragic colors; that it is pretended she has epilepsy, and she is to be made to renounce the throne which indeed has been a terrific curse to her. And heaven and earth have looked calmly on, while the King of France has managed all this with the most unnatural of mothers.

January 27

This morning comes the plan of the Address of the Chamber of Deputies to the King: it contains some passages that are keenest satire upon him, as also some remarks which have been made, some words of truth spoken in the Chamber of Peers, that must have given him some twinges of nervous shame as he read. M. Guizot's speech on the affairs of Switzerland shows his usual shabbiness and falsehood. Surely never prime minister stood in so mean a position as he: one like Metternich seems noble and manly in comparison; for if there is a cruel, atheistical, treacherous policy, there needs not at least continual evasion to avoid declaring in words what is so glaringly manifest in fact.

There is news that the revolution has now broken out in Naples; that neither Sicilians nor Neapolitans will trust the king but demand his abdication; and that his bad demon, Coclo, has fled carrying two hundred thousand ducats of gold. But in particulars this news is not yet sure, though no doubt there is truth at the bottom.

Aggressions on the part of the Austrians continue in the north. The advocates Tommaso and Manin (a light thus reflected on the name of the last Doge), having dared to declare formally the necessity of reform, are thrown into prison. Every day the cloud swells, and the next fortnight is likely to bring important tidings.

LETTER XXIII

March 29, 1848

.   .   .   .

The Romans renounced the *Moccoletti* ostensibly as an expression of sympathy for the sufferings of the Milanese, but really because at that time there was great disturbance about the Jesuits, and the government feared that difficulties would arise in the excitement of the evening. But, since, we have had this entertainment in honor of the revolutions of France and Austria, and nothing could be more beautiful. The fun usually consists in all the people blowing one another's lights out. We had not this; all the little tapers were left to blaze, and the long Corso swarmed with tall fireflies. Lights crept out over the surface of all the houses, and such merry little twinkling lights, laughing and flickering with each slightest movement of those who held them! Up and down the Corso they twinkled, they swarmed, they streamed, while a surge of gay triumphant sound ebbed and flowed beneath that glittering surface. Here and there danced men carrying aloft *moccoli,* and clanking chains, emblem of the tyrannic power now vanquished by the people—the people, sweet and noble, who in the intoxication of their joy were guilty of no rude or unkindly word or act, and who, no signal being given as usual for the termination of their diversion, closed of their own accord and with one consent, singing the hymns for Pio, by nine o'clock, and retired peacefully to their homes to dream of hopes they yet scarce understand.

This happened last week. The news of the dethronement of Louis Philippe reached us just after the close of the Carnival. It was just a year from my leaving Paris. I did not think as I looked with such disgust on the empire of sham he had established in France, and saw the soul of the people imprisoned and held fast as in an iron vise, that it would burst its chains so soon. Whatever be the result, France has done gloriously; she has declared that she will not be satisfied with pretexts while there are facts in the world—that to stop her march is a vain attempt, though the onward path be dangerous and difficult. It is vain to cry, Peace! Peace! when there is no peace. The news from France in these days sounds ominous, though still vague. It would appear that the political is being merged in the social struggle: it is well. Whatever blood is to be shed, whatever altars cast down, those tremendous problems *must* be solved whatever be the cost! That cost cannot fail to break many a bank, many a heart in Europe, before the good can bud again out of a mighty corruption. To you, people of America, it may perhaps be given to look on and learn in time for a preventive wisdom. You may learn the real meaning of the words *"Fraternity, Equality"*: you may, despite the apes of the past who strive to tutor you, learn the needs of a true democracy. You may in time learn to reverence, learn to guard, the true aristocracy of a nation, the only real nobles—the LABORING CLASSES.

And Metternich too is crushed; the seed of the woman has had his foot on the serpent. I have seen the Austrian arms dragged through the streets of Rome and burned in the Piazza del Popolo. The Italians embraced one another, and cried, *Miracolo! Provvidenza!* The modern Tribune Cicero-nacchio fed the flame with fagots; Adam Mickiewicz, the great poet of Poland, long exiled from his country or the hopes of a country, looked on, while Polish women, exiled too, or who perhaps, like one nun who is here, had been daily scourged by the orders of a tyrant, brought little pieces that had been scattered in the street and threw them into the flames—an offering received by the Italians with loud plaudits. It was a transport of the people, who found no way to vent their joy, but the symbol, the poesy, natural to the Italian mind. The ever-too-wise "upper classes" regret it, and the Germans choose to resent it as an insult to Germany; but it was nothing of the kind; the insult was to the prisons of Spielberg, to those who commanded the massacres of Milan—a base tyranny little congenial to the native German heart, as the true Germans of Germany are at this moment showing by their resolves, by their struggles.

When the double-headed eagle was pulled down from above the lofty portal of the Palazzo di Venezia, the people placed there in its stead one of white and gold, inscribed with the name *Alta Italia,* and quick upon the emblem followed the news that Milan was fighting against her tyrants— that Venice had driven them out and freed from their prisons the courageous protestants in favor of truth, Tommaso and Manin—that Manin, descendant of the last Doge, had raised the republican banner on the Place St. Mark—and that Modena, that Parma, were driving out the unfeeling and imbecile creatures who had mocked Heaven and man by the pretense of government there.

With indescribable rapture these tidings were received in Rome. Men were seen dancing, women weeping with joy along the street. The youth rushed to enroll themselves in regiments to go to the frontier. In the Colosseum their names were received. Father Gavazzi, a truly patriotic monk, gave them the cross to carry on a new, a better because defensive crusade. Sterbini, long exiled, addressed them. He said: "Romans, do you wish to go; do you wish to go with all your hearts? If so, you *may,* and those who do not wish to go themselves may give money. To those who will go, the government gives bread and fifteen baiocchi a day." The people cried: "We wish to go, but we do not wish so much; the government is very poor; we can live on a paul a day." The princes answered by giving, one sixty thousand, others twenty, fifteen, ten thousand dollars. The people responded by giving at the benches which are opened in the piazzas literally everything; street-peddlers gave the gains of each day; women gave every ornament—from the splendid necklace and bracelet down to the poorest bit of coral; servant-girls gave five pauls, two pauls, even half a paul, if they had no more. A man all in rags gave two pauls. "It is," said he, "all I have." "Then," said Torlonia, "take from me this dollar." The man of rags thanked him warmly, and handed that also to the bench, which refused to receive it. "No, *that* must stay with you," shouted all present. These are the people whom the traveler accuses of being unable to rise above selfish considerations—a nation rich and glorious by nature, capable like all nations, all men, of being degraded by slavery, capable as are few nations, few men, of kindling into pure flame at the touch of a ray from the Sun of Truth, of Life.

The two or three days that followed, the troops were marching about by detachments, followed always by the people, to the Ponte Molle, often farther. The women wept; for the habits of the Romans are so domestic that it seemed a great thing to have their sons and lovers gone even for a few months. The English—or at least those of the illiberal, bristling nature too often met here, which casts out its porcupine quills against everything like enthusiasm (of the more generous Saxon blood I know some noble examples)—laughed at all this. They have said that this people would not fight; when the Sicilians, men and women, did so nobly, they said: "Oh, the Sicilians are quite unlike the Italians; you will see when the struggle comes on in Lombardy, they cannot resist the Austrian force a moment." I said: "That force is only physical; do not you think a sentiment can sustain them?" They replied: "All stuff and poetry; it will fade the moment their blood flows." When the news came that the Milanese, men and women, fight as the Sicilians did, they said: "Well, the Lombards are a better race, but these Romans are good for nothing. It is a farce for a Roman to try to walk, even; they never walk a mile; they will not be able to support the first day's march of thirty miles, and not have their usual *minestra* to eat either." Now the troops were not willing to wait for the government to make the necessary arrangements for their march, so at the first night's station—Monterosi—they did *not* find food or bedding; yet the second night, at Civita Castellana, they were so well alive as to remain dancing and vivaing Pio Nono in the piazza till after midnight. No, gentlemen, soul is not quite nothing, if matter be a cog upon its transports.

The Americans show a better, warmer feeling than they did; the meeting in New York was of use in instructing the Americans abroad! The dinner given here on Washington's Birthday was marked by fine expressions of sentiment, and a display of talent unusual on such occasions. There was a poem from Mr. Story of Boston, which gave great pleasure; a speech by Mr. Hillard, said to be very good; and one by the Rev. Mr. Hedge of

Bangor, exceedingly admired for the felicity of thought and image, and the finished beauty of style.

Next week we shall have more news, and I shall try to write and mention also some interesting things want of time obliges me to omit in this letter.

April 1

Yesterday I passed at Ostia and Castle Fusano. A million birds sang; the woods teemed with blossoms; the sod grew green hourly over the graves of the mighty past; the surf rushed in on a fair shore; the Tiber majestically retreated to carry inland her share from the treasures of the deep; the seabreezes burnt my face, but revived my heart. I felt the calm of thought, the sublime hopes of the future, nature, man—so great, though so little—so dear, though incomplete. Returning to Rome, I find the news pronounced official, that the viceroy Ranieri has capitulated at Verona; that Italy is free, independent, and one. I trust this will prove no April foolery, no premature news; it seems too good, too speedy a realization of hope, to have come on earth, and can only be answered in the words of the proclamation made yesterday by Pius IX:

"The events which these two months past have seen rush after one another in rapid succession are no human work. Woe to him who in this wind which shakes and tears up alike the lofty cedars and humble shrubs hears not the voice of God! Woe to human pride, if to the fault or merit of any man whatsoever it refer these wonderful changes, instead of adoring the mysterious designs of Providence."

LETTER XXIV

Rome, April 19, 1848

In closing my last, I hoped to have some decisive intelligence to impart by this time as to the fortunes of Italy. But though everything, so far, turns in her favor, there has been no decisive battle, no final stroke. It pleases me much, as the news comes from day to day, that I passed so leisurely last summer over that part of Lombardy now occupied by the opposing forces, that I have in my mind the faces both of the Lombard and Austrian leaders. A number of the present members of the Provisional Government of Milan I knew while there; they are men of twenty-eight and thirty, much more advanced in thought than the Moderates of Rome, Naples, Tuscany, who are too much fettered with a bygone state of things, and not on a par in thought, knowledge, preparation for the great future with the rest of the civilized world at this moment. The papers that emanate from the Milanese government are far superior in tone to any that have been uttered by the other states. Their protest in favor of their rights, their addresses to the Germans at large and the countries under the dominion of Austria, are full of nobleness and thoughts sufficiently great for the use of the coming age. These addresses I translate, thinking they may not in other form reach America:

"The Provisional Government of Milan to the German Nation

"We hail you as brothers, valiant, learned, generous Germans!

"This salutation from a people just risen after a terrible struggle to self-consciousness and to the exercise of its rights ought deeply to move your magnanimous hearts.

"We deem ourselves worthy to utter that great word Brotherhood, which effaces among nations the traditions of all ancient hate, and we proffer it over the new-made graves of our fellow-citizens, who have fought and died to give us the right to proffer it without fear or shame.

"We call brothers men of all nations who believe and hope in the improvement of the human family, and seek the occasion to further it; but you especially we call brothers, you Germans, with whom we have in common so many noble sympathies—the love of the arts and higher studies, the delight of noble contemplation—with whom also we have much correspondence in our civil destinies.

"With you are of first importance the interests of the great country, Germany—with us, those of the great country, Italy.

"We were induced to rise in arms against Austria (we mean, not the people, but the government of Austria) not only by the need of redeeming ourselves from the shame and grief of thirty-one years of the most abject despotism, but by a deliberate resolve to take our place upon the plane of nations, to unite with our brothers of the Peninsula, and take rank with them under the great banner raised by Pius IX on which is written, *The Independence of Italy.*

"Can you blame us, independent Germans? In blaming us you would sink beneath your history, beneath your most honored and recent declarations.

"We have chased the Austrian from our soil; we shall give ourselves no repose till we have chased him from all parts of Italy. To this enterprise we are all sworn; for this fights our army enrolled in every part of the Peninsula—an army of brothers led by the King of Sardinia, who prides himself on being the sword of Italy.

"And the Austrian is not more our enemy than yours.

"The Austrian—we speak still of the government, and not of the people —has already denied and contradicted the interests of the whole German nation, at the head of an assemblage of races differing in language, in customs, in institutions. When it was in his power to have corrected the errors of time and a dynastic policy, by assuming the high mission of uniting them by great moral interests, he preferred to arm one against the other and to corrupt them all.

"Fearing every noble instinct, hostile to every grand idea, devoted to the material interests of an oligarchy of princes spoiled by a senseless education, of ministers who had sold their consciences, of speculators who subjected and sacrificed everything to gold, the only aim of such a government was to sow division everywhere. What wonder if everywhere in Italy, as in Germany, it reaps harvests of hate and ignominy. Yes, of hate! To this the Austrian has condemned us, to know hate and its deep sorrows. But we are absolved in the sight of God, and by the insults which have been heaped upon us for so many years, the unwearied efforts to debase us, the destruction of our villages, the cold-blooded slaughter of our aged people, our priests, our women, our children. And you—you shall be the first to absolve us, you virtuous among the Germans, who certainly have shared our indignation when a venal and lying press accused us of being enemies to your great and generous nation, and we could not answer, and were constrained to devour in silence the shame of an accusation which wounded us to the heart.

"We honor you, Germans! We pant to give you glorious evidence of this. And, as a prelude to the friendly relations we hope to form with your governments, we seek to alleviate as much as possible the pains of captivity to some officers and soldiers belonging to various states of the Germanic Confederation, who fought in the Austrian army. These we wish to send back to you, and are occupied by seeking the means to effect this purpose. We honor you so much that we believe you capable of preferring to the bonds of race and language the sacred titles of misfortune and of right.

"Ah, answer to our appeal, valiant, wise, and generous Germans! Clasp the hand which we offer you with the heart of a brother and friend; hasten to disavow every appearance of complicity with a government which the massacres of Galicia and Lombardy have blotted from the list of civilized and Christian governments. It would be a beautiful thing for you to give this example, which will be new in history and worthy of these miraculous times—the example of a strong and generous people casting aside other sympathies, other interests, to answer the invitation of a re-generate people, to cheer it in its new career, obedient to the great principles of justice, of humanity, of civil and Christian brotherhood."

"The Provisional Government of Milan to the Nations
Subject to the Rule of the House of Austria

"From your lands have come three armies which have brought war into ours; your speech is spoken by those hostile bands who come to us with fire and sword; nevertheless we come to you as to brothers.

"The war which calls for our resistance is not your war; you are not our enemies: you are only instruments in the hand of our foe, and this foe, brothers, is common to us all.

"Before God, before men, solemnly we declare it—our only enemy is the government of Austria.

"And that government which for so many years has labored to cancel in the races it has subdued every vestige of nationality, which takes no heed of their wants or prayers, bent only on serving miserable interests and more miserable pride, fomenting always antipathies conformably with the ancient maxim of tyrants, *Divide and govern*—this government has con-stituted itself the adversary of every generous thought, the ally and patron of all ignoble causes, the government declared by the whole civilized world paymaster of the executioners of Galicia.

"This government, after having pertinaciously resisted the legal expression of moderate desires, after having defied with ludicrous hauteur the opinion of Europe, has found itself in its metropolis too weak to resist an insurrection of students and has yielded—has yielded, making an assignment on time and throwing to you, brothers, as an alms-gift to the importunate beggar, the promise of institutions which in these days are held essential conditions of life for a civilized nation.

"But you have not confided in this promise; for the youth of Vienna, which feels the inspiring breath of this miraculous time, is impelled on the path of progress; and therefore the Austrian government, uncertain of itself and of your dispositions, took its old part of standing still to wait for events, in the hope of turning them to its own profit.

"In the midst of this it received the news of our glorious revolution, and it thought to have found in this the best way to escape from its embarrassment. First it concealed that news; then made it known piecemeal and disfigured by hypocrisy and hatred. We were a handful of rebels thirsting for German blood. We make a war of stilettos; we wish the destruction of all Germany. But for us answers the admiration of all Italy, of all Europe, even the evidence of your own people whom we are constrained to hold prisoners or hostages, who will unanimously avow that we have shown heroic courage in the fight, heroic moderation in victory.

"Yes, we have risen as one man against the Austrian government to become again a nation, to make common cause with our Italian brothers, and the arms which we have assumed for so great an object we shall not lay down till we have attained it. Assailed by a brutal executor of brutal orders, we have combated in a just war; betrayed, a price set on our heads, wounded in the most vital parts, we have not transgressed the bounds of legitimate defense. The murders, the depredations of the hostile band irritated against us by most wicked arts, have excited our horror, but never a reprisal. The soldier, his arms once laid down, was for us only an unfortunate.

"But behold how the Austrian government provokes you against us, and bids you come against us as a crusade! A crusade! The parody would be ludicrous if it were not so cruel. A crusade against a people which in the name of Christ, under a banner blessed by the Vicar of Christ and revered by all the nations, fights to secure its indefeasible rights.

"Oh, if you form against us this crusade—we have already shown the world what a people can do to reconquer its liberty, its independence— we will show also what it can do to preserve them. If almost unarmed we have put to flight an army inured to war—surely, brothers, that army wanted faith in the cause for which it fought—can we fear that our courage will grow faint after our triumph, and when aided by all our brothers of Italy? Let the Austrian government send against us its threatened battalions, they will find in our breasts a barrier more insuperable than the Alps. Everything will be a weapon to us; from every villa, from every field, from every hedge, will issue defenders of the national cause; women and children will fight like men; men will centuple their strength, their courage; and we will all perish amid the ruins of our city, before receiving foreign rule into this land which at last we call ours.

"But this must not be. You, our brothers, must not permit it to be; your honor, your interests, do not permit it. Will you fight in a cause which you must feel to be absurd and wicked? You sink to the condition of hirelings, and do you not believe that the Austrian government, should it conquer us and Italy, would turn against you the arms you had furnished for the conquest? Do you not believe it would act as after the struggle with Napoleon? And are you not terrified by the idea of finding yourself in conflict with all civilized Europe, and constrained to receive, to feast as your ally, the Autocrat of Russia, that perpetual terror to the improvement and independence of Europe? It is not possible for the House of Lorraine to forget its traditions; it is not possible that it should resign itself to live tranquil in the atmosphere of liberty. You can only constrain it by sustaining yourself with the Germanic and Slavonian nationalities and with this Italy, which longs only to see the nations harmonize with that resolve which she has finally taken, that she may never more be torn in pieces.

"Think of us, brothers. This is for you and for us a question of life and of death; it is a question on which depends, perhaps, the peace of Europe.

"For ourselves, we have already weighed the chances of the struggle, and subordinated them all to this final resolution, that we will be free and independent, with our brothers of Italy.

"We hope that our words will induce you to calm counsels; if not, you will find us on the field of battle generous and loyal enemies, as now we profess ourselves your generous and loyal brothers.

"CASATI, *President*	BORROMEO
DURINI	P. LITTA
STRIGELLI	GIULINI
BERETTA	GUERRIERI
GRAPPI	PORRO
TURRONI	MORRONI
REZZONICO	AB. ANELLI
CARBONERA	CORRENTI, *Sec.-Gen.*"

These are the names of men whose hearts glow with that generous ardor, the noble product of difficult times. Into their hearts flows wisdom from on high—thoughts great, magnanimous, brotherly. They may not all remain true to this high vocation, but at any rate they will have lived a period of true life. I knew some of these men when in Lombardy; of old aristocratic families, with all the refinement of inheritance and education, they are thoroughly pervaded by principles of a genuine democracy of brotherhood and justice. In the flower of their age, they have before them a long career of the noblest usefulness, if this era follows up its present promise, and they are faithful to their present creed and ready to improve and extend it.

Every day produces these remarkable documents. So many years as we have been suffocated and poisoned by the atmosphere of falsehood in official papers, how refreshing is the tone of noble sentiment in Lamartine! What a real wisdom and pure dignity in the letter of Béranger! *He* was always absolutely true—an oasis in the pestilential desert of humbug; but the present time allowed him a fine occasion.

The Poles have also made noble manifestations. Their great poet, Adam Mickiewicz, has been here to enroll the Italian Poles, publish the declaration of faith in which they hope to re-enter and re-establish their country, and receive the Pope's benediction on their banner. In their declaration of faith are found these three articles:

"Every one of the nation a citizen—every citizen equal in rights and before authorities.

"To the Jew, our elder brother, respect, brotherhood, aid on the way to his eternal and terrestrial good, entire equality in political and civil rights.

"To the companion of life, woman, citizenship, entire equality of rights."

This last expression of just thought the Poles ought to initiate, for what other nation has had such truly heroic women? Women indeed—not children, servants, or playthings.

Mickiewicz, with the squadron that accompanied him from Rome, was received with the greatest enthusiasm at Florence. Deputations from the clubs and journals went to his hotel and escorted him to the Piazza del Gran Duca, where amid an immense concourse of people some good speeches were made. A Florentine, with a generous forgetfulness of national vanity, addressed him as the Dante of Poland who, more fortunate than the great bard and seer of Italy, was likely to return to his country to reap the harvest of the seed he had sown.

"O Dante of Poland, who like our Alighieri hast received from Heaven sovereign genius, divine song, but from earth sufferings and exile—more happy than our Alighieri, thou hast reacquired a country; already thou art meditating on the sacred harp the patriotic hymn of restoration and of victory. The pilgrims of Poland have become the warriors of their nation. Long live Poland, and the brotherhood of nations!"

When this address was finished, the great poet appeared on the balcony to answer. The people received him with a tumult of applause, followed by a profound silence as they anxiously awaited his voice. Those who are acquainted with the powerful eloquence, the magnetism of Mickiewicz as an orator, will not be surprised at the effect produced by this speech, though delivered in a foreign language. It is the force of truth, the great vitality of his presence, that loads his words with such electric power. He spoke as follows:

"People of Tuscany! Friends! Brothers! We receive your shouts of sympathy in the name of Poland; not for us, but for our country. Our country, though distant, claims from you this sympathy by its long martyrdom. The glory of Poland, its only glory truly Christian, is to have suffered more than all the nations. In other countries the goodness, the generosity of heart, of some sovereigns protected the people; as yours has enjoyed the dawn of the era now coming, under the protection of your excellent prince. [Viva Leopold II!] But conquered Poland, slave and victim of sovereigns who were her sworn enemies and executioners—Poland, abandoned by the governments and the nations, lay in agony on her solitary Golgotha. She was believed slain, dead, buried. 'We have slain her,' shouted the despots; 'she is dead!' [No, no! Long live Poland!] 'The dead cannot rise again,' replied the diplomatists; 'we may now be tranquil.' [A universal shudder of feeling in the crowd.] There came a moment in which the world doubted of the mercy and justice of the Omnipotent. There was a moment in which the nations thought that the earth might be forever abandoned by God, and condemned to the rule of the demon, its ancient lord. The nations forgot that Jesus Christ came down from heaven to give liberty and peace to the earth. The nations had forgotten all this. But God is just. The voice of Pius IX roused Italy. [Long live Pius IX!] The people of Paris have driven out the great traitor against the cause of the nations. [Bravo! Viva the people of Paris!] Very soon will be heard the voice of Poland. Poland will rise again! [Yes, yes! Poland will rise again!] Poland will call to life all the Slavonic races—the Croats, the Dalmatians, the Bohemians, the Moravians, the Illyrians. These will form the bulwark against the tyrant of the North. [Great applause.] They will close forever the way against the barbarians of the North—destroyers of liberty and of civilization. Poland is called to do more yet: Poland, as crucified nation, is risen again, and called to serve her sister nations. The will of God is that Christianity should become in Poland, and through Poland elsewhere, no more a dead letter of the law, but the living law of states and civil associations [Great applause]; that Christianity should be manifested by acts, the sacrifices of generosity and liberality. This Christianity is not new to you, Florentines; your ancient republic knew and has acted upon it: it is time that the same spirit should make to itself a larger sphere. The will of God is that the nations should act towards one another as neighbors, as brothers. [A tumult of applause.] And you, Tuscans, have today done an act of Christian brotherhood. Receiving thus foreign unknown pilgrims, who go to defy the greatest powers of the earth, you have in us saluted only what is in us of spiritual and immortal—our faith and our patriotism. [Applause.] We thank you; and we will now go into the church to thank God."

"All the people then followed the Poles to the church of Santa Croce, where was sung the *Benedictus Dominus,* and amid the memorials of the greatness of Italy collected in that temple was forged more strongly the chain of sympathy and of union between two nations, sisters in misfortune and in glory."

This speech and its reception, literally translated from the journal of the day, show how pleasant it is on great occasions to be brought in contact with this people so full of natural eloquence and of lively sensibility to what is great and beautiful.

It is a glorious time too for the exiles who return and reap even a momentary fruit of their long sorrows. Mazzini has been able to return from his seventeen years' exile, during which there was no hour night or day that the thought of Italy was banished from his heart—no possible effort that he did not make to achieve the emancipation of his people, and with it the progress of mankind. He returns like Wordsworth's great man, "to see what he foresaw." He will see his predictions accomplishing yet for a long time, for Mazzini has a mind far in advance of his times in general and his nation in particular—a mind that will be best revered and understood when the "illustrious Gioberti" shall be remembered as a pompous verbose charlatan, with just talent enough to catch the echo from the advancing wave of his day, but without any true sight of the wants of man at this epoch. And yet Mazzini sees not all: he aims at political emancipation; but he sees not, perhaps would deny, the bearing of some events which even now begin to work their way. Of this, more anon; but not today, nor in the small print of the *Tribune.* Suffice it to say, I allude to that of which the cry of Communism, the systems of Fourier, &c., are but forerunners. Mazzini sees much already—at Milan, where he is, he has probably this day received the intelligence of the accomplishment of his foresight, implied in his letter to the Pope, which angered Italy by what was thought its tone of irreverence and doubt, some six months since.

Today is the 7th of May, for I had thrown aside this letter, begun the 19th of April, from a sense that there was something coming that would supersede what was then to say. This something has happened in a form that will cause deep sadness to good hearts everywhere. Good and loving hearts that long for a human form which they can revere will be unprepared and for a time must suffer much from the final dereliction of Pius IX to the cause of freedom, progress, and of the war. He was a fair image, and men went nigh to idolize it; this they can do no more, though they may be able to find excuse for his feebleness, love his good heart no less than before, and draw instruction from the causes that have produced his failure, more valuable than his success would have been.

Pius IX, no one can doubt who has looked on him, has a good and pure heart; but it needed also not only a strong but a great mind,

> To *comprehend his trust,* and to the same
> Keep faithful, with a singleness of aim.

A highly esteemed friend in the United States wrote to express distaste to some observations in a letter of mine to the *Tribune* on first seeing the Pontiff a year ago, observing, "To say that he had not the expression of great intellect was *uncalled for.*" Alas, far from it; it was an observation that rose inevitably on knowing something of the task before Pius IX, and the hopes he had excited. The problem he had to solve was one of such difficulty that only one of those minds, the rare product of ages for the redemption of mankind, could be equal to its solution. The question that inevitably rose on seeing him was, "Is he such a one?" The answer was immediately negative. But at the same time he had such an aspect of true benevolence and piety that a hope arose that Heaven would act through him, and impel him to measures wise beyond his knowledge.

This hope was confirmed by the calmness he showed at the time of the conspiracy of July and the occupation of Ferrara by the Austrians. Tales were told of simple wisdom, of instinct which he obeyed in opposition to the counsels of all his Cardinals. Everything went on well for a time.

But tokens of indubitable weakness were shown by the Pope in early acts of the winter, in the removal of a censor at the suggestion of others, in his speech to the Consistory, in his answer to the first address of the

Council. In these he declared that when there was conflict between the priest and the man, he always meant to be the priest; and that he preferred the wisdom of the past to that of the future.

Still times went on bending his predeterminations to the call of the moment. He *acted* more wisely than he intended; as for instance three weeks after declaring he would not give a constitution to his people, he gave it —a sop to Cerberus indeed—a poor vamped-up thing that will by and by have to give place to something more legitimate, but which served its purpose at the time as declaration of rights for the people. When the news of the revolution of Vienna arrived, the Pope himself cried *Viva Pio Nono!* and this ebullition of truth in one so humble, though opposed to his formal declarations, was received by his people with that immediate assent which truth commands.

The revolution of Lombardy followed. The troops of the line were sent thither; the volunteers rushed to accompany them. In the streets of Rome was read the proclamation of Charles Albert, in which he styles himself the servant of Italy and of Pius IX. The priests preached the war, and justly, as a crusade; the Pope blessed their banners. Nobody dreamed, or had cause to dream, that these movements had not his full sympathy; and his name was in every form invoked as the chosen instrument of God to inspire Italy to throw off the oppressive yoke of the foreigner and recover her rights in the civilized world.

At the same time, however, the Pope was seen to act with great blindness in the affair of the Jesuits. The other states of Italy drove them out by main force, resolved not to have in the midst of the war a foe and spy in the camp. Rome wished to do the same, but the Pope rose in their defense. He talked as if they were assailed as a *religious* body, when he could not fail like everybody else to be aware that they were dreaded and hated solely as agents of despotism. He demanded that they should be assailed only by legal means, when none such were available. The end was in half-measures, always the worst possible. He would not entirely yield, and the people would not at all. The order was ostensibly dissolved; but great part of the Jesuits really remain here in disguise, a constant source of irritation and mischief, which if still greater difficulties had not arisen, would of itself have created enough. Meanwhile, in the earnestness of the clergy about the pretended loss of the head of St. Andrew in the ceremonies of Holy Week, which at this juncture excited no real interest, was much matter for thought to the calm observer as to the restlessness of the new wine, the old bottles being heard to crack on every side and hour by hour.

Thus affairs went on from day to day—the Pope kissing the foot of the brazen Jupiter and blessing palms of straw at St. Peter's; the *Circolo Romano* erecting itself into a kind of Jacobin Club, dictating programs for an Italian Diet-General and choosing committees to provide for the expenses of the war; the Civic Guard arresting people who tried to make mobs as if famishing, and being searched, were found well provided both with arms and money; the ministry at their wits' end, with their trunks packed up ready to be off at a moment's warning—when the report, it is not yet known whether true or false, that one of the Roman Civic Guard, a well-known artist engaged in the war of Lombardy, had been taken and hung by the Austrians as a brigand, roused the people to a sense of the position of their friends, and they went to the Pope to demand that he should take a decisive stand and declare war against the Austrians.

The Pope summoned a consistory; the people waited anxiously, for expressions of his were reported as if the troops ought not to have thought of leaving the frontier, while every man, woman, and child in Rome knew, and every letter and bulletin declared, that all their thought was to render active aid to the cause of Italian independence. This anxious doubt, however, had not prepared at all for the extent to which they were to be disappointed.

The speech of the Pope declared that he had never any thought of the great results which had followed his actions; that he had only intended local reforms, such as had previously been suggested by the potentates of Europe; that he regretted the *mis*use which had been made of his name; and wound up by lamenting over the war—dear to every Italian heart as the best and holiest cause in which for ages they had been called to embark their hopes—as if it was something offensive to the spirit of religion, and which he would fain see hushed up, and its motives smoothed out and ironed over.

A momentary stupefaction followed this astounding performance, succeeded by a passion of indignation, in which the words "traitor" and "imbecile" were associated with the name that had been so dear to his people. This again yielded to a settled grief: they felt that he was betrayed but no traitor; timid and weak, but still a sovereign whom they had adored and a man who had brought them much good, which could not be quite destroyed by his wishing to disown it. Even of this fact they had no time to stop and think; the necessity was too imminent of obviating the worst consequences of this ill; and the first thought was to prevent the news leaving Rome to dishearten the provinces and army, before they had tried to persuade the Pontiff to wiser resolves, or if this could not be, to supersede his power.

I cannot repress my admiration at the gentleness, clearness, and good sense with which the Roman people acted under these most difficult circumstances. It was astonishing to see the clear understanding which animated the crowd as one man, and the decision with which they acted to effect their purpose. Wonderfully has this people been developed within a year!

The Pope, besieged by deputations who mildly but firmly showed him that, if he persisted, the temporal power must be placed in other hands, his ears filled with reports of Cardinals, "such venerable persons" as he pathetically styles them, would not yield in spirit though compelled to in act. After two days' struggle he was obliged to place the power in the hands of the persons most opposed to him, and nominally acquiesce in their proceedings, while in his second proclamation, very touching from the sweetness of its tone, he shows a fixed misunderstanding of the cause at issue which leaves no hope of his ever again being more than a name or an effigy in their affairs.

His people were much affected and entirely laid aside their anger, but they would not be blinded as to the truth. While gladly returning to their accustomed habits of affectionate homage toward the Pontiff, their unanimous sense and resolve is thus expressed in an able pamphlet of the day, such as in every respect would have been deemed impossible to the Rome of 1847:

"From the last allocution of Pius result two facts of extreme gravity— the entire separation between the spiritual and temporal power, and the express refusal of the Pontiff to be chief of an Italian Republic. But far from drawing hence reason for discouragement and grief, he who looks well at the destiny of Italy may bless Providence, which breaks or changes the instrument when the work is completed, and by secret and inscrutable ways conducts us to the fulfillment of our desires and of our hopes.

"If Pius IX refuses, the Italian people does not therefore draw back. Nothing remains to the free people of Italy, except to unite in one constitutional kingdom, founded on the largest basis; and if the chief who by our assemblies shall be called to the highest honor either declines or does not answer worthily, the people will take care of itself.

"Italians, down with all emblems of private and partial interests! Let us unite under one single banner, the tricolor, and if he who has carried it bravely thus far lets it fall from his hand, we will take it one from the other, twenty-four millions of us, and till the last of us shall have perished under the banner of our redemption, the stranger shall not return into Italy.

"Viva Italy! Viva the Italian people!"

These events make indeed a crisis. The work begun by Napoleon is finished. There will never more be really a Pope, but only the effigy or simulacrum of one.

The loss of Pius IX is for the moment a great one. His name had real moral weight—was a trumpet appeal to sentiment. It is not the same with any man that is left. There is not one that can be truly a leader in the Roman dominion, not one who has even great intellectual weight.

The responsibility of events now lies wholly with the people, and that wave of thought which has begun to pervade them. Sovereigns and statesmen will go where they are carried; it is probable power will be changed continually from hand to hand, and government become to all intents and purposes representative. Italy needs now quite to throw aside her stupid King of Naples, who hangs like a dead weight on her movements. The King of Sardinia and the Grand Duke of Tuscany will be trusted while they keep their present course; but who can feel sure of any sovereign, now that Louis Philippe has shown himself so mad and Pius IX so blind? It seems as if fate was at work to bewilder and cast down the dignities of the world and democratize society at a blow.

In Rome there is now no anchor except the good sense of the people. It seems impossible that collision should not arise between him who retains the name but not the place of sovereign and the provisional government which calls itself a ministry. The Count Mamiani, its new head, is a man of reputation as a writer, but untried as yet as a leader or a statesman. Should agitations arise, the Pope can no longer calm them by one of his fatherly looks.

All lies in the future; and our best hope must be that the Power which has begun so great a work will find due means to end it, and make the year 1850 a year of true jubilee to Italy; a year not merely of pomps and tributes, but of recognized rights and intelligent joys; a year of real peace —peace founded not on compromise and the lying etiquettes of diplomacy, but on truth and justice.

Then this sad disappointment in Pius IX may be forgotten, or while all that was lovely and generous in his life is prized and reverenced, deep instruction may be drawn from his errors as to the inevitable dangers of a priestly or a princely environment, and a higher knowledge may elevate a nobler commonwealth than the world has yet known.

Hoping this era, I remain at present here. Should my hopes be dashed to the ground, it will not change my faith, but the struggle for its manifestation is to me of vital interest. My friends write to urge my return; they talk of our country as the land of the future. It is so, but that spirit which made it all it is of value in my eyes, which gave all of hope with which I can sympathize for that future, is more alive here at present than in America. My country is at present spoiled by prosperity, stupid with the lust of gain, soiled by crime in its willing perpetuation of slavery, shamed by an unjust war, noble sentiment much forgotten even by individuals, the aims of politicians selfish or petty, the literature frivolous and venal. In Europe amid the teachings of adversity a nobler spirit is struggling—a spirit which cheers and animates mine. I hear earnest words of pure faith and love. I see deeds of brotherhood. This is what makes *my* America. I do not deeply distrust my country. She is not dead but in my time she sleepeth, and the spirit of our fathers flames no more, but lies hid beneath the ashes. It will not be so long; bodies cannot live when the soul gets too overgrown with gluttony and falsehood. But it is not the making a President out of the Mexican war that would make me wish to come back. Here things are before my eyes worth recording, and if I cannot help this work, I would gladly be its historian.

May 13

Returning from a little tour in the Alban Mount, where everything looks so glorious this glorious spring, I find a temporary quiet. The Pope's brothers have come to sympathize with him; the crowd sighs over what he has done, presents him with great bouquets of flowers, and reads anxiously the news from the north and the proclamations of the new ministry. Meanwhile the nightingales sing; every tree and plant is in flower, and the sun and moon shine as if paradise were already re-established on earth. I go to one of the villas to dream it is so beneath the pale light of the stars.

LETTER XXV

Rome, December 2, 1848

I have not written for six months, and within that time what changes have taken place on this side the "great water"—changes of how great dramatic interest historically—of bearing infinitely important ideally! Easy is the descent in ill.

I wrote last when Pius IX had taken the first stride on the downward road. He had proclaimed himself the foe of further reform measures when he implied that Italian independence was not important in his eyes, when he abandoned the crowd of heroic youth who had gone to the field with his benediction, to some of whom his own hand had given crosses. All the Popes, his predecessors, had meddled with, most frequently instigated war; now came one who must carry out literally the doctrines of the Prince of Peace, when the war was not for wrong or the aggrandizement of individuals, but to redeem national, to redeem human rights from the grasp of foreign oppression.

I said some cried "traitor," some "imbecile," some wept, but in the minds of all, I believe, at that time grief was predominant. They could no longer depend on him they had thought their best friend. They had lost their father.

Meanwhile his people would not submit to the inaction he urged. They saw it was not only ruinous to themselves, but base and treacherous to the rest of Italy. They said to the Pope, "This cannot be; you must follow up the pledges you have given, or if you will not act to redeem them, you must have a ministry that will." The Pope, after he had once declared to the contrary, ought to have persisted. He should have said, "I cannot thus belie myself, I cannot put my name to acts I have just declared to be against my conscience."

The ministers of the people ought to have seen that the position they assumed was utterly untenable; that they could not advance with an enemy in the background cutting off all supplies. But some patriotism and some vanity exhilarated them, and the Pope having weakly yielded, they unwisely began their impossible task. Mamiani, their chief, I esteem a man under all circumstances unequal to such a position—a man of rhetoric merely. But no man could have acted unless the Pope had resigned his temporal power, the Cardinals been put under sufficient check, and the Jesuits and emissaries of Austria driven from their lurking-places.

A sad scene began. The Pope—shut up more and more in his palace, the crowd of selfish and insidious advisers darkening round, enslaved by a confessor—he who might have been the liberator of suffering Europe permitted the most infamous treacheries to be practiced in his name. Private letters were written to the foreign powers, denying the acts he outwardly sanctioned; the hopes of the people were evaded or dallied with; the Chamber of Deputies permitted to talk and pass measures which they never could get funds to put into execution; legions to form and maneuver, but never to have the arms and clothing they needed. Again and again the people went to the Pope for satisfaction. They got only benediction.

Thus plotted and thus worked the scarlet men of sin, playing the hopes of Italy off and on, while *their* hope was of the miserable defeat consummated by a still worse traitor at Milan on the 6th of August. But indeed what could be expected from the "Sword of Pius IX," when Pius IX himself had thus failed in his high vocation? The King of Naples bombarded his city and set on the Lazzaroni to rob and murder the subjects he had deluded by his pretended gift of the Constitution. Pius proclaimed that he longed to embrace *all* the princes of Italy. He talked of peace when all knew for a great part of the Italians there was no longer hope of peace, except in the sepulcher or freedom.

The taunting manifestoes of Welden are a sufficient comment on the conduct of the Pope. "As the government of His Holiness is too weak to control his subjects"—"As, singularly enough, a great number of Romans are found fighting against us, contrary to the *expressed* will of their prince" —such were the excuses for invasions of the Pontifical dominions, and the robbery and insult by which they were accompanied. Such invasions, it was said, made His Holiness very indignant; he remonstrated against these; but we find no word of remonstrance against the tyranny of the King of Naples—no word of sympathy for the victims of Lombardy, the sufferings of Verona, Vicenza, Padua, Mantua, Venice.

In the affairs of Europe there are continued signs of the plan of the retrograde party to effect similar demonstrations in different places at the same hour. The 15th of May was one of these marked days. On that day the King of Naples made use of the insurrection he had contrived to excite, to massacre his people, and find an excuse for recalling his troops from Lombardy. The same day a similar crisis was hoped in Rome from the declarations of the Pope, but that did not work at the moment exactly as the foes of enfranchisement hoped.

However, the wounds were cruel enough. The Roman volunteers received the astounding news that they were not to expect protection or countenance from their prince; all the army stood aghast that they were no longer to fight in the name of Pio. It had been so dear, so sweet, to love and really reverence the head of their Church, so inspiring to find their religion for once in accordance with the aspirations of the soul! They were to be deprived too of the aid of the disciplined Neapolitan troops and their artillery, on which they had counted. How cunningly all this was contrived to cause dissension and dismay may easily be seen.

The Neapolitan General Pepe nobly refused to obey, and called on the troops to remain with him. They wavered; but they are a pampered army, personally much attached to the King, who pays them well and indulges them at the expense of his people, that they may be his support against that people when in a throe of nature it rises and strives for its rights. For the same reason the sentiment of patriotism was little diffused among them in comparison with the other troops. And the alternative presented was one in which it required a very clear sense of higher duty to act against habit. Generally after wavering awhile, they obeyed and returned. The Roman States, which had received them with so many testimonials of affection and honor, on their retreat were not slack to show a correspondent aversion and contempt. The towns would not suffer their passage; the hamlets were unwilling to serve them even with fire and water. They were filled at once with shame and rage; one officer killed himself, unable to bear it; in the unreflecting minds of the soldiers hate sprang up for the rest of Italy and especially Rome, which will make them admirable tools of tyranny in case of civil war.

This was the first great calamity of the war. But apart from the treachery of the King of Naples and the dereliction of the Pope, it was impossible it should end thoroughly well. The people were in earnest and have shown themselves so; brave and able to bear privation. No one should dare, after the proofs of the summer, to reiterate the taunt, so unfriendly frequent on foreign lips at the beginning of the contest, that the Italian can boast, shout, and fling garlands, but not *act*. The Italian always showed himself noble and brave, even in foreign service, and is doubly so in the cause of his country. But efficient heads were wanting. The princes were not in earnest; they were looking at expediency. The Grand Duke, timid and prudent, wanted to do what was safest for Tuscany; his ministry, "Moderate" and prudent, would have liked to win a great prize at small risk. They went no farther than the people pulled them. The King of Sardinia had taken the first bold step, and the idea that treachery on his part was premeditated cannot be sustained; it arises from the extraordinary aspect of his measures, and the knowledge that he is not incapable of treachery, as he proved in early youth. But now it was only his selfishness that worked to the same results. He fought and planned not for Italy but the House of Savoy, which his Balbis and Giobertis had so long been prophesying was to reign supreme in the new great era of Italy. These prophecies he more than half believed because they chimed with his ambitious wishes; but he had not soul enough to realize them; he trusted only in his disciplined troops; he had not nobleness enough to believe he might rely at all on the sentiment of the people. For his troops he dared not have good generals;

conscious of meanness and timidity, he shrank from the approach of able and earnest men; he was inwardly afraid they would in helping Italy take her and themselves out of his guardianship. Antonini was insulted, Garibaldi rejected; other experienced leaders who had rushed to Italy at the first trumpet-sound could never get employment from him. As to his generalship, it was entirely inadequate even if he had made use of the first favorable moments. But his first thought was not to strike a blow at the Austrians before they recovered from the discomfiture of Milan, but to use the panic and need of his assistance to induce Lombardy and Venice to annex themselves to his kingdom. He did not even wish seriously to get the better till this was done, and when this was done, it was too late. The Austrian army was recruited; the generals had recovered their spirits and were burning to retrieve and avenge their past defeat. The conduct of Charles Albert had been shamefully evasive in the first months. The account given by Franzini when challenged in the Chamber of Deputies at Turin might be summed up thus: "Why, gentlemen, what would you have? Everyone knows that the army is in excellent condition and eager for action. They are often reviewed, hear speeches, and sometimes get medals. We take places always, if it is not difficult. I myself was present once when the troops advanced; our men behaved gallantly, and had the advantage in the first skirmish; but afterward the enemy pointed on us artillery from the heights, and naturally we retired. But as to supposing that His Majesty Charles Albert is indifferent to the success of Italy in the war, that is absurd. He is the 'Sword of Italy'; he is the most magnanimous of princes; he is seriously occupied about the war; many a day I have been called into his tent to talk it over, before he was up in the morning!"

Sad was it that the heroic Milan, the heroic Venice, the heroic Sicily should lean on such a reed as this, and by hurried acts, equally unworthy as unwise, sully the glory of their shields. Some names indeed stand out quite free from this blame. Mazzini, who kept up a combat against folly and cowardice day by day and hour by hour with almost supernatural strength, warned the people constantly of the evils which their advisers were drawing upon them. He was heard then only by a few, but in this "Italia del Popolo" may be found many prophecies exactly fulfilled, as those of the "golden-haired love of Phoebus" during the struggles of Ilium. He himself in the last sad days of Milan compared his lot to that of Cassandra. At all events his hands are pure from that ill. What could be done to arouse Lombardy he did, but the "Moderate" party being unable to wean themselves from old habits, the pupils of the wordy Gioberti thought there could be no safety unless under the mantle of a prince. They did not foresee that he would run away and throw that mantle on the ground.

Tommaso and Manin also were clear in their aversion to these measures; and with them as with all who were resolute in principle at that time, a great influence has followed.

It is said Charles Albert feels bitterly the imputations on his courage and says they are most ungrateful, since he has exposed the lives of himself and his sons in the combat. Indeed there ought to be made a distinction between personal and mental courage. The former Charles Albert may possess, may have too much of what this still aristocratic world calls the "feelings of a gentleman" to shun exposing himself to a chance shot now and then. An entire want of mental courage he has shown. The battle, decisive against him, was made so by his giving up the moment fortune turned against him. It is shameful to hear so many say this result was inevitable, just because the material advantages were in favor of the Austrians. Pray, was never a battle won against material odds? It is precisely such that a good leader, a noble man, may expect to win. Were the Austrians driven out of Milan because the Milanese had that advantage? The Austrians would again have suffered repulse from them, but for the baseness of this man on whom they had been cajoled into relying—a baseness that deserves the pillory; and on a pillory will the "Magnanimous," as he was meanly called in face of the crimes of his youth and the timid selfishness of his middle age, stand in the sight of posterity. He made use of his power only to betray Milan; he took from the citizens all means of defense, and then gave them up to the spoiler; he promised to defend them "to the last drop of his blood," and sold them the next minute; even the paltry terms he made, he has not seen maintained. Had the people slain him in their rage, he well deserved it at their hands; and all his conduct since shows how righteous would have been that sudden verdict of passion.

Of all this great drama I have much to write, but elsewhere, in a more full form, and where I can duly sketch the portraits of actors little known in America. The materials are over-rich. I have bought my right in them by much sympathetic suffering; yet amid the blood and tears of Italy, 'tis joy to see some glorious new births. The Italians are getting cured of mean adulation and hasty boasts; they are learning to prize and seek realities; the effigies of straw are getting knocked down, and living, growing men take their places. Italy is being educated for the future, her leaders are learning that the time is past for trust in princes and precedents—that there is no hope except in truth and God; her lower people are learning to shout less and think more.

Though my thoughts have been much with the public in this struggle for life, I have been away from it during the summer months in the quiet valleys, on the lonely mountains. There, personally undisturbed, I have seen the glorious Italian summer wax and wane—the summer of Southern Italy, which I did not see last year. On the mountains it was not too hot for me, and I enjoyed the great luxuriance of vegetation. I had the advantage of having visited the scene of the war minutely last summer, so that in mind I could follow every step of the campaign, while around me were the glorious relics of old times—the crumbling theater or temple of the Roman day, the bird's-nest village of the Middle Ages, on whose purple height shone the sun and moon of Italy in changeless luster. It was great pleasure to me to watch the gradual growth and change of the seasons, so different from ours. Last year I had not leisure for this quiet acquaintance. Now I saw the fields first dressed in their carpets of green, enameled richly with the red poppy and blue cornflower—in that sunshine how resplendent! Then swelled the fig, the grape, the olive, the almond; and my food was of these products of this rich clime. For near three months I had grapes every day; the last four weeks enough daily for two persons for a cent! Exquisite salad for two persons' dinner and supper cost but a cent, and all other products of the region were in the same proportion. One who keeps still in Italy and lives as the people do may really have much simple luxury for very little money; though both travel and, to the inexperienced foreigner, life in the cities are expensive.

Rome, December 2, 1848

Not till I saw the snow on the mountains grow rosy in the autumn sunset did I turn my steps again toward Rome. I was very ready to return. After three or four years of constant excitement, this six months of seclusion had been welcome; but now I felt the need of meeting other eyes besides those so bright and so shallow of the Italian peasant. Indeed I left what was most precious, but which I could not take with me; * still it was a compensation that I was again to see Rome—Rome, that almost killed me with her cold breath of last winter, yet still with that cold breath whispered a tale of import so divine. Rome so beautiful, so great, her presence stupefies, and one has to withdraw to prize the treasures she has given. City of the soul! Yes, it is *that;* the very dust magnetizes you, and a thousand spells have been chaining you in every careless, every murmuring moment. Yes, Rome, however seen, thou must be still adored; and every hour of absence or presence must deepen love with one who has known what it is to repose in thy arms.

Repose, for whatever be the revolutions, tumults, panics, hopes of the present day, still the temper of life here is repose. The great past enfolds us, and the emotions of the moment cannot here greatly disturb that impression. From the wild shout and throng of the streets the setting sun recalls us as it rests on a hundred domes and temples—rests on the Campagna whose grass is rooted in departed human greatness. Burial-place so full of spirit that death itself seems no longer cold, O let me rest here, too! Rest here seems possible; meseems myriad lives still linger here awaiting some one great summons.

The rivers had burst their bounds, and beneath the moon the fields round Rome lay one sheet of silver. Entering the gate while the baggage was under examination, I walked to the entrance of a villa. Far stretched its overarching shrubberies, its deep green bowers; two statues with foot ad-

* Her child, who was born in Rieti, September 5, 1848, and was necessarily left in that town during the difficulties and siege of Rome.—A. B. F.

vanced and uplifted finger seemed to greet me; it was near the scene of great revels, great splendors in the old time; there lay the gardens of Sallust where were combined palace, theater, library, bath, and villa. Strange things have happened since, the most attractive part of which—the secret heart—lies buried or has fled to animate other forms; for of that part historians have rarely given a hint more than they do now of the truest life of our day, which refuses to be embodied by the pen, craving forms more mutable, more eloquent than the pen can give.

I found Rome empty of foreigners. Most of the English have fled in affright—the Germans and French are wanted at home—the Czar has recalled many of his younger subjects; he does not like the schooling they get here. That large part of the population which lives by the visits of foreigners was suffering very much—trade, industry for every reason stagnant. The people were every moment becoming more exasperated by the impudent measures of the Minister Rossi, and their mortification at seeing Rome represented and betrayed by a foreigner. And what foreigner? A pupil of Guizot and Louis Philippe. The news of the bombardment and storm of Vienna had just reached Rome. Zucchi, the Minister of War, at once left the city to put down overfree manifestations in the provinces, and impede the entrance of the troops of the patriot chief, Garibaldi, into Bologna. From the provinces came soldiery called by Rossi to keep order at the opening of the Chamber of Deputies. He reviewed them in the face of the Civic Guard; the press began to be restrained; men were arbitrarily seized and sent out of the kingdom. The public indignation rose to its height; the cup overflowed.

The 15th was a beautiful day, and I had gone out for a long walk. Returning at night, the old padrona met me with her usual smile a little clouded. "Do you know," said she, "that the Minister Rossi has been killed?" No Roman said "murdered."

"Killed?"

"Yes—with a thrust in the back. A wicked man, surely; but is that the way to punish even the wicked?"

"I cannot," observed a philosopher, "sympathize under any circumstances with so immoral a deed; but surely the manner of doing it was great."

The people at large were not so refined in their comments as either the padrona or the philosopher; but soldiers and populace alike ran up and down singing, "Blessed the hand that rids the earth of a tyrant."

Certainly the manner *was* great.

The Chamber was awaiting the entrance of Rossi. Had he lived to enter, he would have found the Assembly without a single exception ranged upon the Opposition benches. His carriage approached, attended by a howling, hissing multitude. He smiled, affected unconcern, but must have felt relieved when his horses entered the courtyard gate of the Cancelleria. He did not know he was entering the place of his execution. The horses stopped; he alighted in the midst of a crowd; it jostled him as if for the purpose of insult; he turned abruptly, and received as he did so the fatal blow. It was dealt by a resolute, perhaps experienced hand; he fell and spoke no word more.

The crowd, as if all previously acquainted with the plan, as no doubt most of them were, issued quietly from the gate and passed through the outside crowd—its members, among whom was he who dealt the blow, dispersing in all directions. For two or three minutes this outside crowd did not know that anything special had happened. When they did, the news was at the moment received in silence. The soldiers in whom Rossi had trusted, whom he had hoped to flatter and bribe, stood at their posts and said not a word. Neither they nor anyone asked, "Who did this? Where is he gone?" The sense of the people certainly was that it was an act of summary justice on an offender whom the laws could not reach, but they felt it to be indecent to shout or exult on the spot where he was breathing his last. Rome, so long supposed the capital of Christendom, certainly took a very pagan view of this act, and the piece represented on the occasion at the theaters was *The Death of Nero*.

The next morning I went to the Church of St. Andrea della Valle, where was to be performed a funeral service with fine music in honor of the victims of Vienna; for this they do here for the victims of every place— "victims of Milan," "victims of Paris," "victims of Naples," and now "victims of Vienna." But today I found the church closed, the service put off —Rome was thinking about her own victims.

I passed into the Ripetta, and entered the Church of San Luigi dei Francesi. The Republican flag was flying at the door; the young sacristan said the fine musical service which this church gave formerly on St. Philip's day in honor of Louis Philippe would now be transferred to the Republican anniversary, the 25th of February. I looked at the monument Chateaubriand erected when here to a poor girl who died last of her family, having seen all the others perish round her. I entered the Domenichino Chapel, and gazed anew on the magnificent representations of the life and death of St. Cecilia. She and St. Agnes are my favorite saints. I love to think of those angel visits which her husband knew by the fragrance of roses and lilies left behind in the apartment. I love to think of his visit to the Catacombs, and all that followed. In one of the pictures St. Cecilia, as she stretches out her arms toward the suffering multitude, seems as if an immortal fount of purest love sprang from her heart. It gives very strongly the idea of an inexhaustible love—the only love that is much worth thinking about.

Leaving the church, I passed along toward the Piazza del Popolo. "Yellow Tiber rose," but not high enough to cause "distress," as he does when in a swelling mood. I heard the drums beating, and entering the Piazza, I found the troops of the line already assembled and the Civic Guard marching in by platoons, each battalion saluted as it entered by trumpets and a fine strain from the band of the Carbineers.

I climbed the Pincian to see better. There is no place so fine for anything of this kind as the Piazza del Popolo, it is so full of light, so fair and grand, the obelisk and fountain make so fine a center to all kinds of groups.

The object of the present meeting was for the Civic Guard and troops of the line to give pledges of sympathy, preparatory to going to the Quirinal to demand a change of ministry and of measures. The flag of the Union was placed in front of the obelisk; all present saluted it; some officials made addresses; the trumpets sounded, and all moved toward the Quirinal.

Nothing could be gentler than the disposition of those composing the crowd. They were resolved to be played with no longer, but no threat was uttered or thought. They believed that the court would be convinced by the fate of Rossi that the retrograde movement it had attempted was impracticable. They knew the retrograde party were panic-stricken, and hoped to use the occasion to free the Pope from its meshes. All felt that Pius IX had fallen irrevocably from his high place as the friend of progress and father of Italy; but still he was personally beloved, and still his name, so often shouted in hope and joy, had not quite lost its prestige.

I returned to the house, which is very near the Quirinal. On one side I could see the palace and gardens of the Pope, on the other the Piazza Barberini and street of the Four Fountains. Presently I saw the carriage of Prince Barberini drive hurriedly into his courtyard gate, the footman signing to close it, a discharge of firearms was heard, and the drums of the Civic Guard beat to arms.

The padrona ran up and down, crying with every round of shot, "Jesu Maria, they are killing the Pope! O poor Holy Father!—Tito, Tito" (out of the window to her husband), "what *is* the matter?"

The lord of creation disdained to reply.

"O Signora! Pray, pray, ask Tito what is the matter?"

I did so.

"I don't know, Signora; nobody knows."

"Why don't you go on the Mount and see?"

"It would be an imprudence, Signora; nobody will go."

I was just thinking to go myself, when I saw a poor man borne by badly wounded, and heard that the Swiss were firing on the people. Their doing so was the cause of whatever violence there was, and it was not much.

The people had assembled as usual at the Quirinal, only with more form and solemnity than usual. They had taken with them several of the Chamber of Deputies, and they sent an embassy headed by Galetti, who had been in the late ministry, to state their wishes. They received a peremptory negative. They then insisted on seeing the Pope and pressed on the palace. The Swiss became alarmed, and fired from the windows and from the roof. They did this, it is said, without orders; but who could at the time suppose that? If it had been planned to exasperate the people to blood, what more could have been done? As it was, very little was shed; but the Pope no doubt felt great panic. He heard the report of firearms—heard that they tried to burn a door of the palace. I would lay my life that he could have shown himself without the slightest danger; nay, that the habitual respect for his presence would have prevailed and hushed all tumult. He did not think so, and to still it, once more degraded himself and injured his people by making promises he did not mean to keep.

He protests now against those promises as extorted by violence—a strange plea indeed for the representative of St. Peter!

Rome is all full of the effigies of those over whom violence had no power. There was an early Pope about to be thrown into the Tiber; violence had no power to make him say what he did not mean. Delicate girls, men in the prime of hope and pride of power—they were all alike about that. They could die in boiling oil, roasted on coals, or cut to pieces; but they could not say what they did not mean. These formed the true Church; it was these who had power to disseminate the religion of him, the Prince of Peace, who died a bloody death of torture between sinners because he never could say what he did not mean.

A little church outside the gate of St. Sebastian commemorates the following affecting tradition of the Church. Peter, alarmed at the persecution of the Christians, had gone forth to fly, when in this spot he saw a bright figure in his path and recognized his Master traveling toward Rome. "Lord," he said, "whither goest thou?" "I go," replied Jesus, "to die with my people." Peter comprehended the reproof. He felt that he must not a fourth time deny his Master, yet hope for salvation. He returned to Rome to offer his life in attestation of his faith.

The Roman Catholic Church has risen a monument to the memory of such facts. And has the present head of that Church quite failed to understand their monition?

Not all the Popes have so failed, though the majority have been intriguing, ambitious men of the world. But even the mob of Rome—and in Rome there *is* a true mob of unheeding cabbage-sellers, who never had a thought beyond contriving how to satisfy their animal instincts for the day—said, on hearing the protest, "There was another Pius not long since, who talked in a very different style. When the French threatened him, he said, 'You may do with me as you see fit, but I cannot consent to act against my convictions.'"

In fact the only dignified course for the Pope to pursue was to resign his temporal power. He could no longer hold it on his own terms; but to it he clung; and the counselors around him were men to wish him to regard *that* as the first of duties. When the question was of waging war for the independence of Italy, they regarded him solely as the head of the Church;

but when the demand was to satisfy the wants of his people, and ecclesiastical goods were threatened with taxes, then he was the prince of the state, bound to maintain all the selfish prerogatives of bygone days for the benefit of his successors. Poor Pope, how has his mind been torn to pieces in these later days! It moves compassion. There can be no doubt that all his natural impulses are generous and kind, and in a more private station he would have died beloved and honored; but to this he was unequal; he has suffered bad men to surround him, and by their misrepresentations and insidious suggestions at last entirely to cloud his mind. I believe he really thinks now the Progress movement tends to anarchy, blood, and all that looked worst in the first French Revolution. However that may be, I cannot forgive him some of the circumstances of this flight. To fly to Naples; to throw himself in the arms of the bombarding monarch, blessing him and thanking his soldiery for preserving that part of Italy from anarchy; to protest that all his promises at Rome were null and void, when he thought himself in safety to choose a commission for governing in his absence, composed of men of princely blood but as to character so null that everybody laughed, and said he chose those who could best be spared if they were killed (but they all ran away directly); when Rome was thus left without any government, to refuse to see any deputation, even the Senator of Rome whom he had so gladly sanctioned—these are the acts either of a fool or a foe. They are not his acts, to be sure, but he is responsible; he lets them stand as such in the face of the world, and weeps and prays for their success.

No more of him! His day is over. He has been made, it seems unconsciously, an instrument of good his regrets cannot destroy. Nor can he be made so important an instrument of ill. These acts have not had the effect the foes of freedom hoped. Rome remained quite cool and composed; all felt that they had not demanded more than was their duty to demand, and were willing to accept what might follow. In a few days all began to say: "Well, who would have thought it? The Pope, the Cardinals, the Princes are gone, and Rome is perfectly tranquil, and one does not miss anything, except that there are not so many rich carriages and liveries."

The Pope may regret too late that he ever gave the people a chance to make this reflection. Yet the best fruits of the movement may not ripen for a long time. It is a movement which requires radical measures, clearsighted, resolute men: these last as yet do not show themselves in Rome. The new Tuscan ministry has three men of superior force in various ways —Montanelli, Guerazzi, d'Aguila—such are not as yet to be found in Rome.

But should she fall this time—and she must either advance with decision and force or fall, since to stand still is impossible—the people have learned much; ignorance and servility of thought are lessened—the way is paving for final triumph.

And my country, what does she? You have chosen a new president from a slave state, representative of the Mexican war. But he seems to be honest, a man that can be esteemed, and is one really known to the people, which is a step upward after having sunk last time to choosing a mere tool of party.

Pray send here a good ambassador—one that has experience of foreign life, that he may act with good judgment, and if possible a man that has knowledge and views which extend beyond the cause of party politics in the United States—a man of unity in principles, but capable of understanding variety in forms. And send a man capable of prizing the luxury of living in or knowing Rome; the office of ambassador is one that should not be thrown away on a person who cannot prize or use it. Another century and I might ask to be made ambassador myself ('tis true, like other ambassadors, I would employ clerks to do the most of the duty); but woman's day has not come yet. They hold their clubs in Paris, but even George Sand will not act with women as they are. They say she pleads they are too mean, too treacherous. She should not abandon them for that, which is not nature but misfortune. How much I shall have to say on that subject if I live, which I desire not, for I am very tired of the battle with giant wrongs, and would like to have someone younger and stronger arise to say what ought to be said, still more to do what ought to be done. Enough! If I felt these things in privileged America, the cries of mothers and wives beaten at night by sons and husbands for their diversion after drinking, as I have repeatedly heard them these past months—the excuse for falsehood, "I *dare not* tell my husband, he would be ready to kill me" —have sharpened my perception as to the ills of woman's condition and the remedies that must be applied. Had I but genius, had I but energy to tell what I know as it ought to be told! God grant them me, or some other more worthy woman, I pray.

Don Tirlone, the *Punch* of Rome, has just come in. This number represents the fortress of Gaeta. Outside hangs a cage containing a parrot (*pappagallo*), the plump body of the bird surmounted by a noble large head with benign face and Papal headdress. He sits on the perch now with folded wings, but the cage door, in likeness of a portico, shows there is convenience to come forth for the purposes of benediction when wanted. Outside, the King of Naples, dressed as Harlequin, plays the organ for instruction of the bird (unhappy penitent, doomed to penance), and, grinning with sharp teeth, observes: "He speaks in my way now." In the background a young Republican holds ready the match for a barrel of gunpowder, but looks at his watch, waiting the moment to ignite it.

A happy New Year to my country! May she be worthy of the privileges she possesses, while others are lavishing their blood to win them—that is all that need be wished for her at present.

LETTER XXVII

Rome, evening of February 20, 1849

.   .   .   .

The Roman still plays amid his serious affairs, and very serious have they been this past winter. The Roman legions went out singing and dancing to fight in Lombardy, and they fought no less bravely for that.

When I wrote last, the Pope had fled, guided, he says, "by the hand of Providence"—Italy deems by the hand of Austria—to Gaeta. He had already soiled his white robes and defamed himself forever by heaping benedictions on the King of Naples and the bands of mercenaries whom he employs to murder his subjects on the least sign of restlessness in their most painful position. Most cowardly had been the conduct of his making promises he never meant to keep, stealing away by night in the coach of a foreign diplomatist, protesting that what he had done was null because he had acted under fear—as if such a protest could avail to one who boasts himself representative of Christ and his apostles, guardian of the legacy of the martyrs! He selected a band of most incapable men to face the danger he had feared for himself; most of these followed his example and fled. Rome sought an interview with him to see if reconciliation were possible; he refused to receive her messengers. His wicked advisers calculated upon great confusion and distress as inevitable on the occasion; but for once the hope of the bad heart was doomed to immediate disappointment. Rome coolly said, "If you desert me—if you will not hear me— I must act for myself." She threw herself into the arms of a few men who had courage and calmness for this crisis; they bade her think upon what was to be done, meanwhile avoiding every excess that could give a color to calumny and revenge. The people with admirable good sense comprehended and followed up this advice. Never was Rome so truly tranquil, so nearly free from gross ill as this winter. A few words of brotherly admonition have been more powerful than all the spies, dungeons, and scaffolds of Gregory.

"The hand of the Omnipotent works for us," observed an old man whom I saw in the street selling cigars the evening before the opening of the Constitutional Assembly. He was struck by the radiant beauty of the night. The old people observe that there never has been such a winter as this which follows the establishment by the French of a republic.

May the omens speed well! A host of enemies without are ready to levy war against this long-suffering people, to rivet anew their chains. Still there is now an obvious tide throughout Europe toward a better order of things, and a wave of it may bear Italy onward to the shore.

The revolution, like all genuine ones, has been instinctive, its results unexpected and surprising to the greater part of those who achieved them. The waters which had flowed so secretly beneath the crust of habit that many never heard their murmur unless in dreams have suddenly burst to light in full and beautiful jets; all rush to drink the pure and living draught.

As in the time of Jesus, the multitude had been long enslaved beneath a cumbrous ritual, their minds designedly darkened by those who should have enlightened them, brutified, corrupted amid monstrous contradictions and abuses; yet the moment they hear a word correspondent to the original nature, "Yes, it is true," they cry. "It is spoken with authority. Yes, it ought to be so. Priests ought to be better and wiser than other men; if they were, they would not need pomp and temporal power to command respect. Yes, it is true; we ought not to lie; we should not try to impose upon one another. We ought rather to prefer that our children should work honestly for their bread than get it by cheating, begging, or the prostitution of their mothers. It would be better to act worthily and kindly; probably would please God more than the kissing of relics. We have long darkly felt that these things were so; *now* we know it."

The unreality of relation between the people and the hierarchy was obvious instantly upon the flight of Pius. He made an immense mistake then, and he made it because neither he nor his Cardinals were aware of the unreality. They did not know that great as is the force of habit, truth *only* is imperishable. The people had abhorred Gregory, had adored Pius upon whom they looked as a savior, as a liberator; finding themselves deceived, a mourning-veil had overshadowed their love. Still had Pius remained here and had courage to show himself on agitating occasions, his position as the Pope before whom they had been bred to bow, his aspect which had once seemed to them full of blessing and promise like that of an angel, would have still retained power. Probably the temporal dominion of the Papacy would not have been broken up. He fled; the people felt contempt for his want of force and truth. He wrote to reproach them with ingratitude; they were indignant. What had they to be grateful for? A constitution to which he had not kept true an instant; the institution of the National Guard, which he had begun to neutralize; benedictions followed by such actions as the desertion of the poor volunteers in the war for Italian independence? Still the people were not quite alienated from Pius. They felt sure that his heart was in substance good and kindly, though the habits of the priest and the arts of his counselors had led him so egregiously to falsify its dictates and forget the vocation to which he had been called. Many hoped he would see his mistake and return to be at one with the people. Among the more ignorant there was a superstitious notion that he would return in the night of the 5th of January. There were many bets that he would be found in the palace of the Quirinal the morning of the 6th. All these lingering feelings were finally extinguished by the advice of excommunication. As this may not have reached America, I subjoin a translation. Here I was obliged to make use of a manuscript copy; all the printed ones were at once destroyed. It is probably the last document of the kind the world will see.

MANIFESTO OF PIUS IX

"To our Most Beloved Subjects:

"From this pacific abode to which it has pleased Divine Providence to conduct us, and whence we can freely manifest our sentiments and our will, we have waited for testimonies of remorse from our misguided children for the sacrileges and misdeeds committed against persons attached to our service—among whom some have been slain, others outraged in the most barbarous manner—as well as for those against our residence and our person. But we have seen nothing except a sterile invitation to return to our capital, unaccompanied by a word of condemnation for those crimes or the least guaranty for our security against the frauds and violences of that same company of furious men which still tyrannizes with a barbarous despotism over Rome and the States of the Church. We also waited, expecting that the protests and orders we have uttered would recall to the duties of fidelity and subjection those who have despised and trampled upon them in the very capital of our States. But, instead of this, a new and more monstrous act of undisguised felony and of actual rebellion by them audaciously committed, has filled the measure of our affliction, and excited at the same time our just indignation, as it will afflict the Church Universal. We speak of that act, in every respect detestable, by which it has been pretended to initiate the convocation of a so-called General National Assembly of the Roman States, by a decree of the 29th of last December, in order to establish new political forms for the Pontifical dominion. Adding thus iniquity to iniquity, the authors and favorers of the demagogical anarchy strive to destroy the temporal authority of the Roman Pontiff over the dominions of Holy Church—however irrefragably established through the most ancient and solid rights, and venerated, recognized, and sustained by all the nations—pretending and making others believe that his sovereign power can be subject to controversy or depend on the caprices of the factious. We shall spare our dignity the humiliation of dwelling on all that

is monstrous contained in that act, abominable through the absurdity of its
origin no less than the illegality of its form and the impiety of its scope;
but it appertains to the Apostolic authority, with which, however unworthy,
we are invested, and to the responsibility which binds us by the most
sacred oaths in the sight of the Omnipotent, not only to protest in the most
energetic and efficacious manner against that same act, but to condemn it
in the face of the universe as an enormous and sacrilegious crime against
our independence and sovereignty, meriting the chastisements threatened
by divine and human laws. We are persuaded that, on receiving the impudent invitation, you were full of holy indignation, and will have rejected
far from you this guilty and shameful provocation. Notwithstanding, that
none of you may say he has been deluded by fallacious seductions, and by
the preachers of subversive doctrines, or ignorant of what is contriving by
the foes of all order, all law, all right, true liberty, and your happiness, we
today again raise and utter abroad our voice, so that you may be more certain of the absoluteness with which we prohibit men, of whatever class and
condition, from taking any part in the meetings which those persons may
dare to call, for the nomination of individuals to be sent to the condemned
Assembly. At the same time we recall to you how this absolute prohibition
is sanctioned by the decrees of our predecessors and of the Councils, especially of the Sacred Council-General of Trent, Sec. XXII, Chap. II, in
which the Church has fulminated many times her censures, and especially
the greater excommunication, as incurred without fail by any declaration
of whomsoever daring to become guilty of whatsoever attempt against
the temporal sovereignty of the Supreme Pontiff, this we declare to have
been already unhappily incurred by all those who have given aid to the
above-named act, and others preceding, intended to prejudice the same
sovereignty, and in other modes and under false pretexts have perturbed,
violated, and usurped our authority. Yet, though we feel ourselves obliged
by conscience to guard the sacred deposit of the patrimony of the Spouse
of Jesus Christ, confided to our care, by using the sword of severity given
to us for that purpose, we cannot therefore forget that we are on earth the
representative of Him who in exercise of His justice does not forget mercy.
Raising, therefore, our hands to Heaven, while we to it recommend a
cause which is indeed more Heaven's than ours, and while anew we

declare ourselves ready, with the aid of its powerful grace, to drink even to the dregs, for the defense and glory of the Catholic Church, the cup of persecution which He first wished to drink for the salvation of the same, we shall not desist from supplicating Him benignly to hear the fervent prayers which day and night we unceasingly offer for the salvation of the misguided. No day certainly could be more joyful for us than that in which it shall be granted to see return into the fold of the Lord our sons from whom now we derive so much bitterness and so great tribulations. The hope of enjoying soon the happiness of such a day is strengthened in us by the reflection that universal are the prayers which, united to ours, ascend to the throne of Divine Mercy from the lips and the heart of the faithful throughout the Catholic world, urging it continually to change the hearts of sinners, and reconduct them into the paths of truth and of justice.

"Gaeta, January 6, 1849"

The silliness, bigotry, and ungenerous tone of this manifesto excited a simultaneous movement in the population. The procession which carried it, mumbling chants, for deposit in places provided for lowest uses, and then taking from the doors of the hatters' shops the cardinals' hats threw them into the Tiber, was a real and general expression of popular disgust. From that hour the power of the scarlet hierarchy fell to rise no more. No authority can survive a universal movement of derision. From that hour tongues and pens were loosed, the leaven of Machiavellianism which still polluted the productions of the more liberal disappeared, and people talked as they felt, just as those of us who do not choose to be slaves are accustomed to do in America.

"Jesus," cried an orator, "bade them feed his lambs. If they have done so, it has been to rob their fleece and drink their blood."

"Why," said another, "have we been so long deaf to the saying that the temporal dominion of the Church was like a thorn in the wound of Italy, which shall never be healed till that thorn is extracted?"

And then without passion all felt that the temporal dominion was in fact finished of itself, and that it only remained to organize another form of government.

LETTER XXVIII

Rome, evening of February 20, 1849

The League between the Italian States and the Diet which was to establish it had been the thought of Gioberti, but had found the instrument at Rome in Mamiani. The deputies were to be named by princes or parliaments, their mandate to be limited by the existing institutions of the several states; measures of mutual security and some modifications in the way of reform would be the utmost that could be hoped from this Diet. The scope of this party did not go beyond more vigorous prosecution of the war for independence, and the establishment of good institutions for the several principalities on a basis of assimilation.

Mazzini, the great radical thinker of Italy, was on the contrary persuaded that unity not union was necessary to this country. He had taken for his motto, *God and the People,* and believed in no other powers. He wished an Italian Constitutional Assembly selected directly by the people, and furnished with an unlimited mandate to decide what form was now required by the needs of the Peninsula. His own wishes certainly aimed at a republic; but the decision remained with the representatives of the people.

The thought of Gioberti had been at first the popular one, as he in fact was the seer of the so-called Moderate party. For myself I always looked upon him as entirely a charlatan, who covered his want of all real force by the thickest embroidered mantle of words. Still for a time he corresponded with the wants of the Italian mind. He assailed the Jesuits, and was of real use by embodying the distrust and aversion that brooded in the minds of men against these most insidious and inveterate foes of liberty and progress. This triumph at least he may boast: that sect has been obliged to yield; its extinction seems impossible, of such life-giving power was the fiery will of Loyola. In the Primate he had embodied the lingering hope of the Catholic Church; Pius IX had answered to the appeal, had answered only to show its futility. He had run through Italy as courier for Charles Albert, when the so falsely styled "Magnanimous" entered, pretending to save her from the stranger, really hoping to take her for himself. His own cowardice and treachery neutralized the hope, and Charles Albert, abject in his disgrace, took a retrograde ministry. This the country would not suffer, and obliged him after a while to reassume at least the position of the previous year by taking Gioberti for his premier. But it soon became evident that the ministry of Charles Albert was in the same position as had been that of Pius IX. The hand was powerless when the head was indisposed. Meantime the name of Mazzini had echoed through Tuscany from the revered lips of Montanelli; it reached the Roman States, and though at first propagated by foreign impulse, yet as soon as understood was welcomed as congenial. Montanelli had nobly said, addressing Florence: "We could not regret that the realization of this project should take place in a sister city, still more illustrious than ours." The Romans took him at his word; the Constitutional Assembly for the Roman States was elected with a double mandate, that the deputies might sit in the Constitutional Assembly for all Italy whenever the other provinces could send theirs. They were elected by universal suffrage. Those who listened to Jesuits and Moderates predicted that the project would fail of itself. The people were too ignorant to make use of the liberty of suffrage.

But ravens nowadays are not the true prophetic birds. The Roman eagle recommences her flight, and it is from its direction only that the high priest may draw his augury. The people are certainly as ignorant as centuries of the worst government, the neglect of popular education, the enslavement of speech and the press, could make them; yet they have an instinct to recognize measures that are good for them. A few weeks' schooling at some popular meetings, the clubs, the conversations of the National Guards in their quarters or on patrol, were sufficient to concert measures so well that the people voted in larger proportion than at contested elections in our country, and made a very good choice.

The opening of the Constitutional Assembly gave occasion for a fine procession. All the troops in Rome defiled from the Campidoglio; among them many bear the marks of suffering from the Lombard war. The banners of Sicily, Venice, and Bologna waved proudly; that of Naples was veiled with crape. I was in a balcony in the Piazza di Venezia; the Palazzo di Venezia, that sternest feudal pile so long the headquarters of Austrian machinations, seemed to frown as the bands each in passing struck up the

Marseillaise. The nephew of Napoleon and Garibaldi, the hero of Montevideo, walked together as deputies. The deputies, a grave band, mostly advocates or other professional men, walked without other badge of distinction than the tricolored scarf. I remembered the entrance of the deputies to the Council only fourteen months ago in the magnificent carriages lent by the princes for the occasion; they too were mostly nobles, and their liveried attendants followed carrying their scutcheons. Princes and councilors have both fled or sunk into nothingness; in those councilors was no counsel. Will it be found in the present? Let us hope so! What we see today has much more the air of reality than all that parade of scutcheons, or the pomp of dress and retinue with which the ecclesiastical court was wont to amuse the people.

A few days after followed the proclamation of a republic. An immense crowd of people surrounded the Palazzo della Cancelleria, within whose courtyard Rossi fell, while the debate was going on within. At one o'clock in the morning of the 9th of February, a republic was resolved upon, and the crowd rushed away to ring all the bells.

Early next morning I rose and went forth to observe the republic. Over the Quirinal I went, through the Forum to the Capitol. There was nothing to be seen except the magnificent calm emperor, the tamers of horses, the fountain, the trophies, the lions as usual; among the marbles, for living figures, a few dirty, bold women and Murillo boys in the sun just as usual. I passed into the Corso; there were men in the liberty cap—of course the lowest and vilest had been the first to assume it; all the horrible beggars persecuting as impudently as usual. I met some English; all their comfort was, "It would not last a month," "They hoped to see all these fellows shot yet." The English clergymen, more mild and legal, only hopes to see them (i.e., the ministry, deputies, etc.) *hung.*

Mr. Carlyle would be delighted with his countrymen. They are entirely ready and anxious to see a Cromwell for Italy. They too think, when the people starve, "It is no matter what happens in the back parlor." What signifies that, if there is "order" in the front? How dare the people make a noise to disturb us yawning at billiards!

I met an American. He "had no confidence in the Republic." Why? Because he "had no confidence in the people." Why? Because "they were not like *our* people." Ah, Jonathan and John—excuse me, but I must say the Italian has a decided advantage over you in the power of quickly feeling generous sympathy, as well as some other things which I have not time now to particularize. I have memoranda from you both in my notebook.

At last the procession mounts the Campidoglio. It is all dressed with banners. The tricolor surmounts the palace of the senator; the senator himself has fled. The deputies mount the steps, and one of them reads in a clear friendly voice the following words:

"FUNDAMENTAL DECREE OF THE CONSTITUTIONAL ASSEMBLY OF ROME

"ART. I. The Papacy has fallen in fact and in right from the temporal government of the Roman State.

"ART. II. The Roman Pontiff shall have all the necessary guaranties for independence in the exercise of his spiritual power.

"ART. III. The form of government of the Roman State shall be a pure democracy, and will take the glorious name of Roman Republic.

"ART. IV. The Roman Republic shall have with the rest of Italy the relations exacted by a common nationality."

Between each of these expressive sentences the speaker paused; the great bell of the Capitol gave forth its solemn melodies; the cannon answered; while the crowd shouted *Viva la Repubblica! Viva Italia!*

The imposing grandeur of the spectacle to me gave new force to the emotion that already swelled my heart; my nerves thrilled, and I longed to see in some answering glance a spark of Rienzi, a little of that soul which made my country what she is. The American at my side remained impassive. Receiving all his birthright from a triumph of democracy, he was quite indifferent to this manifestation on this consecrated spot. Passing the winter in Rome to study art, he was insensible to the artistic beauty of the scene—insensible to this new life of that spirit from which all the forms he gazes at in galleries emanated. He "did not see the use of these popular demonstrations."

Again I must mention a remark of his, as a specimen of the ignorance in which Americans usually remain during their flighty visits to these scenes where they associate only with one another. And I do it the rather as this seemed a really thoughtful, intelligent man; no vain, vulgar trifler. He said, "The people seem only to be looking on; they take no part."

"What people?" said I.

"Why, these around us; there are no other people."

There are a few beggars, errand-boys, and nursemaids.

"The others are only soldiers."

Soldiers! The Civic Guard—all the decent men in Rome!

Thus it is that the American on many points becomes more ignorant for coming abroad, because he attaches some value to his crude impressions and frequent blunders. It is not thus that any seed-corn can be gathered from foreign gardens. Without modest scrutiny, patient study, and observation, he spends his money and goes home, with a new coat perhaps, but a mind befooled rather than instructed. It is necessary to speak the languages of these countries and know personally some of their inhabitants, in order to form any accurate impressions.

The flight of the Grand Duke of Tuscany followed. In imitation of his great exemplar he promised and smiled to the last, deceiving Montanelli, the pure and sincere, at the very moment he was about to enter his carriage, into the belief that he persevered in his assent to the liberal movement. His position was certainly very difficult, but he might have left it like a gentleman, like a man of honor. 'Twas pity to destroy so lightly the good opinion the Tuscans had of him. Now Tuscany meditates union with Rome.

Meanwhile Charles Albert is filled with alarm. He is indeed betwixt two fires. Gioberti has published one of his prolix, weak addresses in which he says that in the beginning of every revolution one must fix a limit beyond which he will not go; that for himself he has done it—others are passing beyond his mark, and he will not go any farther. Of the want of thought, of insight into historic and all other truths, which distinguishes the "illustrious Gioberti," this assumption is a specimen. But it makes no difference; he and his prince must go sooner or later if the movement continues, nor is there any prospect of its being stayed unless by foreign intervention. This the Pope has not yet, it is believed, solicited, but there is little reason to hope he will be spared that crowning disgrace. He has already consented to the incitement of civil war. Should an intervention be solicited, all depends on France. Will she basely forfeit every pledge and every duty, to say nothing of her true interest? It seems that her President stands doubtful, intending to do what is for *his* particular interest; but if his interest proves opposed to the republican principle, will France suffer herself again to be hoodwinked and enslaved? It is impossible to know, she has already shown such devotion to the mere prestige of a name.

On England no dependence can be placed. She is guided by no great idea; her Parliamentary leaders sneer at sentimental policy and the "jargon" of ideas. She will act as always for her own interest; and the interest of her present government is becoming more and more the crushing of the democratic tendency. They are obliged to do it at home, both in the back and the front parlor; it would not be decent as yet to have a Spielberg just at home for obstreperous patriots, but England has so many ships, it is just as easy to transport them to a safe distance. Then the Church of England, so long an enemy to the Church of Rome, feels a decided interest with it on the subject of temporal possessions. The rich English traveler, fearing to see the Prince Borghese stripped of one of his palaces for a hospital or some such low use, thinks of his own twenty-mile park and the crowded village of beggars at its gate, and muses: "I hope to see them all shot yet, these rascally republicans."

How I wish my country would show some noble sympathy when an experience so like her own is going on. Politically she cannot interfere; but formerly when Greece and Poland were struggling, they were at least aided by private contributions. Italy, naturally so rich but long racked and impoverished by her oppressors, greatly needs money to arm and clothe her troops. Some token of sympathy too from America would be so welcome to her now. If there were a circle of persons inclined to trust such to me, I might venture to promise that trust should be used to the advantage of Italy. It would make me proud to have my country show a religious faith in the progress of ideas, and make some small sacrifice of its own great resources in aid of a sister cause, now.

But I must close this letter, which it would be easy to swell to a volume from the materials in my mind. One or two traits of the hour I must note. Mazzarelli, chief of the present ministry, was a prelate, and named spontaneously by the Pope before his flight. He has shown entire and frank intrepidity. He has laid aside the title of monsignor, and appears before the world as a layman.

Nothing can be more tranquil than has been the state of Rome all winter. Every wile has been used by the Oscurantists to excite the people, but their confidence in their leaders could not be broken. A little mutiny in the troops, stimulated by letters from their old leaders, was quelled in a moment. The day after the proclamation of the republic, some zealous ignoramuses insulted the carriages that appeared with servants in livery. The ministry published a grave admonition that democracy meant liberty not license, and that he who infringed upon an innocent freedom of action in others must be declared traitor to his country. Every act of the kind ceased instantly. An intimation that it was better not to throw large comfits or oranges during the Carnival, as injuries have thus been sometimes caused, was obeyed with equal docility.

On Sunday last placards affixed in the high places summoned the city to invest Giuseppe Mazzini with the rights of a Roman citizen. I have not yet heard the result. The Pope made Rossi a Roman citizen; he was suffered to retain that title only one day. It was given him on the 14th of November; he died the 15th. Mazzini enters Rome at any rate for the first time in his life as deputy to the Constitutional Assembly; it would be a noble poetic justice if he could enter also as a Roman citizen.

February 24

The Austrians have invaded Ferrara, taken $200,000 and six hostages, and retired. This step is no doubt intended to determine whether France will resent the insult, or whether she will betray Italy. It shows also the assurance of the Austrian that the Pope will approve of an armed intervention. Probably before I write again these matters will reach some decided crisis.

LETTER XXIX

Rome, March 20, 1849

The Roman Republic moves on better than could have been expected. There are great difficulties about money necessarily, as the government, so beset with trials and dangers, cannot command confidence in that respect. The solid coin has crept out of the country or lies hid, and in the use of paper there are the corresponding inconveniences. But the poor, always the chief sufferers from such a state of things, are wonderfully patient, and I doubt not that the new form, if Italy could be left to itself, would be settled for the advantage of all. Tuscany would soon be united with Rome, and to the Republic of Central Italy, no longer broken asunder by petty restrictions and sacrificed to the interests of a few persons, would come that prosperity natural to a region so favored by nature.

Could Italy be left alone! But treacherous, selfish men at home strive to betray, and foes threaten her from without on every side. Even France, her natural ally, promises to prove foolishly and basely faithless. The dereliction from principle of her government seems certain, and thus far the nation, despite the remonstrance of a few worthy men, gives no sign of effective protest. There would be little hope for Italy, were not the thrones of her foes in a tottering state, their action liable at every moment to be distracted by domestic difficulties. The Austrian government seems as destitute of support from the nation as it is possible for a government to be, and the army is no longer what it was, being made up so largely of new recruits. The Croats are uncertain in their adhesion, the war in Hungary likely to give them much to do; and if the Russian is called in, the rest of Europe becomes hostile. All these circumstances give Italy a chance she otherwise could not have; she is in great measure unfurnished with arms and money; her King in the south is a bloody, angry, well-armed foe; her King in the north, a proved traitor. Charles Albert has now declared war because he could not do otherwise; but his sympathies are in fact all against liberty; the splendid lure that he might become King of Italy glitters no more; the Republicans are in the ascendant, and he may well doubt, should the stranger be driven out, whether Piedmont could escape the contagion. Now, his people insisting on war, he has the air of making it with a good grace; but should he be worsted, probably he will know some loophole by which to steal out. The rat will get out and leave the lion in the trap.

The "illustrious Gioberti" has fallen—fallen forever from his high scaffold of words. His demerits were too unmistakable for rhetoric to hide. That he sympathized with the Pope rather than the Roman people, and could not endure to see him stripped of his temporal power, no one could blame in the author of the "Primato." That he refused the Italian General Assembly if it was to be based on the so-called Montanelli system instead of his own, might be conviction, or it might be littleness and vanity. But that he privily planned, without even adherence of the council of ministers, an armed intervention of the Piedmontese troops in Tuscany, thus willing to cause civil war and at this great moment to see Italian blood shed by Italian hands, was treachery. I think indeed he has been probably made the scapegoat in that affair; that Charles Albert planned the measure, and finding himself unable to carry it out in consequence of the vigilance and indignant opposition of the Chamber of Deputies, was somewhat consoled by making it an occasion to victimize the "Illustrious," whom four weeks before the people had forced him to accept as his minister.

Now the name of Gioberti is erased from the corners of the streets to which it was affixed a year ago; he is stripped of all his honorary degrees, and proclaimed an unworthy son of the country. Mazzini is the idol of the people—"Soon to be hunted out," sneered the skeptical American. Possibly yes; for no man is secure of his palm till the fight is over. The civic wreath may be knocked from his head a hundred times in the ardor of the contest. No matter, if he can always keep the forehead pure and lofty, as will Mazzini.

In thinking of Mazzini, I always remember Petrarch's invocation to Rienzi. Mazzini comes at a riper period in the world's history, with the same energy of soul, but of purer temper and more enlarged views to answer them.

I do not know whether I mentioned a kind of poetical correspondence about Mazzini and Rossi. Rossi was also an exile for liberal principles, but he did not value his birthright; he alienated it, and as a French citizen became peer of France and representative of Louis Philippe in Italy. When with the fatuity of those whom the gods have doomed to perish Pius IX took the representative of the fallen Guizot policy for his minister, he made him a Roman citizen. He was proclaimed such on the 14th of November. On the 15th he perished, before he could enter the parliament he had called. He fell at the door of the Cancelleria when it was sitting.

Mazzini in his exile remained absolutely devoted to his native country because, though feeling as few can that the interests of humanity in all nations are identical, he felt also that born of a race so suffering, so much needing devotion and energy, his first duty was to that. The only powers he acknowledged were God and the People, the special scope of his acts the unity and independence of Italy. Rome was the theme of his thoughts, but, very early exiled, he had never seen that home to which all the orphans of the soul so naturally turn. Now he entered it as a Roman citizen, elected representative of the people by universal suffrage. His motto, *Dio e Popolo*, is put upon the coin with the Roman eagle; unhappily this first-issued coin is of brass, or else of silver with much alloy. *Dii, avertite omen,* and may peaceful days turn it all to pure gold!

On his first entrance to the house Mazzini, received with fervent applause and summoned to take his place beside the President, spoke as follows:

"It is from me, colleagues, that should come these tokens of applause, these tokens of affection, because the little good I have not done but tried to do has come to me from Rome. Rome was always a sort of talisman for me; a youth, I studied the history of Italy and found, while all the other nations were born, grew up, played their part in the world, then fell to reappear no more in the same power, a single city was privileged by God to die only to rise again greater than before, to fulfill a mission greater than the first. I saw the Rome of the Empire extend her conquests from the confines of Africa to the confines of Asia. I saw Rome perish crushed by the barbarians, by those whom even yet the world calls barbarians. I saw her rise again after having chased away these same barbarians, reviving in its sepulcher the germ of civilization. I saw her rise more great for conquest not with arms but with words—rise in the name of the Popes to repeat her grand mission. I said in my heart, the city which alone in the world has had two grand lives, one greater than the other, will have a third. After the Rome which wrought by conquest of arms, the Rome which wrought by conquest of words, must come a third which shall work by virtue of example. After the Rome of the Emperors, after the Rome of the Popes, will come the Rome of the People. The Rome of the People is arisen; do not salute with applause, but let us rejoice together! I cannot promise anything for myself except concurrence in all you shall do for the good of Rome, of Italy, of mankind. Perhaps we shall have to pass through great crises; perhaps we shall have to fight a sacred battle against the only enemy that threatens us—Austria. We will fight it, and we will conquer. I hope, please God, that foreigners may not be able to say any more that which so many of them repeat today, speaking of our affairs—that the light which comes from Rome is only an *ignis fatuus* wandering among the tombs. The world shall see that it is a starry light, eternal, pure, and resplendent as those we look up to in the heavens!"

On a later day he spoke more fully of the difficulties that threaten at home the young republic, and said:

"Let us not hear of Right, of Left, of Center; these terms express the three powers in a constitutional monarchy; for us they have no meaning; the only divisions for us are of Republicans or non-Republicans—or of sincere men and temporizing men. Let us not hear so much of the Republicans of today and of yesterday; I am a Republican of twenty years' standing. Entertaining such hopes for Italy when many excellent, many sincere men held them as utopian, shall I denounce these men because they are now convinced of their practicability?"

This last I quote from memory. In hearing the gentle tone of remonstrance with those of more petty mind or influenced by the passions of the partisan, I was forcibly reminded of the parable by Jesus of the vineyard and the discontent of the laborers that those who came at the eleventh hour "received also a penny." Mazzini also is content that all should fare alike as brethren, if only they will come into the vineyard. He is not an orator, but the simple conversational tone of his address is in refreshing contrast with the boyish rhetoric and academic swell common to Italian speakers in the present unfledged state. As they have freer use of the power of debate, they will become more simple and manly. The speech of Mazzini is laden with thought—it goes straight to the mark by the shortest path, and moves without effort from the irresistible impression of deep conviction and fidelity in the speaker. Mazzini is a man of genius, an elevated thinker, but the most powerful and first impression from his presence must always be of the religion of his soul, of his *virtue* both in the modern and antique sense of that word.

If clearness of right, if energy, if indefatigable perseverance can steer the ship through this dangerous pass, it will be done. He said, "We will conquer"; whether Rome will this time is not to me certain, but such men as Mazzini conquer always—conquer in defeat. Yet Heaven grant that no more blood, no more corruption of priestly government, be for Italy. It could only be for once more, for the strength of her present impulse would not fail to triumph at last; but even one more trial seems too intolerably much, when I think of the holocaust of the broken hearts, baffled lives that must attend it.

But enough of politics for the present; this letter goes by private hand and as news will be superseded before it can arrive.

LETTER XXX

Rome, May 27, 1849

I have suspended writing in the expectation of some decisive event; but none such comes yet. The French, entangled in a web of falsehood, abashed by a defeat that Oudinot has vainly tried to gloss over, the expedition disowned by all honorable men at home, disappointed at Gaeta, not daring to go the length Papal infatuation demands, know not what to do. The Neapolitans have been decidedly driven back into their own borders, the last time in a most shameful rout, their King flying in front. We have heard for several days that the Austrians were advancing, but they come not. They also, it is probable, meet with unexpected embarrassments. They find that the sincere movement of the Italian people is very unlike that of troops commanded by princes and generals who never wished to conquer and were always waiting to betray. Then their troubles at home are constantly increasing, and should the Russian intervention quell these today, it is only to raise a storm far more terrible tomorrow.

The struggle is now fairly, thoroughly commenced between the principle of democracy and the old powers, no longer legitimate. That struggle may last fifty years, and the earth be watered with the blood and tears of more than one generation, but the result is sure. All Europe, including Great Britain, where the most bitter resistance of all will be made, is to be under republican government in the next century.

God moves in a mysterious way.

Every struggle made by the old tyrannies, all their jesuitical deceptions, their rapacity, their imprisonments and executions of the most generous men, only sow more dragon's teeth; the crop shoots up daily more and more plenteous.

When I first arrived in Italy, the vast majority of this people had no wish beyond limited monarchies, constitutional governments. They still respected the famous names of the nobility; they despised the priests, but were still fondly attached to the dogmas and ritual of the Roman Catholic Church. It required King Bomba, the triple treachery of Charles Albert, Pius IX, and the "illustrious Gioberti," the naturally kind-hearted but, from the necessity of his position, cowardly and false Leopold of Tuscany, the vagabond "serene" meannesses of Parma and Modena, the "fatherly" Radetzky, and finally the imbecile Louis Bonaparte, "would-be Emperor of France," to convince this people that no transition is possible between the old and the new. The *work is done;* the revolution in Italy is now radical, nor can it stop till Italy becomes independent and united as a republic. Protestant she already is, and though the memory of saints and martyrs may continue to be revered, the ideal of woman to be adored under the name of Mary, yet Christ will now begin to be a little thought of; *his* idea has always been kept carefully out of sight under the old regime, all the worship being for the Madonna and saints, who were to be well paid for interceding for sinners—an example which might make men cease to be such, was no way coveted. Now the New Testament has been translated into Italian; copies are already dispersed far and wide; men calling themselves Christians will no longer be left entirely ignorant of the precepts and life of Jesus.

The people of Rome have burnt the Cardinals' carriages. They took the confessionals out of the churches, and made mock confessions in the piazzas, the scope of which was, "I have sinned, father, so and so." "Well, my son, how much will you *pay* to the Church for absolution?" Afterward the people thought of burning the confessionals or using them for barricades; but at the request of the Triumvirate they desisted, and even put them back into the churches. But it was from no reaction of feeling that they stopped short, only from respect for the government. The *Tartuffe* of Molière has been translated into Italian, and was last night performed with great applause at the Valle. Can all this be forgotten? Never! Should guns and bayonets replace the Pope on the throne, he will find its foundations, once deep as modern civilization, now so undermined that it falls with the least awkward movement.

But I cannot believe he will be replaced there. France alone could consummate that crime—that for her most cruel, most infamous treason. The elections in France will decide. In three or four days we shall know whether the French nation at large be guilty or no—whether it be the will of the nation to aid or strive to ruin a government founded on precisely the same basis as their own.

I do not dare to trust that people. The peasant is yet very ignorant. The suffering workman is frightened as he thinks of the punishments that ensued on the insurrections of May and June. The man of property is full of horror at the brotherly scope of Socialism. The aristocrat dreams of the guillotine always when he hears men speak of the people. The influence of the Jesuits is still immense in France. Both in France and England the grossest falsehoods have been circulated with unwearied diligence about the state of things in Italy. An amusing specimen of what is still done in this line I find just now in a foreign journal, where it says there are red flags on all the houses of Rome; meaning to imply that the Romans are athirst for blood. Now the fact is that these flags are put up at the entrance of those streets where there is no barricade, as a signal to coachmen and horsemen that they can pass freely. There is one on the house where I am, in which is no person but myself, who thirst for peace, and the *padrone,* who thirsts for money.

Meanwhile the French troops are encamped at a little distance from Rome. Some attempts at fair and equal treaty when their desire to occupy Rome was firmly resisted, Oudinot describes in his dispatches as a readiness for *submission.* Having tried in vain to gain this point, he has sent to France for fresh orders. These will be decided by the turn the election takes. Meanwhile the French troops are much exposed to the Roman force where they are. Should the Austrians come up, what will they do? Will they shamelessly fraternize with the French, after pretending and proclaiming that they came here as a check upon their aggressions? Will they oppose them in defense of Rome, with which they are at war?

Ah, the way of falsehood, the way of treachery—how dark, how full of pitfalls and traps! Heaven defend from it all who are not yet engaged therein!

War near at hand seems to me even more dreadful than I had fancied it. True, it tries men's souls, lays bare selfishness in undeniable deformity. Here it has produced much fruit of noble sentiment, noble act; but still it breeds vice too, drunkenness, mental dissipation, tears asunder the tenderest ties, lavishes the productions of Earth, for which her starving poor stretch out their hands in vain, in the most unprofitable manner. And the ruin that ensues, how terrible! Let those who have ever passed happy days in Rome grieve to hear that the beautiful plantations of Villa Borghese—that chief delight and refreshment of citizens, foreigners, and little children—are laid low, as far as the obelisk. The fountain, singing alone amid the fallen groves, cannot be seen and heard without tears; it seems like some innocent infant calling and crowing amid dead bodies on a field which battle has strewn with the bodies of those who once cherished it. The plantations of Villa Salvage on the Tiber, also the beautiful trees on the way from St. John Lateran to La Maria Maggiore, the trees of the Forum, are fallen. Rome is shorn of the locks which lent grace to her venerable brow. She looks desolate, profaned. I feel what I never expected to—as if I might by and by be willing to leave Rome.

Then I have for the first time seen what wounded men suffer. The night of the 30th of April I passed in the hospital, and saw the terrible agonies of those dying or who needed amputation, felt their mental pains and longing for the loved ones who were away; for many of these were Lombards who had come from the field of Novara to fight with a fairer chance—many were students of the University, who had enlisted and thrown themselves into the front of the engagement. The impudent falsehoods of the French general's dispatches are incredible. The French were never decoyed on in any way. They were received with every possible mark of hostility. They were defeated in open field, the Garibaldi legion rushing out to meet them; and though they suffered much from the walls, they sustained themselves nowhere. They never put up a white flag till they wished to surrender.

The vanity that strives to cover over these facts is unworthy of men. The only excuse for the imprudent conduct of the expedition is that they were deceived, not by the Romans here but by the priests of Gaeta, leading them to expect action in their favor within the walls. These priests themselves were deluded by their hopes and old habits of mind. The troops did not fight well, and General Oudinot abandoned his wounded without proper care. All this says nothing against French valor, proved by ages of glory beyond the doubt of their worst foes. They were demoralized because they fought in so bad a cause, and there was no sincere ardor or clear hope in any breast.

But to return to the hospitals: these were put in order and have been kept so by the Princess Belgiojoso. The Princess was born of one of the noblest families of the Milanese, descendant of the great Trivulzio, and inherited a large fortune. Very early she compromised it in liberal movements and, on their failure, was obliged to fly to Paris, where for a time she maintained herself by writing, and I think by painting also. A princess so placed naturally excited great interest, and she drew around her a little court of celebrated men. After recovering her fortune, she still lived in Paris, distinguished for her talents and munificence, both toward literary men and her exiled countrymen. Later, on her estate called Locate between Pavia and Milan, she had made experiments in the Socialist direction with fine judgment and success. Association for education, for labor, for transaction of household affairs had been carried on for several years; she had spared no devotion of time and money to this object, loved and was much beloved by those objects of her care, and said she hoped to die there. All is now despoiled and broken up, though it may be hoped that some seeds of peaceful reform have been sown which will spring to light when least expected. The princess returned to Italy in 1847–8, full of hope in Pius IX and Charles Albert. She showed her usual energy and truly princely heart, sustaining at her own expense a company of soldiers and a journal up to the last sad betrayal of Milan on August 6th. These days undeceived all the people, but few of the *noblesse;* she was one of the few with mind strong enough to understand the lesson, and is now warmly interested in the republican movement. From Milan she went to France, but, finding it impossible to effect anything serious there in behalf of Italy, returned and has been in Rome about two months. Since leaving Milan she receives no income, her possessions being in the grasp of Radetzky, and cannot know when if ever she will again. But as she worked so largely and well with money, so can she without. She published an invitation to the Roman women to make lint and bandages, and offer their services to the wounded; she put the hospitals in order; in the central one, Trinità dei Pellegrini, once the abode where the pilgrims were received during Holy Week and where foreigners were entertained by seeing their feet washed by the noble dames and dignitaries of Rome, she has remained day and night since the 30th of April, when the wounded were first there. Some money she procured at first by going through Rome, accompanied by two other veiled ladies, to beg it. Afterward the voluntary contributions were generous; among the rest, I am proud to say, the Americans in Rome gave $250, of which a handsome portion came from Mr. Brown, the Consul.

I value this mark of sympathy more because of the irritation and surprise occasioned here by the position of Mr. Cass, the Envoy. It is most unfortunate that we should have an envoy here for the first time, just to offend and disappoint the Romans. When all the other ambassadors are at Gaeta, ours is in Rome, as if by his presence to discountenance the republican government, which he does not recognize. Mr. Cass, it seems, is required by his instructions not to recognize the government till sure it can be sustained. Now it seems to me that the only dignified ground for our government, the only legitimate ground for any republican government, is to recognize for any nation the government chosen by itself. The suffrage had been correct here, and the proportion of votes to the whole population was much larger, it was said by Americans here, than it is in our own country at the time of contested elections. It had elected an Assembly; that Assembly had appointed to meet the exigencies of this time the Triumvirate. If any misrepresentations have induced America to believe, as France affects to have believed, that so large a vote could have been obtained by moral intimidation, the present unanimity of the population in resisting such immense odds, and the enthusiasm of their every expression in favor of the present government, put the matter beyond a doubt. The Roman people claims once more to have a national existence. It declines further serfdom to an ecclesiastical court. It claims liberty of conscience, of action, and of thought. Should it fall from its present position, it will not be from internal dissent, but from foreign oppression.

Since this is the case, surely our country, if no other, is bound to recognize the present government *so long as it can sustain itself*. This position is that to which we have a right: being such, it is no matter how it is viewed by others. But I dare assert it is the only respectable one for our country, in the eyes of the Emperor of Russia himself.

The first, best occasion is past, when Mr. Cass might, had he been empowered to act as Mr. Rush did in France, have morally strengthened the staggering republic, which would have found sympathy where alone it is of permanent value, on the basis of principle. Had it been in vain, what then? America would have acted honorably; as to our being compromised thereby with the Papal government, that fear is idle. Pope and Cardinals have great hopes from America; the giant influence there is kept up with the greatest care; the number of Catholic writers in the United States, too, carefully counted. Had our republican government acknowledged this republican government, the Papal Camarilla would have respected us more but not loved us less; for have we not the loaves and fishes to give, as well as the precious souls to be saved? Ah, here indeed, America might go straightforward with all needful impunity. Bishop Hughes himself need not be anxious. That first, best occasion has passed, and the unrecognized, unrecognizing Envoy has given offense and not comfort by a presence that seemed constantly to say, I do not think you can sustain yourselves. It has wounded both the heart and the pride of Rome. Some of the lowest people have asked me, "Is it not true that your country had a war to become free?" "Yes." "Then why do they not feel for us?"

Yet even now it is not too late. If America would only hail triumphant, though she could not sustain injured Rome, that would be something. "Can you suppose Rome will triumph," you say, "without money, and against so potent a league of foes?" I am not sure but I hope, for I believe something in the heart of a people when fairly awakened. I have also a lurking confidence in what our fathers spoke of so constantly, a providential order of things by which brute force and selfish enterprise are sometimes set at naught by aid which seems to descend from a higher sphere. Even the old pagans believed in that, you know; and I was born in America Christianized by the Puritans—America freed by eight years' patient suffering, poverty, and struggle—America so cheered in dark days by one spark of sympathy from a foreign shore—America first "recognized" by Lafayette. I saw him when traversing our country, then great, rich, and free. Millions of men who owed in part their happiness to what, no doubt, was once sneered at as romantic sympathy threw garlands in his path. It is natural that I should have some faith.

Send, dear America, to thy ambassador a talisman precious beyond all that boasted gold of California. Let it loose his tongue to cry, "Long live the Republic, and may God bless the cause of the people, the brotherhood of nations and of men—the equality of rights for all." *Viva America!*

Hail to my country! May she live a free, a glorious, a loving life, and not perish like the old dominions from the leprosy of selfishness.

Evening

I am alone in the ghostly silence of a great house not long since full of gay faces and echoing with gay voices, now deserted by everyone but me —for almost all foreigners are gone now, driven by force either of the summer heats or the foe. I hear all the Spaniards are going now—that twenty-one have taken passports today; why that is, I do not know.

I shall not go till the last moment; my only fear is of France. I cannot think in any case there would be found men willing to damn themselves to latest posterity by bombarding Rome. Other cities they may treat thus, careless of destroying the innocent and helpless, the babe and old grandsire who cannot war against them. But Rome, precious inheritance of mankind— will they run the risk of marring her shrined treasures? Would they dare do it?

Two of the balls that struck St. Peter's have been sent to Pius IX by his children, who find themselves so much less "beloved" than were the Austrians.

These two days, days of solemn festivity in the calends of the Church, have been duly kept, and the population looks cheerful as it swarms through the streets. The order of Rome, thronged as it is with troops, is amazing. I go from one end to the other and amid the poorest and most barbarous of the population (barbarously ignorant, I mean) alone and on foot. My friends send out their little children alone with their nurses. The amount of crime is almost nothing to what it was. The Roman, no longer pent in ignorance and crouching beneath espionage, no longer stabs in the dark. His energies have true vent; his better feelings are roused; he has thrown aside the stiletto. The power here is indeed miraculous, since no doubt still lurk within the walls many who are eager to incite brawls, if only to give an excuse for slander.

Today I suppose twelve thousand Austrians marched into Florence. The Florentines have humbled and disgraced themselves in vain. They recalled the Grand Duke to ward off the entrance of the Austrians, but in vain went the deputation to Gaeta—in an American steamer! Leopold was afraid to come till his dear cousins of Austria had put everything in perfect order; then the Austrians entered to take Leghorn, but the Florentines still kept on imploring them not to come there; Florence was as subdued, as good as possible already—they have had the answer they deserved. Now they crown their work by giving over Guerazzi and Petracci to be tried by an Austrian court-martial. Truly the cup of shame brims over.

I have been out on the balcony to look over the city. All sleeps with that peculiar air of serene majesty known to this city only—this city that has grown not out of the necessities of commerce or the luxuries of wealth, but first out of heroism, then out of faith. Swelling domes, roofs softly tinted with yellow moss, what deep meaning, what deep repose, in your faintly seen outline!

The young moon climbs among clouds—the clouds of a departing thunderstorm. Tender, smiling moon, can it be that thy full orb may look down on a smoking, smoldering Rome, and see her best blood run along the stones without one nation in the world to defend, one to aid—scarce one to cry out a tardy "Shame"? We will wait, whisper the nations, and see if they can bear it. Rack them well to see if they are brave. *If they can do without us,* we will help them. Is it thus ye would be served in your turn? Beware!

LETTER XXXI

Rome, June 10, 1849

What shall I write of Rome in these sad but glorious days? Plain facts are the best; for my feelings I could not find fit words.

When I last wrote, the French were playing the second act of their farce.

In the first, the French government affected to consult the Assembly. The Assembly, or a majority of the Assembly, affected to believe the pretext it gave, and voted funds for twelve thousand men to go to Civita Vecchia. Arriving there, Oudinot proclaimed that he had come as a friend and brother. He was received as such. Immediately he took possession of the town, disarmed the Roman troops, and published a manifesto in direct opposition to his first declaration.

He sends to Rome that he is coming there as a friend; receives the answer that he is not wanted and cannot be trusted. This answer he chooses to consider as coming from a minority, and advances on Rome. The pretended majority on which he counts never shows itself by a single movement within the walls. He makes an assault and is defeated. On this subject his dispatches to his government are full of falsehoods that would disgrace the lowest pickpocket—falsehoods which it is impossible he should not know to be such.

The Assembly passed a vote of blame. M. Louis Bonaparte writes a letter of compliment and assurance that this course of violence shall be sustained. In conformity with this promise twelve thousand more troops are sent. This time it is not thought necessary to consult the Assembly. Let us view the second act.

Now appears in Rome M. Ferdinand Lesseps, Envoy, etc., of the French government. He declares himself clothed with full powers to treat with Rome. He cannot conceal his surprise at all he sees there, at the ability with which preparations have been made for defense, at the patriotic enthusiasm which pervades the population. Nevertheless, in beginning his game of treaty-making, he is not ashamed to insist on the French occupying the city. Again and again repulsed, he again and again returns to the charge on this point. And here I shall translate the letter addressed to him by the

Triumvirate, both because of its perfect candor of statement and to give an idea of the sweet and noble temper in which these treacherous aggressions have been met.

LETTER OF THE TRIUMVIRS TO MONSIEUR LESSEPS

"May 25, 1849

"We have had the honor, Monsieur, to furnish you in our note of the 16th with some information as to the unanimous consent which was given to the formation of the government of the Roman Republic. We today would speak to you of the actual question, such as it is debated in fact, if not by right, between the French government and ours. You will allow us to do it with the frankness demanded by the urgency of the situation, as well as the sympathy which ought to govern all relations between France and Italy. Our diplomacy is the truth, and the character given to your mission is a guaranty that the best possible interpretation will be given to what we shall say to you.

"With your permission we return for an instant to the cause of the present situation of affairs.

"In consequence of conferences and arrangements which took place without the government of the Roman Republic ever being called on to take part, it was some time since decided by the Catholic Powers: (1) That a modification should take place in the government and institutions of the Roman States; (2) That this modification should have for basis the return of Pius IX, not as Pope, for to that no obstacle is interposed by us, but as temporal sovereign; (3) That if to attain that aim a continuous intervention was judged necessary, that intervention should take place.

"We are willing to admit that while for some of the contracting governments the only motive was the hope of a general restoration and absolute return to the treaties of 1815, the French government was drawn into this agreement only in consequence of erroneous information, tending systematically to depict the Roman States as given up to anarchy and governed by terror exercised in the name of an audacious minority. We know also that in the modification proposed the French government intended to represent an influence more or less liberal, opposed to the absolutist program of Austria and of Naples. It does none the less remain true that under the Apostolic or constitutional form, with or without liberal guaranties to the Roman people, the dominant thought in all the negotiations to which we allude has been some sort of return toward the past, a compromise between the Roman people and Pius IX considered as temporal prince.

"We cannot dissemble to ourselves, Monsieur, that the French expedition has been planned and executed under the inspiration of this thought. Its object was on one side to throw the sword of France into the balance of negotiations which were to be opened at Rome; on the other to guarantee the Roman people from the excess of reaction, but always on condition that it should submit to constitutional monarchy in favor of the Holy Father. This is assured to us partly from information which we believe we possess as to the concert with Austria; from the proclamations of General Oudinot; from the formal declarations made by successive envoys to the Triumvirate; from the silence obstinately maintained whenever we have sought to approach the political question and obtain a formal declaration of the fact proved in our note of the 16th, that the institutions by which the Roman people are governed at this time are the free and spontaneous expression of the wish of the people inviolable when legally ascertained. For the rest the vote of the French Assembly sustains implicitly the fact that we affirm.

"In such a situation, under the menace of an inadmissible compromise and of negotiations which the state of our people noway provoked, our part, Monsieur, could not be doubtful. To resist—we owed this to our country, to France, to all Europe. We ought, in fulfillment of a mandate loyally given, loyally accepted, maintain to our country the inviolability, so far as that was possible to us, of its territory, and of the institutions decreed by all the powers, by all the elements of the state. We ought to conquer the time needed for appeal from France ill informed to France better informed, to save the sister republic the disgrace and the remorse which must be hers if rashly led on by bad suggestions from without, she became, before she was aware, accomplice in an act of violence to which we can find no parallel without going back to the partition of Poland in 1772. We owed it to Europe to maintain as far as we could the fundamental principles of all international life, the independence of each people in all that concerns its internal administration. We say it without pride—for if it is with enthusiasm that we resist the attempts of the Neapolitan monarchy and of Austria, our eternal enemy, it is with profound grief that we are ourselves constrained to contend with the arms of France—we believe in following this line of conduct we have deserved well not only of our country, but of all the people of Europe, even of France herself.

"We come to the actual question. You know, Monsieur, the events which have followed the French intervention. Our territory has been invaded by the King of Naples.

"Four thousand Spaniards were to embark on the 17th for invasion of this country. The Austrians, having surmounted the heroic resistance of Bologna, have advanced into Romagna and are now marching on Ancona.

"We have beaten and driven out of our territory the forces of the King of Naples. We believe we should do the same by the Austrian forces, if the attitude of the French here did not fetter our action.

"We are sorry to say it, but France must be informed that the expedition of Civita Vecchia, said to be planned for our protection, costs us very dear. Of all the interventions with which it is hoped to overwhelm us, that of the French has been the most perilous. Against the soldiers of Austria and the King of Naples we can fight, for God protects a good cause. But we *do not wish to fight* against the French. We are toward them in a state not of war, but of simple defense. But this position, the only one we wish to take wherever we meet France, has for us all the inconveniences without any of the favorable chances of war.

"The French expedition has from the first forced us to concentrate our troops, thus leaving our frontier open to Austrian invasion, and Bologna and the cities of Romagna unsustained. The Austrians have profited by this. After eight days of heroic resistance by the population, Bologna was forced to yield. We had bought in France arms for our defense. Of these ten thousand muskets have been detained between Marseille and Civita Vecchia. These are in your hands. Thus with a single blow you deprive us of ten thousand soldiers. In every armed man is a soldier against the Austrians.

"Your forces are disposed around our walls as if for a siege. They remain there without avowed aim or program. They have forced us to keep the city in a state of defense which weighs upon our finances. They force us to keep here a body of troops who might be saving our cities from the occupation and ravages of the Austrians. They hinder our going from place to place, our provisioning the city, our sending couriers. They keep minds in a state of excitement and distrust which might, if our population were less good and devoted, lead to sinister results. They do *not* engender anarchy or reaction, for both are impossible at Rome; but they sow the seed of irritation against France, and it is a misfortune for us who were accustomed to love and hope in her.

"We are besieged, Monsieur, besieged by France in the name of a protective mission, while some leagues off the King of Naples, flying, carries off our hostages, and the Austrian slays our brothers.

"You have presented propositions. Those propositions have been declared inadmissible by the Assembly. Today you add a fourth to the three already rejected. This says that France will protect from foreign invasion all that part of our territory that may be occupied by her troops. You must yourself feel that this changes nothing in our position.

"The parts of the territory occupied by your troops are in fact protected; but if only for the present, to what are they reduced? And if it is for the future, have we no other way to protect our territory than by giving it up entirely to you?

"The real intent of your demands is not stated. It is the occupation of Rome. This demand has constantly stood first in your list of propositions. Now we have had the honor to say to you, Monsieur, that is impossible. The people will never consent to it. If the occupation of Rome has for its aim only to protect it, the people thank you, but tell you at the same time that, able to defend Rome by their own forces, they would be dishonored even in your eyes by declaring themselves insufficient and needing the aid of some regiments of French soldiers. If the occupation has otherwise a political object, which God forbid, the people who have given themselves freely these institutions cannot suffer it. Rome is their capital, their palladium, their sacred city. They know very well that, apart from their principles, apart from their honor, there is civil war at the end of such an occupation. They are filled with distrust by your persistence. They foresee, the troops being once admitted, changes in men and in actions which would be fatal to their liberty. They know that in presence of foreign bayonets the independence of their Assembly, of their government, would be a vain word. They have always Civita Vecchia before their eyes.

"On this point be sure their will is irrevocable. They will be massacred from barricade to barricade before they will surrender. Can the soldiers of France wish to massacre a brother people whom they came to protect, because they do not wish to surrender to them their capital?

"There are for France only three parts to take in the Roman States. She ought to declare herself for us, against us, or neutral. To declare herself for us would be to recognize our republic, and fight side by side with us against the Austrians. To declare against us is to crush without motive the liberty, the national life, of a friendly people, and fight side by side with the Austrians. France *cannot* do that. She *will not* risk a European war to depress us, her ally. Let her then rest neutral in this conflict between us and our enemies. Only yesterday we hoped more from her, but today we demand but this.

"The occupation of Civita Vecchia is a fact accomplished; let it go. France thinks that in the present state of things she ought not to remain distant from the field of battle. She thinks that, vanquishers or vanquished, we may have need of her moderative action and of her protection. We do not think so; but we will not react against her. Let her keep Civita Vecchia. Let her even extend her encampments, if the numbers of her troops require it, in the healthy regions of Civita Vecchia and Viterbo. Let her then wait the issue of the combats about to take place. All facilities will be offered her, every proof of frank and cordial sympathy given; her officers can visit Rome, her soldiers have all the solace possible. But let her neutrality be sincere and without concealed plans. Let her declare herself in explicit terms. Let her leave us free to use all our forces. Let her restore our arms. Let her not by her cruisers drive back from our ports the men who come to our aid from other parts of Italy. Let her above all withdraw from before our walls, and cause even the appearance of hostility to cease between two nations who later undoubtedly are destined to unite in the same international faith, as now they have adopted the same form of government."

In his answer, Lesseps appears moved by this statement, and particularly expresses himself thus:

"One point appears above all to occupy you; it is the thought that we wish forcibly to impose upon you the obligation of receiving us as friends. *Friendship and violence are incompatible.* Thus it would be *inconsistent* on our part to begin by firing our cannon upon you, since we are your natural protectors. *Such a contradiction enters neither into my intentions, nor those of the government of the French republic, nor of our army and its honorable chief."*

These words were written at the headquarters of Oudinot, and of course seen and approved by him. At the same time in private conversation the "honorable chief" could swear he would occupy Rome by "one means or another." A few days after, Lesseps consented to conditions such as the Romans would tolerate. He no longer insisted on occupying Rome, but would content himself with good positions in the country. Oudinot protested that the Plenipotentiary had "exceeded his powers"—that he should not obey—that the armistice was at an end, and he should attack Rome on Monday. It was then Friday. He proposed to leave these two days for the few foreigners that remained to get out of town. M. Lesseps went off to Paris in great seeming indignation to get *his* treaty ratified. Of course we could not hear from him for eight or ten days. Meanwhile, the "honorable chief," alike in all his conduct, attacked on Sunday instead of Monday. The attack began before sunrise and lasted all day. I saw it from my window, which, though distant, commands the gates of St. Pancrazio. Why the whole force was bent on that part, I do not know. If they could take it, the town would be cannonaded, and the barricades useless; but it is the same with the Pincian Gate. Small parties made feints in two other directions, but they were at once repelled. The French fought with great bravery, and this time it is said with beautiful skill and order, sheltering themselves in their advance by movable barricades. The Italians fought like lions, and no inch of ground was gained by the assailants. The loss of the French is said to be very great: it could not be otherwise. Six or seven hundred Italians are dead or wounded. Among them are many officers, those of Garibaldi especially who are much exposed by their daring bravery and whose red tunic makes them the natural mark of the enemy. It seems to me great folly to wear such a dress amid the dark uniforms, but Garibaldi has always done it. He has now been wounded twice here and seventeen times in Ancona.

All this week I have been much at the hospitals where are these noble sufferers. They are full of enthusiasm; this time was no treason, no Vicenza, no Novara, no Milan. They had not been given up by wicked chiefs at the moment they were shedding their blood, and they had conquered. All were only anxious to get out again and be at their posts. They seemed to feel that those who died so gloriously were fortunate; perhaps they were, for if Rome is obliged to yield—and how can she stand always unaided against the four powers?—where shall these noble youths fly? They are the flower of the Italian youth; especially among the Lombards are some of the finest young men I have ever seen. If Rome falls, if Venice falls, there is no spot of Italian earth where they can abide more, and certainly no Italian will wish to take refuge in France. Truly you said, M. Lesseps, "Violence and friendship are incompatible."

A military funeral of the officer Ramerino was sadly picturesque and affecting. The white-robed priests went before the body singing, while his brothers in arms bore the lighted tapers. His horse followed, saddled and bridled. The horse hung his head and stepped dejectedly; he felt there was something strange and gloomy going on—felt that his master was laid low. Ramerino left a wife and children. A great proportion of those who run those risks are happily alone. Parents weep, but will not suffer long; their grief is not like that of widows and children.

Since the 3d we have only cannonade and skirmishes. The French are at their trenches, but cannot advance much; they are too much molested from the walls. The Romans have made one very successful sortie. The French availed themselves of a violent thunderstorm, when the walls were left more thinly guarded, to try to scale them, but were immediately driven back. It was thought by many that they never would be willing to throw bombs and shells into Rome, but they do whenever they can. That generous hope and faith in them as republicans and brothers, which put the best construction on their actions and believed in their truth as far as possible, is now destroyed. The government is false, and the people do not resist; the general is false, and the soldiers obey.

Meanwhile frightful sacrifices are being made by Rome. All her glorious oaks, all her gardens of delight, her casinos full of the monuments of genius and taste, are perishing in the defense. The houses, the trees which had been spared at the gate of St. Pancrazio, all afforded shelter to the foe, and caused so much loss of life that the Romans have now fully acquiesced in destruction agonizing to witness. Villa Borghese is finally laid waste, the villa of Raphael has perished, the trees are all cut down at Villa Albani, and the house, that most beautiful ornament of Rome, must, I suppose, go too. The stately marble forms are already driven from their place in that portico where Winckelmann sat and walked with such delight. Villa Salvage is burnt with all its fine frescoes, and that bank of the Tiber shorn of its lovely plantations.

Rome will never recover from the cruel ravage of these days, perhaps only just begun. I had often thought of living a few months near St. Peter's, that I might go as much as I liked to the church and the museum, and have Villa Pamfili and Monte Mario within the compass of a walk. It is not easy to find lodgings there, as it is a quarter foreigners never inhabit; but walking about to see what pleasant places there were, I had fixed my eye on a clean, simple house near Ponte St. Angelo. It bore on a tablet that it was the property of Angela ——; its little balconies with their old wooden rails full of flowers in humble earthen vases, the many birdcages, the air of domestic quiet and comfort, marked it as the home of some vestal or widow, some lone woman whose heart was centered in the ordinary and simplest pleasures of a home. I saw also she was one having the most limited income, and I thought, "She will not refuse to let me a room for a few months, as I shall be as quiet as herself and sympathize about the flowers and birds." Now the Villa Pamfili is all laid waste. The French encamp on Monte Mario; what they have done there is not known yet. The cannonade reverberates all day under the dome of St. Peter's, and the house of poor Angela is leveled with the ground. I hope her birds and the white peacocks of the Vatican gardens are in safety—but who cares for gentle, harmless creatures now?

I have been often interrupted while writing this letter, and suppose it is confused as well as incomplete. I hope my next may tell of something decisive one way or the other. News is not yet come from Lesseps, but the conduct of Oudinot and the formation of the new French ministry give reason to hope no good. Many seem resolved to force back Pius IX among his bleeding flock into the city ruined by him, where he cannot remain, and if he come, all this struggle and sorrow is to be borne over again. Mazzini stands firm as a rock. I know not whether he hopes for a successful issue, but he *believes* in a God bound to protect men who do what they deem their duty. Yet how long, O Lord, shall the few trample on the many?

I am surprised to see the air of perfect good faith with which articles from the London *Times* upon the revolutionary movements are copied into our papers. There exists not in Europe a paper more violently opposed to the cause of freedom than the *Times*, and neither its leaders nor its foreign correspondence is to be depended upon. It is said to receive money from Austria. I know not whether this be true, or whether it be merely subservient to the aristocratical feeling of England, which is far more opposed to republican movements than is that of Russia; for in England fear embitters hate. It is droll to remember our reading in the classbook,

Aye, down to the dust with them, slaves as they are,

to think how bitter the English were on the Italians who succumbed, and see how they hate those who resist. And their cowardice here in Italy is ludicrous. It is they who run away at the least intimation of danger—it is they who invent all the fee-faw-fum stories about Italy—it is they who write to the *Times* and elsewhere that they dare not for their lives stay in Rome, where I, a woman, walk everywhere alone, and all the little children do the same with their nurses. More of this anon.

LETTER XXXII

Rome, June 21, 1849

It is now two weeks since the first attack of Oudinot, and as yet we hear nothing decisive from Paris. I know not yet what news may have come last night, but by the morning's mail we did not even receive notice that Lesseps had arrived in Paris.

Whether Lesseps was consciously the servant of all these base intrigues, time will show. His conduct was boyish and foolish, if it was not treacherous. The only object seemed to be to create panic, to agitate, to take possession of Rome somehow, though what to do with it if they could get it, the French government would hardly know.

Pius IX, in his allocution of the 29th of April last, has explained himself fully. He has disavowed every liberal act which ever seemed to emanate from him, with the exception of the amnesty. He has shamelessly recalled his refusal to let Austrian blood be shed, while Roman flows daily at his request. He has implicitly declared that his future government, could he return, would be absolute despotism—has dispelled the last lingering illusion of those still anxious to apologize for him as only a prisoner now in the hands of the Cardinals and the King of Naples. The last frail link is broken that bound to him the people of Rome, and could the French restore him, they must frankly avow themselves, abandon entirely and fully the position they took in February 1848, and declare themselves the allies of Austria and of Russia.

Meanwhile they persevere in the jesuitical policy that has already disgraced and is to ruin them. After a week of vain assaults, Oudinot sent to Rome the following letter, which I translate, as well as the answers it elicited.

LETTER OF GENERAL OUDINOT

Intended for the Roman Constitutional Assembly, the Triumvirate, the Generalissimo, and the Commander-in-Chief of the National Guard

"General—The events of war have, as you know, conducted the French army to the gates of Rome.

"Should the entrance into the city remain closed against us, I should see myself constrained to employ immediately all the means of action that France has placed in my hands.

"Before having recourse to such terrible necessity, I think it my duty to make a last appeal to a people who cannot have toward France sentiments of hostility.

"The Roman army wishes, no doubt, equally with myself, to spare bloody ruin to the capital of the Christian world.

"With this conviction, I pray you, Signore General, to give the enclosed proclamation the most speedy publicity. If, twelve hours after this dispatch shall have been delivered to you, an answer corresponding to the honor and the intentions of France shall not have reached me, I shall be constrained to give the forcible attack.

"Accept, etc.

"Villa Pamfili, 12 June 1849, 5 p.m."

(He was in fact at Villa Santucci, much farther out, but could not be content without falsifying his date as well as all his statements.)

PROCLAMATION

"Inhabitants of Rome—We did not come to bring you war. We came to sustain among you order, with liberty. The intentions of our government have been misunderstood. The labors of the siege have conducted us under your walls. Till now we have wished only occasionally to answer the fire of your batteries. We approach these last moments, when the necessities of war burst out in terrible calamities. Spare them to a city full of so many glorious memories.

"If you persist in repelling us, on you alone will fall the responsibility of irreparable disasters."

The following are the answers of the various functionaries to whom this letter was sent:

ANSWER OF THE ASSEMBLY

"General—The Roman Constitutional Assembly informs you, in reply to your dispatch of yesterday, that, having concluded a convention from the 31st of May 1849 with M. de Lesseps, Minister Plenipotentiary of the French Republic, a convention which we confirmed soon after your protest, it must consider that convention obligatory for both parties, and indeed a safeguard of the rights of nations, until it has been ratified or declined by the government of France. Therefore the Assembly must regard as a violation of that convention every hostile act of the French army since the above-named 31st of May, and all others that shall take place before the resolution of your government can be made known, and before the expiration of the time agreed upon for the armistice. You demand, General, an answer correspondent to the intentions and power of France. Nothing could be more conformable with the intentions and power of France than to cease a flagrant violation of the rights of nations.

"Whatever may be the results of such violation, the people of Rome are not responsible for them. Rome is strong in its right, and decided to maintain the conventions which attach it to your nation; only it finds itself constrained by the necessity of self-defense to repel unjust aggressions.

"Accept, etc., for the Assembly,

"The President, GALLETTI

"Secretaries, FABRETTI, PANNACCHI, COCCHI"

ANSWER OF THE COMMANDER-IN-CHIEF OF THE NATIONAL GUARD

"General—The treaty, of which we await the ratification, assures this tranquil city from every disaster.

"The National Guard, destined to maintain order, has the duty of seconding the resolutions of the government; willingly and zealously it fulfills this duty, not caring for annoyance and fatigue.

"The National Guard showed very lately, when it escorted the prisoners sent back to you, its sympathy for France, but it shows also on every occasion a supreme regard for its own dignity, for the honor of Rome.

"Any misfortune to the capital of the Catholic world, to the monumental city, must be attributed not to the pacific citizens constrained to defend themselves, but solely to its aggressors.

"Accept, etc.

"STURBINETTI,
General of the National Guard, Representative of the People."

ANSWER OF THE GENERALISSIMO

"Citizen General—A fatality leads to conflict between the armies of two republics, whom a better destiny would have invited to combat against their common enemy; for the enemies of the one cannot fail to be also enemies of the other.

"We are not deceived, and shall combat by every means in our power whoever assails our institutions, for only the brave are worthy to stand before the French soldiers.

"Reflecting that there is a state of life worse than death, if the war you wage should put us in that state, it will be better to close our eyes forever than to see the interminable oppressions of our country.

"I wish you well, and desire fraternity.

"Rosselli"

ANSWER OF THE TRIUMVIRATE

"We have the honor to transmit to you the answer of the Assembly.

"We never break our promises. We have promised to defend, in execution of orders from the Assembly and people of Rome, the banner of the Republic, the honor of the country, and the sanctity of the capital of the Christian world; this promise we shall maintain.

"Accept, etc.

"The Triumvirs,

Armellini

Mazzini

Saffi"

Observe the miserable evasion of this missive of Oudinot: "The fortune of war has conducted us." What war? He pretended to come as a friend, a protector; is enraged only because after his deceits at Civita Vecchia Rome will not trust him within her walls. For this he daily sacrifices hundreds of lives. "The Roman people cannot be hostile to the French"? No, indeed; they were not disposed to be so. They had been stirred to emulation by the example of France. They had warmly hoped in her as their true ally. It required all that Oudinot has done to turn their faith to contempt and aversion.

Cowardly man! He knows now that he comes upon a city which wished to receive him only as a friend, and he cries, "With my cannon, with my bombs, I will compel you to let me betray you."

The conduct of France—infamous enough before—looks tenfold blacker now that, while the so-called Plenipotentiary is absent with the treaty to be ratified, her army daily assails Rome—assails in vain. After receiving these answers to his letter and proclamation, Oudinot turned all the force of his cannonade to make a breach, and began, what no one even in these days has believed possible, the bombardment of Rome.

Yes, the French, who pretend to be the advanced guard of civilization, are bombarding Rome! They dare take the risk of destroying the richest bequests made to man by the great past. Nay, they seem to do it in an especially barbarous manner. It was thought they would avoid as much as possible the hospitals for the wounded, marked to their view by the black banner, and the places where are the most precious monuments; but several bombs have fallen on the chief hospital, and the Capitol evidently is especially aimed at. They made a breach in the wall, but it was immediately filled up with a barricade, and all the week they have been repulsed in every attempt they made to gain ground, though with considerable loss of life on our side; on theirs it must be great, but how great we cannot know.

Ponte Molle, the scene of Raphael's fresco of a battle in the Vatican, saw again a fierce struggle last Friday. More than fifty were brought wounded into Rome.

But wounds and assaults only fire more and more the courage of her defenders. They feel the justice of their cause, and the peculiar iniquity of this aggression. In proportion as there seems little aid to be hoped from man, they seem to claim it from God. The noblest sentiments are heard from every lip, and thus far their acts amply correspond.

On the eve of the bombardment one or two officers went round with a fine band. It played on the piazzas the *Marseillaise* and Roman marches; and when the people were thus assembled, they were told of the proclamation, and asked how they felt. Many shouted loudly, *Guerra! Viva la Repubblica Romana!* Afterward, bands of young men went round singing the chorus,

> *Vogliamo sempre quella,*
> *Vogliamo Libertà.*

("We want always one thing; we want liberty.") Guitars played, and some danced. When the bombs began to come, one of the Trasteverini, those noble images of the old Roman race, redeemed her claim to that descent

pictures, was torn to pieces. I sat alone in my much exposed apartment, thinking, "If one strikes me, I only hope it will kill me at once, and that God will transport my soul to some sphere where virtue and love are not tyrannized over by egotism and brute force as in this." However, that night passed; the next, we had reason to expect a still more fiery salute toward the Pincian, as here alone remained three or four pieces of cannon which could be used. But on the morning of the 30th, in a contest at the foot of the Janiculum, the line, old Papal troops, naturally not in earnest like the free corps, refused to fight against odds so terrible. The heroic Marina fell, with hundreds of his devoted Lombards. Garibaldi saw his best officers perish, and himself went in the afternoon to say to the Assembly that further resistance was unavailing.

The Assembly sent to Oudinot, but he refused any conditions—refused even to guarantee a safe departure to Garibaldi, his brave foe. Notwithstanding, a great number of men left the other regiments to follow the leader whose courage had captivated them and whose superiority over difficulties commanded their entire confidence. Toward the evening of Monday, the 2d of July, it was known that the French were preparing to cross the river and take possession of all the city. I went into the Corso with some friends; it was filled with citizens and military. The carriage was stopped by the crowd near the Doria Palace; the lancers of Garibaldi galloped along in full career. I longed for Sir Walter Scott to be on earth again and see them; all are light, athletic, resolute figures, many of the forms of the finest manly beauty of the South, all sparkling with its genius and ennobled by the resolute spirit, ready to dare, to do, to die. We followed them to the piazza of St. John Lateran. Never have I seen a sight so beautiful, so romantic, and so sad. Whoever knows Rome knows the peculiar solemn grandeur of that piazza, scene of the first triumph of Rienzi, and whence may be seen the magnificence of the "mother of all churches," the baptistery with its porphyry columns, the Santa Scala with its glittering mosaics of the early ages, the obelisk standing fairest of any of those most imposing monuments of Rome, the view through the gates of the Campagna, on that side so richly strewn with ruins. The sun was setting, the crescent moon rising, the flower of the Italian youth were marshaling in that solemn place. They had been driven from every other spot where they had offered their hearts as bulwarks of Italian independence; in this last stronghold they had sacrificed hecatombs of their best and bravest in that cause; they must now go or remain prisoners and slaves. *Where* go, they knew not; for except distant Hungary there is not now a spot which would receive them, or where they can act as honor commands. They had all put on the beautiful dress of the Garibaldi legion, the tunic of bright red cloth, the Greek cap, or else round hat with puritan plume. Their long hair was blown back from resolute faces; all looked full of courage. They had counted the cost before they entered on this perilous struggle; they had weighed life and all its material advantages against liberty, and made their election; they turned not back nor flinched at this bitter crisis. I saw the wounded, all that could go, laden upon their baggage cars; some were already pale and fainting, still they wished to go. I saw many youths born to rich inheritance, carrying in a handkerchief all their worldly goods. The women were ready; their eyes too were resolved if sad. The wife of Garibaldi followed him on horseback. He himself was distinguished by the white tunic; his look was entirely that of a hero of the Middle Ages—his face still young, for the excitements of his life, though so many, have all been youthful, and there is no fatigue upon his brow or cheek. Fall or stand, one sees in him a man engaged in the career for which he is adapted by nature. He went upon the parapet and looked upon the road with a spyglass, and, no obstruction being in sight, he turned his face for a moment back upon Rome, then led the way through the gate. Hard was the heart, stony and seared the eye, that had no tear for that moment. Go, fated, gallant band! And if God care not indeed for men as for the sparrows, most of ye go forth to perish. And Rome, anew the Niobe! Must she lose also these beautiful and brave that promised her regeneration, and would have given it, but for the perfidy, the overpowering force, of the foreign intervention?

I know that many "respectable" gentlemen would be surprised to hear me speak in this way. Gentlemen who perform their "duties to society" by buying for themselves handsome clothes and furniture with the interest of their money speak of Garibaldi and his men as "brigands" and "vagabonds." Such are they, doubtless, in the same sense as Jesus, Moses, and Aeneas were. To me men who can throw so lightly aside the ease of wealth, the joys of affection, for the sake of what they deem honor, in whatsoever form, are the "respectable." No doubt there are in these bands a number of men of lawless minds, and who follow this banner only because there is for them no other path. But the greater part are the noble youths who have fled from the Austrian conscription, or fly now from the renewal of the Papal suffocation, darkened by French protection.

As for the protectors, they entirely threw aside the mask, as it was always supposed they would, the moment they had possession of Rome. I do not know whether they were really so bewildered by their priestly counselors as to imagine they would be well received in a city which they had bombarded, and where twelve hundred men were lying wounded by their assault. To say nothing of the justice or injustice of the matter, it could not be supposed that the Roman people, if it had any sense of dignity, would welcome them. I did not appear in the street, as I would not give any countenance to such a wrong; but an English lady, my friend, told me they seemed to look expectantly for the strong party of friends they had always pretended to have within the walls. The French officers looked up to the windows for ladies, and she being the only one they saw, saluted her. She made no reply. They then passed into the Corso. Many were assembled, the softer Romans being unable to control a curiosity the Milanese would have disclaimed, but preserving any icy silence. In an evil hour, a foolish priest dared to break it by the cry of *Viva Pio Nono!* The populace, roused to fury, rushed on him with their knives. He was much wounded; one or two others were killed in the rush. The people howled then, and hissed at the French, who, advancing their bayonets and clearing the way before them, fortified themselves in the piazzas. Next day the French troops were marched to and fro through Rome to inspire awe in the people; but it has only created a disgust amounting to loathing to see that, with such an imposing force and in great part fresh, the French were not ashamed to use bombs also, and kill women and children in their beds. Oudinot, then seeing the feeling of the people and finding they pursued as a spy any man who so much as showed the way to his soldiers—that the Italians went out of the cafés if Frenchmen entered—in short that the people regarded him and his followers in the same light as the Austrians—has declared martial law in Rome; the press is stifled; everybody is to be in the house at half past nine o'clock in the evening, and whoever in any way insults his men or puts any obstacle in their way is to be shot.

The fruits of all this will be the same as elsewhere; temporary repression will sow the seeds of perpetual resistance; and never was Rome in so fair a way to be educated for a republican form of government as now.

Especially could nothing be more irritating to an Italian population in the month of July than to drive them to their homes at half past nine. After the insupportable heat of the day, their only enjoyment and refreshment are found in evening walks and chats together as they sit before their cafés or in groups outside some friendly door. Now they must hurry home when the drum beats at nine o'clock. They are forbidden to stand or sit in groups, and this by their bombarding "protector"! Comment is unnecessary.

French soldiers are daily missing; of some it is known that they have been killed by the Trasteverini for daring to make court to their women. Of more than a hundred and fifty, it is only known that they cannot be found; and in two days of French "order" more acts of violence have been committed than in two months under the Triumvirate.

The French have taken up their quarters in the courtyards of the Quirinal and Venetian palaces, which are full of the wounded, many of whom have been driven wellnigh mad and their burning wounds exasperated by the sound of the drums and trumpets—the constant sense of an insulting presence. The wounded have been warned to leave the Quirinal at the end of eight days, though there are many who cannot be moved from bed to bed without causing them great anguish and peril; nor is it known that any other place has been provided as a hospital for them. At the Palazzo di Venezia the French have searched for three emigrants whom they wished to imprison, even in the apartments where the wounded were lying, running their bayonets into the mattresses. They have taken for themselves beds given by the Romans to the hospital—not public property but private gift. The Hospital of Santo Spirito was a governmental establishment, and in using a part of it for the wounded its director had been retained, because he had the reputation of being honest and not illiberal. But as soon as the French entered, he with true priestly baseness sent away the women nurses, saying he had no longer money to pay them, transported the wounded into a miserable, airless basement that had before been used as a granary, and appropriated the good apartments to the use of the French!

July 8

The report of this morning is that the French yesterday violated the domicile of our Consul, Mr. Brown, pretending to search for persons hidden there; but Mr. Brown, banner in one hand and sword in the other, repelled the assault and fairly drove them downstairs; that then he made them an appropriate speech, though in a mixed language of English, French, and Italian; that the crowd vehemently applauded Mr. Brown, who already was much liked for the warm sympathy he had shown the Romans in their aspirations and their distresses; and that he then donned his uniform and went to Oudinot to make his protest. How this was received I know not, but understand Mr. Brown departed with his family yesterday evening. Will America look as coldly on the insult to herself as she has on the struggle of this injured people?

Today an edict is out to disarm the National Guard. The generous "protectors" wish to take all the trouble upon themselves. Rome is full of them; at every step are met groups in the uniform of France, with faces bronzed in the African war and so stultified by a life without enthusiasm and without thought that I do not believe Napoleon would recognize them as French soldiers. The effect of their appearance compared with that of the Italian free corps is that of body as compared with spirit. It is easy to see how they could be used to purposes so contrary to the legitimate policy of France, for they do not look more intellectual, more fitted to have opinions of their own than the Austrian soldiery.

July 10

The plot thickens. The exact facts with regard to the invasion of Mr. Brown's house I have not been able to ascertain. I suppose they will be published, as Oudinot has promised to satisfy Mr. Cass. I must add, in reference to what I wrote some time ago of the position of our Envoy here, that the kind and sympathetic course of Mr. Cass toward the Republicans in these troubles, his very gentlemanly and courteous bearing, have from the minds of most removed all unpleasant feelings. They see that his position was very peculiar—sent to the Papal government, finding here the Republican, and just at that moment violently assailed. Unless he had extraordinary powers, he naturally felt obliged to communicate further with our government before acknowledging this. I shall always regret, however, that he did not stand free to occupy the high position that belonged to the representative of the United States at that moment, and peculiarly because it was by a republic that the Roman Republic was betrayed.

But as I say, the plot thickens. Yesterday three families were carried to prison because a boy crowed like a cock at the French soldiery from the windows of the house they occupied. Another, because a man pursued took refuge in their courtyard. At the same time, the city being mostly disarmed, came the edict to take down the insignia of the Republic, "emblems of anarchy." But worst of all they have done is an edict commanding all foreigners who had been in the service of the Republican government to leave Rome within twenty-four hours. This is the most infamous thing done yet, as it drives to desperation those who stayed because they had so many to go with and no place to go to, or because their relatives lie wounded here: no others wished to remain in Rome under present circumstances.

I am sick of breathing the same air with men capable of a part so utterly cruel and false. As soon as I can, I shall take refuge in the mountains, if it be possible to find an obscure nook unpervaded by these convulsions. Let not my friends be surprised if they do not hear from me for some time. I may not feel like writing. I have seen too much sorrow and, alas, without power to aid. It makes me sick to see the palaces and streets of Rome full of these infamous foreigners, and to note the already changed aspect of her population. The men of Rome had begun, filled with new hopes, to develop unknown energy—they walked quickly, their eyes sparkled, they delighted in duty, in responsibility; in a year of such life their effeminacy would have been vanquished. Now dejectedly, unemployed, they lounge along the streets, feeling that all the implements of labor, all the ensigns of hope, have been snatched from them. Their hands fall slack, their eyes rove aimless, the beggars begin to swarm again, and the black ravens who delight in the night of ignorance, the slumber of sloth, as the only sureties for their rule, emerge daily more and more frequent from their hiding-places.

The following address has been circulated from hand to hand.

"TO THE PEOPLE OF ROME

"Misfortune, brothers, has fallen upon us anew. But it is trial of brief duration—it is the stone of the sepulcher which we shall throw away after three days, rising victorious and renewed, an immortal nation. For with us are God and Justice—God and Justice, who cannot die but always triumph, while kings and popes once dead revive no more.

"As you have been great in the combat, be so in the days of sorrow—great in your conduct as citizens, by generous disdain, by sublime silence. Silence is the weapon we have now to use against the Cossacks of France and the priests, their masters.

"In the streets do not look at them; do not answer if they address you.

"In the cafés, in the eating-houses, if they enter, rise and go out.

"Let your windows remain closed as they pass.

"Never attend their feasts, their parades.

"Regard the harmony of their musical bands as tones of slavery, and when you hear them, fly.

"Let the liberticide soldier be condemned to isolation; let him atone in solitude and contempt for having served priests and kings.

"And you, Roman woman, masterpiece of God's work, deign no look, no smile to those satellites of an abhorred Pope! Cursed be she who, before the odious satellites of Austria, forgets that she is Italian! Her name shall be published for the execration of all her people! And even the courtesans —let them show love for their country, and thus regain the dignity of citizens!

"And our word of order, our cry of reunion and emancipation, be now and ever *Viva la Repubblica!*

"This incessant cry, which not even French slaves can dispute, shall prepare us to administer the bequest of our martyrs, shall be consoling dew to the immaculate and holy bones that repose, sublime holocaust of faith and of love, near our walls, and make doubly divine the Eternal City. In this cry we shall find ourselves always brothers, and we shall conquer.

Viva Rome, the capital of Italy! Viva the Italy of the people! Viva the Roman Republic!

"A Roman

"Rome, July 4, 1849"

Yes, July 4th, the day so joyously celebrated in our land, is that of the entrance of the French into Rome!

I know not whether the Romans will follow out this program with constancy, as the sterner Milanese have done. If they can, it will draw upon them endless persecutions, countless exactions, but at once educate and prove them worthy of a nobler life.

Yesterday I went over the scene of conflict. It was fearful even to *see* the Casinos Quattro Venti and Vascello, where the French and Romans had been several days so near one another, all shattered to pieces, with fragments of rich stucco and painting still sticking to rafters between the great holes made by the cannonade, and think that men had stayed and fought in them when only a mass of ruins. The French indeed were entirely sheltered the last days; to my unpracticed eyes, the extent and thoroughness of their works seemed miraculous, and gave me the first clear idea of the incompetency of the Italians to resist organized armies. I saw their commanders had not even known enough of the art of war to understand how the French were conducting the siege. It is true, their resources were at any rate inadequate to resistance; only continual sorties would have arrested the progress of the foe, and to make them and man the wall their forces were inadequate. I was struck more than ever by the heroic valor of *our* people—let me so call them now as ever; for go where I may, a large part of my heart will ever remain in Italy. I hope her children will always acknowledge me as a sister, though I drew not my first breath here. A *contadino* showed me where thirty-seven braves are buried beneath a heap of wall that fell upon them in the shock of one cannonade. A marble nymph, with broken arm, looked sadly that way from her sun-dried fountain; some roses were blooming still, some red oleanders, amid the ruin. The sun was casting its last light on the mountains on the tranquil, sad Campagna that sees one leaf more turned in the book of woe. This was in the Vascello. I then entered the French ground, all mapped and hollowed like a honeycomb. A pair of skeleton legs protruded from a bank of one barricade; lower, a dog had scratched away its light covering of earth from the body of a man, and discovered it lying face upward all dressed; the dog stood gazing on it with an air of stupid amazement. I thought at that moment, recalling some letters received: "O men and women of America, spared these frightful sights, these sudden wrecks of every hope, what angel of Heaven do you suppose has time to listen to your tales of morbid woe? If any find leisure to work for men today, think you not they have enough to do to care for the victims here?"

I see you have meetings where you speak of the Italians, the Hungarians. I pray you *do something;* let it not end in a mere cry of sentiment. That is better than to sneer at all that is liberal, like the English—than to talk of the holy victims of patriotism as "anarchists" and "brigands"—but it is not enough. It ought not to content your consciences. Do you owe no tithe to Heaven for the privileges it has showered on you, for whose achievement so many here suffer and perish daily? Deserve to retain them, by helping your fellow-men to acquire them. Our government must abstain from interference, but private action is practicable, is due. For Italy it is in this moment too late; but all that helps Hungary helps her also—helps all who wish the freedom of men from a hereditary yoke now become intolerable. Send money, send cheer—acknowledge as the legitimate leaders and rulers those men who represent the people, who understand their wants, who are ready to die or to live for their good. Kossuth I know not, but his people recognize him; Manin I know not, but with what firm nobleness, what persevering virtue, he has acted for Venice! Mazzini I know, the man and his acts, great, pure, and constant—a man to whom only the next age can do justice, as it reaps the harvest of the seed he has sown in this. Friends, countrymen, and lovers of virtue, lovers of freedom, lovers of truth! be on the alert; rest not supine in your easier lives, but remember

> Mankind is one,
> And beats with one great heart.

PART V

Letters

Prefatory Note

No book devoted to Margaret Fuller's writings would be complete without a section devoted to her letters. The letter was her second-best medium of expression, and since we cannot recover that conversation which awed and charmed her contemporaries, it is fortunate that we can find its echoes in the great stream of letters that poured from her pen during her lifetime. For it is clear that in her letters she wrote as she talked: all the traits reported of her as a conversationalist are to be found in these missives. And surely few correspondences have been more revealing of the personality that composed them.

This fact has not gone unrecognized. All Margaret's biographers have allowed much of her story to be told in her own words, drawn from the great masses of letters that she wrote at all periods of her career. Since the purpose of this volume is to make available such work of hers as has been inaccessible, this section of letters is devoted to letters newly discovered, previously unpublished, or radically revised from the originals when previously printed. An attempt has been made to illustrate her powers as a letter-writer from the beginning to the end of her life, and the diversity of her correspondents. The selection is not representative, in the sense that the best grapes have been culled by previous workers in the vineyard. The *Memoirs of Margaret Fuller Ossoli* is a storehouse of purple patches, freely edited and rarely identified. T. W. Higginson's biography is a more reliable source. The *Letters of Ralph Waldo Emerson* gives most of the letters to Emerson that have not appeared elsewhere in print. Margaret's letters to James Nathan appear in *Love-Letters of Margaret Fuller*. Many letters of the Italian period were first printed in Margaret Bell's biography. Originals and copies are partly collected in the Fuller MSS. of the Harvard College Library and the Boston Public Library; the remainder are scattered among the descendants of the vast circle of correspondents.

Letters

1. To Timothy Fuller *

Cambridgeport, January 8, 1819

Dear Papa

This paper is blotted but it is not my fault. While I was writing Eugene stood by the table. He laid the point of a penknife he had in his hand on it & in taking it up he made a blot. I do not think he did it intentionally & I should not have told you of it but I was afraid you would think me careless. I wrote a short letter to you as a forerunner to this. I think your maxim with regard to letter writing is good, but it is not easy for me to use it. For anybody whose ideas flow fast it is easy but as mine do not it is not to me. Like you Papa I have no faith in dreams. I want to ask you a question. Whether my manners ought to increase with my growth or with my years. Mamma says people will judge of me according to my growth. I do not think this is just for surely our knowledge does not increase because we are tall. Do you go to the Theatre often. Perhaps Mama has told you that Mr Wheeler is going to be married. He is to be married to the widow Balch of Dorchester. She is a very young widow for she is not more than 25 & is not likely to meet the fate of his former wives. Sarah Hartwell a favorite of Uncle Elishas is married to Mr Peirce. Weddings Balls Parties all are nothing to me, for I am not invited to them. I am soon to have lessons in drawing. Because of these Aunt Elizabeth has changed her mind & we shall go into Town Tomorrow morning so that I must finish this letter to night or else let it lie till Monday which I do not like to do. Mamma & my two Aunts are gone out Betsy is ironing in the kitchen William has got the old brush after vain efforts to get the new one & is pushing the fire out while Eugene is trying to prevent him from doing it.

So Papa I am Your affectionate Daughter

Sarah M Fuller

---

* Fuller MSS., Harvard College Library, Vol. IX, p. 6. Timothy Fuller was in Washington serving as Representative from Massachusetts when he received this letter from his eight-and-a-half-year-old daughter. The Eugene and William of this letter were Margaret's brothers.

2. To Mrs. Almira Barlow *

Groton, March 9, 1834

Are you not ashamed, oh most friendship-less clergywoman! not to have enlivened my long seclusion by one line? You can write to Mistress Mary Hedge, forsooth! to her you confide the history of your intellectual efforts, of your child's mental progress & various maladies, & of your successes in Brooklyn Society. Who is she, that you should prefer her to me as the depositary of all these interesting particulars? Can the Brooklyn Society have exercised so depraving an influence on your heart & tastes? Or does the author of the "Lecture delivered with much applause before the Brooklyn Lyceum," despise & wish to cast off the author of "Essays contumeliously rejected by that respected publication, the Christian Examiner?" That a little success should have such power to steel the female heart to base ingratitude! Oh Ally! Ally! wilt thou forget that it was I, (in happier hours thou hast full oft averred it) who first fanned the spark of thy ambition into a flame? Think'st thou that thou owest nought to those long sweeps over the insignificant, inexpressive realities of literature, when thou wert obliged to trust to my support, thy own opinions, as yet scarce budding from thy heels or shoulders? Dost thou forget,—but my emotions will not permit me to pursue the subject; surely I must have jogged your conscience sufficiently. I shall follow the instructions of the great Goethe, & having, in some degree vented my feelings, address you as if you were what you ought to be. Still remains enveloped in mystery the reason why neither you nor my reverend friend came to bid me good-bye before I left your city, according to promise. I suspected the waiter, at the time, of having intercepted your card: but your long, *venomous* silence has obliged me to acquit him. I had treasured up sundry little anecdotes touching my journey homeward, which, if related with dramatic skill, might excite a smile on your face, oh laughter-loving blue-stocking! I returned home under the protection of a Mr Fullerton, fresh

* *Works of S. M. F. Ossoli,* Harvard College Library, Vol. I, p. 7. Mrs. Almira Barlow, the wife of the Reverend D. H. Barlow, was one of Margaret Fuller's most intimate friends at this period. The letter supplies evidence of the self-pitying mood in which its author regarded her life on the Groton farm and enforced separation from the social and intellectual life of Cambridge.

from London & Paris, who gave me an entirely new view of continental affairs. He assured me that the German Prince was an ignorant pretender, in the face of my assurances that I had read & greatly admired his writings; & gave me a contemptuous description of Waldo Emerson *dining in boots* at Timothy Wiggin's, absolument à faire mourir! All his sayings were exquisite. And then a sui generis *Mother* whom I met with on board the steamboat. All my pretty pictures are blotted out by the rude hand of Time; verily, this checking of speech is dangerous. If all the matter I have been preserving for various persons, is in my head, packed away, distributed among the various organs, how immensely will my head be developed when I return to the world,—not admissible in good society, I fear. This is the first time in my life that I have known what it is to have nobody to speak to, c'est à dire, of my own peculiar little fancies. I bear it with strange philosophy, but I do wish to be written to. I will tell you how I pass my time, without society or exercise. Even till two o'clock, sometimes later, I pour ideas into the heads of the little Fullers; much runs out;—indeed I am often reminded of the chapter on home-education, in the New-Monthly. But the few drops which remain, mightily gladden the sight of my Father. Then I go down stairs & ask for my letters from the Post; this is my only pleasure: according to the ideas most people entertain of pleasure. Do you write me an excellent epistle by return of mail, or I will make your head ache by a minute account of the way in which the remaining hours are spent. I have only lately read the "Female Sovereigns" of your beloved Mrs Jameson, & like them better than any of her works. Her opinions are clearly expressed, sufficiently discriminating, & her manner unusually simple. I was not dazzled by excess of artificial light, nor cloyed by spiced & sweetened sentiments. My love to your reverend husband, & four kisses to Edward, two on your account, one for his beauty, & one abstract kiss, symbol of my love for all little children in general. Write of him, of Mr B's sermons, of your likes & dislikes, of any new characters, sublime or droll you may have unearthed, & of all other things I should like.

Affectionately your country friend, poor & humble, Margaret.

3. To Frederick Henry Hedge *

Boston, April 6, 1837

Dear Henry,

I have been wishing and wishing, trying and trying to write to you this past month and after all can get no hour for the fulfilment of so good a purpose unless at the fag end of a busy eve^g itself the flavorless post-act to a bustling day. So please take my letter kindly and marvel not if there should be nothing in it worthy of you—or me!

Firstly I would scold that you are not coming here till May. Here I have been living these six months and you would not come and now you must needs be planning to come just as I am going away. You manage very ill, to take no thought of me in any of your plans. The end of it will be that we shall not be able to talk when we do meet and that will, I think, be very grievous. For, upon the whole, I have had as satisfactory talks with you as I shall or can have in this world. And why must they end? Just because you will not come where I am.

Secondly Why is it that I hear you are writing a piece to "cut up Mr. Alcott?" I do not believe you are going to cut up Mr. Alcott. There are plenty of fish in the

[page missing]

things as *verses* and be content. I hope you are not so romantic as to think of raising people up to the level of your own tastes.

4thly Why did you not send me your lecture? Have not I a claim as a *literary friend?* I was obliged to *steal* it, which did not look well in me, a school-mistress!—These are all my questions.—

As to my biography, much of it cannot be given on a piece of paper like this. I have learned much and thought little, an operation which seems para-

---

* From a copy in Fuller MSS., Boston Public Library. F. H. Hedge, who graduated from Harvard College in 1825 and the Divinity School in 1828, was one of Margaret Fuller's earliest friends and intellectual companions. His knowledge of German and French literature, gained from five years of study abroad, did much to influence her intellectual development. From 1835 to 1850 he held a pastorate in Bangor, Maine, and made only periodic forays to Boston, although he kept in close touch with the currents of intellectual life there. The Transcendental circle was first known as Hedge's Club from the fact that gatherings were usually held upon the occasions of his visits.

doxical and *is* true. I faint with desire to think and surely shall, the first oppor.^{y}, but some outward requisition is ever knocking at the door of my mind and I am as ill placed as regards a chance to think as a haberdasher's prentice or the President of Harvard University— As to study my attention has been concentrated on the subjects about which I teach. There was a time when my dearest books became detestable to me on account of the duty work I did upon them. But that bad time is passed and I think I could do what I would if I staid here.

As to reading I have read only two books. Coleridge's literary remains and Eckermann's Conversations with Goethe, both very good.

I see many people and some of them are very pleasant but you know the best of them.

I have been very unwell all winter and am now rather worse. If May flowers and fair breezes do no good I must prepare either to leave this scene or become "that extremely common character, a confirmed invalid." But I intend to get perfectly well, if possible, for Mr. Carlyle says "it is wicked to be sick."—When you write tell me how you like his Mirabeau. I am sorry to hear that Mr. Bradford is going to leave you but glad you can hold converse with Mr. Woods.—I daresay I shall not write again, or if I do, no better a letter than this, for I write very bad letters now.

As ever your friend, S. M. Fuller.

4. To Arthur B. Fuller *

Greene St. School, Providence, December 31, 1837

My dear Arthur,

I wish I were near enough to send you some new year's gift tomorrow, but, since I am not, you shall at least have a letter. I thought you would like to have a picture of the house where I pass so many hours, & have therefore taken one of the bills to write upon. I sent one to Richard, & intend writing one to Lloyd in the same way bye & bye.

I was very glad to get your letter, but was sorry it was so short. I want my brother, who can talk so fluently, & who has many thoughts which *I* should think worth knowing, to learn to express himself in writing. It is the more important to me as I may probably be very little with you the remainder of my life, & if you do not learn to write, you & I, who have been such good friends, may become as strangers to one another. It is more desirable that you should write well than I, because you are changing more than I shall change, & because I have many occupations & many claims on my feelings & attention; you, comparatively few. I wish you would begin a letter to me as soon as you receive this; write in it from time to time as things occur worth telling, & whenever the sheet is full, send it me. I will not fail to answer it as soon as I can. You need not pay postage when you write to me, —but I will pay when I write to you,—for I suppose you want all your pocket-money.

You express gratitude for what I have taught you. It is in your power to repay me a hundred-fold, by making every exertion now to improve. I did not teach you as I would: yet I think the confinement, & care I took of you children at a time when my mind was so excited by many painful feelings, have had a very bad effect upon my health. I do not say this to pain you, or to make you more grateful to me (for, probably, if I had been aware at the time what I was doing, I might not have sacrificed myself so;) but I say it

---

* From the original, Fuller MSS., Harvard College Library, Vol. IX, p. 46. Arthur Fuller was Margaret's younger brother, in early life her pupil and after her death her editor. He became a clergyman and died while serving as a chaplain in the Civil War. This letter indicates to what an extent Margaret played the roles of father and mother to the younger Fullers.

that you may feel it your duty to fill my place, & do what I may never be permitted to do. Three precious years at the best period of my life, I gave all my best hours to you children; let me not see you idle away time which I have always valued so much: let me not find you unworthy of the love I felt for you. Those three years would have enabled me to make great attainments, which now I never may. Do you make them in my stead, that I may not remember that time with sadness. I hope you are fully aware of the great importance of your time this year. Your conduct now will decide your fate. You are now fifteen, & if at the end of the year, we have not reason to be satisfied that you have a decided taste for study, & ambition to make a figure in one of the professions, you will be consigned to some other walk in life. For you are aware that there is no money to be wasted on any of us, though, if I live & thrive, & you deserve my sympathy, you shall not want means & teaching to follow out any honorable path. With your sister Ellen's improvement, & desire to do right, & perseverance in overcoming obstacles, I am well satisfied. I feel pretty sure Richard will do well; but I feel greater anxiety about you, my dear Arthur; I know you have both heart, & head,— but you have always been deficient in earnestness, & forethought. May God bless you, & assist you to conquer these faults: & make this coming year a prelude to many honorable years. If Mr Haven is still at Leicester, I wish you to present my compliments to him, & say that I much regret never having had an opportunity of thanking him for his kind care of you when you were there before.

Next time I write, I will not fill my whole sheet with advice; advice generally does little good, but I will not believe I shall speak in vain to my dear Arthur.

Very affectionately your sister,

S. M. F.

5. To Caroline Sturgis *

Groton, March 9, 1839

Dearest Cary,

As this is the last day I suppose that I shall have a half hour's leisure to write to anyone, I heartily wish it were in my power to write you a good letter in return for yours which always have some good thought in them. But as it is not I think I will at least tell you why it is not.

Last night as I was lying awake and thinking in most painful restlessness of all possible things, and among others of your designs for my poems, I thought—thinks I to myself—Cary supposes, I daresay, that I do not love her much.

She always excused my writing her such miserable letters while I was at work with my school, but now, she thinks I am in solitude and at leisure, and, if I thought of her as I ought, would write her many letters full of pictures, thoughts, and sentiments.

Then thinks I to myself I'll tell her how I have passed the time since I came home. It will give her some idea of the way in which my life is drained off, and she will never be surprized at my omissions, and, perhaps, it may make her own leisure seem more valuable to her.

When I came home I was determined to take every precaution to ensure my having the whole time for myself.—I had it mentioned to all the neighbors, that I was worn out, and should not go out. I declined their invites so as not to offend them. Five or six of them who knew me best, made me short calls which I have not yet returned.

I have never been to any house and to church only once. I have not spent two hours in the society of any person out of our own family. I stay in my

---

* From the original in the possession of Mrs. Gorham Brooks of Brookline, Mass. Caroline Sturgis (Mrs. William A. Tappan) was one of Margaret's closest woman friends, along with her sister Ellen (Mrs. Robert William Hooper). She was something of a writer as well as an artist, contributing to the *Dial* and *Western Messenger*. It was with her that Margaret passed the autumn of 1844 at Fishkill on the Hudson, during which time she rewrote *Woman in the Nineteenth Century*. The letter gives a good picture of its author's life when she returned to Groton after teaching for two years at the Greene St. School in Providence. The translation referred to is that of *Eckermann's Conversations with Goethe,* which Margaret made for George Ripley's series of translations from the new German and French writers.

551

own room always till about nine in the eve^g; when very busy, I do not go down then or to meals. I have not seen half as much even of the family as I wished.

I had several loose robes fixed to wear this winter that I might lie down whenever I have severe pain, and apply friction, when necessary. This has really done good, and as I have only had the trouble of keeping myself *neat* without any *fixing,* dressing has not taken a quarter the time it usually does. Mother and Ellen have mended my clothes, when necessary. I have had no duties of the work^g sort except taking care of my own room, paying some attention to Mother and Ellen when sick and teaching Ellen and Richard two afternoons in the week.

Out of this whole time I have not been confined to the bed above four or five days in all. I have had no amusement to take up my time except that I have walked a mile or two those days when the weather permitted and five or six times have played on the piano.

For seven years I have never been able to pass two months so much as I pleased, and never expect it again, and I have been as industrious as any beaver. Why then will you say—no more or better letters?

I have had the curiosity to keep a list of my letters and I have written just 50 before this since the 3rd Jany when I came home—*more to you* than any-one else.

As soon as I came home I arranged the first two days my books & clothes. Then my papers which I had not been able to for more than three years. I haven't a great many, and I sent you those I selected for you.

I settled up the accts of my two little girls, wrote to them & their parents. I wrote about twenty letters then. This took about ten days, at the end of that time I was sick from fatigue. So soon as I was able to sit up, Mother & Ellen were sick. While they were so and I getting better I studied parts of Goethe, and read two of Plato's dialogues, and a no. of the London and Westminster. As soon as I was able, I began on my trans., revised what had been written, & compared with the orig. & wrote out the remainder. All the other writing I have done has been the other letters & a very little in my journal. All the reading I did was occasionally when lying down in day time Mr Very's sonnets & pieces, Jane's letters, the Stirlings in two Black-woods, and little bits of Plato, Coleridge, Goethe and Ben Jonson. After I went to bed I would read myself to sleep with chapters out of Vivian Grey and Marryatt's novels, and I read the debates in Congress. I also had talks with Mother about our future arrangements. This took up all my time till last Monday when before two o'clock, I finished my translation. In afternoon, I began my next piece of work on which I have been engaged ever since all day and all the eve^g, till today, I felt so wearied I thought I must take a holiday.

This is the arrangement of my father's papers, the accumulation of forty years from the time he entered College till now. He brought them all here hoping to arrange them himself.

I had no idea till I began what a labor it would prove, but, though I have been at work a week, and examined more than a thousand letters, I seem scarcely to have made an impression on the great heaps of papers. It is very interesting, though very fatiguing work, and teaches me a great deal.

As soon as I can get through with it, I shall pack the books which we are to take and select those we are to sell, and make many other arrangements for the auction which is to take place on the 19th. After that I shall have much to settle before I escape to Concord where I shall pass a day or two. Then to Boston, where I shall see you for some hours. Then we will talk of Poetry and Personality!—But I see I cannot write again, unless it be some short note. Perhaps you think I might as well have written something on such subjects as all these details, but I never can speculate when I am in practical trim,

> Still planning when
> And where and how the business can be done.

I have read of men who could write of such subjects in all the stir of every day life and yet play well their parts, but I confess this beyond me.

On the whole I feel with some sadness that I can hardly be a real friend to any one more. The claims upon me are now too many. I am always sacrificing myself more than is for my health or fame, yet I can do very little for any one person.

I know that you, my dear Cary, ask nothing, but I cannot help feeling you must expect it. So I think I will now say, Dear Cary, though you are much younger than I, yet I have that degree of respect for your mind and character that I can look on you as an equal friend. I also love you, and, probably, no other person you know could be so much to you as I, with all my shortcomings.—Can you be contented, in consideration of your great freedom and leisure, to do much for, receive little from me. Above all, can you be contented to write to me often and sometimes receive no reply, generally a meagre one. When I see you I shall always, I suppose, be able to talk. But writing is too fatiguing to my body, let alone the constant occupation of my mind. Yet not to hear from you often would grieve me. Indeed the week is darker hued in which I do not receive a letter. Yet they make me feel as if I ought to answer. If I am sure you do not expect it, and that you feel always that my mind answers, I shall write no letter unless I am able and then they will be good, if perhaps few.

I am ashamed when I think what letters I have written you, and I wish you would burn all the useless business scrawls. You deserve better treatment. I think I shall like the designs very much. They are complicated, but not more so than many of the best things in ancient and modern art. Please do them, and I will read you passages from Goethe's Propylea out at Willow Brook, as a fit expression of my gratitude.

I will not tell you now wh I like best for what I think good reasons till I see them in pencil.

I did not ask Mrs Jameson for anything except some local particulars. I still think her conduct ingenuous, but not so much so, since I now think her knowledge more scanty than I had supposed. And the book seems to be addressed to Mrs Austen: I do not wonder she thought it impertinent in an obscure stranger to propose doing what Mrs A, whom she seems so much to admire, did not feel competent to undertake. I have learnt some matters of fact from her book wh will be of use.

I send you my favorite Prince, as I believe you do not own him, and I thought you might like to read about his pictures, castles &c again. If not, only let him lie in your room until I come. He is too refined to be an intruder anywhere, though his coat is not in the best condition.

Will you do me the favor to send the other as directed.

Do write, if you can feel like it to

yrs affly

S.M.F.

6. To William Henry Channing *

Jamaica Plain, January 1, 1840

My dear William,

[first paragraph illegible]

I write to inform you that there is now every reason to hope that a first number of the much talked of new journal may be issued next April and to ask what you will give. I have counted on you for the first number because you seemed so really in earnest and said you had articles ready written. But I want to know what part you propose to take in the grand symphony and I pray you to answer me directly for we must proceed to tune the instruments. Mr Emerson is warmly interested and will give active assistance for a year. Mr Ripley and Mr Dwight are also in concert for others I know not yet. Will not Mr Vaughan give us some aid. His article on the Chartists excited interest here and we should like some such "large sharp strokes" of the pen very much.

This is a business letter—Mr Ripley would have written you a better, but he is too busy fighting the battles of Spinoza and other infidels. I am going to Mr Emerson's lecture and have only one hour to write three letters. So with best wishes for the coming year farewell,

S. Margaret Fuller

At Newport you prophecied a new literature; shall it dawn on 1840.

---

* From the original, Fuller MSS., Boston Public Library. William Henry Channing, a nephew of Dr. William Ellery Channing, was Margaret Fuller's friend from his student days at Harvard and the Divinity School. Graduating from the latter in 1833, he held pastorates in New York and Cincinnati. It was in his company that Margaret inspected the public institutions of New York and wrote pleas for their reformation in the *Tribune*. The present letter is concerned with the *Dial*, whose first number appeared the following July. Channing became one of the leading contributors.

7. To Mrs. Maria Weston Chapman *

Jamaica Plain, December 26, 1840

My dear Mrs. Chapman,

I received your note but a short time before I went to the conversation party. There was no time for me to think what I should do or even ascertain the objects of the Fair. Had I known them I could not by any slight suggestion have conveyed my views of such movements. And a conversation on the subject would interrupt the course adopted by my class. I therefore merely requested Miss Peabody to show the papers and your note to me before I began on the subject before us.

The Abolition course commands my respect, as do all efforts to relieve and raise suffering human nature. The faults of the party are such as it seems to me must always be incident to the partizan spirit. All that was noble and pure in their zeal has helped us all. For the disinterestedness and constancy of many individuals among you I have a high respect. Yet my own path leads a different course and often leaves me quite ignorant what you are doing as in the present instance of your Fair.

Very probably to one whose heart is so engaged as yours in particular measures this indifference will seem incredible or even culpable. But if indifferent I have not been intolerant: I have wronged none of you by a hasty judgement or careless words, and, when I have not investigated a case so as to be sure of my own opinion, have, at least, never chimed in with the popular hue and cry. I have always wished that efforts originating in a grievous sympathy, or a sense of right should have fair play; have had firm faith that they must, in some way, produce eventual good.

The late movements in your party have interested me more than those which had for their object the enfranchisement of the African only. Yet I presume I should still feel sympathy with your aims only not with your measures. Yet I should like to be more fully acquainted with both. The

---

* From the original in *Weston Papers,* 1840, Vol. II, p. 82, Boston Public Library. Mrs. Maria Weston Chapman, the grandmother of John Jay Chapman, was one of the New England women most active in the Abolitionist cause, with which Margaret Fuller was reluctant to associate herself. Mrs. Chapman had a leading part in organizing the annual Anti-Slavery Fairs.

late convention I attended hoping to hear some clear account of your wishes as to religious institutions and the social position of woman. But not only I heard nothing that pleased me, but no clear statement from any one. Have you in print what you consider an able exposition of the views of yourself and friends?—Or if not, should you like yourself to give me an account of how these subjects stand in your mind? As far as I know you seem to me quite wrong as to what is to be done for woman! She needs new helps I think, but not such as you propose. But I should like to know your view and your grounds more clearly than I do.

With respect   S. M. Fuller

8. To Ralph Waldo Emerson *

Boston, April 9, 1842

Dear Waldo,

I understand you have given notice to the Public, that, the Dial is to be under your care in future, & I am very glad of this for several reasons, though I did not like to express my feeling as you seemed reluctant to bind yourself in any way. But a year is short time enough for a fair trial.

Since it is now understood that you are Pilot, it is not needful for me to make the observations I had in view. The work cannot but change its character a good deal, but it will now be understood there is a change of director, too. The only way in which this is of importance to me is that I think you will sometimes reject pieces that I should not. For you have always had in view to make a good periodical and represent your own tastes, while I have had in view to let all kinds of people have freedom to say their say, for better, for worse.

Should time and my mood be propitious, I should like to write some pages on the amusements here this past winter, & a notice at some length of Hawthorne's Twice told tales. I was much interested by the Gipsey book, but dont incline to write about it—Longfellow sent us his poems, and if you have toleration for them, it would be well to have a short notice written by some one (*not* me)—I will have them sent to you & the little prayer book also. If you do not receive the latter, it will be because I could not get it, not because I have forgotten your wish. Please mention in your next, whether you did not find "Napoleon." I do not see it among my papers, and think I must have given it you.

* In *The Letters of Ralph Waldo Emerson,* edited by Ralph L. Rusk. Vol. III, pp. 45–6, note 170. Emerson, "that only clergyman of all possible clergymen who eludes my acquaintance," finally became Margaret Fuller's closest intellectual companion. Their correspondence is one of the most revealing pictures of the ideas and concerns of the Transcendental group, quite aside from its biographical interest. Of it Ralph L. Rusk, the editor of Emerson's letters, says: "After more than two years of irregular correspondence, with some long silences, the letters to Margaret Fuller multiplied until they poured forth in a steady stream during a large part of the period of the *Dial,* lessening after she withdrew from that journal, falling off still further when she migrated to New York and new interests, and ceasing finally shortly before her death in 1850." Almost all of Margaret Fuller's letters to Emerson are in the possession of the Ralph Waldo Emerson Memorial Association.

As to pecuniary matters, Miss Peabody I have found more exact & judicious than I expected, but she is variable in her attention, because she has so many private affairs. She will do very well under your supervision, but a connection with her offers no advantages for the spread of your work whatever it may be. But you have always thought the Dial required nothing of this kind. Much, much do I wish for myself I could find a publisher who is honest, and has also business talents. Such a connexion ought to be permanent. But I can hear of no person in Boston or elsewhere that it is desirable to be connected with, so I suppose I must still jog on as before, this dubious pace. But if ever you get any light in this quarter, pray impart.

I should think the Dial affairs were now in such a state that you could see clear into the coming year, and might economize about it considerably.

Well! I believe this is all I have to say, not much truly.

I leave town Monday eve^g & go to Cambridge for a few days. On Friday or Saturday I go to Canton to board with an Aunt of mine for four or five weeks. I think I shall be there perfectly retired and quiet; it suits my convenience in many respects to go. I wish I could feel as if the Muse would favor me there and then, but I feel at present so sad and languid, as if I should not know an hour of bright life again. It will be pity if this hangs about me just at the time when I might obey inspirations, if I had them, but these things are beyond control, and the demon no more forgets us than the angel. I will make myself no more promises *in time*. If you have any thing to say to me I should receive a letter here as late as Friday morn^g, if directed to Miss Peabody's care. Afterward direct to me at Canton, Care Charles Crane.

I thank you and Lidian for your invitation and know well your untiring hospitality. Should it seem well so to do, I will come. I cannot now tell how I shall feel. After Canton I shall go to Providence, for a few days, then to N. Bedford to pass a week with Aunt Mary Rotch. Farewell, dear Waldo. Yours as ever,

Margaret.

I still have thoughts of going to the West, but shall not know about it for some weeks.

9. To Richard F. Fuller *

Cambridge, August 11, 1842

Dear Richard,

I don't see any way I can do about your money, unless to enclose it in a letter. I am sorry to do this, as you will have to pay double postage, probably, and next time you must take enough to secure you against emergencies. If this sum is not enough, (I could not judge from your letter,) you might borrow a small sum from Mr Lawrence, and send it to him on your return, but I hope this will not be necessary.

Your letter was very pleasant to me, and as to the journal I shall be glad to read, ay, and correct it, too!! You do not speak of Groton. That place is very beautiful in its way, but I never admired it much, both because the scenery is too tamely smiling and sleepy, and because it jarred my mood. My associations with the place are painful. The first passage of our lives there was Arthur's misfortune, my first weeks there were passed in Arthur's chamber. There darkened round us the consequences of our father's ill-judged exchange, ill-judged at least as regarded himself, your mother, and myself. The younger ones were not violently rent from all their former life and cast on toils for which they were unprepared. There your mother's health was injured and mine destroyed; there your father died, but not till the cares of a narrowed income, and collisions with his elder sons which would not have ended there had so embittered his life and made him so over-anxious that I have never regretted that he did not stay longer to watch the turning of the tide, for his life up to 1830 had been one of well-earned prosperity, which, after that time, was rapidly ebbing from him, and I do not think adversity would have done him good. He could not reconcile himself to it, his feeling was that after thirty years labor and self-denial he was entitled to peace and he would not have had it.

You are too young to feel how trying are the disorders of a house which has lost its head, the miserable perplexities which arose in our affairs, the wounds your mother underwent in that time of deep dejection from the

* From the original, Fuller MSS., Harvard College Library, Vol. IX, p. 83. Richard was Margaret Fuller's younger brother and gradually took her place as head of the fatherless family after her removal to New York in 1844.

unfeeling and insolent conduct of many who had been kept in check by respect for your father, her loneliness and sense of unfitness for the new and heavy burden of care. It will be many years yet, before you can appreciate the conflicts of my mind, as I doubted whether to give up all which my heart desired for a path for which I had no skill, and no call, except that *some one* must tread it, and none else was ready. The Peterborough hills, and the Wachusetts are associated in my mind with many hours of anguish as great I think as I am capable of feeling. I used to look at them, towering to the sky, and feel that I, too, from my birth had longed to rise, but I felt crushed to earth, yet again a nobler spirit said *that* could never be, the good knight may come forth scarred and maimed from the unequal contest, shorn of his strength and unsightly to the careless eye, but the same fire burns within and deeper ever. He may be conquered but *never subdued.*

But if these beautiful hills, and wide, rich fields saw this sad lore well learned they also saw some precious lessons given too, of faith, of fortitude, of self-command, and a less selfish love. There too in solitude the mind acquired more powers of concentration and discovered the beauty of a strict method. There the heart was awakened to sympathize with the ignorant, to pity the vulgar, and to hope for the seemingly worthless. For a need was felt of realizing the only reality, the divine soul of this visible creation, which cannot err and will not sleep, which cannot permit evil to be permanent or its aim of beauty to be eventually frustrated in the smallest particular. Ought I not to say that my younger brothers too laid there the foundations of more robust, enterprizing and at the same time self-denying character than the elder had been led to by more indulgent fortune. Ellery is gone to Concord to stay, and you can see him there at any time. He now expects to pass the winter there in writing. Mother and Ellen will return by the middle of Lent. If you defer your visit till the end of the week, or till you are on your way back to Cambridge, you may see me too. I shall probably be there next week. I am glad you like your books. I have been reading Herodotus. I find these Greeks, though I can only read them in translation, the most healthful and satisfying companions. I keep one of them by me always now. You should not have tried Cousin on Locke but his Introduction.

Affectionately your sister M.

10. To William Ellery Channing, Jr.*

[*October* 3, 1842]

Dear Ellery,

I had fixed today as the one on which I would write to you for this third of October has been a saint's day in my calendar, as the birthday of our friend Ward, who for many years seemed born for cheer and companionship to me, the fair child of my hopes. Last year it was his marriage day also. I must always think of him in connexion with you, for almost as early as we were intimate he wished to have me prize you also, and you were the only living man about whom he desired my sympathy, indeed the only one whom he had worthily met. And all along these years, he has copied your verses and quoted your words whenever his own seemed inadequate, esteeming you of clearer insight, and, in some respects, of finer temper than himself. Thus have you been so far made known to me that I feel little doubt how I shall feel toward you. You say you cannot promise me any thing nor tell how any character shall affect you. I had not thought of this for, of a nature which the observer may call vain and presumptuous or affectionate and trustful at his pleasure, it never occurs to me that those I am inclined to love may not receive me till they themselves suggest it. But now I do think of it. There may be much you cannot meet. My character and life have been of various strain and mine is now in a sense a worldly character & one of many sides. You may not like or enjoy meeting me, and I shall not set my heart upon it. It will, however, be easy for me to bear it, if you do not, as I have been long trained to all the forms of separation, and I shall not prize you the less. Should you prove the wise and faithful guardian of my sister's happiness; should you be the means of unfolding what is beautiful in her character, and leading her tenderly to her true aim, you will have conferred on me a benefit, beyond requital, and only to be answered in prayer.

---

* From the original, Fuller MSS., Harvard College Library, Vol. IX, p. 82. William Ellery Channing, Jr., the poet nephew of Dr. Channing and cousin of William Henry Channing, married Margaret Fuller's sister Ellen in 1842. The Channings abandoned the idea of living at Brook Farm and took up residence in the Red Cottage on the turnpike in Concord, after Margaret's attempt to induce the newly married Hawthornes to take them as boarders had been repulsed.

I think still more of Mother than myself in reference to Ellen. Eugene and Ellen are truly Mother's children in all that can adorn and enliven domestic life. Mother's eyes were of the same glistening blue, and she gave herself with the same full heart up to a feeling that Ellen does. Those bright tints are faded now, and Mother's sweetness is more saintly since she is less a wife and mother and more of the lay nun. Yet I could not wish more for Ellen than that she should be as lovely, as happy, and as good as her Mother has been while the springs of life were yet unbroken. I feel sure you will be able to love Mother, and that the bond between her and Ellen will not be weakened by her marriage.

This has been a great shock to Mother for it was an event so important in time and eternity that those at a distance felt as if all was done too hastily, and the thoughts of all that it might lead to thronged too fast upon a Mother's heart. Yet we all feel a greater degree of clearness that you have taken your mutual destiny so decidedly in your own hands: we wish to trust your inward leading which has spoken in tones so determined.—Yet, as to the future, I hope you will advise with your cousin William as to whether it will be for your good to come here. He knows you, and knows Ellen: he has surveyed the ground with reference to himself, and can give you a wise judgment. Of all the plans of which Ellen wrote to me the only one which strikes me favorably is that which projects your connexion with him. In the Ripleys' community you would find a little city, and, *at present,* with less freedom of walk and feeling than elsewhere. It will not be so always if they carry out their original intentions, but at present you would hardly find quiet and an atmosphere sane and genial for young affections. By and by, if you would have a little cottage of your own, and only labor not live with the rest, it might be well for you.—I have written as to my brother, yet I do not know whether the vow has been pronounced in the sight of Man. Tomorrow I trust will bring us a letter. In hope and affectionate goodwill,

Yours

Margaret F.

11. To Ralph Waldo Emerson *

October 16 [1842]

Dear Waldo—I can hardly believe that it is a month this day since I passed a true Sabbath in reading your journals, and Ellery's book, and talking with you in the study. I have not felt separated from you yet.—It is not yet time for me to have my dwelling near you. I get, after a while, even *intoxicated* with your mind, and do not live enough in myself. Now don't screw up your lip to an ungracious pettiness, but hear the words of frank affection as they deserve "mente cordis." Let no cold breath paralyze my hope that there will yet be a noble and profound understanding between us. We have gone so far, and yet so little way. I understand the leadings of your thought better & better, and I feel a conviction that I shall be worthy of this friendship, that I shall be led day by day to purify, to harmonize my being, to enlarge my experiences, and clear the eye of intelligence till after long long patient waiting yourself shall claim a thousand years' interview at least. You need not be terrified at this prophecy nor look about for the keys of your cell.—*I* shall never claim an hour I begin to understand where I am, and feel more and more unfit to be with any body. I shall no more be so ruled by the affectionate expansions of my heart but my hope is great, though my daily life must be pallid and narrow.

I must not try to say to you much that has passed in my mind which I should like you to know. I find no adequate expression for it.

I do not know whether it is owing to this feeling of your mind being too near me that I have not yet been able to finish the ragged rhymes I meant for you. I got along well enough till the point of division came, where I wanted to show that the permanent marriage cannot interfere with the soul's destiny, when lo! this future which has seemed so clear, vanished and left me without a word, yet unconvinced of your way of thinking. There lies the paper, and I expect the hour may come when I can make out my case, if so, it will be sent

---

* In the *Letters of Ralph Waldo Emerson,* edited by Ralph L. Rusk. Vol. III, pp. 89–90, note 334. The letters written by Emerson before and after this epistle are to be found in Rusk's work. See note, p. 558.

Will you have the rhymes I gave Lidian copied & sent me by Ellery, that is, if she wishes to retain the original. *Dont* think this request silly: I want to put them in my journal of that week. They interest me from their connection And will you send my little picture and all the papers you have of mine E. Hooper's & Caroline's letters &—Penknife & key were touching symbols for me to leave, how can L. wish to send them back?—My love to her. I hoped she had had her share of nervous fever. To be sick & lose this weather of Paradise is sad. I have lost it well nigh as much amid my affairs. And yet not wholly for though shut up in the house, I have had the loveliest view from my window the same as from the window where I used to read the Italian poets, in young days. The thoughts of that time come back like an old familiar music at sight of the river & gentle hills; they are fair to me still. Heaven be praised it is the same cadence that I love best now, though then less rich, less deep—

Apropos to the Italians, I am inclined to suspect H. T. of a grave joke upon my views, with his "dauntless *infamy*."—There is also *abstraction* for *obstruction,* which one would have thought such hacknied Shakspeare might have avoided.—I *am a little* vexed, having hoped my notice might meet the eye of the poet. Henry's verses read well, but meseems he has spoiled his "Rumors" &c by substituting

And simple truth on every tongue

for all the poems are unsung, or some such line which was *the* one that gave most character to the original and yet I admire the

tread of high souled men.

The Dirge is more & more beautiful, & others feel it no less than I. S. Ward no less.—I like Parker's piece much; it is excellent in its way, the sneer is mild, almost courtly. Your essay I have read with delight, but it is true the passage about fate is weak; Seek a better. Why cannot the fate behind fate be brought out somehow? Saadi I have read many times. As to my own piece every one praises the few Rhine ballads, none the Romaic. If you could get me vouchers of interest for the Romaics, I should be encouraged to make a rosary of all the rest.—If any thing occurs to me I shall write for your Dial. I think now I should like to write my impressions of Dr Channing. If you go away I should *rather* you would leave the *Record of the Months* to me than to any one else, allowing sixteen or twenty pages for it, but if you are here, will give any thing I may have to your discretion.—The new Essays, come and read to me, if not to Boston, I pray.

Alas! here I am at the end of my paper, and have told you nothing of my stay at Brook Farm, where I gave *conversations* on alternate evenings with the husking parties. But you will come to see me in my new home, & then I will tell you. My first visitor last Sunday was S. Ward. My second next day W. Channing. The following day I expected *you,* & since you were not so kind as to come, observe with pleasure that your letter dates from that day. Adieu, dear friend, be good to me, think of me, and write to me. The days of toil & care are coming when I shall need your ray, mellow if distant. I owe to the protection of your roof, to the soothing influence of your neighborhood, and to the gentle beauty of the Concord woods, some weeks of health and peace which have revived my courage, so unusually dulled last summer. To Lidians unfailing and generous kindness also I owe much. But you must be the better to me for my thanks

"Most welcome they who need him most."

Love to Mamma and Lidian, and salute for me sweet Edith of the dewy eyes

Richter is as you say. I will send you a little notice of the book from my journal.

12. To William Henry Channing *

Sunday evening, November 17, 1844

At last, my dear William, I have finished the pamphlet. The last day it kept spinning out beneath my hand. After taking a long walk early on one of the noble exhilerating sort of mornings I sat down to write & did not put the last stroke till near nine in the evening. Then I felt a delightful glow as if I had put a good deal of my true life in it, as if, suppose I went away now, the measure of my foot-print would be left on the earth. That was several days ago, and I do not know how it will look on revision, for I must leave several days more between me & it before I undertake that, but think it will be much better than if it had been finished at Cambridge, for here has been no headach, and leisure to choose my hours.

It will make a pamphlet rather larger than a number of the Dial, & would take a fortnight or more to print. Therefore I am anxious to the matter *en train* before I come to N.Y. that I may begin the 1st Decr for I want to have it out by Christmas. Will you see Mr Greeley about it the latter part of this week or the beginning of next. He is absent now, but will be back by that time & I will write to him about it. Perhaps he will like to undertake it himself.

The estimate you sent me last summer was made expecting an edition of fifteen hundred, but I think a thousand will be enough. The writing, though I have tried to make my meaning full and clear, requires, shall I say? too much culture in the reader, to be quickly or extensively diffused. I shall be satisfied if it moves a mind here & there & through that others; I shall be well satisfied if an edition of a thousand is disposed of in the course of two or three years. If the expense of publication should not exceed or cover a hundred and fifty dollars, I should not be unwilling to undertake it, if thought best by you & Mr G. But I suppose you would not think that the favorable way as to securing a sale.

If given to a publisher I wish to dispose of it only for one edition. I should

---

* From the original, Fuller MSS., Boston Public Library. See note, p. 555.

hope to be able to make it constantly better while I live & should wish to retain full command of it, in case of subsequent edition.

[rest of letter cut out]

Adieu, dear Friend

13. To Mrs. Sarah Shaw *

Fishkill Landing, November 20, 1844

My dear Sarah,

Two months have passed since I was with you, passed with winged swiftness, yet that swiftness has not been as that of the arrow straight to one mark, but rather as that of the bee who finds time to stop wherever he can collect his honey. Happy and blessed have been the weeks of seclusion, the society of the mountains, so bold and so calm, the long mountain paths that suggest the enchantments of nature, the spells of wisdom waiting in the secret for the approach of patient steps; the river so grand and fair with its two thousand sails, each moving softly as an angel's thought, and looking, *in the distance,* as spotless and glittering; and its great boats advancing now and then with a triumphant stride, like some noble discovery breaking in upon the habitual course of human events to inform and extend it.— Then after the days of exercise, how pleasant the evening of study or writing by the bright wood fire. The days come to an end solid and unbroken by frivolity or conflict.

Next week it ends and I return from this pleasant life of the *free man* to the busy rushing world. But I am willing; after such a pleasant time I feel refreshed for the melée & willing to take my share of the press of life.

If you send the box by the 28th to the office of the N.Y. Tribune directed to me care Horace Greeley, the friendly warmth of your gifts will defend my heart from the cold, as I walk the wide streets of the stranger & meet their foreign gaze.

It pleases me much to combine you two in one gift. I shall think of all that is pleasantest, of my Sarah "the Mother" and of her frank and loving intercourse with me. I shall think of Frank, *the* frank, and his wise plans for the good of injured man.—Cary says the Forbes also are anxiously plotting such means of reform. So if Jesus came here, he would not find all unjust stewards. Say to Anna that her swift and warm response gave

---

* From the original in the possession of Mrs. Pierre Jay of New York City. Mrs. Sarah Shaw, the wife of Francis G. Shaw and the mother of Colonel Robert Gould Shaw of Civil War fame, was active in Margaret Fuller's Conversation classes,

me joy. I shall write to her when I have leisure. Love to Sarah. In the spring she gave me violets, in the autumn grapes, was not that expressive of the promise given by her grand nature? Good angels tend to its proper flower and fruit!

I wish you would write to me fully of yourself and of the children. And tell me also *the news,* which no one writes us. We heard J. King and W. Story were dangerously ill, but not the result. Now in the distance I want some facts as well as thoughts from my friends. As to the letter for Dr El-liot, I am so well now, it seems as if I should never more be ill, but I sup-pose the old causes may bring in the old results, & I want some refuge in case of violent assault from my enemy, so should like the letter to use in case of need.

Is the St. with you & if so, how does the plan prosper? I did what I could for you by persuading the Farrars to try her, but in a few hours Mr F. pro-nounced her a "well intentioned woman of tolerable manners but weak and silly." So of course, she would not answer there. Of other things, too, you were to write me.

I have enjoyed being with Cary. Her relation has been entirely pleasant and to me often profitable. Adieu, dear Sarah, give kisses to the gay little troop, especially the apaso [?] dancer, whose inventions it makes me laugh to recollect.

Always your friend,
M.F.

14. To Elizabeth Palmer Peabody *

New York, December 26, 1844

Dear Elizabeth,

I wished to earlier answer your good letter, but my life begins to be crowded and, à l'ordinaire,—pain in the side or spine follows much exertion. I am obliged to be especially careful not to write too much.

I like my position very well; think I can fill it, and learn a great deal in it. This scene brings me many fresh impressions.

Let me answer, in brief, to the most interesting part of your letter. Probably, I have, as you say, a large share of prudence by nature. It has not, however, been large enough to save me from being much disappointed, in various relations, by a want of delicacy and tenderness from those who had seemed capable of it. But, perceiving similar faults in me, and yet knowing my heart capable of pure and intelligent love, I believe them so, too, and that we shall all be better, and do better as we grow.

The tone of your letter was so mild, and its spirit so comprehensive, that I felt as if you *must* be nearer peace than I had ever expected to find you in this world. Yet your tendency to extremes, as to personal attachments, is so strong, I am afraid you will not wholly rise above it.

The persons whom you have idolized can never, in the end, be ungrateful, and, probably, at the time of retreat they still do justice to your heart. But, so long as you must draw persons too near you, a temporary recoil is sure to follow. It is the character striving to defend itself from a heating and suffocating action upon it.—

A little, only a little less of this in you would give your powers the degree of fresh air they need. Could you be as generous and sympathetic, yet never infatuated; then the blur, the haste, the tangle would disappear, and neither I nor any one could refuse to understand you.

* From a copy, *Works of S. M. F. Ossoli,* Harvard College Library, Vol. III, p. 261. Elizabeth Palmer Peabody anticipated Margaret Fuller's Conversations by similar gatherings in 1833 and 1836, and like her taught at Bronson Alcott's Temple School and served Dr. Channing as literary assistant. She conducted the West Street bookshop, which served as intellectual arsenal to the Transcendental circle, and published Margaret Fuller's translation of the *Correspondence of Fräulein Günderode and Bettina von Arnim,* to which the present letter refers.

I admit that I have never done you justice. There is so much in you that is hostile to my wishes, as to character, and especially as to the character of woman; how could I be quite candid! Yet when I have looked at you, truly, I have also looked steadily, and always feel myself in your debt that you cordially pardon all that must be to you repressing—and unpleasant in me.

To the care of the fair spirit that sometimes looks out so full through your features and your conduct I commend you. It must finally give you back all your friends.

As to Guenderode, I should like much to have the copies boxed up, after having been counted, you reserving some on sale, and sending me *ten,* which I will distribute from time to time. Should I ever get a name, probably I may be able to finish the translation on good terms, but shall, at present, do nothing about it.

As the copyright was taken in your name, I also wish a writing from you relinquishing any title to it, and in the same letter, acquaint me how much is still due you, for the expense for publication. I will not pay you till it is convenient, but *then* I wish to do so, and it is right I should. The ten copies I should be very glad to have the day before New Year's day and with them 2 sets of the etchings I left for sale with you. A set of these makes a pretty present.

My pamphlet on woman is in press at last, and you will receive it ere very long.

Can you with all convenient speed, send the enclosed to B. Randall, and have that to Mrs. F. put into the Post Office. Remember me to your Mother and know me all yours in friendliest good will. Margaret.

15. To Mrs. Sarah Shaw *

New York, February 25, 1845

My dear Sarah,

I do regret never getting time to write letters, but I cannot yet. Do not forget to think of me sometimes. I wish I could have letters to tell me of all your news. I sent my book on Woman &c to my three female friends, in your house, as, indeed, I know no better women. Write me, if any thoughts come to you about it. Also of your own private news. Anna, too, I want to hear from. Next August I expect to see you all. I shall then be in Mass. for several weeks. Meantime I hear much of Frank in Fourierite association. Sarah seems more quiescent in the grand measures of social renovation.

I like living here. All flows freely: and I find I don't dislike wickedness and wretchedness more than pettiness and coldness. My own individual life is easy to lead. No doubt I shall have many stories to tell when we meet.— Could you and Frank know through how many scenes of cold and storm the muff and boa have protected me, you would rejoice in the affectionate gift! What a note this is! wasting [?] N.Y. but it is only meant to convey the loving remembrances of your friend Margaret.

---

* From the original in the possession of Mrs. Pierre Jay of New York City. See note, p. 569.

16. To Eugene Fuller *

[*New York, February* 1845?]

Dearest Eugene,

Your Arkansas letter was received with great joy. It was long since I had heard from yourself and as usual, I cannot obtain much information from the family. It is true I deserve not from them, as the necessity of doing so much other writing makes me a bad correspondent to them and to every one.—

I am glad too to hear of your health, and that with the ennui of so long a journey at such a time, you were able to make some profit. Profit always sounds like your coming back to us, which, amid the whirl of a busy life, I cannot cease to wish, and which Mother has only too much leisure to dream about.

I do not know much of the family, except, that Mother is still troubled with dyspepsia, but, in other regards, not sick. Ellen well, and the child, they say most lovely. Richard doing well. For me I have never been so well situated. As to a home the place where we live is old and dilapidated but in a situation of great natural loveliness. When there, I am perfectly secluded, yet every one I wish to see comes to see me, and I can get to the centre of the City in half an hour. The house is kept in a Castle Rackrent style, but there is all affection for me and desire to make me at home, and I do feel so, which could scarcely have been expected from such an arrangement. My room is delightful; how I wish you could sit at its window with me and see the sails glide by!

As to the public part, that is entirely satisfactory, I do just as I please and as much or little as I please, and the Editors express themselves perfectly satisfied, and others say that my pieces *tell* to a degree I could not expect. I think, too, I shall do better and better. I am truly interested in this great field which opens before me and it is pleasant to be sure of a chance at half a hundred thousand readers.

* From a copy, *Works of S. M. F. Ossoli,* Harvard College Library, Vol. II, p. 765. Eugene Fuller, who was Margaret Fuller's favorite brother, early left home to try to make his way in the West and South.

Mr. Greeley I like, nay more, love. He is, in his habits, a —————— plebeian; in his heart, a noble man. His abilities, in his own way, are great. He believes in mine to a surprising extent. We are true friends.—

It was pleasant you should see that little notice in that wild place. The book is out, and the theme of all the newspapers and many of the journals. Abuse public and private is lavished upon its views, but respect expressed for me personally. But the most speaking fact and the one which satisfied me, is that the whole edition was sold off in a week to the booksellers and $85 handed to me as my share. Not that my object was in any wise money, but I consider this the signet of success. If one can be heard that is enough; I shall send you two copies one for yourself and one to give away, if you like. If you notice it in a N.O. paper, you might create a demand for it there: the next edition will be out in May. In your next letter tell me your address that I may know what to do when I wish to send parcels to you.

I wish you would write a series of letters about what you have seen in Arkansas and the Southwest, that I might use in the Tribune, if I thought best. I think you would do this well. Write one at least, about this late tour, as a sample and tell about Wild Cat &c, *out full.*

I have a great deal of music, having free entrance every where from my connection with the paper. Part of the Italian Opera Corps is now at N.O. and I hope you will hear them perform   with which I was enchanted, I am glad you love music as well as ever. Farewell and Heaven bless my dear brother is always the prayer of

Margaret.

If you see the Weekly Tribune you will find all my pieces marked with a star. I began 1st Dec^r—

I am almost perfectly well at present.

17. To Francis G. Shaw *

Rome, October 25, 1847

Dear Frank,

I write two little notes just like what you and Sarah sent to me. I do not wish to write at all: my mind is too crowded and I get myself too tired. Only I want to hear from you, and see, too, if I can not get your sympathy as to some objects you being a practical man. In first place I want to know how has succeded in America "Les Compagnons" [?], it is a book in which only those who are in earnest and willing to think will take an interest I fancy. Then of the remnant of the Brook Farmites and if you are likely to carry out the thought of which you spoke of an Associate Home near New York.

I want also to take you into sympathy with some of my objects of interest. First there is a painter here, a young American, one of the "right kind of stuff" for a laurel, who has raised himself up from the difficult circumstances of his childhood by sheer force of talent and will to a high position in life and mind, which he is still obliged to maintain by continuous struggles and privations. His name is Hicks: he has rich relations in America, but rich relations seldom aid or sympathize till the hour of effectual aid is passed, that precious moment when men can really help one another, which a few, like Mr Carey in our country and Burke in England, have had the soul to seize and become the protecting angels of young lives. This man will interest you as being perhaps the only artist yet deeply penetrated by the idea of social reform, and especially by the hopes of the Associationists. If he lives, he will illustrate these ideas, in his own way. Your brotherly love for Page makes me think of you as a friend also to this friend of mine. He has in his mind pictures which would really express his thoughts, if he could find time and freedom to paint them.

---

* From the original in the possession of Mrs. Pierre Jay of New York City. Francis G. Shaw, the husband of Sarah Shaw, was active in the Brook Farm experiment and in the Fourierite association movement generally. Thomas Hicks painted a portrait of Margaret Fuller in Rome. The "Mrs. Child" is Lydia Maria Child, whose career had served as an inspiration to Margaret. In one of her *Tribune* letters Margaret had suggested that funds be raised in America to present a cannon to the newly formed Italian National Guard.

In order to this it is very desirable for him to sell some that he has sent to N.Y. to the Art Union. These do not present a sample of his thoughts, but they do of his practical talent. What I want of you is to look at them, and, if they please you, turn the attention of others to them, with a view to their being sold.

Be so good, too, as to write me a little of Mrs. Child. I hear nothing of her for so long. Now, I have asked much of you, but it is blessed to give, and I continue to beg letters to *care* Mas [manuscript illegible because of mutilation here] ny Pakenham & Co Rome.

Ever yours
S. M. Fuller

Reading over my letter I see I have forgot one of my requests. It is that in reading a letter I have sent to the Tribune about an American expression of sympathy for Italy at this moment, you will seriously consider whether it suits you to stir at all in such a matter. If two or three on the spot take an interest, it would be done so easily, and me it would please much, if the Guard, that earnest of National Institutions to Italy, should have something in their possession called the Colombo.

18. To Mrs. Sarah Shaw *

Rome, October 25, 1847

My dear Sarah,

You wrote in May, I answer in October, but that is quick interchange for a life so crowded as mine has been of late. Within this six months, I have seen almost every important place in Italy and begin to know as well as to feel about this country, dream of my heart and realization of my mind.

I cannot write about it in a little letter, a book would be too short. In writing to my friends I aim only to let them see I am thinking of them, and to cause them to tell me of the events of their own lives. With you I am anxious to know if your eyes continue in good condition and whether anything has happened to you, and how you feel. Tell me too of Anna, of Sarah Russel and of Elizabeth, also where Carrie is, for she does not write and nobody writes of her.

You regret not being in Italy at the same time with your sister & me, but when you get here you will feel nothing of that sort. Italy alone will suffice you. Come with all your children and live quietly here: to anyone who can feel, who is not very shallow, it must be torture merely to travel to Italy and give a passing stare at the beautiful body without ever having time or peace to come in contact with its soul. I have returned to Rome to stay six months; do not know exactly where I shall go after that: you will see in the Tribune. For the present I drop all thought of the future seeking to take my share of what lies before me.

It is a most beautiful day, so warm and bright, but I have been very busy. My head begins to ache; I must go to my walk, go to the Villa Borghese. A troop of the Trasteverini in those costumes we admire in Pinelli have just passed, colours flying, drums beating, five minutes earlier, a procession of monks chanting a requiem.

I live in the Corso and every day yields some fine show. Tonight I expect to hear Rubini sing: he is on a visit here, but I do not hear much good music in Italy. Germany or even France are far better for that.

Adieu, dear Sarah, love me, I pray and write sometimes to your friend

M.F.

* From the original in the possession of Mrs. Pierre Jay of New York City. See note, p. 569.

19. To Ossoli *

Rieti, August 22, 1848

I am a little better, dearest, but if I could thus pass a less suffering day—on the contrary it troubles me that this seems to tell me I must wait yet longer.

Wait! That is always hard. But—if I were sure of doing well, I should wish much to pass through this trial before your arrival:—but when I think that it is possible for me to die alone, without the touch of one dear hand, I wish to wait longer. So I hope for your presence on Sunday morning.

I see by the papers that the Pope suspends the departure of the troops—he acts as I thought he would, and I am now very glad that you did not enter the service yet. In a short time these affairs will be more certain, and you can decide more advantageously than now.

Try if you can hear any particulars from Milan, would it not be possible in the Café degli Belli Arti! I am much troubled by the fate of those dear friends, how much they must suffer now.—

I still think so much of you, I hope that you are less tormented. If we were together it would be a consolation. Now every thing goes wrong, but it is impossible it should always be so— Adieu, love, it vexes me that so many days must pass before your coming.—So many, so many. I am glad that I have the little picture. I look at it often. God keep thee.—

---

* From a copy, *Works of S. M. F. Ossoli,* Harvard College Library, Vol. II, p. 133. The original is in Italian and the translation was made by Elizabeth Hoar. Giovanni Angelo, Marchese Ossoli, whom Margaret Fuller first met in Rome during the spring of 1847 and with whom she contracted an alliance in the following fall. This letter was written while she was awaiting the arrival of their child, who was born on September 5. Ossoli was detained in Rome by his duties as a member of the Civic Guard.

20. To Ossoli *

Sunday, September 17, 1848

My love,

This morning I received nothing from you but the journal of Friday. I suppose now I shall have to wait till Tuesday to hear from you, as no post comes tomorrow.

The nurse's child is better, and I feel relieved. We must have courage, but it is a great care to be alone and ignorant with an infant in these first days of its life. When he shall be a month old, I shall feel more quiet. Then he will be stronger for the changes he will have to undergo. Now he is well, begins to sleep well, is very pretty for his age, and all around without knowing what name I thought of giving him, call him *Angiolino,* because he is so lovely. He has your mouth, hands, feet— It seems to me that his eyes will be blue.—For the rest—he is wholly   , understands well, is very obstinate to have his will.

I shall have much to say when you come, and also we shall then have much to plan, because it will be too cold in this room for me to stay here late in the autumn. The 40 days will terminate 15th October, and I wish to leave as soon as possible after that—the 20th or 25th if I can. Adieu, love, always thy. M.—

---

* From a copy, *Works of S. M. F. Ossoli,* Harvard College Library, Vol. II, p. 145. The original is in Italian and the translation by Elizabeth Hoar. See note, p. 579.

21. To Giuseppe Mazzini *

Rome, March 3, 1849

Dear Mazzini,

Though knowing you occupied by the most important affairs, I again feel impelled to write a few lines.

What emboldens me is the persuasion that the best friends,—in point of perfect sympathy and intelligence, the only friends,—of a man of ideas and of marked character, must be women. You have your mother; no doubt you have others, perhaps many. Of that I know nothing: only I like to offer also my tribute of affection.

When I think that only two years ago, you thought of coming into Italy with us in disguise, it seems very glorious, that you are about to enter Republican Rome as a Roman Citizen. It seemed almost the most sublime and poetical fact of history. Yet, even in the first thrill of joy, I felt, "He will think his work but beginning now."

When I read from your hand these words "il lungo esilio testè riciminciato, la vita non confortato fuorchè d'affetti lontani e contesi, e la speranza lungamente protrata e il desiderio che comincia a farmi si supremo di dormire finalmente in pace, da chè non ho potuto vivere in terra mia."

When I read these words they made me weep bitterly and I thought of them always with a great pang at the heart. But it is not so, dear Mazzini. You do not return to sleep under the sod of Italy, but to see your thought springing up all over her soil. The gardeners seem to me, in point of instinctive wisdom or deep thought, mostly incompetent to the care of the garden, but an idea like this will be able to make use of any implements. The necessity, it is to be hoped, will educate the men by making them work. It is not this, I believe, which still keeps your heart so melancholy, for I seem to read the same melancholy in your answer to the Roman assembly. You speak of "few and late years," but some full ones still remain; a century is not needed, nor ought the same man, in the same form of thought, to

* From the original, Fuller MSS., Harvard College Library, Vol. XI, p. 105. Mazzini, the intellectual leader of the Roman Revolution, had been known to Margaret since she met him through Thomas and Jane Carlyle in London in 1846.

work too long on an age. He would mould and bend it too much to himself, better for him to die and return incarnated to give the same truth aid on yet another side. Jesus of Nazareth died young; but had he not spoken and acted as much truth as the world could bear in his time? A frailty, a perpetual shortcoming, motion in a curve line, seems the destiny of this earth. The excuse awaits us elsewhere: there must be one, for it is true, as said Goethe, that *"Care is taken* that the trees grow not up into heaven." Men like you, appointed ministers, must not be less earnest in their work, yet to the greatest, the day, the moment, is all their kingdom. God takes care of the increase. Farewell! For your sake I would wish at this moment to be an Italian and a man of action. But *though an American,* I am not even a *woman of action;* so the best I can do is to pray with the whole heart. Heaven bless dear Mazzini, cheer his heart and give him worthy helpers to carry out its holy purposes!

22. To Ossoli *

[*May or June* 1849]

Mio Caro,

I go out, to the post-office and to the hospitals—I cannot stay so in the house all day.—I feel too much anxiety. If unluckily you come when I am not here, I beg you also to come a moment this evening, and leave word with the porter whether you can do so. M.—

How hard it was for me, love, to miss you yesterday, and possibly also today, if you can come. I am going to Casa Diez, if possible, inquire there, the last floor, if I am still there or have gone to the hospitals. God keep thee— How much I have suffered in seeing the wounded, and I cannot know if any thing should happen to you—but I must hope. I have received the letter from Rieti, our Nino is perfectly well, thanks for this. It does me good that the Romans have at least done something, if only you can remain. In event of the death of both, I have left a paper with a certificate of Angelino, and some lines praying the Storys to take care of him. If by any accident *I* die, you can resume this paper if you will, from me, as from your wife. I have wished Nino to go to America, but you will do as seems best to you— We ought to have planned this better, but I hope that it will not be needed.

Always with benedictions thy Margherita.—

If you live, and I die, be always most devoted to Nino— If you ever love another think first for him, I pray, pray, love.

---

* From a copy, *Works of S. M. F. Ossoli,* Harvard College Library, Vol. II, p. 223. The original is in Italian and the translation by Elizabeth Hoar. See note, p. 579.

Florence, December 2, 1849

Dear William,

It was like you to receive with such kindness the news of my marriage. A less generous person would have been displeased, that when we had been drawn so together, when we had talked so freely, and you had shown towards me such sweet friendship, I had not told you. Often did I long to do so, but I had, for reasons that seemed important, made a law to myself to keep this secret as rigidly as possible, up to a certain moment. That moment came; its decisions were not such as I had hoped; but it left me at least without that painful burden of secret, which I hope never to bear again. Nature keeps so many secrets, that I had supposed the moral writers exaggerated about the dangers & plagues of keeping them; but they cannot exaggerate. All that can be said about mine is that I at least acted out with some tragic thoroughness "the wonder, a woman keeps a secret." All that can be said of my not telling you is that I was keeping the same from my family and dearest friends at home, & had you remained near me a very little later, you would have been the very first person to whom I should have spoken; and you would have been the first on this side of the water to whom I should have written, had I known where to address you. Yet I hardly hoped for your sympathy, dear William. I am very glad if I have it.

May brotherly love ever be returned unto you in like measure. Ossoli desires his love & respect to be testified to you both. Should he meet you sometime in our land I doubt not the light of your eye will be consoling to him. I feel he will feel very strange & lonely there; indeed I feel much more anxious about his happiness than my own. Still his love for our child is so great

---

* From a copy, Fuller MSS., Harvard College Library, Vol. IX, p. 227. William Story and his wife Emelyn were Margaret's closest friends among the Americans in Italy. Story was a Boston lawyer turned sculptor. It was to his wife that Margaret confided the story of her secret marriage and the birth of her child, sometime during the siege of Rome when she feared that both Ossoli and herself might perish. Mrs. Story's manuscript account (Fuller MSS., Boston Public Library) is the chief authority for that little-known period of Margaret's life.

& his pleasure in the woods and fields so simple and profound, I hope he will be able to make for himself a life in the unknown country till changes favor return to his own.

That changes must take place very soon, within two or three years at farthest, there seems great reason to expect. The conduct of the restored authorities is so very unjudicious that it cannot be otherwise.

I am just reading Macaulay's new history which seems even more brilliant and fascinating than his previous writings. He says James II was unable to get beyond this one idea, "My father made concessions and was beheaded, therefore the only way for me to do is to make no concessions." The Cardinals are just as stupid. But it is better for one not to write about these matters through the post. I suppose letters are not opened here as the means of espionage is not likely to reach the same he[at as] in Rome, but cannot feel sure, & we study to give no umbrage, as the Police made difficulty about letting us stay, & the need to move would be a great evil at this time.

The *"Völkersband"* I suppose you will be able to see in Germany, & it will give you tidings of what the great disbanded are hoping & trying. I do not expect to see it while here.

I deeply regret you did not decide on coming here this winter; it would have been such a pleasure to me & others to have you, but you would not have found your marble. If I can do anything about it by & by you will let me know. If I could not see about it myself, I might keep alive the interest of some capable person. Mr. Browning & Mr. Henry Greenough both speak in high praise of the statue: do not be too long before you put it into marble.

I think you will have some opportunity of sending your poems as it is said there is a great tide of travel from Germany into Italy at present. I have been much pleased with Mr. Clough's which he sent me & with those of two of his friends, Burbidge and Arnold. They are of the Emersonian kind, entirely out of all rule, not of high power, but genuine though imperfect reflexes of the higher life of their writers.

I think you will be amazed when you see the Highland   [you] will be hardly able to believe it written by our timid   of leading questions. He is indeed spoken of in England as the coming man. Mr. Browning as was natural in a high professor of the Lyric art was annoyed by the defects in form, while he liked the substance. I scarcely observed them, it is so rare now a days to come so near in contact with the living soul as you may in some of them.

When you go to London do call on Mr. C.

He is superior of University Hall

Garden Square.

Through him you will no doubt come in contact with young men really alive like the best of us in America. Adieu, dear William. If you sometimes write me a little about what you are observing & doing I shall be very glad, but make no claim knowing well how thronged these European days are with claims and fascinations. I trust a solid friendship has now been founded which will last through our lives & that every now and then we shall meet & exchange some thoughtful words. I count it among the gains of these years to subscribe myself with grateful and hopeful affection   Your friend

Margaret

24. To Marcus and Rebecca Spring *

Florence, December 12, 1849

Dear Marcus & Rebecca,

A letter from Mr Doherty, a notice in the paper of Miss Bremer's visit to the North American Phalanx, undoubtedly made in company with you, bring you so forcibly to mind that I must e'en devote the last two hours and the best & quietest ones of the 24 to answering your letters. For I have actually two letters from you to answer & excellent ones likewise—

Your letter, my dear Rebecca, was written in your noblest and most womanly spirit. I thank you warmly for your sympathy about my little boy. What he is to me, even you can hardly dream, you who have three, and in whom the natural thirst of the heart was earlier satisfied, can scarcely know what my one ewe lamb is to me. That he may live, that I may find bread for him, that I may not spoil him by over-weening love, that I may grow daily better for his sake, are the ever recurring thoughts —say prayers—that give their hue to all the currents of my life.

Yet in answer to what you say, that it is still better to give the world this living soul than a portion of my life in a printed book; it is true; and yet of my book I could know whether it would be of some worth or not, of my child I must wait to see what his worth will be. I play with him, my ever growing mystery, but from the solemnity of the thoughts he brings, is refuge only in God. Was I worthy to be parent of a soul with its eternal immense capacity of weal and woe. God be merciful to me a sinner comes so naturally to the mother's heart I think.—But I cannot write much about it; we shall meet sometime & see whether it is natural to communicate on these subjects. Meanwhile I doubt not you will feel for my child somewhat of the affection which I do about yours.

You say you wish I had not left you to hear these tidings from others &

* From a copy, Fuller MSS., Harvard College Library, Vol. IX, p. 219. Marcus and Rebecca Spring were among Margaret Fuller's closest friends during the later years of her life. Their home at Eagleswood was a refuge often sought by her when she was on the *Tribune* staff in New York, and it was with them that she went abroad in August 1846. They parted company in Italy early the next summer, but kept in touch by letter after the Springs returned to New York.

I wish so too, but the fact is never having heard from you of the birth of little Marcus, never any answer to a letter addressed to you in November or December of the past year, under the pressure of heavy care & sorrow, never any line in answer to an effusion of feeling sent you just after Mazzini came to Rome in the spring, I felt as if your friendship to me was, not dead, indeed, but sleeping, & could not resolve to write on a subject so delicate and make my communication to any but hearts that seemed awake in love to mine, at that time worn out and sensitive from much suffering. I wrote to Mr Greeley, my soul all opened towards him by the news of his great calamity—mine too it was—for the lost child was infinitely dear to me. I have been sadly disappointed that he should not answer that letter, but life is full of such things, truly hard is the travel to one who has but the "brain unencompassed by nerves of steel."—

My dear Marcus, your long letter was a grand one and did me good. It was like some few walks we had in our travels, one out of Birmingham I think amid the green shrubberies of Edgbarton,—one climbing the Appenines to Pietra Monta. It imparted much of valuable facts, more of your own true soul. I wish I could answer in kind but can only touch on some topics.

I have become an enthusiastic Socialist; elsewhere is no comfort, no solution for the problems of the times. I rejoice in what you tell of some successful practical study at the N.A. Phalanx. I wish you had told more explicitly why you return to business in the common way. Was it because you needed more money? Or because a truly congenial course was not yet clearly marked out for you? It is an excellent thing you have done about that washing house. Blessed be he who gets one such good thing done while the rest of us are only blundering, observing, perhaps learning something. What you say is deeply true about the peace way being the best. If any one see clearly how to work in that way, let him in God's name. Only, if he abstain from fighting against giant wrongs, let him be sure he is really and ardently at work undermining them, or better still sustaining the rights that are to supplant them. Meanwhile I am not sure that I can keep my hands free from blood. I doubt I have not the strength. Cobden is good, but if he had stood in Kossuth's place, would he not have drawn the sword against the Austrian? You, Marcus, could you let a

Croat insult Rebecca, carry off Eddie to be an Austrian serf, & leave little Marcus bleeding in the dust? Yet it is true that while Moses slew the Egyptian, Christ stood to be spit upon and that Death to Man could do no harm. You have the truth—you have the right—but could you act it, Marcus, in all circumstances? Stifled under the Roman priesthood would you not have thrown it off with all your force? Would you have waited unknown centuries hoping the moment when you could use another method? If so, you are a Christian; you know I never pretended to be except in dabs & sparkles here & there. Yet the agonies of that baptism of blood I felt oh how deeply in the golden June days of Rome. Consistent no way I felt I should have shrunk back. I could not have had it shed. Christ did not have to see his dear ones pass the dark river; he could go alone; however, in prophetic spirit, no doubt he foresaw the crusades.

In answer to what you say of Nino, I wish indeed the little effort I made for him had been wiselier applied. Yet these are not the things one regrets. It does not do to calculate too closely with the affectionate human impulse; we must consent to make many mistakes or we would move too slow to help our brothers much. I am sure you don't regret what you spent on Miani & other worthless people; as the circumstances looked then it would have been wrong not to risk the loss. To be sure one must learn prudence by degrees. If I ever have anything to give again I hope to have better discretion than in past years. Yet I have been very fortunate a number of times when I have tried to help. Efforts not very energetic have been crowned with a good deal of success. The little way I ever travelled on the road to Zion I have been borne along on flowery beds of ease, and other people have been fifty times better to me than I have been to my small pack of Lazaruses.

As to what you say of your wishes to mewards, I want nothing of thee, dear Marcus, in the shape of dollars. I know you are not rich; that you have upon you many claims & make many more paying double tithes to the true church of fraternity-equality. What you have done for me I prize, the acts & the spirit in which they were done. May like love ever be ready to cheer yourself if you should need it. What you may do for me now is—

1stly—Pray to St Margaret, since she hangs in your parlour, that I may somehow escape from the danger of poverty which I have faced much in the same ecstatic mood as she seems to feel and now begin to fear lest it snatch my boy. Pray that I may find some way to earn my daily bread, with milk & pearlbarley for my boy.

2ndly—Go to Wiley & Putnam & ask if all that stuff published as my miscellanies is forever to be unprofitable as well as flat and stale. If so I don't think it is quite fair as certainly worse slate stones turn to gold in some hands. It is now the end of the third year & if you could squeeze for me even a very small sum from his publishing mercies, it would be most welcome. A fifty dollars would at least pay my postage bill when I leave Florence. I am now sore pressed; and we are like to be so for several years. Could we weather through these next years, we might have a little peace, joy perhaps. Yet worry not thyself for me—I dare say God who has got me on thus far through the bog of practical life will never let me sink in more than knee deep, & I shall get off with only a fright or two at last. Write of Miss Bremer. I think she will see many things in the U.S. to please her kind heart, and trust she will give the benefit of many wise suggestions & reproofs. Sauced by her kindly playfulness they will be digested even by the conceit of Jonathan. Love to dear Eddie & Jeanie, a kiss to the baby—it all came right—a Marcus was better than a Margaret.

25. To Richard F. Fuller *

Florence, January 8, 1850

My dear Richard,

I was just making up a pacquet to send home by a friendly hand when this mornᵍ yours of 4th Decʳ reached me. I was very glad, having become saddened & indeed surprized not to hear from you. The way you speak now of my marriage is such as I expected from you. Now that we have exchanged some words on these important changes in our lives, it matters little to write letters. Too much has happened; the changes have been too great to be made clear in writing. I doubt not when we have met face to face, we shall be friends the same as ever, or better than before.

It would not be worthwhile to keep the house thinking of me. I cannot fix precisely the period of my return, though at present it seems to me probable we may make the voyage in May or June. At first we should go & make a little visit to Mother. I should take counsel with various friends before fixing myself in any place, see what openings there are for me &c. I cannot judge at all before I am personally in the U.S. & wish to engage myself noway. Should I finally decide on the neighborhood of N.Y. I would see you all often. I wish, however, to live with Mother, if possible. We will discuss it on all sides when I come. Climate is one thing I must think of: the change from the Roman winter to that of N. England might be very trying for Ossoli. In N.Y. he would see Italians, often hear his native tongue & feel less exiled. If we had our affairs in N.Y. & lived in the country we could find places as quiet as Canton, more beautiful & from which access to a city would be as easy by means of steam. On the other hand my family & most cherished friends are in N. England. I would weigh all advantages at the time & choose as may then seem best. I feel also the great responsibility about a child, & the mixture of solemn feeling with the joy its sweet ways and carefree give. Yet this is only different in degree, not in kind, from what we should feel in other relations; the destiny of all we come in contact

* From the original, Fuller MSS., Harvard College Library, Vol. IX, p. 162. See note, p. 560.

with we may more or less impede or brighten. Much in the child lies in our power; still God and nature are there, furnishing a thousand masters to correct our erroneous, fill up our imperfect teachings. I feel impelled to try for gain for the sake of my child, most powerfully, but if I fail, I trust help will be tendered him from some other quarter. I do not wish to trouble myself more than is inevitable or lose the simple innocent pleasure of watching his growth from day to day by thinking of his future. At present my care of him is to keep him clean body & mind, to give for body & mind simple nutriment when he demands it & play with him. Now he lies playing as we all shall when we enter a higher state. With him my intercourse thus far has been satisfactory & if I do not well for *him,* he at least has taught me a great deal.

My love to your wife. I hear she is very sweet & rejoice she makes you so happy. Ossoli sends his love to you. I may say of him, as you say of your wife, it would be difficult to other than like him, so sweet is his disposition, so without an effort disinterested, so simply fine his daily conduct, so harmonious his whole nature. Add that he is a perfectly unconscious character & never dreams that he does well. He is studying English but makes little progress. For a good while you may not be able to talk with him, but you will like showing him some of your favorite haunts: he is so happy in nature, in sweet tranquil places. Farewell, dear R.

ever yr affec^e friend & sister

M.

Bibliography of Published Writings
of Margaret Fuller

Index

Bibliography of the Published Writings
of Margaret Fuller

I. BOOKS

(First editions, in order of publication)

Eckermann's Conversations with Goethe. (Translation.) Boston: Hilliard, Gray, 1839.

Günderode. (Translation.) Boston: E. P. Peabody, 1842. (First of four numbers, the remainder of which were not issued. The translation was completed by Minna Wesselhoeft and published as *Correspondence of Fräulein Günderode and Bettina von Arnim.* Boston: T. O. H. P. Burnham, 1861.)

Summer on the Lakes, in 1843. Boston: C. C. Little and James Brown, 1844. (Reprinted in *At Home and Abroad.* Boston: Crosby, Nichols, 1856.)

Woman in the Nineteenth Century. New York: Tribune Press, 1845.

Papers on Literature and Art. 2 vols. New York: Wiley and Putnam, 1846. (Reprinted as 1 vol., 1848, and in *Art, Literature and the Drama,* Boston: Brown, Taggard and Chase, 1860. Translation of *Torquato Tasso* first appears in the Crosby, Nichols edition of 1856.)

At Home and Abroad, edited by A. B. Fuller. Boston: Crosby, Nichols, 1856.

Life Without and Life Within, edited by A. B. Fuller. Boston: Brown, Taggard and Chase, 1859.

Love-Letters of Margaret Fuller, 1845-1846, with an introduction by Julia Ward Howe. New York: D. Appleton, 1903.

II. PERIODICAL WRITINGS

Boston Daily Advertiser

Defense of Brutus	November 27, 1834

The Western Messenger

Crabbe and Hannah More	June 1835	Vol.	I, No. 1, p. 20
Bulwer	August 1835	Vol.	I, No. 2, p. 101
Philip van Artevelde	December 1835	Vol.	I, No. 6, p. 398

The Western Messenger

Korner: I	January 1838	Vol. IV, No. 5, p. 306
Korner: II	February 1838	Vol. IV, No. 6, p. 369
Letters from Palmyra	April 1838	Vol. V, No. 1, p. 24

The Dial *

A Short Essay on Critics	July 1840	Vol.	I, No. 1, p. 5
A Record of Impressions Produced by the Exhibition of Allston's Pictures in the Summer of 1839	" "	Vol.	I, No. 1, p. 73
To Allston's Picture, "The Bride" (verse)	" "	Vol.	I, No. 1, p. 84
A Dialogue: Dahlia and the Sun (verse)	" "	Vol.	I, No. 1, p. 134

* Based on G. W. Cooke, *Historical and Biographical Introduction to Accompany the Dial,* Vol. II, Chap. XXXII, pp. 196 ff., by permission of the Rowfant Club.

Richter (verse)	July 1840	Vol.	I, No. 1, p. 135
Some Murmur at the "Want of System" in Richter's Writings (verse)	" "	Vol.	I, No. 1, p. 135
The Morning Breeze (verse)	" "	Vol.	I, No. 1, p. 135
A Sketch: I (verse)	" "	Vol.	I, No. 1, p. 136
A Sketch: II (verse)	" "	Vol.	I, No. 1, p. 136
Did You Never Desire Anything? (verse)	" "	Vol.	I, No. 1, p. 136
Angelica Sleeps (translation from Berni)	October 1840	Vol.	I, No. 2, p. 172
The Athenaeum Exhibition of Painting and Sculpture	" "	Vol.	I, No. 2, p. 260
Meta	January 1841	Vol.	I, No. 3, p. 293
The Magnolia of Lake Pontchartrain	" "	Vol.	I, No. 3, p. 299
Menzel's *View of Goethe*	" "	Vol.	I, No. 3, p. 340
Rodman's *Voice from the Prison*	" "	Vol.	I, No. 3, p. 404
Hawthorne's *Grandfather's Chair*	" "	Vol.	I, No. 3, p. 405
Leila	April 1841	Vol.	I, No. 4, p. 462
A Dialogue: Poet and Critic	" "	Vol.	I, No. 4, p. 494
Goethe	July 1841	Vol.	II, No. 1, p. 1
Carlyle's *On Heroes*	" "	Vol.	II, No. 1, p. 131
Lowell's *A Year's Life*	July 1841	Vol.	II, No. 1, p. 133
Goethe's *Faust*	" "	Vol.	II, No. 1, p. 134
H. Martineau's *Hour and the Man*	" "	Vol.	II, No. 1, p. 134
Tennyson, Sterling, *Festus*	" "	Vol.	II, No. 1, p. 135
The Plain Speaker	" "	Vol.	II, No. 1, p. 135
To Contributors	" "	Vol.	II, No. 1, p. 136
Lives of the Great Composers: Haydn, Mozart, Handel, Bach, Beethoven	October 1841	Vol.	II, No. 2, p. 148
Festus (dialogue between Aglauron and Laurie)	" "	Vol.	II, No. 2, p. 231
Yucca Filamentosa	January 1842	Vol.	II, No. 3, p. 286
Bettina Brentano and Her Friend Günderode	" "	Vol.	II, No. 3, p. 313
Epilogue to the Tragedy of Essex (translation)	" "	Vol.	II, No. 3, p. 380
Motherwell's *Poems*	" "	Vol.	II, No. 3, p. 393
Goethe's *Egmont*	" "	Vol.	II, No. 3, p. 394
Monaldi's *A Tale*	" "	Vol.	II, No. 3, p. 395
Wilde's *Conjectures and Researches*	" "	Vol.	II, No. 3, p. 399
Boston Academy of Music	" "	Vol.	II, No. 3, p. 407
Theory of Teaching	" "	Vol.	II, No. 3, p. 408
Marie van Oosterwich (translation)	April 1842	Vol.	II, No. 4, p. 437
Entertainments of the Past Winter	July 1842	Vol.	III, No. 1, p. 46
Hawthorne's *Twice-Told Tales*	" "	Vol.	III, No. 1, p. 130
Hawthorne's *Stories for Children*	" "	Vol.	III, No. 1, p. 131
Romaic and Rhine Ballads	October 1842	Vol.	III, No. 2, p. 137
Canova	April 1843	Vol.	III, No. 4, p. 454
Fetis's *Music Explained*	" "	Vol.	III, No. 4, p. 533
The Great Lawsuit	July 1843	Vol.	IV, No. 1, p. 1
The Modern Drama	January 1844	Vol.	IV, No. 3, p. 307
Dialogue (Aglauron and Laurie at boarding house)	April 1844	Vol.	IV, No. 4, p. 458

New York Daily Tribune

Emerson's *Essays: II Series*	December	7, 1844
Mrs. Hemans	"	10, "
Mr. Hosmer's Poems	"	11, "

Cranch's Poems	December	12,	1844
Thanksgiving (editorial)	"	"	"
Monument to Goethe (translation from *Schnellpost*)	"	16,	"
Christmas (editorial)	"	25,	"
New Year's Day	January	1,	1845
Miss Barrett's Poems	"	4,	"
Liberty Bell for 1845	"	7,	"
Liszt and Sue (translation from *Schnellpost*)	"	11,	"
North American Review	"	13,	"
Longfellow's *The Waif*	"	16,	"
Lanman's *Letters from a Landscape Painter*	"	18,	"
Lowell's *Conversations on Some of the Old Poets*	"	21,	"
Edgar A. Poe—*Graham's Magazine*	"	24,	"
Deutsche Schnellpost	"	25,	"
Popular Literature in Germany (translation from *Schnellpost*)	"	27,	"
Mrs. Sigourney's *Scenes in My Native Land*	"	28,	"
French Novelists of the Day: Balzac, Sand, Sue	February	1,	"
The Slave: or Memoirs of Archy Moore	"	4,	"
Eliza L. Fuller's *The Child's Friend*	"	5,	"
Life of Beethoven	"	7,	"
Schoolcraft's *Oneota, or Red Races of America*	"	12,	"
J. Stanley Grimes's *Etherology*	"	17,	"
St. Valentine's Day—Bloomingdale Asylum for Insane	"	22,	"
Theodore Parker's *The Excellence of Goodness*	"	26,	"
English Writers Little Known Here: Milnes, Landor, Hare	March	4,	"
New Year's Letter from a Catholic Priest (translation from *Schnellpost*)	"	12,	"
Noel's translation of Richter's Flower, Fruit, and Thorn Pieces	"	"	"
Countess Hahn-Hahn's *Countess Faustina*	"	"	"
Correspondence between Schiller and Goethe	"	14,	"
Our City Charities: Visits to Bellevue, Alms House, Farm School, Asylum for the Insane, Blackwell's Island	"	19,	"
Writers Little Known Among Us: Milnes, Landor, Hare	"	28,	"
Sermons by Theodore Parker and W. H. Furnas	"	29,	"
Undine and *Eothen*	April	4,	"
The Modern Jews	"	21,	"
Hazlitt's *Table-talk*	"	30,	"
Commander Wilkes's Narrative	May	7,	"
Mrs. L. M. Child's Letters	"	10,	"
Charles Anthon's *A System of Latin Versification*	"	12,	"
Saul, a Mystery, by the author of *Christian Ballads*	"	"	"
Headlong Hall and *Nightmare Abbey*	"	"	"
H. Martineau's *Five Years of Youth, or Sense and Sentiment*	"	"	"
Taylor Lewis's *Plato against the Atheists*	"	14,	"
W. W. Lord's *Poems*	"	19,	"
American Facts	"	"	"
Michelet's *History of France*	"	20,	"
The French in Algiers	"	22,	"
Goethe's *Essays on Art*	"	29,	"
Select Tales from Gesta Romanorum	"	31,	"
L. M. Child's *Philothea*	June	5,	"
Courrier des Etats-Unis	"	7,	"
The Crescent and the Cross	"	"	"
Life of Frederick Douglass	"	10,	"
Longfellow's *Poets and Poetry of Europe*	"	17,	"

Condition of the Blind in This Country and Abroad	April 18,	1846
Comte de Monte Cristo	" "	"
Wonders Have Not Ceased in Our Times (translation from *Schnellpost*)	" 24,	"
Headley's *Napoleon and His Marshals*	May 4,	"
Francisco de Noronha	" 9,	"
Christian Dancing, Hunting, Angling	" 16,	"
Victory (editorial on Schiller's *Ode to Joy*)	" 21,	"
Grand Festival Concert at Castle Garden (editorial)	" 22,	"
Wadby Thompson's *Recollections of Mexico*	June 2,	"
J. A. King's *Twenty-Four Years in the Argentine*	" 5,	"
Belshazzar's Feast (Spear's completion of Allston's design)	" 12,	"
J. T. Headley's *Napoleon and His Marshals*	" 18,	"
Hawthorne's *Mosses from an Old Manse*	" 22,	"
George Sand's *Consuelo*	" 24,	"
Hazen's *Grammatical Reader*	" 26,	"
Illustrated Botany		
Children's books and occupations for women		
Mrs. Jameson's *Heroines of Shakespeare*	" 30,	"
Thomas L. M'Kenney's *Memoirs*	July 8,	"
William Smith's *Memoirs of J. G. Fichte*	" 9,	"
Browning's Poems	" 10,	"
Brockden Brown's *Ormond* and *Wieland*	" 21,	"
Count of Monte Cristo	" "	"
Mrs. Jameson's *Memoirs and Essays*	" 24,	"
Dickens's *Pictures from Italy*	" "	"
Farewell to New York City	August 1,	"

(Margaret Fuller's letters from Europe, which appeared in the *Tribune* at irregular intervals from September 1846 to July 1849, are collected in *At Home and Abroad*.)

Index